The Life and Ideas of
James Hillman

The Life and Ideas of
James
Hillman

Volume II
Re-Visioning Psychology

DICK RUSSELL

Arcade Publishing
New York

Arcade Publishing books may be purchased in bulk at special discounts for sales promotion, corporate gifts, fund-raising, or educational purposes. Special editions can also be created to specifications. For details, contact the Special Sales Department, Arcade Publishing, 307 West 36th Street, 11th Floor, New York, NY 10018 or arcade@skyhorsepublishing.com.

Arcade Publishing® is a registered trademark of Skyhorse Publishing, Inc.®, a Delaware corporation.

Visit our website at www.arcadepub.com.

10 9 8 7 6 5 4 3 2 1

Library of Congress Cataloging-in-Publication Data is available on file.

Cover design by David Ter-Avaneysan
Cover photo © 2023 by Margot McLean Hillman / Melanie Jackson Agency
Hillman previously unpublished letters and writings © Margot McLean Hillman / Melanie Jackson Agency
Hillman photographs © Margot McLean Hillman / Melanie Jackson Agency

Print ISBN: 978-1-956763-18-8
Ebook ISBN: 978-1-956763-19-5

Printed in the United States of America

CONTENTS

INTRODUCTION:
AN ARCHETYPAL LIFE

"Each life has its 'feel' to it, the way its time courses, which turns a case history into a soul history, a chain of events into a patterned rhythm. A biography is the exposition of feeling running through time, the feeling of a person and a period."

—James Hillman, Jung's Typology.[1]

This is the second volume of a biography about an American sage most have never heard of. Thomas Moore (author of the bestseller *Care of the Soul* and two dozen more books) unabashedly called him, "the greatest thinker who ever lived: more important than Aristotle, Plato, Heidegger, and Blake."[2] In the pantheon of Freud and Jung, Moore places Hillman at the very top. At the very least, according to the poet Robert Bly, he is, "The most lively and original psychologist we have had in America since William James."[3]

James Hillman, who died in 2011 at the age of eighty-five, didn't provide us self-help directives to change our lives—so that we might get more of what we think we need. In his twenty-five published books and his lectures around the world, he laid out no step-by-step action plan for curing one's neuroses. While the mindset of his field focused on statistics, outcome measures, and evidence-based practices, Hillman went renegade—examining the exceptional, the abnormal, the pathologizing tendency of the psyche. Instead of privileging the Western ego, he set about returning psychology to Soul. This is not a return to Soul in the dogmatic sense, but the return of psychology to its mythic and historical roots, revivifying the gods and goddesses of Mount Olympus and forgotten Renaissance philosophers like Vico and Ficino. Hillman provided no answers, but reopened paths to mystery, while calling us to collective action in the world.

Framed along the wall in James Hillman's rural Connecticut home were his guiding ancestral ghosts—the Hungarian freedom fighter, the radical reform rabbi, the astute Boardwalk hotelier—"a wealth of guardians," as he put it. They peered down upon the bed in a guest room, perhaps similar to the hotel where he'd been born in 1926, to two very different parents: a mother enamored with the world of class, the rich and famous, and a father drawn to the common man, friend to cops and firemen.

Atlantic City was the ideal place to have grown up. The Boardwalk teemed with fantasy figures—flagpole sitters and "High Diving Horses" and "Deep Sea Net Hauls." His family's 400-room establishment hosted odd characters and an "underground" of workers with nicknames like Pete the Plumber. An electric, eclectic world fired the imagination of the tall bright boy who also recognized the sham within the show, the hypocrisy and shadow and false importance. This same boy would spend much time alone, studying maps of the world in his room.

James Hillman came of age, joined the Navy, and took care of blind veterans returning from the Second World War—losing his innocence. Becoming a news correspondent based in postwar Germany, he witnessed the beginning of the United Nations. While enrolled at the Sorbonne in Paris, he came upon an adventurous Swedish beauty in a jazz club, then contracted tuberculosis and spent several meditative months recovering in a Swiss sanitarium. He went on to Trinity College in Dublin and helped start a magazine called *Envoy*. After traveling first across Africa, he lived with Kate Kempe in Kashmir for almost two years working on a novel, then experienced a "breakdown" at their wedding and ended up seeking analysis at the Jung Institute in Zürich.

There, Hillman encountered depth psychology. Despite being a young man of relative privilege, he had already begun to learn that periods of suffering are soul-making experiences. While getting to know Carl Jung during the last decade of his life, Hillman not only graduated from the Jung Institute, he gained a Ph.D. in philosophy from the University of Zürich. At only thirty-three, he was appointed the Institute's first Director of Studies and in 1960 published his first book—his doctoral thesis on *Emotion*.

By the next year, he and Kate would have their fourth and final child, and he would deliver his first public lectures. Hillman's distance from traditional Jungians eventually became more acute, expressed in his second book, *Suicide and the Soul*, where he transgressed the taboo of questioning suicide prevention. He was soon invited to join a group of pathbreaking intellectuals from many disciplines who came together for annual conferences at Eranos.

After writing a seminal essay on "Betrayal," Hillman's life became enveloped in it—he had an affair with a patient who happened to be a minister's wife. This is after Hillman learned that his own wife had an affair with C. A. Meier, who had been her analyst as well as his. With Meier leading a hypocritical campaign against him, Hillman ended up being forced out as the Institute's Director of Studies. That was where volume one of this biography ended: Hillman adrift, uncertain of what would come next—"way out on a branch," as he put it, "[I] like it there very much."

We pick up the story here, as Hillman approaches mid-life, when a young woman from Ohio named Patricia Berry enrolled at the Jung Institute. She became his student, his analysand, eventually his lover and colleague, and then in 1976, his second wife. In Zürich their destinies merged with a flamboyant Cuban, Rafael López-Pedraza. During a trip to London taken together, they gave birth to what came to be called archetypal psychology.

Hillman and his compatriots linked this effort toward expanding Jung's analytical psychology to culture and the imagination, moving psychology away from the dominant scientific/medical model and its focus on the treatment of the isolated individual. Hillman took over a Jungian journal, *Spring*, and began to host passionate discussions in Zürich's bohemian quarter. In both, the archetypalists explored images in literature, myth, alchemy and art, honoring these as living realities. At the annual Eranos conferences in southern Switzerland, bringing together pathfinders across many disciplines, Hillman made mythology and alchemy relevant to our times.

Chosen to deliver the prestigious annual Terry Lectures at Yale, Hillman turned these talks into a pioneering book called *Re-Visioning Psychology*—nominated in 1975 for a Pulitzer Prize. By now divorced, Hillman returned to America after living primarily in Europe for thirty years. To the surprise of many, he and Pat Berry settled in Dallas, Texas—where he became a professor at a Catholic university and then helped found an Institute of Humanities and Culture. In the *nouveau riche* capital of the U.S., Hillman refined his ideas on the *anima mundi*, the "soul of the world"—taking up how to re-vision city planning.

Equally surprising was his subsequent move to rural Connecticut, where he settled into an old farmhouse with a chicken coop out back. From there, Hillman ventured out as a teacher in the mythopoetic men's movement—into the backwoods of Minnesota and California—where deep talk about fathers and sons and male-female relationships offered a new kind of group therapy, a cultural therapy.

Along the way Hillman's discoveries and insights came to encompass dance, theater, art, architecture, all within what he called a "poetic basis of mind." Depth psychology merged with deep ecology, and the importance of the animal kingdom. While drawing upon classical European thought, Hillman was thoroughly American in his restlessness, his pioneering spirit, and his martial energy. American too were his affection for multiple cultures, his pushing of limits, his frontier conscious- ness, and his perpetual need to be young, undefined, and con- tinually self-renewing and self-transcending. He was equally American in his lack of piety toward conventional institutions and established traditions. He relished the challenge of break- ing boundaries, confronting the unknown, scouting out new horizons. His eclectic group of friends ranged from poets to magicians, barbers to bartenders. His books in translation lined reader's shelves in Italy and Japan, where his lectures drew thousands. Yet he disdained having followers and repu- diated being cast as the founder of a "school" of archetypal psychology.

The extremes of his life seemed to reflect a pattern set in childhood—in the contrast between the teeming fantasyland of the summer Boardwalk and the empty and forlorn beaches of the Atlantic City winter. At college, during the day he took classes on "mental and moral science" at Dublin's Trinity College and at night reveled with the likes of Brendan Behan at McDaid's Pub. After analytical training, he moved from the introverted realm of Zürich's Jung Institute to the ultra-extraversion of Dallas, Texas. After settling in Connecticut, you could find him com- miserating with men in the North Woods or holding court with the eclectic scholars at Eranos.

As Thomas Moore also said about James Hillman: "No one pushed the imagination into the world and actual life to the extent that [he] did and with such immediate relevance." He possessed a "genius for taking any theme and shedding serious, fresh light on it."[4]

Come along then as we follow the Hillman roller-coaster from Europe to America and back again, accompanying his excur- sions into the depths and mythic caves of human imagining.

NOTES

---

1. "Each life has its 'feel' to it . . . .': *Lectures on Jung's Typology: The Inferior Function by Marie-Louis von Franz" and "The feeling Function" by James Hillman*, Spring Publications, Zürich, 1971.
2. Moore: "The greatest thinker who ever lived . . . .": "Remembering James Hillman: An Enterview with Thomas Moore," by Rob Henderson, *48 Quadrant XXXXII*, 2012, p. 56 (available online).
3. Bly: "the most lively and original . . . ." Back cover comment for James Hillman's book, *Kinds of Power*, Currency Doubleday, 1995.
4. Moore: "No one pushed the imagination . . . .": "Remembering James Hillman . . . .", p. 56.

CHRONOLOGY
(through Volume I)

1895: Grandfather Joel Hillman acquires his first hotel in Atlantic City.

1923: Grandfather, renowned reform Rabbi Joseph Krauskopf, dies in Philadelphia.

April 12, 1926: James Hillman is born in an Atlantic City hotel room.

Summer 1936: Hillman takes a cross-country auto trip with his brother and other students.

September 1939–February 1943: Hillman attends high school in Atlantic City.

Summer 1942: Hillman travels to Mexico City to study Spanish, begins chronicling his life in letters to his family.

February 1943–June 1944: Hillman attends Georgetown University in Washington, D.C., works part-time as a newsroom copy boy for a CBS radio station.

June 1944: Hillman joins the Navy.

Summer 1945: Hillman's introduction to the therapeutic, tending to blind veterans of World War Two, as part of the Navy Hospital Corps.

June 1946: Hillman accompanies his parents to Europe, becomes correspondent for American Forces Network in occupied Germany.

Early 1947: Hillman enrolls at the Sorbonne in Paris on the GI Bill.

Spring 1947: Hillman meets Kate Kempe at Paris club, falls madly in love. Hillman spends time with philosopher George Santayana.

November 1948: Hillman enrolls at Trinity College, Dublin. Becomes friends with future novelist J. P. Donleavy. Suffering from tuberculosis, spends several months at sanitarium in Switzerland.

1949: Hillman becomes associate editor for *Envoy* magazine, Dublin.

December 1950: Hillman graduates from Trinity College with MA in philosophy.

1951: Hillman travels with Kate and his friend Doug Wilson to Africa.

Summer 1951: Hillman and Kate go to Kashmir and settle there, where he begins work on a novel.

Summer 1952: Hillman meets Gopi Krishna in Kashmir. Hillman has "big dream" in the Himalayas that will send him into analysis eventually.

Fall 1952: Hillman marries Kate in Stockholm.

Spring 1953: Hillman and Kate enroll at the C. G. Jung Institute in Zürich.

1955: The Hillmans' first child, Julia, is born.

April 1956: Daughter Carola is born.

1959: Hillman graduates Summa cum laude from the University of Zürich and receives Analyst's Diploma from the Jung Institute.

1959—1969: Hillman serves as the first Director of Studies at Zürich's Jung Institute.

1960: Hillman's first book, *Emotion*, is published. A third daughter, Susanne, is born.

January 1961: A son, Laurence, is born.

June 1961: Jung dies.

Fall 1963: Hillman goes on lecture tour in America with Adolf Guggenbühl-Craig.

October 1964: Hillman gives new paper on "Betrayal" in London.

1965: Hillman's second book, *Suicide and the Soul*, is published.

Mid-1960s: Hillman learns that Kate has been having an affair with C. A. Meier, the analyst for both of them. Hillman's own affair with a married patient is subsequently exposed publicly, and Meier sides with the woman's husband in a court case against Hillman.

1966: Hillman is invited to be among the lecturers at the prestigious Eranos conference on Lago Maggiore, presenting "On Psychological Creativity."

1967: Hillman's third book, *InSearch: Psychology and Religion*, is published.

Fall 1968: Hillman accepts an invitation to teach at the University of Chicago, bringing his family along.

Early 1969: Hillman is forced to resign as Director of Studies at the Jung Institute.

March 1969: Hillman visits the Warburg Institute in London, and conceives archetypal psychology.

1

MEETING PAT BERRY

"Anima as relationship means that configuration which mediates between personal and collective, between actualities and beyond, between the individual conscious horizon and the primordial realm of the imaginal, its images, ideas, figures, and emotions . . . So, relationship governed by anima will show unstable paradoxes of longing and trepidation, involvement and skittishness, faith and doubt, and an intense sense of personal significance owing to the importance of the imaginal soul at large . . . such relationship reflects her as bridge to everything that is unknown."

—*James Hillman*, Anima.[1]

March 1966: When Patricia Berry arrived in Zürich, she had just turned twenty-three. A recent graduate of Ohio State University, she had plans to enroll at the Jung Institute with the vague notion of becoming a therapist. At that time anyone could attend who wanted, but nobody as young as Pat had ever applied. As a requirement for registration, she needed to be interviewed by the Institute's Director of Studies, James Hillman.

A year earlier, a boyfriend had given Pat a tape recording of a lecture recently delivered to a Ministers' Seminar at a Columbus, Ohio church, by an American psychologist named Hillman who Pat had never heard of.[2] She listened to it while alone in her room—in the house she shared with some other students. She found the voice "raspy, too far up in the head . . . discordant, strangulated as though perhaps his collar is too tight. [Yet] his elocution, certainly a continent away from anything heard in Ohio, is eloquent, elegant."[3] His was "the first voice I heard talking about [C. G.] Jung,"[4] whose writings she had recently discovered. The talk excited her.

That lecture would become the basis for Hillman's third book, *InSearch: Psychology and Religion.* The part that Pat remembered best focused on the anima, "those female images and impulses who pass through the corridors of our psyche—often silent, often neglected, sometimes cheapened, and certainly misunderstood," Hillman said. He elaborated that, as a man gets older, the weight he feels on the heart is the anima state. "This is the time when he is most vulnerable for the love-affair which may or may not solve something . . . *reorienting his usual habitual masculine point of view in terms of all the feminine values of life.*" [In the typescript of his talk, the italicized phrase was underlined for emphasis.] The feminine emotions "which depress and weaken us . . . peel off our crust, they soften our heart, they sap our right arm, in favor of the left where we are awkward and unable to manage."[5]

Pat had never thought of herself in anima terms before, but as Hillman spoke of various types of women, she thought that his description of "a cool distant Nordic type sounds a little like me."[6] A few weeks later, Pat's boyfriend followed up by giving her Hillman's latest book, *Suicide and the Soul*—published the year before. She could barely understand it. In a talk of her own, almost thirty years later, she said: "This isn't English as I've been taught, all the inverted syntax, the strange elliptical turns, arch and over-wrought I think, schizoid too. He seems to say that death is a possibility. You can die if you want, for the sake of your soul. Soul? Whatever soul is, he seems to be saying it can be more important than life."[7]

Although what Hillman expressed about the soul's connection to death eluded her, Pat had already found herself confronting mortality. Tall and athletic, she'd held a summer job as a camp counselor, taking teenagers on canoe outings. In the wilderness of upper Michigan, along a dangerous portion of a river filled with rapids and waterfalls, one of the girls ignored Pat's warnings and fell overboard. She became pinned under a log. Pat tried to wrestle the fifteen-year-old free, but couldn't. The girl drowned.

Pat blamed herself. "I took it as my narcissism, my heroic identification that caused her death," she remembered. "I just collapsed."[8] She returned to the university but found herself unable to finish papers. For a time, she dropped out. At one point, Pat even cut her wrist and was briefly hospitalized. In the course of a year, the drowning tragedy pushed Pat into therapy.

Psychology, she found, captivated her. When she returned to Ohio State, she became a straight-A student.

Early in 1966, Pat read a third piece by James Hillman, a pamphlet titled *Betrayal*. Pat recalled: "In it, he tells a story in which a father encourages a child to jump, to fling himself from the top of the stairs, the father promising to catch him. The boy jumps, and the father lets him fall. That's betrayal. And knowing that this may happen, that's trust."[9] The essential truth about trust and betrayal, Hillman went on to say, is that they contain each other. For her, "this was real psychology. No promises, disaster as a given."[10]

Pat was ambivalent about proceeding to graduate school in clinical psychology, with its heavy emphasis on statistics. She resonated with Jung; his posthumously-published autobiography *Memories, Dreams, Reflections* was captivating many young Americans at the time. In the meantime, Pat wound up spending a couple of evenings with Dr. Otis Maxfield, the Minister at Columbus' First Community Church. He had brought Hillman over from Switzerland to give the tape-recorded lecture that first intrigued her. Maxfield himself had taken some instruction at Zürich's Jung Institute. But there were no Jungian analysts in Ohio to work with, and Pat wasn't interested in Freudian psychoanalysis. So the minister suggested she travel to Europe. She could enroll in courses at the Institute and do the requisite therapy over there.

Pat initially discussed going abroad with the boyfriend who turned her on to Hillman—only to discover that he'd been sleeping with another girl. Here was the trust and betrayal . . . disaster as a given, that Hillman had described. She went instead with a girlfriend who wanted to explore Europe. Arriving in Zürich, Pat cancelled her first scheduled meeting with the Institute's Director of Studies after meeting a ski instructor. She took off with him, only to "get caught in a blizzard in the Alps, a blinding one. Somewhat shaken, and chastened, I return to the gray and dismal lowlands of Zürich and make another appointment."[11]

Pat first encountered Hillman in his ground floor office that had once been Jung's "retreat room" at the Institute—inside a tall Gothic, ivy-covered building of gray sandstone at Gemeindestrasse 27. Hillman was almost forty, wearing a tweed Irish-style suit, Pat remembered. She had long hair, "in Sixties style to conceal as much of myself as possible; what wasn't concealed, I covered with a dark raincoat down to my ankles."[12]

One of the purposes of the interview was to hear her story, and Pat "imagined that, since I was entering the realm of depth psychology . . . I should start by showing the damaged goods. So I opened up and bared what I thought of as my soul with a certain earnestness."[13] She may have spoken of never knowing her real father, and of being raised by a single mother who had Pat walking to nursery school by the age of two. Eventually, her mother remarried a gentleman named Berry and started a new family—Pat's two half-siblings were eight and ten years younger—and she'd grown up middle-class in Middletown, Ohio. But she kept her distance from others, "extremely self-sufficient for good and for ill." By her last year of high school, while elected president of the student council, Pat had "a completely secret life. I smoked, hung out with bad kids, was a rebel. Underneath, I felt lost. I didn't like dishonesty or sanctimoniousness. That quality connected me with Jim [Hillman] later, I think."[14]

Yet in general she found Hillman to be "a rather unsympathetic listener . . . polite, but obviously unimpressed." She arrived in Zürich with only three hundred dollars and, after she informed Hillman of this, immediately he "turned to practicalities. How did I think I was going to live in Zürich with no money? No possibilities for a job—it was illegal for a foreigner to work in Zürich—and no ability to speak the language. He told me I was crazy."[15]

Pat indeed felt she was "so screwed up [that] I needed the deepest analysis possible." So at the end of the interview, after Pat told him she was "interested in existential psychology" (the broadly humanistic approach that her Ohio therapist had practiced), Hillman suggested she go into Jungian analysis—not with himself, but with Hilda Binswanger. Hilda was the daughter of Ludwig Binswanger, who had been a renowned colleague of Jung's and considered the founder of existential psychology. She was also an older woman and a distant relation of Hillman's. And yes, Hillman told Pat, she could go ahead and enroll in classes at the Institute.

"A MASTER AT ANIMATING THE UNSEEN"

The Zürich atmosphere Pat Berry dove into seemed light years away from mid-1960s America. Formality reigned. Pat observed that women on the streets mostly wore dresses and anyone in pants received stares from passersby. Women's liberation was still a few years away in the U.S., but in the patriarchal culture of Zürich, women couldn't even vote (a referendum in 1971 would finally allow this). You didn't flush the toilet after 9 p.m. You didn't run your vacuum cleaner or wash your car on Sundays. Pat recalled getting "in trouble for all of those things, at one time or another, so I learned the rules."

What was it about Zürich and psychology? Adolf Guggenbühl-Craig, a close friend of Hillman's, and among the city's most prominent figures in Jungian psychology, once explained it this way: "England or France can be in this world by just being strong, militarily and otherwise. Small nations like Switzerland cannot dominate; they are always kind of molested and abused. So the only way they can survive is by being psychologically smart. There is a certain atmosphere of trying to figure out, what the hell does that other guy want? This is why the Swiss culture is gifted for psychology."[16]

Hilda Binswanger agreed to be Pat's analyst, and because Pat had so little money, Hilda charged her a mere ten francs (about two dollars) for the hour. But Pat found herself bored to tears. She recalled: "The truth was, I wasn't ready for Binswanger yet. I needed more spark, more challenge, more action."[17] Pat did take Hillman's emphasis on practicality as "a kind of challenge" and ended up living in a woman's basement room in exchange for cleaning the house. She spent her first months "eating a kind of mush paste . . . made by mixing water and *Birchermüesli* in a cup. It was a grim *Les Miserables* existence—grimmer yet because the classes at the Institute were so disappointing."[18]

Jung had died five years before, and most of the classes were taught by his now-elderly female followers—"worshipful people telling stories" rather than the serious academic studies of the great man's work that Pat had anticipated: "I didn't understand the place at all."[19] She recalled striding into the "miniscule library" at the Institute, lighting a cigarette, and saying to herself, "My God, at Ohio State at least we have libraries!" This seemed more like a church—and her personal "childhood experience of organized religion was that it was a breeding ground for hypocrisy."[20] She noted, though, that "just as I said that [about the library], I burned a huge blister in the palm of my hand."[21]

Pat soon fell into a depression, wondering what she was doing there. But she felt that she'd burned all her bridges. She did find one scintillating lecturer in Marie-Louise von Franz, on the archetypal symbolism in fairy tales. Pat recalled: "She would sit up there on the lecture platform with her legs splayed, her dirty fingernails, and hold forth with such passion and sparkle— it was truly exciting. She *was* the psyche."[22]

As Pat considered her second semester, Hillman was offering a class on "The Feeling Function" (which became part of a book co-authored with Marie-Louise von Franz, *Jung's Typology*). Pat enrolled, and found this to be "a whole other world . . . It was obvious from the start that feeling *per se* was not Hillman's strong suit,"[23] because he described feeling not as "a heartfelt emotion, but a coolly discriminating judging impersonal function. Watch out for people with feeling, he seemed to say, they're slick and they'll get you. Which is what I'd always suspected anyway. This man warmed my heart." For Pat, Hillman's words were not "clouded with the quasi-mystical tones and esoteric jargon of the other Institute classes," but "clear, intelligent, and original"[24]—containing both critical and scholarly levels "as well as an incredible symbolic sense."

The next class Pat took of Hillman's focused on animal images in dreams. It became apparent to her that his own instinctual energies were "a little odd." She remembered him "demonstrating baboon behavior to the class by jumping up and down, turning round and rubbing his behind in a way that was maybe not lewd but at least unusual."[25] "He was just so *alive*," Pat reflected, "and I could suddenly make sense of things. I understood his language and respected his way."[26]

After that second semester of classes ended, Pat asked Hillman if she could go into analysis with him. Hillman had been practicing since 1959, seeing several people a day and sometimes half-a-dozen on Saturdays. He had a second-story office with an anteroom, actually "a former servants room with an old iron and tile stove,"[27] overlooking a small courtyard at Zeltweg 16. Pat remembered: "To get to his office you went in through the back door of this very old building and climbed some very old steps, up four-and-a-half flights. Which was half a flight past Jim's office. There you sat on the landing, in a narrow wooden chair, and waited. The point was not to get comfortable. There were no magazines or anything like that."[28]

Upon finishing with one patient, he'd emerge from below, look up, and signal that your time was at hand. Hillman had other ways of prepping his patients, which aimed at ensuring they were emptied out and awake, ready to reveal and hear the unexpected. According to Pat, "First of all the time, it wasn't like the customary fifty-minute hour when you always begin on the hour or half-hour. You went to analysis with him at ten till, or twenty past, or twenty-five past. He had strange ways of deconstructing time . . . And it was also more of a platonic conversation, not always set in a particular room. Some people might have their analysis walking along the street. If Jim wanted a break, he'd take you to Beitner's coffee shop next door. As he ate his strudel, you'd tell him your dreams and do your analysis. Right there in the crowded restaurant! . . . If however he wasn't hungry, which was extremely rare . . . or if he had eaten with his patient before, which is more likely, then you had your analysis in his office."[29]

In his office, she and Hillman sat across from one another, perched bolt upright "on what were surely the most uncomfortable chairs ever invented." The chairs came from a junk give-away furniture place, the Swiss version of the Goodwill called the Brockenhaus. Hillman's private joke, which Pat never learned about until much later, was that the patient's chair had a seat that lifted up and contained a potty underneath.

Over Hillman's desk in fine golden frames were three pictures "of Chinese mythological horse-like animals with whiskers that twirled around into the air, and bits of mane that twirled this way and that, and then these eyes—bright brilliant crazy mythic eyes"[30]—fantastical creatures "*full* of energy and danger," which Pat came to feel "embodied so much of the spirit of what working with him was like." [31]

Her once-a-week analysis with Hillman occurred "much to the dismay" of Hilda Binswanger, a member of the Institute's governing Curatorium, "who didn't think this was a good idea at all." But one thing was immediately clear to Pat: unlike Binswanger, Hillman wasn't going to put her to sleep. "If it was challenge I was looking for, he gave it. In the first session he told me the problem was that I was stupid. I'd been called a lot of things in my life, but not usually that I was stupid, usually too *much* in my head."[32]

"At the very beginning stage, I kept trying to think the way I had in Ohio, in terms of normal psychology . . . where you tell all your bleeding heart stories."[33] But Hillman was "a master at animating the unseen . . . the psychic reality and power of one's images. In so doing, he brought the psyche as imagination to life in a way that I've never seen anybody else do. It was the passion of a fantast. His eyes would glitter, and I as an eager analysand would catch it and be running off to find books or looking up things in books he'd given me with a transferential fervor. He was an unusual analyst, a great one in a way. He certainly possessed a fire in the mind that others in my experience—and I've certainly had a lot of analysis and therapy—did not possess. He wasn't kindly, or even very related. But he *was* passionate."[34]

"He could bring dreams alive. He didn't put every part of the dream together into a structure ('this is because of this') so the whole dream made sense. Hillman would skim through the dream and he'd pick out this and that. He'd get an essence. He didn't try to explain all of the dream because that would put him into an explanation mode. That wasn't what he *did*. He touched the parts that had fire in them. It was astonishing to me that he didn't care about encompassing the entire dream, wrapping it up (as my other analysts had). He didn't explain it terms of types, ego-Self, or in any such ways. It taught me what psychological reality is all about. He made life meaningful, the things he did with my dreams put everything on a whole other level."[35]

One dream Pat recalled bringing to Hillman was "of a bug, a beetle, on my foot. I was horrified, but he said, oh, that's a scarab—the animal that pushes the dung and the Egyptians believed also pushes the sun along its course in the sky. So having that sense that there was something bigger than me, even connected with ancient Egypt but that had meaning for me right now—walking with this beetle on my foot, there was a direction, a stepping along into the future. That was the biggest gift in the world!"[36]

Hillman was himself going through a considerable self-examination over his role as a therapist. May 30, 1967 (during the same period Pat was seeing him), he wrote a letter to his friend Marvin Spiegelman—who'd been a student at the Institute alongside Hillman and then become a Jungian analyst in America: "During March I saw 17 different people in analysis. It was too much. I cut down. Now I see about 10–12 different people, some frequently and regularly and some every now and then . . . I am amazed how much more intense the hours used to be, and how half-assed they seem now. Yet, curiously people seem to find what I do and say has more weight if less brilliance."[37]

Hillman may have cryptically hinted at his impression of Pat at the time—although he does not name her specifically—in another letter written in the spring of 1967 to a different close friend in Jungian practice in America. "[T]he anima made a turn inward," Hillman wrote. "She is sort of a student type and leaves behind the outer involvements which [are] anyway departing for other reasons."[38]

"A HUGE TRANSFERENCE"

Among the Institute's students, Pat "met so many people who were afraid of Jim. Because he had no manners whatsoever in the classroom! Well, people's emotional [nature] was not where he was tuned in. He was interested in the ideas."[39] Audrey Haas, a student at the Institute in the mid-1950s—who also later went into analysis with Hillman—tells this story: "I remember a time when Jim was in the corridor—maybe he'd been lecturing—but I went up to him and was telling him about some problems that young friends of mine were having. And he just wheeled on me and said: 'I'm not interested in all these young people! It's the old ones I care about! The ones with no hope!' I turned and walked away. He was still screaming at me. He would do that. One time I saw him up at the swimming pool, the Dolder, which we all went to in the summer. I went brightly over and said, 'Hi, Jim.' He sort of said 'Hi' back and turned away. At our next analysis, he said, 'What makes you think that I want to see you and I'm so thrilled when you come along.'"[40]

Liliane Frey, who taught at the Institute and had once been Hillman's analyst, used to warn Pat about him. "She said he hadn't been properly analyzed and he hadn't developed his male energy. 'What about his mother complex, his anima stuff?' With Frey, that was something to be careful of. And, you know, he *was* dangerous. And he was also incredible."

To survive in Zürich, Pat took one job after another as an *au pair*. She started with a Swiss family, but was then hired to watch

the four children of Thayer and Anita Greene, who were studying at the Institute and eventually became analysts. Pat was even
flown to the States during the summer with their family. Her
final experience as a live-in *au pair* was for Joan Buresch, at the
time a single mother. Buresch was the daughter of former CIA
director Allen Dulles, who had gotten to know Jung while in
Switzerland during the Second World War. Her mother had seen
Jolande Jacobi for therapy, and in 1964, Buresch herself decided
to train at the Institute to become a Jungian analyst.

Buresch attended some of Hillman's lectures. And it was this
daughter of America's secret-keeper, Pat remembered, who one
night told her about Hillman's affair with a female patient in her
twenties, whose clergyman husband had found out about and
exposed to the Jung Institute's hierarchy. This had taken place
late in 1965, a few months before Pat arrived in Zürich. The
situation had become a full-blown scandal within the Jungian
world in Zürich, a subject explored in depth in Volume I of this
biography.

At her next therapy session with Hillman, Pat decided to tell
him what she'd learned from Buresch about the scandal. "He
called me up that same evening and asked me to meet him for
a beer in town," Pat remembered, "which I thought was very
strange, but I did. And he said, 'Now I don't think you really
told me what you meant to say, about what you thought of that
affair.' And I said, 'Oh no, I did.' I think he'd expected me to say,
'I'm angry about it,' or 'How could you my analyst do that?' But
that wasn't what I felt at all. I mean, really I just wanted to tell
him that I knew about it. So we sat and drank beer and ate food.
After that, I don't think we talked about it again, in the analysis."

Pat was by now experiencing what she later recalled as "a
huge transference" with Hillman. She was starting to fall in
love with him. Sometime during her first year in analysis with
him, she had what she later described as a major individuation
dream—the process of integrating the unconscious with consciousness on the path toward wholeness, or what Jung called
self-actualization. "I was at Bellevue Platz with a crowd of

people and there was a unicorn, and I put the tips of my fingers against the velvety [part] of the unicorn. That was numinous. The unicorn took me through the crowd by keeping my fingers on it."[41] Pat elaborated later that the skin on the unicorn that her fingers were touching "was unmistakably the delicate skin on the head of a penis. It is a bit embarrassing, but it did occur during my work with Jim and did have to do with my being in love with him psychologically and eventually physically."[42]

If Hillman felt similarly at that time, it went unspoken. He remained concerned about Pat having so little money. At one point, she "did get some sort of job in the mountains and Jim thought it was crazy for me to leave the Institute, a real waste of time." So he paid her to come by his office periodically and help him with filing papers. Hillman also hired Pat to come to his home up on the hill by the Zürich zoo and teach sports to his four children. That is where she met his wife Kate. Pat would go there once a week, take the two youngest (Susanne and Laurence) for jaunts in the woods and "run them around the yard." For a time, she even stayed at the Hillman's house after she fell and hurt her back in their yard. The relationship between Kate and Pat took a downturn when Pat sent flowers to thank her hosts, but only addressed them to Jim.

Then, finally, Pat landed a position at the American High School, an English-speaking school for U.S. families temporarily living in Zürich. This came about after Hillman organized a baseball team at the Institute, which included Pat, and they played a game against the high school's teachers. Afterward, the principal, John Mattern, approached Pat and asked if she'd like a job. She would teach English to the boys and sports to the girls.

Pat continued to take classes at the Jung Institute. At that time, you paid only for individual classes, unlike at an American university where you signed up for a semester: "You pretty much just did what you wanted, attended if and when you wanted." She recalled Hillman inviting guest lecturers. He would customarily go to their talks, but often fall asleep in a corner.

During her first semester, one night she attended a student party at the magnificent home of Jungian analysts Heinrich and Linda Fierz-David overlooking Zürich Lake. "On the walls, and even the ceilings, were alchemical and symbolic images, painted all over the place," Pat remembered. "We looked at all this for a while, it was mind-boggling. Then someone . . . put on American music and we began to dance." Suddenly, "a man from across the room started mimicking my movements, gave them back to me with such depth and decisiveness that I was transfixed." He was "a short, bull-shaped Cuban in his forties," and he soon introduced himself. They talked; he was brilliant. That night, Pat dreamt that the man "had sired a huge group of children, of all sizes and ages."[43]

This was, it turned out, Hillman's close friend Rafael López-Pedraza. He had come to Zürich in 1963 from London—where he'd been in Jungian analysis—carrying a letter from his therapist recommending him to Hillman. On his second day in Zürich, López started analysis with Hillman, and continued going three days a week. As time went on, Hillman would remember, "We had many, many discussions about lofty things. Rafael had endlessly inspiring insights, often incomprehensible but remarkable twists. Also, his way of living was so shadowy. He'd left Cuba when the revolution happened [during Fidel Castro's takeover in 1959]. No one knew what he did before he came here, whether he was a drug runner or supposed to have worked for a pharmaceutical company, who knows what."[44] As Pat put it, "Rafael was a huge natural force. And Jim saw Rafael's genius."

Despite their age difference, Pat and López quickly became friends: "I think because Rafael liked to talk a lot and needed somebody to listen to him, and for me because he was not like the Institute. I wanted to learn from him. And I couldn't often grasp what he was saying, so I had to learn to listen, to not know, to have a sense that there was something pulling me beyond my own concepts, my own understanding, and just live with it."[45]

Much of what she learned, Pat reflected later, came "as a maenad under his [López's] direction . . . Our knowledge and experience and levels of culture were radically disparate. He became for me a kind of teacher or guru that I hung out with, practically lived with." López would hold small meetings in an empty room at the Institute and "from him in that time, I learned how to think upside down."[46] Pat would also later call his teaching "water for the soul."[47]

Attending the Institute at the same time as Pat was Valerie Donleavy, whom Hillman had known since he attended Trinity College in Dublin (1948–50). Valerie was married to J. P. Donleavy, Hillman's longtime close friend and by now a world-renowned novelist—author of *The Ginger Man*. (See Volume I for the Hillman-Donleavy relationship.) Valerie's mother, a fervent Jungian, had lived part-time in Zürich during the 1950s. Valerie decided to leave Ireland after she and J. P. separated and sign up for classes at the Jung Institute. There, although she and her husband would not formally divorce until 1969, she fell in love with López-Pedraza.

Valerie was tall, willowy, and beautiful, her long black hair often tied up in a bow. Not long after the party by the lake where Pat encountered López, she and Valerie met and became instant friends. While Pat was young and described herself as "naïve," Valerie "was a sort of older woman with much more experience and embodied in the world," Pat recalled. At the close of her workday at the American High School, Pat was "most often with Valerie or Rafael or both of them. Though I was eating now, I still didn't have a bath or even hot water for that matter, so I bathed in Rafael or Valerie's bathroom. They had adjoining rooms in an apartment building in the Niederdorf, which is Zürich's red-light district. Jim would sometimes come by and, since I was part of the group, I got to know him socially as well."[48]

The personal connection grew between Hillman and Pat. "When we were still having a flirtation, he was explaining to me how to do a chart," she recalled. Hillman had studied astrology in the 1950s with Jung's daughter, Greta Baumann. Hillman's wife Kate had four planets in the zodiacal sign of

Sagittarius, including her Sun sign. Pat was born under the sign of Capricorn, but had Sagittarius rising or Ascendant. Hillman himself had no planets in Sagittarius. "So they fill a gap in my horoscope," he believed, "either a complement to the Aries fire [Hillman's Sun and Moon were closely aligned in Aries] or to my Ascendant opposite [from Sagittarius], in Gemini."[49]

1968 became a tumultuous year. In France and in Germany, university students rioted. In the States, Martin Luther King and Robert Kennedy were assassinated and, while the Vietnam War raged on, in August the Democratic Convention in Chicago erupted in violence. That same month, Soviet tanks rolled into Czechoslovakia to quell rising dissidence there.

That year, Hillman moved part-time to an Italian-speaking region of Switzerland called the Tessin, located several hours' drive south of Zürich in the small town of Ascona. It was one of several stunningly beautiful places that Hillman often found himself blessed to work. The house looked out upon beautiful Lake Maggiore, amid a panoramic vista of glaciered alps commingled with palm trees. "One spends a lot of time fixing ovens and brickets [sic] and ashes, and there are 30 steep steps, outside, to the kitchen two floors below," Hillman described in a letter to his mother.

The property belonged to the Eranos Foundation, which Jung had pioneered in the 1930s. Hillman went there in 1968 to prepare his summer lecture for the annual gathering of multidisciplinary scholars at Eranos. His previous year's talk, titled *The Language of Psychology and the Speech of the Soul*, had been a major success. He had taken up the theme of sexuality and the psyche's craving "to submit in some form, in any form, to Eros—Eros at any price—in order to disengage itself from the imperious materialist inflation of the nineteenth century's insistence that the psyche belongs only to the mind."[50] The "Sexual Revolution" of the 1960s was in full bloom as well.

Talking to Pat over the phone from the Tessin, Hillman suddenly found a scorpion in his shoe; he didn't say what he did with it. When he returned to Zürich, he took Pat and a friend of hers out to dinner after a public event. Pat believed Hillman might be making a play for her friend. She felt shocked, enraged, even physically ill. Later that night, she called and told him so. Hillman took her out the next afternoon for a steak and a glass of red wine. They ended up in his office, where they lay together—nothing beyond that—on the analytical couch. There followed, she would recall, "wild phone calls, tentative meetings, terror over what this might all mean."[51] They went to dinner again at a restaurant called Mövenpick, the German word for "seagull peck." That night, two years after their first meeting, they became intimate. It was early fall. Pat planned to stop seeing Hillman for analysis.

They had only been together for two weeks; nobody knew except Valerie and Rafael. But Hillman was soon to take a leave-of-absence from the Jung Institute and take his family across the Atlantic to the University of Chicago for several months—to teach a seminar positing an alchemical basis for depth psychology. "We had a final meal in a very nice restaurant, Kronenhalle," Pat remembered. (This was where Hillman always dined, alone, after the birth of each of his children). "Then he was at my house in the Niederdorf, and just sort of jauntily went off. All my abandonment stuff from childhood rose up. I went down to the street with him and, as Jim was getting into the cab, he didn't duck down. He hit his head on the door. He made a joke of it. And I thought: 'Serves him right.'"

She also recalled: "As we were first getting together, I had dreamt a dream in which a woman stood in a field poised, slanted forward, with her head forward against a man's head, who with his tongue in her mouth pushed her backwards, making of her a plow that opened the earth."[52]

Asked many years later about the shift from being in analysis to having a relationship with Hillman, Pat responded: "It was wonderful! I have no sense that it shouldn't have happened . . . What was difficult was the fact that he was married. That was awful and I felt terrible about it. But for me it was a natural shift from one state of being to another. I think I knew in my soul that I was going to learn a lot more from him that way."[53]

LETTERS FROM CHICAGO

In autumn 1968, along with Kate and their four children, Hillman took up residence as a visiting professor at the University of Chicago, where he would find the seminar students "a broody lot [with] their minds overblown (pot and ideas)." In a letter postmarked October 21, 1968, addressed to Miss Patricia Berry at 29 Spiegelgasse in Zürich, Hillman began by describing a dream in which they phoned each other simultaneously, "synchronistically communicating." In the dream, Pat had indicated that his "anima mood" was not what she wanted. This, Hillman said, confirmed something inside him, although he felt "seriously disoriented" in Chicago, as though "in a backwater, biding time." He appreciated that she'd also told him in a letter about a dream ("a boy writing about a snake") and that he too "had one important dream of writing." This led him to "believe we have a connection here," and he urged Pat to pursue it further. "You may write me all you can, all you dare," he replied. Hillman closed with a handwritten postscript also referencing a snake, about a young woman who lived next door in Chicago and had a pet python: "We all held it yesterday. Wow."

In Hillman's absence, Pat was teaching English at Zürich's American High School. Apparently responding to something she'd said about how difficult she found the job, he elaborated in a handwritten letter postmarked the same day: "Sorry school is as it is. If you would write & *publish*, you could say 'Fuck-you-all' to the parents & they could say nothing back. Find your love for English & for the kids & never mind the parents." He himself was "trying, today, to do what I came for—write a new book (rewrite senex-puer). So today I begin to work on the *puer* rewrite chapter. I *hate* college atmosphere . . . How do you find the Senex chapter? Indicate your suggestions!! if any."

Handwritten and postmarked October 28, 1968: "I am shocked by your importance. At times I feel—against all my will—that you are the one who now carries a too-large piece of my future." This statement could be interpreted in different ways. He'd been going through difficult times with Kate for some time, certainly since he discovered her affair with C. A. Meier. He often chafed at family responsibilities that interfered with his work. Did Pat offer Hillman a way out against his will? While Hillman remained her teacher—and convinced of her potential—did he intuit that Pat was to become a "too-large" partner in his future work?

Hillman saved some of Pat's letters to him from that period, and at some point returned them to her. Her first response that has survived is handwritten—dated, Sunday, November 3.

"Dear Jim . . . I felt for the first time a communication via mail with you. Connected me to myself and the love, so that I could finally begin psychic work within it. The problem before (and which always threatens me) is the thread of unreality. Then I find myself bombarded with stimuli & unable to cope. Now I have at least a starting point . . .

"In the past I've been so hung up, caught in people & relationship—extraversion, partying, talking (which I love so much)—I was a part of each of them, lost in all of them in the name of soul, comradeship, humanity . . . Now I have a scent which I must follow—and develop until it permeates all through me— Alone, keep it, love it, submit, live it . . .

"Please give care to yourself too—the anima who continually betrays you to the world, can't hold, feels guilty or whatever . . .

"Been doing a lot of writing (speaking of limitations)—*desperately* important to me! Still not enough, never enough time— need rites of entry & departure—keep that fuckin' snake out of my hair . . . Love Pat."

In another letter, typewritten (November 5), Pat reports hearing voices and sets forth a long dialogue between "Voice" and "I," in what Jung had described as an "active imagination." The Voice suggested she move beyond "the animus and being notably Capricornian. You should know better, using that tone of voice, pretending to be talking to an Aries" [Hillman's birth sign]. Pat ("I") wondered: "So maybe I'm not really talking to him," and the Voice concurred, asking her to "give the feminine a chance too, she feels a bit left out." At first, Pat ("I") dismissed this as "her problem. She would only eat it, swallow it, betray it, ride the breeze of it, whiff away on it; least resistance would be the way. I want *lead!*"

> **Voice:** You are all in the head.
> I: I know that I wear myself out that way, besides I never win.
> Voice: It's all so heavy, heavy!
> I: Oh, I know, if only I could float up just once rather than fighting to the top every time.
> Voice: But you like to fight, don't you?
> **I:** I really do—left over from a street gang animus somewhere, not very sophisticated.
> I: Have we reached any agreement?
> Voice: Of course not.
> I: But I hold the typewriter.
> Voice: Today you do, tomorrow perhaps we'll switch places.
> I: I don't mind—just so we get to fight.
> Voice: I might make you speechless, you know.
> I: Yes, you *do* do that, you bastard.
> Voice: Well, at least you'll get a rest.
> I: That's the first nice thing you've said.

Pat's psychological dialogue with her unconscious moved Hillman powerfully. In his response (postmarked November 18, 1968), he called her letter "*superb*," adding:

"I begin to get your originality, not that I haven't felt it, but now it's getting to come over as a distinct personality, a style, of influences mixed in your special way of opposites, (the culture and the rawness, the hick and the subtlety, the complexities and the naivties [sic], and your own use of language. I feel you as a person distinct from my images and memories of you. Great this."

Describing the revising of his work on "Senex and Puer," he concludes: "Yes the historical part of my paper was first rate. You have no idea what it is to *REWRITE* psychiatric history to see it all anew afresh different from all the texts, and to prove your point of view in the welter of all the details of history, and to face the doubts that experts will find you wrong. I did all that this past year in the midst of all else."

In her next responses, Pat tells of needing some help to cope with the difficulties of being in relationship with a married man, and of having begun to see a woman Jungian analyst. Ironically, her choice was Pit Pope, once a student at the Institute with Hillman and who with her husband used to play tennis with James and Kate. Hillman was nonetheless "delighted you took the step," and Pat protected their relationship by lying that her affair was with a married man in Germany named Jason. Pat went on:

"[Pope] seems to have accepted my squeemishness [sic] about details. I explain that I'm terrified that anyone should ever happen to meet Jason; it's my craziness and part of the insecurity I feel concerning the whole thing. She says that is understandable (under her breath: with my mother problem, that is) and pushes me not at all. I rather enjoy the eccentricity of all this . . . I have admitted that the situation is doomed in reality and she caught on strongly at this point. So we move from there."

After the teaching term ended at the University of Chicago in mid-December, Hillman made plans to head with his family to a dude ranch in Arizona for Christmas. "Watch rattlesnakes & sunstroke," Pat had concluded one of her letters. First, Hillman flew to Florida to meet his friend Adolf Guggenbühl-Craig, just arrived from Zürich to give a few days of joint lectures with him. Guggenbühl brought news. "When you come back to Zürich, I think you will no longer be director of studies," he told Hillman. "What happened while you were away is that you've been eased out."[54] The president of the Jung Institute had finally bowed to the pressure of the furor still swirling over Hillman's affair with a patient several years before.

In his last letter to Pat from the road (December 16), Hillman didn't mention what he'd learned about his fate from Guggenbühl. He said only that he was flying west for "3 days of all-day seminars at U. So. Cal. It is not amusing, since I'm often very 'off,' split, manic/or depressed." He also spoke briefly of "2 whopping dreams, (I have few) and you were a *MAJOR* figure. You were either my *daughter* or the *mother of my 2 younger children*. At end of dream we both had trouble with our *shoes*. We must talk of all this . . .

"You cannot guess how much I look forward to returning to Zürich, and seeing you . . . Things have happened to me, but I don't know at all what they are. It's sure not up front."

In her final letter to him from that period, Pat wrote: "I keep having browsing fantasies for you—to spend leisurely days, weeks, months just browsing through a large library—following delightful little snips and waiting, just keeping an eye out for the larger things to come when and if they will."

James Hillman returned to Zürich, to the house on the hill by the zoo with his wife and four children, to submit his forced resignation to the Jung Institute, with "no practice, no teaching, no work"[55] in sight, and to another relationship that almost no one knew about. Pat Berry's "browsing fantasies" would soon prove to be prescient.

NOTES

1. "Anima as relationship. . . .": James Hillman, *Anima: An Anatomy of a Personified Notion*, Woodstock, Ct.: Spring Publications, Inc., 1985, p. 39.
2. Unless otherwise cited, the anecdotal stories and quotes from Pat Berry are taken from interviews with the author in October 2007; August 2008; September 2013, and May 2014, as well as email correspondence.
3. The voice was "raspy. . . .": Transcript made by author of Pat Berry audiotaped talk, "Reminiscences and Reflections," at the Notre Dame Festival of Archetypal Psychology, July 10, 1992.
4. "the first voice I heard talking about Jung. . . .": Robert and Janis Henderson, *Living With Jung*, Volume 1, New Orleans: Spring Journal Books, 2006, p. 165.
5. "those female images and impulses . . . awkward and unable to manage": James Hillman, "The Inner Femininity: Towards the Religious Moment."
6. "a cool distant Nordic type. . . .": Pat Berry talk at Notre Dame.
7. "This isn't English as I've been taught. . . .": Pat Berry talk at Notre Dame.

8. Berry recounted the story of failing to save the girl to Nancy Robinson-Kime, transcript of interview for *Side By Side*, 2014.
9. Berry on *Betrayal* lecture: Notre Dame talk.
10. Berry on *Betrayal*: Notre Dame talk.
11. "We got caught in a blizzard. . . .": Notre Dame talk.
12. Berry's hair and raincoat: Notre Dame talk.
13. Berry telling her story: Notre Dame talk.
14. Berry on childhood: Michael Lerner podcast.
15. Hillman "turned to practicalities. . . .": Notre Dame talk.
16. On the Swiss gift for psychology: Author interview with Adolf Guggenbühl-Craig, Zürich, May 2005.
17. "The truth was, I wasn't ready for her yet. . . .": Berry interview with Lyn Cowan at "These Women," a symposium sponsored by the Institute for Cultural Change, Santa Barbara, Ca., summer 2011.
18. Berry on survival in early days in Zürich: Notre Dame talk.
19. Berry's initial impression of the Jung Institute: interview with Lyn Cowan.
20. "childhood experience of organized religion. . . .": *Living with Jung*, p. 179.
21. "What I found instead . . . palm of my hand": *Living With Jung, p. 166*.
22. On von Franz: *Living With Jung*, p. 177.
23. Hillman on "The Feeling Function: *Jung's Typology*, p. 144.
24. Berry on Hillman lectures: Notre Dame talk.
25. Hillman's class on animal images in dreams: Notre Dame talk.
26. "I could suddenly make sense of things. . . .": Side by Side.
27. "a former servants room. . . ." Hillman letter to J. P. Donleavy, August 2, 1958.
28. "To get to his office. . . ." Notre Dame talk.
29. Hillman's different approach to analysis: Notre Dame talk and Lerner podcast.
30. "of Chinese mythological horse-like animals. . . .": Berry interview with Lyn Cowan, summer 2011.
31. Full of energy and danger. . . ." Side by Side.
32. "embodied so much of the spirit . . . usually too much in my head": Notre Dame talk.
33. "where you tell all your bleeding heart stories. . . .": Side by Side.
34. "a master at animating the unseen. . . .": Notre Dame talk.
35. "He could bring dreams alive. . . ." Side by Side.
36. Berry on her beetle dream: interview with Lyn Cowan, summer 2011.
37. Hillman letter to Spiegelman, May 30, 1967 (Robert Hinshaw files, Einsedeln, Switzerland).
38. "I am in good shape. . . .": Hillman letter to Robert Stein, Spring 1967.
39. "met so many people who were afraid. . . .": Notre Dame talk..
40. Author interview with Audrey Haas, Zürich, May 2005.
41. Unicorn dream: Side by Side.
42. "unmistakably the delicate skin. . . .": Berry email to author, July 4, 2014.
43. Berry meeting Lopez: Notre Dame talk.
44. Hillman on Lopez: Author interview.
45. Berry on her friendship with Löpez: interview with Lyn Cowan, summer 2011.
46. "from him in that time, I learned how to think upside down": Author interview with Berry,
47. "water for the soul": Larner podcast.
48. Berry's friendship with Valerie Donleavy and Lopez: Notre Dame talk.

49. "They fill a gap in my horoscope. . . .": Author interview with Hillman.

50. Psyche's craving "to submit in any form. . . .": *The Myth of Analysis: Three Essays in Archetypal Psychology*, Evanston, Ill: Northwestern University Press, originally pub. 1972; 1997 paperback edition, p. 148.

51. "wild phone calls. . . .": Notre Dame talk

52. Berry dream of woman in a field: Notre Dame talk.

53. "It was wonderful. . . .": Side by Side.

54. "When you come back to Zürich. . . .eased out": Hillman interviews with author, 2007 and 2008.

55. "no practice, not teaching, no work. . . .": JH letter to Marvin Spiegelman, copy provided author by Spiegelman.

2

BEGINNINGS OF ARCHETYPAL PSYCHOLOGY

"When you read the presocratics read them not just in terms of philosophy, but also as fragments that say something about the psyche, about human life, for example Herakleitos is a favorite of mine . . . these old guys were mad and great."
—James Hillman, in a letter to his nephew
Roger Sternfeld, mid-1960s.

"There is nothing permanent except change."
—Herakleitos, 535–475 B.C.

Toward the end of 1968, shortly before Hillman finished his three months of teaching in the U.S., Valerie Donleavy wrote to him from Zürich. She and Rafael López-Pedraza were just back from a trip to London, and she had a dream that Rafael asked her to write about Hillman, "as he felt it might cheer you."

Valerie's recollection of the dream went like this: "In a large wooden room were most of the Jungian people. The classics and you, Rafael and Guggenbühl and others. There was a lot of discussion etc. Then all the classics filed out and while they were doing so, I went over and sat by Rafael. Then you, Guggenbühl, Rafael and I and probably a few others set out on a long journey through a dense forest of spruce and firs. It was a virgin forest. I pointed out a river which was flowing down a ravine over rocks. The water was a deep translucent green . . . I felt a sort of relief after it."[1]

A dense virgin forest with a deep translucent green river . . . This was around the same time as Pat's letter urging Hillman toward "keeping an eye out for the larger things to come when and if they will." Both women knew that Hillman was going through a rough time ("Dear Jim you really have sounded miserable and desolate," Valerie had written him). So describing their dreams and fantasies might be viewed as attempts to make him feel better. Or, perhaps, they presaged something that would soon emerge from one of the most uncertain times in Hillman's life.

Hillman's return to Zürich brought the denouement of his long battle to preserve his reputation and job at the Jung Institute. The previous April of 1968, a Swiss court had ruled that Hillman had misused "in an 'extreme,' 'stubborn' and persistent way a 'pronounced relationship of trust' toward his younger and married patient" and thus "greatly injured" the woman's American minister husband, whose demand to the Institute's governing Curatorium for Hillman's dismissal was "not without reason."[2] Hillman had to pay the man a fine, although less than half of what the husband had demanded. Pressured by several of the Institute's patrons in Zürich's Office of Education, he might not only be ousted by the Institute, he could also be ordered by the police to leave the country entirely.

The situation wasn't just disheartening to Hillman. Glin Bennet, whose father had been close to Jung and was a friend of Hillman's from his Trinity College days, wrote him: "It seems to me tragic and against all but their meanest self-interest that anyone should want you to leave after all you have accomplished. And tragic that this seat of wisdom should be swayed by such pettiness. If the great man [Jung] were still with us, this would never have happened, but a broad view of life seems to have passed with him and the least desirable aspect of Swiss parochialism prevailed."[3]

Hillman himself "felt very relieved to be out, but the transition time is extremely hard for Kate and for me. Everything is 'up in the air again.' One reconsiders the whole life pattern and questions what to do how to do it etc." He was writing daily but "it is not easy, for I am FULL OF DOUBT."[4]

In the book *Inter Views* (1980), Hillman spoke of his simultaneous decision to also cease therapeutic practice. "I thought nothing I had done from '55 to '69 was authentic, that everything I did I had learnt. It was like an illness, a physical illness, and when anybody mentioned patients, my whole body moved away from it . . . I didn't want anything to do with analysis."[5]

Images from past sessions with patients would resurface and nauseate him. "I realized what oppression doing therapy had been, what a burden, how much guilt was involved, how I was carrying people, how I was trying to make them well, how I was . . . oh, my goodness!"[6] All Hillman says about the personal context in *Inter Views* is that this "took place at the same time as my first marriage was untying," but clearly his reaction had to do with the scandal surrounding his affair with the minister's wife—as well as the burgeoning relationship with another former analysand.

The secret affair between Hillman and Berry resumed as soon as he returned to Zürich, primarily in the room where she was staying—a relationship she later reflected was tempestuous "in the beginning, because I was the other woman, and I don't know anybody who knows how to live that [easily]. So during that time, we fought."[7]

In later life, Hillman reflected that, even before encountering Pat, he'd been "torn between two families, split apart. Kate couldn't get tied into my work, so we had the traditional problem of the woman taking care of the children and the house while the man goes out to do his work. Which didn't make Kate happy at all; it wasn't her nature to be a housewife. But she didn't have her own work and she couldn't really work with me. So she was in a trap and couldn't find her way out. If she had, things might have been very different. At least my children sometimes think so. I went with the 'other family,' the writing. That's what ended the marriage, in a deeper sense."[8]

It was an attitude shared by most men with families in the patriarchal world of that era, that it wasn't part of their job to understand the broader interests of their wives. Pat Berry, as a working colleague, provided reinforcement in that sense. Kate was not such a collaborator. And why *should* she have been? In his elder years, Hillman would recall that Kate was in fact an extremely creative person in her own right, but he hadn't valued it. His own psychological development vis-à-vis women would require decades to unfold.

As a younger man, his "other family" of writing disclosed his infidelity to Jungian orthodoxy. Hillman described this in a letter written in the spring of 1969, to a man who'd sent him two letters about defining the ego: "I think Jung for all his getting away from the protestant extraverted ego of will and reason, still has the old ego implied in his introverted techniques: responsibility, *active* imagination, and all the things the ego does in connection with the unconscious. The very notion of developing oneself is hung up with old ego ideals . . . Look, the whole bag has to be re-worked; all of it."[9]

TWO FRIENDS

Re-working "the whole bag" of analytical psychology was initially very much a joint venture between Hillman and his two friends of vastly different temperaments: Rafael López-Pedraza and Adolf Guggenbühl-Craig. López, as noted earlier, had arrived in Zürich in 1963 and immediately entered three-days-a-week analysis with Hillman—upon recommendation of his London therapist Irene Claremont de Castillejo. (López remained fond of quoting Castillejo's dictum: "Emotion always has its roots in the unconscious and manifests itself in the body.") López later reflected: "Hillman was in his best shape at the time, he possessed a very special openness and feeling for psychotherapy."[10]

López had quickly decided to become a Jungian analyst himself, although much at the Zürich Institute was new to him. While taking courses in religious studies, mythology, psychopathology, and Jungian theory, he "learned remarkable notions in anthropology." He studied with the old guard—learning Jolande Jacobi's systems for deciphering patients' paintings and from Marie-Louise von Franz's seminars "that the psyche has what I call a 'fairy tale level' . . . easily noticed in anyone" (and, after someone has lived for a while in a fairy tale psychology, it is followed by its opposite, which is tragedy). He read Greek mythology in Karl Kerényi's books, and a paper about the instincts by Jung that he found "fundamental." In all these ways, he seemed to be following Hillman's earlier path of study.

However, after completing his internship with Hillman's distant cousin Ludwig Binswanger, López started working at the Klinik am Zürichberg soon after it opened, and was put in charge of the painting workshop with "very sick patients." His means of relating were unusual, including Sunday walks in the hills where "some patients threatened to jump off a cliff," weekly dances that proved "a great therapeutic experience," and "a couple of times I even went out to a night club with a group of patients." Therapy was constant; even the Klinik's cook participated.[11]

Pat later wrote about López's unique therapeutic approach in an essay titled *Echo's Passion*: "He'd take people out of hospitals who had been there most of their lives and teach them how to live alone and keep house for themselves. He'd instruct them in shopping at the market, washing dishes, ironing . . . The trick is that for him these mundane chores were full of echo. If someone had been ironing, he'd say, 'Aha, you're ironing? Ironing, hum-uh, ironing!' Echo was there in the word, in the activity. He didn't interpret—'Your ironing is like flattening out your mother' or 'Your ironing is because you were never allowed to iron as a child.' Rather, he preserved the echo in the word and thus in the activity."[12] Pat said elsewhere, only partly tongue-in-cheek: "It was Rafael who taught me that the way to get well was to take on patients, and let them carry the madness for you."[13]

Fellow Jungian analyst Robbie Bosnak, remembered an episode that occurred after López had completed analytical training: "The best Rafael story I remember was when one of his patients called him and said she was going to kill herself. He said, 'Send me a postcard,' and hung up on her. She got so enraged that she came to the next session."[14]

López put it like this in a 2003 interview with Axel Capriles: "I understand the psychic world as being based on the emotions, which are irrational. Emotion has its origins in the classical Greek world: *pathos*/pathology. If psychotherapy does not touch emotional levels, it does not touch what is deeply paralyzed and ill, hence there is no transformation." It seemed to

López that Jung "did not value the whole catalogue of emotions contained in the irrational world." Thus did Jungian psychology become, he believed, "stuck in concepts." By contrast, a study of archetypes focused on symbols and images. "I think our interest was to conceive a psychology focused essentially in the here and now where the life of feeling and emotion is."[15]

The "our" refers to his relationship with Hillman, who recalled in our interviews: "By the time '69 arrived, I had awakened from some psychological idealizations—the sort of thing that anybody who's in a cult wakes up to at some point. It isn't that [the Jungian world] was a cult, it's that the cult mentality affects people who are in such spiritualized groups, who have certain spiritual ambitions like wider consciousness or individuation or whatever. Rafael was extremely important in that regard. López was a shadowy figure in a Swiss world—though he wouldn't be as much so in the Latin world. He was an auto-didact, he taught himself. On the one hand, he was very orthodox. He believed in asylums, in proper psychiatry. He believed in taking Jung's ideas and working them in his way. He was not revolutionary, never offended the establishment, he was very cautious. He just did it differently. For example, anytime anybody said anything about the church or religion, he said 'I have nothing to do with that.' He had a kind of psychic street smarts."[16]

By 1966, Hillman had begun writing letters to Marvin Spiegelman and Robert Stein, his Jewish-American friends from student days at the Institute, revealing the influence that López was having on him. : "The older generation for all their virtues fail somewhere in their emotional reactions. As López says, we must stop talking of the puer problem and begin to speak of the senex problem—that is now the problem in our group."

This letter, written the same month that Pat Berry arrived in Zürich, went on: "The younger students are beginning to wake up, very slowly of course, that there is such a thing as a 'new analysis.' López coined this term."[17]

That same year, Hillman wrote that the people he sees in Zürich "are all outsiders," with López topping the list. And since

"López . . . has neither money nor permit," the Jungians attack him as "the weakest one."[18] Hillman wrote to Rudolf Ritsema, organizer of the prestigious Eranos conferences, introducing López as "a valuable person," and conveying that López wished to attend at least part of the next one but might need some financial help.[19]

In May 1967, he wrote: "Yes, the old Zürich of our 1950s is dead, but there is a new Zürich forming for the 1970s; it's happening very fast too and in many directions. López is a key figure in it all."[20]

He added in another letter: "López and I have done much talking about the Fool . . . just the foolishness makes us human, real psychologists (understanders of the psyche) and on the edge." That edge, Hillman added, was where true insights come from.

López wrote to Hillman about a dream he had (December 13, 1968): "I had the insight that I was a street dog, that that was my actual nature."

According to Pat Berry, Hillman would "shelter somebody who was odd in a way that caught Jim's fancy . . . [whom] he would then protect, or help, in the world. Rafael wouldn't have been an analyst if it weren't for Jim—because he saw Rafael's genius." She herself found López "a huge natural force. And even more dangerous than Jim by far!" Pat would elaborate on the danger in her talk at a Notre Dame festival honoring Hillman in 1992: "Rafael had a breadth of cultural and historical knowing that was remarkable, in that it seemed not to reside in his head but in his very being. He had body, as he called it. And actually this man's head was kind of short and his neck was short, and so his head was very connected to his body." By the time Pat showed up at the Institute, "he had gathered a bit of a following, so I wasn't the only maenad on the scene. Other young women had come to Zürich and had become patients of his, which I never was, thank God. So now there were four or five of us who gathered round Rafael to soak up whatever it was we seemed to be needing and absorbing from him. You know, nowadays psychotherapy would call these complexly personal interconnections incestuous, or at the very least dual relationships. But in those days, that was how you did [it]."[21]

Every Monday, López had lunch with Hillman's closest friend in Zürich, Adolf Guggenbühl-Craig. Over the course of his life, Guggenbühl would have an enormous influence on the development of Jungian psychology in Zürich and around the world. In addition to his work as a psychotherapist and a teacher/training analyst at the Jung Institute, he would serve as president of its governing Curatorium for more than a decade, and as president of both the Swiss Society of Analytical Psychology and the International Association of Analytical Psychology. An independent spirit fascinated by the paradoxes of human existence, his five books (like Hillman's work) turned conventional wisdom upside-down in exploring subjects such as the psychopath, the shadow side of the healer, and the tradition of marriage.

Guggenbühl was three years older than Hillman. The men had become friends in 1959—soon after Hillman was named the Institute's director of studies. "I wasn't very much involved in the Institute," Guggenbühl recalled, "but practically every week we had meetings over lunch and talked about the challenges and opinions and happenings."[22] In 1963, they toured the United States together for five weeks, giving a series of joint lectures. The next year, Guggenbühl was instrumental in pushing Hillman to publish *Suicide and the Soul* (Guggenbühl's younger brother had killed himself).

Guggenbühl called his relationship with Hillman "a soul connection": "When I think I have an insight, he understands it before I say it. And that's a tremendous relief in a relationship. I don't have to go on with endless explanations of what I mean. We all have that with very few people. Jim would say, that's a gift of the gods." Guggenbühl was fascinated by the way Hillman "could play with mythology. He could use it for his work, or for his [own] development." Guggenbühl also "admired very much his ability to formulate, his language mastery. He's a tremendous writer. And that's even a bit of a danger, because he's such a good writer that maybe he might lose a bit of the struggle. I don't have that at all. I am not jealous of that, I just admire it." He did challenge Hillman's adherence to "orthodox Jungianism" at the time, and believed that his influence helped Hillman break free from it. "For me, he is archetypally [the] younger brother," Guggenbühl said.[23]

Hillman described both Guggenbühl and López as "somehow older brothers to me. They each, from very different points of view, were very gifted psychologists in the sense of 'seeing through,' the way I used that term in *Revisioning Psychology*. Rafael was gifted in thought, Adolf was gifted in feeling. Rafael was very much an outsider; Adolf was a complete insider. The three of us would often go off to someplace for a weekend to bathe in the hot waters and talk."[24]

López remembered sometimes calling Hillman three or four times a day "to exchange impressions about the ideas we were working on."[25] In letters to Hillman when he was teaching in Chicago, López made a number of references to his weekly lunch dates with Guggenbühl.[26] "A lot of connection and recognition," López wrote in one (October 22, 1968). He and Guggenbühl had "talked about J. C. and Psych. and about old and new. My feeling is that 'new' things are coming along having their own pervading effect from underneath and will be seen more in the open in due time. But I know very well that if we push on anything like signing a manifesto the whole movement will die, losing its body aspect by way of offering a 'new' point of view that rejects the 'old': 'New' things are coming along and we only need to take care of ourselves."

November 20, 1968, López wrote: "The other day I also told Adolf that, if we can knead patiently the material of new little things probably we can bake good bread in due time. Avoiding hastiness that kills those little things and can kill us too . . . Adolf and I need each other's level of Psyche and shadow."

After having coffee with Guggenbühl the day before heading off to Spain for a rest (December 13, 1968), López reflected:

"I began to realize for the first time something very danger-ous, that probably what I say in relation to Psychology could be important, more dangerous than was the idea that probably my ideas have a revolutionary tint. If it is so I have to be very careful. I know by instinct how to survive a revolution (outer) not to be devour[ed] by the revolution archetype" [a reference to having left Castro's Cuba].

López held a unique view of the contemporary world situ-ation, which he expressed in a letter to Hillman (December 1, 1968): "Thanks to the Gods we are living in decline and analysis provides us with the right instrument in the right time. I myself accept decline as the condition of our times and the need of my soul. Otherwise I'd be in Cuba dressed with a militia uniform and having the fantasy of changing the world." He continued, "It came to me the other day that St. Paul is at the back of L.S.D. and the fantasy of the sudden change by a sudden revelation ... [which was] never deep in terms of internalization."

Guggenbühl remembered López once saying: "I will take care of the inertia." That word could never be applied to Rafael himself. "People at the Institute are upset because my name is at [sic: on] the program," López wrote Hillman—after hear-ing this from Guggenbühl. Hillman said: "He was always pro-tected by Adolf and me, because we had power in the system, but he was—not a drag but a blemish, because he was sort of underworldly."

When I asked Guggenbühl about López in one of our interviews (2005), he reflected: "He was very much inclined to destroy himself. He did strange things; he was always coming into the foreground, where he should have been discreet and hidden. He was very exuberant and open. He had a very deep, loud voice. You never knew what he was going to say. He always could take a completely unexpected twist. That's why he was so stimulating. Many people thought he was mentally deranged, but he wasn't at all. He couldn't say things so that the other person really understood it, [so] he was talking in some way to himself ... always very unexpected, very fruitful things. But if you are not willing to listen, or to interpret them positively, then you would be taken aback."[27]

Later in life, Hillman said Guggenbühl and López represented two different parts of himself—the family man and professional psychiatrist who fit into society (Adolf), and the "wild shadow figure Cuban" (Rafael), with Hillman the self-described "renegade" in the middle. During their always intense conversations, "that split manifested in three friends challenging each other—mostly López and me shouting . . . Being in association with Rafael opened my eyes to many things. I lost some of my naivete." Like Guggenbühl, López had supported Hillman all through the turmoil of the scandal-plagued late 1960s—and not just supported, but helped him see through "the way everybody manipulated; underneath it, the power plays and hiding of truth. As Pat put it, 'You survived a terrible corruption there.'"

Soon after, Pat became part of "the almost daily conversations over wine and dinner or lunch, two or three or four of us, or Jim with Adolf Guggenbühl and then reporting the discussion back to us, or Rafael; among us all, the discussions got reported and we were excited in sort of fantasizing this evolving thought. For me it was fascinating to learn the twists and turns, to witness the leaps to the unexpected, which leaps really were Jim's specialty from the beginning . . . Rafael always started with the unexpected and then just barreled it through. Jim generally started with . . . a lot of scholarly layout and then he finds a place where he sort of turns on something, turns it upside down, and then he's off and leaping. This was all very heady, very exciting stuff, to a by now . . . 25-year-old."[28]

THE COMING OF *SPRING*

Looking back at the time, Hillman said: "It's an insult to Pat to see her simply as a student of mine—because she was far more than that, she was a very bright collaborator."[29] The collaboration bloomed soon after his forty-third birthday in 1969. That was when a letter came to Hillman from a wealthy woman in New York. Jane Pratt, whose husband was descended from one of the original owners of Standard Oil, had long been a patron of Jungian efforts. She provided the backing for *Spring* in 1941, initially an annual mimeographed journal for members of the Analytical Psychology Club of New York and later a forum for scholarly pieces by Jung and his followers (the 1965 issue had included Hillman's essay, *Betrayal*). Pratt also served as *Spring*'s primary editor since the beginning, along with occasionally publishing small books under its auspices.

"Jane Pratt was very literary, and supported the translation of Jung's work into English," Hillman recalled. "She and I had talked all through the '60s, when she would come to Zürich to look for essays and articles by Jung that hadn't been published before. She was a whole generation older, and we liked each other very much; we had a natural connection."[30]

An overlapping connection existed. J. P. Donleavy, Hillman's friend from Trinity College, lived with his wife at the time, Valerie, in the Connecticut lodge house on the property of "Jeep" and Jane Pratt in the 1950s—when Donleavy was writing *The Ginger Man*. This apparently came about through Valerie's mother, also a Jung acolyte.

Later, Jane Pratt aided Hillman in establishing the Aion Foundation, a tax-exempt organization "for the purpose of supporting Jungian activities of all sorts." She'd recently underwritten costs to create an Archive for Research in Archetypal Symbolism at New York's Jung Foundation. By 1969, she was tired of running *Spring*, which had just gone from mimeographed to a printed journal-style format. According to Hillman, she wrote "saying she wanted to give it up, and would I like to be the editor? For the first couple of years, she would supply the money. That got me very excited—an opportunity to have a whole new vehicle for the thoughts that were just coming up at the same time."[31]

Publishing ventures had been a theme for Hillman since childhood, when he started a weekly hand-written magazine called

Pulse on his own little printing press. While at Trinity College, he'd been among the founding writers and editors of an Irish periodical called *Envoy*. Now, for the previous three years, since delivering his first lecture at Eranos in 1966 ("On Psychological Creativity," which returned him to Plato and to myth in the form of Eros and Psyche), Hillman had been moving simultaneously in two directions: deepening his knowledge of classical images and myths ("Senex and Puer," at Eranos 1967) and critic of the medical history of his field ("On Psychological Language," as it was called in *The Myth of Analysis*, at Eranos 1968). He had also begun a study of alchemy with lectures at the Jung Institute and the University of Chicago, again working toward a new approach to therapeutic practice. By Spring 1969, he'd started on an essay about the Greek god Dionysus, while López steeped himself in Kerényi's studies of mythology that had previously influenced Hillman.

Hillman and López were in the midst of conversations about "the differences between the symbolic view of the Jungians and the imagistic view of images (as in poets)."[32] López recalled: "I had already read many of the works on the history of culture written by the scholars of the Warburg Institute; I also studied art from the viewpoint of iconology, an approach to history from within the complexities of its relation to art."[33]

For the past decade, *Spring* had used images of gods and goddesses on the majority of its covers, and these intrigued Hillman greatly. He was interested in finding more of these, appropriate for *Spring* or books that it might publish. While attending the Eranos gatherings, he'd heard about London's Warburg Institute, once the private library of Aby Warburg, an art historian from a wealthy family of Jewish bankers in Hamburg, Germany. Warburg's primary interest was the Renaissance period. What, Warburg wondered, had the Medici circle in Florence found so compelling about antiquity, when its pagan symbols suddenly reappeared with renewed vitality in fifteenth-century Italy? In a curious connection to both Hillman and López, Warburg had spent several years at Ludwig Binswanger's Swiss clinic during the early 1920s—hospitalized for symptoms of schizophrenia.

Following Warburg's death in 1929, his vast collection of texts and images had been moved to London after Hitler came to power in Germany. By the end of the sixties, the Warburg Institute was drawing scholars from around the world, who were immersing themselves in how European thought, literature, art, and institutions harkened back to the ancient world. Hillman was aware that the Warburg also housed a portion of Eranos's collection of some 7,000 photographs of Jungian archetypes, "images of the gods of Egypt, symbols like crosses, images of certain animals and trees"[34]—from Tree of Life to Hermes Trismegistus, the Great Mother, and many more.

So a visit to London was planned. It seems fitting that John Layard was the man to whom Hillman first wrote about the upcoming trip, which would change the shape of post-Jungian psychology. In our interviews, Hillman described Layard as "a real ancestor," and included him in a list of his mentors (along with Jung, mythological scholar Kerényi, philosopher George Santayana, poet Patrick Kavanagh, and Father Gerry Yates of Georgetown University).[35]

Layard, thirty years Hillman's senior, was from an upper-class British family (son of the essayist George Somes Layard), a fellow at the Royal Anthropological Institute of Great Britain and Ireland, and a psychologist. While Layard married and fathered two children, in 1920s Berlin he was part of the expatriate gay community where he mentored the poet W. H. Auden and novelist Christopher Isherwood. Layard also suffered from depression. After miraculously surviving a suicide attempt—he shot himself in the mouth—he ended up in analysis with Jung. He'd already documented the language and myths of the indigenous inhabitants of the New Hebrides islands (today called Vanuatu) in a classic work, *Stone Men of Malekula*. As one of the first ethnologists to use methods of "participant observation," Layard recognized aspects of Jung's theory of transference. This fueled a desire to become an analyst. After working with several—including C. A. Meier—Layard started his own practice. His book of dream-analysis (*The Lady and the Hare*) was considered unique in the field.

Hillman couldn't recall how he first met Layard when he was a student at the Jung Institute. "John was one of the few people who gave me intellectual recognition and support very early. He was a peculiar genius, highly educated, aristocratic, and brilliant. A real rebel, too, with his own agenda. He was very annoyed with the narrowness of the analytical approach, partly because he was bisexual and Jung had never accepted [that in] him. John was a handsome man, tall with white hair. He liked me very much, and I think he probably had designs on my body, but he did stay in our house on a few occasions in a little guest room out back. His birthday was the same day as Kate's."[36]

In a letter to Layard (early 1969), Hillman wrote: "I believe that the Jungian thing is in great crisis, as I am . . . mine is a long one, with much depression, a sense of limitation . . . well, maybe something new will come later on out of it." [37]

Hillman followed up in March with: "I am surviving, and the changes wrought internally and in feeling, lifestyle and the like are good and deep. So on the main score, no worry. What goes on at the Institute and Jungian field as a whole . . . well that's another sadder matter. It's a time of restriction, but I am writing every day . . . The whole thing has been very hard on [Kate], and on Adolf who is now quite alone at the Institute and on Rafael."

Hillman added that he planned to definitely be in England in the spring and would try to come see Layard there. He hoped to be in London on March 20, and "I expect to come back to England to use libraries for maybe two weeks during the first half of April while Kate is in the mountains with children . . . I might come alone, I might come with López, maybe he will have a friend with him."

INSIDE THE WARBURG

The stated reason for the trip was that Hillman had been invited to London take part in a two-day symposium by the Centre for Spiritual & Psychological Studies, focusing on the scientific approach to the study of religious experience alongside such British luminaries as Professor Sir Alister Hardy and Francis Huxley. (In a letter, Hillman wrote he was "to give a paper at a highstyled queer academic setting clublike thing.")[38] Hillman prefaced his talk on "the psychological approach" by saying: "When I told a friend of mine in Zürich what I was coming to London for—and he comes from one of those Caribbean cultures mentioned by Francis Huxley—he said 'Ah these English, they still want to take photographs of ghosts.'"[39] The "friend of mine" seemed to be a reference to López, and Hillman's own journey here was very much about "photographs of ghosts."

Neither Hillman nor López were alone when they arrived in London late that March. López was accompanied by Valerie Donleavy, with whom he'd been together for a while but still referred to her (rather cryptically in letters to Hillman, as if afraid someone else might read them) as "Mrs. Donleavy," a "candidate" at the Jung Institute among twenty-two new students, "reading books, etc. . . . She sends you her love."

Hillman had brought along Pat Berry. "So it was a cheating escapade at the same time," he later said. "And Valerie left her children in the care of Kate, so she could get away. The whole thing . . . had a very dark shadow in it . . . I remember going to Fortnum and Mason's to have tea, and who's in the tea room but Mike Donleavy, her former husband!"[40] (J. P. Donleavy remained Hillman's close friend. The affair between Valerie and Rafael "didn't seem to bother him at all,"[41] Hillman remembered— even though they were not yet officially divorced.)

The two couples would stay in London for ten days, in a hotel not far from the Warburg, whose five-story brick building occupied a full city block at Woburn Square. Pat, however, became quite sick for a couple of those days, "apparently from a bad bit of crab in a salad—the only thing the others had not eaten as well," she recalled. "Perhaps at that moment I carried the pathology of the revolution that was gurgling underneath?"[42]

Both Hillman and López were working at the time on themes related to the Greek god of wine and religious ecstasy Dionysus (renamed Bacchus by the Romans). Hillman wrote to Kate of their visit to the British Museum: "The first day here I went with Rafael to look at the Greek gods and heroes . . . It is not yet all opened, but I had very powerful experiences and I am more and more sure that I have got my new direction even if it now will occupy me for the next years . . . Mythology and Psychology and my own 'psychopathy' all go together."

Hillman had always loved working in libraries. In Zürich, he would do research in the stacks of the huge Zentralbibliothek in the center of "Old Town." Pat remembered: "He talked about his 'hawk,' that there was some magical thing that would happen, where he'd open a couple of books and boom!, what he wanted was right there. He was amazed by this, because it was otherwise a very slow process to actually look up things in the card catalogue."[43]

On another afternoon in London, Hillman went alone to the Warburg Library. The Warburg constituted "a giant vault of psychic archaeology," he would recall. A *New Yorker* article later described how, amid four floors of steel shelves overlooked by fluorescent lights, were "signs pointing toward 'Magic Mirrors' and 'Amulets' and 'The Evil Eye.' Long shelves of original medieval astrology, huge texts on modern astronomy . . . the books are available to be thumbed through at will."[44]

Hillman really had no idea what he wanted to look for, but perhaps, he said in one of our interviews, "a 'dig' would reveal a buried tradition on which psychology and psychotherapy could build a different approach from the medical-scientific and its terminology."[45] The gods and goddesses of antiquity were all catalogued and, as Hillman pulled out the large drawers and perused the images of Aphrodite and Apollo, Hestia and Hermes, he felt something mysterious happening inside him. It didn't occur all at once, as some overwhelming visionary experience, rather the dawning realization that "there was a trove of occult knowledge buried here."[46]

There were associated texts to peruse, by contemporary scholars like Edgar Wind and P. O. Kristeller, as well as earlier authors.

Hillman was aware of Plotinus, the preeminent Roman philosopher of late antiquity, "but all these Neo-platonist ideas and philosophers I really knew nothing about." Among the obscure writers from the Renaissance era was Marsilio Ficino—"a loveless, humpbacked, melancholy teacher and translator who lived in Florence,"[47] Hillman would later write. As chief translator in the court of Cosimo di Medici, Ficino revived interest in Plato, Plotinus, and other Neo-platonists. Ficino's villa was modeled on Plato's Academy; here the Renaissance scholar conducted rituals singing ancient Orphic hymns to the accompaniment of his lyre. He also brought to light the *Corpus Hermeticum*, the ancient works of the Egyptian sage Hermes Trismegistus.

For Ficino, soul was "the centre of nature . . . the bond and juncture of the universe"; everything was "known via the soul, i.e. transmitted through psychic images, which is our first reality."[48] According to Hillman, Ficino offered "an incentive to plumb the depths of one's own soul so that the whole world may become clearer in the inner light"[49]—a way of seeing that had deeply influenced Michelangelo. Ficino's work spread through Renaissance Europe, then went underground with the advent of Rationalism and the Enlightenment. Now it spoke to Hillman from across the centuries as though he'd found an ancestral "soul brother."

In the Warburg, Hillman had the overwhelming feeling that "something was beginning and something was over."[50] "All these new thoughts about Western psychology came pouring into my head, and I was writing little notes to myself on everything I could find, thoughts about the Gods, about polytheism, about images, the Renaissance, I wanted to find out who were Ficino, and Gemisto Pletho. I suddenly saw a foundation. Other things were no longer interesting—I remember walking into the Asian section of the Warburg Library and walking out of it saying, that's finished. I can close that off. What a relief."[51]

"Looking back," he reflected in 2007, "much of what I had been floundering around with in this lecture or that seminar were pieces that the Warburg pulled together into a single tradition—and that is what I was searching for: a tradition prior to Jung and Freud which could found the work and which was a tradition in which soul was the central trope."[52]

Hillman and López took their lady friends to other London museums and to the theater. Pat later reflected: "Jim used to get diarrhea whenever he went into a bookstore . . . I used to faint whenever I heard a siren. Rafael and Valery, suffice to say that among us we amply represented most pathologies. And so pathologizing became one of our banners."[53]

The two men also went to a library dedicated to the history of medicine, founded by Sir Henry Wellcome. There they spent some time talking with other visiting scholars. "We never knew how all those things from the Warburg Institute and the Wellcome Library entered our psyche," López said in 2003.[54]

By the end of their stay, the impact of the trip was clear. Pat remembered: "Over a meal in a rather fancy English pub, some-one—Rafael I think—made the first moves toward what would come to be archetypal psychology. Rafael was on about how the problem in psychology, and western thought in general, was monotheism. This notion caught fire and we went on all after-noon, drinking wine, trashing monotheism, and intuiting how things might be different in a more pagan polytheistic world."[55] Later, Pat elaborated: "Where I grew up in Ohio, polytheism was pagan and bad. Rafael reversed it all—meaning the gods are coming from many different directions, and multiple perspec-tives on anything are okay!"[56]

Hillman remembered the same event as "a late lunch, sitting in a booth drinking some beer, when I said something about polytheism versus monotheism. And López exclaimed, 'Now you've got it! Now you see it! That's it!' That is the way he would say things, with a grunt or something. He had already seen the power of the church and its domination of Western thinking. I didn't see it the same way; I saw it as the power of monotheism. And from that came the essay in *Spring*, 'Psychology: Polytheistic or Monotheistic?' Which is really a crucial beginning. Out of the Warburg."[57]

Both Hillman and López conceded their debt to Jung. He had created analytical psychology, a new approach with its pioneering concepts of the complex, the introvert and the extravert, self and shadow, the collective unconscious shared by everyone (including the timeless archetypes). He had focused upon exploring the psyche through dreams, mythology, art, philosophy, and religion. He had delved deeply into the esoteric realms of alchemy, astrology, physics, and the Eastern texts. As the phrase goes, Jung broke the mold, taking the depth psychology that Freud initiated to a deeper level and wider horizon.

Hillman and López believed, like Jung, that psychotherapy needed to reach down to the emotional, irrational, and historical levels of existence. Yet while Jung paid homage to the pagan past, and often referenced the Greek myths, the key tenet of his psychology was self-knowledge gained through progressive life-stages of individuation. Unity and integration were viewed as an advancement from the multiplicity and diversity once exemplified by Zeus and all his offspring. As López later pointed out, Jung had fainted in Zürich's Hauptbahnhof just as he was about to board a train to Rome—and never in his life would he try again to go there. Jung's psyche, it seemed, would not allow him to "go south" into the classic conflict which Rome symbolized: ancient polytheism versus Catholic monotheism. Jung's brilliance and accomplishments, didn't preclude him from having limitations.

Many and different gods—in contrast to one—offer a variety of ways to look at someone's psychic condition. Hillman described what this means: "Depression, say, may be led into meaning on the model of Christ and his suffering and resurrection; it may through Saturn gain the depth of melancholy and inspiration, or through Apollo serve to release the blackbird of prophetic insight. From the perspective of Demeter depression may yield awareness of the Mother-Daughter mystery, or, through Dionysos, we may find depression a refuge from the excessive demands of the ruling will."

A polytheistic psychology "obliges consciousness to circulate among a field of powers. Each God has his due as each complex deserves its respect in its own right." Rather than progressing through hierarchical, unifying stages of development, the "non-growth, non-upward, non-ordered components of the psyche" are given their say. Every phenomenon of the psyche—every symptom, complex, or fantasy has an archetypal background—a god it pays homage. "Better and worse," can no longer apply to the psyche's expressions, when the basis for such judgments in theological morality and monotheism are left behind.[58]

On that memorable afternoon in the London pub, López is said to have exclaimed: "Restore the pagan gods and goddesses to their psychological domain!"

Pat felt excitement building inside her, as if López *was* Dionysus and Hillman *was* Apollo. None of them could specify what had happened. Not yet. It would be some months before archetypal psychology was given a formal name. All they knew then—as López and Donleavy left for the Bourgogne in southern France, and Hillman and Berry went to visit the Greek ruins at Paestum in Italy—was that a turning point had been reached in the way they approached the psychological.

"What started at Warburg in 1969," Hillman wrote in 2009, "became organized in the syllabus at the Univ[ersity] of Dallas for graduate students, ten years later, 1979, with the topics and expanded reading list of my seminar 'Psychological tradition.'"[59] It also developed into the four Terry Lectures Hillman delivered at Yale (1972), and culminated in his Pulitzer Prize-nominated 1975 work, *Re-Visioning Psychology*.

Archetypal psychology, that which "can give sacred differentiation to our psychic turmoil,"[60] had been born.

NOTES

1. Valerie Donleavy's dream: Letter to JH, December 12, 1968, Hillman archive.
2. Swiss court ruling against Hillman: "Aide-memoire concerning the Present situation of analytical psychology in Switzerland," Hillman archive.

3. "It seems to me tragic. . . .": Glin Bennet letter to JH, February 4, 1969, Hinshaw archive.
4. "felt very relieved to be out. . . .": JH letter to Robert Stein, February 6, 1969.
5. Hillman on "physical reaction" against continuing as a therapist: James Hillman with Laura Pozzo, *Inter Views*, p. 107.
6. "I realized what oppression doing therapy had been. . . .": *Inter Views*, p. 108.
7. Tempestuous "in the beginning. . . .": Author interview with Pat Berry.
8. Hillman on Kate, Pat, and the work: Author interviews with JH.
9. Hillman on Jung and ego: JH letter to Paul Wallace, Spring 1969, Robert Hinshaw files, Einsedeln, Switzerland.
10. "Hillman was in his best shape. . . .": "Post-Jungian Movements: Conversations with Rafael López-Pedraza," by Axel Capriles, 2003, sent to author.
11. "very sick patients. . . .": Capriles interview.
12. On López-Pedraza's approach to therapy: Patricia Berry, *Echo's Subtle Body*, p. 116.
13. "It was Rafael who taught me. . . .": Berry talk at Notre Dame Festival of Archetypal Psychology, July 1992.
14. "The best Rafael story I remember. . . .": Author interview with Robbie Bosnak, October 2006.
15. López background and early years in Zürich: Capriles interview.
16. Hillman on López: Interviews with author.
17. "The older generation for all their virtues. . . .": JH letter to Marvin Spiegelman, March 29, 1966, Spiegelman archive.
18. "are all outsiders . . . López has neither money nor permit": JH letters to Robert Stein, June 1, 1966; July 1966.
19. JH introducing López: Letter to Rudolf Ritsema, July 5 1966, Eranos Archive.
20. "Yes, the old Zürich of our 1950s is dead. . . .": JH letter to Marvin Spiegelman, May 30, 1967, files of Robert Hinshaw.
21. "Rafael had a breadth of cultural. . . .": Pat Berry talk at Notre Dame Festival of Archetypal Psychology, 1992, transcribed by author.
22. "I wasn't very much involved. . . .": Author interview with Adolph Guggenbühl-Craig, May 2005.
23. "a soul connection. . . .": Author interview with Guggenbühl, May 2005.
24. "somehow older brothers to me. . . .": Author interviews with JH.
25. "to exchange impressions about the ideas. . . .": López interview with Capriles.
26. López' letters to Hillman: Opus Archive at Pacifica Graduate Institute.
27. "He was very much inclined to destroy himself. . . .": Author interview with Guggenbühl, May 2005.
28. "the almost daily conversations. . . .": Pat Berry talk at Notre Dame, 1992.
29. "It's an insult to Pat. . . .": JH interview with author, July 2009.
30. "Jane Pratt was very literary. . . .": JH interview with author.
31. "saying she wanted to give it up. . . .": JH interview with author.
32. "the differences between the symbolic view. . . .": JH fax to author.
33. "I had already read many of the works. . . .": López interview with Axel Capriles.
34. "meaning images of the gods. . . .": Author interview with JH, July 28, 2009.
35. Hillman mentors: JH interview with author, June 2007.
36. "John was one of the few people. . . .": Author interview with JH.

37. Hillman's letters to John Layard: the John Willougby Layard Papers 1897–1974, Mandeville Special Collections Library, University of California, San Diego. Archive # 0175S, MSS 84, Box 8, Folder 1.
38. "to give a paper. . . .": JH letter to Marvin Spiegelman, undated, Spring 1969.
39. "When I told a friend of mine. . . .": Centre for Spiritual & Psychological Studies, "Report of a Two-Day Symposium at the Royal Overseas League," Opus Archive, Pacifica Graduate Institute.
40. "so it was a cheating escapade. . . .": JH interview with author, June 2009.
41. Affair "didn't seem to bother him at all. . . .": JH interview with author.
42. "apparently from a bad bit of crab. . . .": Pat Berry email to author, August 2, 2014.
43. "He talked about his 'hawk'. . . .": Author transcript of Pat Berry's talk at alchemy conference at Pacifica Graduate Institute, August 2017.
44. "signs pointing toward 'magic mirrors'". . . . "In the Memory Ward," by Adam Gopnik, *The New Yorker*, March 16, 2015.
45. "A giant vault of psychic archeology. . . .": JH Email to Author, October 18, 2009.
46. "there was a trove of occult knowledge buried here. . . .": Author interview with JH, July 2009.
47. "a loveless, humpbacked melancholy teacher. . . .": Hillman, *Re-Visioning Psychology*, 1992 paperback edition, p. 200.
48. Soul was "the centre of nature. . . .": Ficino, quoted in Hillman, *Loose Ends* (1986), pp. 155–56.
49. "an incentive to plumb the depths. . . .": Ibid, p. 201.
50. "something was beginning and something was over. . . .": Author interview with JH, July 2009.
51. "I was writing little notes to myself. . . .": Hillman, *Inter Views*, p. 148.
52. "Looking back. . . .": JH Email to Author, October 18, 2009.
53. "Jim used to get diarrhea. . . .": Berry talk at Notre Dame.
54. "We never knew how all these things. . . .": López interview with Axel Capriles.
55. "Over a meal in a rather fancy. . . .": Berry talk at Notre Dame.
56. "Where I grew up in Ohio. . . .": Berry podcast with Michael Lerner, January 16, 2015.
57. "a late lunch. . . .": JH interview with author, May 2008.
58. "Depression, say, may be led into meaning . . . better and worse": Hillman essay, "Psychology: Monotheistic or Polytheistic?," *Spring 1971*. The essay also appears in David L. Miller's *The New Polytheism*, 1981.
59. "What started at Warburg in 1969. . . .": JH fax to author, October 18, 2009.
60. "can give sacred differentiation. . . .": Hillman, James (1989). Thomas Moore, ed. *A blue fire: Selected writings by James Hillman*. New York: Harper Collins. p. 41.

3

ACUTE TRIANGLE: THE EMERGENCE OF DIONYSUS

"The monogamous view of marriage corresponds with the monotheistic view of God . . . if my thesis is correct, the more we rigidly insist upon unity the more will diversity constellate . . . The situation that then occurs is called a triangle *. . . Until then, the marriage conjunction has served as a defensive or transformative mandala, keeping out all others, providing a set of habits, a delusional or transformative system in which the force of love could be contained. The third releases love from this psychic structure."*
—James Hillman, *"Schism," 1971, in* Loose Ends.[1]

Along the coast of southern Italy, in the Campania region some twenty-five miles south of Salerno, the ancient town of Paestum (originally settled by Greek colonists in the sixth century BCE) possessed three well-preserved Doric temples. Unlike crowded Pompeii, Paestum was off the beaten path and often devoid of tourists. After viewing the images at the Warburg, and absorbing what happened in the London pub, it was an appropriate place for Hillman and Pat Berry to take their first private journey together.

She recounted: "This trip was important, in that it gave us a geography from which to further our imaginings of the polytheistic world. We saw a structure said to be the marriage chambers of Zeus and Hera, which was a square little building partly hidden underground. Marriage was an archetype I hadn't had much to do with, from the inside anyway, and Hera—whom I saw as a guardian of the status quo—was perfectly terrifying to me. I had identified as an outsider, an Artemis perhaps, which with Jim's Apollo made of us a fitting though sometimes warring brother-sister pair. Hera to my mind threatened the purity of this brother-sister bond. Social rules and codes, responsibilities, the establishment, bringing things into the world, all that seemed a crushing weight to me. But sooner or later we would have to enter the world more publicly, build things, take on responsibilities, and bear offspring of a sort."[2]

Hillman first publicly referenced this geography some twenty-five years after the trip, in two talks he gave on "Hera, Goddess of Marriage," where he said: "In Paestum you can see a low covered shrine, with a huge heavy slab of roof on it, and there Zeus and Hera are underground in the dark making love and have been forever and forever and ever after. Eternally coupled and at the same time he's out the window. Why does it occur to the important, successful man to be philanderer or a womanizer . . . ? We have to connect the sexual, generative powers with his imaginative powers because out of the Zeusian imagination came such a variety of other forms. He was chief among the gods because he could imagine the nature of Dionysus and imagine the nature of Apollo and of Hermes and of Athene . . . The imagination must go out, must follow its dangerous dream."[3]

In Hillman's psyche, might Hera be equated to his wife Kate, at the same time that he identifies with Zeus' following the "dangerous dream" embodied in the imagination? Perhaps it wasn't an accident he took Pat Berry to Paestum? Yet, polytheistically, she must also be drawn into Hera's domain. In one of our interviews, Pat reflected: "I'd never respected Hera. I was a self-made woman. But Hera was important, to be able to take care of things, because this was a role I was going to take on. I'd never ironed sheets and I was actually ironing sheets for Jim. Linen sheets, because that's what he liked. I thought, that's what Hera does. That's what my mother would have done, too. Still, the Paestum trip was very romantic, just the two of us—and a lot of mosquitoes in the room that we had to squash all over the walls."[4]

One night at Paestum, amid so many mythological reverberations, Kate called Hillman from Zürich. The call lasted a while; she was clearly upset about something. While Pat lay on the bed listening, she remembered Hillman giving "this long amplification of a dream Kate had—about having ants all over her. His voice was very serious, but he didn't say too much afterward. Just that, 'She had a dream.'"[5] The subject did not come up again.

Not long after returning to Zürich that April of 1969, Hillman took Kate to London for five days. They "had a very good time with each other, slow and quiet,"[6] he wrote in a letter to his friend Bob Stein, and went on to muse: "About marriage: I have given 20 years to it. I do not want to have on my tombstone, here lies a man who successfully was married. That's no goal for me. I am tired of 'doing' what's right, householder. For me, there is just one intense hideous struggle to keep the spirit and keep alive as a man, which goes by way of softening, but marriage has so much matriarchy in it that its softening only produces littleboy in me . . . But it's moving man, it's moving . . . and the fantasy moves out and the guilts move to new places."

Was the fantasy moving out into mythological formulations? While in London with Kate, Hillman wrote to Pat: "Found two small private scholar institutes where one can sit & read & think. But [a] dream says Dionysos is the way to cure. So I'm perplexed."

In the Greek pantheon, Dionysus is customarily said to have been the son of Zeus, and the only deity with a mortal parent, Semele—daughter of a king of Thebes (Cadmus). Zeus visited her secretly on many occasions. She was a maiden often tricked by divinity, including Hera, who discovered the affair when Semele became pregnant. Hera planted doubt in the younger woman's mind as to her lover's divine origin. When Semele demanded Zeus offer her proof, the god reluctantly released a thunderbolt that consumed her. Zeus then rescued the fetal Dionysus from her body, sewing him into his thigh. When Dionysus entered the world a few months later, he was called "the twice-born." When he came of age, he would rescue Semele from Hades and she would preside over Dionysian festivals.

Dionysus stirred the pot wherever he went. He presided over the grape harvest, winemaking and wine; the god of ritual madness and fertility, religious ecstasy and theater. Dionysus and his drum presided over the Athenian dramas. Attending the theater was not a leisure activity. It was a civic action, involving not only the arts, but politics and religion. Ultimately, Dionysus would be torn apart by the Titans—dismembered before eventually being put back together. The underlying archetypal message? Those who do not respect Dionysus may expect to be ripped apart by him. Or, perhaps, the dismemberment is inevitable.

Hillman's first recognition of the Dionysian occurred while a student at the Jung Institute in the mid-1950s. "What grabbed me was [Elvis] Presley. I went to a movie of his in Zürich, with the Spiegelmans, and I said afterward: 'This is Dionysus, this is fantastic. Look at this movement, look at his soft face and all!'"[7]

In 2008, Hillman would reflect that Dionysus had been a primary focus of his published books, from the first to the last. "The Dionysian is already there, if not named, in the 1960 book, *Emotion*; in the sublime horrifying attraction of the Underworld in *Suicide and the Soul* (1964); *Dream and the Underworld* (Dionysus, Hades, Pluto); the Eranos Lecture (1969) where he is the concluding final movement; and . . . in *A Terrible Love of War*" [2005].[8]

So perhaps, indeed, Dionysus was "the way to cure," as Hillman had written in 1969. Soon after that, Hillman dove into reading everything he could about the Greek god. He collected all the books on Dionysus written in the eighteenth and nineteenth centuries, even in Italian and French. "It was a hunger coming out of my own psyche,"[9] he said later.

He'd been invited to give a fourth lecture at Eranos. The ten-day long annual conference had been held since 1930 along beautiful Lago Maggiore at the southernmost edge of Italian-speaking Switzerland, facing the Italian Alps. Jung had given fourteen lectures here and helped plan the programs, which brought together philosophers, theologians, anthropologists, mythologists, ethnologists, and more—in a kind of modern-day Platonic symposium. The word "eranos" derived from the ancient Greek, meaning a "picnic" or "spiritual feast" where guests presented a gift in the form of song or poem or improvised speech. Each speaker gave formal two-hour lectures in the mornings and late afternoons, around a specific archetypal theme. These often explored the relevance of myth and symbolism to history and modern culture.

For the previous three years, despite being twenty years younger than most of the other nine lecturers, Hillman had been invited to address whatever psychological subject he chose. This time, though, he hesitated. Having just been exiled by the Jung Institute, he had reason for caution. He wrote Stein: "It's like a blow that is a blessing. Not many of us get a chance to really start afresh in midlife . . . I have courage, but worry about the inflation that anything new for me always brings."

His plan was to "write about the secondary position of woman and how this has been the age old view."[10] In this, Dionysus became a focal point. He would call his lecture "First Adam, then Eve: Fantasies of Female Inferiority in Changing Consciousness"—later changing the title to "On Psychological Femininity." The lecture would become the third and concluding section of his book *The Myth of Analysis*, published in 1972. The feminist revolution, referred to by some as "women's liberation," was only beginning to manifest at the end of the sixties, and presciently Hillman set out to reveal psychiatry's misjudgments against women as well as classical studies that denigrated the Dionysian impulse. Hillman came to believe that "our misogynist and Apollonic consciousness has exchanged him [Dionysus] for a diagnosis."[11]

"These angers were something very deep," he said in the book *Inter Views* (1983). "There was an outrage and, looking back, I think my own spirit, my ram-headed Mars, was finally coming up and out of a long sleep, a kind of long anima-sleep, you know, autoerotic self-concern, symptoms, wanting to be loved, wanting success."[12] In one of our last interviews, Hillman provided a more personal context: "It was tied with Pat and Kate, tied with not knowing what I was going to do, that I felt somehow beat. I think the Eranos paper about feminine inferiority, sinking into the Dionysian lower level, goes [along] with that."[13] At the time, though, as Pat Berry recalled, "he didn't say that he was wrestling with the problem of Kate and me. I think he just dissociated the whole thing. He was good at that."[14]

In May 1969, Hillman wrote to Stein: "I am still going through the violence and madness of my change. I feel both 'lost' and 'found,' in that from time to time great sense of being connected with the real basic current of what I am to do with myself . . . [O]ther times I am desolate. It's great . . . I have never been in such a stage of thorough upheaval since I began analysis. It affects all parts of my life, including writing . . . and my ideas in the interrelation of psychology and mythology fill me with joy."[15]

THE "SENEX FORCES"

At the same time, Hillman remained under fire from many in the Jungian world for the earlier affair that resulted in his dismissal from the Institute. Laurens van der Post, the author/ adventurer and Jung's close associate whom Hillman had once brought to lecture there, wrote to him about all the personal difficulties: "Whatever the circumstances have been, that makes no difference to the personal regard I have for you . . . [I] hope that you will take this setback as the opportunity which I am certain it is, to fulfill your own greater self."[16]

Hillman responded: "[T]he ugliness continues here as a kind of obsession, with the Curatorium under a sort of revengeful attack, not from youth and students as in most other institutions, but from the 'senex' forces, who it seems to me want to take all of Jung back into the fold of academic, scientific, medical respectability."[17]

Those "senex forces" were marshaled by C. A. Meier's nine-page diatribe against Hillman that included "long quotes from the lawsuit about my character,"[18] which Meier dispatched to all sixty members of the Swiss Society for Analytical Psychology. Hillman chose not to address the hypocrisy—that Meier was known for having affairs with a number of his patients, including Kate (as described in Volume One). Meier wasn't an isolated case. When Hillman was a student, Thomas Kirsch—future president of the International Association of Analytical Psychology (1989–1995) and author of *The Jungians* (2001)—was his doubles partner in tennis. Kirsch would recall learning about the situation in 1967 and feeling "extremely sympathetic to Jim, because I knew that most of the [Institute's] Patrons had been involved in sexual acting out themselves, and they had never been reprimanded or forced to resign any position because of their behavior."[19] The two most vehement of the cabal seeking Hillman's ouster were Meier and Thomas's own father James Kirsch, who had been a close associate of Jung's. While the younger Kirsch thought of Meier as "an excellent analyst, who I saw three times a week," he added in our interview that "one of the biggest things with my father growing up was his acting out with his female patients; it drove my mother and me crazy. So I found this [situation] absolutely duplicitous."[20]

In the midst of this, Pat sent Hillman a letter, leading with a description of a party she'd attended where the guests were making a mockery of his situation. "I wanted *desperately* to leave but it was a smallish sort of party and my leaving would have been most conspicuous. It was just terrible! I know now why I have stayed so far from the institute. It would have been murder not to. I have always greater awareness of what you have had to take . . .

"There's no turning back, Jim, we've got to forge ahead with everything into the new thing, countryless (so far as I'm concerned) and instituteless. And believe me, they are not going to let it be easy (once they get wind that anything new is cropping up). Even if you get your residence thing, my fear is that the Swiss can find a way to block you from doing any teaching, i.e. seminars connected with the association, etc. We've got to make sure everything is legally covered. And I'm sure, unless we can think of a way to cover him, it's only a question of time before Rafael gets canned. This sounds pessimistic but after my crash with reality last night, I'm convinced my fears are not ill-founded. Those people have God on their side! And that spells b-l-o-o-d."[21]

So it went that summer of 1969. With his lecture at Eranos looming, Hillman told Spiegelman that he felt "like a rich pile of lava or shit, trying to get out a narrow controlled uptight faucet" as he read, took notes, and wrote. Simultaneously he was spending more time with his children. And still playing baseball once a week at the American School where Pat taught and participated. Hillman wrote enthusiastically in the same letter: "and last week got the longest hit, a homer, out of the park, me, the oldest man there. (miss the flies though when I stagger around under them, calling 'mine' which it turns out to be not)."[22]

Hillman, in another letter to Pat from Sweden that summer, described riding a bicycle with his eight-year-old son Laurence to pick up the mail. Suddenly, they passed a black viper that curled up "as we sped past. I leapt off, but it was off in the bushes. They are poisonous, I killed one with a board three years ago, and we used to kill one a year, but last three years haven't seen one."[23] (While it was common to kill snakes at that time, they have since been added to Sweden's list of endangered animals and are protected by law).

The advent of the serpent is associated with Dionysus in one tradition of the Greek Orphic mystery cult, in which Dionysus was conceived in an incestuous relationship between Zeus (in the guise of a serpent) and his daughter Persephone.

Early in 2011, during one of our interviews, Hillman addressed the question of when Kate first realized what was going on between him and Pat. Hillman recalled: "She knew about that, I guess, in 1970." It may have been the summer before, perhaps after Kate came across one of Pat's letters to her husband. Pat remembered: "It must have been right after [Kate's] return to Zürich that Valerie Donleavy and I went to speak with her privately at their house. I myself was mostly withdrawn and non-communicative during the evening, like a teenager, Vee said."[24]

DIONYSUS REINVIGORATED

As late August approached and Eranos drew near, Hillman must have been buoyed by receiving a letter from Rudolf Ritsema, the man responsible for bringing speakers to the symposium, and who had also stood by him through the several years of personal crisis. Ritsema wrote to thank Hillman "for the kind words about the psychic strain of believing and putting love into Eranos. It is quite true. Two things help to recharge the battery: the contact with nature as we have it here in the mountains and some true good friends. Among the latter you are of great value for me. It is the communication with somebody who is engaged in things and in a life-struggle that makes sense. That breaks the feeling of loneliness."[25]

Each Eranos conference had a theme, and 1969's was "Meaning and Transformation of the Image of Humanity." The lecture roster included Henry Corbin, scholar of Islamic mysticism, on "Le Récit du Nuage Blanc" (The Story of the White Cloud); Gershom Scholem on "Three Types of Jewish Piety," and Toshihiko Izutsu on "The Structure of Selfhood in Zen-Buddhism."

Kate Hillman decided not to attend, remaining with the children in Sweden. Pat Berry went to Eranos for the first time. She remembered that Hillman identified her as his secretary. Though most of the lectures were delivered in French or German, she "listened to all of them and watched facial expressions."[26] Later, reflecting back, Hillman would write Pat: "When I see all I thought and wrote during the first half of 1969 I think it is amazing. Big part is yours."[27]

Hillman had written that same summer to Marvin Spiegelman: "Above all I am unsure that Aphrodite is the key. Sexual love under her aegis is 'too much'; she should be propitiated in all sorts of ways, and given her due, but I think sexuality, ritualized, and experienced through other archetypes, with less of the divine, ascending, inspired and passionate (jealousy, witchery, etc.) gives us a better chance. Do you not think that the brotherhood/sisterhood of man may come more through the psychic connection of common visions, through the shared imagination (Blake's idea) and not through natural love, which as Hegel points out is only a few moments now and again and cannot account for the history of humanity. We cannot be fucking everyone all the time, not even in fantasy, nor even carry that feeling of sexual participation into life. It becomes programmatic, no?"[28]

Hillman believed that this subject raised "psychological questions of the most profound sort [that] lie waiting to be released from centuries of concretization."[29] He began his Eranos talk by examining the biblical myth where Eve is derived from Adam's rib, thus making the male "the precondition of the female and the ground of its possibility."[30] The Western scientific tradition, beginning with Aristotle, continued to place woman on a lower plane: "The ovaries are inferior testes; female seed is inferior to male."[31] Hence, woman supposedly "also has less soul and less mind."[32]

Pat would recall sitting in the audience "very much impressed with the scientific writings Jim dug out reporting the ovum as seen through a microscope misshapen or inferior compared with sperm. Astonishing how a scientist could see through a microscope what he believed to be true! That point really struck me."[33]

Century after century, Hillman went on, right through Freud and woman's alleged "penis envy" reflecting "her inborn structural inferiority,"[34] the same misogynist perspective dominated. Psychoanalysis had begun as treatment for hysteria, "a woman's disease" that viewed "the woman as preponderant source of 'case material' . . . and the transference fantasies as supposed root of psychoanalysis."[35] Hysteric and witch, he added, were always closely associated.

This led Hillman back to Dionysus, who "is mainly a god of women. His cult was mainly a woman's preserve . . . This figure and his spirit can inform consciousness so that it can at last move away from the line we have been following from

Adam and Apollo."[36] While Jung's analytical perspective tended toward divisions—"conscious from unconscious, cure from neurosis, individuation from collectivity, even eros from psyche . . . Dionysian consciousness proceeds otherwise."[37] One of Dionysus' names was "The Undivided," and a child was one of the god's primary representations.

Hillman continued: "The Gods are not persons who each rule over a different area of human activity," but "each archetype informs consciousness so that another kind of world shines through." The gods "require one another" and "call upon one another for help." He referenced the Renaissance's Ficino, to whom "it is a mistake to worship one god alone."[38] Thus did Hillman take up the hubris of monotheistic consciousness and psychology, with "the ego as sole center of consciousness." We needed to move not merely away from the highest gods (whether called Yahweh, Zeus, ego, or self), but toward "an archetypal psychology that would give proper due to many dominants."[39]

This marked Hillman's first public definition of archetypal psychology, and was also a point of intellectual departure with friends like Guggenbühl, who retained the Christian concepts of salvation and redemption. "I was always a bit taken aback by his thoughts about gods," Guggenbühl said in one of our interviews. "I thought it was psychologically thin. You can pray to God, or if you're a Christian to Jesus Christ, but you cannot pray to *the* Gods. How can you relate to Zeus? Or Hera? How can a religious connection exist? That for me was a kind of a barrier. It was very stimulating, useful, and psychologically fruitful but it didn't touch my heart. This was never my experience of life, so if I would have gone for it, it would have been an escape. So we sometimes had arguments."[40]

Hillman, however, after the powerful experience at the Warburg Institute where he studied ancient images of Dionysus, realized the archetypal forces were alive to the extent that "in the *psyche* . . . in a certain sense God is dead—but not the Gods"[41]—as he put it at Eranos. To "mad Dionysus is attributed the origin of tragedy . . . indispensable for any depth psychology that

would be a cultural humanism."[42] Yet, along with his cult following of maenads, Dionysus is considered inferior: "Psychiatry
and classical scholarship rely upon each other's misogyny."[43]
Discussing the childlike nature of Dionysus, Hillman added:
"The force of life, like the child, needs nursing. The Dionysian
experience transforms women not into raving hysterics and reb-
els but into *nurses*. They become nurse of the natural, giving
suck to all life."[44]

Eventually dismembered by the Titans, Dionysus returned to
life and (not unlike Jesus) remained present among his followers. "If Dionysus is the Lord of Souls, he is the soul of nature,
its psychic interiority. His 'dismemberment' is the fragments of
consciousness strewn through all of life."[45]

Toward the essay's close, Hillman took up another theme
that he'd been through personally and which would remain a
dominant motif of his psychology. "With the return of passivity to consciousness, the inertia of depression and the helplessness of suffering would take on another quality. Depression
and suffering would belong to consciousness, be part of its
composition, not afflictions coming to it unconsciously, making
it unconscious, dragging it away and down, lowering its level.
Depression would then no longer be a sign of inferiority or be
felt as defeat."[46]

He concluded, "therapeutic psychology is over and done
with."[47] And "the end of analysis coincides with the acceptance
of femininity."[48] In the image of Dionysus is "the bisexuality of
consciousness, which means, as well, conscious bisexuality, that
incarnation of durable weakness and unheroic strength . . . [49]

"As we cannot go it alone, so we cannot know it alone.
Our consciousness cannot be divided from the other. Another
is implied, not only because the soul cannot exist without its
'other' side, but also because consciousness itself has an erotic,
Dionysian component that points to participation. Pressed far
enough, this line of thought means that we are conscious only
in some form of related sharing and that man, when he is alone,
reflecting or becoming conscious or individuating, may in fact

be unconscious. Although Dionysus may be a solitary stranger, even somber, depressed, and of the forests and mountain tops, his entourage indicates a style in which awareness is at one with life as it is lived by others."[50]

"Dionysian consciousness requires a *thiasos*, a community; and this community is not only exterior, in other people, but is a communal flow with the complexes, a commingling of consciousness with the 'other' souls and their Gods, a consciousness that is always infiltrated with its complexes, flowing together with them . . ."[51]

"The effect of the Gods on the psyche is the *re-vision of psychology in terms of the Gods* . . . It is so difficult to imagine, to conceive, to experience consciousness apart from its old identifications, its structural bedrock of misogyny, that we can hardly even intuit what this bisexual God might hold in store for the regeneration of psychic life."[52]

No one had ever envisioned Dionysus in quite this way. Ginette Paris, a mythological scholar who came to know Hillman well in his later years, addressed the thorny topic in an essay she wrote about him in 2015. "I happen to think that one of the most powerful feminist texts written by *any* man is his chapter on The Myth of Feminine Inferiority (in *The Myth of Analysis*.) Unfortunately this text leads to many misinterpretations by some feminists who misread it as if he was saying women are inferior. On this particular issue, I was on his side, and against their infuriating misreading of Hillman. I was disappointed to see their refusal to admit that a man can be a feminist champion. Some attacks on Hillman were not only misinformed, some were mean, unfair and justly angered him. Yet, I am a feminist and I could at times feel the gap of generation [with Hillman]."[53]

Paris would use Hillman's essay with her students as an example of the approach of archetypal psychology, examining the field's history as akin to a battle between Dionysus and Apollo. Hillman would later elaborate his personal views about feminism, saying: "I steer clear of it. Once you see the whole world in terms of gender you close your mind in a set of blinders, caught in a pair of opposites, and you lose the particular person . . . So I don't want to answer any questions about the feminine, feminism, or so on. I will talk about certain structures of consciousness that have been called feminine and what happens when they are called feminine; we can talk about hysteria or about Dionysus, because Dionysus was considered a Lord or God of women, and the way that works."[54]

In his 1973 essay on "The Great Mother, Her Son, Her Hero, and the Puer," Hillman would reflect upon the mythical opposites of Dionysus: "The great figures on whose pattern we build our ego strength—Oedipus and Hercules, Achilles, Hippolytus, and Orpheus—in different ways opposed the feminine and fell victim to it. Could we not turn another way? Could we become conscious without that struggle? Ego development has so long been conceived through the heroics of tough aggression, paranoid misogyny, selfishness, and distance of feeling so typical of the mother's son that we have neglected other paths opened by the puer."[55]

Years later, Hillman would write in a fax to the author that, with Dionysus coming onstage, "the anima returns but not as such, but as the feminine aspect of the god of emotion, showing that the whole venture of scientific psychology is aimed at repressing the Dionysian which is at the same time the main content of people's psychological problems." This Dionysian aspect also follows through my subsequent work, for instance in *The Dream and the Underworld* [at Eranos] in 1972, and after, but also in my life with the eruption of Spring House in 1970, disruption of my marriage, book on Pan (1971). No matter how researched and scholarly the works were, they were transparently biographical on the level of thought."[56]

FURTHER PAGAN MEDITATIONS

Hillman would precede his foray into *The Dream and the Underworld* (to be covered later in this book) with an essay on

"Dionysus in Jung's Writings" that he published in *Spring* (1972). While "the principles of light, order, and distance" character- ized the Apollonic, the lodestone of the Dionysian was "emo- tional involvement." And while Dionysus was "never central to Jung's focus," Hillman pointed out a decade later in *Healing Fiction* (1983) that "by turning to dreams for the creative nature in the soul, Jung was also turning to the God of this nature, Dionysos . . . Jung pointed to Dionysos also by stating that the dream had a dramatic structure. Dionysus is the god of theater: the word *tragedy* means 'his goat song.'"[57]

Hillman goes on to spend several pages suggesting that psychotherapy needs turn to "theatrical logic" in order "to understand the dreaming soul from within." The structure of Dionysian logic is dream, and its embodiment is the actor. "Dionysian logic is necessarily mystical and transformational because it takes events as masks, requiring the process of eso- tericism, of seeing through to the next insight." All the world's a stage, Shakespeare told us, and we are such stuff as dreams are made on.

Hillman's friend López-Pedraza, with whom he discovered the Warburg images, was so taken with the God that he published *Dionysus in Exile: On the Repression of the Body and Emotion* as his last book in 2000. It had been López who first piqued Hillman's interest in a letter in August 1968, writing him: "I believe that Persephone and Dyonissos [sic] have their own laws. That these laws are feeling laws. The soul has laws more implacable than the established and to transgress feeling is psychopathy."

López wasn't Hillman's only colleague drawn to Dionysus. Ginette Paris would become close to Hillman in the mid-'80s, when she was a professor of social psychology at the State University of Quebec in Montreal. She had just published *Pagan Meditations: The Worlds of Aphrodite, Artemis and Hestia*, and had embarked on a sequel about their male counterparts, *Pagan Grace: Dionysus, Hermes and Goddess Memory*. So she and Hillman had an immediate affinity, as evinced by her defense of his 1969 Eranos lecture to feminist critics. Paris was herself a self-proclaimed pagan and feminist, writing that for 2,000 years "women could have neither goddesses in their image nor priestesses at their service. No wonder the Christian church cannot understand that birth control and abortion can be an extremely evolved form of feminine conscience and consciousness. The future equilibrium of the human community may depend on the use and refinement of that consciousness by women and couples."[58]

And Paris found Hillman's ongoing insights into Dionysus to be stimulating food for thought. In one handwritten letter to her, Hillman wrote: "Regarding Diony. His physical appearance needs to be remembered: soft belly or plumpness; *long hair & fair skin* (Bacchae). These are also metaphors, psychological qualities that are not his 'other' side; but appear together with his *complete physicality* (not heroic) that is soft & wild at once. *Brando? Presley?*"[59]

As ever, Hillman was compelled to see through to the shadow. He would also write Paris: "As for Dionysus. Here is an image. It helps me dislike the God. I think it is time we see not the violent side of him (the vision of Apollo who projects his own murderousness) . . . but that we see the soft, flabby, love-needy (where are my women, where are my nursemaids, where is my milk?) . . . that sort of Mediterranean psychopathic unscrupulous loverboy, like a male prostitute, seductress of women (out of the house, out of the normal life of chores and duties)—in other words, we need also . . . the disgusting aspect of the God for he is also a serpent, a loosener . . . etc. All things we have 'raised on high' (especially I have) because I am so Apollonic. There is a hysteria in D. and we should not merely whitewash that."[60]

A few years prior to that letter, Hillman had seen this shadow up-close-and-personal while living in Dallas (1978–84). Young men coming into analysis had already identified themselves with Dionysus, but with no awareness of the god's less appealing side. Pat would remember complaining to Hillman about this, after which in a *Spring* article he moved from archetype to archetypal, from noun to adjective, a direct response to that concern. (You cannot identify as readily with an adjective as with a noun).[61]

To Paris, Hillman passed along more thoughts, "*strong* ones," for her book. "1) Dionysos is called Zoe. Biological life. So there must be a Dionysian ecology, not just a scientific one of Apollo, or Artemesian one. D. ecology might be celebration, and a passivity to nature, a 'doing very little'—I suspect.

"2) Dionysian dismemberment. Dionysos excites or invites the Titanic element of EXCESS in others. A person under the 'influence' of D. will find Titanic excess in his own behavior, or around him. But D. himself is *not* excessive. Even the scholars and researchers become 'excessive' when talking about D. Then D. is torn apart by the Titanic element. One feels exhausted, worn out, 'shredded' by the behavior of others who are so excited (drunk, wild, orgiastic, demanding) when a person represents the Dionysian aspect."

In late life, Hillman would still be inviting his audience to wrestle with Dionysus when he gave a talk on "The Ethics of Quality," originally written for the 100th anniversary catalogue of an Italian fabric maker (Anna Zegna). In mentioning Dionysus' "disruption of common conventions," he might well have been describing himself. Hillman went on: "Ancient Mediterranean culture gave to this botanical force, this urge to luxuriate, the name Dionysus—this figure whom our minds have learned to associate with tumult, riots and orgy. The God of wild places . . . Perhaps this disfigures his nature and results from repression . . . Our notions of civilized culture are Athenian and Apollonian, or derived from the family domesticity of Hera. But we should not fully trust the philosophers who have filled our imagination with Olympian ideas to look down on Dionysus. As God of the ordinary people he is called the *Zoe*, from which comes out zoology, the animal force and vitality. There is more purpose to him than the destruction of civilized habits.

"The question now becomes, what would this god of the people do for the people? Was he popular merely because he offers liberation—the wine, the dance, the crowd—or did he have a psychological function required by the Mediterranean soul? Primarily Dionysus invokes and even demands the conjunction of emotion and protection, at the same time—the awakening of both passions and defenses together."[62]

> *"We have not killed anything; we have 'sacrificed' with a knife, like cutting a rope or a navel cord, for the sake of freeing something, and giving it to the Gods. They will let us know what is happening."*
> —*James Hillman, in a letter to Pat Berry, 1970.*

NOTES

1. Quotes from "Schism": James Hillman, *Loose Ends: Primary Papers in Archetypal Psychology*, Spring Publications: Dallas, Texas, 1975, p. 89.
2. This trip was important. . . .": author's transcript from audio of Pat Berry talk at Festival of Archetypal Psychology, Notre Dame, 1992.
3. "In Paestum, you can see. . . .": James Hillman, "Hera, Goddess of Marriage," in *Mythic Figures, Uniform Edition V. 6.1*, Spring Publications, Inc., Putnam, Ct., 2007, p 252.
4. "I'd never respected Hera. . . .": Author interview with Pat Berry, September 2013.
5. "long amplification of a dream Kate had. . . .": Author telephone conversation with Pat Berry, May 2014.
6. "had a very good time. . . .": JH letter to Robert Stein, undated.
7. "What grabbed me was [Elvis] Presley. . . .": Author interview with Hillman, November 2007.
8. Divergences *A propos* of a Brazilian Seminar on Giegerich/Hillman, 2008, unpublished, JH private archive.
9. "It was a hunger coming out. . . .": Hillman, *Inter Views*, p. 94.
10. "accepted Eranos again after long reflection. . . .": JH letter to Robert Stein, February 6, 1969.
11. "Our misogynist and Apollonic consciousness. . . ." James Hillman, *The Myth of Analysis: Three Essays in Archetypal Psychology*, Evanston, Ill., Northwestern University Press paperback edition, 1977, P. 274.
12. "These angers were something very deep. . . .": Hillman with Laura Pozzo, *Inter Views*, p. 147.
13. "It was tied with Pat and Kate. . . .": JH interview with author, May 2008.
14. "he didn't say that he was wrestling. . . .": Pat Berry interview with author, September 2013.

15. "I am still going through the violence. . . ." Hillman letter to Robert Stein, Hillman private archive.
16. Laurens van der Post letter to JH: April 18, 1969, Robert Hinshaw archive, Einsedeln, Switzerland.
17. Hillman letter to van der Post: May 18, 1969, Hinshaw archive.
18. "with long quotes from the lawsuit. . . ." Undated JH letter to Spiegelman, Spring 1967.
19. "extremely sympathetic to Jim. . . .": From unpublished memoir of Thomas B. Kirsch, provided to author.
20. Thomas Kirsch's comments about Meier and his father came in an interview with the author, November 2013.
21. "I wanted desperately to leave. . . .": Pat Berry letter to Hillman, undated, Berry private archive.
22. "like a rich pile of lava. . . .": JH letter to Spiegelman, undated, Spring 1967, Hinshaw archive.
23. "as we sped past. . . .": JH letter to Pat Berry, August 9, 1969, Berry personal papers.
24. "It must have been right after. . . .": Pat Berry email to author, June 4, 2017.
25. "Thank you for the kind words. . . .": Rudolf Ritsema letter to JH, June 21, 1969, Hinshaw archive.
26. "he called me his secretary": Author phone call with Berry, May 16, 2014.
27. "When I see all I thought. . . .": Hillman letter to Pat Berry, Berry private archive.
28. "Above all I am unsure that Aphrodite. . . .": JH letter to Spiegelman, undated, Hinshaw archive.
29. "psychological questions of the most profound sort. . . .": James Hillman, *The Myth of Analysis: Three Essays in Archetypal Psychology*, Northwestern University Press paperback edition, 1997, p. 219.
30. "the precondition of the female. . . .": James Hillman, ibid, p. 218.
31. Ibid, p. 238.
32. Ibid, p. 230.
33. Berry "very much impressed with the scientific writings. . . .": Pat Berry email to author, October 1, 2014.
34. "penis envy. . . .": P. 240.
35. "a woman's disease. . . .": pp. 251–2.
36. Dionysus as "mainly a god of women. . . .": p. 258–9.
37. Analytical viewpoint tending toward divisions: p. 263.
38. "But another God is not merely another point of view. . . .": p. 264.
39. "an archetypal psychology. . . .": p. 265.
40. Guggenbühl "always a bit taken aback. . . ." Interview with author in Zürich, September 30, 2006.
41. "in a certain sense God is dead. . . .": p. 265.
42. "mad Dionysus. . . . p. 266.
43. "Psychiatry and classical scholarship. . . ." p. 270.
44. "The force of life, like the child. . . ." p. 276.
45. "If Dionysus is the Lord of Souls. . . ." p. 280.
46. "With the return of passivity to consciousness. . . .": pp. 283–4.
47. "therapeutic psychology is over and done with. . . ." p. 288.
48. "the end of analysis coincides. . . ." p. 292.
49. "the bisexuality of consciousness. . . ." p.293.

50. "As we cannot go it alone. . . ." pp. 295–6.

51. "But Dionysian consciousness requires. . . ." p. 296.

52. "The effect of the Gods on the psyche. . . .": p. 298.

53. Ginette Paris' unpublished essay was sent to the author in 2015. Hillman originally wrote the piece on femininity for his Eranos lecture in 1969.

54. "I steer clear of it. . . .": Hillman, *Inter Views*, 1983, pp. 72–73.

55. "The great figures on whose pattern. . . .": James Hillman, in *Senex & Puer, Uniform Edition #3*, Spring Publications: Putnam, Ct., 2005, p. 146.

56. "the anima returns but not as such. . . .": Hillman fax to author, 2008.

57. "by turning to dreams for the creative nature. . . .": Hillman, *Healing Fiction*, pp. 36–40.

58. "women could have neither goddesses. . . .": Article in Montreal Gazette about Ginette Paris,May 27, 1990, "Perky rebel decries 'male' religions, rules."

59. "Regarding Diony. . . .": JH letter to Ginette Paris, undated, Paris private archive.

60. "As for Dionysus. . . .": JH letter to Ginette Paris, January 3, 1988, Paris private archive.

61. Dionysus' shadow and Dallas: Pat Berry email to author, January 15, 2019.

62. The quoted lecture on "Ethics of Quality" was given by Hillman on June 4, 2009, at the Great Mother Conference in Maine, taped and transcribed by the author.

4

"THE ARCHETYPAL DOMINANCE OF THE GODS"

"She mystifies, produces sphinx-like riddles, prefers the cryptic and occult where she can remain hidden: she insists upon uncertainty. By leading whatever is known from off its solid footing, she carries every question into deeper waters, which is also a way of soul-making. The deeper we follow her, the more fantastic consciousness becomes."

—*James Hillman,* Anima.[1]

After Eranos, in October 1969, Hillman turned his attention to his new position as General Manager of Spring Publications. He expected the *Spring Journal* to pass into his hands—with funding—for at least five years. The first new edition wasn't scheduled to appear until sometime in the spring of 1970, so there was ample time to solicit articles and prepare for publication. Hillman also decided to replace "that abstract Indian mandala"[2] which had long been the journal's cover logo.

As he later described it, the new logo depicted "a ram and a goat, and they are butting heads over a small pool of water with a few reeds in it, perhaps papyrus . . . The ram is facing forward, and it is the new sign of life, Aries, and Spring. And the goat is the conservative, looking backward. It's a Renaissance idea. 'In order to move forward, you must look backward' . . . There's also a theme of conflict in regard to Jungian psychology . . . it has to do with continuing the Jungian classical tradition—that's the goat—but fighting against it at the same time."[3]

Pat Berry further reflected in 1992: "The new and the old, spring and winter, was also secretly Jim, an Aries ram, and me, a Capricorn goat. This was the sub-text."[4] Pat quit her teaching job at the American High School and, "joined him in trying to make a go of this new venture," as she described it. *Spring* began in her one-room studio apartment on Rennweg, off Bahnhofstrasse.

Hillman recalled in one of our interviews: "The collaboration between Pat and Valerie Donleavy happened immediately, about how to edit and produce these [journals]. So it was a new life."[5] "We were getting support from [Jane Pratt in] New York.

We had to find a printer and a cover designer, we had to have stationery, do a whole thing."[6]

An IBM compositor, "an ungainly precursor to the word processor" as Pat put it, would set type. "Murray Stein's wife at the time, Mary Kay, came to my room and worked all day long at the desk on this machine while I sat in bed and edited all the manuscripts."[7] Murray Stein had formerly been the book review editor at Yale Divinity School, when a copy of Hillman's *InSearch* arrived from the publisher. Stein's very positive review prompted a letter back from Hillman. Since Stein was already thinking about coming to study at Zürich's Jung Institute, he wrote again asking about requirements. "It was really on his encouragement that I ventured over upon my graduation, for a long shot at best," Stein recalled.[8] Sailing for Europe with his wife in the fall of 1969, he began training as a Jungian analyst. When *Spring* started up, Hillman offered Stein's wife a job as a bookkeeper and typesetter. Murray, as Pat remembered, "complained of his wife making only a few cents an hour—which was all any of us made, of course."[9] But, in the course of his four years at the Jung Institute, he would later join the *Spring* team, doing some translating of Karl Kerényi's books and, with his wife, taking care of the business end of things.

Hillman asked Marie-Louise von Franz if *Spring* could publish a couple of her seminar lectures, which became the first printing of her work on fairy tales.[10] According to Pat, von Franz had been searching for someone willing to do this, but "everyone has turned it down because typing and manuscript are in bad shape."[11] Years later, Pat recalled: "What we got were mainly just typed notes on these lectures from Uma Thomas, one of the women who'd taken the seminars. I laboriously put the notes together and then went back and forth to von Franz's house in Küsnacht to go over the editing with her. Sitting with von Franz and her dog, I'd say, 'You said this earlier.' 'Well then, I meant it earlier,' she'd say. Or I'd say, 'You said it twice.' 'Well, I meant it twice,' she'd respond. That's what editing von Franz was like."[12]

Eventually, bringing out three of von Franz's lecture courses in an English-language paperback would be a momentous event in the Jungian world: *An Introduction to the Interpretation of Fairy Tales*, *The Problem of the Puer Aeternus*, and *A Psychological Interpretation of The Golden Ass of Apuleius*. By the end of the year, *Spring* was in the process of publishing a new edition of Emma Jung's classic book, *Anima and Animus*.

Late that fall, Hillman brought Kate along with him again to England where he gave eight talks—"*not* to Jungians; they went well,"[13] he emphasized in a letter. One was titled "The problem of Fantasies and the Fantasy of Problems," given at a conference at Brighton's Centre For Spiritual & Psychological Studies. Toward the close of the lecture, he spoke of how "psychology could go a long way were it to move itself into a more precise understanding of the fantasy world, the imaginal world, the world of angels or the world of archons, the world of powers, demons."

In November 1969, one demon at least was exorcised. At long last and seemingly miraculously, Hillman's permanent Swiss residency permit came through! He no longer had to worry about whether he could remain in Zürich. He was, at the time, attempting to turn three of his Eranos papers into a single volume (later *The Myth of Analysis*). His book *InSearch* was coming soon in paperback, his commentary on Kundalini was published in London and soon would be out with a Berkeley press. His "*main book*" on the puer, as yet untitled but on which he'd been working off-and-on for two years, crept slowly forward. He wrote Robert Stein about the latter: "Psychotherapy has been killing the puer for the sake of adaptation to Hera's culture. So we have lost spirit. And psychology has lost its adventure, hope and eros."[14]

He wrote to Marvin Spiegelman: "I worry a good deal about not having a place in the world, that my star has fallen below the horizon & that I'm very much out & even a taboo person." On the other hand, "It's a 'leader' inflation, but not serious since I have no followers. Anyway the shepherd who cares for the flock and the wolf who eats them are the same figure."[15]

Hillman's vision for the forthcoming *Spring Journal* was captured by "a figure (Etruscan and later) called Eros the Carpenter, who simply fitted pieces together, shown with tools and implements of joinery."[16]

CRISIS

Hillman had never said much, if anything, to his American friends about Pat. But early in 1970, addressing Spiegelman about a piece that he'd submitted to *Spring*, Hillman wrote: "I was very glad that you took our editing. I do not do it all alone, you know, so that a trained hand with English is also at work in it. Pat Berry, who is Asst Editor."[17]

Shortly thereafter, he wrote similarly to Bob Stein about his essay: "It's a touchy thing, to edit especially friends. I don't do it all alone, but have Pat Berry who is more objective and competent in some ways than I."[18]

Was this a kind of introduction on his part, one that he knew would need to happen sooner or later? He also wrote Stein that "students (47 of them) wrote a letter asking me to come back. But my dreams show my attitude of return to be all wrong." What Hillman did not say was that the petition drive had been organized by Pat. He would only hint to Stein: "My emotional life is highly *volatile* & unpredictable."

He added in another letter: "As for men friends, I see mainly Adolf and Rafael. They too change. Adolf is struggling with the opposites of his nature: President and Oddball. The Curatorium doesn't appreciate him at all. Rafael is narrowing down . . . his insights are genius, and I continue to learn a great deal through him, even if he gets so fucking rigid and guruish and paranoid it sometimes is hard to take. But for moving the psyche, for moving the ideas, he is incomparable."[19]

The new journal was still almost three months away from publication when Hillman wrote to Spiegelman early in April 1970: "*Spring* is now a massive book of over 225 beautifully prepared pages, with 17 articles. The printer is way behind, and the whole organization teeters and totters . . . Don't ask me where I'm at, I haven't a clue. I work like hell, but am also falling apart. Not physically, but am queer and unknown to myself, probably deluded, too old, unpsychological as can be. Let us say, a mess. SPRING has become a major project, I do every bloody detail myself. Silly. But I don't know how otherwise."[20]

Pat Berry was also a mess. To understand more about the milieu in which that occurred, consider this overview of Zürich from Audrey Haas, an American analysand of Hillman's and a friend of Pat's. "I have lived here since 1954," Haas said in our interview in Zürich fifty years later. "It's a wonderful place to work in. You can be yourself in a sense, keep away from the crowd. Maybe I'm saying this because I'm an expatriate in a way, I'm terribly happy that I was not born Swiss. It seems to me an awful, awful burden to bear. I have a feeling they pay a very high price for their neutrality. The fact that they've never been in wars means that you never have the highs and the lows. And this creates somewhere in them, I think, a guilt. But it also creates, to a certain extent, a smugness—'ah, we have it so good.' It's a very tricky thing. And what I also find frightening is the shadow—that underneath, there is a devastating shadow that very rarely comes up, but probably makes a lot of people suicidal. It's something that, when you've lived here for a while, you're aware of—and it becomes very, very disturbing."[21]

Some nine months after Pat became involved with Hillman, the "devastating shadow" seemed to close in on her. In one of our interviews, she reflected: "It became too much, really on a number of counts. It was not just the constant work. Emotionally I needed a break. All of the incestuous tangles, *sub rosa* connections, had become too much for me. I'd been an innocent abroad, and I was catching up. I felt sort of like Daisy Miller, and that if I stayed any longer I was gonna die in the Coliseum."[22]

So Pat went home to Ohio. This meant that she wouldn't be around to witness the publication in late June of the new *Spring,* with the trickster god Hermes on the cover. And on the masthead, "Edited by James Hillman . . . with the editorial assistance of Patricia Berry." She didn't know when, or if, she would return to Zürich. Pat recalled in 2014: "Jim was against ultimatums of any sort. He believed in leaving relationships open, as I did too. I don't know that either of us thought it was the absolute end. We certainly knew, however, it was the end for now."[23]

Late that March of 1970, in need of "the fresh air of some normal academic program somewhere,"[24] Pat found a small apartment and began sitting in on graduate psychology classes at Ohio State University. It was similar to the Jung Institute, she recalled, "If you were interested in something, no one seemed to bother whether or not you were actually enrolled."[25]

Pat sent Hillman a postcard, and he wrote her back a kind of apologia: "You did the right thing, leaving. Just too abrupt since it's like pulling a plug out, and all the lights got turned off . . . I fight, through work, to stay above water . . . So many reflections and insights now. How we all used you, and sucked energy from you. How right many of your reactions were."[26]

In another letter, a different tone: "You did leave here with us holding the bag. Not easy to manage SPRING alone. I don't quite see how it can and will be done." Yet he'd given Pat some money to help with the trip and now sent her some more for a car. Hillman added that he and Kate had spent two days cleaning his office and storing the case histories, dream research, and old manuscripts in his home attic—"all that mess beginning to make way for the '70s and whatever is now to come."

He envisioned Zürich's Jung Institute becoming "a little dentistry school sooner or later . . . taught by special technicians, no one is in doubt. Comfortable, secure, unexperimental. Mediocrity confirmed by mediocrity. Little people push out big people so they can feel big . . . Yet I cannot plot my course, and find it hard to steer a ship alone. However, I do know that the puer thing must be kept alive, the idealism, the exaggerated sense of one's worth, the inflation, the preposterous thing . . . at the same time depression."

However, Pat responded that being in Ohio "gives me a chance to *find my own life*. If either of us will be interested after that—I don't know."

Then on May 1, shortly after her classes began, all hell broke loose in Ohio. In a televised national address, President Nixon announced that U.S. troops were invading Cambodia, an expansion of the unpopular war in Southeast Asia. The National Guard had already been called out at Ohio State to quell campus unrest, as some 4,000 students took to the streets. In pitched battles in the state capital of Columbus, more than 400 were arrested and over 100 injured. Subsequent days saw armed checkpoints manned by troops. The campus was already cordoned off from the rest of the city when, at nearby Kent State University, National Guardsmen shot and killed four unarmed students and wounded nine others on May 4. Two days after that, Ohio State cancelled all classes.

"When the riots broke out, tear gas flooded my apartment as well as everything else in the surrounding area," Pat recalled. "Then when Kent State happened right up the road, and school closed, I thought, man this isn't my deal. I didn't come here for this. So I gave up my apartment and took my stuff back home, to Monroe, Ohio, several hours away."[27]

When Hillman invited her to meet him in Paris, Pat flew across the Atlantic for what she remembered long afterward as "a wonderful, romantic time."[28] Hillman wrote to her about it later that summer: "the reunion in May . . . strangers . . . and yet so dear." What would Pat do now? In Columbus, a fellow student had told her about a Liberal Arts master's degree program at St. John's College, held during summers in Santa Fe, New Mexico. She needed such a degree if she wanted to eventually be certified as an analyst by the Jung Institute. Hillman offered to pay her tuition.[29]

THE "ARCHETYPAL EYE"

With his friend Guggenbühl now president of the Institute's governing Curatorium, Hillman would begin lecturing there again in June. His new book had swollen to 450 typed pages (in shortened form, this would later become *The Myth of Analysis*.) *Spring* would also soon go to the print, subtitled "An Annual of Archetypal Psychology and Jungian Thought." Hillman had written an eight-page Editorial Postscript headed: "WHY 'ARCHETYPAL' PSYCHOLOGY?"

This marked his first basic attempt to define the ideas that he, López, and Pat had been developing for more than a year. The piece began by listing "the three generally used terms for the psychology represented in this publication during the past thirty years"—Jungian, analytical, and complex. The first, Jungian, was "intensely subjective" and riddled with internecine rivalries. Jung used "complex psychology" to describe the theoretical side of his work, and "analytical psychology" in discussing its practice. However, none of these terms were "ever happy choices nor were they adequate to the psychology they tried to designate," Hillman wrote. Yet the concept of the archetype, "which Jung had not yet worked out when he named his psychology," nonetheless "follows from its historical development."

Hillman went on: "This designation reflects the deepened theory of Jung's later work which attempts to solve psychological problems at a step beyond scientific models and therapy in the usual sense because the soul's problems are no longer problems in the usual sense. Instead, one looks for the archetypal fantasies within the 'models,' the 'objectivity' and the 'problems' . . . Placing archetypal prior to analytical gives the psyche a chance to move out of the consulting room . . .

"According to Jung myth best represents the archetypes. But myth proceeds from a realm which cannot legitimately be considered altogether human. Like the mythical, the archetypal too transcends the human psyche, which implies the psyche's organs do not altogether belong to it."

The "archetypal eye" brings more into view than the "focus upon persons and cases," provides. "This eye needs training through profound appreciation of history and biography, of the arts, of ideas and culture . . . Amplification can be a method of soul-making, by finding the cultural in the psyche and thereby giving culture to the soul."

Ultimately, Hillman concluded, archetypal or "what might be called a polytheistic psychology . . . provides for many varieties of consciousness, styles of existence, and ways of soul making, thereby freeing [Jung's idea of] individuation from stereotypes of an ego on the road to a Self. By reflecting this plurality and freedom of styles within the structures of myth, the archetypal perspective to experience may be furthered. In this spirit *Spring* hopes to proceed."[30]

In one of our interviews in 2008, Hillman reflected: "As that little paper says, the idea of calling it 'archetypal' was an absolutely crucial move—because, if you call it analytical, then the whole psychology depends on being in analysis. And you've limited the power of Jung's work to the analytical. He took his term 'analytical' in distinction to Freud's psychoanalysis. It was a mistake, wasn't a good term, but he hadn't come upon archetype at that time. Anyway, the idea of archetypal is also a move of mine to dethrone the analyst. A big move. Analysis is only one mode in which archetypal life occurs."[31]

The first issue of the new *Spring* also contained Hillman's piece, "On Senex Consciousness," derived from one of his Eranos lectures, which Pat had then edited. The issue also included: articles by friends from his student days, Robert M. Stein, J. Marvin Spiegelman, and Adolf Guggenbühl-Craig; Eranos president Rudolf Ritsema's "Notes for the Usage of the *I Ching*"; two posthumous tributes to former Institute director Franz Riklin; and several articles by and about Jung, including "Fragments from a Talk with Students"—notes taken by Hillman while attending the Institute.

On June 23, Hillman wrote to *Spring*'s seventeen listed Advisors (including Layard and López, as well as the various old friends who contributed articles) that "we now have six people helping: editing manuscripts, organizing the card catalogues, mailing and stuffing envelopes, recording checks," adding that the printers were "two small, owner-operated firms who are not knowledgeable in English."[32]

WRESTLING WITH THE MYTHS

The correspondence with Pat continued after she arrived at her new school in New Mexico that summer. In her first letter to Hillman, she described a dream about being pregnant with his child, deciding to go ahead and give birth, and walking the streets of Columbus looking for a secret room to do so. In the hospital afterward with a baby girl, Hillman's presence was "somehow vaguely to my left. I reach to right to embrace baby and my hand closes on an enormous phallus. Shock! So, I guess things aren't so bad."

There followed a period of acrimonious exchanges before Hillman shifted the tone: "Read many more of Jung's letters: he insists on the impersonal; won't analyze the personal; insists on the mythic aspect. Will print letters of this sort. Everyone delighted with *Spring* around here." Another letter spoke of "Orders for *Spring* coming in very well, continuous. I think we have actually *sold* 400, even if not all paid for."

He wrote Pat that his dreams had returned, too: "mainly my Hillman family, father, his sister, my grandfather, and wine again, several dreams of wine." As well: "Some big dreams that KNOCKED ME OUT. First time in some long while, that a dream got to me. This had an old fat huge *ram*, my companion, & it was tired out. And the animals were 'leaving the field'— complicated end-of-puer dream; then last night 2 small pigs & Persephone/Demeter sacrifice. I write them down now regularly. Maybe you will help me with them?"

Animal dream images, a preoccupation during his years as the Institute's Director of Studies, would remain a lifelong fascination—including a 1982 Eranos lecture on "The Animal Kingdom in the Human Dream," the 1997 book *Dream Animals* in collaboration with Margot McLean, and a collection of essays in the Uniform Edition volume of *Animal Presences* (2008).

Hillman's opening essay in *Dream Animals* (1997), titled "A Snake Is Not a Symbol," begins with a description of a workshop he once held on animal images that worked toward "freeing people of their insidious notions of snake symbolism." The essay condenses a dozen replies to his questions asking for people's definitions, after which he asks: "Why must we exchange the living image for an interpretative concept? Are interpretations really psychological defenses against the presence of a God? Remember most of the Greek Gods, Goddesses, and heroes had a snake form—Zeus, Dionysus, Demeter, Athene, Hercules, Hermes, Hades, even Apollo. Is our terror of the snake the *appropriate* response of a mortal to an immortal?"[33]

In mid-July 1970, when Hillman arrived in northern Sweden with his family to stay for a month, he wrote Pat: "Lots of snakes this summer, smokey black poisonous vipers . . . all the neighbors report them, and last evening when driving in the old Ford with the kids there was one on the road."

This was where Hillman customarily put the finishing touches on his papers for Eranos, but in 1970 he wasn't giving one. Here, besides working on *The Myth of Analysis*, his writing on *The Puer Papers* manuscript was steadily advancing, and Pat seemed the only confidante with whom he could share his latest revelations.

Hillman wrote her: "Found a remarkable statement of Jung's. Creativity is both construction and destruction. We have always spoken of the creative and the destructive as opposites, but here he makes the creative a principle in itself with two poles. I would like to think about the destructive. What really is it? Evil, Death, division, unconsciousness, acting out, breaking apart . . . what is it. We use the term so quickly."

In another letter to Pat, he added: "I am rewriting or rethinking the whole fucking field of psychology! For example narcissism and donjuanism . . . what are they and what are they from a puer positive view, rather than the old guilts about such things? Or the child and childishness and what role that is in rebirth, and what a mistake it is to talk of goals, a typically puer thing to be interested in goals of the process . . .

"The hard part is keeping my own mad vision of it all as I have done before in regard to suicide. At the same time, keeping in touch with people younger than me in my arguments and aims, rather than arguing against the old senex people in mythology or institute or Jungians . . . [Y]ou see, I tend to fall into the rebel young Jungian analyst against Jacobi or Meier, instead of a 'leader of youth.'"

He felt Pat pulled him into the classics through what she was studying at St. John's: "It's as if we read myth and study and write for each other." She was looking ahead to September and the possibility of auditing courses in Greek and Philosophy at the University of London. Valerie Donleavy had offered Pat her house in the city's Fulham district, where her son was living but came and went. Although Pat still had no plans to return to Zürich, London wasn't all that far away.

Hillman wrote her: "If we could only get rid of the usual images of how lives should be lived, usual images of couples, of procreation, of chicks and mistresses, how relationships all *should* be, and find the freedom (that killed Shelley and his crowd), then there could be such a long association between us, years of fruitfulness and such fun and cherishing, where everyone accepts everything and the hatred goes against enemies, outside . . . O, what a fant[as]y, but could it not be aimed at, at least, partly actualized?"

While Hillman had little use for, and even disdained, the new generation's notion of "everybody get together try to love one another right now" (as a pop lyric by the Youngbloods put it), the above paragraph indicates his fantasy was not all that far removed. But rather than "right now," the work harkened back to the gods of the ancients for guidance.

He wrote Pat after mentioning his expansion of the essay "On Psychological Creativity": "I keep running into Apollo when I write. I mean he turns up again and again in the chapters as the enemy, what I am writing against. Curious how the expert scholars see him as the 'most moral of the gods,' when I see him as a killer, raper, destroyer wolfman. Did you know his first deed was killing Python and Artemis' first deed was killing Orion? . . .

"You're right about Athene and glory and victory. I don't know how to win, not the right connection to Athene that's why I lose the crucial battles. I take winning too subjectively and not for the goddess or the cause of the city. Must learn about that."

Was it sheer romanticism, perhaps of the foolish kind, to view his own modern struggles in the light of the ancient Greek pantheon? It's not, if one keeps in mind how ancient myth facilitates soul-making as Hillman described near the end of "Why 'Archetypal' Psychology?": "The problems of the psyche were never solved in classical times nor by archaic peoples through personal relationships and 'humanizing', but through the reverse: connecting them to impersonal dominants. The dominants in the background permit and determine our personal case histories through their archetypal case histories which are myths, the tales of the Gods, their fantasies and dreams, their sufferings and pathologies."[34]

In his writing about the puer at the time ("a civilization without puer is without spirit," he told Pat), he came to terms with his own style—"which aims to evoke and summon, all writing and writers have a fantasy, most disguise it with objective methods which too is a style and fantasy. I want to write a new kind of psycho[logy] book which includes treating my method as a style, and that all the tricks (polemics, strawmen attacks . . . word-conjury) are part of the method, necessary to deal with the matter."

That definition distinguished all of Hillman's work through the second half of his life, during which he became what some consider the greatest writer in the history of psychology. He wrote Pat at the time: "Being in touch with the writing, even on neg[ative] days, keeps the keel and balance. Had the fantasy the other evening of a handbook for psychologists (?) of myths, on the other hand it is too abstract a thing to write, and better would be to write from the Ares that wants to win points (puer book). One writes where one is driven."[35]

POSEIDON'S STORM

> *"Our Greek topology is a topology of islands, of sailors and travelers, of nostalgia for Ithaca, and of winds and wind-Gods that blow one off course, a topology that is like that of the individuation adventure through unconscious waters."*
> —James Hillman, *"Pothos: The Nostalgia of the Puer Eternus,"* 1974.[36]

While Pat moved into Valerie Donleavy's house in London that October, Hillman went with his family on a trip to Greece, his fourth. He and Kate, their four children, and two close friends would spend nearly two weeks on a motorized sailboat. John Mattern, principal of the American High School in Zürich, was on board, along with Martin Strauss, a Hillman family friend from Israel.

They had initially sailed out of Piraeus, happily island-hopping while nine-year-old Laurence sat with Mattern on the deck, writing a film script together. On one isle, the two of them bought some black-and-white fabric and sewed a pirate flag for their onboard set. Then the weather closed in, a ferocious storm that lifted the waves higher than the boat—"easily fifteen feet if not more," Laurence recalled years later. Hillman poured a libation of wine into the sea before dinner, exhorting: "Poseidon, protect us."[37] His son would never forget the moment. "It made a huge impact on me," Laurence said in 2014, "made me feel like the gods were really alive. And it was as natural to him as speaking to a presence."

The group found themselves stranded on Delos, an island near the center of the Cyclades archipelago containing some of the most extensive excavations in the Mediterranean. In Greek mythology, Delos was the birthplace of Apollo and

Artemis—twins sired by Zeus whom Hillman and Pat had mentioned in letters in reference to their own relationship. (When Pat was hurt by his plan to take Kate and the kids to Greece, he accused her of thrusting at him from afar "Artemis elusive, distant arrows.") Delos was crowned by a sanctuary to Zeus. The "House of Dionysus" still stood as well, a luxurious second-century private home named for the floor mosaic of the Greek god riding a panther.

Hillman's third daughter, Susanne, who was approaching her eleventh birthday at the time, later remembered: "Delos only permitted day visits, but due to the storm we were stranded for several days without any other tourists and had all the ruins to ourselves. We slept on the boat and wandered around the island in the daytime. There was just a little café, and the people who worked there had to go out and shoot some wild rabbits so we'd have a meal. It was all very exciting."

Once the storm subsided, the voyagers began to act their parts of the script while Mattern shot an hour-long color film with his 8-mm camera. Laurence recalled that "my father hated being in it. He played a mean horrible pirate with one painted tooth, an eye patch, and a bandana over his head. He wore a long black T-shirt and we put a snorkel where his hand should be, so it looked like a hook."[38] According to Susanne, "We three daughters were all screaming. My brother played a shepherd-boy from the hills, who finds us and saves us from the pirates. The film was mostly without sound, so we played some Greek music in the background."[39]

Hillman wrote in a letter about the trip soon afterward: "Terrible storms, and scary, but splendid."[40]

They returned to Zürich late in October, when Hillman wrote in a letter defining his current life there: "I do not see patients. I do not administer at the Institute. I see people as a sideline, usually without charge and for sorts of talks and 'supervision.' I do not train analysts, which the Institute seems to have become, a dental technicians place, where old analysts train new ones, turning them out like new priesthood. I hate it. I hate the dogma, and the cute quick answers they have. I am instead wrapped up in writing and editing . . . I have two long books underway. I am trying to rethink the whole business of psychology; at times the energy flags. I can't practice, and it hurts to admit it, I can't use the old words that worked before, and haven't found the new ones . . .

"The struggle is with one's myth and fulfilling the 'necessity' imposed by the Gods, and to discover which one wants what."[41]

He wrote to Bob Stein: "Can't practice analysis, worry about my marriage and whether to stay in it . . . everything seems in the same condition of doubt, which acts like a paralysis on action . . . I am fucked up these days, but the new big book is tremendous. I am sure of that."[42]

Soon after, Hillman told Stein he was "in London for a bash at the Warburg Ins[titute]. Reading and note taking," and going over material for *Spring 1971* with Pat Berry, "who lives there now." (A rare mention of Pat's presence in his life, even to his longtime friend).

Early in 1971, Hillman flew to New York where he gave almost daily lectures on archetypal psychology for two weeks. He wrote Pat on the backs of postcards from the Metropolitan Museum of Art, one of the ambush of Silenus by the henchmen of King Midas as depicted on a sixth century B.C. Greek vase.

"Took a slow solitary morning at the museum. Greek vases only. Think puer figures are in the air and that is important in both dreams and in vases: eros, tryptolemy, Bellophon, Ganymede. Not satyrs. The sexual is NOT pronounced in the Athletes, Heroes, Puer; but in the Dionysian, it seems, only. How does that figure, with puer sexuality. Is it only airy (mental) & power & heroic contest athletic)? . . . Also, enjoyed the terra cotta little statues of heroes, all phallic exposed, masks, grotesque, delightful, all fat-bellied, even those playing women's parts. Several vases show warriors fighting, between 2 cocks. Cock-Rooster motif associated with *fighting & victory* . . .

"I feel old, lost, sober, curled up inside, timid. Hope you are *working*. It's crucial."

Early in January 1971, Hillman wrote Stein that "the whole point of the 'movement'" was "to find place within archetypal world for analysis . . . people need connection to archetypes, analysis only one route." The letter concluded: "I will have got 12 things into print in 1970! Wow what an exhausting compulsion."

"WHY NOT MOVE FORWARD BY LOOKING BACKWARD?"

In a page of typed notes concerning his upcoming student lectures at the Jung Institute (January 28, 1971), Hillman began: "Jung said that the archetypes reveal themselves in two ways. He said this in several places in his writings, and again in a long letter to Upton Sinclair in 1955. Man's treasure is hidden on the one side in the symbols of our mythological tradition and on the other in man's unconscious psyche. This course shall explore this interrelation."[43]

Hillman would give four more talks in New York in April, and another at the Centre for Psychological and Spiritual Studies in Malvern, England. The latter was a two-day symposium with a theme of "Guide-Lines for the Future," and Hillman was one of seven speakers. He began by quoting the opening lines of T. S. Eliot's *Four Quartets*: "Time present and time past/Are both perhaps present in time future." The last was what he wanted to talk about, admitting he was not happy with the title of the gathering: "[F]or it is, after all, a fantasy telling us rather about time present which we project as 'future.' In psychological work we know that when people begin to talk about time future they are already out of it in some peculiar way; they have already jumped into something else, and discussions of the future are really projections of their present state of mind." As had been discussed at the symposium the previous night, this meant "either Utopia or Nightmare."

What Hillman wanted to offer was not "ideas of progress" like those of philosopher Teilhard de Chardin or the way that some viewed Jung's individuation process. "When we talk about the future we tend to turn against our own depression, our own melancholy, our own inherited limitations, our own decay," he pointed out. But the practice in Rome, which was echoed by "a similar pattern in the Renaissance," was to look to classical antiquity—to the past, reviving the pagan gods. Why not move forward by looking backward?

In today's society "all the guide-lines of the past have fallen apart"—customs, law, behavior, manners, patterns in family and relationships, in business. These were no longer believed in. However, despite the obvious breakdown of this belief system, people clung to its notion of moral order. As for polytheistic paganism, a multiplicity of gods, "the difficulty of this idea for many people is that it threatens morality with chaos." It was argued that Greek religion "is notoriously amoral" whereas "what is moral is single and good, true and upright, whole-hearted, single-minded."

People "fear the loss of the controlling central figure," the ego—which means, "morality becomes a support for the ego" and brings puritanical or Victorian "psychological regression." Effective guide-lines, on the other hand, "would have to appeal to the psyche in its entirety—the fact that we are each many people—and they would have to capture the imagination."

"From Hercules through St. George to the hero role in Freud and Jung we have had a hero archetype moving in the ego. We believe the ego should be strong and just and overcome death, depression and decay and stand for culture and civilization." But what if Dionysus was instead the archetypal God influencing the ego: "Then rout and intoxication, then coming and going rather than stability . . . would belong to the ego and be its moral values, and the good would not be the word of choice but the dance of movement." Or what if Hermes governed the ego? Then "morality would all depend on the relationship. There would not be a mission as with the hero, but there would be a message." Morality would differ with each god or goddess, but specific guidelines would still apply: "Justification not by faith, by deed, or by love, but by myth. It might sound highly immoral or amoral," but Hillman believed "this position has a morality and with quite important effectiveness for us today."

He concluded: "By recollecting the role of the Gods as archetypal influences upon our ways of perceiving and doing things, we are remembering them in our lives, recollecting, reminiscent of them as living realities, laying our acts and dilemmas at their altars. This was once called piety—discharging an obligation to the Gods. The worst sin in classical Greek religion was impiousness, that is, neglect of their existence; and our morality, which has been so sure of itself in its heroic St. George Christian model considering all else pagan, immoral, etc. is perhaps highly impious in its neglect of wider and other realities."

Let us look back then, Hillman told his audience, a long way back, past the ego, "at what has always supported us most widely and inclusively, in the time of Rome, of Greece and in the Renaissance—the archetypal dominance of the Gods."[44]

From here on out, Hillman's new approach to psychology was articulated through variations on this theme.

NOTES

1. "She mystifies, produces Sphinx-like riddles. . . .": James Hillman, *Anima: An Anatomy of a Personified Notion*, Woodstock, Ct.: Spring Publications, 1985, pp. 133, 135.
2. Replacing "that abstract Indian mandala. . . .": JH letter to Robert Stein.
3. "a ram and a goat. . . .": "The Erotics of Publishing: A Conversation with Iconoclastic Psychologist James Hillman," by Clarissa Pinkola Estes, *The Bloomsbury Review*, September/October 1989. (Opus Archive, H396).
4. "The new and the old. . . .": Pat Berry talk at Festival of Archetypal Psychology, 1992.
5. Hillman on Pat Berry's role with *Spring*. JH interview with author.
6. "We were getting support. . . .": Author interview with JH, May 29, 2008.
7. "I sat on the bed editing. . . .": Pat Berry email to author, October 1, 2014.
8. "It was really on his encouragement. . . ." Author interview with Murray Stein, Zürich, October 8, 2006.

9. Murray "complained of his wife. . . .": Pat Berry email to author, October 2, 2014.

10. On beginnings of Spring: Author interview with JH. The book, published in 1972, was titled *The Feminine in Fairy Tales*.

11. "Everyone has turned it down. . . .": Pat Berry letter to JH, undated, from her private collection.

12. "What we got were just notes. . . .": Author interview with Pat Berry, email of October 2, 2014.

13. "not to Jungians. . . .": JH letter to Robert Stein, December 1969.

14. "Psychotherapy has been killing the puer. . . .": JH letter to Robert Stein, April 1, 1970.

15. "It's a 'leader' inflation. . . .": JH letter to Spiegelman, November 1, 1969.

16. "a figure, Etruscan and later. . . .": JH letter to Robert Stein, undated.

17. "I was very glad that you took our editing. . . .": JH undated letter, early 1970, to Spiegelman.

18. "It's a touchy thing, to edit. . . .": JH letter to Stein, February 6, 1970.

19. "As for men friends, I see mainly. . . .": JH letter to Robert Stein, April 1, 1970.

20. "*Spring* is now a massive book. . . .": JH letter to Spiegelman, April 7, 1970.

21. Audrey Haas on Zürich: Interview with Author, Zürich, May 2005.

22. "It became too much, really. . . ." Author interview with Pat Berry; also, email to author, October 1, 2014.

23. "Jim was against ultimatums. . . .": Pat Berry email to author, October 2, 2014.

24. "the fresh air of some normal academic program. . . .": Pat Berry in Side by Side interview.

25. "It was a very easy thing to do. . . .": Pat Berry email to author, October 21, 2014.

26. All the letters quoted from Hillman to Berry in this chapter are undated and are from her personal archive.

27. Berry's description of her decision to leave Ohio again after the student riots is drawn from interviews with the author and what she told Side by Side.

28. "a wonderful, romantic time. . . .": Pat Berry email to author, October 21, 2014.

29. St. John's: Pat Berry email to author, October 21, 2014.

30. James Hillman, "Why 'Archetypal Psychology?'": *Spring* 1970: 212–19. Hillman archive, Pacifica Graduate Institute.

31. "As that little paper says, the idea of calling it archetypal. . . .": Author interview with JH, May 29, 2008.

32. "We now have six people helping. . . .": JH June 23, 1970 letter to *Spring* advisors, Hinshaw archive.

33. On the snake: James Hillman with Margot McLean, *Dream Animals*, San Francisco: Chronicle Books (1997), p. 26.

34. "The problems of the psyche were never solved in classical times. . . .": James Hillman, "Why 'Archetypal' Psychology?," *Spring* 1970, p. 218.

35. All the quotes from Hillman's letters to Pat Berry, generally undated, are from her private archive.

36. "Our Greek topology is. . . .": James Hillman, *Senex & Puer, Uniform Edition #3*, Spring Publications: Putnam, Ct., 2005, p. 184.

37. "Poseidon, protect us": Author interview with JH.

38. Laurence Hillman on play: Telephone interview with author, December 5, 2014.

39. Stranded on Delos and the film: Author interview with Susanne Hillman, Zürich, 2005.

40. "Terrible storms, and scary. . . .": JH letter to Anne Bedford Ulanov, Robert Hinshaw archive.

41. "I do not see patients. . . .": Letter from JH to Stephen Burgess, October 1970, attached to Burgess letter to JH, 1985, Opus Archive.

42. "I work like a manic madman. . . .": JH letter to Robert Stein, October 22, 1970; Hillman private archive.

43. "Jung said that the archetypes. . . .": Opus Archive, A756, Hillman Box 108.

44. "Guide-Lines For the Future": Centre for Spiritual & Psychological Studies, Summary of a Two-Day Symposium, April 23—25, 1971 at The Abbey Hotel, Great Malvern, Woros. Hinshaw Archive.

5

SPRING SEMINARS: RENAISSANCE MAGIC IN A ROOMFUL OF PUERS

"The Puer eternus is that structure of consciousness and pattern of behavior that (a) refuses and struggles with the Senex—time, work, order, limits, learning, history, continuity, survival and endurance—and that (b) is driven by a phallicism to inquire, quest, travel, chase, search, to transgress all limits. It is a restless spirit that has no 'home' on earth, is always coming from somewhere or going to somewhere in transition. Its Eros is driven by longing"
—James Hillman, *Pothos: The Nostalgia of the puer Eternus*, 1974.[1]

Prolific is too small a word for Hillman's productivity during the early 1970s. The main book he was working on, Hillman wrote Pat Berry, was *"a kind of reworking of the entire Jungian dogma."* He didn't specify which book, but he would later describe *The Myth of Analysis* as "a companion book" to a work-in-progress on the Puer, which would continue to emerge as key lectures but never did appear between two covers. Hillman later described the puer project as "a prolonged and still incomplete defense of my traits and behaviors."[2]

As Gustavo Barcellos, a Hillman scholar from Brazil, has said: "Along the years, the *puer* seems to have been, if not the main theme in his work, certainly the strongest. In it, this archetype appears, not divided (as Hillman himself denounces as happening in culture), but forming a harmonious whole, albeit opened . . . One that gets involved with the *puer* gets necessarily involved with the *Senex* and, afterward, with *Soul.*"[3]

The 1960s can be seen as the struggle between the Puer's thrust into the new and the forces of the Senex determined to maintain the old—an epic battle. Hillman began analyzing this at Eranos in 1967, just as he was facing such circumstances in his personal life. By the early seventies, his continued elucidation of archetypal psychology—inspired by his involvement in a nascent love triangle and its uncertainty—proved stunning. "The puer aspect of meaning is in the *search*," writes Daniel Joseph Polikoff in a biography of the poet Rilke that carries

101

many Hillmanian overtones. "The quest, or questioning, seeking, adventuring, which grips the ego from behind and compels it forward . . . [is] thereby opening the way and leading the Soul towards further questing."[4]

It is not surprising then that Hillman's own puer makeup and themes would attract a collection of young people during those halcyon days in Zürich. In January 1971, he wrote his friend Robert Stein that he had started a weekly seminar on archetypal psychology in his new Spring office room—"but I feel I don't know how to connect to world and make a place with followers and students. That is the main problem now."

Hillman, who grew up in the era of Swing music, did not readily relate to the youth culture that exploded in the sixties. However, the Dionysian quality of Elvis Presley had fascinated him when he saw one of his movies in Zürich. And when he first heard the Beatles on the radio at the impetus of J. P. Donleavy's sons, Hillman wrote his nephew Roger Sternfeld (at the time a university student): "I think the Beatles are the best group . . . only original . . . the others doors, stones, monkees are derivative and too *loud*, or too adolescent. Beatles have originality and sophistication. I am rabidly against LSD and blowing the mind. I could talk hours on this, having had too much to do with the dead-ends of bad trips, and even the good trips are trivial compared to real-life experiences. Study, yes! Use the good head god gave us!"[5]

Years later, in one of our interviews, Hillman would elaborate on the more personal reasons behind his opposition to drugs: "I remember saying to one young Jewish kid, 'You've got a 5,000-year-old mind, what do you want to blow it for?' The people I saw who had been involved, like Alan Watts, were not improved. I think I was more afraid of a bad trip. Now you can see it negatively, that I didn't want to give up control, I was still very rational and all that. But on the one hand, I didn't feel a need. Another thing: once on a trip to New York, one of my lady friends I visited had made some cookies for me that she'd loaded with something. I didn't enjoy that. Another time, at Eranos a patient did the same without telling me, and it pissed me off enormously."[6]

He'd been speaking in October 1967 at a San Francisco conference on death and suicide, when a parade walked past his hotel "burying the hippie" of Haight-Ashbury, which seemed apropos. By the early seventies, he recalled, "People would come to Zürich looking for Jung; they'd seen a Beatles record with his picture on it." What to do? Hillman set about forming his own "underground" within the staid Jung Institute, bringing the counter-culture to Zürich in a unique manner that carried the richness of esoteric thought from the Renaissance and the Greeks forward—and where the intentionally darker undercurrents kept it from being labeled New Age.

Early in the spring of 1971, a year since she departed Zürich, Pat decided to leave London and return to her studies at the Jung Institute. According to what she told an interviewer in 2014, her relationship with Hillman wasn't the primary motivation. "I was so depressed," Pat said. "I thought the relationship wasn't going to develop anymore, but I had to get something for the debacle—a certificate from the institute saying I was an analyst. And all I would need to do was go back and take the exams, go to classes for another couple years in Zürich. Even though I didn't know if I wanted to be an analyst, I thought I at least wanted to get this piece of paper."[7]

In one of our interviews, Pat added: "Being a good practical Capricorn, this is what I told myself." She also said that her conflict over Hillman and all the shadows of Zürich "were the experiences that created me. They were the crucible."[8]

At the time, Hillman had larger plans for Pat. He soon designated her as his Literary Executor in the event of his death, to carry out publication of two books he was then concluding (one then titled *Analysis Revisioned* and the volume on the Puer). "She should have a free hand with this," Hillman wrote.[9]

Spring Publications, which had to move from Pat's apartment when she left, initially changed its headquarters to a bathroom in Adolf Guggenbühl's office, "a soundproof room because it was actually in a vault of a bank," Hillman remembered.[10] Now it was occupying the storefront basement of a Christian Science Reading Room, a few doors further down on Untere Zäune. "For some reason I can't quite recollect," Pat said in 1992, "perhaps the unavailability of apartments, I moved my bed in—and once again Spring and I are roommates. In addition, there are now weekly seminars taking place in the room, and a fairly constant stream of traffic . . . the continual comings and goings of all sorts of curious Souls."[11]

FORMING THE TEAM

In several of our interviews, Hillman kept returning to what he believed was a central thread in his approach to psychology. "What always gets missed is how I really work in Eros," he said. "What held all these different groups together was the erotic connection with people. It's an old Greek idea, a belief I got from Plato and Socrates, that there is no teaching and no learning without Eros. What a symposium meant, really, was a drinking party. They lay on couches and drank and talked. They gave speeches partly lying down. There has to be Eros with the logos. Everything should have that in it, or it doesn't work. It's not a conference—it's a festival or a dance or a ball game."[12]

It started when Hillman was still Director of Studies, when he brought some baseball gloves and softballs back after a trip to the States. The American High School in Zürich hosted the regular gatherings; Pat had become part of the squad. By 1971, the athletic endeavors had expanded. Thayer Greene, attending the Institute at the time (taking Hillman's class on animals and dreams), recalled their team being challenged to a touch football game by a school across the lake. "Jim Hillman was quarterback and I was playing I guess you'd say end. I still remember dashing across the goal line and pulling in a pass which he had put right in my hands."[13]

Another who found himself drawn to these games was Robert Hinshaw. Coming from a Midwestern family of college math professors and musicians, Hinshaw had graduated from Northwestern University with a degree in psychology, which he hated "because it was behaviorism—white rats and T-mazes and statistics—and not about people and Soul."[14] So, like thousands of his generation. Hinshaw had taken off to hitch-hike around Europe. Amid the serendipity of those times, one of his lifts gave him a copy of Jung's *Man and His Symbols*. Another chance acquaintance soon thereafter told him, "You belong at the Jung Institute in Zürich, I can feel it."

Hinshaw wrote to inquire about enrolling, received an affirmative response, and backpacked into the city. He was a couple of blocks from the Institute when he spotted a group of Americans playing touch football in a park and stopped to take some pictures. "At some point somebody was tired and asked if I wanted to take their place," he remembered. Hinshaw had become part of the Hillman team unawares, only discovering the connection to the Institute when he joined them for a beer afterward.

Today a Jungian analyst and the publisher of Daimon Books in Switzerland, Hinshaw recalled: "You'd be working together at a seminar and suddenly go play softball for an hour. I would not say Jim was a very athletic type, but it was a different way to relate to the people around him. For once it wasn't going through thought and intellect, [but to] get more into the body. We played basketball, too. He was a little gangly and awkward, and I made a point of passing to him so that he could make a basket sometimes. And he was *so* happy when he could do that. Throwing a pass or dropping the ball or whatever you did, it didn't matter who won. We were just out there running around having a good time together."[15]

Pat Berry saw another advantage to Hillman introducing physical sports to his students. They "helped assuage some of the intellectual wounds and to redress damaged egos. Though you may have been pummeled in the seminar, you could pummel back with pigskin. If you went down swinging in class, on the diamond you might get a hit."[16] Hillman, by then forty-five, was along with Valerie Donleavy the eldest of the group. Donleavy and Pat were the lone females.

Joining in was Tom Kapacinskas. In later years, he would become a founding faculty member of the Chicago Society of Jungian Analysts, with a therapeutic practice in South Bend, Indiana. He was in law school at Notre Dame late in 1968 when a friend from the counseling department suggested they go hear a lecturer from Zürich's Jung Institute, speaking at the University of Chicago—about an hour's drive away. Kapacinskas knew a little about Jung through a Great Books course that he was simultaneously teaching. So he went along, discovering Hillman "giving a series of lectures on alchemy, wearing his Irish tweeds and looking very professorial." Wangling an invitation to meet him at a reception, Kapacinskas "felt a certain affinity." Eventually he received a grant to study at the Zürich Institute, where he immediately sought Hillman out.[17]

Pat remembered Kapacinskas being the prime impetus for the softball games, which they called baseball. "He organized our activities and with his van shepherded us to our weekly playing. Tom was the real heart and Soul in creating the *Gemeinschaftsgefühle* in this aspect of our activities."[18] In one of his letters to Pat, Hillman described how, dividing up into seven on a side, he'd pitched four innings and "struck out Kapachinski [sic] twice!!!!!!!!!!!!! He hit a homer off me though." (Hillman's team won, 14 to 13, in the last inning.)

Paul Kugler also showed up. In our interview, Kugler considered himself one of "a number of young psychologists my age who were looking for answers to questions of the '60s. Some went to Paris to work with Jacques Lacan, another group went to London to work with R. D. Laing in existential psychoanalysis. And some, like myself, went to Zürich to work with Jim."[19]

After graduating from the University of Buffalo, Kugler arrived at the Institute in April 1971. Entering the library, he noticed a young fellow around the same age with whom he began talking about poetry. Also present was a tall older man. This turned out to be Hillman. "Of all the persons who should be in the library that day!" Kugler recalled. While in school, he was told he *had* to meet Hillman by the distinguished American classicist and poet Al Cook. Now Kugler and Hillman "talked a bit, and he indicated he was giving a private seminar on alchemy that fall, and he invited me to attend."[20] Pat would remember "wily, wiry Paul Kugler" quickly joining the sporting world promoted by Hillman.[21] He would later become an Executive Committee member of the International Association of Jungian Analysts, residing in Buffalo, New York—and the author of several books.

Many years afterward, Pat remained "impressed with how [Hillman] helped particularly young men get their spirit. He really had the ability to let them do their own thing, and encouraged them in such a way that they were able to. It was amazing, really, and I don't know if Jim was conscious of that; I actually think he wasn't. He could set them on fire, and then push them out of the nest. A mentoring quality, but of an unusual sort. There is probably more variety in the people who worked with him as young men than with any other analyst I can think of."[22]

It is noteworthy that all of the later Jungian publishers—Murray Stein (Chiron), Robert Hinshaw (Daimon), and Daryl Sharp (Inner City Books) basically started as students or apprentices of Hillman and *Spring*, and then later set up their own publishing houses, modeled after *Spring*. Basically, these small, still-extant publishers are distributaries of Spring Publications.

DISCOVERING THE *PICATRIX*

Paul Kugler would find value in his classes at the Jung Institute, "but it was more on a kind of eternal plane, I wouldn't call it cutting edge. The Spring seminars were the only place where I felt that questions were being asked, and philosophical attitudes being articulated and woven into Jungian psychology in interesting new ways. They were great evenings, certainly one of the highlights of my time in Zürich."[23]

The seminars, operating out of a storefront basement in the beginning, were led by Hillman and López. They were free, and by word-of-mouth invitation—"open to anyone [among the Institute students] who walked in with a bottle of wine," Pat remembered.[24] Sometimes, as various arcane texts got dissected, there might be "screaming fights among the participants." Hillman recalled "raucous evenings with wine, and López shouting and sputtering. What's important is realizing that, in the beginning of something, it's not a time of order, it's almost surrealist. And there's an enormous amount of crazy Eros around."[25]

Along with the ball games, this resulted "among the disaffected and the expatriates . . . in this little community that formed," said Kapacinskas. "Jim enabled you to feel welcome. At the seminars, trying to open up the imagery to metaphorical Soulfulness was critical for learning, because the Institute courses were generally much drier. This was colorful and alive."[26]

The *Spring 1971* journal being assembled would feature an essay by Hillman titled "Psychology: Monotheistic or Polytheistic," with his eloquent emphasis upon the latter. So it seemed appropriate that the first text discussed at the seminars was the *Picatrix*, an encyclopedic work that contained the ancient wisdom of hermetic and platonic philosophy. The original *Picatrix* was a treatise on astrological magic derived from talismanic symbols—first composed in Arabic around 1000 A. D., translated into Latin at the end of the thirteenth century, and said to combine the spiritual knowledge of Egypt, Greece, Persia, and India.

As early as December 1968, López had written Hillman that he was trying to find an English copy of *Picatrix*: "There is none. We need this book."[27] After visiting the Warburg Institute with Hillman the following spring, López read Frances' Yates book, *Giordano Bruno and the Hermetic Tradition*. "In it, she made reference to the influence of the *Picatrix* and other books during the Renaissance period," López would recall. A Greek cleric had brought some manuscripts to Florence, where Lorenzo the Magnificent asked Ficino to put aside translating Plato to concentrate on the *Picatrix*. More recently, Aby Warburg "was fascinated by it, as it appeared in Medieval Islam, where it is connected to astrological signs. Warburg saw in astrology the connection between rational mathematical logic, and magic." And now López "had fantasies about the *Picatrix*, so we began to search for it."[28]

It wasn't an easy quest. During the Spanish Inquisition, anyone with a copy was often accused of practicing black magic and led to the stake. Casanova, who in his memoirs described the *Picatrix* as a "book of instruction on the planetary hours," got arrested in the eighteenth century for possessing it. Even until modern times, it had been circulated only in manuscript. Some claimed that just keeping a copy on the shelf produced uncanny effects.

Somehow López came upon a rare German edition. At the seminars, *Picatrix* would be read aloud and simultaneously translated into English by Audrey Haas "in a lovely lilting reading voice,"[29] as Pat recalled. Haas recalled that "Jim liked for me to sit beside him, because he said I always knew the latest gossip but mostly because I kept him to the time. I was the one who said, 'I think we've reached the end for tonight.'" The *Picatrix* was "concerning the way in which one related to the gods— what sacrifices they demanded, what atmosphere surrounded them, the places you were likely to meet them."[30]

López later reflected: "This reading constituted a revelation for us, as well as a formidable psychological experience, for it opened feelings among the group that participated in it. We said very strong things to each other. The reading of the *Picatrix* brought an emotional explosion with it. There's no doubt the *Picatrix* unexpectedly touched the complex in all of us, and people reacted according to how much their complexes were shaken. There were times when we were near to personal aggression, and others when people ran away from the meeting, unable to bear the arousing of such strong emotions. But the *Picatrix* is ultimately a rhetorical reading of the different archetypes, what

I like to call archetypal rhetoric . . . [W]e were most influenced by the book's rhetorical possibilities differentiating each arche-type, bringing a different feeling and emotional connection. It is not the same to read rhetorically the ritualistic approach to Venus, with all her symbolic attributes, the perfumes, the dress, the make-up, etc., moving us into feelings of softness and well-being, [rather] than the raging emotions constellated by Ares. This is what is really the most relevant and useful aspect of the book, a very complex book, with relation to astrology, tal-ismanic medicine and alchemy. There are some passages very similar to Paracelsus' writing . . . I think our interest was to con-ceive a psychology focused essentially in the here and now . . . Possibly, the Untere Zaune and [later] Spring House experiences were an opening that helped value irrationality, where the Soul was the field of emotions."[31]

Pat said that after these evenings, there was "almost always a fight between Jim and Rafael.[32] A couple of big ones as we were leaving and went down the walk. It was all just part of sorting out craziness and projecting on this text, as a way of figuring out what it was we were trying to do . . .[33] One of the gods we went through in the *Picatrix* is where Jim started to talk about Mars. We spent a great deal of time talking about the finery, the dress, the pomp and circumstance, all the battle regalia that was part of it. It was kind of eye-opening, because I didn't ever think that broadly about Mars. But Jim, because of his own martialness, really liked talking about this. In fact, I think much of what is in his last book, *A Terrible Love of War*, came out of talking about Mars and the *Picatrix*."[34]

Bob Hinshaw remembered: "Sometimes you might get off the track, because it was anything *but* a straight academic presentation—it was chaos. Rafael's English was not that under-standable, because he had a very heavy accent. He'd say some-thing off-the-wall that nobody would get, and then you'd come around and realize it was brilliant."[35]

Tom Kapacinskas, looking back on those early days of dis-secting the *Picatrix*, shook his head and said: "The main thing about those meetings was the chemistry between López and Jim. The thing about Rafael—the most prickly Cuban since Castro—was that he had these very, very unusual takes on things, that you just had to listen to carefully so you could understand the metaphorical impact. Many of these were based on bullfight metaphors, the *corrida* that he was so fond of talking about, and he found these metaphors for life and for analytic work. He was very colorful, he would grunt and snort, clear his throat, he was unabashedly authentic. He and Hillman had a kind of Don Quixote-Sancho Panza look to them, and their chemistry was always a little delicate, but well worth paying attention to."[36]

MONOTHEISM OR POLYTHEISM?

Spring 1971, published early that summer, represented the next step in formulating archetypal psychology. Hillman wrote of moving away from wholeness, from concepts of "better and worse," from "ego towards self," by leaving "theological thinking and its monotheistic bias" behind.[37] Instead, a "polytheistic psychology obliges consciousness to circulate among a field of powers . . .

"We would consider Artemis, Persephone, Athene, Aphrodite, for instance, as a more adequate psychological background to the complexity of human nature than the unified image of Maria, and the diversity expressed by Apollo, Hermes, Dionysos and Hercules, for instance, to correspond better with psychological actualities than any single idea of self, or single figure of Eros, or of Jesus or Jahweh. Focus upon the many and the different (rather than upon the one and the same) also provides a variety of ways of looking at one psychic condition."[38]

Following Hillman's fifteen-page essay came a section headed "Discussion." This included comments from López, for whom the images of the "Classic World of polytheism" represented "significance as psychic movers." He noted that the psychology of Jung and most of his followers "came geographically from the Northern hemisphere with another mythology at the back of their minds" tied to "the Protestant geography of Europe . . . We know that Jung could not go to Rome; he just fainted in the station," an image that had remained in López's mind all through his eight years in Zürich. There was no resolving this "historical shadow of *all* that we call modern psychology . . . Northern and Southern European mythology reappeared in Western civilization coming out of different fountains of regression. The Renaissance was a regression to the classic images. The Northern European Reformation opposed this regression by borrowing for its own regression the monotheism of the Old Testament."

López concluded: "A few days ago reading *Picatrix* with a group of friends, we found to our surprise that only Jupiter of the pagan gods carries within his archetype the principle of growth, balance, order and dream interpretation, etc., and also Christianity . . . Out of this reading I have exactly the opposite insight into what Jungian psychology has taught me. It is this: the many *contains* the unity of the one *without losing* the possibilities of the many."[39]

Among the others in the "Discussion" was Hillman's friend from his student days, J. Marvin Spiegelman, who took exception to the polytheistic emphasis. Writing from his new home in Beverly Hills, Spiegelman disagreed that "monotheism must be so rigid and authoritarian, or that Protestantism must also be so narrow . . . The one and the many can exist together, as long as the authority is not tyrannically held, is not in Senex hands." Within himself, he'd discovered that "Greek consciousness can co-exist with Jewish, Christian and Buddhist awareness, among others." His own approach—which he knew Hillman would undoubtedly find too idealistic if not simplistic—was "each of us pursuing his own individuation in a brotherhood of sharing and building a world where the authority lies within each of us. This is happening gradually, I think, even though we all repeatedly fail."[40]

In our interviews thirty-five years later, Spiegelman's viewpoint had not changed. "See, if you're related to all these archetypal gods, it's real enough but not *that* real. So there's a rejection involved, and I suspect it's like Freud with Jung—in order to do your thing, you have to reject what the master [did]. It's very oedipal. I think in order to go his own way, Jim had to cut somebody off. And I think it limited him."[41]

For Hillman, it had started long before *Spring 1971*—and he did not see this as tied to the rejection of his forbears in psychology. "My polytheism belongs to my character as a hill-man, a pagan," he reflected a quarter-century after. "My earliest excitement in philosophy came from reading Plato at Trinity University in Dublin and Plotinus at the University of Zürich, and from the overwhelming emotional impact that the physical places of Greece and Sicily had on me, unlike any I have felt anywhere including the Himalayas or Jerusalem. It was never hard for me to sympathize with Freud in regard to his pathological incident on the Acropolis, and with Jung's fainting at the Zürich railroad station intending to go to Rome, to which he never came. Particular places have singular spirits, and they call us."[42]

Nonetheless, as Spiegelman knew well from their personal exchanges, a part of Hillman's psyche remained haunted by the elder Jungians, particularly the ones who'd betrayed or turned against him—like his former analysts, C. A. Meier and Liliane Frei. This seemed to resurface when Pat left in June 1971 for her second eight-week-long summer of courses at St. John's College in New Mexico, for which Hillman again paid her tuition. Hillman may have been triggered when Pat told him of a younger man with whom she "fell in love immediately," although she added that they weren't having an affair. She described running around with several guys, which sounded to Hillman like it had a "terrible American desert speed to it,"—as opposed to their own "five years of terrible slowness."

This may have stirred his memories of Meier's affair with Kate, and his own with the young analysand, because in several letters to Pat that summer Hillman addressed the longstanding conflict erupting in his dreams. In one of these, he described how it was "embarrassing to dream again last night of Meier and Liliane. He had made many brilliantly coloured beautiful paintings which I was looking at . . . one of which was of a baby, rather surrealist, long legs viewed from below, and it had many divisions in it, as if in two . . . organic forms . . . Liliane said at one point in a low voice that 'she loves me,' and I rejected it. Who are these people who invade my Soul, are they my Soul parents, and what is it all for . . . One thing about dreams: we may be classic in interpretation of motives and so on, but we have yet to get hold of the personal style of dreams, which, like handwriting and styles of walk and dress reveal in their motives and atmospheres certain kinks and bents of personality over and above the collective motives."

In another letter to Pat, he wrote: "Second dream of Meier: this time he wanted gratitude, recognition, reconciliation . . . and I felt the old guilt over spoiled relationships, only then, in dream, to recollect that again he was putting it all on me, and where were his steps in this direction, his admission of fault, etc. He is a spiritual father, representing my troubled relation with the tradition, my combat and unreconciled pain that drives me into rancor and sarcasm with the tradition. How much better Freud took his transference defeat with Fleiss (his 'father'); how brokenly hurt is the psychoanalytic tradition of fathers and sons . . . what are we fighting over?"

He also dreamed that Marie-Louise von Franz, whose seminal work on fairy tales he had just published, criticized his editing: "We had done some stupid little things, but she was picky. She was a dark, rouged, very attractive young girl (25 or so!) And as we talked she and I kept maneuvering our positions to get on the left side of each other, I wanted her on my left and she wanted me on her left."

By summer's end, Hillman appeared to be coming to terms with the dreams. "For years my aim has been to reach outside and turn my back on the locals. They got me in the back, I have resented it, but I have forgotten (when looking at the wounds) that my main aim has been outside, the 'world.'"[43]

Then came a breakthrough. Hillman wrote excitedly to tell Pat about what an artist friend in New York had sent him in a letter. It was a quote from Jung's "Seven Sermons to the Dead," first published in 1962 as an appendix to his posthumous auto-biography, *Memories, Dreams, Reflections*. About the appendix, Hillman said, "Jung wrote while he was 'batty' around age 38, and gave his friends-pupils as if a Gnostic document, and kept secretly underground for years . . . Jung's sort of private active imagination vision and also a joke on his gang (given out as if a historical text), well he says in sermon four, all about the Gods and demons:

"'But woe unto you, who replace these incompatible many by a single God. For in so doing ye beget the torment which is bred from not understanding, and ye mutilate the creature whose nature and aim is distinctiveness. How can ye be true to your own nature when ye try to change the many into one? What ye do unto the Gods is done likewise unto you. Ye all shall become equal and thus is your nature maimed . . . Gods are mighty and can endure their manifoldness . . . Men are weak and cannot endure their manifold nature . . . the Multiplicity of the Gods correspondeth to the multiplicity of man.'

"Well it is too long to go on with. But what a cannon load when they begin to storm my keep, my parapet, I shall blunder-buss them like Davy Crockett and Kit Carson."

Almost forty years would pass before the publication of Jung's *Red Book*, long denied by his heirs, in which the "Seven Sermons to the Dead" comprised the original closing pages in the manuscript. While Jung shared the "Seven Sermons" pri-vately during his lifetime, he ascribed authorship to the early Christian Gnostic religious teacher, Basilides, rather than him-self. The *Red Book* would become a publishing sensation and inspire Hillman to revise his thinking about Jung—realizing how parallel the essence of their psychologies had actually been.

THE MOVE TO SPRING HOUSE

While Hillman discovered that he and Jung were not on such different wave-lengths, his letter exchanges with Pat burgeoned with mythological references. He told her he was reading about the "labours of Herc[ules] . . . where he goes to hell to get the dog and to get the girdle of the amazon queen. In that tale, it is the King's daughter who wants the girdle. The King sets him on all the tasks, but it is the king's daughter this time who sets the task. He gets the girdle easily, but just then Hera appears disguised as an Amaz[on] and raises trouble and brings about the battle. So some new amazon riddles: why does the girl-anima-princess need the amazon belt? And why does Hera constellate the fight? This Admete, the princess, was a priestess of Hera. We have yet to work out something on Hera and the amazons. This might be of particular importance to you."

Some years later, in an essay on "Echo's Passion," Berry would write: "Though Zeus and Hera are the veritable archetype of marriage, most of the fruits of that union are occurring in the hollows beneath (or apart from) their married intention, not apart from their marriage necessarily, but apart from its constant intention.

"And now we have to give Hera more credit. She, too, is a divinity; even her inability to understand what's happening is important. Perhaps it's important that the established *not* understand the unformed and the unestablished. In this way, a tension is maintained—a tension between form, continuity, the manifest, the past, the tradition on the one hand, and the miscreant, the upstart, the bastardly, the new on the other. This tension is what gives the new its sense as something odd (and original) and also requires of the new that it too come formally to terms, at some time or another, in one manner or another."[44]

Were Hillman's letter and Pat's piece mirror images of how each had made sense of their triangular relationship with Kate? Hillman went on to tell Pat that he "would love to do a play on Herc[ules] in the underworld. Imagine him facing Persephone . . . imagine their meeting. Hades is supposed to have fled the throne (disappeared) in the face of storming heroic consc[iousness]. That's not his thing and he takes off; but Persephone abides and looks this monster (called ego consciousness) Herc[ules]

in the face. Some tales hold that he had been previously initiated at Eleusis. Hades is the last labour of Herc[ules]. From the
upperworld interpret[ation] he overcomes death. But from the
psych[ological] interp[retation] there is no longer a possibility
of heroic labour because he has met perseph[one]. He has captured the dog which too is connected to Hera, the death-drive
that has made him heroic all along. Now come the remarkable
non-ego or psychic events, after the twelve labours: his madness, his service of women, his sins and suffering torments and
his end."

Late that summer, Pat returned to Zürich and accompanied
Hillman to his fifth Eranos conference, where he lectured on
"Abandoning the Child"—which he finished writing in northern Sweden. It struck him that their connection involved her
dream about conceiving a child—but might they have already
generated one? "In other words we have become parents, psychological parents. It's happened! And we must use our heads
to find out what . . . the intimacy, emotional level is not enough
anymore."[45]

Pat settled again in Zürich, where by day she worked toward
her diploma as an analyst and became part of a supervision
group at the Klinik am Zürichberg. Meanwhile, more and more
American students began showing up to do part-time typing
work for *Spring*, and attend the wild, customarily weekly seminars at a new location now called Spring House. The three-story
building, built around 1900, was on Bellerivestrasse 13 down by
the lake. Kate had found it, and Hillman leased it from "an old
woman named Pravetcha and her son and his kids, who lived
in a house in front."[46] Most recently it had been a plumbing
company office and, before that, a leather factory. Up some
stone steps to the main floor, a large, heavy oak table—used at
one time for cutting and sewing leather gloves—remained the
centerpiece of the Spring House meetings and seated anywhere
between five and twenty people. (Hillman would later bring the
table across the Atlantic and place it in his home office in Dallas,
and then Connecticut).

Hillman wrote his mother that autumn: "We have been busy arranging the painting and cheap furnishing of a seven room very busted up house which I rented for five years for my seminars, for the offices of SPRING Publications, and for two or three friends who will practice in the building. Nina [what Kate's family called her] scoured the town for busted chairs. It used to be a glove factory, and the floor has so many waves and curves one can't cross the room without getting nauseous, but it's charming and practical."[47] (*Spring Journal* was put together on the same floor as the seminars.)

In the basement, and on the upper floor of the Spring House, several candidates at the Jung Institute rented rooms to do analysis. "A lot of Jungians who are now in the States worked here," according to Hillman. In the attic, Pat recalled, "a sometimes psychotic artist lived. After the artist departed, Jeff Satinover laid out the index of one of the first *Spring* books to have such." (Satinover went on to be a well-known American psychiatrist, neuroscientist, and eventually physicist, author of *The Quantum Brain*.)[48]

Hillman's daughter Susanne remembers: "When my father started Spring Publications, he brought the mailings home to us and we sat in the kitchen stuffing gray envelopes for days. I liked the feel of a 'family business.' I also loved being at the Spring office and picking up on the exciting creative intellectual atmosphere and freewheeling American 1970s way in which people there related, so different to Zwingli's Switzerland. Pat Berry was very welcoming to me there. They listened to some new American music records, which I felt strongly drawn towards."[49]

Pat remembered that "Kate designed the space, and decorated it wonderfully. She paid for the painting and the curtains. It was her attempt, I think, to be part of things."[50] Hillman recalled in 2010: "At one point, Kate had said she didn't want me to start doing *Spring*; she foresaw that it would be a whole new leaving [her] alone. Then she tried to join in, but she couldn't do it, it tore her apart. To sit at the same big table in the Spring House with Pat there . . . It was very cruel to Kate."[51] Pat, in fact, had moved into a room next door in a children's art studio, where she had use of a kitchen and bathroom, with the larger Spring House building right off her backyard.

Valerie Donleavy took young Bob Hinshaw under her wing, giving him Jungian reading lists and putting him to work on the journal with what he described as "an office in a cubbyhole, a dark little room just off the entrance, but actually a wonderfully cozy place."[52] According to Pat, "Valerie was absolutely central to that period, at Spring every day, always carrying around plastic sacks with manuscripts in them."[53]

Among the group, too, was Adam Diment, who attended the ongoing seminars and helped handle *Spring*'s business affairs. Originally from London, Diment had risen to early fame at age twenty-three after publishing a best-selling novel called *The Dolly Dolly Spy* (1967). He followed that up with three other espionage thrillers, none of which did very well. According to Hinshaw, when Diment arrived in Zürich in 1971, "He was down and out. He didn't study at the Jung Institute, but he got into the Spring House circle and ended up playing a vital role." (Diment never wrote another book; once in Zürich, he disappeared from public view; he eventually went back to England, drove a taxi, and finally moved with his family to a farm where he still resides)

Another new participant in the seminars was tall, long-bearded Austin Delaney, an Irish-Canadian recently arrived from an ashram in southern India. And there was a young Dutchman named Robert (Robbie) Bosnak. His wife, Deanne, had been studying at the New School in New York when her teacher wrote on a note card that, since they planned to move to Europe, she and Robbie should try and get to an Eranos conference. That's where the newlyweds went for their honeymoon in August 1971, and where Bosnak introduced himself to Hillman by saying: "Dr. Hillman, I used LSD and I have these strange experiences that I'd like to talk with you about."[54]

The conversation continued that fall after Bosnak enrolled at the Jung Institute. He would later pioneer a radically new method of re-entering one's dreams, based on Jung's active imagination and alchemy. At the time, like Hinshaw, Kapacinskas, and Kugler, Bosnak found the Spring House gatherings a mind-bending experience. The meetings around the table would begin around 8 p.m. and continue until the last tram departed shortly before midnight. Either Hillman or López would often stand by a blackboard and draw diagrams of how different images fit together. López would puff on big cigars, rub his belly, and drink wine—or whatever suited his fancy that night. But, Bosnak reflected, "his mind would never go fuzzy. It was in context of libations, but really an intellectual feast." Bosnak felt that Hillman "very much deferred to López, whose boldness he seemed to trust more than his own." But "the process was steered from underneath somewhere; many, many sparks that suddenly became *one* fire. *The Art of Memory* was a central book—and the Memory Theater was always referred to."[55]

RESURRECTING RENAISSANCE (AND GREEK) MYSTERIES

> *"This Plato foretold: he said to King Dionysius that a time would come after many generations, when the mysteries of theology would be purified by penetrating discussion, as gold is purified by fire. This time has come indeed . . . May the spirit of Plato, we, and all his followers rejoice at this exceedingly!"*
> —Meditations on the Soul:
> Selected Letters of Marsilio Ficino.[56]

In his 1968 Eranos lecture on psychological language, Hillman had devoted some time to Frances Yates's book *The Art of Memory*, and how "through the imagination man has access to the gods." Then, when he first entered the Warburg Library nine months later, at one point Yates walked through. Approaching seventy, she'd been conducting research there for more than three decades, including for her classic work on Renaissance figure Giordano Bruno. "She was all bent over, almost like a hunchback, a real scholar's look," Hillman would remember.[57]

The Memory Theater that Yates studied came out of the Renaissance, "a time when the imagination was liberated," as Paul Kugler put it. "A very important time, when a revolution was occurring in terms of an understanding of the external universe, that the Earth was not the center. But at the same time, Giordano Bruno was burned at the stake because he suggested there was an inner sun and that sun was the imagination. It would still be 250 years before it was safe for mainstream Western philosophers to talk about the creative imagination without being considered heretics."[58]

Don Giulio Camillo, creator of the Memory Theater, had been briefly among the most renowned thinkers of the sixteenth century. The wooden structure, first displayed in Venice and Paris, was never completed and did not survive long after Camillo's death in 1544. It was said to have allowed one or two people at a time within its interior, which was inscribed with a variety of images, figures, and ornaments, and lined with small boxes arranged on various levels. "Following the order of the creation of the world," Camillo wrote in his posthumously published *L'idea del Theatro* (1550), "we shall place on the first levels the more natural things . . . those we can imagine to have been created before all other things by divine decree. Then we shall arrange from level to level those that followed after, in such a way that in the seventh, that is, the last and highest level shall sit all the arts."[59]

The entire Theater symbolically rested, Camillo said, on Solomon's Seven Pillars of Wisdom, above which were the planets that governed cause and effect. The upper levels, arranged in an ascending order and affected by planetary influences, depicted a gradual upward progression from nature to art and were called The Banquet, The Cave, The Gorgons, Pasiphae, The Sandals of Mercury, and ultimately Prometheus.

The idea, as Yates wrote in *The Art of Memory*, was that upon entering the Theater, the "spectator will be able to discourse on any subject no less fluently than Cicero,"[60] while looking out from a stage towards the auditorium with its images placed among the seven pillars or levels. According to Yates in another book, *Theatre of the World*, the construction of the Globe Theatre during Shakespeare's time was a result of Camillo's influence, as passed along in *L'idea del Theatro* through two Elizabethan hermetic philosophers.

As with the *Picatrix*, the Memory Theater had been long forgotten when Rafael López recalled he "had an amplified replica of the Theatre made and we set off to study the correlations between the different archetypes. Basically, Camillo's theatre presents archetypal combinations." It had taken him years, López said, to differentiate between "a memory of recollections and an emotional memory, which is very different and extremely important in the psychic world."[61]

According to Hillman, "the seven planetary figures were all displayed in symbolic images in a great semi-circular map that had once been an actual theater. If you remember any single thing, then through chains of memory you remember everything through images, rather than through words necessarily. It's a whole theory of [how] the psyche [works]."[62]

Bob Hinshaw remembered that inside the big amphitheater "each of the different gods would be seated with lines of relationship drawn between them, and then we would take a particular section of the theater and just talk it through. Rafael said the whole memory could be organized in terms of the different gods."[63]

Hinshaw was stunned by the diversity of it all: "Jim knew the Greek gods inside and out. So he would say something and then Rafael would disagree and say 'But!' and shout at him 'You're forgetting this whole aspect!' So a whole thing would follow about what are the characteristics or qualities of Hermes, for example. Then people would come in with all their associations.[64] Another time it might be about sulfur, when we were into alchemy, or some other substance." (Years later, Hillman was reminded by an attendee that "one evening I was beating on the desk with a chicken drumstick and shouting about sulfur!")[65]

For López, the most important experience of the seminars was reading *The Hieroglyphics of Horapollo*. The text consisted of two books, ascribed to one of the last leaders of the Egyptian priesthood (fifth century, A.D.), but dating back to a much earlier translation into Greek of 189 explanations of ancient Egyptian hieroglyphic symbols. It had been rediscovered in 1419 on the island of Andros and taken to Florence, where during the Renaissance it was translated into Latin and became widely popular.[66] López loved going through the English translation (1950), he said, "because it was not me who did the reading, it was something autonomous, something that worked up in my psyche and whose existence I had never noticed. What I mean is that these readings made it possible for all of us who were there to connect with very strong and unique emotions. They shook us, and could only be somewhat assimilated after many years."[67]

That summer, before Pat returned from St. John's, Hillman had written her of one seminar "speaking of differentiating qualities of night, connection in Horapollo between Soul and night and twilight and time . . . I thought that insomnia might give Soul a chance to differentiate the qualities of the night, the spectrum of divinities that rule the different hours and their qualities; Audrey took night up into the psychic darkness, rather than literal night."

Audrey Haas would "never forget the night in that little room in the Old Town section of Zürich. It was on street level. It had windows and you could see people walking by, but they didn't usually look in. We were discussing Dionysus very avidly when a drunk fell into the room—I mean, literally crashed through the window! And Rafael said: 'You see? We constellated!'"[68]

In the language of archetypal psychology, 'constellate' meant clustering together, like stars in a constellation. Dionysus' presence had clearly opened up the gathering. As Hillman put it, "Rafael would break the usual pattern. When we would see something symbolically, he would try to get rid of it—force everyone to stay with the image, what is the image saying, stick to the image!"[69] (It was Jung who first expressed this idea, writing:

"The fundamental facts of existence are fantasy images of the psyche. Stick to the image."[70])

Years later, Hillman said in one of our interviews: "Who knows what we actually learned? I'd already been giving courses in alchemy, back to the mid-sixties, following from Jung. And this was tied to alchemy, but we were not studying alchemical symbols so much as trying to read these images. They were all very weird, but we immersed in Greek mythology and Renaissance imagery. People didn't know what the hell we were doing, these texts were so obscure. But all of this was part of archetypal studies, you might say."[71]

CIRCLING BACKWARDS WITH THE DANCER

Everyone had their fond memories of Spring House, nights that engrained themselves in private memory theaters. Naomi Goldenberg, today a renowned Professor of Religious Studies at the University of Ottawa, came later and remembered the gatherings growing "louder and more insightful" as they went on; of López speaking of how "sometimes as an analyst, there's a bull you know you can't deal with," and that Hillman was "very accepting of everyone's associations and arguments, not moralistic at all."[72]

Ed Casey, future president of the American Philosophical Association, also came for a couple of weeks and "realized that these folks were really doing active imagination through this sixteenth-century Memory Theater system. I mean, it was like free association but in a collective setting. People would yell out or call out directions, and then there would be a kind of response—almost parallel to the African American gospel church, in that it had a very powerful communal spirit. Coming from Kansas and education mostly in very austere schools in the Northeast, I'd never experienced anything like this. It was altogether one of the most lively occasions I've ever been at."[73]

Lyn Cowan, later to become known for her books *Tracking the White Rabbit* and *The Blue Lady*, recalled Hillman once after dinner going upstairs to change, unusual for these customarily informal get-togethers. He came down wearing a bow tie and black velvet jacket over a pair of blue jeans and asked how he looked. "Well, you look very handsome," Cowan remembered saying, with Pat Berry concurring. But why had he gotten all dressed up for the seminar? "Well," he replied, "we're going to invoke Aphrodite."

Cowan added that around Hillman and López there was "a kind of penumbra . . . as if in a kind of intellectual zone, the way I would imagine if Einstein had been collaborating with somebody on the theory of relativity." The near-sighted Hillman would have his books open, pull off his glasses and peer, "literally put his nose in the book." López would sit next to him in deep thought, muttering something occasionally that caused everyone to stop and stare at him. "That's it! Now there's an insight," Hillman would say.[74]

In her talk two decades later at the Festival of Archetypal Psychology at Notre Dame, Pat Berry elaborated on the stylistic differences between López and Hillman, and what she learned from each. As a kind of summation of the two men's remarkable relationship, and what they brought to that roomful of Puers, it is worth quoting at length.

López, Pat said, "required my learning how to put aside whatever common sense I had, in order to entertain his less common sense. I learned simply to receive his lengthy didactic monologues. His monologues were punctuated by grunts, sort of ahhhhuhhh hmmmm and a bunch of others. A lot of this learning was non-verbal with Rafael. I learned to hold the spaces . . . without questioning or commenting on the apparent lack of reason in what he was saying. This holding, waiting, actually taught me a great deal about psychological thinking. What is immediately apparent is not what things are about anyway—so to wait is to give time for things to interconnect. Eventually I learned to make the kinds of comments, or returning grunts, that encouraged Rafael's thoughts. Since he was a guru, Yoda-like, to relate to him one had always to be a student, a disciple. And for some years, this willing suspension of myself was worth it, in exchange I suppose for the kind of uncommon sense I was learning.

"Jim thought quite differently and in a mode I found far easier to cope with. Whereas Rafael circled ideas in a Cancerian backward manner—[astrologically] he was a Cancer, a crab—clasping insights and ingesting them back into himself, into his own being, Jim moved more like a dancer: quick and clear with sudden spins, pirouettes and somersaults that seemed always to land on somebody's feet. Both men were polemicists. They thought oppositionally and generally worked off an other, an enemy, that was stereotyped and placed out there, which was then either preached at, derided, or battered against. This battering was more Jim's mode, because of his martial nature . . . But Jim is also Apollonic, so he was able to step back, to separate himself from his spars and lunges, then frame the battle, the issue, within an intellectual ideational context and present it. Rafael was Dionysus, if not Silenus [the wine god's tutor], Jim Apollo. This contrast between the two styles, Rafael's mode of being and Jim's brilliance in saying, was fruitful for many years. Jim said what Rafael was, and in so doing nurtured Rafael's originality—and nurtured him as a person, too."[75]

Amid the Eros and among the Puers on those unforgettable evenings, Pat would recall that "the tenets of this new psychology were beginning to take shape . . . [but] I think most of us in the seminar didn't really know what these tenets were, or what they exactly meant. They were vague maxims that we heard all the time, such as 'stick to the image'—Rafael's maxim—or 'save the phenomena' which was Jim's maxim. But what was that? We had a much clearer idea of what archetypal psychology was *not*, and so the learning was a kind of *via negativa*. You were whacked with Rafael's stick, so to speak, if you got it wrong, so you'd try something else. Archetypal psychology was not monotheistic, not ego-personal, not transcendent, not structural, not linear, not Christian, not normal, not mediocre, not about getting better, not balanced. And anyone who was, or who inadvertently expressed any of these more traditional values or assumptions, was shouted down and used as a foil for the rest of us. See, this form of pedagogy was not for the weak . . . Not everyone made it through these entanglements unscathed. But it was also rich and full, and so totally involving that if you did make it through, you were changed forever, for good or for ill."

As one example, Pat cited Tom Kapacinskas as "constantly battered for his at that time more structural habit of mind and Christian background." When asked about this in a 2006 interview, Kapacinskas expressed no regrets. "Yes, I'd grown up in the Roman Catholic tradition, as the grandchild of Lithuanian immigrants who used Catholicism as a bulwark against Bolshevism. So I was formed, and deformed, by that. Part of my analysis and interest in the psychology of religion was trying to find my way through, to make sense of it, to see into it. And one of the things that Jim provided was this idea of seeing through. Being Jewish, and a very Soulful person, he had an approach to and a view of Christianity from the outside. So he gave me some vistas into Christianity that were very helpful to me personally and in developing my own work. Jim always used to say, 'You go where you get something.' And we got something from hanging out together, from what the ideas opened for us, from thinking also about what they were not useful for, what their limitations were."[76]

During the Spring House period, Hillman received a letter from an acquaintance at Yale University, Daniel J. Levinson—a psychologist best known for chronicling the life-stages of what became known as "positive adult development." Levinson wrote: "I am especially pleased that you have come to see the Mentor as an archetypal figure. I have long felt that the depth psychologies have had too limited a view of the 'senior adult male'—almost the only images are those of the Oedipal father (who must, after all, be a young man if he exists mainly in relation to a four year old son) or the aging tyrant, guru or lost soul. Moreover, I don't think that a man at 40 can do much for himself by attempting a synthesis of puer and senex archetypes. We need to clarify further the archetypal possibilities for mature adulthood (which turns out to be a form of middle age). Finding a Mentor in early adulthood is tough; and becoming one is tougher yet."[77]

The kind of mentorship that first flowered at Spring House would come to fruition a dozen years later in Hillman's extensive work within the American "mythopoetic men's movement."

NOTES

1. "The puer eternus is that structure. . . ." James Hillman, essay in *Loose Ends*, p. 58.
2. "a prolonged and still incomplete defense. . . .": referenced by Glen Slater *in A Tribute to James Hillman: Reflections on a Renegade Psychologist*, Edited by Jennifer Leigh Selig and Cailo Francisco Ghorayeb, Mandorla Books, Carpenteria, CA., 2014, pp. 99–100.
3. "Along the years, the puer seems. . . ." Essay by Gustavo Barcellos, ibid. p. 34.
4. "The puer aspect of meaning. . . .": Daniel Joseph Polikoff, *In the Image of Orpheus: Rilke, A Soul History*, Chiron Publications, 2011.
5. "I think the Beatles are the best group. . . .": Hillman letter, undated, to Roger Sternfeld, provided author by Margot McLean.
6. "I remember saying to one young. . . .": Author interview with JH, August 2007.
7. "I was so depressed. . . .": Pat Berry interview with Nancy Robinson-Kime, for *Side by Side*.
8. "the experiences that created me. . . .": *Side by Side* interview.
9. Berry as Literary Executor: Hillman private archive, dated April 22, 1971 and confirmed a second time on March 8, 1975.
10. Spring office "a soundproof room. . . .": Author interview with JH, May 2005.
11. "For some reason I can't quite recollect. . . .": Transcript of Berry talk at Notre Dame Festival, 1992.
12. Hillman's comments on the importance of Eros came in interviews with the author in July and September 2009 and in June 2011.
13. "Jim Hillman was quarterback. . . .": Author interview with Thayer Greene, July 2015.
14. "because it was behaviorism. . . .": Author interview with Robert Hinshaw, May 2005, Einsedeln, Switzerland..
15. "Jim was always playing touch football then, too. . . .": Hinshaw interview.
16. "The meetings. . . .ere free and open. . . .": Pat Berry talk at Notre Dame Festival, 1992.
17. Tom Kapacinskas on meeting Hillman: Interview with author, June 2008.

18. "Like a big brother he organized. . . .": Pat Berry talk at Notre Dame, 1992.
19. The author's interview with Paul Kugler took place in Pittsburgh, in June 2008.
20. Ibid.
21. "wily, wiry little Paul Kugler. . . .": Pat Berry talk at Notre Dame, 1992.
22. Pat Berry on Hillman's mentoring qualities: Author interview, October 17, 2007.
23. Author's interview with Paul Kugler, June 2008.
24. "open to anyone. . . .": Pat Berry talk at Notre Dame Festival.
25. Haas "would read passages. . . .": Author interview with Hillman, May 2005, in Zürich.
26. "There was this little community that formed. . . .": Author interview with Tom Kapacinskas, June 2008.
27. "There is none. . . .": Letter to Hillman at University of Chicago from Rafael López-Pedraza, December 1, 1968, Hillman archive.
28. López on the *Picatrix*: Interview with Axel Capriles.
29. Berry on Haas and texts: Notre Dame talk.
30. Hillman "used to seat me next to him. . . .": Audrey Haas email to author, February 22, 2014.
31. "This reading constituted a revelation. . . .": López interview with Axel Capriles.
32. "almost always a fight. . . .": Berry, Notre Dame talk.
33. "A couple of big ones as we were leaving. . . .": Author interview with Berry, September 2013.
34. Berry on Mars, Hillman, and the *Picatrix*: Author interview with Berry, September 2013.
35. "Sometimes you might get off the track. . . .": Author interview with Robert Hinshaw, May 2005.
36. "The main thing about those meetings. . . .": Author interview with Tom Kapacinskas, June 2008.
37. James Hillman, "Psychology: Monotheistic or Polytheistic," *Spring 1971*, p. 201.
38. "polytheistic psychology obliges consciousness. . . .": Ibid, p. 198.
39. López' comments on "Psychology: Monotheistic or Polytheistic," *Spring 1971*, pp. 212–214.
40. Spiegelman comments: *Spring 1971*, pp. 221–223.
41. The author's interviews with Marvin Spiegelman were conducted in Los Angeles in January 2005 and January 2008.
42. "My polytheism belongs to my character. . . .": James Hillman, "Twenty-Five Years Later," p. 125.
43. "For years my aim has been to reach outside. . . .": JH letter to Pat Berry, 1971, undated.
44. "Though Zeus and Hera are the veritable archetype. . . .": *Echo's Subtle Body*, p. 110.
45. "In other words we have become parents. . . .": JH letter to Pat Berry, summer 1971, Berry private archive.
46. "an old woman named Pravetcha. . . .": Author interview with Robert Hinshaw, May 2005.
47. "We have been busy arranging the painting. . . .": JH letter to his mother, undated, 1971.
48. "a sometimes psychotic artist lived. . . .": Pat Berry email to author, November 22, 2014.

49. "When my father started Spring. . . .": Susanne Hillman, "Memories of my father," sent author September 2020.

50. "Kate designed the space. . . .": Author interview with Pat Berry, email to author, November 22, 2014.

51. "At one point, Kate had said she didn't want me to start. . . .": Author interview with JH.

52. Hinshaw's "little office in a cubby hole. . . .": Author interview with Robert Hinshaw.

53. "Valerie was absolutely crucial. . . .": Author interview.

54. "Dr. Hillman, I used LSD. . . .": Bosnak interview with author.

55. Robert Bosnak on Spring House: Interview with Author, October 19, 2006.

56. "The Plato foretold. . . .": Meditations on the Soul: Selected Letters of Marsilio Ficino, London: The School of Economic Science, 1997 paperback edition, p. 83.

57. "She was all bent over. . . .": Author interview with JH.

58. "a time when the imagination was liberated. . . .": Author interview with Paul Kugler, 2008.

59. Camillo, Giulio, L'Idea del Theatro (Florence: Lorenzo Torrentino, 1550), pp. 10–11.

60. "spectator will be able to discourse. . . .": Francis A. Yates, The Art of Memory (Chicago: The University of Chicago Press, 1966) pp. 130–131.

61. "an amplified replica of the Theatre made. . . .": López-Pedraza conversation with Axel Capriles.

62. "the seven planetary figures were all displayed. . . .": Author interview with JH.

63. "each of the different gods would be seated. . . .": Author interview with Hinshaw.

64. Regarding Hermes, Hillman wrote in a letter to Paul Wallace (Spring 1969, Hinshaw files) that this particular god "who moves between two worlds and who is never in one place, and who has no fixities of position, no ego to overthrow. . . .is the guide of Souls, for it is the function of awareness moving among the sheep of the complexes, now nudging this one, now nipping the heels of that, and inseparable from the sheep. It's a hovering attention, but no special aim,no overthrow. Flow is the better way, just watching and living the flow, or being with that flow."

65. "One evening I was beating on the desk with a chicken drumstick. . . .": Author interview with JH, June 2011.

66. Background on Hieroglyphics of Horapollo: http://en.wikipedia.org/wiki/Horapollo

67. López on Hieroglyphics: Capriles interview.

68. "never forget the night. . . .": Author interview with Audrey Haas, Zürich, May 2005.

69. "Rafael would break the usual pattern. . . .": Author interview with JH.

70. Jung, "The fundamental facts of existence. . . .": "The Soul of the World: Exploring Archetypal Psychology," by Susan C. Roberts, Common Boundary, November/December 1992.

71. "Who knows what we actually learned?....": Author interview with JH, May 2005..

72. "louder and more insighftful. . . .": Author interview with Naomi Goldenberg, July 2015.

73. "realized that these folks. . . .": Author interview with Ed Casey, May 2015.

74. Lyn Cowan: Interview with author, July 2007.

75. "the tenets of this new psychology. . . . and nurtured him as a person, too.": Pat Berry talk at Notre Dame festival, 1992.

76. "Yes, I'd grown up in the Roman Catholic tradition. . . .": Author interview with Tom Kapacinskas, June 2008.

77. "I am especially pleased that you have come to see the Mentor. . . .": Letter from Daniel J. Levinson to Dr. James Hillman, March 29, 1973, Hinshaw archive.

6

AMERICAN RETURN:
THE TERRY LECTURES

"Jim Hillman wrote and told me he has received THE CALL. He has been invited to give the Terry Lectures at Yale University."
—*Letter from Kenny Donoghue to J. P. Donleavy, 1972.*

Late in the summer of 1971, Hillman went to Eranos to deliver his fifth annual lecture to the invited gathering of "underground" scholars from various disciplines. That year's theme was "The Stages of Life in Creative Process," and the other English language speakers included Gilles Quispel on "The Birth of the Child: Some Gnostic and Jewish Aspects," and Geoffrey S. Kirk on "Old Age and Maturity in Ancient Greece."

Hillman took a more radical direction in his talk on "Abandoning the Child," maintaining that "the thinking of psychotherapy and of psychology of personality has been captured by the child archetype and its growth fantasy . . . The dominance of the child archetype in our psychological thinking, besides softening our intellect, has deprived adults of our imagination. This 'inferior' activity has been relegated to childhood, like so much else unreal, autoerotic, and primitive . . . Preferable to the division into child and adult and the consequent patterns of abandonment . . . would be a psychology less given over to the child, its woes and romanticism. We might then have a psychology descriptive of humanity, an aspect of whom is perennially child, carrying an incurable weakness . . . but bearing the child, the child contained."[1]

Without this shift in perspective, Hillman said, "a restoration of the mythical, the imaginal and the archetypal implies a collapse into the infantile realm of the child. Our strong ego-centered consciousness fears nothing more than just such collapse. The worst insult is to be called 'childish,' 'infantile,' 'immature.' So we have devised every sort of measure for defending ourselves against the child—and against archetypal fantasy. These defenses we call the consciousness of the strong, mature and developed ego."[2]

Pat Berry, who accompanied Hillman, believed "that it was and is really an excellent paper but was actually too psychological and phenomenological for the Eranos crowd—which were given to more spiritual, high-flying, noble lectures."[3] Hillman came away from the lecture feeling that "it wasn't well-received, or it didn't work."[4] In the 1983 book, *Inter Views*, he spoke of having "wanted to keep it all a series of images touched lightly, water colors . . . [But] I felt the mode—the rhetorical style didn't work. It seemed too soft. Or my thinking was weak. I said to myself, now there you screwed up because of that aesthetic water-color fantasy. I attacked my fantasy of the forms—not the ideas. Actually, the essay has since worked very well as a written piece. It's been taught and translated and photocopied and so on. But when I delivered it, I felt awful."[5]

Yet Hillman had no sooner returned to Zürich that September when he received a surprise phone call from William Sloane Coffin Jr., Chaplain at the Yale University Divinity School. Would Hillman like to teach a seminar there based on his 1967 book *InSearch: Psychology and Religion*? As Hillman recollected in one of our interviews: "I said I would much like coming, but a seminar workshop thing wasn't my main 'shtick,' I like the more formal longwinded lecture. He said, 'How about the Terry Lectures then?' Wow, I thought, knowing Jung had given them in the 1930s. Anyway, he got the wheels turning."[6]

Hillman's memory may have reversed the way the wheels began turning. When plans were taking a while to firm up, Coffin wrote him late that September: *"I guess I feel guilty but not that guilty, seeing it was you who suggested the Terry Lectures!"*[7] However the invitation was initiated, the Terry Lectures were extremely prestigious. Established by a gift from Connecticut philanthropist Dwight H. Terry in 1905, they were intended to invite both scholars and the general public to consider religion from a humanitarian perspective, taking into account modern science and philosophy. Customarily, the same visiting lecturer gave four free talks over the course of a month or less.

Hillman joined august company indeed. Since John Arthur Thomson delivered the first Terry Lecture in 1923 (*Concerning Evolution*), other guest speakers had included John Dewey (1933–34), C. G. Jung (1937–38, on "*Psychology and Religion*"),[8] Reinhold Niebuhr (1941–42), Erich Fromm (1949–50), Paul Tillich (1950–51), Rebecca West (1955–56), Margaret Mead (1957–58), Paul Ricoeur (1961–62), Norbert Wiener (1961–62), and Loren Eiseley (1966–67). Their chosen topics usually turned into widely-read books.

Coffin, the prime mover behind Hillman's selection, had been the Ivy League college's Chaplain since 1958. Originally a graduate of Yale's School of Music (and a friend of George H. W. Bush since his youth, who brought him into the university's Skull and Bones secret society), Coffin began his working life by joining the CIA as a staunch anti-communist. Disillusioned after the CIA's involvement in overthrowing leaders of Iran and Guatemala in 1953–54, Coffin quit and enrolled at the Yale Divinity School. By the 1960s, he was using his pulpit as a platform for Martin Luther King and Nelson Mandela, among others. He soon became a crusader against America's escalating involvement in Vietnam, preaching civil disobedience. In 1968, along with Dr. Benjamin Spock and two others, Coffin was indicted by a federal grand jury for "conspiracy to counsel, aid and abet draft resistance." Like Hillman, he was a man compelled to stir the pot.

THE COFFIN CORRESPONDENCE

The Coffin papers at Yale contain a series of letters between the two men revealing considerable humor and a growing camaraderie. While Hillman still awaited official word, Coffin wrote him: "You will be glad to know that the soul of the Secretary's office is polytheistic to say the least. In fact, the archetypes are held in such tension that forward progress is a bit slow. However, I am happy to report that the Secretary told me that the Terry Lectures and fifteen hundred dollars are just about yours."[9]

When Coffin informed Hillman that Colin Williams, Dean of the Divinity School, had finished reading *InSearch* and liked everything but the last chapter, Hillman replied (October 4): "The polytheism will come out—cannot be disguised, so if the Dean of Div School has hesitations about *InSearch* (part IV), I wonder how he will take what's going on in me now." The prospect of giving the lectures, Hillman added, had him not only "pleased, excited, awed," but also "afraid."[10]

Coffin wrote again on October 28: "First of all, let me say that your willingness to come, which seems to match our eagerness to have you, constitutes the best news since the invention of the wheel!" Now they needed to figure out a mutually acceptable schedule. Besides the $1,500 fee (generous for those days), Hillman would have all travel expenses covered, plus room-and-board. "I gave your puer and Senex to Erik Erikson," Coffin continued (the famous psychologist's son, Kai, was a Yale faculty member). "He was just delighted with it, and thought you wrote so beautifully that he read parts of it aloud to his wife, Joan." The synchronicity must have delighted Hillman, who had recently started reading Erikson in the course of writing "Abandoning the Child."

However, Coffin cautioned that while he personally thought *Puer and Senex* "difficult but very on target," many undergraduates had found his wife's use of it in a creative writing course "very heavy going . . . Our campuses this year are filled with burnt-out puers, and if you pay a lot of attention to the problem of 'translation,' you will be most helpful on this theme."

While Hillman's analysis of polytheism and monotheism "would be very pertinent" for the Divinity School: "Certainly I would like to discuss that further with you as I think in treating monotheism you give primary significance to religious beliefs instead of recognizing that the integrity of love is more important than the purity of dogma. My own inclination would be to argue that it is precisely an orthodox—as opposed to a conventional—understanding of monotheism that makes for the possibility of polytheism in the fashion you eloquently describe."

Coffin added that, at the Yale Medical School, they're "all a bunch of Freudians . . . so they need to hear everything you have to say." No matter which department, "everything you have to say about the soul would be heard well. Also there is no question about the importance of talking these days to the feminine side of human nature. This may be particularly true at Yale. Here we have admitted only a few girls. Here Aphrodite has reluctantly released Eros. And here when Eros gets burned he tends to take off for Mother Yale!"

Hillman, in his reply on November 5, noted a slip in Coffin's secretary typing. Instead of Jungian thought, she'd mistakenly written "onion" thought. Hillman noted, tongue-in-cheek: "Often it comes out union thought. She is not so off the beam: there are the layers (as in the mystical images), the tear-jerkings and the persistent stench contaminating whatever is touched by it . . .

"Your point about the integrity of love as the core of monotheism turns things around in an excellent new way for me, and I am delighted with that perspective. It touches also upon the jealousy of the [Old Testament] God, and the raging human problem of jealousy. I can't just now press this further, as I am still wrestling with what is here called 'grippe', and get a recurrent fever, as if I had fought once in malarial swamps. The mind is mushy. But during the times in bed I have been cooking the lectures, and the entire prospect of Yale, with much anticipation, not the last is the new-found companionship you offer in your letters. Thank you."

Speaking to Coffin's concerns about "translation," Hillman replied: *"I won't speak down, but I will try to speak out, and over."*

The official invite came on November 15, and Hillman quickly responded that it *"is a fearful joy and I accept willingly."* Coffin proceeded to send six faculty members some of Hillman's "heavier material" to digest. After a two-hour lunch with them, he wrote Hillman that "they are all struggling manfully (if I may use the word) with your Eranos papers. 'It's great stuff but it ain't easy' seems to be the general reaction." Coffin signed his latest epistle "the local padre," and sent Hillman a couple of his sermons to peruse.

Coffin wrote to Hillman, December 9: "People now are experiencing their powerlessness, their isolation and alienation, their disillusionment—which is obviously their fault for having illusions in the first place—and a general lack of much community. The old forms of community no longer obtain, new forms of community have not organically arisen. Intimacy is being sought, rather desperately, with too many demands being made on too few to carry the whole burden. All this you understand beautifully because I hope you realize that the things you write about are things that are now being very deeply experienced. In other words, you are a few years ahead of the times."

Hillman wrote to Coffin, January 5, 1972: "A lot of madness here as year turns . . . hope you're not expecting the wrong man for this one is in the midst of his polycentrism (meaning fragmentation), and would be happier if he were only eccentric for at least being off center indicates a center somewhere. Perhaps I have insulted the God of the Old Order too much and he is revenging himself by withdrawing order from my life altogether, but order becomes worthwhile when it is a matter of survival, rather than a plan, an ambition, a system. Your letters have been a focal point and like you I use the letter now as a means of having a catcher at the other end in which to try out the low pitches and wild curves just to let fly, let fly."

Toward the end of February 1972, Hillman said he would first stop in New York and then arrive at the New Haven, Connecticut railroad station on the 28th, "probably bags i'hand, freezing, hoping to be met and told what to do . . . What shall I bring you in my satchel? A bottle of Kirsch? Swiss Cheese? The lectures are shaping up, Hah. Fond regards, Jim Hillman."

In an undated letter to Coffin written shortly before his departure for Yale, Hillman informed him: "Regarding the Terry-toons themselves, I shall have three prepared, and possibly a fourth. The tentative title is PSYCHOLOGICAL IDEAS: Psychologizing, Pathologizing, Personifying, Dehumanizing.

(The fourth can be dropped, and used in the book, should there not be enough time in your schedule, and should I not get it written.) Please do not be dismayed by these titles."

PREPARATION AND ARRIVAL

Almost three years earlier, soon after the Warburg Institute visit in the spring of 1969, Hillman would recall: "I had already rented a room down at Eranos where I could go and write. I wanted to start and just see what came out. That's where I began to write these notes or passages on pathology, that everything begins with pathology and not with healing or cure or something else . . . That was the beginning of the thoughts."[11]

While working on the initial draft of "Pathologizing"—to become the first of his four lectures at Yale—Hillman placed on the wall in front of his writing table in the Tessin a sentence from the Spanish philosopher and psychological essayist Ortega y Gasset: "Why write, if this too easy activity of pushing a pen across paper is not given a certain bull-fighting risk and we do not approach dangerous, agile and two-horned topics?"[12] Hillman perhaps identified this quote with his friend López, for whom the bullfight was a frequent metaphor. And the forthcoming talks were undoubtedly to be "dangerous, agile and two-horned." As Hillman wrote to his friend Bob Stein: "I tried manfully to make the Terry Lectures simple. I worked 'til I cried at them. I never had such despair as sitting in the Tessin trying to get them ready."[13]

It was a time "that the larger opus I was engaged in seemed to be in a pit."[14] As the lectures loomed closer, he added on a postcard to his friend Marvin Spiegelman, "I'm crazed with midlife crises."[15] From Zürich, Hillman flew first to the West Coast of Florida "for a few days . . . to store strength for the Terrys."[16] Unbeknownst to Kate, Pat Berry accompanied him. As Pat remembered it, the purpose of the Florida stop was "mostly to relax and get a little sun-tan and swim and lie on the beach before going and taking on the world. I mean, this was the revolution!"[17] But some of the writing still wasn't done, and Hillman recalled working on one of the lectures in Florida up to the last minute.[18]

Then the pair flew to New York, where he had scheduled a talk on polytheism to the annual meeting of the American Society of Arts, Religion and Culture. It was there, as Hillman described in the opening chapter of *The Dream and the Underworld* (1979), that he first began articulating "an archetypal approach to the whole business of dreams" and their "distinct mythic geography . . . that tries to keep a sense of underworld always present."[19]

The event was chaired by Stanley Hopper and had been arranged by David Miller, a young professor of religion at Syracuse University who met Hillman at an Eranos conference in 1969 and was soon to publish his own first book, *The New Polytheism*. The Society, Miller remembered, consisted of "a fairly distinguished group of people that included [playwright] Edward Albee, and a lot of well-known artists and architects."[20] Renowned thinkers including Harvard Divinity School professor James Luther Adams and German philosopher Hans-George Gadamer were in the audience. Existential psychologist Rollo May was there as well, with whom Miller recalled Hillman having "a wonderful discussion about dreams in the question period."[21]

Hillman wrote Kate in Zürich that his lecture to "many big-shots went extraordinarily well. I met one after another people whose books I read and use and admire, and was frightened before I talked, since I was the only speaker at a day's meeting and everyone was to talk on my paper, but once I got into my stride I managed it all easily."

Hillman and Pat then took the ninety-minute train ride to New Haven. She was officially given a room at the Yale Divinity School, but has no memory of actually moving in there. Pat does have clear memories of the guest suite at one of the Yale colleges where she recalled they both stayed. "She was, so to speak, my assistant," Hillman said in 2008.

Pat had no idea he was simultaneously writing letters to Kate:

"It is Monday and I am in my guest suite, two modern rooms with thin walls through which the wind blows, modern windows and sheets with holes (thin sheets, thin blankets). I have a rented typewriter and I have spent this morning rewriting. The schedule they have prepared is fierce, and so 'outer,' so hectic, so much the same kind of close personalness that is altogether impersonal . . . well today I feel very much not liking it . . . I feel not only [do I] not belong here, but not belonging in this historical period . . .

"I feel old, set in my ways, disturbed by the little things . . . the wave of depression here that hits me is too much. I look forward to starting the talks & to getting into it."[22]

Perhaps part of that "wave of depression" had to do with his conflict over the two women in his life—maintaining an intimate relationship with Kate while accompanied by Pat. He seemed to still be in love with Kate, yet knew it was not going to endure. And it impacted his preparation for the Terry Lectures. As he wrote to Bob Stein: "[I]n New Haven I tried every morning from 7:30 on to change the style so that [the lectures] would come over clearer. Nothing worked. They were as if cast in iron—I could change and fix nothing."[23]

The two weeks leading up to the lectures were packed, including spending nearly every evening with Coffin and his wife Harriet. Pat found the activist Yale chaplain and Presbyterian minister to be "a sort of numinous figure. I can see how he could mobilize a student body—handsome, well built, and he had charisma."[24] Hillman felt Coffin "a very splendid person." Only later did he realize that the private reason behind Coffin's bringing him to Yale was to seek some marriage counseling. "He'd read my book *InSearch* and said that's what he needed—more in-search. At least that's what his wife told him."[25]

"PATHOLOGIZING, OR FALLING APART"

Hillman's four Terry Lectures constituted a cohesive initial draft of the 1975 book based upon them, *Re-Visioning Psychology*, which would be nominated for a Pulitzer Prize and remain, to many, his most significant work. "The title, and the four parts came into my mind all at once, clearly," he recalled in 2007.[26] Although the central themes stayed the same, the lectures would undergo numerous revisions. In a later Prefatory Note, Hillman wrote: "In preparing the book for print, I have kept the texts substantially as they were presented. However, I have restored some cuts that had been made to meet the time limits of a lecture, omitted some verbal embellishments evoked by the spirit of the moment and of the audience, and added some phrases and paragraphs, even pages, to make my meaning clearer or to carry an idea deeper."[27]

The order of the lectures differed from what would appear in *Re-Visioning Psychology*. As the Yale brochure advertised, Hillman would open with "Pathologizing—or Falling Apart," later to be the second section of the book. On February 29, 1972, shortly before four o'clock, Hillman arrived at Becton Hall's spacious Davies Auditorium—after Pat Berry "helped me find my way around the campus, because I'd get immediately lost."[28] He was "wearing a European suit and a pretentious beard,"[29] as he put it. The hall was filled to overflowing with several hundred people. It was "standing-room-only, they were just about hanging from the rafters," recalled Naomi Goldenberg, then a graduate student studying the psychology of religion.[30]

As Hillman stood at the lectern ready to begin, Coffin came over to introduce him. Pat was stunned at what transpired. "Jim did this thing he was so good at, a graceful gesture. He put his head down, so that Bill put the microphone under his head, and it was like a benediction or something—it was wonderful."[31]

Thus blessed, some of Hillman's fear may have lifted, for he would describe himself in a letter that spring as "quite terrified doing them, since they have such huge reputation."[32] As outlined in the following day's edition of the *Yale Daily News*, Hillman's shakeup of conventional thought began by asserting that psychopathology "should be a source of insight to the inner self: it should integrate the conscious and unconscious

. . . We have denied the value of psychopathology in three ways, through gnoseology, nihilism, and the transcendental denial of humanistic psychology. This is a fundamental betrayal of the soul and its afflictions."[33]

It was heady stuff, but the auditorium quickly fell silent as Hillman went on to maintain that denial of our individual pathology meant taking "our fantasies to an incurable end; to immediately interpret a stiff neck as meningitis and a lump as cancer," leading to the contemporary view of the world as "poisoned, decaying, and falling apart." Where the clinical view of psychology "creates patients by taking pathology at face value," psychologists needed to recognize the mind's need to pathologize. "The psyche can do without analysis, but not without pathology," Hillman said. It was "a way of seeing [that] cannot be cut off without deforming the healthy." All therapy begins with pathology; if the soul didn't "get sick," therapy wouldn't exist.

Such ideas seemed to strike a chord with a largely student audience wrestling with the huge questions that had emerged from the turbulent 1960s—questions of psychedelic drugs and political upheaval, individuality and community, religion and science, spirit and soul. Everything was being questioned. Pat remembered the responses evoked during Hillman's presentation: "For anybody who's used to intellectual things, certainly at Yale it was like, *where* is he coming from? There was outrage, there was disbelief, there were people saying he was crazy—and there were kids who thought this was the most stimulating talk they'd ever heard."[34]

In the audience was Ed Casey, then in his early thirties and an assistant professor of philosophy at Yale who'd begun a parallel clinical program in classical Freudian psychoanalysis in New Haven. A self-described "fairly reclusive person," Casey was originally from Topeka, Kansas. There both his parents were affiliated with the famed Menninger Clinic (his father was their legal counsel), and since many of their friends were psychiatrists and psychologists, "from an early age, I was enclosed in that world of largely Freudian origins." Casey had attended the previous Terry Lectures given nine years earlier by the eminent Paul Ricoeur (*Freud and Philosophy*) which left "a deep impression." He'd never heard of Hillman, but when a friend suggested the psychologist was worth a listen, Casey decided to go. "This was rather adventuresome, to see what Jungian or neo-Jungian thought might be like. I was curious to see what it might deliver."[35] He was not disappointed: "This was a voice speaking in a different way than anything I had encountered."[36]

As the Yale newspaper reported, "Hillman cited religion, love, and nature as other ways in which we might reach the 'soul,' but said it is 'the flavor, the experience' of pathology which gives it value" . . . 'The pathologizing is there, happening inside each of us. It's unnecessary to reach for it' . . . The importance of pathology in psychoanalysis was also emphasized. 'The task of depth psychology now is a careful exploration of the parts into which we fall. It should keep us in touch with the sick and the soul in extremis.'"

In a message faxed to the author in 2008, Hillman emphasized the idea that "the soul naturally pathologizes"—stating that it's "the crucial one of the four [lectures/chapters]." He went on: "This makes the medical model a literalization of something the soul 'just does,' and even the Gods also just do (*Eranos 1974* "Necessity of Abnormal Psychology"); and it justifies all the strange behaviour of the Romantic tradition of writers and their writings, of artists, etc. Again the Dionysian, but couched in the language of psychotherapy: 'pathologizing' . . . [T]he symptom is the base of the whole business, and mythically, the symptom is how the Gods enter, how the myths reach us."[37]

The first night, toward the end of what Hillman later called his rather "chaotically and intensively" delivered ninety minute "harangue,"[38] Ed Casey watched mesmerized as the exhausted speaker lay down on the floor of the auditorium while continuing to hold the microphone and talk. Was there a doctor in the house? Someone to check out Hillman's symptoms? Nobody thought to ask. Indeed, Hillman may simply have been borrowing a page from his spiritual ancestors. "Plato and Socrates gave speeches partly lying down," he once reminded this author, in a different context.[39]

Flat on his back, Casey recollected that Hillman managed to tell the audience: "Any questions you're going to have to ask me here." Casey would later learn that, amid his physical exhaustion, Hillman's back was in fact killing him. "It was really quite extraordinary—people swarming up there around his *corpus delecti*, hoping to get a question in. I was not daunted, because I did have something I felt I had to ask him. What it was, I'm not sure. But I'll never forget posing the question standing *over* his body and, despite his fatigue, he immediately shot back an absolutely brilliant response, letter perfect, as if he'd prepared it. And then I realized—this guy has a mind that doesn't sleep. The ideas were flowing even as the pain had literally floored him!"

"PERSONIFYING—OR SEEING SOUL EVERYWHERE"

The headline of the next day's edition of the *Yale Daily News* read: "Hillman Defends Pathology." This proved too much for some people. Pat remembered being taken to dinner by a graduate student in the psychology department and asking what he thought of the lectures. "He said, 'Well, I'm worried about Dr. Hillman.' Like he was borderline psychotic, dangerous. Because this was so different from the way psychology was [taught] in university. People there were doing rat studies! I mean, there was really no slot for what Jim was creating. There had been Jungians before, and Jung himself, who came to America—but that was another kind of depth psychology. What Jim was doing was a whole new kettle of fish."[40]

Hillman wrote to Kate from Yale: "Dear Dar, It's a real American show . . . I stagger up early, make my food in my kitchenette, shower and am picked up or go off to one thing or another nearly every morning, phone calls all over the place, lunches, then a moment or two to rest then another show in the afternoon or evening, or talk with Coffin until 2 am . . .

"The work load on me is horrendous. And the level here is very very good, better than Chicago [at the university in 1968], and the mood less disintegrative than that crazy drugged too young world. What I say is taken with great seriousness, and so far I have been a little afraid and so not relaxed and warm enough. Too European, and in contrast with Coffin who is so fantastically extraverted and brilliant (and who never dreams).

"Today Daniel Ellsberg speaks . . . I speak at 4 p.m. . . . [Ellsberg had gained notoriety at the time by leaking the Pentagon Papers to the press].

"The idea of shopping, looking at books, swimming is faded. Chained to work. Yesterday morning for instance, 3 hours on *Puer and Senex* with psychiatrists, then in the afternoon 3 hours with theology students on *Insearch*. What pleases me most is my range . . . that I have enough range to answer on so many areas of human thought and action, but the struggle is to keep witty warm concrete and not too wordy in this academic world.

"Trying also to make the contacts with people more open and alive, less paranoid, less isolated . . . so much of me is based on anxiety and sense of being a fake."

Four days after his talk on pathologizing, Hillman took the stage to address the topic of personifying. The Yale brochure advertising the lectures listed "Psychologizing—or Imagining Things" as the second lecture. However, on the typed manuscript of "Personifying—Or Seeing Soul Everywhere" found among Hillman's papers at the Pacifica Graduate Institute, he'd crossed out the third roman numeral at the top, turning it into a 'II.' And that is where he began, apparently shifting the order at the last minute—noting that personification is fundamental "to the thinking about experience of archetypal psychology."

Ed Casey was present again. So were many others who'd attended the first lecture. Once more, the auditorium was Standing-Room-Only—"an enormous audience for those days," according to Casey. "Somehow he was striking a rare note and with a rare voice they'd never heard before. At moments, James would pronounce one of his very poetic, very sustained and remarkably convoluted sentences at which the audience was aghast. You could actually hear people drawing in their breath."[41]

Hillman elaborated on the Cartesian and Christian ideas that had coalesced in the philosophy of Frenchman Marin Marsenne in the late sixteenth century, who embarked on a "holy war" dating back to the Age of Constantine: "the battle to maintain Christian psychology against the psychology of polytheistic paganism." (In *Re-Visioning Psychology*, Hillman would change "paganism" to "antiquity.")

He went on to describe how "in psychiatry words have become schizogenic and in politics have degenerated into the Newspeak of Orwell." What "began as a 'talking cure' [was] now abandoning speech for a process of touch, cry, and gesture." Personification is "considered a stage of thought that has been left behind." As Hillman saw it, "this push of progress has strewn corpses in its wake. Totems, idols and the personages of myth were the first to be mocked and scorned; then followed images of every sort, Gods, demons, saints, the forces of nature, the qualities of character, the substantives of metaphysics." Yet in our epoch, psychopathology had reminded both Freud and Jung "of the psyche's propensity to personify."

Hillman continued: "We wrestle with a dark counter-personality who shadows our life with his intentions. We hear at moments guiding voices that hint at other selves, other psychic inhabitants—Jung calls these complexes 'the little people'—who are of more importance than our usual I. And especially a soul factor intrudes with moods and desires, and with this anima a man may converse as a poet with his muse, a philosopher with his daimon, a mystic with his tutelary angel, or a madman with his hallucination."

Hillman spoke of how "paganism personified Fame, Insolence, Night, Ugliness, Timing, Hope." He quoted the Greek philosopher Plotinus on how "those ancient sages, who sought to secure the presence of divine beings by the erection of shrines and statues, showed insight into the nature of the All." He highlighted Freud's "closest woman pupil," Lou Andreas-Salomé, "with whom Nietzche had fallen in love and who became Rilke's lover," for having "taught Freud about love: that it requires personification." This was not "inferior thinking," but "part of the method of feeling." The "mythopoetic understanding of the world . . . begins in nature, in psychic states, in demons and Gods which are in themselves, from the beginning, presented to our experience in the substantially real form of persons."

This was central: "Personifying serves the psychological purpose *of saving the diversity and autonomy of the psyche* from domination by any single power." We see these secondary personalities in dreams, where "various styles of consciousness embodied as persons are brought to bear on one another" and present "a critique of the ego complex."

So "personification and polytheism require each other," Hillman stated as he approached his conclusion. Approach psychological knowing in this way and "we would no longer be alone in our own house, now sharing it with a community of other voices in other rooms, and nature would echo again with Great Pan, alive. There would be a mass uprising, a resurrection of the dead, as the angels and archons, demons and nymphs, powers and substances, virtues and vices, released from the chains of small-letter descriptions and conceptual prisons return from the mental reservations whence such primitivities had been banned, to enter again into the commerce of our daily action."

Again from a prone position at the end, Hillman took psychology to task for its "withdrawal of soul into the narrow confines of the human skin," while the "countermovement [was] the attempt of the soul to break out again and revive the lost provinces, as the personifications encountered in and supported by depth psychology." We are all "embedded in metaphorical existence," simultaneously "intensely personal" and impersonal. Only the soul's existence "posits me and makes me possible as a personification of the psyche."

Among the audience was Charles Stacy, then an undergraduate at Harvard who was there with a group of friends. In what might be viewed as an example of soul breaking out of its inner confines, Stacy went on to be a renowned neurologist affiliated with Mt. Sinai Hospital in New York. There in the mid-1980s he began seeing a patient named Margot McLean. She would meet Hillman a few years later and become his third wife. In the mid-2000s, Margot suggested that Hillman should see her neurologist. "[Dr. Stacy.] told us to come into the examining room," Margot remembered, "and then mentioned that he took the train from Boston to New Haven to hear James give the Terry Lectures. We were both stunned!"

Stacy recounted how he'd gone through "the psychedelic revolution and then become interested in Eastern religions—but I had a healthy respect for depth psychology and Jung was a way back to my more correct identity." He read some of Hillman's articles before journeying to Yale for the Terry Lectures, and had a sense that Hillman "was going to be freshening things up a bit." But Hillman exceeded his expectations, so Stacy made the three-hour commute between Boston and New Haven for all of his talks.

"I thought he was not only very clever, but very deep at the same time," Stacy said in 2015. "His way of expressing things was memorable and original. It was the entire enterprise, the way of seeing psychology. Put it this way, Jung brought in respect for the psyche which I think Freud had tended to denigrate in a way, where everything else was inferior to ego. But Hillman showed a contrarian and impish quality, saying 'Wait, it's not our psyche, we're just inhabitants among all these animate entities. So let's talk from their point of view for a while, give them their due.' I thought, that's carrying it to its logical conclusion. I didn't have the perspective at the time to realize that most of the orthodox Jungian community thought of this as a kind of heresy."

When they finally met in the examining room, Stacy recalled: "He'd maybe mellowed a little, but not that much. Always, a very lively playfulness about him. He had this great grasp of his material, but at the same time didn't take it with the wrong kind of seriousness. Yes, a bit of a prankster. The main image he had in *Re-Visioning Psychology*, I thought, was of Pan, who was responsible for the feeling of panic. I thought, that's kind of Hillman's role, to spread a little chaos around; he enjoyed shaking things up."[42]

Margot recalled that Hillman gave Dr. Stacy one of his favorite ties as a gesture of appreciation. It was patterned with tiny chickens. He would remain Hillman's neurologist for the rest of his life.

"PSYCHOLOGIZING—OR IMAGINING THINGS"

The third lecture at Yale took place on March 7, 1972. Judging from notations on his original manuscript, Hillman had previously considered using this talk as his opener under a broad heading of "PSYCHOLOGICAL IDEAS." Here the typed roman numeral 'I' has been expanded to a handwritten 'III.' Further evidence of this shift appears about two-thirds of the way through the talk, in a bracketed sentence Hillman eliminated which said: "Psychologizing is thus personifying—but we cannot yet say that until we have cleared up that term in a later lecture."

While this third chapter in *Re-Visioning Psychology* (subtitled "Psychologizing, or Seeing Through") would begin with a quote from Plotinus, Hillman opened the lecture with the first definition of psychology in the English language from 1653. Psychology was described as "a doctrine which searches out man's Soul, and the effects of it; this is the part without which a man cannot exist."

Hillman continued, that it is "by means of psychological ideas [that] the psyche reflects upon itself." In contrast, "the psyche becomes blinded by the dazzling illuminations coming to it through ideas of nature, of history or religion"—resulting in the soul being the reflection of political processes (Marxist psychology) or religious evolution (Chardinesque psychology) or simply the mechanical. Yet the soul *needs* ideas—"the archetypal first step of therapy"—ideas as fields "of vision, speaking of perception, of seeing, viewing, regarding, reflecting." As in Homer and the Presocratics, then in Plato, 'idea' meant what one sees and how. The soul reveals itself in the ideas "through which we envision our lives."

Hillman went on: "Archetypal psychology envisions the fundamental ideas of the psyche as persons—hero, mother, nymph, amazon, senex, child, and other mythical prototypes, the Gods. [Today] even with the best moral intentions, political goals and philosophical methods, we exhibit only psychological naivete." Hillman pointed out that the depth psychology of Freud and Jung couldn't fit into the universities "as one department among others," because psychology "is going on everywhere" and perhaps best "where it is less evident, that is, through 'negative learning' as the underground, interior reaction." He emphasized one sentence, (it was underlined in his typed lecture): "*Psychologizing goes on whenever the mind attempts to reflect in terms other than those presented*"—when "it suspects an interior, not evident intention, or searches for a hidden clockwork, a ghost in the machine, something more than meets the eye."

There are a series of steps to the process. First, the moment of reflection—"wonder, puzzlement, suspicion which moves through the apparent to the less apparent"—followed by the effort "to unmask or expose or show why," and then concluded by the task of seeing through the identification with a particular psychological dogma: "the psychologist's task starts on home ground, seeing through his own psychological literalisms which coagulate the flow of soul." "Seeing through" has become a distinctive Hillmanian concept with ongoing resonance. Most of what is called therapy, in Hillman's view, is really an ideology: "thus better spoken of as a theology or a science or a movement."

Again, with soul-making, it's not about *solving* the problems of "what it is to be human, how to love, why to live, and what is emotion, value, change, body, God, soul and madness in our lives." Psychology becomes its own worst enemy through taking itself literally. "It not only cannot have axioms and laws as axioms and laws; it cannot even have hypotheses, but instead, must be built on fictions."—in other words, *myth*. "[P]articularly in Classical mythology from which the highest points of our culture drew their psychologizing—Classical Greece, Florentine Renaissance, Romanticism," wherein "these myths present the archetypal dramas of the soul, all its problems presented as fiction, 'the tragical, monstrous and unnatural' given sense and importance, providing the models for as it is on earth . . .

"Thus the soul finds psyche everywhere, recognizes itself in all things, all things providing psychological reflection, and the soul accepts itself as one more such metaphor (more real than this there is nothing) enacting a myth." (Hillman inserted "more real than this there is nothing" after the first draft.)

Both Jung and Freud had shown this, as had earlier thinkers (Sallust said of myth: "Now these things never happened but always are."). To Hillman, "[T]he Gods don't stand still; they cannot be defined, or approached directly. They intermarry, intermingle . . . They set us off looking for hidden meanings, and our search, our attempts to see through are prompted by the hidden myth trapped in a problem appealing for release. Yet myths may not be interpreted into practical life, becoming applied psychology for solutions to personal problems. They simply give the invisible background which starts us imagining, questioning."

And here Hillman imagined "a Knight Errant picking up insights as he moves"—perhaps imagining his own wandering "off course away from the true logos of intellectual reasoning and intuitional revelation"; his own following of emotion and regarding "desire as also holy, listening to the deviant discourse of the imagination." If the main task of the Knight Errant was helping the poor, "so does psychologizing liberate the parts of the soul trapped in the poverty of the material." This is the work of "a renegade like Cain who can never return within the structures of concretism, seeing through the walls, the definitions."

In all this, Hillman unequivocally declared himself psychology's renegade. He concluded the third lecture by comparing the Knight Errant to an "odd-job-man"—to "Eros the Carpenter who joins this bit with that, a handyman . . . psychologizing about and upon what is at hand, not a systems architect, a planner with directions."

As noted in Chapter 2, Hillman's vision for *Spring Journal*—was embodied in "*a figure (Etruscan and later) called Eros the Carpenter, who simply fitted pieces together, shown with tools and implements of joinery.*"[43] This image is reminiscent of Hillman's childhood in the Chelsea Hotel that his family owned in Atlantic City, where he loved joining the workers in their "underground city" below the lobby. As Hillman put it in a 2006 letter to the author: "What the 'working people do,' is fascinating because they handle things, make things, and come from odd places (like Poland or Ireland). So one's experience of life and people is immediately extended beyond the confines of the known (family). It's like the 'unconscious realm' of the psyche in a way."[44]

Hillman concluded his third Terry Lecture: "And leaving, before completion, the suggestion hanging in the air, an indirection, an open phrase . . ."

For yet a third time, he ended up on the floor—a suggestion hanging in the air. . . .

KNIGHT ERRANT MEETS WOMEN'S LIBERATION

In a letter to Kate, penned soon after giving the Terry Lecture on "Psychologizing," Hillman starts with an apology for not writing more often. His language in noteworthy: he was "obliged to say yes to everything, *and so go like a Knight from department to department*, [emphasis added by author] hall to hall, lunch to lunch, evening to evening, talking to talking. It is marvelous to be so warmly accepted by an inner circle . . . and to be in the wave of the time (zeitgeist), for my lectures are packed, kids on the floor, even some faculty who have read *all* my books and papers and know my work intimately. It is not quite 'me' but something I represent. There were, for instance, more people at the Divinity School where I talked on Polytheism (very heretical) than had been there since the memorial meeting for Karl Barth (the most famous theologian). It's not that I am someone, but that the time is ripe, and I ride the time with my Hermes opportunism.

"But the animal suffers. I have much fear, I feel ashamed that I do not fulfill what I want (lots of shame), I have the shits often, and sleep fitfully and much too short for the Coffins stay up till 2 . . . Then there are the usual students who want private talks, which I must give since that is the style here, and also necessary for keeping in touch for their sake and mine.

"So far I have given three terry talks, and the audience is still as full as ever, even though I do not consider them to be my best work . . . too difficult and with too little content. I had wished to write more simply and give more substance . . . but complexes intervened, even though I continue to work on them all the time. Sometimes in questions I am uptight and tormented, other times, charming spontaneous strong. Unfortunately as I get tired, it gets harder to be relaxed and have access to my wits . . .

"I won't ask you about yourself because of perhaps striking the wrong chord. But you know I always wish you well and hope the best.

"The main thing about me is that I am able to carry what is now on me, the size of it, but have trouble with the American physical reality, and miss the supportive habits and warmth of the family."

He signed the letter warmly, "*love, Jimbo.*"

Pat Berry had a difficult time at Yale. She recalled once becoming ill with a stomach ache: "Bill Coffin took me upstairs and let me lay down, sat and sort of soothed me and talked to me, while Jim sat downstairs and talked to [Coffin's] wife. He had a heart, Bill Coffin did."[45]

According to Hillman, Coffin had been very moved by his essay on "Betrayal" and once used it for a sermon. The irony wasn't lost on Hillman that while at Yale, "in one of the little groups we were in was, I think, Bill's girlfriend at the time—hidden—and I was there with Pat. So there was this erotic transgressive aspect, breaking bounds."[46]

In another letter to Kate, Hillman discussed his growing camaraderie with colleagues in America:

"I am back from Syracuse, just rushed up there for a day and a half to lecture and a seminar, and had an extraordinary connection with a few faculty people, *equals*. [David Miller was one of the faculty who would become a lifelong friend]. That's the point, there are equals at least, in Zürich I am either always superior or inferior . . . guilty an outcast, not a good analyst, all those inferiorities, also at Eranos not scholarly enough, or superior above the others in mind, reputation achievement . . . but here, so many [who] can do as well as I are not threatened by me, and it is so much easier. The intellectual contacts are superb, and the students are completely different from the nut Eastern spirit/ trip types who come to Zürich for Jung. More learning in them here and more intelligence."

He went on: "The lectures are very successful. I could not have asked for anything better. Even to the third one they all came, the room still packed and some on the floor. About 500 people, they say, but I guess 300. And I don't feel the need of 'success', fame, crowds or any of that . . . I am not specially 'up,' simply over working, by letting everything happen as it comes, without controlling it. So I speak a lot, and see many students, and carry the weight of the job . . .

"This coming week: two evening talks (one to womens liberation), two puer senex seminars, one terry lecture, and a psychiatric lunch, and two talks in the psychology department. (all in four days).[47]

"Tell Julia I am all for Womens Lib (in my way), and that the students here are now hard workers, not like the American types she sees in Zürich. But they work in another way, more softly

. . . but all the girls make themselves terribly ugly . . . they haven't nearly the style she and Carola have."

The new feminism had been on Hillman's mind since his 1969 Eranos lecture, "First Adam, Then Eve." He had continued his contemplation of the subject in letters to Pat the previous summer of 1971: "Been reading about womens lib and their dislike of being used as sexual objects. This is no easy matter, for men do 'objectify' their sexuality in an impersonal way (as women do when they want a man, any man to fecundate them) the rape fantasy of man, as well as the priapos, etc. is part of the autonomy of the hardon, that it has to do with his connection with the male gods, not with the woman, just as woman's ovarian cycles have nothing to do with personal relationships. The real equality is as D. H. Lawrence said wholly impersonal, when man is connected to maleness and woman to femaleness; at the same time sexuality is the most personal intimate expression of loving . . . wow how to make this point to the womens lib. I think of all this in connection with my fantasies regarding you; do I misuse you, abuse you in my desires. The above is my answer."

Hillman also wrote about it to Kate, noting that "womens liberation is much in the air here, and no joke, for it is really trying to change women's attitudes inside towards a new confidence in themselves . . . of course much of it is ridiculous, but the aim is important."

Whether this undated letter preceded his meeting with a group of young feminists is not known. Ed Casey remembered "sort of shepherding him around, and helping arrange spontaneous seminars and discussions. So a couple of women who were friends of mine invited him up to what was supposed to be just a very nice conversation. But in fact, they were lying in wait—like the Furies—to attack him for what they saw as a chauvinism of the worst sort in his writings and in the lectures. It was really merciless, I mean he was beaten back. Jim was consternated, speechless. It was one of the rare places I've ever seen him not knowing what to say."

Casey elaborated: "I think they felt he favored the male archetypal figures—Hermes, Dionysus, Apollo—at the expense of female archetypal figures who they discussed. Anima, certainly as an archetype, was very important to Jim already, which they felt was secondary. I thought it was unfair—and missed the mark, because Jim explicitly brings up the theme of bisexuality and Dionysus himself is bisexual. I think Jim was listening and wanted to learn, but it's hard to know what exact lesson could have been learned that day."[48]

Pat wasn't there that night to observe what happened; Harriet Coffin had invited her over to the house to meet a few faculty women who could acquaint her with feminism. As Casey recollected, one of his students at the time—Naomi Goldenberg—had organized the Hillman gathering and helped lead the charge against Hillman. Today, she is a well-known professor of religious studies at Canada's University of Ottawa, and author of *Changing of the Gods: Feminism and the End of Traditional Religions*. At the time of Hillman's Terry Lectures—all of which she attended—Goldenberg was a graduate student in Yale's Department of Religious Studies. And her memories of what happened differ considerably from those of both Hillman and Casey.

Goldenberg said in our interview in 2015, that the Terry Lectures themselves were "like a fireworks display." She'd done graduate work in the classics at Princeton before switching to Yale, "so I got a lot of the analogies he was making, and the literary references. I couldn't believe what he was combining—psychoanalytic theory with Greek mythology, and all kinds of intuitive insights. Also, it wasn't a superficial feel-good type of discourse. Not like the Christianized psychology that I got in a lot of religious studies courses—which is very repressive in so many ways—and it wasn't scientistic and narrow the way some psychology can be. What you felt listening to him was that the world was expanding. It was intoxicating really."

Goldenberg learned it was possible to register for a special informal session focused on Hillman's 1969 paper, "First Adam, Then Eve: Fantasies of Female Inferiority in Changing Consciousness." She was active in the nascent women's movement, searched out the paper, "read it thoroughly and made all kinds of notes. Then the night came. It was a smallish, very nicely appointed Yale room with comfortable couches and chairs. There must have been a maximum of about thirty people. I brought one of my friends, a woman from the philosophy department. This was the beginning of feminist thought and philosophy, what you might call psychoanalytic theory. We were all thinking it through, we didn't have a position. And we all admired him, because I think everybody had been to at least one of the Terry Lectures.

"So we listened to Hillman talk and, the way I remember it, he was seeing everything within a paradigm of Greek myth. We loved the idea that women could have something else other than these fantasies of female inferiority, but then his solution for it seemed to be a Dionysian experience. Okay, well, it's another male god who's supposed to be leading women to some kind of frenetic freedom. All of us didn't see Greek myth as something located in a sort of disembodied psyche, we saw it as products of social history. And we're trying to come up with some new possibilities for women, rather than being crazy critics of a male order where after dancing a couple nights, you go back to being whatever you were in some Dionysian way.

"Somehow it just got very heated, though I don't remember it being really aggressive.

"I don't think he was used to bringing his ideas out into that kind of an audience, particularly women. Hillman seemed to be defending Greek myth being so basic to us all, coming up with one after another paradigm that we were responding to. But I thought we were in a really good discussion. I don't know why Ed Casey recalls it as attacking him. I remember Hillman was ill that night, somebody told me later that he had a fever. Toward the end I remember him coming up to me and saying, 'Well, aren't you worried about the Eastern influences on religion.' I said, 'No, I don't care about that at all.' I didn't understand what his concerns were, but they weren't our concerns. On the other hand, I think that by calling the paper 'Fantasies of female inferiority in a changing consciousness,' he kind of knew that something new was happening and that's why we were all there. We knew what a great intellect he was. Honestly after the evening was over, I didn't feel like we had had a big argument."[49]

Hillman's most direct public reference to what transpired appears in a Preface to the 1992 paperback edition of *Re-Visioning Psychology*, where he invoked the fate of Dionysus—"I suffered my first dismembering encounter with radical feminists and my first paralyzing encounter with Freudian interrogation in seminars at Yale."[50] Asked about this in June 2011, Hillman remembered being invited to three different events (including "some Christian thing at the Yale Divinity School"). But Hillman chose to elaborate in our interviews only on the discussion with Freudians—"the atmosphere of reduction, getting rid of the ideas and putting them back into the old systems of psychoanalysis. These people were the big guns, and there was a certain amount of pompousness."[51]

The Yale event was not the last that Hillman and Goldenberg would see of each other. After her first year at the university ended, Goldenberg wound up in Zürich for the summer. She made an appointment to see Hillman there, only to learn "how difficult he had found the whole evening. When I walked into his office, he pointed at me and yelled—'you—you are the one who did' . . . I forget what it was he said I did. I was very surprised by his reaction. I remember I said—'well, I forgive you, don't you think you could forgive me?' Then he settled down and agreed to consult with me about Jungian theory—one of four exam topics that I was working on for my doctorate in religious studies at Yale."[52] Goldenberg soon became part of the Spring House crowd, entered analysis with Hillman, and saw her first published paper appear in the *Spring Journal*—on archetypal theory.

"DEHUMANIZING—OR MAKING SOUL"

For the first three Terry talks, Pat Berry had reoriented Hillman on his often errant path from the guest suite to the Yale lecture hall. This gave him pause in later years. He said in 2008, in what might be described as his *mea culpa* to the feminists at Yale: "You see, there's this basic projection onto the anima in the woman, which becomes necessary for my whatever-it-is. Like my going to India with Kate [in 1951]—if she hadn't gone on that trip, it wouldn't have been the same. So that is an abuse of the woman, which so many men who do things—write books or paint pictures—use their women for. And if the woman doesn't profit from it, it's terrible. Because she's not obliged to stay in the relationship, so she has to get something from it. So I think Pat was very important for my sense of, I can't do this alone."[53]

When it came to his writing, however, Hillman didn't think that he took advantage of Pat. She had worked with him on his book about the Puer. "I wanted her to read my chapters and correct my English or improve my style," he said, "but when I was doing the Terry Lectures, although she was with me, I don't recall her reading or discussing parts of it. She wasn't involved, I don't think, in the thought—but maybe I would have an idea and say it, and that she would remember."[54] (Pat responded that this was a fair enough assessment. "At the time of the Terry Lectures I had not reached intellectual maturity . . . I sure do remember reading those pages . . . But it was really, as he says, just to support him.")[55]

Hillman's final Terry Lecture on March 14 took place after his encounter with the Yale feminists. "[T]he exhilarating strain of these talks had me confusedly on campus so I arrived lost and late for the fourth lecture unable to again locate the hall,"[56] he would write almost two decades later. That, it turns out, was an understatement. For whatever reason, Pat had been occupied elsewhere late that afternoon, and took her own route to the lecture hall—so Hillman was left alone. She remembered: "The audience waited with increasing uneasiness (for me, terrifying alarm!) until way after the hour for him to show. Turns out he had got lost, again. I couldn't believe it. He told me later he finally asked a groundsman to show him the way."[57]

The first draft of the "Dehumanizing" talk is filled with crossed-out phrases and penciled-in changes. It's obvious that Hillman had labored long and hard over it. In one margin he wrote after the sentence: "Where indeed does psychology belong?"—"STUDY OF SOUL NOT OF MAN."[58]

He began the talk by saying: "As archetypal psychology is not a science or a religion, so too it is not a humanism." It took a while before he moved from the Greeks to the Renaissance thinkers. Petrarch came first. His statement that "nothing is admirable but the soul" Hillman cited as marking the symbolic beginning of the Renaissance. It was an "inward turning" that stunned Petrarch while descending Mount Ventoux in 1336, as he "opened his tiny pocket copy of Augustine's *Confessions*" to a random page that read: "And men go abroad to admire the heights of mountains . . . and pass themselves by."

Hillman didn't draw any parallels to his own life, but he too had a life-changing experience while seeking spiritual enlightenment in the mountains. While traveling in the Himalayas with Kate twenty years before—he had a disturbingly banal dream about his mother and grandmother lying in bunk beds. But it was a powerful enough soul experience to send Hillman in the direction of Jung and the Institute in Zürich shortly thereafter. The dream, Hillman said, "made me go back, and down."[59] What had so struck Petrarch by way of Augustine, as Hillman described it, was "the wonder of the interior personality, which is both inside man and yet far greater than man."

Hillman also spent time in the lecture on Marsilio Ficino, whom he'd first come across in London's Warburg Institute library three years before. Now he went so far as to call Ficino a "Doctor of Soul" who "was writing, not philosophy as has always been supposed, but an archetypal psychology." Ficino's Platonic Academy in Florence was "best conceived as a flourishing underground movement," not unlike that which Hillman had established at the Spring House in Zürich and was bringing forward to an American audience for the first time at Yale. He was moving away from "humanism's psychology [that] follows

Aristotle" to "a movement downward and inward"—dehumanizing—where "archetypal psychology follows Plato and the examination of soul." In keeping with this tradition "the Renaissance and its psychology is a fantasy about the possibilities for a renascent psychology today." From this "we have learned . . . that rebirth is coupled with defeat, failure is its precondition, Hades its deepest secret." Myth and imagination—never a concern of psychology along with "history, beauty, sensuality, or eloquence"—needed to come to the fore.

In one of our interviews (2009), Hillman elaborated on how his discourse on dehumanizing was "very radical, because all the good psychology at that time—the people who were closest to me like Rollo May and [Abraham] Maslow—were humanists. This was an attempt to say, it's not just getting your feeling right and your relationships right, it's something deeper. I have about four pages in there about the cruelty and tragedy of the Renaissance, the murders and the betrayals. It really knocks the shit out of this idea that we can get everything right if we get beautiful thinking going. Actually, it's like Shakespeare's plays. All those people murder and poison each other, pull out their eyes—in this incredible language! It seems that aspect is always missing in America. Not in the black world—their music is full of tragedy and poverty. But you know, one of the sad things about America is this paranoid idea that the enemy is out-there, and all the badness like a magnet gets attracted to the Communists or the Terrorists. It's sucked out of our actual human life."[60]

At Yale almost forty years earlier, Hillman had invoked the Renaissance practice of engaging "in imaginative discourse with persons of antiquity . . . in the company of ancient heroes, poets and legendary figures." Now, as he neared the conclusion of his series of talks delineating four functions of the soul, something remarkable occurred. He would call it "A Processional Exit." He began: "Soul-making needs adequate ideational vessels, and it equally needs to let go of them . . . By holding to nothing, nothing holds back the movement of soul-making from its ongoing process, which now like a long Renaissance processional slips away from us into memory, off-stage and out of sight."

Hillman did not lie down this time, as he went on to imagine: "They are leaving—even the Bricoleur and the Rogue Errant who put together the work and charted its course; there goes Mersenne in his monk's dress, and Lou, and Hegel; the Cartesians depart, and the transcendent refusers of pathology, and Heroic Ego who had to bear such brunt; now Anima in all her marvelous veils moves off southward smiling."

The packed-house audience in the Davies Auditorium leapt to its feet, applauding wildly, "a spontaneous thunderous ovation and cries of Bravo!" Ed Casey remembered. But Hillman was not done.

"Going too are Freud and Jung, side by side, psychologized, into the distance, and the mythical personages from Greece, the Greek words and Latin phrases, the footnoting authorities, the literalistic enemies and their troop of fallacies; and when the last image vanishes, all icons gone, the soul begins again to populate the stilled realms with figures and fantasies born of the imaginative heart."

It was a grand performance, evaporating time, the imaginative heart racing back to those boyhood moments on the Atlantic City "Boardwalk of Dreams," the fantastic disappearing act of Harry Houdini and the young lady on the High-Diving Horse, the dazzling lights of night masking the pervasiveness of vice. And racing far forward to late-life friendships with the actor John Cleese and the film director Elia Kazan . . . encapsulating the Renaissance Memory Theatre of Don Camilo and the contemporary Pan Theatre of his friend Enrique Pardo.

From the audience, Ed Casey watched as all the figures were "ceremoniously ushered off the stage, in such a moving way. Leading to a standing ovation which, for that historical moment 1972, was unprecedented. In an academic setting, never! This was really something, totally unique. And it indicated that Jim's words, and I would say his voice, were really getting through to people as a message of new thought—not just about psychology but about life, how to reorient yourself in relation to the world in a different way. Just quite extraordinary."[61]

Casey would write to Hillman several years later: "I listened to an extant tape of the end of your Terry Lectures the other night, and your voice was transmuted into a form uncannily indistinguishable from that of the students who were asking you questions!"[62]

After the lectures, Hillman had written Kate of plans to return to Zürich by around the end of February, when they could take a holiday with the children over Easter or right after. That fall, Hillman would write to his friend Bob Stein that, while at Yale, he was able to make several new relationships which he expected would be long-lasting. One of these was assuredly Ed Casey from Kansas.

Years later, asked what struck him as so original about the Terry Lectures, Casey replied: "I think the theme of listening to the symptoms for a unique message that you needed to hear and stay with. Similarly, what depression could achieve, being very careful to note he wasn't recommending that people *get* depressed, but if you were. Also his critique of what I would call pure mentalism, really coming out of Descartes. That notion of pure mind intact, self-authenticating, needing nothing else, was very much in question by Jim's ability to say there is always more at stake than pure thought. Yet on the other hand—this is what made him subtle and interesting—you have to respect greatly the notion of ideas as themselves having unique perspectives for psychology that you can't get anywhere else. So he very ingeniously navigated the Scylla and Charybdis you could say, the twin dangers of Cartesian separation of mind and body, and on the other hand a Platonic idealism of ideas. No one could say that ideas don't remain indispensable for philosophical and psychological work. You can't simply say, well, it's all about emotion or it's all about history. In *Re-Visioning*, this is the big thing, and it would first come out in the lectures very clearly."[63]

Hillman wrote Stein in a different vein of his introduction to Yale: "I was very open there, on one side, but ruthlessly closed psychically to people who wanted to use me analytically. I balked at all soul connections that had a therapeutic angle. Reason: self-protection. I was on a survival course, exposed like never before with very tender new shoots of ideas in which I had invested my whole soul. I suffered a great deal of lonely doubt right in the midst of the work, at night . . . quite horrendous."

And later in the same letter: "Now as I prepare them into a book, I begin to see why and am grateful as hell for the impotence of my ego and the rigidity of the writing (or writer) in sticking to what came out. And the odd thing is that they were an extraordinary success—for all their difficulty, and I have been just now asked back as a visiting lecturer to Yale for a semester next year. Quite a special honour, all owing to the success of the lectures, and my human warmth . . . hah!"[64]

In 2007, Hillman elaborated in a fax to the author: "I am, or my work is, so often ahead of myself. At the time I had no idea that what I was doing might actually start up a revisioning of psychology and put it all on another footing, or another direction altogether. Already *Suicide and the Soul* indicated that possibility, and the works at Eranos (four lectures or five to that time) but the Eranos thrust seems to me now to have been more an encounter with Jung and the Jungians and revisioning that psychology, not all of psychology!"[65]

The Terry Lectures had set him on that circuitous, and momentous, path.

NOTES

1. Hillman's essay on "Abandoning the Child" appeared in his book *Loose Ends*, published in 1975, and in the Uniform Edition Vol. 6.1 (*Mythic Figures*) of his work.
2. "a restoration of the mythical, the imaginal. . . .": *A Blue Fire*, edited by Thomas Moore, p. 237.
3. Berry on *Abandoning the Child*: Email to author, November 10, 2014.
4. "it wasn't well received. . . .": Author interview with JH, May 2008.

5. "I remember writing Abandoning the Child. . . .": Hillman with Laura Pozzo, *Inter Views*, 1983.

6. "I said I would much like coming. . . .": JH fax to author, August 26, 2007.

7. All quotes from the correspondence between William Sloane Coffin, Jr., and James Hillman are taken from the Coffin papers, Box 4, at the Yale University Library's Manuscripts and Archives division.

8. According to Sonu Shamdasani in his book *Jung and the Making of Modern Psychology* (2003), Jung's Terry Lectures presented "a historical survey of the attitude of the medieval church towards dreams."

9. "You will be glad to know. . . .": Coffin papers, September 29, 1971.

10. "The polytheism will come out. . . .": Coffin papers, October 4, 1971.

11. "I had already rented a room. . . .": JH interview with author, May 2008.

12. Quote from Ortega y Gasset on Hillman's wall: Hillman, Introduction to *Re-Visioning Psychology*, pp. xv-xvi.

13. "I tried manfully. . . .": JH letter to Robert Stein, autumn 1972, Hillman private archive.

14. "that the larger opus. . . .": Hillman, *Re-Visioning Psychology*, Preface for 1992 edition, p. xiii.

15. "I'm crazed with midlife crises": JH postcard to J. Marvin Spiegelman, January 25, 1972, Spiegelman private archive.

16. Vi "to store strength for the Terrys. . . .": Hillman, *Re-Visioning Psychology* Preface, p. xiii.

17. "mostly to relax and get a little sun-tan. . . .": Author interview with Pat Berry, August 2008..

18. "working on one of the four lectures. . . .": Author interview with JH, May 2008.

19. "an archetypal approach to the whole business of dreams. . . .": Hillman, *The Dream and the Underworld*, Harper & Row, 1979, p. 3.

20. "fairly distinguished group. . . .": Author interview with David Miller, March 2009.

21. "a wonderful discussion about dreams. . . .": Miller interview.

22. "so many bigshots [that] went extraordinarily well. . . .": JH undated letter to Kate, Hillman private archive.

23. "In New Haven I tried. . . ." JH letter to Robert Stein, fall 1972.

24. "a sort of numinous figure. . . .": Author interview with Pat Berry, September 2013.

25. "Coffin was a very splendid person. . . .": Author interviews with JH, May 29, 2008 and September 2009.

26. "The title, and the four parts. . . .": JH fax to author, August 26, 2007.

27. "In preparing the book for print. . . .': Hillman "Prefatory Note," Opus Archives, Pacifica Graduate institute, Box 108 A756.

28. "helped me find my way. . . ." Author interview with JH.

29. "Wearing a European suit. . . .": Hillman, draft of Preface to 1992 edition of *Re-Visioning Psychology*, Opus Archive, A75b.

30. "Standing-room-only. . . .": Author interview with Naomi Goldenberg, July 2015.

31. "And Jim did this thing. . . .": Author interview with Pat Berry, September 2013.

32. "quite terrified doing them. . . ." JH letter to Robert Stein, May 10, 1972, JH personal archive.

33. "should be a source of insight to the inner self. . . .": "Hillman Defends Psychology," Yale Daily News no. 97, March 1, 1972.

34. "And for anybody who's used to intellectual things. . . .": Author interview with Berry, September 2013.

35. "This was rather adventuresome. . . .": Author interview with Ed Casey, May 2015.

36. "a fairly reclusive person. . . ." Author interview with Ed Casey, January 2006.

37. "I think that chapter. . . .": Hillman fax to author, 2008.

38. "chaotically and intensively. . . .": Author interview with JH.

39. "Plato and Socrates gave speeches partly lying down....": Author interview with JH, September 2009.

40. "He said, 'Well, he was worried about Jim'. . . .": Author interview with Pat Berry, August 2008..

41. "Somehow he was striking a rare note. . . .": Author interview with Ed Casey, May 2015.

42. Dr. Charles Stacy: Interview with author, April 2015.

43. "a figure, Etruscan and later. . . .": JH letter to Robert Stein, undated.

44. "What the 'working people' do. . . .": JH letter to author, June 12, 2006, first referenced in *The Life and Ideas of James Hillman* vol. 1, pp. 27–28.

45. Berry "immediately got sick. . . .": Author interview with Berry, September 2013.

46. "in one of the little groups. . . .": Author interview with JH, September 2009.

47. Hillman's extracurricular talks, according to the Yale University brochure about the 1972 Terry Lectures, were on "One Soul or Many: Psychological Polytheism," at the Divinity School on March 1, and "The Problem of Fantasy and the Fantasy of Problems," at the Yale Medical School on March 6. Hillman wrote to Coffin, prior to arriving, that the first of those "would be relevant also for pastoral counseling to examine the limitations of monotheistic psychology. . . .regarding that branch of the visit, I am at least easy."

48. "sort of shepherding him around. . . .": Author interview with Ed Casey, January 2006.

49. "like a fireworks display. . . .": Author interview with Naomi Goldenberg, July 2015.

50. "that I suffered my first dismembering encounter. . . .": Hillman, *Re-Visioning Psychology*, 1992 HarperPerennial paperback edition, "Preface: A Memoir from the Author," p. xiii.

51. "the atmosphere of reduction. . . .": Author interview with JH, June 2011.

52. "how difficult he had found the whole evening. . . .": Naomi Goldenberg email to author, June 4, 2015.

53. xii "But she was, so to speak, my assistant. . . .": Author interview with JH, May 2008.

54. "I wanted her to read my chapters. . . .": Author interview with JH, May 29, 2008.

55. "At the time of the Terry Lectures. . . .": Pat Berry email to author, November 19, 2016.

56. "[T]he exhilarating strain of these talks. . . .": Hillman, Preface to new edition of *Re-Visioning Psychology*, 1991.

57. "The audience waited with increasing uneasiness. . . .": Pat Berry text to author, November 20, 2016.

58. "Study of Soul Not of Man": Opus Archive, Hillman papers, Box A756.4.4

59. "made me go back, and down. . . .": For the full account of Hillman's experience in the Himalayas, see *The Life and Ideas of James Hillman*, Volume I, pp. 340–42.

60. "very radical, because all the good psychology. . . .": Author interview with Hillman, July 2009.

61. "ceremoniously ushered off the stage. . . ." Author interview with Ed Casey, May 2015.

62. "I listened to an extant tape. . . .": Ed Casey letter to James Hillman, October 30, 1977, Opus Archive.

63. "I think the theme of listening to the symptoms. . . .": Author interview with Ed Casey, January 2006.
64. "I was very open there, on one side. . . .": JH letter to Robert Stein, autumn 1972, Hillman private archive.
65. I am, or my work is, often ahead of myself. . . .": JH fax to author, August 26, 2007.

7

FALLING APART

"For the 'return to Greece' offers a way of coping when our centers cannot hold and things fall apart . . . 'Renaissance' (rebirth) would be a senseless word without the implied dissolution, the very death out of which the rebirth comes."
—James Hillman, *An Essay on Pan, 1972.*[1]

Perhaps after the great triumph of the Terry Lectures, an enantiodromia was inevitable. "Critics miss the validity and necessity of regression,"[2] Hillman wrote that same year of 1972. Upon his return to Zürich that spring, he recounted in a letter to his old friend Marvin Spiegelman how his sojourn in the U.S. came to a dismal end:

"I got exhausted [giving a lecture] at Harvard, fever and cold, performed not too well, and then had a weekend with my brother and sisters and inlaws, all in crises, separating divorcing alcoholism, mess-ups, and I was supposedly the sane one . . .

"I now am supposed to get the lectures in order for printing by Yale, but have no energy on returning here. Don't feel like working at the pace I was during all of 1971—and these last days I took a couple of patients for the first time. We'll see if that is more relaxing and soul-filling than writing and editing. I have been pouring out so much, teaching and writing and ideas, that I feel soulempty."[3]

He continued that he'd dreamt of seeing Spiegelman and "suddenly bursting into tears over my problem. And was shocked over my emotion not recognizing how much it hurt (in the dream)." He wondered if perhaps Marvin and his wife Ryma might "have some answers somewhere. So far I don't know them and continue to live in a triad, with Kate getting little emotion, and little eros, and little spirit too from me. I see no way out but to go on, with both women getting not enough, and I not having enough soul in the midst of it. But I cannot move out of either situation without doing even more damage it seems."

Yet it was something Hillman believed needed to be seen through. He concluded the letter: "I trust my healthy fear of magic and dislike of the occult taken literally. Behind it is the witch, I suppose, with whom I am still not on good terms."

PORTENTS OF DISSOLUTION

In retrospect, it seems possible that Kate's willingness to stay in the marriage despite knowing about the relationship with Pat might not have lasted as long without Berry's periodic absences from Hillman's life. He had continued to express the struggle in letters to Pat, during her previous second summer of studying at St. John's University in New Mexico. In one of these, he wrote that he was most interested to hear what she learned from the nascent women's liberation movement then spreading across the U.S. The classical problem, he noted, was how to have both "marriage and spirit"—amid the physical limit of child-bearing with its huge pressures, along with the social pressures of being a Mrs. It was different for men, who could conceive and father into their sixties, "even if they are grotesque as old fathers often are. So how to bring these two things together: biology and spirit. And if you do take the marriage and child bit, then a sacrifice for many years just to do diapers and blow noses . . . and is there a way out?"

Hillman was then working on a paper to be delivered at Oxford, aptly titled *Schism*. On the one hand, he found Kate's family place in Sweden to be "magical. Feel the extreme wonder of this nature, the botany, the trees and lights and colours. Always the same even when I am blue in mood, or any mood, the silence, air, light; this room where I work suits me . . . quite miraculous as a place, haven . . . nowhere ever do I sleep like this, even in a hammock, yet, somewhere in my emotion I feel its past."

This led him to address something he felt Pat had never understood: "You do not get that I WILL to put energy into lots of dead or half dead customs and habits like these summers, or so many other family and bourgeois events partly because I *fear* what will happen if I don't, and partly because of *principles*. At my age, so much of my life seems an obligation to others."[4]

He wrote later: "My attempts to connect at home fail. I ponder for hours over 'what's wrong' with me that I cannot shift my emotion to where it 'should be' and where a genuine affection exists as ground for other sorts of emotion . . . The emotion does not go there; and even with the children I cannot be bothered. I bear your absence badly. Maybe this is no solace to you for you would say: go where the emotion is, but that too can be a cheat, as you know. Much guilt, there at home; towards you for hanging you up, and I really use every trick in the book to hang you up, you know; towards children for not being 'better' with them; towards self whom I tend to dislike more and more."

In another letter, he added: "You are the image of my erotic inhibitions; I am unable to give where society and sanctification of rite would have me give, because I feel a betrayal towards you; and with you cannot let myself flee into fun because I feel a betrayal of the status of the upright man, bound. So, I use you two women-images to inhibit myself from full participation in either direction. Is this psychic laming? Is this to keep from 'developing' split feeling, and so on? It troubles me immensely that I cannot be wholeheartedly with either [Pat or Kate] . . . Much depression here."

Hillman reflected on how his relationship with Pat had changed dramatically from the summer before, when he was still ambivalent and they were "honestly trying to separate." He'd sent her to New Mexico in pursuit of an M.A., he wrote, "to give you every chance to have as free a life as possible in our circumstances. You see, Pats, I think you are BIG, with more potential . . . even than I (I feel terribly old & used up this summer), and I want you to exercise it by travel, learning, tasting & seeing."

The schism in Hillman became acutely apparent in those letters. Kate represented stability and family, taking him away from work. In that sense, he felt imprisoned in the 1950s, while the relationship with Pat carried the collegiality and freedom of the liberated 1970s. From this perspective, Hillman inflated Pat, and deflated Kate. Yet internally, he wrestled with having dealt Kate a losing hand.

GRAPPLING WITH MULTIPLICITY

On the one hand, by spring 1972 the new annual edition of *Spring* was hot-off-the-press, including Hillman's essay on "Dionysus in Jung's Writings." He'd begun "timidly to practice again, after 3 years of refusal."[5] Soon after, Yale's Psychology Department Chair wrote Hillman that the impression he'd left at Yale was "so favorable . . . I am now at the request of a number of us taking the rather unusual step of extending to you an invitation to return again" as a visiting faculty member either that fall or the following spring.[6] Hillman's new friend Ed Casey was thrilled, writing him that even though the Psychology Department was "often out of touch with such things . . . there was something remarkably catalytic about your being here . . . It's not so much a question of Jung—though he continues to be a neglected source of ferment here—as of your own unique style of search and your powers of articulation . . . So come."[7]

Hillman wasn't sure about the timing. Autumn seemed premature. He thought it would be better to join the Psychology Department around the time that Yale would be publishing the book based on his Terry Lectures. He figured that wouldn't happen until the following spring. Besides, he had other commitments in Zürich and couldn't subject his wife and four children to "too much uprooting"—and so suggested the fall of 1973 instead.[8]

In a letter written that spring, reflecting on what teaching at Yale might be like, Hillman said: "Honestly, what I don't want is a 'Talk show,' regular academe, question and answer thing, too up in the head. I am anyway up in the head, and work best in an all-out scene where I can be farthest out and outrageous. We must be able to bring in our pathology, our crazedness. I had trouble internally when in Chicago at the Univ[ersity] there 3 years ago, trying to be the cool polite professor. It was awful, and I just don't want that to happen again."

Meantime, he set about trying to get the Terry Lectures "into book shape. Very slow."[9] Hillman also wrote Jane Pratt that he was "rather well along with finishing both Chapters Two and Three," and planned to write the other pair "while in Sweden this summer, our place on a Bergman island where I go with the family."

Pat Berry headed back to New Mexico for the last summer semester of her Master's degree from St. John's. What Hillman went through that summer of '72, wrestling with how to complete the book to meet a late September deadline from the Yale press, is chronicled in his letters to Pat—often painfully so. Early on, while still in Zürich, he described how he became "derouted in the library, possessively looking up irrelevancies" about Nietzsche and Dilthey based on "some deep intuition about 'introspection' . . .

"But am filled with doubt, worse: a sense of fate having closed in, all earlier forms going (analysis, family, businessman success) and I am left with being a psychological writer who is very uncertain psychologically and can't analyze. I have no Vorbild . . . no one to pattern myself after. Feel uncertain. Even for the first time, tragic. Caught by my own fate."

He found himself drawn to dine alone at Zürich's renowned Kronenhalle restaurant, a ritual he'd always followed after the birth of one of his children, but it wasn't something he'd done "for long long time." Was a different kind of birth on the horizon? This was shortly before leaving for the northern Swedish island. While en route and running around Copenhagen with the kids, Hillman recalled that the previous night he "dreamt about Freud's ideas, which were continuation of my thoughts on Freud following reading of [Paul] Ricoeur. Main thing is Freudian psychol[ogy] is a psychol[ogy] of conation . . . a will job. (control), (motivation), what are the unconscious motives, how to develop ego control, or relax ego control etc. Will fantasy, behind which is of course hero—Jung should be an imagination psychol[ogy] . . . this is the real diff[erence]. They are based on two diff[erent] faculties of the psyche."

In a P.S. to another letter, Hillman wondered: "How does Soul realize itself—or is it a *form* and already *all* actualized?"

There followed a remarkable letter from Sweden, dated (July 11) unlike most of his epistles, and worth quoting at length. Hillman wrote: "The real Jewish difficulty is adaptation. We can live anywhere—and at same time we are not rooted, truly belonging, anywhere. So, here I am, adapted so terribly well to this Northern melancholy, this completely, utterly, historically, archetypally un-Jewish place. My very adaptability makes me not know who I am, what I truly need, want; but that I can survive anywhere. It is a fate without a fate . . .

"It is for this reason that I cannot keep a journal (a diary, or *journal in-time*, the classical method of the writer or thinker). I can write a letter and tell of things that pass through my life, but I cannot communicate directly with myself about myself, for I do not have one. I am adapted. I have adapted myself so that there is nothing other than the existential adaptation.

"Jungians would call this over-extraversion, and shallowness, hollowness of introversion. But—as Rafael would say—I can't take that for a minute . . . it is more likely historical. The price of Jewish survival: not to sense who one *is* in order to be at every instant on guard, vigilant, about where one is. Who one is devolves into Where one is.

"All my writing about soul, imagination, and about multiplicity reflects this fundamental aspect of my nature. You can see why I get utterly dependent on writing (in order to find Who) and on other very close people (You) . . .

"The program of writing up here now looks like I'll have to finish Pathologizing and Dehumanizing while here. I have got most of Personifying and ¾ of Psychologizing done. The latter has more notes by far than text. Recently I came across even more material on personifying. It is a major theme evidently, and since I have been ambitious enough to review the literature, I have to include even more references. I hope to put everything in the footnotes that lays out my positions, even rather academically. It is of course a senex endeavor, but it is necessary if I am to live into the 'call' that is represented by Eranos and Yale. It's really quite a big undertaking to work out one's own thing; even if it seems unnecessary and old fashioned, it is at the same time required by the image of my ambition (archetypal psychology, my own views, my distinction from Jungianism). If I do not do it, I remain more dilettante than ever, more puer, a commentator, a critic on the side, skirting. I do not want to skirt in this book, but *confront*. But don't get me wrong, I am not changing the lectures, only I am explaining lots of things in the notes. Partly the notes are exhibitionist, to demonstrate my versatility, partly to show that I do have scholarship behind the bravado, partly to work out thoughts that cannot be skirted.

"This is my adventure. I enjoy it too."

The sun never seemed to abate on the island—"There is not enough night here," as Hillman put it in another letter to Pat. He would "spend part of each day at a regular spot on sand alone thinking, like a ritual, of myself and future, marriage and divorce, ageing and fathering, work and wandering, etc. I am making progress, at least in thought."

More of this progress concerned the background that Hillman came from, as alluded to at the beginning of the letter quoted from above, concerning the adaptability he associated with being Jewish. On a trip back to Zürich, Hillman took Kate to see the latest film directed by Vittorio de Sica, "The Garden of the Finzi-Continis." It's "set in Ferrara during the Mussolini epoch and told of the Jews there and the slow decline and imprisonment of their life by fascism," as Hillman described it in a letter to Pat. He added that it was "not a good film, but it touched me because of the Jewish thing," and because it reminded him of a medieval alchemist (Bonus of Ferrara) whom he had quoted at length in an alchemy course but had forgotten about.

Hillman went on: "I had one new angle into my conflict over family, what this conflict is. I have been putting it into the yoke of [the Greek goddess] Hera, but after the film I have been thinking of the Jewish aspect of family. It is really where the religion is. You know that I instituted Friday night ritual, and the only overt jewish thing I do, besides go to funerals (and sit in on one or two circumcisions) is that Friday night with family. To leave family for the sake of self (that is the opposition I have it in) seems sacrilegious. That's the trouble. It seems like the ultimate anti-religious act, a sin, and the final rupture with Jewish soul. And, when I use the word soul as I do so much, I see it carries a mystique of Jewishness . . . This side of me is deep and buried but potent in my ulterior personality."

It was a theme that connected Hillman to his grandfather, the renowned reform Rabbi Joseph Krauskopf who died three years before James was born, and to an essay Hillman wrote at Trinity College on "The Jew as Scapegoat" in the writings of Joyce, Mann, and Eliot—where the Jew is "representative of the new age without religion [and] what all three are working towards is some new order profoundly human."[10] The de Sica film also had a character—"the boy was a tubercular jew"— who reminded Hillman of what he'd suffered through and survived when confined for months to a TB sanitorium in his early twenties.

Among Hillman's spiritual ancestors, Freud was Jewish and Jung a Christian minister's son. Then there was C. A. Meier— Jung's leading assistant and Hillman's analyst, who later betrayed Hillman in having an affair with Kate. Meier was quietly anti-Semitic. Further along in the same letter that Hillman wrote about "the Jewish aspect of family," he said: "I believe also that the Meier I hate so much is me, my own academic dried up senex thing. When this book is done, I hope I can turn to something more liquid. That will be the problem in the next years, keeping the liquids flowing." (Hillman added that his 1967 book on Kundalini—very much about the flow of energetic liquids— was about to come out in paperback).

On a postcard to Pat, he wrote: "Keep dreaming of my father and his family—some strange changes in my senex taking place—makes me afraid."

THE MOIST SPOT IN THE FIRE

Hillman's unusual book, *Anima: An Anatomy of a Personified Notion*, wouldn't be published until 1985. On the left side of each page appear relevant quotations from the works of Jung, a kind of archaeological excavation juxtaposed with Hillman's essay on the right, about the same subject. The essay had first appeared in two parts—in *Spring 1973* and *Spring 1974*—but Hillman had begun working on it simultaneously with *Re-Visioning Psychology* in the summer of 1972. Even before that, starting with his first book on *Emotion* (1960, the subject of his doctoral thesis), and then continuing in the essay on *Betrayal* (1965), and followed by the Psyche/Eros tale in *The Myth of Analysis* (1972), "it seems my work has always been anima-based," Hillman wrote in the Preface to *Anima*.[11]

Anima is Jung's term for the feminine part of the male personality, or the inward-directed portion of the psyche that's in touch with the unconscious. For Hillman, "isn't *devotio* to anima the calling of psychology? . . . Anima attaches and involves. She makes us fall into love. We cannot remain the detached observer looking through a lens. In fact, she probably doesn't partake in optical metaphors at all. Instead, she is continually weaving, stewing, and enchanting consciousness into passionate attachments away from the vantage point of a perspective."[12]

Hillman noted that the essay started as "an excursion that I felt was essential to the body of *Re-Visioning Psychology* (1975), but soon anima claimed more display than the proportions of that work would allow."[13] This "claiming" is evidenced in numerous letters to Pat during that long summer. In one, Hillman discussed how the anima was affecting his efforts to complete *Re-Visioning Psychology*: "I feel depressed and leth-argic. Thoughts about death, about my unconsciousness, lost in regard to my interiority. A heavy anima mood. It began on Sunday when I more or less finished the incredible highpoint of the book the end of the IV chapter on Renaissance, and the summary of the whole book. I have not read it over, but feel that the whole part went very well, and I enjoyed it. (The first half of 'dehumanizing' is still to be written, but less research and less difficult). Then I started on some long notes on the anima, and what it means as a term and a perspective, etc. and have been worse and worse as if she has me altogether."

He goes on to confide to Pat his fear of "losing you if I get too old, too jewish, too boggy." Yet the reality is that he is in fact an aging balding man with toothaches. "I tend to put you in an old highschool uncultivated anima image, yet your feeling sophistication and much more is far different and far better than mine in many places . . . Your friendliness (eros) is most valuable to me. So I'm not against it. Yet I call it psychopath and am afraid. What's that all about? . . . I fear touching the book that I may spoil it."

In Pat's absence, he comes to further realizations—not only about their relationship, but the deeper meaning behind another aspect of it: "I find that the hours of waste in your company (as I often attack you for) are not such waste after all. That the slowness we have, the midday sleeps and the food and tea, the service we give to non-accomplishment each day has kept me more productive than the direct Nietzschean way. I hate admitting this. I still am a wolfchild of Mars, eating the world, wanting to master every area I touch, with footnotes, with knowledge, with proof of superiority."

In later years, taking it slow would become one of Hillman's central messages. He would write: "Just stop for a minute and you'll realize you're happy just being. I think it's the *pursuit* that screws up happiness. If we drop the pursuit, it's right here."[14]

Another anima dream in Sweden revealed "giant beautiful paintings. Strange how recurrent that motif of painting is in my dreams, and for so many years." But alongside the anima is also the animal, a theme that was already and would remain a primary focus of his work. From the man born in the Year of the Tiger (1926) in Chinese astrology: "My own dreams are weird. Get this: tigers on trapezes. Each tiger on one trapeze not liking other tigers to be on the same one with it. They are very orange and young. Then I am lying talking with a large furry bearish animal and then I see a man with a salamander on his nose. Very rare animal the salamander and plays big role in alchemy. In dream I get idea of the salamander being the moist spot in the fire. You know the story is that the salamander couldn't burn in fire . . . now as I am not so hot and crazed with work, and drying up in the fire I make here in this office, and in the arid way I live my emotional life, I have this tiny intuitive salamander keeping a moist spot. No longer the tiny spark or flame to keep alive, for in the conflagration that I have become, the thing to keep alive is the moist salamander."

Hillman took "36 pounds of books and papers, or more" to the island—among these a biography of Petrarch, the fourteenth-century poet. He references Petrarch in several letters to Pat from that summer, often because of Hillman's personal identification with him: "He was subjected to terrible fits of melancholy and the worst despair. Although his life shows balance and good cheer and many many friends and travels. He really was a pioneer." And this identification included their shared experiences of the anima. Petrarch "was a priest, but refused all pastoral responsibility . . . And spent his life tormented by the image of Laura whom he only saw once or more in his youth. The anima aspect of the Renaissance has to be understood. Both the Beatrice [Dante] and Laura figures play an extraordinary role." Hillman would write about Petrarch and Laura in *Re-Visioning*, and speak of anima as "that person by means of whom we are initiated into imaginal understanding."[15]

Hillman was seventeen when he bought a silver bracelet in Guatemala to offer his future fiancée—whoever she might be. Eventually he would give the bracelet to Kate. But that summer of *Anima* and *Re-Visioning Psychology*, he wrote Pat Berry from

Kate's family's summer home: "I do not wear my ring. Took it off first day here. Finished [reading] Petrarch's life."

July 11, 1972: "What kind of a future do I really want, how to build it, where, which way does my life go in the next years, in what place, doing what, life-style, money, relation with children . . . what will I be giving up."

Everything was being re-visioned.

YALE'S RELUCTANCE; A FAMILY TRIP TO PERSIA

In one of his last letters to Pat before her return, Hillman reflected: "I expect this is my last summer of this sort. I think the transition years are closing now 1968–1973. Before 68 I was a proper man, Director of Studies, after 73 [at age 47] I will be into another phase. These four-five years have been the re-vision years. But curiously every time I try to *think* a future, I get nowhere . . . I will go to Yale, and I will spend more time in Tessin . . . but a blank wall when I try to think more. Where you fit in is very strong, but I fear putting it in letters."

At the Spring House, a wine cellar was being rented for a photo darkroom; Von Franz's book on fairy tales was being shipped. Of *Spring*'s management style, Hillman wrote: "Seems the main thing is to treat the organization . . . so that no single individual has more power than any other really. Then the organization never becomes a thing over and against individuals who work in it. I am quite pleased really that I have found enough space in myself (womb) to carry the tension of the chaos of *Spring*. That's one place where the style is right."[16] Along with a clipping from the *International Herald Tribune* headlined, "Lady ump quits after first game," Hillman wrote Pat that when she returns: "Don't forget our baseball equipment."

Directly after her graduation on August 18 with a Master's in Liberal Arts, Pat flew to Europe and accompanied Hillman to the Eranos conference for its first five days. Hillman did not present that year. While he went back and forth with the other lecturers to the afternoon Round Table, the couple stayed in a hotel in the town of Ascona. Beside the swimming pool, they sat with new colleague David Miller and his wife. Miller recalled having "a discussion [of] Goethe's color-theory with Jim."[17] Pat recalled: "We talked about Zen—the image I remember is the blows from the stick of the master."[18]

In early September, Hillman submitted what he anticipated would be the final draft of *Re-Visioning Psychology* to Yale University Press. He'd described the finishing touches to Pat in a letter from Sweden: "Putting everything in, seeds, flowers and husks. I'll be sorry that I used so much of my thoughts up in this, maybe; maybe I'll run out, dry up, and all will have been out in this book put too soon, too fast, too badly. But I'd rather go all out and take my chance and follow the compulsion. I hear no cautionary demon, but then I never do, much."

The outcome of Hillman's earlier discussions with Yale about possibly teaching there in the fall is described in an article published in the *Yale Daily News* (October 11, 1972: "Psychology at Yale: 'Rats or Jung?'"). It began by noting that psychology students had been complaining about the lack of humanistic psychology within the curriculum, and several undergraduates had approached department Chairman Bill MacGuire about Hillman, since the Terry Lectures had indicated "a concrete enthusiasm for the humanist's presence on campus." Even though Hillman had been invited to join the department as a visiting lecturer, "when he did not materialize, some students became angered, thinking that the psychology department had impeded his appointment. MacGuire declined to give any such details about the Hillman affair, citing 'grossly personal reasons.' He was adamant, however, about his department's willingness in extending the offer to Hillman, who is still at the Jung Institute in Zürich. 'I was the one who invited him on the flimsy excuse that his union card was in psychology,' commented MacGuire, stressing that in his opinion, Hillman might just as well have been invited to Yale by either the Philosophy, Religious Studies, or Anthropology departments. MacGuire did go on to emphasize that 'the psychology department has done heroic things for James Hillman.' One informed source speculated that the inability of Hillman and the psychology department to coordinate the invitation had been due to a problem of 'intellectual definition.'" MacGuire said he suspected Hillman would eventually be back, but would not "give any hostages."

Nothing came of the plan to return to Yale—that year (Hillman did not address this in our interviews). Instead, that same October, he took Kate and the children on a two-week trip to Iran—which both Hillman and his daughter Susanne referred to as "Persia." The immediate family was also accompanied, Susanne remembered, by Hillman's mother ("my grandmother Nana"), her older sister Julia's then-boyfriend, and Roger Sternfeld, a cousin from Philadelphia.

"It was really an adventure," recalled Susanne, who at the time was approaching thirteen. "We had a driver who was blind in one eye, and he would drive through the night—sometimes off the road. He would fold up his coat and put it in the refrigerator so it would be cool the next morning. We also took a bus ride from Isfahan to Jazd and on to Shiraz, which is out in the desert in the Zoroastrian hills and we saw some beautiful mosques."[19]

Visiting mosques was a key reason for the trip. After visiting one in Isfahan, Hillman had a powerful dream experience that he described in two of our interviews. "The mosque there is one of the great wonders of the world, and the ceiling is really extraordinary—all tile, these blue tiles. But during the night, I was awakened. I couldn't stop seeing this blue world. A blue-tiled vault, so to speak, over this great mosque. It was very powerful, like a vision. And it kept me awake.

"[Henry] Corbin was in Persia then and I had lunch with him two days later. Now the interesting thing about these mosques, as I learned there, here's this big beautiful door"—Hillman demonstrated entering by moving his body ninety degrees to the side—"and as you walk in, you change direction to go inside.

Very different from our churches. It's a reorientation of your direction, turning completely opposite from where you were planning. Only two turns, but you're utterly disoriented.

"Corbin said, 'Well, the mosque did to you what it's supposed to do. It opens up the heavenly vault.' Years and years later, I wrote a paper called *The Azure Vault*" [delivered at a 2004 Jungian conference in Barcelona].[20]

Hillman had gotten to know Henry Corbin at the Eranos gatherings, so it's likely that the trip to Persia developed from his conversations with the French scholar of Islamic mysticism that summer. Corbin taught Islam & Islamic Philosophy at both the Sorbonne and the University of Tehran. As a champion of the transcendent power of the imagination, he had a powerful influence on Hillman, who called him "the second immediate father of archetypal psychology" after Jung.[21] We shall have more to say of the Hillman-Corbin relationship, but for now it is noteworthy that the *Spring 1972* journal included Corbin's essay, "*Mundus Imaginalis Or The Imaginary and the Imaginal.*" The next year's *Spring* would include a Corbin piece on "Mysticism and Humour" ("*it tells a few Sufi jokes,*" Hillman had written Pat). A few years after Corbin died in 1978, Hillman published an essay called "*Alchemical Blue and the Unio Mentalis.*"

In *The Azure Vault*, Hillman makes no reference to his personal experience in Persia, but does recount Jung's encounters including one that took place upon entering a different style of church, the Baptistry of the Orthodox in Ravenna, Italy: "Here, what struck me first was the mild blue light that filled the room," Jung wrote. He and a companion had envisioned "four great mosaic frescoes of incredible beauty . . . and to this day I can see every detail before my eyes: the blue of the sea, individual chips of the mosaic." And yet, as Hillman goes on, "these mosaics on the wall of the Baptistry did not exist, simply not there—though they were seen and remembered in detail by both viewers. The light which introduced the vision was blue; the most vivid of the images, 'the blue of the sea.'"[22]

Early in the same essay, Hillman writes: "We are headed to the edge."[23]

After returning from Persia, a letter awaited Hillman in Zürich. It concerned *Re-Visioning* and came from the Director of Yale University Press, Chester Kerr. Hillman was informed of the Committee on Publications' "keen disappointment" over the manuscript after a "searching discussion." They weren't turning the book down, but felt that only "some hard work and revising" could still turn the Terry Lectures "into an exciting and important book." In a rather caustic paragraph, the Director continued: "Sure, you could get it published elsewhere. Hillman's name is one to conjure with. But that isn't good enough, is it?" Yale would be pleased to tell him how the book could be reframed.[24]

Later, his Yale colleague Ed Casey would write Hillman: "I could almost have predicted that there'd be problems at Yale Press, but I kept my mouth shut. It's a paranoiac outfit, with Chester Kerr surrounding himself with yes-men to bolster his ego. A number of these underlings are flatly incompetent, and I suspect that you were dealing with one of them."[25]

However, what Hillman felt about the rejection is underscored in a handwritten "Biographical Outline" for 1972 that exists in the Opus Archive. Under the phrase "Summer: Terry Rewrite," appears a single word: "Failure."

In November, Hillman wrote to Marvin Spiegelman: "Have come to a dry choleric and sad depression that rarely lifts and is filled with self hatred and fantasies of sin, poverty paralysis and ageing, classical depressive experiences. My lectures just now at Institute are a disaster. I am blocked while talking. I hate the questions and attack them as soon as they open their mouths, and my mouth is dry, shouting and bodiless. I am doing my best to be hated. I find contentment neither alone, with family, with friends, working nor with Pat . . . My ideas move radically. My life also changed. My soul dry."

He then elaborated: "Also have trouble getting Terry Lectures printed. Yale doesn't like them. Of course they don't, for the book is in style and attitude and content against the whole usual thing. But what a job it was to do this book; Major Opus, and now I don't know where to go with it."[26]

THE EMPTY CLOSET

Hillman also didn't know where to go with his marriage. In an undated typed letter to Kate from this period, he wrote: "Bird, look . . . We bear each other real good will and real love and get so wasted in this struggle. I know you need closeness to me and also independence from my domination. But when we try to get each other to connect through the weak side, it's useless: I can't connect through the feeling side to you directly . . . The relationship as such, the sex, eros, etc are not where I am at with you. I would want you to react to my work with ideas (and feelings), get interested and excited in it with me, carry it on in your mind further, as a living relationship, for that's where I am at. OK . . . probably that's too much demand on you, on top of everything else you have. But that's the kernel of the issue: what you want I am not there, and what I want you are not there.

"But it doesn't matter really (or does it?) if we don't press in these two opposite directions. If we stop the demand on each other, let's see what happens, where the libido goes, where the relationship goes.

"Whatever, do not BLAME yourself that something is wrong with *you* in your needs and wishes or your sensation that I am not 'in' the relationship with you. Your perceptions are right. But I don't blame myself either, or get guilty and then hateful, and try to force myself to feel what I don't feel. I have spent too many years trying Jungian methods of correcting myself from above with my mind: it's useless and makes me hateful. Don't you do it either to yourself. You're great as you are."

It's impossible to say whether this letter was sent before or after what is described below. During our interview in January 2011, some nine months before his death, Hillman recalled: "I didn't move to the Tessin until January of '73. I would go down there, but I was living at home. Then one day, Kate was so furious she packed everything I owned, emptied my closets, put them all in hundreds of suitcases and shipped it all to the Tessin. One day I was sitting down there and I got [atrial] fibrillation, it was one of the first times. What was so sad was, I think she did it in a fury and then was sorry she did."

Hillman gave the first public hint of what happened in a letter to Spiegelman two months later. It was a single, unexplained line: "I no longer live at Klosterweg, so write me at Zeltweg." Klosterweg was the home by the zoo where he'd lived with Kate and his children for almost twenty years. Zeltweg was the street where Hillman maintained his office.

He soon thereafter wrote to his other American friend, Robert Stein: "Kate sent all my stuff down to me one day in the Tessin thereby booting me out." Since early February, he'd resided either there or at a hotel in Zürich or at Pat's—occasionally returning to take care of the kids while "letting Kate get away." Hillman recapitulated to Stein: "Curiously the whole thing began to go wrong in 1968, really wrong, and at the same time I began to find my own direction then. It started in Chicago in that hideous long depression, in Arizona, in abandoning practice, in beginning with Pat, in being fired from the Institute, and then in April 69 I found a line of thought, my own spiritual direction, and that's kept me going."

But about his life with Kate, he had "the feeling that fate says all that family stuff is over, and that the sterile, perhaps, and dry driven, work seems more interesting to me than the burden of her psyche." Yet the older children, he added, were angry over his desertion.[27]

Indeed they were. The author asked the three children who were willing to be interviewed about their memories of what happened. "When I was twelve, he started like the 'French Exodus,' sneak away without saying what's going on," Carola Hillman said in 2005, at her apartment in a Swiss town a couple of hours from Zürich. "I had just started puberty. And my mom was very depressed. I learned later that in the beginning, my mom hoped this was an affair. She also thought he could have the affair, as long as he wouldn't leave the family. This went on for years, and those were very difficult years. I was also very introverted, and it's at a time when you want to start to leave your parents and you don't want their problems.

"Until I was sixteen, he kept this a secret. My mom almost had to beg him on her knees to tell us. It was the only thing she asked of him. He wanted *her* [Pat] to tell us. She said, 'You have to do this.' He was so helpless and awkward in all these things. But she got him to. So we had to go see him. Basically he just said he was going to Tessin, the southern part of Switzerland where Eranos is. He had a workplace there.

"In the closet, he had his clothes. And then there was no key there. One of those times you realize, 'Oh my God, something has changed.'"[28]

Susanne Hillman, the third oldest, also sat for an interview in Zürich: "I remember not realizing he had moved out until I opened his closet, and all his ties were gone. I remember my mother sitting down and telling us, 'He's moved out.' He did tell me he moved out so that we don't yell at each other so much anymore."

What yelling? I wondered.

"During those years, my brother and I had developed these tics. My brother blinking all the time like he couldn't see or was just waking up. And whatever anybody said, I said, 'What?' It drove my family crazy. They'd say, 'You heard exactly what we said, don't keep saying What!' They'd have to repeat everything. It was like a physical protection, we weren't hearing or seeing what was going on.

"He'd met Pat when I was six. I was thirteen when he moved out, and fifteen when they divorced. My mother said she blamed him for moving out, because she was quite progressive. She didn't mind an affair, what she minded was breaking up the family. The French style, you might have your lover here and there, but you stay and the family is together."[29]

The youngest child, and only male, Laurence Hillman, said at his home in St. Louis in 2007: "I remember sort of this stupidity. I remember one conversation, 'Your mom and I fight so much, we think it's better if I spend more time down at the office, I have a bed down there.' Instead of saying, you know what?, we're not going to be together, it was vague. I wasn't dumb. I'd just turned twelve, but I figured it out. But Julia and Carola got the brunt of this and realized it as teenagers. I was kind of saved from that."[30]

The following summer of 1973, Hillman wrote to Kate: "I feel always a great deal of sorrow about you and me. I always have fantasies that it could be different, but I know that for now I go into craziness when we get into contact. I know you believe it is your 'fault' that you failed and all that. It is probably part of the archetype to feel those things, as I do, but the facts are that *I* failed and was destructive much more than you. It is a bitter thing to see that one's neurosis eventually does become one's fate and is more strong than even one's wish to change. The neurosis finally won out, and I feel a great deal of shame. The future as I have said many times is still blank. I want to be separated for now. I need the time apart to see where I am. The official phrase is separated or living apart. But I don't want to hang you up in some sort of hope that when I come back from America everything will return to where it was, it can't . . . it is this sort of hope that I am most vicious about, I do not like people living their lives in terms of me. It's the dependency thing. You have every right to feel as you wish, but hoping needs to be analyzed to the root. Think what the Greek myths said of it (an evil, blind hope, they called it . . . If there is no hope there is no despair or disappointment, there is just actual living)."

*   *   *

James Hillman in *Failure and Analysis*, 1972: "When I am in despair, I do not want to be told of re-birth; when I am aging and decaying and the civilization around me collapsing from its over-growth that is over-kill, I cannot tolerate that word 'growth', and when I am falling to bits in my complexities, I cannot abide the defensive simplistics of mandalas, nor the sentimentalities of individuation as unity and wholeness. These are formulae presented through a fantasy of opposites—the disintegration shall be compensated by integration. But what of cure through likeness, where like takes care of like? I want the right background to the failure of life; I want to hear with precision of those Gods who are served by and thrive upon and can hence provide an archetypal background and even an eros connection with the defeat, decay and dismemberment."[31]

James Hillman, in *Re-Visioning Psychology*: "The soul sees by means of affliction . . . The wound and the eye are one and the same. From the psyche's viewpoint, pathology and insight are not opposites—as if we hurt because we have no insight and when we gain insight we shall no longer hurt. No. Pathologizing is itself a way of seeing; the eye of the complex gives the peculiar twist called psychological insight. We become psychologists because we see from the psychological viewpoint, which means by benefit of our complexes and their pathologizings."[32]

NOTES

1. "For the 'return to Greece' offers. . . ." James Hillman, *Pan and the Nightmare*, Spring Publications paperback edition, Thompson, Ct., 2000, pp. 2–3.
2. "Critics miss the validity. . . .": Ibid, p. 3.
3. "I now am supposed to get the lectures. . . .": JH letter to Marvin Spiegelman 1972, undated.
4. All quotes from Hillman's letters to Pat Berry are from her private archive. Unless other specified, the letters are not dated.
5. "timidly to practice again. . . .": JH letter to William Coffin, August 1, 1974.
6. "So favorable. . . .": Letter to JH from William J. Maguire, June 9, 1972, Opus Archive.

7. "often out of touch. . . .": Letter to JH from Ed Casey, June 9, 1972, Opus Archive.

8. "published closer to my arrival there. . . .": JH letter to William J. Maguire, June 16, 1972.

9. "into book shape. . . .": JH letter to John Layard, MSS 84, Box 8, Folder 1, Layard papers.

10. "The Jew As Scapegoat": See Volume I, *The Life and Ideas of James Hillman*, pp.257–59.

11. "It seems my work has always been. . . ." James Hillman, *Anima: The Anatomy of a Personified Notion*, Spring Publications, Inc., Woodstock, Ct., 1985, p. ix (Preface).

12. "Isn't *devotio* to anima. . . .": Ibid, pp. ix and x.

13. "an excursion that I felt was essential. . . .": Ibid, p. ix.

14. http://www.scottlondon.com/interviews/hillman.html

15. "that person by means of whom. . . .": Hillman, *Re-Visioning Psychology*, p. 43.

16. "Seems the main thing is to treat the organization. . . .": JH letter to Pat Berry, undated, Summer 1972.

17. "a discussion of Goethe's. . . .: David Miller email to author, May 20, 2017.

18. "We talked about zen. . . .": Pat Berry email to author.

19. "It was really an adventure. . . .": Author interview with Susanne Hillman, May 2005.

20. Hillman described the "heavenly vault" in interviews with the author in June 2007 and again in 2008.

21. "the second immediate father of archetypal psychology": James Hillman, *Archetypal Psychology: Uniform Edition Volume !*, Spring Publications, Inc.: Putnam, Ct., p. 15.

22. Jung's vision and Hillman's comment: "The Azure Vault," in *Alchemical Psychology: James Hillman Uniform Edition #5*, Spring Publications, Putnam, Ct., 2010, p. 325.

23. "We are headed to the edge": ibid, p. 318.

24. "keen disappointment. . . .": Letter to JH from Chester Kerr, Director of the Yale University Press, October 20, 1972, Opus Archive.

25. "I could almost have predicted. . . .": Letter to Hillman from Ed Casey, April 4, 1973.

26. "Have come to a dry choleric. . . ." JH letter to Marvin Spiegelman, Spiegelman private archie.

27. Kate sent all my stuff. . . ..: JH letter to Robert Stein, Hillman private archive.

28. Carola Hillman: Interview with author, May 2005.

29. Susanne Hillman: Interview with author, May 2005.

30. Laurence Hillman: Interview with author, July 2007.

31. "When I am in despair. . . .": Hillman essay on "Failure and Analysis" quoted in *Soul-Making: Interweaving Art and Analysis*, by Francesco Donfrancesco, Karnac, 2009, pp. 100–101.

32. "The soul sees by means. . . .": Hillman, *Re-Visioning Psychology*, p. 107.

8

SEEING THROUGH

"In another attempt upon the idea of soul I suggested that the word refers to that unknown component which makes meaning possible, turns events into experiences, is communicated in love, and has a religious concern. These four qualifications I had already put forth some years ago; I had begun to use the term freely, usually interchangeably with psyche (from Greek) and anima (from Latin). Now I am adding three necessary modifications. First, 'soul' refers to the deepening of events into experiences; second, the significance soul makes possible, whether in love or in religious concern, derives from its special relation with death. And third, by 'soul' I mean the imaginative possibility in our natures, the experiencing through reflective speculation, dream, image, and fantasy— that mode which recognizes all realities as primarily symbolic or metaphorical."

—*James Hillman,* Re-Visioning Psychology.

Toward the end of his life, Hillman reflected: "If I could go anywhere again, I'd like to go to Egypt and Persia."[2] He'd first seen Egypt with Kate in 1950, at the start of a long period abroad together that culminated in Kashmir and ultimately landed them both in Zürich. Now, upon separating from Kate early in 1973, he almost immediately returned to Egypt with Pat Berry.

The tombs in Luxor's Valley of the Kings captivated him, he said, like few places he'd seen. In 1987, Hillman told interviewer Jonathan Cott: "I thought: 'My God, it's all *right here*, we're *in* it!' . . . It was as if I were walking into the unconscious—that ridiculous term we use for the kingdom of Hades/Pluto . . . The tombs give a depiction of how the whole psyche works. The ancient Egyptians were much more psychological than we are— they lived in the psyche, and their paintings and poetry reveal that . . . They're metaphors of how human existence really is."[3]

Pat recalled: "It was wonderful traveling with him, because he could adapt to a culture so readily. One of his amazing talents was an ability to pick up language. I remember him speaking Arabic with this cab driver in like a *minute*. How did he do it?

He knew how to slip money. All these things that just impressed the bejesus out of me. This was a worldly man!"[4]

They took a sailboat ride from Luxor up the Nile, and after going ashore on an island, Pat was frightened by a mob of women rushing up and grabbing at her clothes, "because I was tall blond, and from another world." Another time, taking a camel ride, they were crossing over a sand dune when a young boy raced over: "He wanted to sell me a dried hand!" For Pat, "the underworld really came alive in the pyramids. The deeper you descended, the more vibrant became the colors along the wall, and then a bright, maybe red, mythical serpent appears on the wall wending down toward the sarcophagus. In some strange way this descent was like going toward rather than away from life. Actually I think the term sarcophagus for the Egyptians meant life. Egypt was fabulous for this kind of foreign although quintessentially earthy, deeper-than-deep sense of reality. And of course for Jim it must have prepared the way for his consequent *The Dream and the Underworld*."[5]

In fact, Hillman would immediately use this as the main theme for his lecture at Eranos the next summer, first published in Eranos' *Correspondences in Man and World* and expanded into a book bearing the title *The Dream and the Underworld* in 1979. He would begin by asking: "To what mythological region, to what Gods, do dreams belong?"[6] On a later page, he would reference "how the Egyptian underworld turns the dayworld upside down."[7] No wonder, then, that he abandoned two earlier potential titles: *The Dream Bridge* or *The Dream Between World and Underworld*.[8]

Upon returning to Zürich from Egypt, Hillman had resumed "timidly . . . after 3 years of refusal"[9] taking patients for analysis. "I see only one woman, the rest men," he wrote Bob Stein. Analysis felt different to Hillman this time: "has to do with putting the openendedness of the archetypal perspective into actual [session] hours." In a letter to Spiegelman, he elaborated: "Trying to find another way, without references to personal life relationships choices, decisions moves etc of the analysands conscious life. A completely away from ego analysis. Following only dreams and the intrapsychic scenes. Of course I get detoured into the upperworld, but I try to keep altogether in the lowerworld . . . a practice of archetypal psychology." He added: "Out of the marriage is a grand relief. Less sadism" "—and yet: "Sadness over failure sits forever heavy."

Pat remembered: "After Jim's marriage ended, he and I needed a place to live so we rented the floor beneath his office, which had been a publishing company, and which was just a block from the institute. We made it into a fabulous, funky livable space. Livable then was different from livable in the U.S. or nowadays. The toilet was in an unheated hallway on the floor below. We had a shower installed in the kitchen and sanded the wood floors to their original gleaming parquet. It was a crazy, wonderful space . . . Both of our offices were right there, his above, mine on same level. We ate all our meals together and talked constantly. Every day at *Mittagessen* (the noon, main meal with a 2 hour break after) we drank wine and figured out archetypal psychology primarily using our own dreams from the night before as well as those our patients had just brought to us. It was a highly productive and rich time. Really that's when archetypal psychology was created as a practice."[10]

Yet *en famille*, Hillman remained oblique in what he revealed to his mother about what had transpired in his personal life. That summer, he wrote her from Casa Gabriella by the lake in the Tessin: "Nina [Kate] and I live more separately now. I am either down here or have room just under my office at Zeltweg, when the former tenants moved out. She will not be coming over with me to the States while I'm at Yale, although the children will come over . . . My collaborator, Patricia Berry, who works with me in Zürich and will be my teaching assistant at Yale will be keeping whatever housing we get (nothing available yet) and driving the car (my endless problem in the states). It will be a grand job, but probably, as usual, too much to do."

VISITING PROFESSOR AT YALE

The previous December (1972), Hillman went back to the drawing board for *Re-Visioning Psychology*—even though its publication remained uncertain as far as Yale University Press was concerned. Nonetheless, late that month, he wrote to Yale's psychology department chair: "I believe we are getting near the time when you wanted some more precise thoughts in regard to the semester's teaching." He still hoped to start there the following fall and sent suggestions for two courses, one on some of Jung's Collected Works and the other a seminar covering "The Dream and Its Interpretation." Hillman concluded, in a gesture of humility: "Please let me know what you think."[11]

Yale hired Hillman as a visiting professor for the fall term. Earlier in 1973, he'd addressed "The Mythology of Psychopathology and the Psychopathy of Mythology" for the annual William James Lecture Series at the Harvard Divinity School, another feather in his cap. But it was Ed Casey who'd been the prime mover in getting Hillman to Yale. "I appealed to a very open-minded figure named Irving Child in the psychology department, who secured the appointment," Casey would remember.

Casey assumed that arrangements for lodging were taken care of. But when Hillman arrived with Pat Berry, they had no place to live. They scrambled to find a small apartment in New Haven on Chapel Street—"one of the tougher streets in town, filled with prostitutes and drug dealers," Casey recalled. The newcomers didn't seem to mind a bit. "Others would find this incongruous, to find this great psychologist writing at the kitchen table while he was cooking. Jim found it all perfectly natural, liked the coziness and even the rough-hewn character."[12]

Hillman proceeded to teach the two courses he'd suggested nine months earlier—lecturing twice a week on Jung to undergrads and leading a graduate seminar on dreams once a week. So many students signed up for the latter that "they needed another section," Pat remembered—"and there was nobody else who could teach archetypal psychology. So I, a graduate of lowly Ohio State, suddenly found myself teaching students nearly my own age at Yale! I was absolutely terrified—immediately got sick and went to bed, missed the second class."[13]

Once she got herself together, Pat drew up a chart illustrating a method of "what sticking to the image" could look like in working with a dream. The chart showed various columns depicting, for example, a narrative reading as part of "amplifying, and filling out as one moved farther from what was actually in the dream at the level of image."[14] From what she learned by figuring out how to handle the course, she then wrote "An Approach to the Dream," a long essay first published in *Spring 1974* that would later appear in her 1982 book, *Echo's Subtle Body*. Teaching that class, Pat believed, marked "the turning point in my own development."[15] At the same time, she was seeing fourteen student patients in analysis.

Hillman wrote in a letter: "We are enjoying it more than I ever could have thought possible. I love each day of it and have an easy relaxed time lecturing, almost extemporaneously to a beautiful hall (architecturally) with about 150 students. The course is popular, and the students of good level and from all faculties even mathematics. But I have yet to meet many of my colleagues in psychology. I understand my appointment caused some dissension."[16]

So it was a turning point for Hillman as well. His children came overseas to visit, attending one of his lectures and a Yale theater company production of Shakespeare's *The Tempest*—while staying in one of the student dorms. Over long discussions at the dining table, Hillman also grew close to Ed Casey. "He says we often discussed the intersection between phenomenology and archetypal psychology," Casey reflected in 2011. "I think the common term for both is 'appearance.' The gods come forward as phenomena from whatever source, and then the phenomenologist is interested in what appears out of a description of a circumstance. So the body is appearing, as is the place. In that very large sense, we are both phenomenologists."[17]

On one memorable occasion, Casey observed Hillman's uncommon eye for phenomena. "Jim and I were walking and talking around campus when we happened upon Sterling Library, and he said to me, 'Ed, look up at that.' He was pointing to two words sculpted in stone on the north façade of that building that took up a whole city block: '*Festina Lente.*' Translated: 'make haste slowly' . . . It was exemplary of Jim's watchful eye. I had walked by that same façade hundreds of times and never noticed this saying."[18] (According to a woman who met them at the time, "Make Haste Slowly" was also a bumper sticker on one of Hillman's and Pat's cars).[19]

Yet unlike the atmosphere at Zürich's Spring House seminars, there was something about Ivy League academia that ultimately didn't sit well with Hillman. As he put it in one of our interviews: "What's wrong with all these academic things is, the eros is absent in the relations with the students. As Bill Coffin said, 'We are supposed to be a community of scholars. We have the scholars, but no community.' It's all rivalry and prestige and putting the other guy down, and knowing more than everybody else. And I hated it."[20]

It wasn't only this. Long before Yale, from his boyhood in Atlantic City to his student days in Paris and Dublin and thereafter, he could find no continuity. "I don't have a steady stream of career; nothing builds out of something else," he reflected in another interview. "It's as if I'm never really there on earth. In my horoscope, I have no earth [signs]. But it's a very deep thing about maintaining, you know, brick upon brick upon brick. A different kind of daimon, and I don't know quite what that is. There's a great deal of activity or ferment or life in these various scenes, and then I'm elsewhere."[21]

He spoke of another insight he gained from teaching at Yale in a fax to the author (2007): "I think these 'elevations' made me feel both inflated, and very seriously underprepared: Director of Studies, Eranos Lecturer, Yale Terry Lecturer were 'callings' and I had to work like crazy to raise myself, I felt, to the level I imagined these positions required. I believe I have been pulled from ahead more than pushed from behind; and pulled by lucky breaks, which are on-time signal events that did not put me onto a particular career ladder. I seemed still to have remained a lone gunman. Yale for instance did not lead to another invitation, or a post elsewhere. I did not even keep up with Bill [Coffin]. But inward, within myself, I may have longed to be an elite member of Yale, in one sense, I did nothing about it, and didn't really feel well, even there. I seemed never to have networked."[22]

Or, as he put it to John Layard in a letter just before departing Yale for Europe in 1974: The university was "a treasure house of learning, like Alexandria must have been. Yet it is work with such ill-ease, so little leisure and elegance. Such shame at being high up." Yes, the semester there had been "a grand success, but I long to hole up again and get down to the work that matters, writing Archetypal psychology as a deviation and a recapitulation and a resemination of Jung and Freud."[23]

The feeling was reciprocal, as Ed Casey described the aftermath of Hillman's time at Yale in a letter to him: "There is no question as to the massive impact of your courses. About every other paper written for my seminar last fall was in fact an extension of *your* seminar or lecture course. This was true both for graduates . . . and for undergraduates. The latter, of course, were most deeply affected. One girl in my office yesterday said simply, 'I'd never seen the *point* in psychology until I took Hillman's course.' So you've left a remarkable wake, which will continue to spread for years to come . . . Whatever the harassments may have been for you two, for all of us it was more than memorable: your presence was extraordinary. I only wish it could continue."[24]

In the early 1970s of Atlantic City, shortly before the casino boom and the construction of Trump Taj Mahal, the old hotels were being dynamited and demolished for urban renewal. The city fathers granted a permit to knock down The Breakers, once owned by Hillman's family and where he had been born in 1926. A photo of the venerable hotel's hour of demise, on May 22, 1974, appeared in the *Philadelphia Inquirer.*[25]

Three days before his birthplace crumbled to the ground, Hillman had delivered a lecture in France that he titled *Pothos: The Nostalgia of the Puer Eternus*. "The question which shall be engaging us in our wanderings this morning is the psychological one of nostalgia," he began and later said: "Our lives follow mythical figures. We act, think, feel, only as permitted by primary patterns established in the imaginal world . . . The puer eternus . . . is a restless spirit that has no 'home' on earth, is always coming from somewhere or going to somewhere in transition." His essay concluded: "Our longings and sea-borne wanderings are the effects in our personal lives of the transpersonal images that urge us, carry us, and force us to imitate mythical destinies."[26]

A NEW PUBLISHER FOR *RE-VISIONING*

Sometime in the late summer of 1973, Hillman wrote his mother: "I believe Harper and Row will publish my Yale lectures of last year, but we have not yet signed a contract." The letter is undated, but makes reference to his plan to teach at Yale between September and Christmas. That fall, in a letter to Ritsema, Hillman elaborated that he was "getting a good contract and have an editor assigned to me for collaborative work."

The connection had been made by David Miller, the professor of religious studies at Syracuse who'd established something of a synchronistic connection to Hillman shortly before the Terry Lectures. Miller, knowing nothing about the Lectures, had called Zürich to see if Hillman might speak at a conference he was helping arrange with the American Society of Arts, Religion and Culture. Miller couldn't afford to pay travel expenses, but Hillman said that was alright because New York wasn't that far from Yale. Miller, taken by surprise, asked what subject he'd like to address. "Well, I'd like to talk about polytheism," Hillman replied. After a pregnant silence, Hillman asked whether Miller was still on the line. "Well yeah," Miller responded, "but I have a manuscript with Harper & Row called *The New Polytheism*."

So Hillman went and spoke at the conference. When Miller found himself not far from Zürich giving a lecture in Strasbourg. the following summer, Hillman returned the favor, inviting Miller to come to Spring House and address any topic he chose. Miller said, "Well, I want to talk about butterflies, psyche of the butterfly." Well and good. Hillman gathered together his disparate collection of friends, including López and Guggenbühl, and invited Eranos' Rudolf Ritsema up to hear Miller as well.[27] Miller's presentation became the lead essay, "Achelous and the Butterfly: Toward an Archetypal Psychology of Humor," in the *Spring 1973* journal. Based on this work, Miller would eventually be invited to join the prestigious and iconoclastic presenters at Eranos, appearing every year between 1975 and 1988.

In *The New Polytheism*, first published by Harper & Row in 1974, Miller included a chapter on Hillman's work, the first discussion of archetypal psychology in a book not written by Hillman. In Hillman's radical view, wrote Miller, "It is not that we worship many Gods and Goddesses (e.g., money, sex, power, and so on); it is rather that the Gods and Goddesses live through our psychic structures. They are given in the fundamental nature of our being, and they manifest themselves always in our behaviors. The Gods grab us, and we play out their stories."[28]

Miller approached Clayton Carlson, then head of the religious division of Harper & Row, to see if the publishing gods might also smile on Hillman's archetypal opus. Carlson, according to Hillman, "imagined its final typographical format and concluded the contract."[29] According to Miller, "there was a lot of negotiation because they weren't sure about the format."[30]

The manuscript was first dispatched to an outside woman editor who, as Hillman recollected, "tried to get me to rewrite some of my paragraphs in the correct way. That is, you open with what the paragraph is about and then expose this in the same paragraph. Well, that isn't how I write at all, because then there's no discovery! Why write, if you know what you're going to write about? Then you're didactic; you've already got the idea, you're not trying to *get* the idea. It's a completely different approach.

"Mine is not an attempt to be obscure or deliberately difficult. But the experience of reading my books is much closer to the experience of writing them. The editor said, 'Your main thought is buried here in the middle of the paragraph.' Well, the reader discovers that main thought there, too, just as I discovered it when I wrote. So the whole thing has that quality of adventure, and forward motion. That's really I think an important aspect of the life in the writing—my life in the writing and the life in the actual prose." In that sense, Hillman believed, his style is similar to that of poetics, where the reader is required to slow down and take in the words again because they can't be fully absorbed the first time.[31]

With the initial battle fought, and largely won, Hillman's next encounter occurred with an in-house editor. "That woman was a Quaker and she sent me back a shoebox with slips of paper of things she objected to and corrected. Many of them being thoughts that she couldn't take!"[32]

Indeed, Hillman's polytheistic thinking and style of writing struck a nerve. In the Opus Archive of his papers, there exists a six-page, single-spaced letter to him from Annabel Learned, Copy Editor. While praising Clayton Carlson's "splendid work" on the manuscript, and despite Hillman's writing being "far and away superior to most people's," her "query slips" were many. Certain errors "are of a kind that no one who has English in his bones would be apt to make, and they recur fairly often. This is possible, I imagine, if you are profoundly steeped in the literature of other languages; but perhaps you ought to try to lose them."

Learned takes a while to get to her primary objection to "a fascinating book, though I found it repellent in certain respects. I'm a Christian (or try to be), so perhaps not the right audience for it." But she was bothered by his capitalizing of Gods and Goddesses, which "seems a real perversion of language, quite aside from religious or philosophical preferences." Couldn't

Hillman see that he was depriving Christians "of the use of their major and central word . . . The same is true with *soul* and *spirit*, both vital to Christianity. Your meanings are quite remote from those we usually think of, and you insist on them. What puzzles me is your unawareness of the ways in which the New Testament meets some of the distresses you deal with, and indeed the whole basic outlook on life. In fact, I get a feeling here of rather cursory, possibly even secondhand acquaintance . . . Your presentation of the essence of Christianity seems to me, alas, a travesty."[33]

This wouldn't be the last time that Hillman would face such accusations. But to its credit, Harper & Row passed the ball back to David Miller for further review, with Miller making suggestions in support of what Hillman called "Excursions" in formatting the book. It went through four or five revisions, Hillman estimated.[34] Pat Berry remembered: "I did no more than listen to him huff and puff, sympathize and read things over for clarity. I wasn't trying to make him normal, as the editors seemed to think he should be."[35]

Back in Zürich, Hillman asked a newcomer named Lyn Cowan to type the final draft and compile the index. Cowan had arrived at the Jung Institute in September 1973, "after nearly three years of analysis, one divorce, and two college degrees." After reading Hillman's book *InSearch* in her Minnesota backyard, she started "feeling my sluggish academically-deadened mind beginning to expand as if frantically growing billions of new cells."[36] Upon arrival in Zürich, she'd called Hillman after hearing he needed a typist. He asked if Cowan knew how to hyphenate and whether she understood Latin and, apparently satisfied with her affirmative response, Hillman hired her sight unseen. She began by operating the composer for Spring Publications, which she dubbed Mephistopheles "because it was a devil to keep running properly." Cowan was also charged with answering hate mail "received from irate subscribers who inexplicably resented waiting six months or more for their copy of *Spring Journal*." She tried to respond poetically: "If winter comes, can Spring be far behind?"[37] For her services Cowan was paid the equivalent of two dollars an hour, but there were perks: Hillman would call and say he'd bought too much at the market and was baking a new dish that couldn't keep and would she come over? "Once every few days, I was sure to get a good meal." And when Jim and Pat went to the Tessin for the summer, Cowan was given their apartment to house-sit.

By that time, Cowan was immersed in typing *Re-Visioning Psychology* on a Swiss brand typewriter aptly called Hermes, using a Helvetica type-face (Latin name for the pre-Roman tribes in what became Switzerland). As Cowan fell more deeply into the prose, "It was like climbing inside another person's remarkable mind and watching it work, hearing it use language that kept opening up wondrous new realms of ideas, of learning, of ways to think mythically, to live psychologically . . . I began to feel like Dante being led out of a dark wood by the poet Virgil. I began to see countless mysteries of the world and all its hidden places, the endless varieties of psychic life."[38]

When stalled at a new perspective or odd angle, Cowan would simply dial up her Virgil and ask him to explain. Once she called to query Hillman about a passage on "psychological faith," which he came by to explain while pacing around the wooden table at Spring House. "It was about having faith in, trusting, giving credence to, the reality of imaginal fantasies, to the figures and movements in an imaginal world that is hidden from the eye that sees only literally."[39]

When Cowan was working on the galleys, Hillman rushed over one day saying he had to get a few more lines into the text. She said that wasn't possible, as all the pagination would be thrown off (this was pre-computer). Hillman insisted on reading her a passage about "casting Perls before swine"—a reference to Fritz Perls, the inventor of Gestalt Therapy. Cowan couldn't help but laugh. "You see, it's really good!" she remembered Hillman saying. "It'll be worth the time, I promise." As he left the room, she shouted: "Don't get any more inspiration!"[40] and proceeded to painstakingly add the change.

From Hillman, Cowan later said, "I learned you could live the passionate life. I'd never met anybody with the kind of passion he had, and the fearlessness with which he would put something. When he said something, he stood fiercely for it. And if you didn't like his idea, too bad. He wasn't dogmatic but, as he said once, 'I'm an Aries, I am blood lust, I love the battle of argument.' For me, he became a model in that sense, of the best sort."[41]

Almost a decade later, Hillman would publish Cowan's first book, her Jung Institute thesis on *Masochism: A Jungian View*. He accompanied her into a bookstore in New York seeking a place for it, calling the book a "radically new approach." The skeptical store owner asked, "Well, what's the author's position?" Cowan recalled Hillman's quick response: "Submissive." The two were hastily shown the door.[42]

Hardly submissive, Cowan returned to Minneapolis, where she finished her training by attending seminars at the Chicago Jung Institute. Eventually she built a therapeutic practice, became an international lecturer, was president of the Inter-Regional Society of Jungian Analysts, and the author of two more books: *Tracking the White Rabbit: A Subversive View of Modern Culture* (2002) and *Portrait of the Blue Lady: The Character of Melancholy* (2004).

Late in 1974, with the page proofs for *Re-Visioning Psychology* on the floor of his Zürich apartment, Hillman had written to Spiegelman: "The book reads badly, I feel disgust (like shit smells after it's out), it's badly designed and printed too, but it's my baby which I slaved over more than anything."[43] To his mother, Hillman added that the publisher had a 45-day U.S. tour of lectures lined up after the book came out in March; since Harper & Row had given him a big advance, "they have to spend a lot on pushing it to make their money back. But the book is difficult, and I doubt if it will be the success they think."[44]

Notwithstanding Hillman's doubts, *Re-Visioning Psychology* would sell well and be nominated in 1975 for a Pulitzer Prize. Casey wrote him that the original Terry Lectures had "seemed

written to be spoken . . . I keep *hearing* you as I read the book."[45]
About its impact, Hillman had written presciently to his mother:
"Actually my works don't have success, they have echo. They are
read by kids, intellectuals, young college profs, and then are used
and quoted in their works. A kind of underground, which is just
what I aim for."[46]

Fellow members of that underground were among the
reviewers. Murray Stein, a colleague from the Zürich days, wrote
one for the *Houston Chronicle*. He placed Hillman in the vanguard of something that "has nothing to do with enrichment
weekends, meditation techniques, human potential movements,
or any other of the nostrums currently available for improving the human condition. Not fantasies of self-improvement
or better mental health or centeredness and tranquility guide
Hillman in his quest for 'soul-making,' as he calls the task by
which modern consciousness must be transformed, but rather
images of deepening—deepening consciousness, deepening
experience—dominate these reflections. In Hillman's view, psychology should be disentangled from religion and spiritual disciplines on the one hand and from physiology and medicine on
the other; neither of these disciplines, the one oriented toward
spirit, the other toward body, give the psyche (soul) its due."[47]

Robert Sardello, later to become a close friend of Hillman's,
seized a reviewing opportunity to take contemporary psychology to task: "Psychology has become a discipline that has eliminated strife from its speaking. The heated controversies of the
days of the 'schools' of psychology are said to be of historical
concern only. The days of learning theorists making bold assertions concerning man's behavior are past . . . The terrain of
the discipline has become flat. Everything has equal visibility.
Under such circumstances no one knows or cares where he
stands, and this lack of standing in and for anything is termed
objectivity . . .

"Hillman's re-visioning is a psychology of the soul, based in a
psychology of image, founded in a poetic basis of mind, in the
processes of imagination . . . The method of imagination is to

follow soul wherever it leads, to become its servant, to listen to the story it wishes to tell."[48]

RE-VISIONING RELATIONSHIPS

Robbie Bosnak, recently arrived in Zürich at the time, remembered years later: "I was working with him in analysis when he got divorced from Kate. So I think that *Re-Visioning Psychology* was very much about his process of falling apart and the important things he had found in that—a state that was to be welcomed and that you didn't have to be destroyed by. He was really exploring psyche as a multiplicity of selves."[49]

Hillman himself, in the book *Inter Views*, reflected on the period when he framed *Re-Visioning*—starting with five-day stretches of writing in the Tessin. "I didn't have a purpose in mind: but I began to see the importance of psychopathology in the whole psychoanalytical business, for all of the work begins in pathology. And slowly I began to write about what we really are doing in this work, why pathology is so important, and the idea of seeing into and seeing through. So I had those thoughts in my head and some on paper already in 1970. That was the period when I had stopped practicing. Stopped for two years. Maybe I had written my way out of being a disciple who had been 'trained.'

"I wasn't burned out as they say now. I was embarrassed, ashamed. I just hated the psychoanalytical business too much and myself in it—like a scalding or an acid or something that made it impossible. I had also been in a scandal and that broke many of my relationships. I saw they were frauds, I was a fraud. Breakdown. A whole world collapsed . . . All of these things went into *Re-Visioning Psychology*."[50]

It is noteworthy that, as publication of the book neared, Hillman seemed to be coming to terms with the many changes in his personal life. Although Kate did not join him at her family's island in Sweden in the summer of 1974, the four children "and their innumerable friends" came with Hillman "up in the Northwoods for my fifteenth summer."[51] That September, he wrote his mother: "I hope you have ceased worrying about Nina [Kate] and her life and my life. She is a generous deep and loving person and we speak regularly on the phone about all sorts of things and saw each other over essentials just recently too. There is little harshness or conflict, and the children move back and forth between Zeltweg and Klosterweg, Sweden and the Tessin without complications. Pat and I are driving to London this time, taking Carola and Laurence."

In January 1975, Hillman put himself in the dock in a letter to Bob Stein: "With Kate there is much goodness on her side, so that the relationship by phone and letters goes regularly and rather well. The complex in me is still totally unsolved. I am still enraged and sadistic internally towards her despite the other feelings. I do nothing about 'working it out' except to stew and brood and suffer it, occasionally—and watch. I still feel I'm in the midst of working out a whole new vision of psychology."[52]

Changes were afoot with friendships, too, including the Americans he'd gone to school with in 1950s Zürich. After Hillman sent Stein pre-publication material from *Re-Visioning*, his friend responded: "I'm still not sure what I feel is missing. Perhaps it has to do with the fact that your task seems to center primarily around the need to free the archetypal perspective from the narrow confines of psychotherapy."[53] In a letter to Spiegelman, Hillman conveyed refusal to adapt himself to the expectations of others, even his friends: "As I get older I like living in an odd way with a small bunch around me, tho without program or manifesto. As for failing to grasp individual relations . . . I repeat, that's what my fucking life is overburdened with, and life will never be cleared up in and through personal relations. Let's *do* things together but not analyze each other."[54] In another letter to Spiegelman, Hillman added: "Relationships that once were BIG now are ashes (but without regret)."

In November 1974, Hillman had starkly informed John Layard: "Rafael [López] moved back to Venezuela."[55] That same month, Hillman made note of a dream: "Nov 16. Rafael walks with two women on either side of him. He has completely short, almost shaven brownish hair. He does not recognize me."[56]

López obliquely hints at a possible split with Hillman over *Re-visioning*, in a 2003 interview with Axel Capriles. After Capriles suggested, "You didn't attempt to leave a mark in history by breaking away," López responded: "The book by Hillman made me take my first step back. The psychology Hillman presents in it is controversial . . . To be controversial should be studied as a psychology in itself."[57]

López certainly didn't leave archetypal psychology behind upon moving to Caracas. There he told Capriles he "was lucky enough to work in the School of Literature at the Universidad Central de Venezuela," where he "had the chance to assimilate the knowledge and emotions which had accumulated during my years in Zürich." There he gave seminars introducing students to Greek tragedy. The early days of archetypal psychology, López told Capriles, had been "exciting times." About the period of his departure, he only added: "Hillman dedicated himself increasingly to his publications, and when they asked what I was going to do, I said something like . . . I will take care of the inertia."[58]

This wasn't the last López and Hillman would see of each other. In 1977, Spring Publications would bring out his book, *Hermes and His Children*, and he would continue corresponding with and visiting Hillman and Pat after they moved back to the U.S. But in Zürich, new younger colleagues were entering Hillman's orbit: Ed Casey, David Miller, and Mary Watkins would remain close friends to the end of his life.

Watkins had finished her senior undergraduate thesis at Princeton (later the basis of her first book, *Waking Dreams*), and in 1972–73 was living in a therapeutic community and working nights in Massachusetts' Cambridge City Hospital. Around three o'clock in the morning, she encountered a woman in the process of a suicide attempt. Although Watkins stopped her, the experience proved "very traumatic for a 21-year-old" already suffering some depression of her own. When she went the next morning to see her analyst, the woman suggested a book: James Hillman's *Suicide and the Soul*. Though it had been stolen out of every library in Boston, Watkins finally tracked the book down in North Carolina through an inter-library loan.

"Towards the middle, it got very radical," she recalled, "and one passage in particular really struck me. He was talking about the images people have when they're deeply suicidal, and how most treatments try to cut them off from those death dealing images because it's assumed people will only get worse if they articulate them. But Hillman said, the paradox is that even though the images might be horrible, dark, and often grotesque, if you engage with them coming forward you release a sense of liveliness. The life energy is in these images of death! And therapists may be starving the patient of a potential source for reconnecting with the importance of being alive."[59]

Before long, Watkins was "trying to scrape together money to go to the Jung Institute in Zürich" where Hillman taught. She made her way there only to find that he'd just left for a teaching term at Yale. Her first semester at the Institute proved "one of the most boring intellectual experiences" she'd ever experienced—the worst being "a seminar by a dentist who'd become a Jungian and was following dreams about when teeth fall out." Hillman's return in January 1974 marked a welcome turning point, as Watkins attended his lectures based on *Re-Visioning Psychology* and the content that would become his *Dream and the Underworld*. "All of a sudden, where there'd been a sprinkling of people, the room was now packed and you could have heard a pin drop. I mean, it was just completely electric."

Watkins was simultaneously in a psychodrama training group with a fellow student, Robbie Bosnak, whom she told about her thesis on waking dreams and who apparently passed that along to Hillman. During a break at Hillman's next class, he walked up to the "shy and introverted" Watkins, said he'd learned about her work and would she consider letting him read some of her thesis and possibly even publish a chapter? She was floored. Her essay, "The Waking Dream in European Psychotherapy," would occupy twenty-two pages of the *Spring 1974* journal, in between Edward S. Casey's opening "Toward an Archetypal Imagination" and Patricia Berry's "An Approach to the Dream."

Watkins remembered: "At that time, in the academic world, women weren't particularly respected. Certainly in my own family, there was no support for going off and following your intellectual direction. So he provided a sort of mentoring fatherly presence that was quite crucial for me. At one point he called me up about my article and said, 'What's wrong with you? You haven't gotten the references in the right order yet!' He was always challenging, but very deeply accepting at another level—that the young people around him had something to offer that was different from what he offered, young people who could be put in conversation with his work but had a value of their own."

David Miller, then in his late thirties, was ten years younger than Hillman. Born in Ohio, he was the son of an Anabaptist clergyman in a family that moved all around the U.S. Miller had two passions—tennis (he became a teaching pro) and unorthodox religion. At Syracuse University, studying under Stanley Hopper who had known Jung, Miller wrote his doctoral dissertation on Aristophanes and Greek religion. By the time he first encountered Hillman at Eranos in 1969, he was as taken by psychology and mythology as theology.

In the summer of 1975, after Miller helped shepherd *Re-Visioning* into print, his academic connection to Hillman burgeoned into a personal one when Hillman invited Miller and his family—who were traveling in Europe at the time—to spend a week at the island retreat in northern Sweden. The property had a tennis court, and Miller informed Hillman that he was a retired tennis pro. "I'm not much into tennis with its white lines, short white pants and fuzzy balls," Hillman wrote him in a note that Miller never forgot. They played nonetheless.

Miller also recalled taking a trip to the mainland to buy some fresh-caught salmon from a fellow in a pickup truck. Back on the island, Hillman gathered all of his kids and Miller's two, killed the fish and showed them how to clean it—then sliced it into lox and taught them how to smoke salmon. He also instructed Miller's son in how to build a fire, standing the logs upright, "the way trees grow." The two men talked for hours on end.

With Miller scheduled for a writing sabbatical in Strasbourg that fall semester, Hillman arranged for Miller to also teach two courses at the Jung Institute, a three-hour train ride away. "Ironically, one course was on 'Termination and Problems of Endings'—at the same time I was trying to kill myself," Miller recalled in 2007, not entirely tongue-in-cheek. After his lecturing debut at the Eranos conference, Miller had what he described as "a pretty serious breakdown." He told Hillman: "I'm in desperate shape, I really need help." Hillman wasn't seeing patients at the time, but agreed to take on Miller twice a week before and after when he came to lecture in Zürich. "I was the first patient really for him to practice what he'd written about in *Re-Visioning Psychology*," according to Miller.

"What did I learn from James Hillman? I learned how to die. I was successful in what I did when too young, and there seemed no place to go after that. I'd been suicidal, literally. Little by little working with him but also reading him, I learned what the psyche really wanted was to refocus itself in Soul and in Self, not in ego. That Christmas of '75, the woman who was then my wife was a soprano soloist and singing Mozart's Requiem. I was sitting in this church listening when it came to the *Dies Irae*—the part of the mass where the soul is given up forever. I heard a sound snap and it was loud. The people sitting on either side of me in the pew both turned and looked at me, so they apparently heard it, too. I knew immediately what had happened. I'd died. But not in the sense that I was trying to die six months earlier. Then I thought about all of those philosophers who say philosophy is learning how to die, starting with Socrates. William Blake once signed an autograph album, 'William Blake born some year died many times since.' Or St. Paul saying, 'I die daily.' I was thinking, that's the thing to watch, the different ways that we displace the structure of the Self out of ego's economy into larger frameworks. Hillman taught me to do that, or at least he started me on the path."[60]

CRITICAL ACCLAIM

Even before *Re-Visioning* came out, Hillman had made further inroads in Europe. The Italians published his paper on Plotinus, Ficino, and Vico. At a university in Chambéry, France, in May 1974, he gave a talk on "Pothos: The Nostalgia of the Puer Eternus," about which he wrote his mother: "I even had to defend my paper and argue in French. It's a *long* way from the early days in Paris" [Hillman had attended the Sorbonne in 1947]. Pat, who accompanied him to both Sicily and Chambéry, recalled: "He went into an altered state; he had no idea what he said after the lecture."[61] In October, he gave lectures in London and then Rome.

Then came the big American promotion tour for *Re-Visioning*'s publication. He wrote his mother: "I have now connections in different university departments in many places in the States. I am such a freelancer that I am invited by an art department in New Mexico, to talk on the Renaissance in Pittsburgh, on philosophy in Tennessee, on death at MIT in Boston . . . a strange mix."[62] That August, Hillman couldn't help but wax on to his mother about how *Re-Visioning* "seems to be making a very big impression . . . In Dallas there was a whole course this summer on the Works of James Hillman, at Syracuse a graduate course on [Norman O.] Brown and Hillman," while the book was assigned to students at Yale, the University of Connecticut, and the University of New Mexico. "In San Francisco a book store had a whole window of Hillman books (and Spring books)," and the journal was now turning over $60,000 a year. "You cannot imagine how many letters I have to deal with in a week."[63]

As the future unfolded, Hillman took time to revisit the past. En route to the lecture tour, he went to Florida with Pat to visit her parents. Later, in southern California, the two of them drove through the part of town in Long Beach where she was born. After the tour ended, he harkened back to his childhood in writing his mother that the Marx Brothers' movies had finally come to Zürich; "they are marvelous and undated," and daughters Susanne and Carola went to see all of them. He drove with Pat through Germany, where he lived with his parents in the early post-war years. "My thoughts were constantly in Hofheim and our Summers in the forties. It's such a powerful captivating country, and the first time I had been really 'in' it for many years," he wrote his mother.[64] In London, where he'd discovered the archetypal treasures of the Warburg Institute, he attended "a little party off Kings Road with Eminent Painters, Writers and Revolutionaries."[65] He also went back to Dublin for the 25th reunion of his Trinity College class and to attend his novelist friend J. P. Donleavy's party celebrating a new book. "In Ireland I lived it high, the jet set, for at the party was Mick Jagger of Rolling Stones fame, and international bigwigs."[66]

In the final months of 1975, the most important part of Hillman's past reached its denouement. He wrote his mother: "Nina and I were at the lawyers to sign our agreement and on Friday the official court divorce takes place. It's all with tolerance and understanding, which sows seeds for a better future. In fact the other evening I took Laurence to a concert, and Nina was there with a friend who then drove us all home in the rain (only to have a car crash, tho not serious). So don't be too sad about the divorce."[67]

In writing Stein about the divorce, Hillman said: "My whole book talks of *involvement* and staying in the valley. But one stays there knowing that it is a valley, and that is not the whole scene . . . It is the barriers, the personal individual differences and hang-ups that make for uniqueness of each individual Soul, not the totality and union."[68]

Nineteen seventy-five was also the year that Hillman's own Spring Books published *Loose Ends*, a collection of his essays on betrayal, schism, failure and more—"building the idea of a sophisticated classicism to counter what he feels is the primitive romantic psychology prevalent today," reviewer Margaret Boe Birns wrote for *P.M. New York*.[69]

But after the publication of *Re-Visioning*, not all the critics rallied to Hillman's vision. Robert H. Davis, in the 2003 book *Jung, Freud and Hillman: Three Depth Psychologies in Context*, reflected: "To some, Hillman's ambitious goal to re-vision psychology by reintroducing soul suggests a level of hubris not seen in the field since John B. Watson's famous boast that, using behaviorist methods, he could shape the character of any infant in accordance with whatever specifications the parents or society desired."[70]

Such charges were aptly refuted in a review by Thomas Moore, then a young professor of religion. "In recent years, for all of its branchings, psychology has become an ever narrower discipline," Moore concluded his analysis of *Re-Visioning*. "Where it was once inseparable from religion, philosophy, and mythology, it is now being stuffed into the shell of an exact science or squeezed into attitudes of personalism, communications, or mental health. By exploring the non-human reaches of psyche, Hillman is again blurring the boundaries of psychology moving not toward a field of study but toward a comprehensive style of living. He is sculpting a psychology of religion and a religious perspective on psychology."

And where it most counted, among the elders in his realm, Hillman had assuredly arrived. He must have been delighted when Eranos' Rudolf Ritsema informed him of the reaction that *Re-Visioning* elicited from Mircea Eliade—the renowned mythological scholar whose classes Hillman had attended as a neophyte student at the Jung Institute. Eliade reportedly told Henry Corbin that he considered the book "*trés importante et meme revolutionnaire*"[71] [very important and even revolutionary].

Marianne Jacoby, a pioneer in training Jungian analysts in Zürich, admitted that initially the book's advocacy of multiplicity caused her apprehension: "'If I tossed away my sense of unity, would I not have to pay for it with madness.' But presently, when no daimon seemed to play havoc with me, I went on reading as if *Re-Visioning Psychology* were an essay in active imagination." She ended up calling it "a pioneer's book and written with considerable dash."[72]

Rudolf Ritsema summed it in a personal letter: "You have found your own position. I think it is a major contribution to the necessary evolution from 'analysis' and 'unconscious' to the new way of dealing with man's destiny, a new way that is in line with the oldest traditions."[73]

NOTES

1. "In another attempt upon the idea of soul. . . .": Hillman, *Re-Visioning Psychology*, p. x.
2. "If I could go anywhere again. . . .": Author interview with JH, May 2008.
3. "I thought, my God. . . .": "Conversation with James Hillman," in *The Search for Omm Sety*, by Jonathan Cott, 221–25 (New York: Doubleday, 1987).
4. "It was wonderful traveling with him. . . .": Pat Berry interview with author, September 2013.
5. "because I was tall and blond. . . .": Pat Berry interview with author, September 2013, and email to author, December 8, 2017.
6. "To what mythological region. . . .": James Hillman, *The Dream and the Underworld*, Harper & Row, N.Y., 1979, p. 2.
7. "how the Egyptian underworld. . . .": Ibid, p. 174.
8. Abandoned two earlier titles: Ibid, p. 1.
9. "timidly. . . .after 3 years of refusal": JH letter to William Coffin, August 1, 1974, Yale University Coffin papers.
10. "After Jim's marriage ended. . . .": Pat Berry email to author, December 8, 2017.
11. "I believe we are getting near. . . .": Letter from JH to Yale Department Chair, December 20, 1972, tech. notes—letters, series Q,H203, Opus Archive.
12. "I appealed to a very open-minded. . . .": Author interview with Ed Casey, January 2006.
13. So many students signed up. . . .: Author interviews with Pat Berry.
14. "what sticking to the image looks like. . . .": transcript of Pat Berry Podcast with Michael Lerner, January 16, 2015.
15. "the turning point in my development. . . .": Pat Berry email to author, November 19, 2016.
16. "We are enjoying it. . . .": JH letter to Rudolf Ritsema, October 9, 1973, Eranos archive.
17. "He says we often discussed the intersection. . . .": Author interview with Ed Casey, January 2006.
18. "Jim and I were walking. . . .": Ed Casey email to author, June 2017.

19. "Make haste slowly" as bumper sticker: Author communication with Wendy Orange, 2017.
20. "What's wrong with all these academic things. . . .": JH interview with author, September 2009.
21. "I don't have a steady stream of career. . . .": JH interview with author, September 2006.
22. "I think these 'elevations' made me feel. . . .": JH fax to author, August 26, 2007.
23. "a treasure house of learning. . . .": JH letter to John Layard, January 2, 1974, Layard archive.
24. "There is no question as to the massive impact. . . .": Ed Casey letter to "Dear Jim and Pat," 17, 1974.
25. Demolition of The Breakers: Dick Russell, *The Life and Ideas of James Hillman Volume I*, pp. 40–41.
26. Hillman, "Pothos: The Nostalgia of the Puer Eternus," in *Loose Ends*, pp. 49–61.
27. Miller's recollection of the beginning of his relationship with Hillman came in an interview with the author in 2009.
28. "It is not that we worship many Gods and Goddesses. . . .": David L. Miller, *The New Polytheism*, Spring Publications: Dallas, Texas, 1981 edition, p. 76.
29. "imagined its final typographical format. . . .": Hillman, Preface to 1992 edition of *Re-Visioning Psychology*, p. xiii.
30. "There was a lot of negotiation. . . .": David Miller interview with author, March 2009.
31. "tried to get me to rewrite some of my paragraphs. . . .": Hillman interview with author, May 29, 2008.
32. "That woman was a Quaker. . . .":
33. Letter to Hillman from Annabel Learned, Copy Editor, undated (Editorial Material, A-756, *Re-Visioning Psychology*, Opus Archive.
34. Four or five revisions: Hillman letter to William Coffin, August 1, 1974, Coffin archive, Yale.
35. "I did no more than listen to him. . . .": Email to author from Pat Berry, September 8, 2017.
36. "after nearly three years of analysis. . . .": Lyn Cowan, "The Archetype of the Personal: A Memoir Scrap," unpublished and provided the author.
37. "If winter comes, can Spring. . . .": Author interview with Lyn Cowan, July 16, 2007.
38. "It was like climbing inside. . . .": Cowan, "The Archetype of the Personal."
39. "It was about having faith. . . .": Ibid.
40. "casting Perls before swine. . . .": Author interview with Cowan.
41. "I learned you could live the passionate life. . . .": Author interview with Cowan.
42. On *Masochism: A Jungian View*. Ibid.
43. "The book reads badly. . . .": JH letter to Marvin Spiegelman, undated, Spiegelman private archive.
44. "they have to spend a lot. . . ." JH letter to "Dear Mother," December 10, 1974, Hillman private archive.
45. "seemed written to be spoken. . . .": Ed Casey letter to Hillman, August 3, 1975.
46. "Actually my works. . . .": ibid.
47. "has nothing to do with enrichment weekends. . . .": Murray Stein review of *Re-Visioning Psychology*, Houston Chronicle, May 25, 1975, Page 12, Opus Archive.

48. "Psychology has become a discipline. . . .": Review by Robert Sardello, *Contemporary Psychology, 1976, Vol. 21, No. 3*, Opus Archive.

49. "I was working with him. . . .." Author interview with Robbie Bosnak, October 2006.

50. "I didn't have a purpose in mind. . . .": Hillman, *Inter Views* (1980), p. 148.

51. Four children "and their innumerable friends. . . .": JH letter to William Coffin, August 1, 1974, Coffin archive, Yale.

52. "With Kate there is much goodness. . . .": JH letter to Robert Stein, January 5, 1975, Hillman private archive.

53. "I'm still not sure what I feel is missing. . . .": Robert Stein letter to JH, February 11, 1974, Hillman private archive.

54. "As I get older I like living. . . .": JH letter to Marvin Spiegelman, undated, private Spiegelman collection.

55. "Rafael moved back to Venezuela. . . .": JH letter to John Layard, November 1974, undated, Layard papers.

56. "Nov 16. Rafael walks with two women. . . .": Hillman papers, Oopus archive, Dreams: A75b:2.26

57. "separates Jungian psychology. . . .": "Post-Jungian Movements: Conversations with Rafael López-Pedraza, with Axel Capriles, unpublished manuscript sent to author, pp. 8–9.

58. "lucky enough to work. . . .": Ibid, p. 21.

59. Mary Watkins' story and quotes are derived from her interviews with the author, January 2006 and August 2015.

60. "What did I learn. . . .": Author interview with David Miller, March 2009.

61. "He went into an altered state. . . .": Author interview with Pat Berry, September 2013.

62. "I have now connections. . . .": JH letter to his mother, December 10, 1974, Hillman private archive.

63. "seems to be making a very big impression. . . .": JH letter to his mother, August 13, 1975.

64. "My thoughts were constantly. . . ." Ibid.

65. "a little party off Kings Road. . . .": JH letter to JP Donleavy, October 15, 1975, Donleavy private archive.

66. "In Ireland I lived it high. . . .": JH letter to mother, undated.

67. "Nina and I were at the lawyers. . . .": JH letter to mother, undated, but sometime between September and December 1975.

68. "My whole book talks of. . . .": JH letter to Robert Stein, September 1975, Hillman private archive.

69. "building the idea of a sophisticated classicism. . . .": Review of *Loose Ends* by Margaret Boe Birns, Opus Archive, Hillman 109 Criticism folder.

70. "To some, Hillman's ambitious goal. . . .': Robert H. Davis, *Jung, Freud, and Hillman: Three Depth Psychologies in Context*, Praeger, Westport, Ct. and London, 2003, p. 161.

71. "*tres important et meme revolutionnaire*": Letter from Rudolf Ritsema to JH, July 22, 1975, Eranos archive.

72. "If I tossed away my sense. . . .': Typescript of Marianne Jacoby review of *Re-Visioning Psychology*, Opus Archive.

73. "You have found your own position. . . .": Letter from Rudolf Ritsema to JH, June 12, 1975, Eranos archive.

9

THE ERANOS CIRCLE

"The spontaneous expression of the psyche in images, thoughts and emotions has been most appropriately termed the 'speech of the soul' by James Hillman in his 1968 lecture, where he contrasted it with the rational language of psychology as a science. Throughout the 56 Eranos conferences, this spontaneous speech of the soul has been studied in its innumerable expressions: dreams, fantasies, myths, religions, poetry, scientific theories, fine arts and alchemy."
—Rudolf Ritsema, 1988 Eranos yearbook.[1]

"The Platonist inspiration at Eranos, its concern for spirit in a time of crisis and decay, the mutuality of engagement that transcends academic specialization, and the educative effect of eros on soul were together formative in the directions that archetypal psychology was to subsequently take."
—James Hillman, Archetypal Psychology.[2]

The annual ten-day-long late summer gatherings at Eranos, where Hillman gave fifteen talks between 1966 and 1987, were seminal for him on numerous levels. He might work on many projects during the year, but the Eranos lecture was the one that counted. Like many of the unique and often eccentric individuals he'd been drawn to since his youth in Atlantic City, even as he moved into middle age, the men Hillman encountered at Eranos were intellectuals with impeccable academic credentials—but at the same time, as he put it in 2005, "each marginal figures in their fields, as I am marginal in a strange way in psychology. That's what united them, and why I realized one time at Eranos I belonged among them."[3] The ten to twelve speakers across various disciplines formed a kind of underground that was Hillman's deepest source of inspiration during the 1970s into the late 1980s. Hillman believed that "Eranos was one of those things that invented the modern world, intellectually."[4]

The general conference topic was set forth a year in advance, but nothing else was prearranged. As the gathering's co-hosts Rudolf Ritsema and Adolf Portmann wrote: "The Eranos

Conferences may perhaps be said to stand for a type of productivity devoid of public acclaim. They often embody the work of individuals who—quietly tilling their own soil—take courage in the idea that others of similar persuasion are doing likewise. The fruits of these labors come to light and are passed on to others in the August meetings, furthered as they are, by an attitude of open-minded receptivity on the part of speakers and audiences alike."[5]

It was a stunningly beautiful place to gather. A long stretch of land on a steep hillside, Eranos included three simple houses—the 300-year-old Casa Gabriella and two others built in 1928 in the Bauhaus style. Layered paths ran between the residences—a sculpted figure of the Hindu god Vishnu presided over one them. Secluded spots to talk or meditate were surrounded by seas of flowers including a Chinese variety of climbing rose and a wide variety of big trees, from a lone redwood to a bamboo forest.

The Tessin region was, Hillman wrote in a letter, "the Italian, lowest in altitude part of Switzerland, a strange tropical region—palms, bamboos, and other tropical plants, heavy wet air, often misty here on the lago Maggiori in which we swim daily, a view stretching to Italy in one direction, to the Alps in the other. Very much a soul place."[6]

Windows on one side of the Casa Eranos lecture hall overlooked the patio garden with its "Round Table" where the speakers took their meals, while the opposite side of the hall offered a view of Lake Maggiore. The meetings on the squeaky wooden floors followed a traditional Swiss model. An elevated speaker's podium in the corner stood to the left of an audience crowded together in a small room with a low ceiling, seated in straight rows on stiff-backed wooden folding chairs. No more than a hundred people could attend. The elder generation had their reserved seats. All would come together for "ten days of common hours meant for interpenetration of the minds."[7]

Pat Berry recalled: "There was no lighting, no amplifiers, no making the sounds bigger. Everything was *so* old-fashioned.

And simple. There was an incredible closeness because of that. Even though the lectures were erudite and often in a language you couldn't understand, you had to sit and figure it out from the expressions and the tone of voice. Then after the lecture, everyone went down to the lake and swam, these skinny guys in their little bathing suits." (For his part, Hillman was impressed that men in their seventies would climb out onto the rocks and dive right into the deep lake.)

Pat elaborated: "The wives were there too. We'd all go back up for lunch. There were usually two tables, including the Round Table just outside. And when it rained, we moved inside. We all sat and drank wine while excellent Swiss-Italian courses were served to us by the same family that had prepared the meals for decades. We drank a lot, so after lunch always went to sleep! Another two-hour lecture would happen at four o'clock before dinner. Toward the end of the conference, an evening concert would be scheduled, generally including a Mozart piece."[8]

Hillman's connection to Eranos seemed fated. Mircea Eliade and Gershom Scholem had been participants at Eranos since the 1940s. As a student at the Jung Institute in 1953, Hillman had studied with Eliade, the Romanian scholar who blended mythology, alchemy, yoga, and shamanism into his texts on religion. In a letter years later, Hillman recalled seeing Eliade when he first arrived in Zürich—"and all the greats were there, including the Jungs, and [Eliade] talked about the Dogon and primitive philosophy. His face was red, he spoke fast and I saw an image of the passionate head, the passion of intellect and it had a tremendous effect on me."[9]

In early 1953, Hillman was visiting old friends in Israel after living in India for almost two years—trying to figure out what he wanted to study. He called Scholem to ask a question (Hillman didn't recall about what). The first Professor of Jewish Mysticism at Hebrew University in Jerusalem, Scholem initiated the modern academic study of Kabbalah, a metaphysical branch of Judaism. Hillman had never read any of Scholem's books, nor did he speak a word of Hebrew. "The pretention [in calling Scholem] was enormous," Hillman would recall. "But it shows that somehow I thought I belonged in that group, even though it had nothing to do with time."[10] A generation later, he and Scholem would end up sitting at the same table at Eranos. Scholem didn't become a direct influence on Hillman, but served for him as an embodiment of the freedom to forge new paths.

Hillman said in 2009: "These people were mammoth, huge figures. I never felt I knew enough. There were two things I needed to do. One was to stay within my own field, Western psychology, not try to talk of things I didn't know about. The second was, I needed to educate myself more. I had a doctorate, but I now had to get like a second one. So I had to read a lot of mythology. I didn't know Greek, I had to figure things out with a dictionary. There would be an image and then I'd find a corresponding word from Plato."[11]

For Hillman, the conferences also represented "what old Europe really looks like," as he put it in a letter to his writer friend J. P. Donleavy. He described his lecture as "a two hour solo flight, very intellectual, to a group that goes back to 1933 and meets annually, the most old fashioned timeless and select body in Europe, though seemingly very old fogey, nobel science winners and that sort together with oddities left over from the 1930s."[12]

As it had been for Jung, who "considered the Eranos conferences the best possible sounding board for his newly developed discoveries and ideas,"[13] so it was for Hillman. He mentioned this in a letter to Eranos' director Rudolf Ritsema: "I envision Eranos lectures as work that is emerging, still in the wood of the branch in part, not yet differentiated into twig and leaf and flower, and that is what Eranos is for. But then many in the audience 'don't get it' and are disappointed. Yet, as it is worked out later, or printed, it becomes a good solid piece of construction."[14] Many of Hillman's books emerged from his Eranos lectures, starting with *The Myth of Analysis* and parts of *Re-Visioning Psychology*, and later including *The Dream and the Underworld* (a lecture given in 1973) and *The Thought of the Heart* (in 1979).

Rudolf Ritsema, director of the Eranos Foundation since 1962, was a tall, distinguished Dutchman who would walk around during the conferences in a butler's jacket. He and his wife Catherine lived on the grounds year-round. Ritsema had begun studying the *I Ching* at the age of eleven and ultimately developed an archetypal way of reading the Confucian-era "Book of Changes," that would allow a Westerner to understand it without knowing anything about Chinese culture. He attended Eranos since the early 1940s. After taking over the conference from founder Olga Frobe, Ritsema was stringent in his evaluation of potential lecturers. No invitation would be offered until he was convinced someone was mature enough to present—which could sometimes take years. Once enlisted, as Hillman had been at forty in 1966, the lecturers weren't allowed to talk about something they'd discussed before; it had to be new, creative, and go beyond the limits of their specific field. Since they didn't receive any compensation, they came only for "the cause" and rarely saw each other in between.

THE PRICE OF THE TICKET

According to Pat Berry, Hillman's lectures could both surprise and mesmerize. "The first half would be all scholarly layout, but at a certain point he would make a sudden twist almost tangibly in the air, turn things upside down and take off running toward a leap at the finale," she recalled.[15]

What Hillman went through to prepare those talks is expressed poignantly in his letters to Pat—beginning his paper on "Abandoning the Child" in summer 1971. He described "combating the fears of Eranos (wow what fear that thing evokes)," and of "concentrating on how I work, rather than the work. I futz too much owing to senex internalized professors; much anxiety coping; too much energy for too little result. Am now at new system of shorter clearer attacks on the work, rather than the long hairy sweat, working less 'against myself,' trying to enjoy it rather than as guilt and duty."[16]

In another letter, Hillman wrote that he was seeking "the fantasy of the eranos paper, eager to change from the four previous styles of heavy learning, big structure, intricacy . . . This is a rather crucial thing . . . Too soon to tell what will come, but I fear a lot, afraid that it will be 'weak', unstructured, sentimental, not powerful and forceful as I have been in the past . . . but I must experiment, and cannot write til I get the right fantasy. I do know that I use learning and quotes and references as defenses and to please the inner figures . . . partly OK but partly not."

He described managing to turn out "about three pages a day, if that" while seeking "not a linear development but a series of angles." He added that "Writing is mining and smelting, hours 'till one gets clear idea from the mixture." He spoke of the difficulty of both beginnings and endings: "the first four days of not knowing where you are, wallowing, depressed, dark, and the last days trying to get out, cut it off, end it, stop the doubts and new thoughts that seem 'so important.'"

His colleague David Miller, after getting a glimpse one of Hillman's typed Eranos manuscripts, "was astonished at what some would take to be the disarray of it." Observing how Hillman would Scotch-tape together the various pieces, Miller realized that the form of the notes was true to the content—open, fragmented, polytheistic, and circular.[17]

Hillman often began preparing the lecture for the next conference during the winter months at Eranos itself, when he and Pat would stay there as part of his arrangement with Ritsema. Ascona was warmer than in Zürich, and Ritsema would store wood and briquettes for them at Casa Gabriella. Hillman would ship his reference books to Eranos. (The one consistent book David Miller remembered seeing was *The Collected Poems of Wallace Stevens*, "imagination about imagination.")[18]

Hillman's daughter Susanne remembers: "It was fantastic visiting him there. The weather was much milder than in Zürich, and the light was different. A large Eucalyptus tree hung over the house and garden and my father would take a few sprigs and put them on the stove when he would heat up my room. I'll never forget the lovely smell. He cooked all the meals and we ate in the sunroom overlooking the lake. He would cook a small cup of hot chocolate flavored with a vanilla bean for dessert, and we would get sweet Italian blood oranges at the market in Ascona."[19]

At the lakeside retreat where "lemons grow on the wall, and camellias, and old crud too,"[20] Hillman wrote at a small, unadorned table. The view from the room—occupied during the conferences by zoologist Adolf Portmann—includes a tall eucalyptus above the lake, and below "German power boats go by, occasional rowers, a hydrofoil to Italy carrying the tourist trade, private planes come into the airport five miles away, coming low over the lake." Hillman was up at 6 a.m., and writing "at 6:45 after breakfast of dark bread and heather honey and Fortnums Tea. (Second breakfast of ham, swiss bread and more tea at 9:30). Lunch at 1:15 after resting & exercising on balcony."[21]

When present, Pat stayed in the room that was reserved for Henry Corbin, the French scholar of Islamic mysticism, during the conferences. Hillman and Berry would do stretches on the balcony in the morning, then go swimming later. He sometimes saw patients during the day, who would stay at another house in Ascona.

During the winter in southern Switzerland, and at Kate's family's island retreat in northern Sweden in the summer leading up to Eranos, Hillman could reach a more remote, hinterland part of himself—even in the midst of what was otherwise a hullabaloo of travel and engagements. In the little white room on the Swedish island, while finishing those long papers, Hillman had the "sense of being physically enveloped by the material I was working with." He described it as an alchemical process, like "building a head of steam, unless the work builds a tremendous heat I can't get at what I'm really working on, why I'm writing it at all."[22]

At the same time, this required him to repress or suppress the aesthetic of his environment, as he noted later. Though—often working in tight spaces while surrounded by beauty—like writing *Suicide and the Soul* in 1960s Ireland and writing his failed novel in 1950s Kashmir—his letters rarely describe the landscapes of these exceptional places. It was the same with all the remarkable men he encountered at Eranos. He never kept a diary or took any notes on what they talked about. Hillman couldn't remember a single conversation, something he considered "a really interesting biographical fact."[23]

For years, Hillman was puzzled by his own diffidence toward Eranos. He always considered himself to be the learner, that the others were the "larger people." When it was suggested that perhaps he absorbed them, he replied: "Yes, but it's beyond human history. It's the psychic biography, the psyche of being present in these places at these times."[24]

At the same time, Hillman remembered that while preparing his Eranos talks, he sought to "get away from the internalized Portmanns and Scholems and Meiers whom I am always proving myself to."[25] The Hillman-Ritsema correspondence in the Eranos archive documents the doubts Hillman had to repeatedly overcome so he could continue to participate. In the autumn of 1974, he wrote: "The matter is that I cannot rely on my psyche (or spirit) to produce on schedule. I am too puer. I drive the spirit right out when I ask it to work for me. If I make the wrong moves in regard to it, it refuses cooperation . . . There are other things beginning to stir in the psyche and they need emptiness and foolishness, and if I don't give enough waste time to them, I may kill the goose and find the eggs not golden after all.

"It is a great mistake for me to carry on with something that is not where the mercurius is. I can return to it, some years later, but to push it beyond where it wants to go, now at my age, doesn't work . . . I sense resistances that must be heeded, it's the conflict between Jupiter and Saturn, and I am choosing Saturn as the protector of the puer."

He was not alone in experiencing such trepidation. During an interview in 2009, David Miller recalled his own introduction to Eranos forty years earlier. At a lunch break, he turned to an elderly British woman sitting next to him and asked whether there would be a discussion period. "You must be an American," she began, and Miller asked, "Why do you say that?" The woman replied: "The Americans all think there should be a discussion period. It must be something about democracy. Look, these speakers are chosen because they're at the edge of something. If they manage to speak at this edge, they don't know the answers to the questions yet any better than the audience does. It would be premature. On the other hand, if they don't manage to speak at the edge, then they're not worth asking questions of in the first place!"[26]

"The lectures that have stayed with me are ones where, in the end, it was difficult to know where Hillman stood on something," Miller reminisced. "Like the ones at Eranos on paranoia and abandoning the child: he just dove into a mystery, a psychological problem, and you didn't know where he came out. That frustrated the hell out of some listeners who would say, 'What's the solution?' That's precisely the answer. There isn't any."[27]

Miller, a skier, knew what it meant to traverse such edges—how you wouldn't make it down the mountain if you couldn't. But that didn't make it any easier. Miller's first Eranos talk in 1975, on polytheism, was titled somewhat ironically, "Images of Happy Endings." He was beyond nervous. Pat Berry sensed his anxiety and asked what was wrong. Miller told her that he had diarrhea. Pat responded: "Oh, that's just right. You want to get rid of all the crap—and then it won't be you talking."

According to Miller, Hillman added his own advice: "Now here's what you do. Don't talk to those people out there. Don't talk to Corbin, or Scholem, or Portmann. Talk only to dead people. Talk to Jung. Talk to Augustine. Talk to Luther, Erasmus. That's where the conversation is." Miller later felt that was the best teaching advice he ever received. It wasn't communication of a subject to an object, but more like being part of an alchemical vessel. When Miller told Henry Corbin what Hillman had said, the Frenchman nodded and replied: "That's the best we can do, to talk to the ghosts."[28]

Hillman confirmed in one of our interviews: "I used to say to my friends Miller and Kugler, 'I'm speaking to the dead, the former lecturers here, not the actual people in the room. This is talking to the tradition, not trying to convince the public, and that's what makes the talks sort of arcane and difficult."[29]

HENRY CORBIN

Perhaps no one had as powerful an influence on Hillman during these years as the French scholar who spent most of his life in Iran and other Middle Eastern countries. As noted earlier, Corbin was a Professor of Islam & Islamic Philosophy at both the Sorbonne and the University of Tehran. While often a harsh critic of mystically-infused spirituality, Hillman revered Corbin's "great cosmology of the imagination, which refuses any chasm between psyche and world."[30] Hillman wrote that Corbin's Eranos lectures epitomized the creative imagination's "theophanic power of bringing the divine face into visibility"[31] And, in turn, Corbin called Hillman's *Re-Visioning* "the psychology of the resurgence of the Gods."[32]

Corbin addressed the Eranos gatherings for twenty-seven years between 1949 and 1976. He was bespectacled, rather squat and slightly overweight. But no one at the lectern was more charismatic and dramatic—he reminded many of a Sufi mystic. Imaginal beings felt present. As Robbie Bosnak, a regular attendee in the 1970s, put it: "One of his passions was angelology, and it seemed he was seeing them as he spoke about them."[33]

Corbin wasn't easy to understand. He spoke in rapid French interspersed with Persian words. If you were sitting in the first few rows, he would spit and sputter all over you. A generation older than Hillman, he was deaf in one ear. Corbin wore an old-fashioned hearing aid with a head-set and a wire that threaded down to an electrical device about the size of a cigarette pack attached to his chest. The hearing aid had an on-off switch, and when he was onstage Corbin turned it off, thus emphasizing "that he was always talking up to the audience, to the angels,"[34] Paul Kugler remembered. (Other speakers would watch to see which way Corbin maneuvered the hearing aid during *their* presentations).

He interwove Persian visionary tales of spiritual initiation and practice, with the works of Iranian theosophers like Suhrawardi and Ibn'Arabi. Upholding their metaphysical perspective, Corbin maintained that "any *history* that happens in this visible world is the *imitation* of events that happened first in the soul, in Heaven, and hence the place of hierohistory . . . [which] cannot be perceived by the senses, for their signification refers to another world."[35] To Corbin, images were just as real, if not more so, than external reality. Above all, he sought to free the religious imagination from fundamentalisms of any kind.

Corbin impressed Hillman as "a person who *was* what he talked about." In terms he rarely used, Hillman said: "You felt you were in the presence of almost a mystical inspiration."[36] Inspired by Corbin's view of imagination, in *The Thought of the Heart*, Hillman described "the thought of the heart as sovereign and noble . . . forming a beauty in the language of images."[37] Jungian dialogues in active imagination were thus "a form of prayer. In other words, it's realizing that the figures you engage with are numinous, not only pieces of your complexes."[38]

Some came to refer to Hillman's archetypal psychology as "imaginal psychology." But imaginal does not mean imaginary, which is generally associated with the unreal. Hillman refined his conception of imagination using distinctions drawn from Corbin's idea of the *Mundus Imaginalis*, a realm in between thinking and sensation where the senses, imagination, and intellect correspond to matter, soul, and spirit. The imaginal realm is where matter and spirit meet and make their claim on the soul in the images that mediate their messages. The body's instincts, urges, emotions, moods disclose their character and intentions in imaginal form. We have no way to honor them as they wish until we divine the fantasy hidden in their flesh, and flesh out their guardian divinity. Spirit condenses as imagination too. Its revelations are ineffable until they become imaginal. Images are angels conveying the sacred to the soul.

Even this is too dichotomous a description, because in Corbin's view, matter and spirit don't just meet in the imaginal, in soul, they are expressions of each other through soul, through image. In descending levels of emanation, spirit takes form in the imaginal and the imaginal takes form in the physical world. Every image is an angel—a messenger—from spirit, made manifest in the flesh of the world. The cosmos, then, is spirit imagining itself into material form. The world is the physiognomy of angels, their self-display. We too are the embodiment of an image, an angel—in whose face we behold our truest, deepest form. Loss of imagination, then, blinds us to the real significance of everything—the material world, the world of spirit, and ourselves—because we can no longer see the depths of things, their soul, their image, their angel. We are left with only the literal—a reduction and distortion of everything. So, without imagination—without fantasy—we are lost in the illusory. We are only truly adapted to reality when we have come to terms with the *Mundus Imaginalis*. . . . .

For Hillman, as Tom Cheetham (author of several books about Corbin's thought) has written, Corbin was part of "the effort to loosen the grip of dogmatic monotheism on Western consciousness by disclosing the polytheistic faces of Divinity."[39] Hillman writes in *Archetypal Psychology* that the "therapeutic aim [is] neither social adaptation nor personalistic individualizing but rather a work in service of restoration of the patient to imaginal realities. The aim of therapy . . . is the development of a sense of soul, the middle ground of psychic realities, and the method of therapy is the cultivation of imagination."[40]

Corbin would often have Pat Berry sit next to him at meals. She recalled that Corbin could sometimes act like a clown. He watered down his wine because otherwise he thought he'd get too tipsy. Once Pat remembered Corbin explaining to her: "It's not that something is symbolic *of* something, it's symbolic *with*." That wasn't a Jungian way of thinking, she recalled him saying, tapping the Round Table and adding: "This is not only something you put things on, but it's symbolic with things that structure, on which you can hold and arrange things." For Corbin, according to Pat, "the concrete world and the more imagistic or even more platonic world were all of a piece." That idea became basic to her own understanding of archetypal psychology.[41]

In the 1983 book *Inter Views*, Hillman recalled a remarkably prescient statement: "Corbin said to me one time, 'What is wrong with the Islamic world is that it has destroyed its images, and without these images that are so rich in its tradition, they are going crazy because they have no containers for their extraordinary imaginative power.' His work with mystical philosophical texts, the texts that re-establish the imaginal world, can be seen as political action of the first order: it was meeting terrorism, fanaticism, nihilism right at its roots in the psyche."[42]

Since Hillman could speak French, frequently he bantered at the dining table with Corbin and his compatriots like Gilbert Durand, known for his work on mythology and the imagination.[43] David Miller, also conversant in French, generally joined the conversation. Immediately following Miller's Eranos lecture on polytheism—on the importance of many gods and their differences ("a radical thing to begin with," Hillman later reflected, "because we say on everything over here in the States, *E Pluribus Unum*, out of many one")[44]—none other than Corbin glared across the table and asked, "But Monsieur Miller, what is beyond the many? What is the one behind the many?" Miller said he didn't know. Corbin asked the same question twice more, the finale spoken while red in the face and at the top of his voice. Both times, Miller gave the same answer, curiously finding himself completely at ease as he said in a quiet voice, "I don't know." Corbin leaned over, grabbed the younger man around the neck, and said, *"Tu es mon frère"* [You are my brother].

Later, Miller recalled Corbin telling him: "The first time you answered, it was unconscious, you didn't know what you were saying. The second time you answered, you were too conscious, it was calculated. The third time you answered, it was from the heart. And that's where we have to get."[45]

In a subsequent letter, Hillman discussed another implication of Miller's talk on polytheism:. "It could as well be put the other way: from the multitude of ancestors and Gods, my particularity begins, following a unifying fantasy of identity and individuality (the heroic ego making significance of itself) to dissolve into a multitude of remnants, images, effects, components."[46]

Eranos demanded the relinquishment of expectation. As Miller experienced by facing Corbin's questions about "the one behind the many," once you could relax into not knowing, things might open up. However, if you came *looking* for profound content at those Round Table conversations, Miller observed, you would often be disappointed. Hillman once said to his younger colleague: "If Leonardo and Michelangelo are having lunch together in Florence, what would they talk about? They would talk about how do you clean your brushes."[47]

Corbin and Hillman didn't completely converge in their approach to the imaginal. Hillman viewed pathology as key to opening up the imagery—in therapy, "we must begin where we have fallen, flat on our backs in personal pain."[48] Corbin's theological vision viewed pathology as a starting point, but according to Corbin scholar Tom Cheetham, he believed that "many in the modern world seem to revel in darkness for its own sake, and this is antithetical to any spiritual quest."[49] For Corbin, the Islamic sages never lost sight of the fundamental unity of the Divine; the individual is not inhabited by multitudes, but ultimately has a single supreme "Unknown and Unknowable God of Gods." The soul to Corbin has a "hierarchical architecture," where "the primary metaphor is orientation towards the figure of the Angel, who is both the source and the goal for each of us."[50] This, of course, differs from Hillman's view of our poly-theistic nature. Cheetham writes: "Hillman in the end abandons the kind of spiritual quest that lies at the heart of Corbin's work in favor of a much less oriented and goal-directed approach to human life, one far more accepting of the inevitability of human failings than Corbin's theology could ever be."[51] Yet Corbin did say that "Active imagination is the *mirror par excellence*, the epiph-anic place for the Images of the archetypal world."[52]

Robbie Bosnak, who would go on to formulate a new approach to understanding dreams, experienced working on one of his own, first with Hillman and then Corbin. Both men, Bosnak related in an interview, had "something very important to say, but so completely different." In the dream, Bosnak was walking along a river. Across the other side stood a city entirely comprised of white Middle Eastern domes. He jumped into the river, swam across, came to the city, and began to explore it. The city felt more real than anything in his daily life. Hillman saw this as indicating he needed more reality in that daily life, which Bosnak realized was absolutely true. Then he relayed the dream to Corbin, who said in response, according to Bosnak: "You were in that city because that city exists, walking through that city because it is there."[53]

Two years after his final appearance at Eranos, Corbin died on October 8, 1978. Upon receiving the news in a letter from Ritsema, Hillman wrote back: "The loss of Corbin is terrible. There is no way to replace the gap or to equal his stature and gifts to Eranos. We must all do all we can to continue and to find new younger persons to go on with the work. It is very very important."[54]

ADOLF PORTMANN

In a chapter titled "Animals" in his 1983 book *Archetypal Psychology*, Hillman writes: "Besides C. G. Jung and Henry Corbin, a third 'father' deserves honoring: Adolf Portmann, the eminent Swiss zoologist whose originality, judgment and inspiration led the Eranos conferences from the early 1960s until his death in [1982]. Portmann's approach to biology opened the way to an aesthetic reading of life's phenomena."[55]

A lecturer at Eranos since 1946 and its President for twenty years (1962–1982), Portmann was a professor at the University of Basel, in the Swiss city where he was born in 1897. Jung and Portmann attended the same school, but a decade apart—though they took biology courses from the same professor (Frederich Zschokke). About that experience, Jung would write in *Memories, Dreams, Reflections*: "I could never free myself from the feeling that warm-blooded creatures were akin to us and not just cerebral automata . . . My compassion for animals did not derive from the Buddhist trimmings of Schopenhauer's philosophy, but rested on the deeper foundation of a primitive attitude of mind—on an unconscious identity with animals."[56] When Portmann later came to know Jung at Eranos, he described how Jung "appeared to me as a powerful 'natural force,' possessing the extraordinary capability of raising to consciousness the spiritual ways of functioning in all of us."[57] (Portmann's essay, "Jung's Biology Professor: Some Recollections," appeared in *Spring 1976*.)

Portmann was always the concluding speaker at Eranos, and always spoke in his native German tongue (no simultaneous translation in those days). A good-looking man, tall and solid, dry and intellectual, Hillman called him "a philosopher of nature."[58] In bringing aesthetics and biology together, Portmann took his listeners "out of the dictatorship of evolution," as Robbie Bosnak put it.[59] Portmann was fascinated by things that could not be explained, like a beautifully-colored fish swimming at oceanic depths where no light existed.

Pat Berry recalled: "He would go through these very precise biological explorations and explanations of the way a bird made a certain kind of song, and then the question would be why? There's no evolutionary reason, no adaptive reason. So he went beyond scientific explanations, it was for some other incredible reason that that bird made this crazy kind of sound! Jim loved that."[60]

While speech may distinguish humans from animals, we needed their "animal eye" to *aesthetically* perceive and respond. To Portmann, animal physiognomy and expressiveness—what shows on their faces and in their bodies—was just as important as their actual traits. This resonated deeply with Hillman, who wrote: "Form, color, pattern, movement, interrelatedness reveal the self-display of animals as living images."[61]

In *Kinds of Power* (1995), Hillman elaborated on Portmann's idea that "self-presentation (*Selbst-darstellung*) for animal life is as primary as self-preservation. Because we have learned to think of animals within a competitive capitalist framework of scarcity and predation, we look at what they do only functionally. Portmann disagrees.. He insists that display is not reducible to any single function and is, for instance, narrowly sexual only in particular circumstances. Each species shows off its style without any purpose other than to show itself (as some birdsong), to manifest its essential capacity, and perhaps for its own pleasure. For us human animals, this implies that exhibitionism is not only a sexual act but a display of one's innate nature. It displays one's power: how you come on shows who you are."[62]

David Miller felt this provided a conceptual framework and also a vocabulary for Hillman to talk about his notion of beauty in a psychological way. Portmann, of course, was focused on zoological and biological phenomena, but had discovered that tropical butterflies, for example, apparently display themselves not for any utilitarian purpose but simply for the sake of show. Self-presentation focuses on the aesthetic of a life, rather than the practical sociology of it. Applied to depth psychology, this dimension goes beyond the ego's concerns for self-preservation. The self-presentation of the psyche in feeling, in fantasy, in pathology doesn't serve another purpose—these are simply the colors of its wings displayed for their own sake. There is no hidden meaning or agenda, the psyche is what it shows. Such psychological faith was always characteristic of Hillman, expressed even in his first book *Emotion*, but also later on in *Suicide and the Soul* and *Re-Visioning Psychology*. In the relationship between therapist and patient, struggling with questions of the soul, what's important is "a participatory awareness, rather than a detached consciousness that's often associated with the goals of psychotherapy."[63] If self-presentation is regarded as a *sui generis* aim of the psyche, the purposes of therapy shift altogether.

Here is how Hillman put it years later in the book, *Dream Animals*, co-authored with Margot McLean and dedicated to Portmann: "You know, people come to therapy really for blessing. Not so much to fix what's broken as to get what's broken blessed. In many cultures animals do the blessing since they are the divinities. That's why parts of animals are used in medicines and healing rites. Blessing by the animal still goes on in our civilized lives, too. Let's say you have a quick and clever side to your personality. You sometimes lie, you tend to shoplift, fires excite you, you're hard to track and hard to trap; you have such a sharp nose that people are shy of doing business with you for fear of being outfoxed. Then you dream of a fox! Now that fox isn't merely an image of your 'shadow problem,' your propensity to stealth. That fox also gives an archetypal backing to your behavior traits, placing them more deeply in the nature of things. The fox comes into your dream as a kind of teacher, a doctor animal, who knows lots more than you do about those traits of yours. And that's a blessing. Instead of a symptom or a character disorder, you now have a fox to live with, and you need to keep an eye on each other."[64]

At Eranos in 1978, David Miller gave a talk on the "Rhythms of Silenus," a figure in Greek mythology representing the archetypal image of a great teacher. Considered a precursor of Socrates, little is known about Silenus—except that he was a devotee of the wine god Bacchus and was, thus, often intoxicated. During lunch, the day after Miller's lecture, Portmann took out a framed photograph of a wild flower and asked if Miller knew what it was called. He didn't. "It's a *Silenus*," Portmann said, "do you know why?" Miller had no idea. "First of all it's fat, like

Silenus was. You open it up, and you know what's inside?" Miller again shook his head. Portmann nodded. "That's right—nothing's inside. That's what was inside Silenus, and Socrates. He was the world's wisest man because he said, 'I know nothing. And as a result, everything.'" Portmann handed the photograph of the *Silenus* flower across to Miller, saying: "I went out and found this flower in the mountain, took a picture, had it developed overnight, and framed. It's for you."[65]

ENGAGING A NEW GENERATION

In the summer of 1972, the Spring House seminars remained in full swing in Zürich. When the younger participants kept talking far into the night, Hillman suggested they continue at Eranos. Pat Berry organized a weekend retreat. Few had even heard of Eranos when about two dozen headed to Ascona for three days of playing with ideas and cooking meals together. Ritsema's wife Catherine became upset "because there were too many American hippies in sleeping bags"[66] sprawled across Casa Gabriella. Hillman managed to calm her down, and everyone was allowed to stay. He was writing a book on the puer at the time, expanding a lecture he gave at Eranos in 1969. He read sections aloud during what came to be remembered as the "Puer Weekend."

Pat would later organize other weekends there around alchemy and animal dreams. Students from the Jung Institute would pile into vans or onto trains, and gather in the Eranos meeting room—playing baseball in the afternoons. This led to several students obtaining summer jobs—selling tickets to the conference, helping clear tables, and wash dishes.

The first and most involved of the younger group, Robbie Bosnak and his wife Deanne, lived at Eranos between 1972 and 1975. They worked as secretaries for the Eranos Foundation, which included helping put together the annual yearbooks containing reprints of the different lectures. In his book *Embodiment*

(2007), Bosnak reflected on Hillman: "He stayed in his room at Casa Gabriella, while Deanne, our tiny children and I lived next door in Casa Shanti. Outside our frequent psychoanalytic sessions we often tended to run into one another, especially in the large downstairs conference kitchen where, by himself, he indulged his pleasure in lentil soup . . . We often floated together in the Lago. Many ideas come up while swimming or hanging off a buoy, bobbing about in a huge mountain lake below the southern Alps."[67]

Hillman wrote to Ritsema toward the end of 1973: "I believe Eranos is moving towards sterilization if there is no place for younger people to come while the great old ones are still active. It's because I was able to be present when Corbin, Portmann, Scholem, etc spoke, that I grew into the tradition." There needed to be "some rule about letting in at least 2 or 3 newer ones each year, and the regular ones make a place for them—to come and gain experience and the spirit from the older 'masters.' There is an ideal there. It is one of the last places with ideal. This ideal needs revivification with top quality newer people."[68]

It didn't happen overnight; Ritsema reportedly resisted the idea at first. But as the 1976 conference approached, when Hillman asked that among others Paul Kugler, Wolfgang Giegerich, and Tom Kapacinskas all be invited, they were.[69] Ritsema enthusiastically wrote Hillman: "The number of young participants includes some 20 names! Very nice, indeed."[70]

Kugler and his Persian friend Gita would sell the lecturers' books. Jerry Donat, a former seminary student from Chicago, set up the tables and chairs. Robert Hinshaw served as the taxi driver, heading back and forth to the train station or the airport to pick up speakers. In exchange, they and others in the younger group received free room-and-board. They would meet after dinner on the piazza in town and continue their dialogues until the restaurant closed at midnight. Kugler recalled being struck by how many of the talks traced a theme in their discipline through the past 2,000 years.[71] Kapacinskas remembered struggling to comprehend the lectures in German, Italian, or

French—but "you got a sense of how Europeans had carried culture, how they imagined cultural life; it was kind of rigid and uncomfortable for an American, but it was an experience."[72]

Deanne Bosnak observed that in his lectures Hillman was "very tuned in to how people were receiving what he was talking about, and giving them time to digest information."[73] After Hillman's 1973 lecture on "The Dream and the Underworld," Robbie Bosnak remembered walking up to Aniela Jaffe, part of the Jungian old guard, and exclaiming: "Isn't this amazing? Isn't it fantastic?" To which Jaffe replied: "It was very brilliant, but it was one-sided." Hillman was giving imagination its own paradigm. The beings in a dream had intentions of their own, sometimes completely unconcerned with our waking life, with an existence that's important for *them*—and intentions that *we had to serve*. However, Hillman's emphasis on the importance of such an underworld, at the height of most psychology stressing the importance of the daylight world of the ego, didn't sit well with Jaffe (Jung's collaborator on *Memories, Dreams, Reflections*).

Eranos wasn't for everybody. Hillman's close friend in Zürich, Adolf Guggenbühl-Craig, attended only once, finding it "too inflated . . . absolutely strange."[74] Audrey Haas, part of the older Spring House crowd, worked at the Eranos cash desk for about five years at Pat's suggestion. Haas recalled the actress Paulette Goddard once showing up, while everyone in the hall stared at her. During one Hillman lecture, when he was talking about where the soul abides—"always in the weakest part of the body"—Haas, who felt her throat and neck to be that weakest part, fell into a coughing fit and couldn't stop. She walked down to the lake and slowly recovered. When she told Hillman what had happened, he gave her a recording of the lecture so she could hear what she'd missed.[75]

Kugler remembered an even more profound physical reaction. It happened in 1979, about halfway through Hillman's talk on "The Thought of the Heart." While he began describing the circulation of blood in the heart and what happens if the imagination is clogged, a man in the audience suddenly rose to his feet and grasped his chest. According to Kugler, "They stopped the lecture because they thought he was having a heart attack." He wasn't, but Hillman didn't resume for forty-five minutes.[76]

As Hillman once wrote: "Archetypal psychology embeds human existence within an animalized, animated world, not because the human has fallen into it owing to sin or is evolving out of it toward a higher condition, but because the psyche, as Aristotle said, is the forming idea of a living body."[77]

That too was Eranos, an animated, enchanted place where "you have stepped into a magic circle and you are caught," as one participant described it and added: "how better to describe this magic than a conjunction of opposites; a place of intellectual excellence and of relaxed conviviality . . . a place nourishing not just to the mind, but to the senses."[78]

NOTES

1. R. Ritsema, "Encompassing Versatility: Keystone of the Eranos Project," in *Eranos-Jahrbuch/Yearbook/Annales 57/ 1988*, /Eranos Foundation/Insel, Ascona/Frankfurt am Main, 1990, pp. VII-XXII (p. XIX).
2. "The Platonist inspiration at Eranos. . . .": James Hillman, *Archetypal Psychology*, p. 54.
3. "each marginal figures in their fields. . . .": Author interview with JH, April 2005.
4. "Eranos was one of those things. . . .': Author interview with Hillman, July 2008.
5. "The Eranos Conferences may perhaps. . . .": Adolf Portmann and Rudolf Ritsema,"Eranos and Its Meaning," in *Spring: A Journal of Archetype and Culture*, Vol. 92, Spring 2015, p.292.
6. "The Italian, lowest part. . . .": Hillman letter to Pat Berry, August 14, 1982, Berry personal archive.
7. "ten days of common hours. . . .": Letter from Rudolf Ritsema to JH, December 10, 1973, Eranos archive.
8. "There was no lighting, no amplifiers. . . .": Author interview with Pat Berry, August 2008.
9. "and all the greats were there. . . .": JH letter to Murray Stein, May 16, 1977, Stein private archive.
10. "The pretension was enormous. . . .": Author interview with JH, April 2005.
11. "These people were mammoth, huge figures. . . .": Author interview with JH, June 2009.

12. "what old Europe really looks like. . . ." JH letter to J.P Donleavy, June 1977, Donleavy private archive.

13. Jung "considered the Eranos conferences. . . .": John von Praag, "The Spirit of Eranos" pamphlet, p. 15.

14. "I envision Eranos lectures. . . .": JH letter to Rudolf Ritsema, October 9, 1973, Eranos archive.

15. "The first half would be all scholarly. . . .": Author interview with Pat Berry, August 2008.

16. "combating the fears of Eranos. . . .": This, and other quotes from letters to Pat Berry, come from her private archive.

17. "was astonished at what some people would take. . . .": Author interview with David Miller, March 2009.

18. "imagination about imagination": Author interview with David Miller, March 2009.

19. "It was fantastic visiting him. . . .': Susanne Hillman, "Memories of My Father," sent author September 2020.

20. "lemons grow on the wall. . . .": Hillman letter to J. P. Donleavy, undated, 1975, Donleavy private archive.

21. "German power boats go by. . . .": Hillman letter to J. P. Donleavy, June 1977, Donleavy private archive.

22. "sense of being physically enveloped. . . .": Hillman lecture on writing, February 16, 1982, Dallas.

23. "a really interesting biographical fact. . . .": Author interview with JH, July 2007.

24. "Yes, but it's beyond human history. . . .": Author interview with JH, July 2007.

25. "get away from the internalized. . . .": Hillman letter to Pat Berry, 1971, undated.

26. "You must be American. . . .": Author interview with David Miller, March 2009.

27. "The lectures that have stayed with me. . . .": Author interview with David Miller, 2009.

28. Miller quoting Berry, Hillman and Corbin on talking at Eranos: Ibid.

29. "I used to say to my friends. . . .": Author interview with JH, July 2006.

30. "great cosmology of the imagination. . . .": Tom Cheetham, *Imaginal Love: The Meanings of Imagination in Henry Corbin and James Hillman*, Thompson, Conn.: Spring Publications, 2015, p. 177.

31. "theophanic power of bringing the divine face. . . .": James Hillman, *The Thought of the Heart*, p. 3.

32. "the psychology of the resurgence. . . .": Henry Corbin, *Words of the Heart*, p. 105.

33. "One of his passions was angelology. . . .": Author interview with Robbie Bosnak, October 2006.

34. "so that he was always talking up. . . .": Author interview with Paul Kugler, June 2006.

35. "any *history* that happens. . . .": Corbin quoted in Woutter J. Hanegraaff, *Esotericism and the Academy: Rejected Knowledge in Western Culture*, Cambridge University Press, 2013, p. 299.

36. "a person who was what he talked about": Author interview with JH, April 2008.

37. "the thought of the heart. . . .": James Hillman, *The Thought of the Heart and the Soul of the World*, (Putnam, Conn.": Spring Publications, 2014, 9)

38. "a form of prayer. . . .": Author interview with JH, April 2008.

39. "the effort to loosen the grip. . . .": Tom Cheetham, *The World Turned Inside Out: Henry Corbin and Islamic Mysticism* [publisher], 2003, p. vi.

40. Xxxi: Hillman, *Archetypal Psychology*.

41. Pat Berry on Corbin: Author interview, August 2008.
42. "Corbin said to me one time. . . ."" James Hillman, *Inter Views: Conversations with Laura Pozzo* (Dallas: Spring Publications, 1983, 142–43.
43. Gilbert Durand: Hillman would publish his "Exploration of the Imaginal" in *Spring 1971* and "The Image of Man in Western Occult Tradition" in *Spring 1976*.
44. "a radical thing to begin with. . . .": Hillman interview with Jay Kugelman, KPFK Radio, November 1978 (transcribed by author).
45. The exchange between David Miller and Henry Corbin was recounted by Miller in an interview with the author, March 2009.
46. "It could as well be put the other way. . . .": Hillman letter to Murray Stein, undated, 1977.
47. "If Leonardo and Michelangelo are having lunch. . . .": Author interview with David Miller, March 2009.
48. "we must begin where we have fallen. . . .": Hillman quoted in Tom Cheetham, *After Prophecy: Imagination, Incarnation and the Unity*, Spring Journal, 2007, p. 108.
49. "many in the modern world. . . .": Ibid, p. 108..
50. "hierarchical architecture. . . .": Tom Cheetham, *After Prophecy*, New Orleans: Spring Journal Books, 2007, p. 107.
51. "Hillman in the end abandons. . . .": Ibid, p. 109.
52. "Active imagination is the *mirror par excellence*. . . .": Henry Corbin, "Mundus Imaginalis, Or the Imaginary and the Imaginal," *Spring 1972*, p. 9. Hillman also published Corbin's "The Imago Templi and Secular Norms" in *Spring 1975*
53. "something very important to say. . . .": Author interview with Robbie Bosnak, October 19, 2006.
54. "The loss of Corbin is terrible. . . .": JH letter to Ritsema, November 1, 1978, Eranos archive.
55. "Besides C. G. Jung and Henry Corbin. . . .": Hillman, *Archetypal Psychology, James Hillman Uniform Edition I*, Spring Publications, Putnam, Ct, p. 71.
56. "I could never free myself from the feeling. . . .": Jung, *Memories, Dreams, Reflections* p. 101 quoted by Adolf Portmann in "Jung's Biology Professor: Some Recollections," *Spring 1976*, p. 150.
57. Jung "appeared to me. . . .': Essay by Portmann.
58. "a philosopher of nature. . . .": Hillman, *Kinds of Power: A Guide to Its Intelligent Uses*, Currency Doubleday, 1995, p. 127.
59. "out of the dictatorship of evolution. . . .": Author interview with Robbie Bosnak, October 2006.
60. "He would go through these very precise. . . .": Author interview with Pat Berry, August 2008.
61. "Portmann's approach to biology. . . .": *Archetypal Psychology, Uniform Edition of the Writings of James Hillman Vol. 1*, p. 71.
62. Lxii: "self-presentation. . . .": *Kinds of Power*, p. 127.
63. "a participatory awareness. . . .": David J. Dalrymple, Restoring Soul: The Contribution of James Hillman's Archetypal Psychology to the Study of Religion, Ph. Dissertation, 2007, Chicago Theological School Library
64. "You know, people come to therapy. . . .": James Hillman and Margot McLean, *Dream Animals*, pp. 2 and 5.
65. Silenus flower: Author interview with David Miller, March 2009.

66. "because there were too many American hippies. . . .": Author interview with Tom Kapacinskas, June 2008.
67. Hillman "stayed in his room. . . .": Robert Bosnak, *Embodiment: Creative Imagination in Medicine, Art and Travel,* Routledge, 2007, pp. 14–15.
68. "I believe Eranos is moving towards sterilization. . . .": JH undated letter to Rudolf Ritsema, late 1973, Eranos archive.
69. Hillman suggestion: JH letter to Ritsema, March 25, 1976, Eranos archive.
70. "The number of young participants includes. . . .": Ritsema letter to Hillman, July 12, 1976, Eranos archive.
71. Author interview with Paul Kugler, June 2006.
72. "You got a sense of how Europeans. . . .": Author interview with Tom Kapacinskas, June 2008.
73. "very tuned in to how people. . . .": Author interview with Deanne Bosnak, October 2006.
74. "too inflated. . . .": Author interview with Adolf Guggenühl-Craig, May 2005.
75. "always in the weakest part of the body. . . .": Author interview with Audrey Haas, May 2005.
76. "They stopped the lecture. . . .": Author interview with Paul Kugler, June 2006.
77. "Archetypal psyhchology embeds human existence. . . .": *Archetypal Psychology, Uniform Edition of the Writings of James Hillman,* p. 72.
78. "you have stepped into a magic circle. . . .": Essay by Shantena Augusto Sabbadini, in *Spring 2015* special issue on Eranos, p. 297.

10

AMERICA BECKONING: THE DREAM AND THE UNDERWORLD

"The dream is a little hidden door in the innermost and most secret recesses of the soul, opening into that cosmic night which was psyche long before there was any ego-consciousness."
—C. G. Jung.[1]

"In my lecture at Eranos on Lago Maggiore in the summer of 1976 . . . I proposed a depth psychology of extraversion. Rather than conceiving 'depth' to be only interior to the subject, depth could also be found in the object, in the images presented by the world. They, too, are faces to be read as displays of soul."
—James Hillman, "Aesthetic Response as Political Action."[2]

As early as 1964, in a reply letter to his nephew Roger Sternfeld, who had written him asking about dreams, Hillman touched on themes he would often contemplate in the years to come. "You spoke of dreaming of your religious school, or of your camp, as if I were to dream of something of yours I had not seen . . . No, I meant *psychological* information, for example dreams show you what things you want, what things you are attracted to or by, what things you are afraid of, what symbols appear again and again repetitively in your soul (which animals, which people, which situations, which landscapes), and these things then become a sort of inner world which is a 'family' or atmosphere or 'home' just as your outer one. Sometimes even dreams solve major difficult problems about ideas, or even choice of career, what to do, what to be, whether to do something or not to do it. This is the kind of information I meant, psychological information. You can certainly die in your dreams without dying. People dream of death, of dying, of being dead very often. It means of course that a real basic change is taking place in one's life; let's say the old you is dead and maybe a new you will come along."[3]

Amid much other work, *The Dream and the Underworld* occupied Hillman for five years between 1972 and 1977. It was the subject of his 1973 Eranos lecture and, as he wrote in the book's first chapter, "though now much wider and fuller, it yet bears the mark of Eranos, where for several years I have been elaborating specific archetypal themes and the ways they influence our consciousness."[4] He gave due credit, in "the recall of phenomena to their imaginal background," to "the work of Henry Corbin, a friend at Eranos."[5] And Hillman would devote several pages to a longstanding fascination fueled by Adolf Portmann, the appearance of animals in our dreams. Rather than depth psychology's customary interpretation of animal images as "instinctual, bestial, sexual, part of human nature," Hillman wrote, "I prefer to consider animals in dreams as Gods, as divine, intelligent, autochthonous powers demanding respect."[6]

At the time the book appeared, Hillman had been keeping his own dream journal for thirty years, saved in a cardboard box of diary-style notebooks that he chose to keep private, then and afterward. He did not want his dreams (or anyone else's) subject to future interpretation. However, among his papers at Opus Archive, on the grounds of Pacifica Graduate Institute, there are ten typed pages recounting dreams from the 1974–1976 period when he was preparing *The Dream and the Underworld*. Several speak to his belief that "every night we are inside a dream, walking around, meeting other figures and they have effects on us . . . The soul wanders, they used to say, during the night."[7]

One of these wanderings took Hillman to the realm of Eranos: "I have hit a gold ball too far, outside of the course, into a confused building area. It has to do with Eranos, in that other players, or those who go off to look for the ball, are Eranos lecturers . . . I realize that I should go to look, not just let it be looked for by them, and am in this flatish open area, nearer the course than they. I think they are looking too far out, and I am covering the area that I have a sort of after-image of where the ball went. Next I am climbing around a partly-constructed white building, part of this area clambering, jumping . . . foolish getting stuck in sections where I have either to retrace my steps, or jump down and start again. It too has Eranos people in and on it.

"Then I am going up a newly constructed, under construction ramp . . . It is flat slat boards on which is red earth, padded down. The building site is whitish and to the left. Half way up this ramp, there is a sort of gap; not enough earth over or under the boards, seemingly risky. I move toward the left thinking there is a way up and through, but it looks hardly possible. The work is simply not finished here."[8]

The gold ball, the unfinished work, was about to carry Hillman in a parallel but new direction—back to the red earth of American soil with increasing regularity, until finally he uprooted from Zürich after living there for twenty-five years. Where he chose to settle would surprise almost everyone.

NEW BLOOD

Early in 1975, Hillman received a letter from Robert Sardello, chairman of the psychology department within a recently-formed Graduate Institute of Philosophic Studies at the University of Dallas. Years later, Sardello would recall a trip he made a few months prior to writing the letter, accompanying others from the school to several ruins in ancient Greece. "It completely changed me," Sardello said. "I came back knowing I couldn't do psychology the same way. I started writing some very strange things, and actually thought I was going crazy. I'd bought Hillman's book, *Pan and the Nightmare*, but it had been on the shelf for a year or so. For some reason, I picked it up and read it. And I felt I wasn't crazy anymore. It gave a kind of imagination for what I'd experienced."[9]

Sardello's letter informed Hillman that reading his study of the Greek goat-god's relationship to the multi-faceted human psyche proved "exactly the kind of work I have been moving toward in the past several years." After working through *Insearch*, *Suicide and the Soul*, and *The Myth of Analysis*, Sardello was now "searching for someone who might be interested in teaching" in the university's Ph.D. program—"I now believe that imagination and myth will begin to be more important, particularly if it is possible to find someone besides myself with these interests." If Hillman had any plans to come to the U.S., might he be interested in giving a "short course?"[10]

Hillman was traveling regularly to give talks on *Re-Visioning Psychology*, with plans for a 45-day tour starting toward the end of March. So, early that May, he and Pat journeyed to Dallas to give a public lecture and then a seminar at the university.[11] While there, he attended a dinner party at the home of Joanne Stroud, an oil heiress who was funding Hillman's appearance. She discovered Jung while attending Sarah Lawrence College and, upon graduation, moved back to Dallas, "casting around to find people who had some spark of imagination."[12]

One of these was Gail Thomas, a warm, smart close friend of Joanne's whose husband, like her own, was a prominent attorney. Gail had been intrigued by mythology since childhood (one of her earliest memories was looking up at the sky to learn the constellations and being fascinated by Pegasus), and became enamored with Jung while earning a degree in philosophy.

Both women were connected to the University of Dallas through Don and Louise Cowan, to whom Sardello made sure Hillman was introduced that night at Joanne Stroud's. The Cowans were a power couple at the co-ed Catholic school founded two decades before on a barren, windswept hilltop in suburban Irving. Built on one of the highest points in Dallas County, the university resembled a medieval citadel. From the moment Don Cowan arrived, he sensed "a spirit that walks these hills." He was appointed president in 1962 by the head of the Dallas diocese, who was determined to create a stellar liberal arts program in a conservative milieu. The first faculty consisted of six nuns and nine monks.

Cowan's wife Louise took on the task. She was a spellbinding English teacher who tossed away standard textbooks in favor of reviving what she called "the great tradition," which started with the Greeks and went through Shakespeare to Dostoevsky and Faulkner. One of Louise's pupils, Randy Severson, recalled her "very musically cadenced voice, bardic really, as if not her own but a shared vision of her guardian spirits, an incantational quality. Anybody who ever took a class from her, it marked them in one way or another."[13] To instruct a growing enrollment that soon passed a thousand students, Don set about recruiting an international faculty (eventually, thirty percent European), including the mesmerizing metaphysical philosopher, Frederick Wilhelmsen.

"We didn't want to change only Catholic education," according to Louise, "we wanted to change American education." Her husband "was certain that our society was soon to enter a time of breakdown, which would precede, he felt, a new 'middle ages,' a time of slow growth and development when the kind of education we espoused would be needed. He felt very strongly that the main function of a liberal education was to develop the imagination."[14]

Eager to forge a larger connection to the city, at a cocktail party Louise accepted an invitation from a woman to teach "some of her tennis friends" the classics. About a dozen came together to read *Moby Dick*. As word spread, ultimately well over a hundred of "Louise's Ladies" gathered for ten Tuesdays a semester in a special lounge created for them by the university. These included the wives of conglomerate manager James Ling, and Stanley Marcus of Dallas' upscale department store Nieman-Marcus; Margaret McDermott, whose husband co-founded Texas Instruments; and women from the Hunt and Murchison oil families. They would "come out in their Cadillacs with their chauffeurs carrying silver trays of finger food for lunch," Louise recalled, and many would generously endow the growing university.[15]

So, too, came Joanne Stroud and Gail Thomas, who both enrolled in Louise's class to pursue advanced degrees in literature. By the mid-1970s, Thomas had become the school's Dean of Students and then assistant to the president. Stroud would eventually earn the university's first interdisciplinary Ph.D. in literature and psychology. Both women had been pushing to incorporate psychology, a department the Cowans were initially suspicious of bringing into the school "because all we'd heard about were behaviorists" running rats through mazes, as Louise put it. Don Cowan finally agreed to bring Robert Sardello, then a luminary in Duquesne University's phenomenological psychology program, out for an interview. Patrick Kelly, the Dallas university's drama instructor, remembered Sardello "looked exactly like Montgomery Clift playing Freud [in the 1962 movie]. His hair was jet-black, he wore a full beard, and had this incredible intensity."[16] Sardello joined the team after passing muster with Stroud and Thomas as well.

Hillman had no idea of the milieu into which he arrived. Louise remembered of the dinner party: "He walked in so irenic, so peaceful in his approach, as opposed to stimulating arguments and differences. We were amazed because from his books, we'd expected somebody who would be difficult. At first it also surprised Don and me that such a person would be a psychologist, because we had an enormous distaste for Freud and Skinner and all those who simply stamped patterns on things. And if there was ever anybody who *didn't* do that, it's Jim Hillman. He read the patterns *in* things, and never imposed an idea on anything."[17]

Afterward, Sardello wrote Hillman that "the time was all too short." At Hillman's public lecture titled "Peaks and Vales: The Soul and Spirit of Jung's Psychology," Sardello said that "there were also many opposing forces in your audience and one could feel the tension. Two days after you left I received a letter from Dr. [James] Hall offering to present a seminar on dreams here next year to straighten out the confusion of your approach." Hall was a dogmatic Jungian whose antipathy toward Hillman would only increase. However, Sardello went on, "You have a marvelous way of seeing through the crap . . . and deepening the discussion." Indeed, the university would later offer its facilities and sponsor a larger gathering in the future on depth psychology/phenomenology. Sardello had also spoken to Dr. Cowan and the bookstore manager, both of whom agreed "that there would be no difficulty in becoming a distributor for Spring Publications."[18]

Hillman seemed to be inwardly weighing the meaning of his unexpectedly warm reception. "I believe it crucial to throw away the positions one holds, else the soul can't flow on," he'd written his friend Robert Stein soon after that first trip to Dallas. Later that year, he wrote to Stein again: "I'm in a waiting desert area . . . sabbatical . . . doing foolish nothings, watch and waiting, but so far nothing has come through . . . or at least I can't sniff the wind."

That wind was rapidly shifting. Hillman's excitement about a change in his life proved evident in another letter to Donleavy: "This autumn I'm taking another of those USA jaunts. Last time during the seven weeks on the road I pocketed 20,000 dolls, of which about $41.69 cents went for necessary expenses. We [Hillman and Pat Berry] are given houses and cars (old Oldsmobiles), and pools, and the like to recline in between talks, though at some places we are met by grubby grad students with beards, old Vulva cars (Swedish), and bad breath and shunted off to a professors house [in] his 'department.' This time we're staying mainly West. Denver, Minneapolis, Taos, and the Golden State."

In the course of that trip, Hillman spoke at a workshop on the image, arranged by the art education department at the University of New Mexico. It took place at the former D. H. Lawrence ranch in Taos. Howard McConaughey, the department chair, had previously brought Hillman there to give four lectures on "Soul in Alchemical Imagery" (salt, sulfur, mercury and lead)—"which was new to most New Mexicans, of course, but it was successful," McConaughey recalled.[19] Hillman had written afterward: "Saw the Pueblo Jung visited, but found the Indians stiffly taciturn, though one old squaw did sing me a traveler's song to the accompaniment of the drum. It was a fine present."[20]

Then, for the autumn workshop, fellow travelers Sardello, Stroud, and Thomas made plans to join Hillman and Pat at the house where D. H. Lawrence once wrote *The Plumed Serpent*. They bonded in what Stroud remembered as an "us-against-them experience. We were confronted with all these art historians who were determined that we knew *nothing* about an image. In fact, when we got there, they gave us each several pounds of clay so we could make figures and be able to understand. We sat there defending the way psychology looks at image. But we were out-numbered and sort of beleaguered, and failed to convince them."[21] The four did begin discussing, however, the possibility of holding in Dallas the first conference specifically devoted to archetypal psychology.

MARCHING INTO MARRIAGE—AND TOWARD TEXAS

As 1975 drew toward a close, Hillman recorded several more dreams. In one: "There is an enormous mass of military men marching to a depository for old field weapons trucks, tanks, artillery etc. I am in their number. Tires of trucks are being burnt, right on the wheels, as all this gear is being dismantled, and put up. The wind blows very strongly at our backs, and yet from the water, so that the flag blows backwards . . . my echelon moves quickly through the marching men so that we are by the time the dream ends up near the front, and as we march into this wind, or toward the sea, all of us in grey olive drab colour, and our gear, our faces, covered with sand, become like stone."

In another dream: "A grey-white haired diamond merchant tells me the rank of diamonds or about their value, instructing me to keep to the very best sorts, *blue-white*. There are some small fragments and splinters that glitter, and I have a flat rectangular piece, a stone slab, that is opaque or like unpolished or clouded over. This is a diamond."

Noting one more, Hillman described, "A dream where I am all dressed in a pinkish-apricot suit. I have five children."[22]

In life, he had fathered four—but there was also Pat Berry, seventeen years his junior.

Hillman penned a handwritten letter to Kate (January 7, 1976): "My situation has finally come to marriage. There is no way Pat can stay in Switzerland unless we marry. Her permit was stopped Nov. 30 and only temporarily 'put off' for another few months. Or, we move to US—and I can't work, as a foreigner. And I don't want to move abroad while the whole family lives in Zürich and is still in need of Father—if ever, I mean, I don't feel like leaving here anyway. So, law and the Freudenpolizei become instruments of fate, and we will marry in the next month. I wanted you to hear about it from me, not just see it in the Tagblatt [newspaper]. With very much love, Jim."[23]

It was a curiously unromantic letter, as if he wanted his former wife to understand something about his relationship with Pat. Hillman wrote to Donleavy: "We marry on groundhog day." On that day, the groundhog comes out of its hole at the end of hibernation; if it sees its shadow, there will be six more weeks of winter weather as the tradition holds. Almost a decade after they met as analyst and student, Hillman and Pat joined in a quiet ceremony on February 2, 1976. "Unfortunately we set the date at the very last minute, never wanting to finally go through with this," he wrote his mother.

In a taxi on the way to the registry, his friend Adolf Guggenbühl-Craig would recall saying to Hillman: "Look Jim, it's never too late, you can even now say no."[24] On their wedding day, Hillman was accompanied by Guggenbühl and Pat by Audrey Haas, into a room with stained-glass windows at the Zürich City Hall. "The guy who married us," Pat recalled, "was Herr Eisenring, 'Iron Ring.' He gave us a lecture about how important it was for each of us to let the other do our separate things."[25] Hillman described the wedding to his mother as "great fun," after which "we had champagne and oysters and caviar for about a dozen people. And a drunk man to open the oysters."

In the meantime, the pull of Dallas increased. In January, after an acquaintance at the Rockefeller Foundation expressed interest, Hillman proposed a conference on "Archetypal Backgrounds: Psycho-Mythical Approaches to Consciousness," lasting at least four days "in a civilized, hospitable, leisurely, peripatetic setting, with the barest of 'arrangements,' schedules, and officiality." Although a friend had offered the D. H. Lawrence ranch in Taos, Hillman liked the idea of Dallas—"because it is geographically central" and because Sardello as chair of the psychology department "would necessarily be an active participant."

Hillman assessed the need for the occasion: "It is strange how obdurate I have been about this. I have so many hesitations about 'going big,' yet I know, from the continual correspondence that I get, that this sort of meeting is what this beginning field, and the few already deep into it, need—perhaps to keep from 'solipsism'"[26] [the theory that the self is all that can be known to exist].

Then in April, Sardello wrote to Hillman that he'd been appointed Director of the Institute of Philosophic Studies, replacing Louise Cowan at her request. Yet, "as I now teach totally in the area of imagination, myth, and your work, it has become increasingly difficult to continue at the University here. My work in archetypal psychology has split our graduate program in two. Some students resent it terribly because they come here expecting a program in phenomenology and suddenly find themselves reading James Hillman. Others find themselves dedicated to this work . . . [but] I have been severely depressed over this all year." Sardello was considering moving elsewhere.[27]

Hillman' response may have surprised Sardello. "Don't abandon ship, is the first thing I'd cry out. It always looks better elsewhere; the body of scholars and workers in our field doesn't exist; there is no true Jungian community either . . . Part of what you want is an archetypal Ficinian-Platonic academy that everyone wants, but this is an age of decline and dispersion, we live in exile, let us learn to hold our seats (chairs), and work it slowly from where we are each at. You are in an excellent position there . . . That there is a split is not the worst thing, provided the split can be used generatively."[28]

Clearly, Hillman already felt a strong kinship with Sardello, one that he didn't wish to see jeopardized just as it was starting to blossom. He went on to say that he reached out to the Rockefeller group about Sardello chairing a conference hosted by the university. In another letter, Hillman described what he sensed about the potential significance of Dallas.

"The social aspect, I think, is extremely important. It must have largesse, belle epoch fantasy which Dallas can do so well. It mustn't get grim protestant hard work academic. We are to be 'South.' It must be amplified and carried by fantasy and images—by this I mean the actual physicality of it . . . Now here I am not speaking about sumptuous expensive luxury. I am not speaking about venery and greed, laxity and improper sphincters, but I want desperately to be free of the usual academic verbiage, imagelessness, and constriction. In other words, the hosting must have a style, for it will be in the fantasy of that style that the whole thing will be carried."[29]

That summer of 1976, Hillman would focus his annual lecture at Eranos on the question of whether psychology had been caught in introversion. Could there be a depth psychology of extraversion? His work, as often happened, was a step ahead of his life. Dallas would become, as he later reflected, "the actual laboratory of that."[30]

RETURN

> "Today is CG [Jung]'s birthday. The actual day. One hundred years ago his big mom labored to bring him forth."
> —Letter from James Hillman to Lyn Cowan, July 26, 1975.[31]

Hillman had realized for a while that a long life-chapter in Zürich was ending. The Spring House gatherings had dissipated after López departed (he was now practicing psychotherapy and lecturing on mythology at Caracas University; *Spring 1976* would include his submission from there, derived from his book *Hermes and His Children*). In Zürich, Hillman remembered, "there wasn't enough for me really to do besides my practice."[32] With

Re-Visioning Psychology nominated for a Pulitzer, he was spending more and more time in the U.S. According to Pat, "since I first knew him, he had lots of fantasies about becoming an academic. He wanted a post somewhere."[33] His work was now being taught in a number of universities, and he wrote his mother: "How I would like to sit in on one of these courses to hear the students complain, argue, and grapple."

Hillman's wish was granted by his friend David Miller, who convinced department chair Jim Wiggins at New York's Syracuse University to bring him in September 1976 to instruct students on "Religion, Psychology and Alchemy." Hillman would earn $12,000 for the semester as a Visiting Professor in the Department of Religion. "Shades of Grandfather Krauskopf," Hillman wrote his mother, referring to his renowned rabbi ancestor. Pat would teach a course on dreams, and they would also co-lecture in California in the fall on "Animal Images and Dreams," enlarging themes from Eranos and *The Dream and the Underworld.* Pat's 1982 book, *Echo's Subtle Body,* would also contain two lengthy essays on dreams.

At Syracuse, "the course on alchemy was absolutely brilliant and everybody loved it," Miller recalled. "But after the first two sessions, he told me one day: 'This is dreadful, I hate it.' I said, 'Jim, I've noticed for years that you have this fantasy about what a professor is, and what university academic life is. You didn't like it before you started playing it out, so how could you like it now? So don't be a professor, they're all in their heads and mostly bullshit, just go into the classroom and be a therapist.' Well, a couple of weeks later he said, 'You know, that's true, that's what I'd been doing. And now it's going much better.' Actually, it was going just the same. Of course, he'd done so much schooling in Europe, and the professors in Germany and Switzerland and Paris and even Dublin were a completely different scene. So I think he had a notion about professors that didn't go with his Atlantic City sense of things. Anyway he was a terrific teacher, and a lot of people sat in. It was maybe one of the first times he integrated a lot of his alchemy material."[34]

Nevertheless, even late in life, Hillman still looked back upon his re-entry at Syracuse as "very depressing, that American academic side of life. Little houses and little parties with cubes of cheese and jug wine, oh God! The house we were put in belonged to a professor who was away in Europe, and it seemed made of cardboard, with these low ceilings and crappy beds. I remember saying to David Miller toward the end, 'I really am not a teacher.' I felt I'd failed completely."[35]

That autumn, he attended a political rally in downtown Syracuse for Democratic presidential nominee Jimmy Carter. It was sparsely attended, but in the crowd was a young graduate art student from Virginia named Margot McLean. It would be another dozen years before their paths crossed again.

With the Syracuse semester over, in early January 1977 the University of Dallas hosted the first American conference on archetypal psychology. Fifteen months prior, Hillman wrote down a dream: "I find myself at a large meeting of writers, poets, scholars . . . Distinguished sober people. I am surprised this is taking place and that nobody told me, since I am living or staying right on the premises, as if Eranos (but not Eranos) . . . Am I unwanted, excluded, not for me? Two men complement me on two of my books—how well written . . . Someone like a publisher discusses my way of handling Jung, that he was doctrinaire and mightn't have liked what I did, good that he is dead, didn't want to be 'seen through' only confirmed with similar studies based on him . . . Next there is a discussion in a room at a long conference table. Woman poet reads some lines. I had read same lines but her emphasis changes passage to metaphor, and I had not done it right, had not got the thing of it. It's like poetry itself."[36]

For the gathering at the university, the Rockefeller Brothers Fund donated $15,000. That was enough to bring Rafael López and Valery Donleavy from Venezuela, Stephanie de Vogt from Amsterdam; Neil Micklem from London; David Miller and Stanley Hopper from Syracuse; the poet Charles Boer from Connecticut; Paul Kugler, Tom Kapacinskas, Robbie Bosnak,

Thomas Moore, Murray Stein—and Ed Casey and Mary Watkins (who met here for the first time and eventually got married). Altogether some twenty-five people gathered for a five-day "extravagant thing," Gail Thomas remembered, "where we put people up in wonderful homes."[37]

The most lavish dwelling was reserved for James and Pat. They stayed in the house that Joanne Stroud's mother had built during World War II—designed by the famed architect Edward Durrell Stone—when she took over her husband's oil companies. It was filled with courtyards, sun screens, polished white marble, hand-carved mahogany and Italian walnut, columns wrapped in gold anodized aluminum, and an indoor pool. Golden images of Aphrodite graced the lamps, and a white terrazzo screen on the second story enclosed an immense bronze sculpture by Fernando Botero. The *pièce de résistance* was a circular platform for the dining room table that floated on a pool of water called "the lagoon." Hillman labeled it all "Aphrodite's house."

For the conference itself, Miller remembered, "One of the things I've always enjoyed with Jim is his aesthetic sense. We used to talk for hours about the psychological feel—how the chairs were set up, where to put the tables, should there be flowers? Today people call it *feng shui*. This was something like it, but a Western version, and that conference was run consummately; the taste was just right."[38]

It was held in the Faculty Room in the old Science Lecture Center, ordinarily furnished "in a sort of medieval Spanish style with ornate painting and stern, high backed chairs, but not that night, when it was ringed with magnificent easy chairs,"[39] recorded Randy Severson, by then a second-year graduate student in psychology at the university. "It was sumptuous, splendid, leather chairs, brandy, cigars."[40]

The speakers had all pre-submitted their papers. López led things off with a Friday night presentation on Priapus, the Greek god of fertility. Gail Thomas later reflected: "When Rafael came in with that paper, even demonstrating all the different angles [of masturbation]—well, it was shocking and amazing. In the

Seventies, people weren't even saying 'shit' out loud in Dallas. I'd not met people like this. And I loved it."[41]

Hillman had earlier written to Sardello: "López is the true 'founder,' the hidden leader of the whole business. A very odd man, who is not a partner, dialoguer, but must be given a platform to be his own King for a Day."[42] Now, as López finished his talk, from across the room Hillman rose and extended an arm to toast his old friend. According to Severson, "In unison, all stood, raised their glass: 'to Hermes and to Rafael.'"[43]

Hillman and Berry presented a paper on "Archetypal Therapy." Hillman engaged in a dialogue with Casey on archetypal psychology, and then later did the same with Sardello on "What Next?" Matching the elevated conversations, Thomas and Stroud hosted sumptuous dinners at their homes. "It was a chance for all of us as a community to meet for the first time," said Paul Kugler.[44] Hillman described it in a letter as "much fun, and the academicians, and few 'Jungian archetypalists' managed to get on with one another extremely well. There was much eros flowing, even if it was bitter cold weather, and Dallas an odd place, so odd that I like it."[45]

Odd was a term equally ascribable to one of the city's temporary inhabitants. When David Miller arrived at the airport, he ran into López standing in the American Airlines terminal with his suitcase. Finding the Cuban quite relieved to see him, Miller realized this was perhaps Rafael's first trip to the U.S. and certainly to Dallas. As they walked together toward the baggage claim, suddenly López stopped in his tracks and set down his bag. Miller asked him what was wrong. "He said, 'These people are all crazy.' I said, 'What?' He said, 'They're all smiling. They're manic. Everybody is manic here.' I said, 'Oh Rafael, yes. And when we come to Venezuela we think everybody is depressive, because nobody smiles. It has to do with toothpaste here, we're into toothpaste.' He said, 'Oh, okay,' and we walked on."

During the proceedings, when one of the speakers was droning on and on, Miller, sitting next to López, nudged him after twenty minutes and suggested they go have a beer. Rafael raised a finger to his lips: "Shhhhh, shhhhh," he counseled. After an hour went by, Miller tried again but received the same rejoinder. When the talk finally ended, he turned to López and asked why he kept shushing him, when that might have been the worst lecture of all time. "Oh, but David," Miller remembered López responding, "did you see that? Here comes the bull. The man waved his cape and he missed it. Then the bull came from the other side, and he missed it again. That man missed the point every time! I became so interested in the many ways that you can miss the point." Miller took a deep breath and replied, "Rafael, you have probably saved many lectures for me, because I will now watch to see how they're missing the point!"[46]

Pat Berry in retrospect viewed the event as "a lot of talking and excitement, but there was no structure hardly. It ended up being basically a party. I thought there should have been some proceedings, or maybe a book that came out of it. Here was this Rockefeller backing, why not give them in return something that they could see happened out of this and can go on being created?"[47]

Yet for Ed Casey, what was being created could not be qualified that way. Today a Distinguished Professor of Philosophy at the State University of New York and the author of eight books, Casey remembered: "There we were, in an ice storm, about twelve of us all riding in a van and flipping dangerously across the highways. One of our jokes was, if we had an accident the entire movement would be wiped out at one swipe. Which is interesting, because it showed that even then, there was some sense that this was an unusual venture. We were going somewhere. We couldn't say where, but definitely a sense that this was already percolating. Not that *we* were so important, it's just that something unique had been started, something singular."[48]

The audience hadn't all been sympathetic. Sardello had written Hillman earlier that: "[James] Hall has got to be included, somewhere, somehow. It would be disastrous politically to invade big D. with a bunch of Jungian colleagues and not pay him any recognition." Hall was invited to attend the conference, but his silence during the proceedings spoke volumes to Hillman and Pat.

Overall, though, in a revealing letter responding to Stephanie de Vogt—a speaker at the conference from Amsterdam—Hillman had this to say: "If you recall, at Dallas, the attempt . . . to find out what archetypal psychology was, to define it, was roundly defeated . . . no one wanted to be in a movement, etc . . . but there is an eros there, a *gemeinschaftsgefühl* [community feeling] and that is the whole difference from Freud and his followers and Jung and his ladies and adulants, and this thing that is much more collegial, much more fragmented, much more autonomous . . . There is an even deeper reason. Freud and Jung were rather large figures, in a time of large men. I am not at all of that stature and it is a time of self-mockery. The people in Freud's and Jung's circles were lesser than they, by far. The persons who were at Dallas are in many cases more than I and by far."[49]

That's not the way Hillman was viewed by his new colleagues at the event. To Sardello, it felt like the university's popular Ph.D. program "had come to its limit of creativeness and you have to really risk and see where psychology would go if it had Jim Hillman." The same week of the conference, the Cowans offered Hillman a chair as visiting professor of psychology. He'd received several other offers in the U.S., and said he needed to think about it. "I think I'll be much more in the States in the future, maybe eventually returning for longer periods," he hedged in a letter to Robert Stein.

While in the U.S., "all in all I gave 46 different talks & seminar sessions—some of them lasting 4 hours straight," Hillman wrote his mother. Early in February 1977, writing from Zürich to German colleague, Wolfgang Giegerich, Hillman summarized the trip: "Back after five months away—and quite a time it was. Of the many things, visits, discoveries, travels, at least 'archetypal psychology' is alive and kicking . . . there are degree programs at at least two universities, and the thought is proceeding in all sorts of directions, in many schools and practical persons (prisons), and so on. The Jungians, here and there are 'finding out' about it, but they are the last. This sounds like the report of a missionary, but it is not meant as such, since our trip was less spreading the word than enjoying the role of entertainer, and learning more about the art of teaching."[50] Giegerich responded: "It is astonishing how much more lively and open the intellectual scene is in America than it seems to be here."[51]

But before returning to Switzerland, Hillman and Pat flew to Venezuela to spend more time with López: "Rafael is in the best shape I've ever seen him, he is quite a remarkable person." Once back, Hillman described how constricted he felt in Zürich. He wrote Stein: "It is so close here. The flat so dingy, damp. The days so bound to work. Hours seem shorter, every little bit is portioned out. I like seeing the patients, surprisingly, for they give me a direct engagement. I seem to have sharpened and become more immediate while in the States."[52]

He soon went back. He wrote Donleavy about taking in the New York Mets season opener on his birthday. From there, Hillman and Pat went again to Dallas. After spending nearly five months lecturing all over the country, the university's offer to help with his publishing company remained a temptation. "*Spring* becomes my property in Sept.," he wrote Murray Stein. "I have no more access to funding. It's going to be tough to keep afloat."[53]

That same spring in Dallas, they were invited to stay at the home of Helen Corbett, the famed Neiman-Marcus chef who prepared menus for the luncheons of "Louise's Ladies." Hillman's daughter Carola joined them there and, he remembered, "We celebrated her 21st birthday in April. I was sitting out on the lawn thinking, would this really be a good place to come?"

He could easily have chosen other locations to resettle. A group of archetypalists in San Francisco lobbied strongly for Hillman and Pat's attention, "one being an astrologer who did a whole chart to show why we needed to come there, because we would have Sagitarrius rising," Pat recalled. Pat preferred an offer

from Sonoma State University in Northern California. Howard
McConaughey wanted them both to come to New Mexico and
teach courses, "but to make a living there was tough."[54]

Musing on the manicured grass, Hillman said he "went over
all the other possibilities, and I made up my mind. This is so
radically different, completely experimental. Here was this little
university with people who were all extremely simpático, and
full of high ideals. They didn't offer a great amount of money—
around $20,000 a year—but I could have a [therapeutic] practice
immediately. Gail and Joanne had said they'd give us a place to
house Spring [Publications]. Pat was very excited because she
could get her Ph.D. at the university and teach as well. And we'd
still have the summers in Europe. It just seemed like a great
adventure to go to Dallas."[55]

Gail Thomas remembered the ensuing conversation at the
McDermott apartment on campus. "He said, 'You know, Dallas
is Aphrodite's city, I want to explore this.'" He identified Dallas
this way, Thomas later wrote, "because of its allure, and possibly, because he felt Dallas to be psychologically fascinating with
its focus on ornament and display while aspiring toward power
and control."[56]

After deciding on Dallas, Hillman and Pat journeyed to
Ireland together for the first time in June 1977. It was a return
to his memorable past at Dublin's Trinity College, where he
stayed upon arrival almost three decades before in the shadow
of James Joyce's legendary Martello Tower. In writing Donleavy,
with whom his friendship began at Trinity, the novelist in
Hillman always came to the fore: "We had only greyness, but
then at the end taking PBee out to Sandycove to show her Mrs
Godwins at 9 Sandycove Ave where once I resided, my window looking out onto the Martello, and where once you helped,
or actually did, build me a bookshelf, and where I contracted
TB, there was immense bright sun, children galore in the filthy
waters with dogs barking, and paleskinned Irish schoolgirls and
a man selling ices. The fortyfoot [tower] still reserved for men,
but now suited, no longer pinkbottomed priests in cold water,

continuing its frigid tradition. We ate before we left at the Lord Edwards and the seafood there is as fine as you get in Dublin since Jammets."[57]

Eranos came in August, attended by his mother, who "heard her son the Dr. give his talk on her eightieth birthday." The subject: "Psychotherapy's Inferiority Complex." From there, Hillman went on to attend the annual Jungian Congress in Rome, which he wrote Robert Stein "was a big social event, though the papers for the first time seemed somewhat better, more divergent, less based on repetition of Jung, even sometimes controversial. There was a good day on psychiatry . . . Adolf [Guggenbühl] is now President of the whole bag and he made me Hon. Secretary which had an element of sweetness in it after having been almost booted out by the old guard nine years ago. Few of the old guard left, the two Joes, Meier, Fordham and Cohen is about it. Lots of ageing in our generation and hundreds of new people—470 persons signed up, and there will be some 700 members in the world soon."[58]

All seemed to be moving from past tense into future possibility. He didn't get the Pulitzer, but "Rev. Psy selling too well to be believed," Hillman wrote in a letter. "Not only the hardcover sales which have now covered the original 5000 dollar advance royalty, but paperback advance orders were 2200, and since then another 2200 have sold to bookstores."[59]

Yet, in Texas, a shadow was already descending over the university he'd committed to. Late in 1977, following the death of a wealthy board member who had supported all that Don Cowan had been implementing, the rest of the trustees turned on him. As Louise later recalled "that painful, painful time, my husband walked into a board meeting one day and they said, 'Thank you, we have a new president,' just like that."[60] (He continued on the faculty).

Hillman reflected in 2008: "I didn't know about all the Catholic background, that it had really been a priest-ridden school. And it was at a turning point, after Don Cowan's benefactor died and he was dismissed as president. The Texas Instruments people were inventing all this new equipment and they were really behind the board of directors, and wanted to shift the university away from this classic cultured education to something more [to emphasize] computers. Sardello knew all that and he thought what was going to happen was tremendously dangerous."[61]

The letter Hillman received from Chancellor Bryan F. Smith was welcoming enough: "We are indeed honored to have such distinguished persons in the field of psychology teaching on our faculty and are grateful to Dr. Joanne Stroud for the generous gift which brings you here."[62] Yet as Hillman and Berry packed their bags to depart Zürich in January 1978, how the university's theologians would take to a psychology professor who favored polytheism with its pantheon of gods over Christianity remained very much an open question.

In a letter to Donleavy, Hillman addressed the shadow side: "Dallas is Big D., Assassination City, a kind of grandiose Zürich because of the banks. Gnomes become Giants."[63] The dream—and the underworld.

FINISHING TOUCHES

In the months leading up to the move, Hillman had been putting the finishing touches on *The Dream and the Underworld*. It was scheduled for publication by Harper & Row and promoted as "the first new view of dreams since Freud and Jung." But the last leg was slow-going. In a letter, Hillman described "slogging through the bog of footnoting for this rewrite of the dream and the underwear which I am trying to complete, and which is heavy, heavy, heavy."[64] According to Robbie Bosnak, "he didn't want to write the whole second part of the book, but the publisher wanted to have a practical part to it."[65] Concluding it, Hillman later said, was "somewhat of a regression" from where his thought was taking him.[66]

The book approaches dreams through the mythologies of the underworld, and is an attempt to make readers see that dreams have to do with the soul and directing our attention towards its life, not ours. As Hillman described to an interviewer shortly before the book's publication: "What goes on in dreams is not how to get on better with your father, or whether or not to buy the car, or working out a childhood sexual problem that got hung up. But that your dreams are a way of taking events that happen in the day out of the world and digesting them into new mythical patterns."

Hillman went on: "Dreams have always been connected to the soul, and the soul has always been connected to death, but none of the theories of dreams ever make that move, they don't ask the question—to what kind of myth do dreams belong? So it's a move in a way to stop—because there's a very strong polemical side to the book—our misuse of dreams. We deceive ourselves and our dreams by trying to turn them into practical answers for life. That's part of it. There's a long part also on various images in dreams, like clocks and wheels and mushrooms and all kinds of underworld symbolism."

But how, the interviewer asked, did his interpretation of dreams differ from the classic one of Freud? "I start off with trying to keep the dream alive. The dream is more important than the interpretation. If I dream of a black snake and in the morning I'm told through the interpretation [that] black snake means your mother, your anxiety, your sexuality—and then you walk home thinking about your anxiety, your sexuality and your mother, you forgot the black snake. And the black snake's been stopped, and it's a concept. For me it's the black snake. You walk home with the black snake. And the black snake will tell you what it is, if it wants to. And you'll be living with the living imagination. Dream interpretations have translated dreams into concepts. And by doing that, they've *killed* the dream. In fact we even have got so far in our imagination that we translate everything from the night world into the day world. When we wake up in the morning, we say 'I had a dream.' Well all night long, the dream had me. And I want to keep us back in the place where the dream *has* me."[67]

It wasn't a black snake, but a mouse and an old man about whom Hillman dreamed in the midst of this turning point— divorce from Kate, marriage to Pat, turning fifty, prominence in his field, an unknown future looming as America beckoned him back to his roots. This was the dream that had him then, the dream he kept alive:

"Looking for an image, looking for a soul figure. I climb the tower into the keep. An empty room . . .

"A mouse. I laugh. It has nothing to say, though I marvel at its quickness, whiskers. It's busy looking, too, for crumbs.

"It's over. It's all over, and I don't have to go up there anymore, and mainly because the 'she' has left it.

"Descending into the grounds. An old man with clothbound feet, feet wrapped in felt, a vague figure, like the hooded man in the Michelangelo self-portrait. We walk in the grounds to and fro, two old men, caretakers, taking care.

"For that is what he has to say. There is nothing to do anymore. Some gardening, some helping of this and that as it comes up.

"I do not know what to do when there is nothing to do. That is precisely what the old man wants to teach me, to show me how ignorant I am when it comes to nothing to do—and nothing I know of what to do about doing can help me in this season. Summer and Spring have nothing to teach winter.

"My mother. Here is where she still has me. I am the embodiment of her energy, her animus. As long as I am doing, being busy, I am driven by her; her son. To be still is to be free of her; myself.

"And I must learn to let the anima go. To let the daughter go, says the old man. That's what is hard: to wait and do this and that, without towers and being holed up, and excitations. Let the Kore come, and go, neither holding on, nor even waiting, as if the time without her were dead waste time, Godot time. Independently, she and I. I have known this for some time; yet each time it re-occurs, it is hard to take.

"To be an explorer, without She. To be a gardener . . . a caretaker . . . For the sake of the exploration, the garden, the care of the grounds themselves . . . not for the sake of me, my work, my publications, my reflections.

"Integration of the anima: loss of the figure, loss of the feeling, loss of the function. Integration as letting go. She will come as she wants. Independently.

"It is because the keep is empty, except for a nervous scurrying small-toothed gnawer, that I cannot 'get,' 'hold,' 'keep' my dreams.

"I go up there to get them. Either they do not come in there, or the mouse chases them away. Then I feel empty: 'I had a dream but lost it.'

"More: when I do let the dream play about me . . . when walking to and fro through the day, I feel that this way of handling it, is cheaper, cheating, less earnest.

"I have not found out how to be with the dream. Nor have I found where to receive them, since I cannot receive them in the tower. I think I am asking them to come up too high, into the mind. The Anima seems no longer to want to climb the winding stair. The dreams are her, or hers, 'bridge to the unconscious' is her title. As I cannot keep her, so I cannot keep the dreams: by the indication that I do not know how to receive the dreams, I do not know how to receive her—let her come and go.

"Sabbatical now is no longer a rest for a return, but a whole new style of *life*, of living soul, living dream, in the garden with the old man in felt feet. Giving it all away: keeping nothing. Limitation comes from the feet not the hands.

"This has come to life. Its presence pressed all day. *Felt feet*, seems the key, a moving image. Curious how myth is now in metaphor, in language itself. As Vico said, a metaphor is a mini-myth. Still, we are in the Tower's grounds, that garden. But the question, old man, is vocation . . . He is encouraging of work, not worried about it for me. 'It would be a good thing to do the animal book,' or the alchemy book, but not the puer book. Poems can be written anytime, maybe should be.

"I haven't been able to get to work on anything because work still meant the tower, the tour, the tour de force. Could I walk to work like a pigeontoed bear, like a man with his feet wrapped? But, I'm pretty stupid down below in the garden, in the grounds, and pretty brilliant up top.

"I'd have to spend a lot of time with the old man to be able to do anything of consequence. Maybe now I'd be doing it for its sake.

"Climbing the stair
Nobody there
A mouse eating air."[68]

> *"Consider the household mouse: it has not merely a single function and its image in a dream is not merely a symbolic representation of that function. That flattens the mouse, making its incursion into the dream too understandable . . . If you put yourself inside the mouse, you can sit there quiet as a mouse and hear the world, its little tonalities, its whispers, and to do this you must remain very nearby and yet very hidden."*
> —James Hillman, "The Animal Kingdom in the Human Dream," 1982.[69]

NOTES

1. "The dream is a little hidden door. . . .": C. G. Jung, *Psychological Reflections: A New Anthology of His Writings*, 1905–1961, edited by Jolande Jacobi & R.F.C. Hull, Bollingen Series, Princeton, 4th printing 1978, p. 53.
2. ". . . .in my lecture at Eranos. . . .": James Hillman, "Aesthetic Response as Political Action," in *City & Soul*, Uniform Edition 2, Putnam, Ct.: Spring Publications, 2006, p. 143.
3. "You spoke of dreaming. . . .": Hillman letter to Roger Sternfeld, July 31, 1964, provided author by Margot McLean.
4. "now much wider and fuller. . . .": *Hillman, The Dream and the Underworld*, Harper & Row, 1979, p. 3.
5. "in the recall of phenomena. . . .": Ibid, p. 4.
6. "instinctual, bestial, sexual. . . .": Ibid, p. 147.
7. Every night we are inside a dream. . . .": Hillman interview with Jay Kugelman, KPFK Radio, November 1978, transcribed by author.

8. "I have hit a gold ball too far. . . .": Oct. 27, 1975, Dreams, A75b:2.26, Hillman papers, Opus Archive, Pacifica Graduate Institute.

9. "It completely changed me. . . .": Author interview with Robert Sardello, November 2008.

10. "exactly the kind of work. . . .": Sardello letter to Hillman, January 3, 1975, Opus Archive.

11. Hillman's public lecture at the University of Dallas was on "Peaks and Vales: The Soul and Spirit and Jung's Psychology," and his seminar course (for credit) was entitled "Re-Visioning Psychology."

12. "casting around to find people. . . .": Author interview with Joanne Stroud, November 2008

13. "very musically cadenced voice. . . .": Author interview with Randolph Severson, November 2008.

14. Author interview with Louise Cowan.

15. "We didn't want to change only Catholic education. . . .": Author interview with Louise Cowan, November 2008..

16. "looked exactly like Montgomery Clift. . . .": Author interview with Patrick Kelly, November 2008.

17. "he walked in so irenic. . . .': Author interview with Louise Cowan, November 2008.

18. "the time was all too short. . . .": Sardello letter to Hillman, July 30, 1975, Opus Archive.

19. "which was new to most New Mexicans. . . .": Author interview with Howard McConaughey, June 2006.

20. "Saw the pueblo Jung visited. . . .": JH letter to Murray Stein, August 22, 1975, Stein private archive.

21. "us-against-them experience. . . .": Author interview with Joanne Stroud, November 2008.

22. The dream references all appear in the Opus Archive.

23. "My situation has finally come to marriage. . . .": JH letter to "Dear Kate," January 7, 1976, Hillman private archive.

24. "it's not too late. . . .": Author interview with Adolf Guggenbühl-Craig, May 2005.

25. "The guy who married us. . . .": Author interview with Pat Berry, August 2009.

26. "in a civilized. . . .": JH letter to Rockefeller Foundation, January 19, 1976.

27. "As I now teach. . . ." Sardello letter to Hillman, April 1976, Opus Archive.

28. "Don't abandon ship. . . .": Hillman letter to Sardello, April 1976.

29. "The social aspect is, I think. . . .": Hillman letter to Sardello, December 1976.

30. "the actual laboratory of that. . . .": Hillman interview with author, November 2008.

31. "Today is CG [Jung]'s birthday. . . .": Hillman letter to Lyn Cowan, Cowan private archive.

32. "there wasn't enough for me really. . . .": Hillman interview with author, November 2008.

33. "Since I first knew him. . . .": Author interview with Pat Berry.

34. "The course on alchemy was. . . .': Author interview with David Miller, March 2009.

35. "very depressing, the academic side of life. . . ." Author interview with Hillman, May 2008.

36. "I find myself at a large meeting. . . .": Hillman papers, Opus Archives, Dreams, A75b:2.26, Oct.29, 1975.

37. "extravagant thing. . . .": Author interview with Gail Thomas, November 2008.

38. "One of the things I've always enjoyed. . . .": Author interview with David Miller, March 2009.
39. "with ornate painting. . . .": Randolph Severson paper on "Hillman, Lopez, and Duende," sent author September 2017.
40. "It was sumptuous. . . .": Randolph Severson email to author, December 2017.
41. "When Rafael came in with that paper. . . .": Author interview with Gail Thomas, November 2008.
42. "López is the true 'founder'". . . .Hillman letter to Robert Sardello, May 1976.
43. Severson, "Hillman, Lopez, and Duende."
44. "It was a chance for all of us. . . .": Author interview with Paul Kugler, June 2006.
45. "much fun, and the academicians. . . .": James Hillman letter to his mother, undated.
46. David Miller on López: Author interview, March 2009.
47. "a lot of talking and excitement. . . .": Pat Berry interview with author, August 2008.
48. "There we were, in an ice storm. . . .": Author interview with Ed Casey, January 2006.
49. "If you recall at Dallas, the attempt. . . .": Hillman letter to Stephanie de Vogt, October 1977 (undated).
50. "Back after five months away. . . .": Hillman letter to Wolfgang Giegerich, February 14, 1977, Giegerich private archive.
51. "It is astonishing how much more lively. . . .": Giegerich letter to JH, February 16, 1977, Opus Archive.
52. "Rafael is in the best shape. . . .": Hillman undated letter to Robert Stein.
53. "*Spring* becomes my property. . . .": Hillman letter to Murray Stein, July 17, 1977, Stein private archive.
54. "one being an astrologer. . . .but to make a living. . . .": Author interview with Pat Berry, August 2008.
55. "We celebrated her 21st birthday. . . .": Author interview with Hillman, October 2008.
56. "because of its allure. . . .": Gail Thomas interview with author.
57. "We had only greyness. . . .": Hillman letter to J. P. Donleavy, June 1977, Donleavy private archive.
58. "was a big social event. . . ." Hillman letter to Robert Stein, September 15, 1977.
59. "*Rev. Psy.* selling too well. . . .": Hillman letter to Pat Berry, undated, Berry personal archive.
60. "that painful, painful time. . . .": Author interview with Louise Cowan, November 2008.
61. "I didn't know about all the Catholic background. . . .": Author interview with Hillman, 2008.
62. "We are indeed honored. . . .": Letter to Hillman from Chancellor Bryan F. Smith, December 28, 1977.
63. "Dallas is Big D. . . .": Hillman letter to J. P. Donleavy, spring 1977, undated.
64. "slogging through the bog. . . .": Hillman response to Stephanie de Vogt, October 22, 1976.
65. "He didn't want to write. . . .": Author interview with Robbie Bosnak, October 2006.
66. "somewhat of a regression. . . .": Author interview with Hillman, June 2007.
67. "What goes on in dream. . . .": Hillman interview with Jay Kugelman, KPFK Radio, November 1978, transcribed by author.
68. "Looking for an image. . . .": Hillman papers, Dreams, A75b:2.26, Autumn 1975, Opus Archive.

69. "Consider the household mouse. . . .": James Hillman, "The Animal Kingdom in the Human Dream," in *Animal Presences: Uniform Edition Volume 9*, Putnam, Ct.: Spring Publications, 2008, pp. 43–44.

11

CITY AND SOUL

"Curious that just as I leave Europe, Europeans begin to turn to the writings (though not Zürich, of course), and this being one of the reasons I believe I go to the States (because, if there are 'becauses,' in the States there are excitements and a feeding into the work)."
—James Hillman in a letter to Wolfgang Giegerich, December 11, 1977.[1]

"The desert he rode was red and red the dust he raised, the small dust that powdered the legs of the horse he rode, the horse he led. In the evening a wind came up and reddened all the sky before him. There were few cattle in that country because it was barren country indeed yet he came at evening upon a solitary bull rolling in the dust against the bloodred sunset like an animal in sacrificial torment. The blood red dust blew down out of the sun. He rode with the sun coppering his face and the red wind blowing out of the west across the evening land and the small desert birds flew chittering among the dry bracken and horse and rider and horse passed on and their long shadows passed in tandem like the shadow of a single being. Passed and paled into the darkening land, the world to come."
—Cormac McCarthy, All the Pretty Horses.[2]

Texas. Red Texas. Red dirt, red neck, red state, a red granite capitol, the blood-red sunset. In time it would have Hillman seeing red—stoking "the outrage that gave rise to his best thinking, a martial thinker, a child of Mars, the angry red planet," as Randolph Severson later wrote.[3]

In January 1978, as Hillman and Pat packed their belongings in Zürich, he wrote J. P. Donleavy to send future correspondence to the Institute for Philosophic Studies at the University of Dallas. "It is all very pukka [British slang for high society]," Hillman said, "catholic with priests about and Braniff airlines and Texas Instruments behind scenes. I am not afraid of Assassination City after all I was born in Atlantic City which has the highest syphilis rate official in the state of New Jersey which is no mean state for the Syph, and the highest crime rate for smalltown in all of USA."[4]

A sudden snowstorm delayed their flight. Hillman wrote Robert Stein that it was "very weird leaving Zürich. Very hard, emotionally."[5] Yet the university had called, having "found us a place to put our bags: turns out to be an architectural monument, on market for 550,000 dollars, has an atrium open to sky in middle, wholly furnished and with art collection. We expect the burglar alarm system to be fantastic, having seen several such Texas things already."[6] The house belonged to one of Joanne Stroud's friends.

That "high sense of style," as Louise Cowan called it, had long characterized Dallas. As a little girl growing up in the "cow town" of Fort Worth thirty miles away, she had felt self-conscious about going to the big city: "We thought Neiman-Marcus and Dallas's sophistication was terribly impressive." Donald Cowan had once written an article comparing the founding of the two cities, where the first settlers both encountered tribes of Indians. "Don maintained that there were two ways to deal with a different ethnic group," Louise said. "Either you fight them—and Fort Worth *was* a fort—or you trade with them, and that's what Dallas did. It was mercantile from the beginning, when the Jewish merchants came and gave it that sense of style."[7]

There was another facet to this, one that local architect James Pratt traced back and later discussed with Hillman. Among those very first arrivals were members of a community inspired by the Utopian thought of French philosopher Charles Fourier. In 1855, a couple hundred colonists calling themselves La Réunion arrived by boat in Houston and, hauling their possessions by ox-cart for more than two hundred miles, settled near the forks of the Trinity River about three miles west of today's downtown Dallas (the Reunion Tower, a city landmark, was named after them).

"They didn't understand frontier," Pratt recounted. "They were writers and astronomers and ceramicists and love-makers, all those communal social skills which the frontier didn't have and wasn't yet ready for. So it failed, one primary reason being agitation about the coming Civil War. They very naively said they wanted to educate the Negroes, which antagonized slave-holders further south. It was that, plus a seven-year drought. The poor ones stayed and the rich ones went home. But they were responsible for a number of things in Dallas, including the first abattoir, when a Swiss member figured out a way to process meat."[8]

As Donald Cowan described in a piece he titled *The Myth of Dallas*, "Many of the French stayed in Dallas, giving the city a cosmopolitan air and an infusion of the lofty hopes of Utopianism."[9] This more communal spirit was what his wife Louise sought to tap. She had studied as a doctoral student under Donald Davidson, founder of the Agrarians, at Vanderbilt University. There she had learned about "the potency of groups" when doing her dissertation on the Southern "Fugitive Poets," (Ransom, Tate, Penn Warren, and others)—"a little group of college professors and students that met every two weeks to read poems to each other, but inspired a movement in literary criticism that lasted for half-a-century."[10]

Gail Thomas felt similarly inspired. "It was a tribal feeling," she recalled, "that we belonged to a very small tribal group, who really believed that there were things at work in the universe shaping our thought and our gathering. We were a young bunch of aspiring intellectuals and fervent believers that we could make a difference in the world."[11]

For Thomas, this meant applying the epic nature of Cowan's plans for the University of Dallas to a focus on re-visioning Dallas itself. During the mid-1960s, a new Mayor named Erik Jonsson had initiated a program he called "Goals for Dallas," and invited the Cowans to be among the sixty citizens on his planning team. They met regularly, including a yearly week-long conference at a resort. "I remember Doxiadis, the city planner from Greece, came here and said that cities all over the world are dying," Louise Cowan said. "Yet there was this feeling that

Dallas didn't have to be like other modern cities, that somehow we could become great."[12] (Hillman believed that "part of the motivation was to overcome the shame of the Kennedy assassination [in 1963]. They were chagrined over this blemish put on their city.")

Despite the lofty goals, Thomas remembered that in the 1970s "downtown Dallas was really in bad shape. The banks and law firms and insurance companies had started moving out to surrounding centers that were then being built, and many buildings were just boarded up."[13] With the Cowans' blessing, in 1976 Thomas formed a Center for Civic Leadership at the university, funded by a grant from Neiman-Marcus. "You see, Gail had the idea that cities have souls," according to Louise. "In our program, we were thinking about it poetically. So I began to study the great cities of the world—Athens and Rome and Paris—analyzing what made them immortal. And I went on then to teach a course called 'The Eternal City' in Gail's program and gave lectures in various organizations, maintaining that Dallas was aspiring to become an eternal city."[14]

With her training in "the mythic imagination," Thomas said she realized "that in city-making, there's something else available to work with than a flow chart and economic statistics. History and culture, the story of Romulus and Remus laying out the boundaries of Rome—who were those augurs and how were they able to determine what the boundaries are? It's to be guided by presences, and awareness of the many forces involved."[15] According to Joanne Stroud, "The students would do theoretical work at the university, then serve as interns doing practical work in the city."[16]

It seemed a milieu tailor-made for James Hillman. His arrival happened to align with a building boom, influenced by architects of national acclaim. The oil industry had largely relocated to Houston, but Dallas became the beneficiary of the burgeoning computer and telecommunications industries—while remaining a locus of banking, business, and the law. As Louise Cowan was fond of saying, "The people in Dallas are all deal-makers."

Following the opening of the Dallas-Fort Worth International Airport in 1974, at the time the world's largest, Hillman recalled that "they created a kind of tax-free zone around it and a lot of companies began to move their headquarters to Dallas, including American Airlines. It wasn't politically cramped by old regulations or internal fighting like Chicago or Pittsburgh. It was like a colony, a completely free place."[17] Besides American Airlines, JC Penney, Greyhound, Blockbuster Video, and many other corporations relocated here.

"It was a whole new way of thinking," Hillman said, "not about people but about *place* in imagination." He had come here, as Thomas recalled him telling her, "to move the furniture around"—and the décor turned out to be far richer than he'd anticipated. Already at the university, Sardello had brought in a phenomenological psychologist he'd known at Duquesne, Robert Romanyshyn. The department was unlike any other, "where you were not conducting experiments but actually using the fields of philosophy, literature, art, art history, and so on, as a way of reflecting psyche."[18]

Hillman taught a course to students in psychopathology, along lines he'd pursued in Zürich. But he was also being instructed: "Sardello and Romanyshyn opened my eyes there to thinking about the psyche of the world. They were talking about buildings in a phenomenological way. And Gail made the opportunities where I could talk about such things that I'd never thought about."[19]

THE DALLAS CITY-SCAPE

In April 1978, Thomas' Center for Civic Leadership sponsored a seminar on "Planning the City." In the council chambers of the newly-opened Dallas City Hall designed by I. M. Pei, before an audience comprised largely of local planners and other bureaucrats, Hillman commenced his seminal talk, *City and Soul*.[20] It was customary to blame psychic illness on city life, he began.

Indeed, "one of humankind's favorite fantasies is that the soul is best off in nature and needs to slow down to nature's pace . . . I do not at all accept this anti-city view . . . We restore the soul when we restore the city in our individual hearts, the courage, the imagination and love we bring to civilization."

If there were a few raised eyebrows in the audience, wondering if perhaps they were listening to a sermon, Hillman soon dispelled their misapprehension. "The soul has always been associated with a reflective part in us or the reflective function. This is built into our cities as pools, ponds, malls, shades, shadows, where reflections occur. Glass and mirrors especially make reflection possible. But mirrors always have had another association in traditional symbolism, not only of reflection, but also of vanity and narcissus. So there is a danger of empty vanity and superficiality in the use of mirrored glass surfaces, that is, if they only reflect themselves or if they reflect each other."

Since the early Greeks, Hillman went on, soul had also been associated with the idea of depth. "It's very hard for this city, I understand, to go concretely deep: the shale resists and the ground temperature changes are extreme. So we would have to imagine the creation of depth by means of levels . . . such as levels of light, shadings of light." And who would speak in favor of alleys? Hillman would—"The city alley as the place of depth, the heart, is the dark part of the city, the mystery of the city. The alleyway and the narrow way, bending and twisting, is one of the modes of intensifying and adding a depth dimension." Dallas' skyscrapers were manifestations of up-thrusting power, but "there's always a danger to soul if one goes up only, that is, if one emphasizes skylines, towers, and does not keep the heights relative to depths."

There was also the city's story as told through its memorials, parks, statues, cemeteries—"even sites where fateful assassinations have occurred . . . soul keeps nothing out." The human hand seemed to want to leave its touch (in graffiti if no other opportunities were presented), and public meeting places where eye contact and greater intimacy become possible were "crucial to the soul." What else could Dallas be calling for, by naming the new airport Love Field and a boulevard Lovers Lane?

"A city of the magnificent spirit is not enough," Hillman told the assemblage of its fashioners. "A city that neglects the soul's welfare makes the soul search for its welfare in a degrading and concrete way, in the shadow of those same gleaming towers . . . The barbarian is that part of us to whom the city does not speak." He concluded: "For our psychic health and the well-being of our city, let us continue to find ways to make place for soul."

Like much of his writing which had its origin as oral presentation, this was no exception. But there was something very different on display that day, a straightforwardness to the eloquence, a more earthy tone tailored to a new audience. "There was an incredible freedom," he recalled. "I was leaving Zürich behind. I was not writing as a Swiss for other intellectuals."[21]

It was something in the elemental nature of the two places. In a later lecture, Hillman would elaborate: "The external limitlessness of Dallas is what strikes one first on arrival here from Switzerland: where are the hills? And the sky, so opened out! No rivers, lakefronts, woods—nothing to force geographical boundaries."[22] Reflecting on the regions years later in one of our interviews, Hillman added: "With the Swiss, everything is internalized. When the Swiss would buy a fur coat, they wore the lining out; the fur was hidden next to the body, you didn't show off. Dallas was *total* ostentation. I used to say, if you need a lift, they mean a *face*-lift. Dallas was the main place in the country for plastic surgery. If you walked down the street in the morning when people were going to work, the smell of perfume on the girls going into these office buildings was extraordinary. Once I said to a woman who'd invited us to go somewhere, 'Do we have to dress?' She replied, 'Have to *dress*? We *love* to dress!'"

The dinner parties at Margaret McDermott's mansion were customarily black-tie and long dresses. When Hillman and Pat attended the funeral of Gail Thomas' father, they wore dark clothes a la Zürich, only to find the church "filled with women in hats and brightly-flowered dresses. They were completely from another tribe, it was like going to an anthropological event," he marveled. "I remember Gail's brother gave a testimony and his parting words were, 'It was nice doing business with you.'"[23]

The 1978 debut of the hit television program called *Dallas* coincided precisely with Hillman's arrival. He and Pat used to watch "the first of those huge TV serial shows about power and corruption and family relations," as Hillman described it. "That's what people knew Dallas for. The filming location—J. R. Ewing's Southfork Ranch—became the main tourist attraction in the area. Did art imitate reality, or did reality copy art?"[24] In 1980, a then-record-setting eighty million viewers would tune in to find out "who shot J. R."

Around the same time, Hillman mailed Donleavy a newspaper clipping about a South Dallas man whose son lost his temper while building a chicken coop. "Father slays son who hammered chicks to death," the headline announced. Hillman didn't find anything further to say; the shadow spoke for itself.

FINDING A HOME, BUILDING A COMMUNITY

Late in March, Hillman wrote to Ritsema at Eranos: "We have bought a house, 20,000 dollars, must pay another amount equal, for fixing it to be livable. It's at the edge of black district, black neighbors, hence cheap. Old house."[25]

It was in the State-Thomas District north of downtown, a two-story wood-frame at the corner of Routh and Hibernia and part of a gentrifying, but still predominantly African American neighborhood. Originally called Freedman's Town, it had been first settled by freed slaves after the Emancipation. "Here we'd been put up in these mansions," Pat remembered, "and a lot of people

were quietly horrified that Jim wanted to be in a black district."[26]
One of Hillman's students, Stella Rodriquez, recalled it as "a scary
neighborhood, nobody drove down there."[27] Bob Thomas, Gail's
husband, observing the many doors leading from rooms to the
outside, believed the house had more recently been a "dosshouse,"
or flophouse. A patient of Pat's was robbed sitting in her parked
car while waiting to come into the house for analysis.

Interestingly, this wasn't the first time Hillman had chosen such a place. Almost ten years earlier, while teaching at
the University of Chicago, he'd written Donleavy late in 1968:
"We live in a huge, redbrick filthy, magnificent house—negroes
(blacks) all around (across street & on either side as neighbors).
We integrated the neighborhood, it having been all black 'till we
moved in."[28]

Now in Dallas, according to Gail Thomas: "Well, they wanted
to be in a part of town that had sidewalks. And Jim said, 'This
is perfect.' That was the other thing about Jim that was so good
for us—he could talk to the people. He became close friends
with all of the black neighbors. They'd stand out on the stoop
and talk back and forth."[29]

Hillman later described the neighborhood as "old-fashioned, with wonderful talk. Everything happens on the
porches, out in the street: phoning, music, visiting, shouting.
Plenty of depression, too. And there is courtesy there and that
way of joking and that way of walking in the heat. I'd get all
kinds of images from my neighbors, all kinds of feelings. You
know it was from the blacks that we got the word 'soul' back
into our language."[i]

Because Pat was now the one with U.S. citizenship, she had to
buy the house. Then they set out to do a major renovation, most
of which Hillman paid for. University instructor Patrick Kelly
remembered that "Jim and I had conversations about plumb-
ers, sheetrock sources, things like that." Hillman picked out the
paints and decided which molding was going to stay. Louise
Cowan recalled "they restructured the interior so it had high
ceilings and lots of bookshelves, and a room upstairs converted

into a study for Jim." This was in addition to an office for Pat and a guest room for visitors.

Hillman's daughter Susanne recalled: "My father planted many trees in the garden on Routh street. He had already planted a couple of beautiful Japanese type trees outside the dining room window in the garden of the rental house on Klosterweg in Zürich. Now he began spending many happy hours in the garden, watering and trying to get the trees to grow in the dry desert soil of Dallas. He said he needed to get his hands in the soil as he lacked earth in his astrological chart. And he had a deep love for trees, we often spoke about that."[30]

Getting his hands into the earth reconnected Hillman to his own soil, his roots, and genealogy. Pat found it "kind of a joke" that when they redid the downstairs hallway, he decorated the walls not only with photos of his ancestors dating back several generations—but added framed articles from old newspapers about the lives of Rabbi Krauskopf, hotel magnate Joel Hillman, and others. "I missed what was really happening," Pat reflected in 2021. "I realize now that wasn't his vanity. When we returned to live in America, he was getting back in touch with his ancestry."

The university was more than twenty minutes away, and Hillman didn't like to drive. So, on the days Pat didn't go, Thomas was among those who would swing by in the mornings to pick him up. Hillman's entry into the faculty's inner circle was greeted with open arms, because of what Louise Cowan called the "galvanizing effect" of—listening and taking seriously other's ideas. "He would take some idea you didn't think was so great, and give a new twist, and then you basked in that. He made us think more deeply, with greater insight. He made us better than we were."[31]

Hillman's persona, she felt, was perfect "for a communal sharing," the kind Louise was always looking to expand upon. He had always found inspiration among small groups—in Dublin during his student years and at the Spring House gatherings—but this was the first time American academia seemed to suit him. Patrick Kelly, then a young drama instructor, first met Hillman at a party at Sardello's: "I remember the first thing I ever heard him say was wondering how the little organisms in beer could stay alive in a can." Where faculties elsewhere were often marked by intense jealousies and rivalries, with this one "for a lamentably short period, the teachers were learning from each other, changing each other's minds on a daily basis. When you're dealing with minds on the level of Hillman, Cowan and Sardello, that's quite something to be around. Jim wasn't totally responsible for this important dialogue, but he created and established a tone."[32]

While Kelly incorporated the use of mythic figures into his classes, Lyle Novinski—who ran the art department but was also responsible for the campus landscape—credited Hillman with giving him "a locus" for his own thinking, by asking what it means to walk or breaking down the etymology of the word "entrance" to find its deeper meaning. "Bob [Sardello] did it in his work as well," Novinski remembered. "Ideas about moving from one space to another, that there are thresholds where you change thought—like when you come out of a classroom, and hold what you've been listening to by the sidewalk. That slows you down and then there's some kind of aperture that you pass through, to enter the idea of the next class you're anticipating. So I got rid of all the straight sidewalks on campus, which had been laid out by the architects geometrically from overhead, and made them all curving walks so that it's analogous to changing perspectives."[33]

The university held a medieval atmosphere, punctuated by a soaring bell-tower that pealed hourly throughout the day. Dominican priests taught the theology classes, nine hours required for every undergraduate student. Yet Marshall McLuhan, the charismatic pioneer of communication studies ("the medium is the message")—who predicted the Internet thirty-five years before its time—had spent a month at the university in 1975 and described it as "an ideal learning environment." As Randolph Severson later wrote: "It was certainly one of the few universities in the '70s where students got into drunken fist fights, not over girls or politics, but over fine points in Medieval philosophy . . . [surely] the only university . . . where one could study both Thomism with Sir Frederick Wilhelmsen, one of the great existential Thomists of the last century, and alchemy and neo-Platonism with James Hillman."[34] (Thomism is the theology of Thomas Aquinas and his followers.).

The students never walked straight sidewalks in Hillman's classes. Dennis Slattery, later a professor of archetypal psychology at Pacifica Graduate Institute, was then at the university taking courses from both Hillman and Louise Cowan. Hillman's required reading included six works of Plato and others by Plotinus and Sallustius, "One thing that excited the students about Jim's class was understanding the Greek divinities as forms of consciousness through which one sees the world," Slattery recalled. "When it came time to do my dissertation, I knew I wanted to write it on Dostoevsky but didn't know what angle. And Jim brought into the vocabulary the word 'fantasy,' which carries such a negative charge in the culture. But his working of that term made me begin to think differently. I wound up writing on fantasy as a mode of consciousness in Dostoevsky's *The Idiot*."[35]

Stella Rodriquez, who became the director of a counseling center near Dallas and a national speaker on therapeutic issues involving Hispanic families, recalled "taking every class [Hillman] taught; I've never met a man with more elegant ideas. What I took away was that the life of the mind and one's soul was important, and you needed to tend to that no matter what."[36]

The tending wasn't only about the past. At a time when anorexia was being diagnosed in more and more young people, Hillman gave a course he called "Food Disorders." Going beyond the then-current theories about a patient's bad parenting and other Freudian fantasies, Hillman traced the etiology to a cultural/historical pathology rather than placing the blame on the individual suffering from it. He recalled: "I went into the whole meat industry. I brought forth the history of frozen food and bakeries in America—how they're all owned by three companies—how we bake bread and fake the brown loaf that's actually painted on."[37]

As Jung once put it: "There is in the psyche some superior power, and if it is not consciously a god, it is the 'belly' at least, in St. Paul's words."[38]

YOUNG BLOOD FOR *SPRING*

As he had with the young American pilgrims coming to Zürich in the Spring House era, Hillman kept his eye out for solid assistants in Dallas. Randolph Severson, a 22-year-old psychology undergrad when Hillman gave his 1975 public lecture there, remembered coming early to the hall. The only other person present was a tall, thin man in a sport coat who was moving from chair to chair passing out catalogues. Severson later recounted: "My image of Hillman, based on reading a couple of his things, was of this Jung-like, massive physical presence who wore a beard. Well, I saw this fellow and we exchanged civilities and then he left—only to come back in with an entourage twenty minutes later. And it's Hillman! For me, that was a big part of Jim's appeal, that he was not above doing something like putting out catalogues, which he could easily have asked somebody else to take care of."[39]

Severson himself would eventually become what he called Hillman's "Man Friday" with Spring Publications. Hillman had acquired full ownership of Spring from Jane Pratt in September 1977. After Sardello started making arrangements to house it on the Dallas campus, and Hillman began shipping boxes and then furniture from Zürich, Sardello arranged an interview with Severson. Hillman hired him away from the university post office and, the next thing Severson knew, two-ton crates of books were scheduled to arrive at the port of Houston and he was to take care of this. "No further instructions. His trust was breath-taking," Severson later said. Soon he was establishing the new Spring office on campus "literally in the cellar of a building, at the *back* of the janitor's office." Hillman called it "a boiler room," not unlike one of its earlier homes in Guggenbühl's bathroom in Zürich.

Also joining the team was another 22-year-old, Michael Sipiora. He came to the university with a Master's in philosophy to study phenomenological psychology. His first year, Sipiora took Hillman's class in Psychological Traditions (Heraclitus, Plotinus, Ficino, Vico, and others). Hillman not only gave him an A on a paper about Camus and Aphrodite, but published it in the *Spring Journal*—that is, after editing out all of Sipiora's references to his phenomenological hero, German philosopher Martin Heidegger, who Hillman (like Jung) felt was "that most un-psychological man." (Yet when a scholarly comparative work by Roberts Avens titled *Hillman, Heidegger, and Angels* came out, Hillman handed Sipiora a copy asking for his opinion).

Sipiora needed a job his second year. He started off stocking books in Spring's storage basement at the university, and ended up becoming director of marketing and sales with his wife hired on as Hillman's accountant. Sipiora recalled learning "how to negotiate and cut a deal" from Hillman, when the half-dozen employees approached him about the fact they had no health insurance. Ultimately, according to Sipiora, "he said 'okay, you go out and find me the very best policy that will include Pat and me, and I'll do it.' He paid for it, too. He put his money where his mouth is." On the side, Hillman had Sipiora work on the complicated index for *Puer Papers*—by writing it out by hand. When he complained about falling behind in his course work, Hillman helped out, and then suggested he take a break by participating in the Sunday baseball games, which Sipiora did. It was Spring House redux.

At the time that Spring Publications reorganized as a Texas corporation, besides the annual journal "it offered a list of nearly forty titles," Hillman wrote, "having been the first to produce, not only Jung's *Visions Seminars*, but also Freud's *Cocaine Papers*, Kerényi's works *Hermes* and *Athene* in English, as well as seven volumes of Marie-Louise von Franz's seminars. *Spring* itself had expanded to a full-size book; it is now . . . quoted in scholarly works, as well as still being stand-by reading for individuals engaged in depth analysis or pursuing the unicorn along the borderlands." *Spring Journal,* having sold for a dollar when Hillman first started publishing it ten years before, now cost ten dollars and paid article contributors $125; for books, royalties were negotiated. Between $160,000 and $190,000 of books a year were being sold.[40]

"The move to Texas emphasized even more than usual our eccentric style of service,"[41] Hillman remembered. Indeed, he hired other student assistants who were Severson's friends (including Stella Rodriquez) and, before long, Severson would be part of the discussions on what to publish, and was even allowed to assist with the editing. He was there as Hillman worked in the study at a "gigantic two-door table that he used as a desk, with piles of stuff all over the place." Hillman kept a little pot of glue on his desk, and would get down on the floor to cut-and-paste together issues of the journal, a method he told Severson he'd learned from observing Karl Kerényi work—"a way that wasn't linear but was scholarly and reputable."[42]

Arriving at his classes, Rodriquez remembered Hillman carrying bulging manila folders with colored strips of paper marking various ideas that had come to him for a lecture—"but every time he'd open them to try to find something, it would elude him. He never really needed them anyway, he *was* the ideas." According to Severson, Hillman "couldn't file things away in a drawer and remember they were there, he'd have to see it all laid out. He'd always say he had to have his mind visible. I spent a lot of time growing up on my grandparents' ranch, so I remembered what it was to walk through a barn stable and watch every step; in Jim's study, it was the same. He'd be liable to fly out of the chair saying 'Don't touch that! Watch it, watch it, watch it!' His books lined the study all the way around up to the ceiling, and he had a ladder so he could immediately grab what he needed."

Probably no one besides Pat spent as much time with Hillman during his first years in Dallas as Severson. He would chauffeur Hillman to *Spring*'s printer on the far south side of town, a drive of more than an hour (according to Severson, "he'd want to go nearly every day initially, he was very hands-on"). The young man liked the air conditioning on full blast—it was his car, after all—but Hillman didn't care for that. So they reached an unspoken compromise. Hillman would simply roll down the window on his side. "He could easily have pulled rank, but instead he was going to do it his way and let me do it my way. Could mean a little 'suffering' on both sides, but okay, we'll agree to disagree. That was very telling about him."

On Severson's birthday in 1978, Hillman gave him a copy of his first book *Emotion*, then out of print and difficult to find. Today Severson regards it as "a kind of talisman," and still vividly recalls the inscription: "Partner—pupil—colleague—coworker, in appreciation of his appreciation of what this work is all about." That, Severson believed, "is so Hillman. It sounds personal but it's not really, it's an acknowledgment of a certain collegiality, more like a coach saying to an athlete, 'good play' or 'good run.'"

It was good enough for Hillman to promote Severson to Executive Editor of *Spring*, and suggest he do some fundraising. "There was a fella here in Dallas, Pat Howell, now passed on, who was heir to a considerable fortune and very sympathetic to Hillman," Severson reflected in 2016. "So I, a 27-year-old Dallasite, knowing exactly who the Howell family was—a street in Highland Park, the ritzy exclusive enclave, where Dallas 'old money' resides, bears the family name—swallowed hard and called him. A little chit chat, and then, 'Mr. Howell, I'd like to ask you for some financial help for Spring.' Howell: 'That'd be just fine, Randolph. How much?' I had no idea what to ask for, so I said (how I came up with this figure the gods only know—and remember this was 1980), '$20,000?' Howell: 'You want to come get it now?' So I immediately drove over to his house, he ushered me into his study and wrote out a personal check. It was never that easy again, but it sure made [asking] easier."[43]

Hillman and Pat also signed on as Contributing Editors to a short-lived new journal with Sardello as Editor and Thomas as Consultant. *Dragonflies: Studies in Imaginal Psychology* would publish Hillman's essay on "Therapeutic Value of Alchemical Language" in 1978.

Spring 1978 printed his "Further Notes on Images."

By early 1979, Spring Publications had a dozen new books planned. Hillman wrote Murray Stein, a colleague in Zürich who worked on the publication, that "orders come from more & more odd places. Truly National & International—no longer just counter-culture or 'Jungians.'"[44] However, as another colleague remembered, somehow the list of subscribers vanished. Hillman wrote in *Spring 1979* that "the move [to Dallas] caused agonies and delays and enraging mistakes. For the fourth time in its history, Spring had to spring forth anew: new persons, new authors, new printers, new systems and laws, new postal regulations, new editorial grammars, new psychological soil. We are not altogether out of the woods, and according to our history can't expect ever to be fully free and clear. But our readership continues to expand, and more and more excellent papers are being submitted. We do believe we embody an indefinable though definite direction in contemporary thought—what some have called post-modern consciousness, imagination as a way, psyche as existence. You, readers, are this consciousness, this psyche, and we invite your responses, by letters, by replies to articles, by sending in your manuscripts. Thank you."

Michael Sipiora sometimes drove Hillman on road-trips to book fairs ("he didn't like chain restaurants") and recalled: "We were keeping important books in print, like a mission. He always insisted these had to be high quality in their composition—the paper, the binding, the design. He would refer to von Franz as the last remnant of the Austro-Hungarian empire, but her books were Spring's bread-and-butter."[45]

At the time, Hillman had a private practice of about ten analysands. When he sensed that Severson might want to do analysis with him, he told him one day: "I just don't think business and analysis mix."[46] Hillman did take on another young fellow in 1978 named Sven Doehner, today an archetypal therapist in Mexico City.[47] Doehner was then an artist/photographer who had recently discovered Jung. He was passing through Dallas from Mexico en route to New York, where he hoped to enter analysis and save up enough money to "knock at the door of the Jung Institute in Zürich and say, 'I've got some great dreams if somebody will help me.'"

Doehner planned to take a bus onward the next morning when he walked into a bookstore and found himself standing next to Hillman. "I had no idea who he was. He was interested in my being part Mexican, so we struck up a conversation and ended up adjourning to a coffee shop. At the end of two hours, I discovered *he* was a Jungian analyst. I said, 'Well, maybe I can see you instead of pursuing this in more complicated ways.' He said, 'I've just arrived from Zürich. So why don't you go back to Mexico, see if you have a good dream, and here's my number.'"

Within two days, Doehner had a dream that began with needing a haircut and finding a barbershop in a basement. The moment he sat in the chair, however, he felt violently ill, fell onto the floor, and crawled his way to a small bathroom. It was covered with other people's similar problems but, too weak to care, he proceeded to release his own. When he was finally exhausted, the barber walked in, helped him up and said, "Look, you need a little time in a sanitorium." So Doehner passed through an opening where, at the end of a hallway, a woman told him, "This is your bed." As he approached closer, he saw that her blouse was open and she was offering him a breast dripping with milk.

Transfixed by this dream, Doehner called Hillman, made an appointment, flew back to Dallas, and arrived at the office in his home on Routh Street to relate the nocturnal event. Hillman took it all in and asked simply, "What's a barber?" Doehner replied,

"Well, it's somebody who picks through your head"—clearly a metaphor for a psychoanalyst. He remembered Hillman walking over to a bookshelf, where he reached for what Doehner thought was "an ancient alchemical text—I, of course, idealized this, it was actually Jung's book on alchemy—but he opened right to the page of a woman, sitting on a whale and offering her breast dripping with milk."

Doehner would end up spending nine years off-and-on in analysis with Hillman, who also put him and his wife to work designing book covers for Spring. Doehner would become a fringe member of the small group that gathered regularly in Hillman and Pat's living room. He remembered that Hillman was asked why he came to Dallas, and Hillman responded: "It's the wound of America. It's where it hurts the most."

THE WOUND OPENS

Hillman told a reporter for the *Dallas Morning News* that the city was "developing a consciousness about itself, just like a Renaissance city." In June 1979, he spoke on "Goals for Dallas" to the city's department heads and subheads. He began by congratulating them for this "extraordinary thing"—"the unknown faceless bureaucrats at City Hall, the administrators and all powerful paper-pushers meeting with the absentminded professors, the impractical useless fuzzy arcane academics. You are the hard-boiled and we are the eggheads."

He proceeded to talk of the importance of realizing that "the less literally we take the goals, the more inventive we become, searching and trying alternatives or exploring wider horizons and new images." Why not conceive of aesthetic goals, such as different types of billboards? We were encouraged to see waste, but taste was being neglected. Beauty *could* belong in government. Hillman asked the audience to think about: "What specific images and fantasies come to mind with such words as efficiency, optimizing, enhancing, improving?"[48]

Later in the year, he offered his "Psychological Fantasies in Transportation Problems" at another seminar. He delved into phrases that implied disdain for public transportation ("being taken for a ride . . . getting railroaded"), and descriptive terms such as thruways, highways, and freeways "that reinforce fantasies of unburdened freedom and liberty when we are driving our vehicles measured by horse-power." It was all about "quicker equals better . . . a world with little place for slowness," and the "universal sameness of our contemporary utopias, the no-where everywhere of our shopping centers and roads to and from them." But what about conceiving it all differently? What about a shift of perspectives "not only from space to place, but as well from city center to community, public to persons, homogeneity to differences, geometry to geography, from quick and easy to slow and interesting, from private driver to civic passenger, that sense of transiency which accepts that the wheel on which we turn can never truly be in our own hands."[49]

Judith French-Kelly, who founded the university's drama department, recalled that "inevitably Jim's questions to the city leaders were profound, stirring, and completely unexpected."[50] Her husband Patrick described the lectures as "always very simple—and devastating. Because Jim had no jargon, but a man-on-the-street quality that he brought to these events. Asking common-sense questions that an educated alert person would ask, if only they had the guts or the inspiration. It was very interesting to see the city officials have to stop and think about what they would answer; to see them off-script always got the effect Hillman hoped for. The thing was, Jim always seemed to ask with no idea about what the answer would be. That was unsettling to begin with."[51] Stella Rodriquez said that, unlike his demeanor with the students, in public venues "if somebody asked a stupid question or they were spouting off or challenging him, he was always polite and gracious but—you know that aquiline nose he has—he'd literally turn into a hawk: attack from afar and just pick 'em off."[52]

Stirring the pot like this was not without its potential perils. Lyn Cowan, then in private practice in Minneapolis after her time with Hillman in Zürich, wrote a letter to him expressing what she sensed while visiting there. "Wasn't there a famous outlaw named Texas Jim? Seems to me there was a fellow, 'bout '88 or so, who rode around on a mule and wore too-tight boots, but was fast with a gun and used silver bullets. Seems to me this gold-hearted outlaw was finished off in an ambush by a mean marshal who didn't hold with anything new-fangled like Eateemollogies [sic] and such like and laid into Texas Jim while the outlaw was dreaming and they buried TJ with his boots on . . . Watch it. Big D is a Dangerous Place, even if they don't ride mules anymore."[53]

Lyn Cowan seemed to have tuned in to an aspect of the *genius loci*, the soul of Dallas, which according to a reporter was described by Gail Thomas like this: "Something of that soul can be glimpsed in the stereotype of the wild west gunslinger—unbridled, macho, explosive. Restlessness and aggression run deep in the Dallas psyche, flaring up not only in constant clashes between the city's different ethnic groups but also in the geology of the region. The city is situated at the confluence of the three branches of the Trinity River, and at the convergence of the region's three geological strata—farmlands, chalky hills and pine forests. This kinetic, swirling geological vortex infuses Dallas with a spirit of upheaval that sometimes manifests in tragic ways, from the Cherokee Indian massacre of 1820 to the assassination of John F. Kennedy."[54]

By all appearances, the dawn of the eighties remained a heady time. Hillman's latest book, *The Dream and the Underworld*, was reviewed favorably in the *New York Times* and *Newsweek*. "This has helped the sales very much," Hillman wrote in a letter to Ritsema at Eranos, "for these popular journals make a huge difference in America, despite the book being highly intellectual and difficult."[55]

A university colloquium arranged by Sardello, "On the Necessity of Liberal Education," brought together such luminaries as Marshall McLuhan, Malcolm Muggeridge, Mortimer

Adler, and Jacques Barzun, and was attended by several thousand people over a three-day period. López wrote Hillman after
a visit that he now believed Hillman's conversations with the city
powers-that-be were "something tough and needed," and that
he himself had been invited in Caracas "to talk about the city to
a group of architects who have founded an institute to discuss
urban problems."[56]

It seemed fitting that Hillman was asked in June to serve a
three-year term as Dean of the university's Braniff Graduate
School. Yet Hillman wrote López in a 1980 new year's mis-
sive: "My main anxiety is loss of soul . . . the Jungian soul that
comes through silence despair sickness meditation and inability.
Instead we work, go to the spa, rarely have pain, and dream
only on occasion. I can't find any problems! Except—that. It
implies the usual American situation of loss of some dimension
without noticing it. Besides, I watch football games on TV, again
and again and again. Still drink wine, sometimes twice a day, and
sleep afternoons as before."

Shortly thereafter, he wrote to the poet Robert Duncan,
whom he recently met and felt an instant camaraderie with:
"Between bouts of activity, efficiency in the Dallas style, I sink
into an iron anger mixed with lead: a bitter barren hardness,
not true depression, not need, not even despair, simply a dreadful hatred, hard, and incredibly oppressed by 'work.' Everything
they said from Aristotle through Burton and Ficino about the
intellectual's melancholy is true. Fierce. Black. Acrid."[57]

After Hillman and Pat returned from a jaunt to Mexico, he
sent this to David Miller:. "I came back clear headed, and hating
the USA, and this Texas world too. But it is so easy to hate it
here that the joy is finding out how to live in it."[58]

Not far into 1980, events at the University of Dallas suddenly took an ugly turn. This had been building ever since, as
Patrick Kelly put it, "the board gave Don Cowan his golden
handshake—and not much of a golden one either." As Kelly's
wife Judith added: "When we lost the visionary, our philoso-
pher-king, the whole place was in turmoil."[59]

The intellectual leaders of the school were no longer the administrators—except in the case of Hillman, whose appointment as Graduate Dean had been successfully promoted by Louise Cowan. However, the undercurrents against him seethed just below the surface. "A lot of the turmoil was actually because of Jim," Gail Thomas remembered. "The head of the Cistercian seminary had started reading his books." Also, as Hillman recalled, "I gave a seminar on Neoplatonic Psychology (to the chagrin of the priests)." Patrick Kelly remembered being stunned to hear Hillman being labeled as the worst kind of polytheist by the Hungarian priest in charge of the theology department, where Kelly sensed a "deep-running element of anti-semitism" as well.

Dennis Slattery recalled: "There was a lot of academic envy because students were flocking to the psychology program. The Greek gods were entering, and this made the Catholic fundamentalists real nervous. I think out of envy, not out of any sense that someone's going to lose their faith. It was the gravitational pull of myth."[60]

The catalyst that brought all this out from the shadows was an invitation to a Dutch psychologist, Jan Hendrick van den Berg, to teach a six-week course. He had been Robert Romanyshyn's mentor at Duquesne, and was the author of a textbook titled *Medical Power and Medical Ethics*. In one section, van den Berg discussed the possibility that euthanasia, or "mercy killing," might become more legitimized in medicine for babies born with severe physical or mental defects. "He wasn't promoting euthanasia," according to Sardello, "but simply stating this could be the case in the future."[61] (The textbook was in the school bookstore and already being used in one of the classes).

A few of the faculty and priests then protested that such views were contrary to church doctrine, and asked that van den Berg be disinvited. The priests concurred. John Sommerfeldt, a medieval historian who had replaced Don Cowan as the university's president, became worried that unwanted publicity could jeopardize the school's fifteen million dollars capital campaign drive. Hillman tried to intervene. He wrote Sommerfeldt in March stating: "The only 'politic' course, it seems to me, is to stand firmly for the academic integrity and humanity of the University against terrorism, blackmail, lobbying and whatever other pressures are brought to your office." Should van den Berg's invitation be withdrawn, Hillman added that he himself "would be obliged also to reconsider my association with the University."[62]

Gail Thomas remembered driving Hillman to a meeting of the graduate council, where "Father David would start asking direct questions of Jim and his beliefs," basically an inquisition into whether archetypal psychology was immoral.[63] The Faculty Senate proceeded to come together for a vote and overwhelmingly condemned "the approval of euthanasia and the killing of defective children advocated" by van den Berg "as being contrary to Christian morality and the public conscience of Western Civilization."[64]

That this weighed heavily on Hillman was evident in a letter he wrote to Don Fredericksen, a film professor at Cornell University who had arranged a Hillman seminar there in mid-April. Expressing the "feeling of failure I have over what I brought to you," Hillman confessed: "I am not able right now to do what I used to do: mammoth historical heroical lectures. I am old, tired, depressed, dry, changing, new things in the offing but not yet on the horizon. Meanwhile what I 'have done' all seems dead and 'has been' making me feel 'has been.' So I didn't deliver what I wish I could have, and probably left you disappointed. Perhaps it is not the time for me to be in the public: but then, perhaps somebody got something somehow anyway."[65]

A week later, at the end of April 1980, university president Sommerfeldt broke the contract with van den Berg and terminated his invitation. "A few of us on the faculty were outraged at what we considered censoring of academic freedom," Hillman recalled. "None of us liked this president. So we got together with phone calls and a lot of excitement."[66] A big meeting was called at Lynch Auditorium, where almost 500 students (out of an enrollment of over 2,000) added their names to a petition against the president's move.

Rodriquez recalled a series of break-ins to the Spring Publications on-campus warehouse, where boxes were up-ended and invoices scattered everywhere. Hillman then called a meeting and began by asking his student employees if they felt in any danger. "He said he didn't think there was," Rodriguez remembered. "He just said, 'It's obvious somebody wants to be on the inside.' He turned it into something kinda funny and not scary. After that, we'd just come in and pick up the papers off the floor and go on with our work. And it stopped after awhile."[67]

Then came what Gail Thomas would look back on as "Black Thursday." Hillman recounted: "At eight o'clock one morning, about 20 of us [out of 110 faculty] walked into the president's office to present a letter saying that we humbly requested his resignation. He then called the board, which also disliked him because they thought he was inefficient (we didn't like him because he was so stupid)."

Hillman foresaw what was coming next in a letter to Ritsema. He described being "completely engaged in the Palace Revolution, or coup d'etat," which he anticipated would result in the removal of himself and others on "'our side' (entire admin-istration and eight of twelve department chairmen)." Behind the president "are the Business senex people and the Church. Two more powerful allies cannot be imagined . . . Reagan, heli-copters, Khomeini—these are the signs of the '80s. Nixon was held back by hippies and liberals and the commonfolk, to some extent, but nothing will hold back the militarism and catholi-cism/islamicism fanatics in the next period I fear."[68]

Here's what happened: Sommerfeldt resigned, saying that he wanted to return to scholarly pursuits—a move the *Dallas Times Herald* noted "relieves tension."[69] The chairman of the econom-ics department and dean of the graduate school of management, Svetozar Pejovich, was named acting president for up to a year.

He proceeded to demote seven administrators, removing Sardello as head of the Institute for Philosophic Studies and Hillman as Graduate Dean. Louise Cowan, calling this an attempt to "intimidate an entire faculty," submitted her resignation.[70]

Hillman responded in a letter to Pejovich, noting that he was "peremptorily dismissed by you . . . before a hastily summoned meeting of the Faculty. That this took place in full public [view] and without my presence requires an explanation which I request from you personally so that I do not read your behavior as an act of willful disgracing, or intimidation by example, or simply unconscionable ignorance concerning the dignity of academic ritual and human manners on the part of a man who has a University in his trust."[71]

Privately, writing to Donleavy, Hillman was more browbeaten:. "Ran into a reef at the University here. We ganged up on the President. Handed him a revolver at 8am one morning by surprise and he had to be fired by the Board, which then, lickety-split, fired yours truly and a few other scaliwags. I'm still around, but no longer a 'power' in academe."[72]

And to Wolfgang Giegerich, he wrote: "Yes we have had tremendous troubles with the Trustees of our small school, fights that go back to long before I came . . . The trustees are a combination of parochial catholics, priests (old and irish), and tough Texas business types . . . no one with a decent education in the lot. The people who brought me have slowly lost power, so that Camelot is over as far as academic life is concerned though our group of friends is lively enough."[73]

Nonetheless, as he put it to Ritsema, "I am enjoying good health and this active life immensely and still feel delivered from the oppression of Zürich despite the many days and hours of dryness and rust. Depression simply comes in different styles according to the Gods of the place. But the opportunity to take part in 'world' means a great deal to me, and is so much more significant than the little arguments with the Jungians."[74]

With no such background to fall back on, Don and Louise Cowan were "heartbroken over the university," according to Thomas. She herself would resign in another six months. Sardello remembered: "To control them, the board then told each chair-person they could have their position back if they would not do anything like this again. In my case, they then turned around and asked Romanyshyn to take the job, which he did. So I left the university and took a sabbatical."[75]

Hillman was told he could retain his teaching post, but in a note to the psychology graduate students he wrote that he could not "accommodate with the moral collapse of the University . . . the deceit . . . the incompetence of the Board," despite his affection and loyalty to the students and their work. "I didn't come here to work with the University of Dallas, or lend my reputation to its archaic Catholicism, or to endorse its stands in politics, dogma, and intellect. I enjoyed working within it to continue the ancient battles between paganism and christianity . . . It is hard for me to live with the shame of a hypocritical business minded university. I could do it when I felt my ideals were affecting something. But to do it merely for the sake of teaching you all, no."[76]

Severson remembered that, for the students, "the majority were there to study archetypal psychology and they felt abandoned by Hillman. Most didn't finish the program and gradually scattered. It left a bad taste with some people. But Hillman didn't see it as abandoning anybody, because that didn't belong in his *weltanschaung*, his world-view: "you're not children, not my kids, not foundlings, follow your karma, you know?"[77] Rodriquez said it took years before she could bear coming onto the campus again.

Hillman wrote to an alumni: "As a latecomer, and even an outsider, I fought as I could," amid "retrenchment, cost efficiency, doctrinal compliance—maybe even worse: purge."[78] To Guggenbühl, Hillman wrote: "Sad how quick it went, and how America can change so fast."[79] To López, whom he soon went to Venezuela to visit, he wrote: "Losing the University, of course, was a loss, because it was a further isolation. When I get into these states, I dry up in anger (Mars) and then must get away for new love and new images."[80] To David Miller, he wrote: "We lost . . . Let it go, let it go. The fortress has been penetrated, and that's enough."[81]

They still owned a house, and Pat was immersed in her thesis, and out of the ashes perhaps some phoenix could still rise. Hillman had been here before. It was, in fact, part of the recurring pattern of his life, the mysterious eruptions that destroyed the existing structures—from his youthful days turning renegade at a summer camp, through the affair that threatened to end his career in Zürich, to being "booted for leading a rebellion at the University against the President," as he described it to Donleavy.[82] The more conservative Romanyshyn who found himself for a time at the top-of-the-heap, saw Hillman as bringing "a wildness to the place and a certain kind of genius, but he didn't belong in an academic setting."[83]

If Hillman didn't belong in academia, then where? That was what seven people—Thomas, Stroud, the Cowans, Sardello, Pat, and Hillman—all sat down together one day trying to figure out. They met on June 10, 1980, in downtown Dallas's North End on the top floor of the old four-story White Swan Coffee Roaster warehouse. It was owned by a developer acquaintance, John Tatum, who remembered the meeting ensuing while a thunderstorm roiled outside "and everyone thought the university might call a lightning strike down on them."[84] There they sat, under a massive skylight designed to keep an eye on the color of the coffee beans in the roasting ovens below, drinking scotch and bourbon out of the bottle with straws—and mapping out their rebirth into independence.

A DEATH IN JERUSALEM

The terrible uncertainty of the time even carried over to the Eranos gatherings. In a letter to Rudolf Ritsema, Hillman addressed "the dreadful condition of our world's intellectuals. No one knows where we are going . . . we are in a ship without a rudder, not just a political absence of captaincy, but a most profound lack of spirit, that affects everything."[85]

That wasn't the letter's only sorrow. Hillman had news about his wife of twenty years, Kate, from whom he'd divorced four years earlier. "It was told me finally clearly by the children that their mother is surely dying, and soon," Hillman wrote. "It had been half suspected for some months, but she had kept it to herself, and none of us wanted to broach it openly, respecting her desire for privacy. She is in Jerusalem, and the children have been with her in turn. She is impressively managing, and it is profoundly sad."

In the summer of 1979, Kate had departed Zürich with a man that she and her son Laurence had been living with for a few years. A World War II survivor from Poland, he was a painter who fought in the Israeli war of independence in 1948 and, now seriously ill, wished to return to Israel to spend his last days. Before she left, Kate told Anne Guggenbühl-Craig, her longtime friend in Zürich, that she herself had incurable cancer. She would be "tending a flat" in Jerusalem. Kate said she'd been reading a book, *Life After Life*, a 1975 bestseller investigating over a hundred case studies of people who went to the "other side" and came back (now called Near-Death-Experiences), and she felt prepared and unworried. "Kate seems to have reached a serenity," Anne wrote to Hillman.[86] Kate died a little over a year later, in October of 1980, at the age of only fifty-two.

She had found a Swedish Lutheran cemetery in Jerusalem where a handful of Protestants from Sweden were buried on Mount Scopus, and talked her way into a burial plot there.[87] In a letter to J. P. Donleavy, who had known Kate longer than any of his friends, Hillman described attending the funeral with their four children: "That beautiful extraordinary woman turning into a haggard dried corpse: dreadful, a horror you cannot imagine. Still violently active in spirit to the end: ordering, fighting, engaged. The sadness is overwhelming. The children nursed her at home, then washed the body at her death, and wrapped it in linen sheets, and two went off to buy the coffin from the Arabs, and Laurence nailed his mother in the box, and we carried it through the old city of Jerusalem at 8 am to the Swedish church, like one on the island of North Sweden, with Swedish choir and ministers out of Bergman, a kind of procession and show that Kate herself could have staged, in fact partly did stage in her arrangements for the funeral, all this in Jerusalem, right by the holy of holies, and then back through the bazaar because no cars can go through, to the graveyard, where she had arranged a burial place (no foreigners ever can get buried in Jerusalem since half the religious of the world wish to be) and the arabs had dug the soil out, box didn't fit, lowered and adjusted and lowered, and the children and sisters and I standing there, with our little flowers, an olive branch . . . To think that woman is dead. I have been in her death now for weeks and weeks."[88]

Hillman gave the eulogy at the funeral. He spoke of Kate's laughter and hospitality, "her lyrical melancholy" and musical gift, "her superb fantasy embedded in Northern nature, its tenderness and wildness, her strength of solitary will, and a sensitivity, which though poetic, sometimes romantic, was never sentimental." He spoke of her "originality of spirit in the smallest details of life . . . For all her modesty, embraced by the simplicity of her little intimate name, Nina, and other pet names so many had for her, she was large and grand because of a largesse and grandeur of soul."

He spoke of her passion for family, and as someone who taught "how to enjoy the good things of life, whether eating her fresh bread and butter, riding a horse, or receiving a gift of flowers. She did not chase sensations but knew how to choose among them. By this she taught economy: the recognition of value as sensate delight in the quality of things."

He spoke of "the enigma of her person and her fate, that she was so beautiful, that she endured so much, that she died not old after pain and ugliness, and died here. The mystery of her: as if there was in her an angel from another world that had to come to Jerusalem to leave this world, so that, despite her realism—that obsession with practical organization, that fearless salty tongue and penetratingly critical eye—she, or that angel, never quite found its home on earth. Now we must read her life from its death, from Jerusalem, backwards."[89]

NOTES

1. "Curious that just as I leave. . . .": Hillman letter to Wolfgang Giegerich, Giegerich private archive.
2. "The desert he rode was red. . . .": Cormac McCarthy, *All the Pretty Horses*, Page One of Texas Border Trilogy, 1992.
3. "the outrage that gave rise. . . ." And quote from *Myth of Analysis*: Randolph Severson, *Seeing Red: A Tribute to James Hillman*, November 20, 2013 presentation at Dallas Institute Symposium.
4. "It is all very pukka. . . .": Hillman letter to JP Donleavy, January 24, 1978, Donleavy private archive.
5. "very weird, leaving Zürich. . . .": Hillman letter to Robert Stein.
6. "having found us a place to put our bags. . . .": Hillman letter to JP Donleavy.
7. "high sense of style. . . .": Author interview with Louise Cowan, November 2008.
8. "They didn't understand frontier. . . .": Author interview with James Pratt, November 2008.
9. "many of the French stayed. . . .": Donald Cowan essay in *Imagining Dallas*, Edited by Gail Thomas, Dallas Institute of Humanities and Culture, 1982, p. 1–14.
10. "the potency of groups. . . .": Author interview with Louise Cowan, November 2008.
11. "It was a tribal feeling. . . .": Author interview with Gail Thomas, November 2008.
12. "I remember Doxioadis. . . .": Author interview with Louise Cowan, November 2008.
13. "downtown Dallas was really. . . .": Author interview with Gail Thomas, November 2008.
14. "You see, Gail had the idea. . . .": Author interview with Louise Cowan, November 2008.
15. "in city making, there's something else available. . . .": Author interview with Gail Thomas, November 2008.
16. "The students would do theoretical work. . . .": Author interview with Joanne Stroud, November 2008.
17. "they created a kind of tax-free zone. . . .": Author interview with Hillman, Oct. 31, 2008.
18. "where you were not conducting experiments. . . .": Author interview with Ron Schenk, November 2008.
19. "Sardello and Romanyshyn opened. . . .": Author interview with Hillman, Oct. 31, 2008.

20. *City and Soul* by James Hillman: All lecture quotes are from a monograph published by The Center for Civic Leadership, University of Dallas, 1978.
21. "There was an incredible freedom. . . .': Author interview with Hillman, October 2008.
22. "The external limitlessness of Dallas. . . ." Hillman essay, "City Limits," in *Imagining Dallas*, pp. 59. Dallas: The Dallas Institute of Humanities and Culture, 1982.
23. "With the Swiss, everything is. . . .": Author interview with Hillman, October 2008.
24. "the first of those huge TV. . . .": Author interview with Hillman, October 2008.
25. "We have bought a house. . . .": JH letter to Rudolf Ritsema, March 21, 1978, Eranos archive.
26. "Here we'd been put up. . . .": Author interview with Pat Berry, August 2008.
27. "a scary neighborhood. . . .": Author interview with Stella Rodriguez, February 2009.
28. "We live in a huge. . . .": JH letter to JP Donleavy, undated 1968, Donleavy private archive.
29. "Well, they wanted to be in a part of town. . . .": Author interview with Gail Thomas, November 2008.
30. "My father planted many trees. . . .": Susanne Hillman email to author, November 2020.
31. "a galvanizing effect. . . .": Author interview with Louise Cowan, November 2008.
32. "I remember the first thing. . . .": Author interview with Patrick Kelly, November 2008.
33. "a locus. . . .": Author interview with Lyle Novinski, November 2008.
34. "It was certainly one of the few universities. . . .": Randolph Severson, "Seeing Red: A Tribute to James Hillman."
35. "One thing that excited the students. . . .": Author interview with Dennis Slattery, June 2007.
36. "taking every class he taught. . . .': Author interview with Stella Rodriguez, February 2009.
37. "I went into the whole meat industry. . . .": Author interview with Hillman, June 2009.
38. "There is in the psyche some superior power. . . .": C. G. Jung, *Collected Works*, Vol. 7, p. 71.
39. The Randolph Severson story and quotes come from his interview with the author, November 2008.
40. "between 160 and 190 thousand dollars of books a year. . . .": Hillman letter to "Dear Charles," October 5, 1980.
41. "It offered a list of nearly forty titles. . . .." Hillman, "Letter From the Editor for an Anniversary," *Spring 1979*.
42. All Severson quotes, unless otherwise noted, are from the author's interview, November 2008.
43. "There was a fella here in Dallas. . . .": Randolph Severson email to author, June 26, 2016.
44. "orders come from more and more odd. . . .": Hillman letter to Murray Stein, undated, Stein private archive.
45. "I saw him create archetypal. . . .": Author interview with Michael Sipiora, November 2016.
46. "I just don't think business and analysis. . . ..": Severson interview.
47. All Sven Doehner quotes are from an author interview, September 2007.

48. "Goals for Dallas" delivered June 7, 1979, is reprinted in *City & Soul, James Hillman Uniform Edition No. 2*, Thompson, Ct: Spring Publications, Inc., 2006, pp. 274–82.

49. "Psychological Fantasies in Transportation Problems" was delivered by Hillman at a seminar on "Transportation" held at the University of Dallas on December 3, 1978. The quotes are taken from a monograph published by the university's Center for Civic Leadership.

50. "inevitably Jim's questions to the city leaders. . . .": Author interview with Judith French-Kelly, November 2008.

51. "always very simple—and devastating. . . .": Author interview with Patrick Kelly, November 2008.

52. "If somebody asked a stupid question. . . .": Author interview with Stella Rodriguez, February 2009.

53. "Wasn't there a famous outlaw. . . .": Lyn Cowan letter to Hillman, Cowan private archive.

54. "Something of that soul. . . .": Article "Searching for the Soul of Dallas," by Mark Gauvreau Judge, in *Common Boundary*, November/December 1992, p. 45.

55. "This has helped the sales. . . .": Hillman letter to Rudolf Ritsema, September 11, 1979, Eranos archive.

56. "something tough and needed. . . ." Lopéz private archive, letter provided to author.

57. "Between bouts of activity. . . .": Hillman letter to Robert Duncan, courtesy of Duncan archive.

58. "I came back clear headed. . . .": Hillman letter to David Miller, Miller private archive.

59. "the board gave Don Cowan. . . .": Author interviews with Kellys, November 2008.

60. "There was a lot of academic envy. . . .": Author interview with Dennis Slattery.

61. "He wasn't promoting euthanasia. . . .": Author interview with Robert Sardello, November 2008.

62. "The only 'politic' course. . . .": Hillman letter "To the President From the Graduate Dean," March 22, 1980. This and other letters and minutes of meetings were in the University of Dallas Library archive, Hillman Collection, Box 183.

63. "Father David would start asking. . . .": Author interview with Gail Thomas, November 2008.

64. Faculty Senate: University of Dallas archives.

65. "feeling of failure I have. . . .": Hillman letter to Don Fredericksen, April 20, 1980, Fredericksen archive.

66. "A few of us on the faculty were outraged. . . .": Author interview with Hillman, October 2008.

67. Stella Rodriguez: Author interview.

68. "completely engaged in the Palace Revolution. . . .": Hillman letter to Rudolf Ritsema, May 13, 1980, Eranos archive.

69. "relieves tension. . . .": "UD president's resignation relieves tensions," *Dallas Times Herald*, May 29, 1980, University of Dallas Hillman archive.

70. The story of the events at the University of Dallas are derived, in part, from an article in the *Fort Worth Star-Telegram*, June 1, 1980, "UD struggling in program upheaval," found in the University of Dallas' archives.

71. "peremptorily dismissed by you. . . .": Hillman letter to Svetozar Pejovich, July 18, 1980, University of Dallas Archives.

72. "Ran into reef at university here. . . .": Hillman letter to JP Donleavy, August 4, 1980, Donleavy private archive.

73. "Yes we have had tremendous troubles. . . .": Hillman letter to Wolfgang Giegerich, postmarked July 28, 1980, Giegerich private archive.

74. "I am enjoying good health. . . ." Hillman letter to Rudolf Ritsema, May 13, 1980, Eranos archive.

75. "To control them, the board then. . . .": Author interview with Robert Sardello, November 2008.

76. "accommodate with the moral collapse. . . ." Undated, unaddressed letter by Hillman beginning, "About my position," in University of Dallas Hillman Collection, Box 183.

77. "the majority were there to study. . . .": Author interview with Randolph Severson, 2008.

78. "As a latecomer. . . .": Hillman letter to "Dear Mr. Perrier," January 8, 1981.

79. "Sad how quick it went. . . .": Hillman letter to Adolf Guggenbühl-Craig, December 18, 1980, Guggenbühl private archive.

80. "Losing the university, of course. . . .": Hillman letter to Rafael López-Pedraza, undated, López private archive.

81. "We lost. . . .": Hillman letter to David Miller, undated, Miller private archive.

82. "booted for leading a rebellion. . . .": Hillman letter to JP Donleavy, undated, Donleavy private archive.

83. "a wildness to the place. . . .": Author interview with Robert Romanyshyn, May 2006.

84. "an everyone thought the university might call. . . .": Author phone interview with John Tatum, February 2009.

85. "the dreadful condition of our world's intellectuals. . . .": Hillman letter to Rudolf Ritsema, October 17, 1979, Eranos archive.

86. "Kate seems to have reached a serenity. . . .": Letter from Anne Guggenbühl to Hillman, September 5, 1979, Hillman private archive.

87. Background on Kate going to Israel and the burial plot: Email to author from Laurence Hillman, December 20, 2017.

88. "That beautiful extraordinary woman. . . .": Hillman letter to JP Donleavy, Donleavy private archive.

89. "Eulogy for Kate," Jerusalem, Old City, October 28, 1980. Hillman private archive.

12

THE DALLAS INSTITUTE:
ANIMA MUNDI

"If the soul, as Plotinus says, is always an Aphrodite, then it is always concerned with beauty, and our aesthetic responses are evidence of the soul's active participation in the world. Our sense of beauty and ugliness draws us out, into the polis, activating us politically. Simply by noticing what is about us and responding to it with naïve recoil or desirous advance, we are involved. Our personal psyches are in tune with the presentation of the world's soul."

—*James Hillman,* Aesthetic Response
as Political Action, *1999.*

Hillman possessed, as Ed Casey once described it, "a very special form of courage, one that's hard to define because it doesn't fit in the typical categories. It's not military or moral courage in the usual sense. To him, it may seem perfectly natural. In Dallas, he had many friends among the wealthy and well-established, but he couldn't join the sybaritic or hedonistic life they lead or seem to lead. 'Diving into the wreck' is a phrase that Adrienne Rich called a collection of her poems, and that's what I think Jim does. Where other people would keep a distance, he dives into it."[1]

Randolph Severson saw in Hillman a "personal physical courage" as well, and recounted a story of what happened one day on an interstate highway in Missouri, where he was accompanying James and Pat to a conference when the car broke down. "There were no cell phones in those days, and we were stuck trying to figure out what to do. A car passed us going the other way carrying three or four black guys, then turned around and pulled over and parked about three car lengths in front of us. They all got out. You need to remember that black-white relationships were often still very volatile at that time. Jim sent Pat back into the car, and told me to go stand on the other side of the car. Then he walked right out to meet them. After a moment, they got back in their car and drove off. When Jim returned I asked him, 'What was that?' He shrugged and said, 'Oh, I don't know, just asking for directions, they were lost.' But I think his action disarmed them and earned their admiration. He performed a strategic second lieutenant-type decision."[2]

After the debacle at the university, Hillman and his colleagues would need all the strategy and courage they could muster. "Hillman was what UD pretended to be: cosmopolitan, international, world class,"[3] Severson has written. And Hillman left the university "restless, disappointed, angry, perhaps justifiably so, at UD's obtuseness—but nonetheless, re-oriented in outlook."[4]

When in 1980 those seven refugees from the university faculty gathered together in an empty old warehouse being pelted by rain, straddling crates and commiserating over what had happened, at first they figured the most they could probably do now was sit around and read their papers to one another. They went around the room, each person expressing themselves. "I remember Hillman said what he wanted was revenge," Robert Sardello recalled, with a smile.[5] Hillman, hearing of this remark in 2009, nodded affirmatively and added: "I wanted revenge on the philistines, on the church, on the business mind. This had been like a little Harvard in the middle of the desert, and they'd destroyed the possibility of this unique place. They didn't realize what was there—or who the Cowans were, exceptional people that don't come around often."[6]

Then, suddenly on that wet night in Dallas, Gail Thomas had walked in with an announcement. "Look!" she exclaimed, holding up a charter for a new organization that her lawyer husband had applied to the state for; it had arrived in the mail that afternoon. (It helped that Bob Thomas was head of the Dallas Bar Association). Hillman, Gail Thomas, Stroud, Sardello, and the Cowans were now to be Founding Fellows of a Dallas Institute of Humanities & Culture.

It had come about, fittingly enough, through the auspices of the woman who invented Liquid Paper. Her name was Betty Graham, a close friend of Gail's mother and once a legal secretary who got tired of erasing copies. Also a weekend artist, she'd come up with the idea of pouring liquid gesso into little jars and using it to white-out mistakes. Before long, other

The Jung Institute, Zürich

James Hillman in the doorway of his office
at Zeltweg 16.

Pat Berry

Marvin Spiegelman with his wife Ryma and
children.

© Robert Hinshaw

Adolf Guggenbühl-Craig

Rafael López-Pedraza

Rafael López-Pedraza and Valerie Donleavy, Einsiedeln, Switzerland (1992).

Valerie Donleavy with her typewriter at Spring House.

© Robert Hinshaw

Hillman at Spring House "Alchemy Evening."

After a Spring House softball game: (lying down) Pat Berry; (second row) James Hillman and Angie Wierwille; (third row) Murray Stein, Valerie Donleavy, and Mary Kaye Stein; (standing) Robert Hinshaw and Jonathan Wierwille.

Adam Diment standing on a table, with Audrey Haas, at Spring House gathering.

© Robert Hinshaw
Hillman holding forth at Spring House.

© Robert Hinshaw
(from left to right) student of Hillman, Hillman, and Dr. Joel Brence at Spring House.

Kate Hillman with their four children: (left to right) Julia, Laurence, Carola, and Susanne.

The four Hillman children: (left to right) Carola, Julia, Susanne, and Laurence.

Poster for the Terry Lectures, Yale University (1972).

Hillman exploring a Persian ruin, on a family trip to Iran (October 1972).

CASA ERANOS   CASA GABRIELLA   CASA SHANTI

Postcard of the Eranos houses along Lago Maggiore.

Hillman and Rudolf Ritsema at Eranos (1969).

Hillman at the "Puer Weekend" in Eranos (1971).

© Robert Hinshaw

Spring Journal editorial staff in front of Casa Gabriela at Eranos—with Lago Maggiore behind them—New Year's Day, 1972: (left to right) James Hillman, Pat Berry, Adam Diment, Valerie Donleavy, and Robert Hinshaw.

© Jan Marlan

Mary Watkins, Robbie Bosnak, Wolfgang Giegerich, and Nor Hall.

Hillman, Gilbert Durand, and Henry Corbin at Eranos.

Adolf Portmann and Kate Hillman at Eranos.

Hillman, Marianne New, and Adolf Portmann at Eranos.

Gershom Scholem and Catherine Ritesma, with David Miller, Rudolf Ritsema, and Hillman at Eranos.

Staff card for Hillman, University of Dallas.

The house at Routh Street and Hbernia, Dallas.

Attendees at first conference on archetypal psychology, University of Dallas (January 1977): (top row) Ed Casey, Rafael López-Pedraza, Richard A. Underwood, David Miller, Tom Kapacinskas, Charles Boer, Wes Churchman, Niel Micklem; (second row) Gail Thomas, Valerie Donleavy, Murray Stein, Charles Scott, Gordon Tappan, James Hillman, Pat Berry, Robert Bosnak, Robert Romanyshyn; (bottom row, seated) Mary Watkins, Stephanie de Voogd, Howard McConeghey, Paul Kugler, Joanne Stroud, Robert Sardello.

Hillman, Gail Thomas, and Robert Sardello.

Poet Robert Trammell with Hillman, Dallas.

Randolph Severson

Hillman in action.

Attendees at Ivan Illich Conference, Dallas Institute, 1982: (top row, left to right Tom Moore, Dennis Slattery, unidentified, Lyle Novinski, Mickey Bright, Robert Romanyshyn, Robert Sardello, Sven Doehner, Bill Burford; (second row) Randolph Severson, Robert Kugelman, Gordon Tappan, Louise Cowan, Don Cowan, Father Don Fisher; (third row) Wes Churchman, Brice Howard, Ann Patrick; (bottom row) Gail Thomas, Ivan Illich, Nor Hall, Joanne Stroud, unidentified.

Hillman delivering "Anima Mundi" lecture at the Pallazio Vecchio, Florence (October 1981).

Pat Berry and Hillman in Dallas.

Charles Boer and Hillman, on the balcony at Eranos.

James's mother, Madeleine, at his sixtieth birthday party in Thompson, Connecticut (April 1986).

Son Laurence tap-dancing with his father at the sixtieth birthday celebration.

© Paul Kugler
Hillman and Enrique Pardo at Eranos.

Hillman making a point at men's gathering, with Michael Meade on drum.

First multicultural men's conference in Buffalo Gap, West Virginia (May 1991). Hillman sitting front row, alongside Malidoma Patrice Somé, Robert Bly (pointing), and Michael Meade (next to Bly)

Enjoying the multicultural gathering: Hillman, Meade, Malidoma, and others.

Presenters and organizers at "Anima, Animal, Animation: A Conference on the Poetic and Bestial Faces of the Soul," Buffalo, New York (November 1980): (top row, left to right) Robert Duncan, Robert Creeley, David Miller, Tom Kapacinskas, Paul Kugler; (bottom row) Pat Berry, Patricia Cox-Miller, and Hillman.

Hillman, Robert Bly, and mythological scholar Joseph Campbell, sharing a stage in San Francisco (1981).

overworked women were knocking at her door. Graham and her son converted their garage and started selling a new product. She sold the company for $40 million the day before attending a conference on "Myth in Community," at which she approached Thomas and said: "I want you to dream a big dream. Let's meet in two weeks." Graham had formed two foundations to help innovative women found such things as a mid-city Institute to think about culture and ideas.[7]

Louise Cowan remembered: "We all talked excitedly of what an Institute could be about. My husband said it should be about language. Gail was already interested in the city and its structures. I was interested in the tradition the liberal arts carry on, particularly poetry; Sardello and Joanne in psychology. Of course, Jim was interested in *everything*."[8]

Sardello recollected that "to bring the imagination to bear on the difficulties of the world in the city was the major part of what we came up with. And not to be academic, but to begin to find other ways that were still public ways."[9] According to Hillman, "There was talk about affiliating but it never was a formal curriculum, and never offered a degree or certificate of any kind."[10] Nor would they be answerable any longer to a board like the university's which could pull the rug out from under them.

Gail Thomas had already been looking for a site to house the Dallas Institute and, within a week, a friend of her husband's called to say he'd found one. It was a gray Prairie-style place on Routh Street, only a block away from where Hillman and Pat lived—"a wonderful old house surrounded by trees, and just rich with stories and culture," Thomas recalled. "It was amazing. But we had no money, so I had to sign a personal year's lease. Then a friend who was in the Center for Civic Leadership program made a donation of $25,000, and that's what we used for a down payment. We put a group together of ten couples who bought the house over a ten-year period, after which we donated it to the Dallas Institute."[11]

The Institute proclaimed itself dedicated to "awakening a sense of sacredness in the world." Hillman, however, discussed

its inauspicious beginnings with a touch of sarcasm in one letter: "The new institute may give us new focus for our alienation and allow our civic hatred to manifest in a Swiftian mode."
In another letter, this one to López, he added a more realistic
tone: "We are trapped in Dallas for a while. It is terribly lively
here. Our Institute is like Zürich in the old days . . . but there
is no money for it, no one of the power structure cares about
it, even though we are already notorious in the city. What we
are attempting is a 'revolution from above'—affecting a citystyle
from above—since there is no way to do anything here from
below."

Thomas became the Institute's director, merging her Center
for Civic Leadership into it. "Gail had a tough row to hoe,"
recalled one of the Institute's followers. "She was trying to
bridge the moneyed Dallas world and her intellectual interests,
and she got flack from all sides." Hillman would now teach
classes at the Institute, with Joanne Stroud continuing to pay his
stipend. He rented from Thomas a new space there to house
Spring Publications, and soon was giving talks to numerous
groups around the city. "For a couple of years," Thomas said,
"we were always just taking him off for events and to meet people too. I just booked him all over, whenever I could, to speak to
the community of churches, the real estate people. I think this
helped solidify and give him a new field to mine."

As Hillman wrote to Wolfgang Giegerich in Germany:
"My psyche is more and more in the world, differentiating the
'unconscious' there . . . a curiously dense area . . . But both Pat
and I are feeling 'very alive' as they say. For once, I seem to own
my own time."

RE-VISIONING THE CITY

Dallas by 1980 was ranked the nation's seventh largest city (then
at 900,000-plus residents), when innovative planning came to
the fore. Bryan Place, for example, was a bold effort by one

developer to pioneer an intimate, neighborly community in the East Dallas inner city—attractive homes, minimal traffic, and pedestrian-friendly streets.

For a seminar on "Imagining Dallas," Hillman wrote a speech called *City Limits*. Images, he noted, provide limits; but in a place where "the sky's the limit," where there was "nothing to come up against that turns us back on ourselves—total availability, endless action to the horizon, the spirit of Texas space," what do you do? He drew a comparison with psychotherapy: "We are always very careful with a person's void and empty place, his or her feeling of nothingness." And he spoke of how one shouldn't rush in to fill the space with programs, but ought to "let the emptiness imagine itself out." Perhaps this meant "that the greatest drawbacks of Dallas are its blessings in disguise . . . the natural emptiness, flatness and aridity of geography becomes a perpetual challenge to which we continually imagine new responses. Trees, lakes, landscaping emerge from within their arid absence. The cultural dearth leads to intensification of cultural fervor." The desolation of downtown at evening, at "its 5:00 o'clock shadow," could yet "draw our city's greatest efforts of creative imagining . . .

"And last, the very hugeness of the metroplex reminds us of the value of intimacy, personal relations, knowing each other. The social formalities of Dallas give it form: fashion, manners, style in speech, rhythm, respect for the heart's charm, grace—these belong to the image of Dallas and provide definite patterns and limits." In the heart of its citizens is "where the future of the city resides."

In finding that future, some also saw the importance of preserving the past. Atop the eastern roofline of the Old Red (renamed the Dallas County) Courthouse, remained a series of now-crumbling terracotta gargoyles dating back to the building's origin in 1892. Large winged mythological griffin, the gargoyles gazed down upon Dealey Plaza, the site where President Kennedy had been assassinated. Perhaps, since gargoyles are thought to ward off evil, the city fathers didn't want to see this simply fall into oblivion. They sent the fractured gargoyles to an artist's studio in Hoboken, New Jersey, where the terracotta would be cast in fiberglass and replicated. The commission called for the sculptor's girlfriend, a painter, to develop the precise baked earth color of the original.

The sculptor and his artist girlfriend then flew together to Dallas for the installation. Her name was Margot McLean. Less than two miles to the north, and less than a decade away from when they would meet, James Hillman had begun "imagining Dallas" at the new Dallas Institute of Humanities and Culture.

For the Institute, Gail Thomas flew to Toronto five times to court a very shy Jane Jacobs, the urban-planning writer renowned for her book *The Death and Life of Great American Cities*. Jacobs' mentor, William H. ("Holly") Whyte (author of *The Organization Man*, a classic 1956 study of postwar suburbia), also came out to discuss Dallas' city design. So did architect Christopher Alexander, author of *A New Theory of Urban Design*.

Each May, Thomas organized an annual conference titled "What Makes a City?" The idea was to bring together philosophers, poets, and architects, and mix archetypal psychology with urban development. During the first three years (1982–1984), the events bore the titles: "Architecture and Poetry," "The Economics of Taste," and "Water and Dreams." Jim Lehrer, later a renowned newscaster with PBS and at the time a political reporter in Dallas, participated along with African American novelist Albert Murray (a specialist in jazz), British poet and William Blake scholar Kathleen Raine, Norwegian architectural historian Christian Norberg-Schulz, and cultural critic Ivan Illich. All these mingled on panels with Hillman, the Cowans, Sardello, and Thomas.

Those yearly gatherings would kick off with a weekend retreat at a dude ranch owned by a local Congressman, Jim Collins, about thirty miles outside of town. "It had a hot tub, which were big in the Eighties," Thomas remembered. "All the guests would give papers. On the last night, we'd invite the mayor and other civic leaders out, then give a public conference at the Dallas Public Library the next day, to present the best of what we'd come up with."[12]

It was cutting-edge stuff, "bringing something to Dallas that the city had no experience with," said Stroud. Dallas had been "a blank canvas," as Thomas Moore recalled Hillman describing it to him: "Would Boston invite us in to talk to their city council about putting in a lake? I don't think so."[13] Yet at the Dallas Institute's Wednesday evening free lectures, people would pack the place, even standing on the stairways or outside listening through the windows. As Stroud remembered: "Dallas, it seemed to me, had always been very much of an island, keeping the world out as much as possible. I think we opened things up a lot, although Robert Sardello used to always say, 'We keep trying to plant these seeds, but the soil is so shallow here, it's hard to make them grow.'"[14]

Lyle Novinski, the university landscape architect/artist who also became one of the Institute's fellows, recalled some of the seed-planting producing dramatic results. "Holly" Whyte was brought to town during a controversy over a downtown mall park where it was thought "the unsightly people" might congregate. Yet, according to Novinski, Whyte convinced an assembly of building owners and architects that his work in New York "showed that such civic places were enormously attractive, while empty plazas killed business. At the time, it was illegal to eat outdoors in Dallas and you couldn't even sell anything outdoors that wasn't wrapped in cellophane. Gail, Whyte, and the Institute succeeded in getting the City Council to change the law. So today you have sidewalk vendors, and at lunchtime a thousand people eat outdoors on those plazas."[15]

As Hillman told a reporter for the *Dallas Downtown News* in 1982, his conception of the ideal city was "a place where intense conversation is going on that is not useful" (expressed with "a mischievous smile," the article noted). He wasn't opposed to growth, but urged questioning about whether to tear down old buildings: "A building is a concrete embodiment of memory, and the mind lives in places." "Dallas is an invention," Hillman went on. "It is not here because of its geography, but because the city fathers were able to get the railroad to come through. It is part of the fabric of Dallas that there's no reason for it to exist geographically. It's not really true of course, because the Trinity River was a port here. But the fable is what's important, not whether it's so or not. And the fable is that this city exists only as a mental event. It starts off with the mind; it starts off with enterprise. So it has a huge potential for mental life, and that's what one wants to see here. It could be marvelous. So far it isn't fulfilled. But it could be. It could be." [16]

Toward this end, Hillman had lunch several times with architect James Pratt.[17] A large-boned, handsome man with a no-holds-barred reputation around town, Pratt built luxury homes, managed construction for the Dallas Museum of Art, spent twenty years doing core projects for developer Trammell Crow "and seven years consulting about how to pull the State Fair of Texas out of the swamp." Two years younger than Hillman, Pratt's home was only a few blocks from his. There were other parallels between the two men. In 1953, the same year Hillman arrived in Zürich, Pratt had gone there also, "to stay twelve months in the attic of a prime architectural philosopher. So I was not far away from the Jungians, but not part of it." Later he would travel to Egypt, Greece, and India, and "spend three months in Japan living in temples."

Pratt recalled in an interview: "I didn't fully understand the character of what I was doing now, until Jim Hillman came along." Thomas had invited him to hear Hillman deliver a lecture at the Institute on "Walking." Pratt said he "had just recently finished a little project for a shopping center, where I'd organized everything for walking and more or less shielded from the automobile. He reinforced my actions nicely."

Pratt had also set about creating a boulevard to try to ease the way in which traffic worked through the city. "I wanted to emphasize cross streets that were important. Jim made the suggestion that I have some large image sculptures at those intersections that could be seen from a distance, which would allow you to know where you were and make a turn with more ease."

Over their lunches, Pratt said, Hillman "always gave me fresh insights: how to relate soul to depth in architecture, how to relate history to it, how to relate reflection. All those things are part of what I do as an architect. For one thing, you keep clear of the profit motive being the prime goal. You organize it to include these other qualities, such as face-to-face, eye and body contact. You organize it to try to give the city a view of itself that's more than just a shabby bunch of buildings."

Pratt later put together a book, *Dallas Visions*, funded by a large grant from the National Endowment for the Humanities and which Dallas developer John Tatum said "ultimately became a vision for a 25-year master plan in the city."[18] What Pratt sought to embody in his work was reflected in what Hillman once spoke of in a Dallas lecture about moisture: "The moisture that gives pleasure to the soul is the flow of life, of people, of juices, of ourselves crowded with dreams, our streets pleromatic, full of folk."[19]

Hillman gained a position on the civic committee that dealt with bus transportation. Asked whether the city fathers were nonplussed by his ideas or receptive to them, Stroud responded: "Well, he can sometimes say outrageous things for the shock value, and does have a sort of mischievous sense of humor. But I always felt that was good for our community."[20]

Thomas made sure that Hillman met all the city's movers-and-shakers, from tycoon Ross Perot to real estate developer Trammell Crow. He even had lunch once at the exclusive Petroleum Club. While he appreciated Gail and Joanne's "wonderful Renaissance idea" that the Institute could impact the city, he personally "always felt very estranged from those people."[21] According to Thomas, "I think he loved it, and yet he's so opposed to so much of what they stand for."[22] The way Randolph Severson saw it, "because it was very much the city's elite, I don't think he could ever really fit comfortably in the role that his imagination placed him, as a kind of Renaissance Humanist lecturing the leaders of the *polis*."[23]

Hillman was more at ease bringing together poets like Robert Duncan with Dallas' own Robert Trammell and Gerald Burns, or setting up a performance by a new friend, Enrique Pardo of France's Roy Hart Theatre. Thomas arranged one workshop with Hillman and Ivan Illich, the charismatic critic of modern Western culture who became a Fellow of the Institute. Ron Schenk, then a student of Hillman's who was in the audience, recalled that "it turned out to be a dialogue between them, with amazing ideas firing back and forth across the room. Afterwards I heard Gail say, 'This is really the ultimate, this is what I've been living for.'"[24]

These were "the golden days," as described independently by all three of the triumvirate of women (Thomas, Stroud, and Cowan) without whom none of this would have happened—overflowing with new ideas and remarkable conversations.

DOWN-HOME DALLAS

Many evenings after a lecture at the Institute, a group would walk the short block to James and Pat's house and talk far into the night. Hillman did much of the cooking at the get-togethers. There were even Sunday afternoon softball games, another tradition Hillman had carried over from the Spring House days in Zürich. A number of Hillman's friends and colleagues from elsewhere would often show up in Dallas, finding themselves somewhat in awe of what was transpiring. As Guggenbühl wrote Hillman after one trip from Zürich: "I am still profiting from my stay in the United States, especially Dallas. I think about the things and the people I saw and meditate over the opinions and insights I heard . . . It has something extremely uplifting."

Kathleen Raine, the poet and Blake scholar from London, wrote Hillman upon her return home: "The time at Dallas was most valuable, certainly to myself, in meeting and exchanging ideas with the group you have assembled in the Institute. I hope it was effective in the way you had intended also—moving the cement and glass mountain of Dallas! But Dallas is after all the very type and symbol of all that in the 1980s somehow has to be moved and I am filled with admiration for the work you have taken upon yourselves."[25]

Hillman looked back upon it all rather simply, saying: "I like being with similar spirits. A small group where the eros is very alive among the people. We had that in Dallas. We listened to each other, we fed each other."[26]

Joseph Cambray was drawn to Dallas because of Hillman. Formerly a successful chemistry researcher and later a Jungian analyst with practices in Boston and Providence (elected President in 2008 of the International Association for Analytical Psychology), Cambray ran the bookstall at the Dallas Institute meetings. He even typed Pat's dissertation for her on a huge computer that the Institute had put in one of its rooms. "Because Hillman was there," said Cambray, "a group of scholars came through from around the world—people like David Tacey and Peter Bishop and Ralph Maud."[27]

Thomas remembered that when López and Valerie Donleavy would fly in from Venezuela, staying with Hillman and Pat for a couple of weeks at a time, "we would party *every* night. It was raucous. We'd just sit on the floor and drink beer and wine or whatever." Pat's recollection was that "after Jim went to bed, I'd stay up and dance and drink and carouse with everybody." Severson remembered, "He would excuse himself at 10 o'clock or thereabouts, just as the evening was getting rolling, and go to bed." (Hillman maintained "it's because after ten o'clock, I get tired and begin to hate everybody for disturbing my rest. So instead of staying up and getting into all kinds of nonsense, I disappear.")[28] Severson, an early riser, would sometimes come by his house before dawn. "It would be pitch-black, and I'd see the lighted window on that second floor, and I knew he was up and working. My impression was, the work was really everything and all else was secondary." [29]

Sven Doehner, who heard stories of the Spring House years, said that "some of us tried to recreate that for ourselves." One night, when he was enlisted by Hillman as a waiter and serving Guggenbühl a beer, he recalled the Swiss psychiatrist looking at him and asking sardonically, "Would you like to be a butcher?" Doehner replied, "Why a butcher? I don't think so." Guggenbühl shrugged and said, "Well, you're not going to make a very good psychoanalyst then."

According to Doehner, "It was the Dallas way of life—the back porch, the barbecues—but it often felt like a medieval or Platonic dialogue. I mean, within that Texas environment, the level of discourse was unbelievable."[30] For example, Ed Casey remembered "a free-wheeling conversation around the color blue. It started with my just looking at the wall of his dining room—a deep, very distinctive blue—and being very struck by it. I said something like, 'How in the world did you choose this?' and soon we were pursuing the question of what it is for *anything* to be blue. We spent a whole evening, hour upon hour, in the discussion. It was memorable because we both really got into it, in a way we never would have done on our own. Jim went on to write wonderful things on the alchemical nature of blue; I'd like to believe it came out of that night."[31]

Sardello said that the evenings in Hillman's and Pat's living room were "where my thinking was transformed, just by getting together and working through a certain theme. It was always this kind of turning things upside down and inside out." Thomas recalled that Hillman was also "fascinated with Robert's thought. On one of the blurbs for Robert's book, he wrote: 'I've thieved from his mind for many years.' I think he did in some cases. And then we all thieved from Jim."[32]

According to Thomas Moore, then a professor of religion at Southern Methodist University and later the author of numerous popular books with archetypal themes, Sardello "could give things a *gravitas* they may not have had otherwise, although his imagination can fly in all directions all the time. He was at a party once at my house in Dallas, when a woman came up to me and said, 'I'm a little worried about a friend of yours over there—he's talking about the soul of the air conditioner.' I said, 'Don't worry, that's just Sardello.' We gave talks together more than once at computer conferences, which were just beginning to happen. I remember mine being on medieval theology and Sardello talking on the soul of the computer. I also remember audiences storming out of the place, because he was really *out* there."[33]

At a lecture Hillman delivered on "Interiors in the Design of the City: The Ceiling,"[34] he discussed the "remarkable, thought-provoking paper" Sardello had given at an Institute retreat on Architecture and Poetry. In it, Sardello "examined the place of the right angle in the design of modern cities. He pointed out that the right angle is an abstract expression for the ancient archetypal directions of heaven and earth, Sky God and Earth Mother, the vertical and horizontal dimensions reduced to a simple pair of intersecting lines, much like the tool used by carpenters, the square, the Greek word for which is *norma* (from which we have norms, normal, normalcy)."

Normalcy was definitely not the watchword for the poets, "all of whom came to the Institute because of Jim," according to Thomas. One was William Burford, whose mother was a Shamrock Oil heiress and grew up in The Mansion, today the most exclusive hotel in Dallas—"the ne'er-do-well son who needed to have a trust put in his name, because he was a poet."[35] Another was Gerald Burns, a graduate of Dublin's Trinity College (fifteen years after Hillman attended), considered a leading practitioner of long-lined, thickly-textured verse; "a fantastic scholar and unique genius," according to Hillman. Pat remembered that people from the Institute, including herself, provided Burns support money every month. Every day when he finished a new poem, he'd come knock on the door and hand it to her. He also helped edit some of her papers.

A third poet was Robert Trammell, a fifth generation Texan—former fry cook, carpenter, bartender, and taxi driver who spent a year in jail for possession of marijuana—with whom James became good friends. Tall and lean, long haired and bearded, Trammell looked like a cross between a cowboy and a biker. Largely self-taught, he was considered "the essential, grass-roots poet in Dallas," as onetime Texas poet laureate Jack Myers put it. Trammell's epic, *The Book of Fire*, filled eight volumes and was based upon "philosophical alchemy, the idea of turning something base into something better."[36]

Interacting with Trammell could be challenging. Thomas recounted: "I think the Institute was seen originally by Robert Trammell and Gerald Burns as effete and breathing too rarefied air. Our dark side—'they're all full of themselves over there.' Because we were, we really were. I mean, we thought we had a cause and a mission and understood things in a new way, and we were fervent. So someone just off the street might walk in and turn right back around. But Jim had a way of bringing people in, and one night I was giving a talk on our imagination theories. It was much too long—I can't believe we used to do this to people, an hour and fifteen minutes reading a paper! Mine specifically was on the transformation of Paris after they took out its heart, the Les Halles market. As I'm reading along, I hear a voice saying, 'What in the hell is she *talkin'* about!' Louise was sitting in the front row and she said, 'Gail, just keep going, just keep going.' So I did. 'What is she *sayin'*!' the voice came again. Just as drunk as he could be. That was Robert Trammell." (Hillman remembered Trammell hollering out "Bullshit!" more than once).

According to Thomas, "A friend went over and took him by the scruff of his neck out to the porch, and I continued. Well, we all ended up that night over at Jim and Pat's. And I sat on the floor and talked to Robert Trammell with a beer in *my* hand. We became good friends, and his second wife Adrienne was my employee at the Institute, which is where they met."[37]

SHADOW-LAND

*"Idea for a course: Subjectivism . . . How the West Was
Lost in Subjectivism: birth of ego for Augustine's confessions
through Descartes, for it is the promise of an Ego that con-
quered the world (not West. Technology) and that we must
now yield up."*

—*James Hillman, in an undated letter to
David Miller sent from the Dallas Institute.*

Amid all the inspired moments and camaraderie, the wolf was
never far from the door. Ronald Reagan, the B-movie actor,
had been elected America's president just as the Dallas Institute
was forming. In a letter to López not long after, Hillman wrote:
"Reagan runs the country, and the people love it. They do not
want messyboy [Jimmy] Carter, they want a fake actor who says
what they expect according to the script. It is slowly a military
regime. Everything is showbusiness, including showbusiness
itself which has invented itself into a certain style. This is the
most interesting phenomenon of the age, not technology but
the new mode of imagining oneself and others and the world as
'show': all the world a stage."[38]

Such thoughts were elaborated on in a talk that Hillman
delivered in Dallas called "On Show Business Ethics," a topic
he believed was "one of the most important of our times. If
politics and government, terrorism, peace and war, popular religion and the High Church, starvation and revolution, as well as
the models for how to be a person in looks, gesture, voice, and
word derive from and depend on media images, then we must
consider the principles that govern the rights and wrongs of the
media; i.e., are there ethics in show business, and if so, what are
they?"

At the very beginning of the Reagan era, what Hillman saw
through remains remarkably prescient. "When P. T. Barnum
supposedly said that 'a sucker is born every minute,' he was

referring to us, for we are each suckers. Each of us 'falls' to show-biz. And why? Isn't there in us each a desire for living theater, to see myth enacted, to enter the illusions and delusions of suspension of disbelief? We want to be taken in just as we want the delusions and illusions of falling in love. We are suckers for the power of the mask."

Among a list of his reflections, item seven reads: "Therefore, erotic behavior has another ethic and other taboos than the conventional attitudes of usual morality. Sexual life is also depersonalized. The 'out-there' dominates: looks, earning power, fame. The clothing consultant, cosmetician, and hairdresser replace the advisor and confessor . . . Sexual relations are part of the set, the deal, and the play."

Toward the end of the list, Hillman said: "The old ethics, with its heroic insistence upon the lone individual who went inside himself to make his moral choices, never grasped the nature of the mask. So moralists of the old school, and Europeans especially, can't read our President. They want to know who he really is, what he really thinks behind the showman. But there is nothing there behind . . . The President is false only when we regard him through the false lens that conceives a man apart from a mask."[39]

Despite its well-intentioned founders and followers, the Dallas Institute was, of course, not immune to this syndrome. Hillman wrote to López in 1981: "Here is the letter paper of our new Institute. It is a bit highflying a bit inflating. The people here do not understand inflation and its horrors. It is the city of assassination. They are not neurotic here, only psychopathic and psychotic. The gun is the instrument of psychopathy and psychosis—neurotics are not gun people. Did you know that Richard Speck who killed all the nurses about 12 years ago in Chicago, was also a Dallas lad?"[40]

To Ritsema, Hillman wrote: "Dallas is the place of assassination, like an ancient city of bloodguilt, a shadow that no one here wants to see."[41]

In another letter, he added: "Dallas does *not worry*. It acts out. No one is Jewish or Italian or torn to pieces by internal conflicts.

No Woody Allens here. It's acted in the world. Conversion in Church. Guns in the car pocket. Shoot the husband. Shoot the son. Drink like a fish. All pre-psychological. Murder. Perversion in the sense of dressing up."[42]

Hillman saw through it all, but being in the midst of it still carried its internal price, particularly in the aftermath of Kate's death. "My depressions were worse this winter than ever," he wrote López. "Very sudden and very suicidally sharp, and then gone in a moment. Like a Mars madness. Iron. Not connected with overwork and hyperactivity, but more with rigidity and iron. Actually, I had a peaceful not hurried winter."[43]

By the summer of 1981, things were even worse: "If you just sit in your room as I do, with the air conditioner on, and the deadly sunlight, and the heat, and the emptiness, you go cabin-crazy as they call it here. A ironlike, rustlike bitter willful aggressive depression. A senex hatred . . . a paralysis. Dreadful. Unbearable and several times suicidal. Writing does keep one free of it . . . but only when it flows . . . eating helps too. And wine, otherwise nothing but talking, and shopping."[44]

Yet he always seemed to create from such depths, and this time was no exception. Indeed, his therapeutic practice had become uplifting for a change. James and Pat both saw patients in different rooms of their house, who entered through different doors and left by separate exits, so that they never saw each other—even though in reality the patients were very intertwined. Sardello had started out as Hillman's patient, then started working with Pat. In exchange, Sardello served as an adviser for her thesis on the aesthetics of doing analysis.

Joanne Stroud, who stayed in analysis with Hillman, said he "was always challenging me to not stay stuck someplace, to move on. When I wrote a book called *The Bonding of Will and Desire*, he kept saying, 'Now what do you mean by will, is that ego?' He forced me into defining, made me figure it out."[45] Gail Thomas analyzed with Hillman and was close friends with Pat.

Hillman wrote at the time: "I love working with patients here. No trainees, no students. Only a few cases, that are cases. Old ex alcoholic bachelor man. Crazy young ex airline hostess woman who sees auras, my salesman of swimming pools, everybody incurable . . . and the work goes well . . . best thing I do in Dallas is therapy. Even if it is very little of it."[46]

"RETURN OF SOUL TO THE WORLD"

Hillman was able to break away in the summer and return to his European "roots." "We stayed a very long time in Europe," Hillman wrote to Jane Pratt in the autumn of 1981. "I was there ten weeks, and Pat about six. It was a marvelous time being able to withdraw to the place at Eranos and get a good deal of writing done. We were both extremely happy—it felt like 'stolen days.'"

His work during this period included three Eranos lectures ("Thought of the Heart," "Imagination of Air," and "Animal Kingdom") and several other long, scholarly pieces. In 1980, he published in the *Spring Journal*, "Silver and the White Earth, Part One"; in 1981, "Alchemical Blue and the Unio Mentalis"; and in another publication, "Salt: A Chapter in Alchemical Psychology." "These were as deep and scholarly and compli-cated as anything," Hillman said. "Which was strange, because it's almost like a retreat from the whole [Dallas realm]. Especially the silver pieces, which were really complex."[47]

While in southern Switzerland the first summer after the establishment of the Dallas Institute, Hillman also began writ-ing a landmark essay he would come to call, "Anima Mundi: Return of the Soul to the World." From Ascona, Hillman wrote to Donleavy: "Now I go to Florence where I give a major paper in the big ol Palazzo Vecchio—best building in the world they say—and I'm reading it out in Italian. I've been practicing—and still I sound like Chico Marx with a Jersey City Italian accent. Well, I'll wear a blue suit."[48]

Pat Berry recalled Hillman taking lessons in the language. "He had somebody translate his speech into Italian and then he worked with her, learning enough to read his paper in Italian and do some responding. He was good at languages."[49] But it didn't necessarily come easily. As he later wrote to his poet friend Charles Boer (tongue in cheek) about his efforts learning Italian, "Each night, like tonight, I work on getting my cheeks loose and tongue agile for wrapping around such phrases as *e un dispiegarsi di forme imagistiche* . . . It's the ending 'e's that are hard for me for I sound them like French, while all the rest I sound like Pavarotti or Chico Marx . . . I fear being egged and tomatoed for sounding Roman in Florence, or worse, Neopolitan, when actually it's Jersey City USA."[50]

The October 1981 lecture was sponsored primarily by the city of Florence and its local university. Pat had already returned to Dallas from Zürich. Hillman, not anticipating what an event it would be, hadn't thought of inviting any of his family. It would turn out to be, in fact, as momentous an occasion as the Terry Lectures delivered at Yale nine years earlier. As those had marked the genesis of his pioneering book *Re-visioning Psychology*, the Florentine talk heralded another step in archetypal psychology—a step toward a depth psychology of the outer world, a cultural psychology.

The idea of a "world soul," *anima mundi* as Neo-Platonic philosophy once espoused it, was new to contemporary psychology. Jung had introduced the concept of the collective unconscious, that the individual psyche lives inside a larger realm that is also ensouled. Jung's therapeutic emphasis, however, remained focused on the self and the process of individuation. To Hillman, this was missing an essential truth that soul lives beyond the interiority of subjectivity, is in fact in everything including "man-made things of the street." We are *in it*, this *anima mundi*, and it thus demands attention beyond our private dramas. As he had journeyed south to Dallas to begin formulating it, now in the European "south" of Mediterranean Italy would come its first full articulation. Hillman called it at the time an "attempt to restore Florentine psychology (Ficino) to the mainstream of thought."

He wore a blue coat and khaki trousers to the all-day affair in the Palazzo Vecchio. This massive, fortress-like Romanesque building crowned by the Arnolfo Tower dates to the thirteenth century and is the most important civic monument in Florence, still serving as its town hall. Hillman described it as "that amazing building that seems Kabbalistically rooted in the air."[51] Hillman would speak in the tapestry-covered Great Hall. "In come the Gonfalones," he wrote to Rafael and Valerie, "men dressed in Renaissance vivid costumes with huge hats, carrying great banner and silver trumpets. Blow trumpets. Some people stand up thinking it is a mass. They leave." (To Wolfgang Giegerich, he wrote: "They blew silver trumpets, so now I do not have to go to heaven.")

"I am introduced and given the medal of the city (silver in a box . . .). Six hundred people in the room . . . two hundred on their feet . . . not enough chairs. The Roman Jungians prowling and scowling like leopards, hating it, envious, enraged that it was done without them, and not real Jungian psychology . . .

"Then I stood up to talk. First time I had a tremor in the hands. Very difficult to do because I had promised to do it in Italian as a gesture. So I gave my paper that had been translated for me for one hour and twenty minutes in almost faultless Italian. I had practiced a great deal to get the rhythms and the accents and the intonations . . . and came off OK, though toward the end I felt like Mohammed Ali in the eleventh round being hit and hit and hit and covering the body to keep standing up. Exhaustion . . . especially because I had to embody each word with my presence (for that is what a good lecture is . . . the embodiment of the words . . . but in a foreign language, very difficult.)"[52]

Hillman said near the beginning of his talk that he had come there to "speak as a psychologist, a son of soul, speaking to psyche. To say 'son of soul' is to speak in a Renaissance, Florentine mode, following Marsilio Ficino who was the first to place the soul in the center of his vision, a vision which excludes nothing of the world's affairs because the psyche includes the world—all things offer soul."[53]

The starting point for this psychological renaissance was "in psychopathology, in the actualities of the psyche's own suffering." And he soon quoted from his "colleague and friend in Dallas, Robert Sardello," who had written: "The individual presented himself in the therapy room of the nineteenth century, and during the twentieth the patient suffering breakdown is the world itself. The new symptoms are fragmentation, specialization, expertise, depression, inflation, loss of energy, jargonese, and violence. Our buildings are anorexic, our business paranoid. Our technology manic."

Now depth psychology had to come out of denial "after one hundred years of the solitude of psychoanalysis . . . Not only my pathology is projected onto the world, the world is inundating me with its unalleviated suffering." In a decaying marriage, one needed to consider also "the materials and design of the rooms in which the marriage is set, the language in which it is spoken, the clothing in which it is presented, the food and money that are shared, the drugs and cosmetics used, the sounds and smells and tastes that daily enter the heart of that marriage."

It was a call for a "new sense of psychic reality" where business could be borderline, consumption narcissistic, agriculture bulimic. In another unspoken allusion to Dallas: "To call a building 'catatonic' or 'anorexic' means to examine the way it presents itself, its behavioral display in its skinny, tall, rigid, bare-boned structure, trimmed of fat, its glassy front and desexualized coldness and suppressed explosive rage, its hollow atrium interior sectioned by vertical shafts."

What was needed was a response from the heart, the awakening of "an aesthetic response to the world." A move "southward," yes even bodily so, moving "the seat of the soul from brain to heart and the method of psychology from cognitive understanding to aesthetic sensitivity. With the heart we move at once into imagination." He did not mean beautifying things like planting sidewalk trees or clipping hedges. Rather, it's something "closer to an animal sense of the world—a nose for the displayed intelligibility of things, their sound, smell, shape, speaking to and through our heart's reactions."

The aim is not the resurrection of man, but the restoration of the world, using a "larger sense of therapy [that] begins in the smaller acts of noticing" the once-mundane. "That vast insensate edifice—the doctrine of a soulless world—now streaked with acid rain and stained by graffiti has, in our fantasies, already exploded into dust. Yet that cataclysm, that pathologized image of the world destroyed, is awakening again recognition of the soul in the world. The *anima mundi* stirs our hearts to respond . . . The things of the world again become precious, desirable, and even pitiable in their millennial suffering from Western humanity's hubristic insult to material things."

This was *not* part of "the tradition from which psychotherapy believes it stems: eighteenth-century enlightenment and nineteenth-century science." A return to an earlier tradition was required, back to the Greeks and the Renaissance, and found in isolated streams of later thought such as the American Transcendentalists—. to refill "the emptied sense of our words" with "concrete images, our talk, an animal talk, echoing the world."

In this pivotal essay, Thomas Moore would note in his commentary on a selection of Hillman's writings that he edited (*A Blue Fire*), Hillman moved "even farther from ego-psychology and personalism." Henceforth, "His writing takes on concreteness and context that were implied in previous works. Now he studies gardens, waterworks, streets, buildings, show business, bombs, racism, ecology, work, education, and architecture."[54]

Moore added in his commentary: "The temptation always is to deal with social ills from the spirit: find out what is going on, develop a plan of attack, and get it under control. Hillman's way is to take the labyrinthine way of the soul, to find a cure by entering into the symptom with unrelenting imagination . . . On one hand, he invites planners, designers, and social and political activists to regard themselves as imaginative psychologists, even as therapists of soul. On the other, he counsels the professional therapist to move into the street where, Hillman claims, today's major unconsciousness now lies."[55]

According to Ed Casey, "We all recognized this as a radical turning point. It was, philosophically, a move toward realism, toward the notion that the mind—important, interesting, and inspiring as it is—is not where the action is ultimately. It still is caught up in the web of subjective identity, what matters to *me*. I think this came together with his experience of America and seeing where subjective idealism had ended disastrously, in a self-serving collective narcissism—entertainment values, pleasure values, all of that. Especially in Dallas, he saw the full force of this. In New York or other more sophisticated places, it might have been harder to detect."[56]

Dallas had provided not Southern comfort, but a road-map into a psychoanalysis of—and for—the street.

THOMAS MOORE

Dallas also marked the beginning of Hillman's long collaborative friendship with Thomas Moore. Some years later, in 1992, Moore would publish *Care of the Soul*, a book that would spend weeks at the top of the *New York Times* bestseller list and be described by one reviewer as "a clearer, more direct translation of Hillman's ideas."[57] Moore had discovered those ideas while spending a dozen years as a monk in a Catholic religious order, collecting the essays Hillman was then publishing in Europe, and initiating a correspondence while a student of David Miller's at Syracuse.

Moore was fourteen years younger than Hillman, but the two men had much in common. Moore's forbears came from Ireland, and he spent two years there in his religious order's monastic school of philosophy. In Dublin, the Director of the National Gallery, Thomas McGreevy, was once an intimate of Joyce, Beckett, Yeats, and Lawrence, and had taken the young Moore under his wing. As Hillman often had, Moore followed an invisible *daimon*—deciding to leave the seminary six months short of being ordained—which then led him to Syracuse and David Miller a year before Hillman taught there, then to Dallas and Hillman himself.

Moore had reviewed *Re-Visoning Psychology* and introduced Hillman at an April 1977 conference on Jung at Notre Dame University, where Hillman gave two lectures on archetypal psychology. Moore had already written an article for *Spring Journal* called "Music in Therapy," by which he (a composer himself) meant the musical *qualities* of doing therapy—a "music without sound," an attempt to de-literalize the arts.[58] As Moore introduced himself to Hillman: "The very first words out of James' mouth were: 'No violins.'" (Meaning, according to Moore, that life itself is musical).

When Hillman ended up in Dallas, Moore had just begun teaching religious studies there at Southern Methodist University (SMU). They quickly struck up a friendship. "I learn so much from your spontaneous reflections on things," Moore wrote Hillman in 1980, and "thoroughly enjoy your company. There aren't too many people I know who keep me in touch with my Seat of Laughter steadily, and you're one of them . . . I hope we have more opportunities this year to sit around drinking wine discussing the differences between virginals and virgins."

Moore added: "SMU has stopped giving me anything except security." He'd been having difficulties at the school for a while, especially since associating with the Hillman crowd. The religion department's chair, Lonnie Kliever, was interested in Hillman's work but, according to Moore, very suspicious of its "rounded edges, he didn't like that style." Moore recalled, when he was still the up-and-comer at SMU, Hillman once told him: "'The soul always loses.' He wanted to warn me that, if I stayed with this work and close to him, he didn't expect I could survive there."

In the Bible Belt, where homilies were the accepted form of instruction, Moore's psychological approach to religion didn't sit well for long. When he was denied tenure at SMU because of his unorthodox ideas, Sardello remembered how Moore felt "totally bereft and didn't know what he was going to do." That was when Moore began a series of lectures at the Dallas Institute that became his first book (*Rituals of the Imagination*). He was soon part of the inner circle. A dream group consisting of Moore, Sardello, and Thomas, along with Hillman and Pat, began meeting once a week. Another group gathered regularly to discuss the import of various fairy tales. Moore, starting to practice therapy, met with a small supervisory group at Hillman's house to discuss issues that came up with patients.

Moore recalled: "I felt the most important thing I learned from Jim was an appreciation for the range of the soul or psyche, what he called 'the quirky expressions of the soul,' the odd things that it does. And instead of judging and labeling these things, or pathologizing them in a bad sense—simply taking interest in how the soul manifests in people's lives, how they get into these messes. Fixing things so you are 'healthy' is not the ultimate criterion. Not too far from the Dallas Institute, you could walk down this street and see these cross dressers, men with beards and mustaches wearing wonderful gowns. Jim was fascinated by all that kind of thing. I learned from him how to appreciate the fringes of behavior."

Being with Hillman, Moore went on, "was almost like Castaneda with Don Juan, where the simple things were the teaching. I don't think he was doing it consciously, but I learned so much just from watching how he shopped or how he ate. In restaurants he was very adventurous, I don't think he'd ever order the same thing twice, where I was rather habitual. We went to Nieman's, which was otherwise so expensive, when the half-price sales were on. I'd be looking at the shades of gray and brown, and he'd look at me with disgust and say, 'You're not gonna *buy* that.' He'd be looking at all these bright-colored yellow shirts and I'd say, 'You're not gonna *wear* that.' That kind of represented who we were. I was this muted kind of person and he was a right-in-your-face person in many ways, although he had another side to him."[59]

SEEKING THE UNCONVENTIONAL

Hillman's daughter Susanne remembers: "When my father lived in Dallas, I came to visit him one time and brought a tape of Swans music with me. They were a band from New York, famous for being the loudest underground musical group, and I was married to their drummer at the time. My father listened to it and said: 'ok, I get it, think Hades! Think underworld!' He played it to some Dallas friends who came to the house, explaining that this was the sound of the underworld!"[60]

In the fall of 1982, Hillman wrote to Gail and Bob Thomas, noting that the direction of the Institute "is very different from where it was, and we each were, two years ago or more . . . It will do what Bob said we do: institute, as a verb. I am glad you have me in reserve as jack-of-all trades, and not engaged in any specific single part of the thing. This fits better with my polytheistic nature."[61]

The latest project to be instituted was Louise Cowan's brainchild. After the university shut them out, the Cowans had gone into retreat for a while, buying a house seventy miles away in the small town of Bonham. But once they re-emerged in Dallas, it was with a vengeance. Thomas recalled Louise arriving for a staff meeting, pounding her fist, and exclaiming: "I want a Teacher's Academy!" She had recently taken part in a Dallas Institute conference revolving around a proclamation called "A Nation at Risk" issued by the National Endowment for the Humanities (NEH). Educators Jacques Barzun and Mortimer Adler took part, concurring with the document's statement that, according to Cowan, "the condition of our public schools is so terrible that if our enemy had done this to us, we'd call it an act of war." She proceeded to write a grant application that resulted in the NEH funding an intensive summer course at the Institute, where fifty Dallas high school teachers came to study the classics for their own edification, "not as material for instruction." It proved a remarkable success. "When we started, they weren't even teaching literature anymore in the schools," said Thomas. "The Academy made an enormous change."[62]

It was these unconventional approaches of his circle that intrigued Hillman. At one conference sponsored by the Institute, held at a funeral home that was formerly the mansion of a colonel, Judith French-Kelly had been asked to give a speech about the current season on Broadway. She chose to focus on the Tony-winning musical, *Sweeney Todd: The Demon Barber of Fleet Street*, replete with rapes and throat-cuttings and featuring a killer who turns his victim's remains into meat pies. "I could sense a definite uneasiness in the audience," she recalled, "like how could anybody make a musical like this that I was extolling? I hadn't thought of it as being particularly in-your-face, but in Dallas it was *not* palatable. But Jim was *thrilled* by my talk. He came running over, picked me up, and swung me around shouting, 'Hurrah! Hurrah!'"[63]

Her husband, Patrick Kelly, remembered staging a performance of *King Lear*, "with a wonderful actor from the Royal Shakespeare Company playing Lear and the rest of the cast were students and very good. Still, I had begun to believe this was not a play I'd do again, because it's so dark and nihilistic. Jim came and saw it, and after the performance he walked up to me and said simply, 'Nothing.' He was experiencing how much the play was about nothingness. He said he'd never heard the word 'nothing' spoken so eloquently."

Hillman and Kelly worked out regularly at a health club, where James mostly swam and "we'd lament the state of plasterers in Dallas and compare hardware stores, the merits of various toilets—very high thoughts!" as Kelly put it sardonically. They also discussed theater and movies, "and he could talk about fictional characters exactly as you would about a real person. As a director, that helped me a great deal, in getting actors to that vulnerability to impression."[64]

Not surprisingly, none of this sat well with the conventional Jungian world. Thomas Moore, while still trying to teach at SMU, had been confronted by a core group of Dallas analysts over becoming Hillman's friend. "Eventually they said, 'You've got to choose, you're either with us or against us.'"[65] Moore chose Hillman, who had himself joined the growing Inter-Regional Society of Jungian Analysts a year or so after Pat did. Its president at the time was James Hall, an MD who had done some of his training in Zürich under Marie-Louise von Franz and adhered fairly strictly to classical Jungian ideas.

Hall was among a number of Jungians who back in the States "formed their own little fiefdoms," as Ron Schenk put it—a Jungian analyst in Dallas and Houston and the author of four books. "He was an enemy of Hillman's before, which created quite a tension especially when a number of followers of Hillman in Zürich started showing up—not only Pat, but Paul Kugler and Lyn Cowan and others. The clique around Hillman ran into what they called 'the Texas Mafia.' Another way of looking at it was, they were 'the Zürich Mafia.' But Hillman won out. There was a big meeting of the Inter-Regional Society in Birmingham [Alabama] with a whole slate of Hillman candidates, including Hillman who ran successfully to be on the Ethics Committee. In a typical Hillmanian way, he said, 'Well, who best would be qualified than someone who had himself been the subject of an ethics investigation?'"[66]

When Randolph Severson first began working for Hillman, he'd been in analysis with Hall, "who would gossip about Hillman and this scandal in Zürich that supposedly forced him to beat it out of town." Severson quickly realized the conflict-of-interest and stopped seeing Hall. At the same time, Hillman occasionally expressed concern over how something Spring Publications was doing would be received in Zürich. "One year we published a catalogue that listed our main authors, but not in alphabetical order. He said, 'This will cause riots because we appear to be ranking Jungian analysts.'"[67]

Severson added: "He was Martin Luther to the established church, a heretic, and met with that kind of fury. There was something else, too, because Jim was welcoming people into the Jungian world from other roads than analysis. If the Jungian world was not going to be a church with this approved and costly means of catechism, it threatened their careers and financial stability."

In truth, Hillman said in 2009, "when we had those evenings at the house talking about cases, there was always a lot of interest in the clinical way. We used the language of the official psychiatry, talking about obsession or compulsion in people who had anorexia or were 'cutting' or transvestites or whatever. There wasn't a desertion of the clinical methodology, but it was trying to see through and work it in new ways. That was going on, as well as this opening freedom."[68]

The situation with Hall's Jungian crowd felt like déjà vu to Hillman after what he faced from the conservative theologians at the University of Dallas. Now, at the Dallas Institute, he was still teaching—indeed, an entire course devoted to the subject Jung concentrated the most on toward the end of his life: Alchemy. Thomas Moore took the course. Ron Schenk did as well, and saved tape recordings of all the lectures, and remembered: "He was like a conductor with an orchestra. He would elicit from the strings, and then over here to the brass, and on to the percussion—by this, I mean his openness to everything and bringing a sense of depth and expansion. At the same time, it was not some free-flowing bullshit session, and he was not someone who suffered fools gladly. He could be very cutting in his responses, dismissive of an uncreative or unoriginal contribution, and turned some people off for that reason. But for most of us, it was a marvelous spectacle to be a part of."[69]

LÓPEZ

That wasn't the only marvelous spectacle they experienced. Often in their midst during those years was the most unconventional personality of them all—Rafael López-Pedraza. His and Valerie's periodic visits to Dallas from Caracas, when they would often stay at least a week, proved memorable for the Institute cadre. During his early months as a therapist, Thomas Moore found himself becoming uncomfortable "when patients would present me with images of violence or aggression, and I didn't know what to do." One afternoon, Moore was walking down the street with Hillman, López, and their two wives, describing his dilemma to Rafael. The Cuban suddenly elbowed him into an alleyway, looked him in the eye and uttered a single word: "Sada." At least that was how he seemed to pronounce it. A baffled Moore resumed the walk and whispered to Valerie: "What does Sada mean?" She replied, "I think he means Sade." Moore immediately bought all the works of the Marquis de Sade "to read mythologically." This led to his writing a book-length study he called *Dark Eros*. After a major prospective publisher blanched at the idea of putting Sade and theology into the same package, Hillman said Spring would put it out. According to Moore, "Today a lot of therapists tell me that's the most important book of mine that they've read."[70]

Severson remembered the multiplicity of López's character— "a healthy drinker and eater, very warm and funny, really a kind of archetype or stereotype; the idea of the Spanish picaresque, a somewhat grotesque presence. When he traveled—I know this to be true because I had to carry the luggage—it was with every medicine known to man, his own personal pharmacy."[71]

In a piece Severson wrote for a Dallas Institute seminar on Hillman and mythology in the fall of 2017, he remembered "chauffeuring Hillman and Rafael to the gym, to a Health Club, down in deep Oak Lawn, in Dallas, not far from where the Hillmans lived. We worked out together. I say 'worked out' with some poetic license. Rafael surveyed the scene like a bull entering into an unfamiliar pasture. I half expected him to lower his head, paw the dust and bellow. He didn't. But what he did do was amble to a bicycle, hoist his bulk atop the small triangular seat, glare in front of him, and for the next hour remain there, periodically and indifferently pedaling once or twice. Hillman obviously knew his way around a gym. We worked out then headed to the pool where Rafael soon followed. Again, Hillman and I did a few laps while Rafael waded into and then sat in the small whirlpool. Again, for the life of me, I couldn't help but think of Brahma bulls I'd seen on my grandfather's ranch, wading in the creek shallows to drink and bask in what can only be described as their almost Paleolithic glory."[72]

Another time, Severson continued, at a University of Dallas seminar "the conversation had wandered into contemporary politics. Rafael, as usual, said little, but at some point intervened to dismiss with a wave of his hand just about everything that had preceded, with the comment that the real contemporary issue, the only issue dividing, or that would divide, the West, the one issue upon which the future of Western Civilization hung as upon a thread: was 'would the Spanish Armada stay sunken?' 'Would Elizabeth or Phillip prevail in the end?'"[73]

Michael Sipiora remembered taking a course from Sardello on the body that included "all kinds of esoteric stuff, and there's this Latin guy hanging around that we think is the janitor. No idea it's Rafael. Then we have our class and López suddenly makes a comment. 'Body is body,' he says. The look on Sardello's face was like the world collapsed. After that I had lunch with Rafael and some Spring people. He said, 'Freud and Jung were like Columbus, they thought they discovered the New World but they only got to the Caribbean. There was so much more.'"[74]

Severson's impression was that, although López was six years Hillman's senior, "Hillman was kind of like the older brother, calming down his occasional fits of anger, terribly supportive and encouraging. I never heard Hillman in any way suggest that there was anything other than an absolutely unique genius about Rafael. He was always effusive in his praise, saying 'I owe him a debt I can't repay.' But I always got the feeling that Rafael was a little resentful of Hillman, because he obviously could not write the way Hillman could."[75]

Was that resentment partly why, after returning to Caracas from a visit to Dallas in early 1983, López called Hillman to inform his friend that he wanted nothing more to do with him? López wouldn't specify what had gone wrong. Hillman responded quickly by letter, which curiously addressed López in the third person——. "so now I am the new one on his list of people he must break with, cut with, and I think what incredible paranoid images is he holding of me?" Hillman continued: "I (J.H.) am such a blind and unconscious person, that there must be something that I have been stupid about and have seriously offended this friend of many years. *Very* seriously offended—and I do not know what it is. I think of all kinds of misdemeanors—neglect of his letters, being isolated for long periods in my depressions and my hyperactivities—but I can't believe it is anything that small or simple. It must be something terrible. Maybe he is too decent to tell me what my fault is?"

Then Hillman addressed López directly: "But at least to honor that past of which you said our relationship belonged to, you might let me have some little light on what my sin is. Even if it is hard for you to tell me, I ask you kindly to let me know, and of course, if I can set it straight, I will do my utmost to try."[76]

There was a second phone call attempted by Hillman, to rectify the situation, followed by a telegram from López telling Hillman flatly to "forget any idea of a new edition of [his book] *Hermes and his Children*," which Spring had originally published in 1977. In a letter, López elaborated: "I have told you that my psyche has moved our relationship into the past. By this I mean that you, or whatever you say, has no psychological connection with my present. This is something you must understand." Should Hillman "insist" upon going ahead with the new edition, López had instructed his lawyers to "take care of the situation," though he added: "But surely we both want to avoid this because it would be boring and expensive, not to mention a shame."[77]

Pat tried to get Valerie to tell her what had caused the rupture, but to no avail. Pat later reflected: "Rafael was incredibly demanding. It took a great deal of patience to deal with him and serve his needs (including to be continuously listened to). It could be like taking care of an overgrown child. Jim, all of us, had served this because Raf's unique points of view and ideas were worth it. Sometimes Jim would blow up at him, and sort of talk down to him, and Rafael always took it. On that last trip, I remember Jim having snapped at him and this time it made me cringe. And then something apparently snapped in Rafael. I think also perhaps he was annoyed that Jim was becoming archetypal psychology. Jim was in another place now, leaping light years in his thinking, writing, influence. Rafael was important to archetypal psychology, and still is. But this was like one of those *Henry the IV* Prince Hal/Falstaff moments—Jim had now more to attend to than Raf. And Raf was probably feeling left behind, slighted, demeaned? Or maybe it was really just time; they were two extremely creative men and the time of working together had passed."[78]

López had a history of breaking ties with men close to him. Hillman could remember four, including Guggenbühl. Reflecting back on the rift between the two of them more than two decades later, Hillman still considered it "a weird thing. I think Rafael was projecting too much. He didn't like America. He didn't like the extraversion, and I think he saw this as all my ambition. But there was another reason: Rafael was very paranoid and it was difficult for him to be treated as an equal. He had to be the guru-teacher. When people made a criticism, he'd explode. He knew I could see through him about a lot, and that bothered him."[79]

López left hints in his last letter to Hillman, written after Hillman reached out to him prior to a planned visit to Caracas in 1994. "Dear Jim, For sure your trip to Venezuela constellates a lot of emotion in me, and they are emotions that are better kept in the past from where they can nourish my psyche today. But I would have wanted to meet you privately to talk about old friends. I imagine that you have a tremendous programme of events, so it won't be possible. To meet you in the collective atmosphere you are going to be involved in is beyond me, since my psychosomatic apparatus protests bitterly in front of such psychological group activities, a clear sign of ageing. These days my psyche becomes bored with discussions about psychology.

"You will receive a warm welcome here and will be well taken care of. Good luck and best wishes, Rafael."

When approached for an interview for this biography in 2007, López declined, but did send photocopies of the remarkable letters that Hillman had written him from Dallas. López died in Caracas at the age of ninety-one in January 2011, nine months before Hillman's death.

DICHOTOMIES

"This archetypal longing and rejection can be seen as the dynamism which makes psyche and life move."
—*Rafael López-Pedraza,* Hermes and His Children.[80]

The irreconcilable break with the friend to whom he could confide his darkest thoughts marked another turning point for Hillman. Something, once again, seemed to be ending. Dennis Slattery, later a professor of mythology at Pacifica Graduate Institute, remembered being in a meeting around this time on the second floor of the Dallas Institute. "There was a Xerox machine in the room, and Jim suddenly came in and stopped the meeting because he was so upset that he couldn't get the copier working. He complicated the matter by immediately biting off the head of anybody who came forward to help him. This might be my fantasy, but—did he kick it? He was definitely in a mood to, even if he didn't. I thought to myself, lionizing the man the way I did then, how can someone with this majestic way of thinking get so caught in the non-machinations of a Xerox machine? I spent the rest of the day trying to balance out my puzzlement at seeing this new side of him—just Jim being who he was and wanting to get something done and being blocked by technology."

Slattery continued: "I sensed that he would become frustrated—certainly at the Dallas Institute—when he began to hear so many echoes of himself and realize that clones were basically gathering around him. That was a point of contention, because to fall into his ray really cancels out what he's attempting to do in his work—for one to find their own imaginal groove and get into it. That's the tricky part of being a leader, with the kind of power that a Joseph Campbell had, and that Jim continued to have."[81]

Thomas Moore remembered asking Hillman whether he was going to try to create something here like Jung had with the Zürich Institute, a permanent training program or educational center. "He said, 'No, I don't want to do that.' Then I said, 'Well, what are you going to do about being a father figure, because it's there.' As I remember it, he told me something like, 'No, the way to deal with it was not to create an institution, but do things in a different style—and when you see the father archetype developing, nip it in the bud.' But I wondered, could he just decide to do that? He *was* fathering something. I didn't trust his solution to that, at the time. Today I think I was probably wrong and he was right. Look what happened to Jung, with the Jungian orthodoxy. I think what Jim was telling me was, he simply didn't believe this was the best way to create anything."[82]

The "father figure" wasn't the only issue. Louise Cowan recalled that Hillman "really liked [her husband] Don, but I think he never quite approved of me. I was always just a little too bold, and a bit fanatical about my literature program." Pat, who took Louise's literature course, found it tremendously inspiring—"but I learned from other people that she didn't like me so much, because she thought I was too common. Whereas Jim was arch, and that sort of fit her fantasy of things."[83]

Louise reminded Hillman of other powerful older women he had known—those in the Jungian coterie like Jolande Jacobi and Esther Harding, and the poet Kathleen Raine. He felt it necessary to keep an—arm's-length distance from all of them. To Hillman, Louise was "an amazing person, who inspired an enormous number of people. But I felt I had to be cautious, to watch out in some way."[84] Louise remembered his resistance when she tried to interest him in the Old Testament, because she believed "he would discover things that nobody else had seen. And it is magnificent poetry."[85]

There was also, perhaps, the long arm of Hillman's power-house mother, still very much alive during the Dallas era. For years, Madeleine Hillman had helped her son financially, as often referenced in his letters to her. About his writing retreat near Eranos, a house Hillman leased in the Tessin, he'd written her in 1974: "I am enormously indebted to you for having made this place possible." In another letter, he thanked her "most warmly for your continued generosity . . . as so many of my patients are students, I can't claim big fees. The philosophy is that it's better to live low and spend little so that one isn't always having to keep up payments on houses, cars, things, places, and the like. Still, food and travel, remain the luxuries. The linen will be terribly welcome . . . The napkins have been grand."[86]

Pat remembered that "Madeleine volunteered at a Jewish thrift shop and was continually sending us 'fine' things—embroidered pillow cases, linen sheets and napkins, which I then had to iron. But I also enjoyed the fantasy of it all. It was like upper-class living in an earlier part of the century. And much about it was for Jim, without doubt, simply *the* way to live. But he was quirky, and also down to earth as those raised upper class people so frequently are. With Madeleine he was both continually at war and of course she was also part of his aesthetic. She had terrific influence, and the struggle with her was a large part of who he was—for good and for ill."[87]

This all traced back to having grown up in an Atlantic City household where finances may have been meager, but appearances provided more than ample compensation. Hillman reflected on economic factors at some length in June 2009, while discussing his Dallas years. When he was a young boy growing up during the Great Depression, "my parents sat once a month at a card table, going through their bills together deciding what they could pay. My father earned $5,000 a year from the hotel, along with laundry for the family and a lot of food free. My mother actually earned more than my father, once her shop got going. That was right up to the war [almost a decade later].

"So there was no money, but that didn't phase the style—a style that looks like you're rich. We had black servants, Willie and Annie, and during the depression Willie was dressed up as a chauffeur. I was raised high class—nurses, the whole thing. Then I married a woman who was raised in an even higher-class style. That's been my whole life. It's also part of [being] the Puer, because I never had any money put aside. I did manage Kate's money, and the children's money when we divorced. When Kate and I split, I had a bank account and was earning as an analyst, but I had maybe $100,000 in my name. Yet I never thought [about] money. I carry my cash to this day in the pocket, loose, dollars folded up. And Pat had no money.

"Now in Dallas, we come to another aspect of it. I was resentful the entire time about the enormous amount of wealth these people had—the Institute had a lot of rich backers—but we were tremendously underpaid in that atmosphere. Something like $15,000 or $20,000 a year by the Dallas Institute. Yet because of my style, my dress, my language, my way, and the class that I grew up in—this Jewish sophisticated class—I *looked* rich. So they all *imagined* that I'm rich! That's a whole complex that needs to come in [to the biography]."[88]

The money complex is evident in one of Gail Thomas's comments on that time. "I thought he was an extraordinary therapist. I never did have a transference thing with Jim, never did fall in love with him, as I'm sure many did. But you see, I was also Jim's employer. When he didn't pay his rent for Spring Publications, I would not say it during the analytical hour, but two hours later when he came to the Institute: 'Jim, you can't get away with this!' He'd argue with me about how many square feet his office was. Well, we'd bought a Compugraphic—one of the first computer machines in Dallas, it took up an entire room!—and it cost $12,000 and then we had to hire a typesetter to run this huge machine."[89]

Randolph Severson had a different impression. It "was so true but also so unbelievable for most people: that this man of consummate richness of ideas and in personal presence and style wasn't rich, not Dallas rich at all, and it bothered him [and] gave rise to the canard that he was 'cheap.' He was immensely generous to me: paid me well, gave me stock in Spring, always 'put it on Spring' when we ate or I filled up with gas. He knew I was a graduate student, married, 3 soon 4 kids already, and I always felt he thought about that. When I left he bought back the stock he had gifted me which had no real value then and he certainly didn't have to. He said, 'Consider it a bonus.'"[90]

Stella Rodriquez also addressed dichotomies that she believed few people saw in Hillman: "He had really nice luggage but it was thirty or forty years old, so road-worn we didn't think it was going to make it home from the airport. Then he was so dapper, with elegant suits and beautiful shirts and what I'm sure were hand-made silk ties."[91]

Perhaps that dichotomy derived, in part, from something Hillman described in a letter to his old friend Robert Stein at the end of 1982. He had just returned from making his first lecture trip to Japan, spending three weeks in Kyoto with Pat. "Japan had a huge impact. Nothing in years has so hit me, now that I am back I am filled with energy and trying to live right. What was the impact? It spoke continually to my aesthetic sense, to anima, to beauty, to a withdrawn and yet emotional way of being . . .

"Now the question is how to live with beauty or bring it in or live from it. I have so little actual talent. I can't write poems, I can't paint, I can't really garden or dress or decorate my house . . . I am stuck in this aggressive Mars fate and suffer from longing for Venus."[92]

All Hillman could do, ultimately, was ask the question: "Where exactly is the money complex hidden?" He did so, elegantly as always, in a piece he published in *Spring 1982*, titled "A Contribution to Soul and Money." Hillman's intention was to "step altogether out of the dilemma that divides money (and soul) into spiritual and material oppositions." This could only occur by asking and addressing another question: "finally, what does money do for the soul: what is its specific function in pos-sibilitizing the imagination? It makes the imagination possible in the world. Soul needs money to be kept from flying off into the Bardo realm of 'only-psychic' reality. Money holds soul in the vale of the world, in the poetry of the concrete, in touch with the sea as *facts*, those hard and slippery facts, so perdur-ing, annoying, and limiting, and ceaselessly involving one in eco-nomic necessity. For economy means originally 'householding,' making soul in the vale of the world, charging and being over-charged, crimping and splurging, exchanging, bargaining, evalu-ating, paying off, going in debt, speculating . . . To find the soul of modern man or woman, begin by searching into those irre-ducible embarrassing facts of the money complex, that crazy crab scuttling across the floors of silent seas."[93]

DALLAS DENOUEMENT

Hillman couldn't make up his mind about Dallas. At the end of their first year in Dallas in 1979, Hillman wrote: "Pat keeps wanting to 'move.' For me that is an impossible image." Then the next year, when things were falling apart at the university, Hillman wrote in another letter: "Many times, Pat and I imagine living in the East, more countryish, working, and coming 'out' to earn as we need to." Yet in 1982, working on a book of con-versations called *Inter Views*, he described Dallas as "*the* cultural challenge for psychology . . . the ideal place to be immersed in the syndrome of one's time."[94] As Pat advanced toward complet-ing her doctoral thesis, which Hillman called "a milestone" in one letter, she began pushing harder to leave. In 1983, Hillman started feeling a similar urge.

There were, after all, other city's souls to contemplate. Paul Kugler, one of the young men Hillman had mentored in Zürich, went on to start a Jungian practice in Buffalo and teach at SUNY-Buffalo's Center for the Psychological Study of the Arts. Hillman had visited Kugler there several times and, early in 1983, the *Buffalo Arts Review* published a conversation between them. "Buffalo, like Dallas, is in the midst of deep-rooted changes," the introduction said. While "going through severe economic decline, the city is also witnessing a growth in artistic and cultural life"—and that "inner city" lay "hidden in our everyday perceptions"[95]

The deep contrast with Dallas ignited Hillman's fantasy. Both were "marginal cities ruled by images"; he would define Dallas's as manic, Buffalo's as depressive. At the same time, the eastern city's architectural soul was internalized; home interiors were "some of the most beautiful in the country." That November, Hillman would keynote a conference on "Imagining Buffalo," organized by residents calling themselves "The Spirit of the City Study Group"—"a gathering for story-telling in which, through some twenty local speakers, Buffalo regarded itself in all its strangeness and familiarity."[96] He wouldn't move there, but because of Kugler Hillman shared podiums and struck up relationships with poets like Robert Duncan and Robert Creeley.

In September 1983, Hillman wrote to Thomas Moore from Ascona, where he was once again lecturing at Eranos: "What seems mainly on my mind is that I am finally finding the reasons why I am leaving Dallas for the Northeast . . . It's the fact that success counts, and growth and money and development, and society. These things really do count in Dallas. I walk past property and think I should have bought . . . I see everybody (like at SMU you saw) successful in the business way and I feel such a schlemiel. I worry about *Spring* all the time in terms of its business (instead of its editorial policy and new ideas and writers and designs) . . . It is a city on the march uphill and I am an older man on the slide downhill. I don't want to make it and prove myself. I want to go to seed, vegetate, rot . . . and be among my own kind, and also to be in a rotting place, for culture, reflection, ideas, and that sort of thing comes from rot, so they say.

"If this were the only case, then how come Dallas did produce so many ideas (for me anyway), and was so fertile even for you these last years? Perhaps it had to do with the 'movement,' the little revolutionaries. But I feel now older and don't want the revolution. I am preparing for the sixties (my sixties that is), and thinking much more about what they are all for and about. I feel that Dallas from now on would become programmatic: I'd have to produce certain sorts of things for certain fixed results . . .

"Also hope that if I move and Pat moves, that you may move not too far away. That's putting it selfishly."[97]

He and Pat would move East, and Moore would soon follow, as would a number of people from the Dallas circle including Gerald Burns, Sven Doehner, and Joseph Cambray. The dream of Gail Thomas, to establish a "Dallas School" of Jungian/archetypal psychology at the Institute, would not be fulfilled. For many in the Institute's circle, it came as a shock. "Here were all these people moving to Dallas to be around Hillman," as Ron Schenk put it, "and here he is pulling up stakes and moving to the Northeast. There was something of a feeling of disillusionment. Certainly Sardello and Gail respected Hillman, but I remember Sardello would make comments like, 'You know, you can't always rely on Jim to come through with what he says he will.'"

As he had so many times in his life, Hillman was marching to the dictates of his inner drummer. "His going-away party was, I think, emblematic," Schenk said. "He even invited the Jungian analyst who hated him, James Hall. Everyone was there who Hillman had any kind of connection with. His black neighbors, his students and analysands, everyone from the Institute. It was like a micro-cosmos of all the different parts of his world."[98]

Years later, Hillman would reflect in a letter to the author: "I believe it is a pattern worth considering: I am in the scene, very active, even generative, and yet without trace afterwards, as if invisible . . . Very few lasting relations from these periods. Dallas too: again a foreigner, jewish in a very *tight* world (like Zürich in that respect, and like Dublin).

"I believe an astrologer once told me that I sow seeds but do not stay around for the harvest."[99]

Hillman would return to Dallas on a number of occasions in the ensuing years, and remain close to the prime movers he came to know at the University and the Institute. For them, the fruits of the harvest would be largely local. Gail Thomas said in 2008: "After Jim and Pat left, and then Robert [Sardello], I felt like I'd been abandoned. But I soon realized there was so much to carry on." She served as director of the Dallas Institute until 1997, with an annual budget that went from $60,000 to $600,000 and supported a dozen full and part-time staff. She was, at the same time, a practicing therapist, as well as a published author of books on water and the ancient healing traditions. She and Joanne Stroud continued to sit on the Institute's Board of Directors.

By the late 2000s, Thomas had become President and CEO of the Trinity Trust Foundation, overseeing the largest public works project in Dallas' history, revitalizing a twenty-mile stretch of river and open space. At the epicenter of downtown is Pegasus Plaza, featuring a steel-and-neon monument to the Flying Red Horse on its roof. "When we started the project," Thomas said, "all the buildings around Pegasus Plaza were mothballed. Now you see the cranes again, buildings going up, the older ones have been renovated for condominiums. People want to live downtown, young people. I remember Jim saying, 'The city is for lovers.' He maintained that an erotic imagination pervades great cities and that we need to become re-enchanted with them. That's what I've tried to help make happen."[100]

Stroud edited two books with Thomas including *The Olympians: Ancient Deities as Archetypes*, while writing a pair of her own as well, and serving as executive editor of the Gaston Bachelard Translation Series published by the Dallas Institute. She provided support for a projected ten-volume Uniform

Edition of Hillman's previously unpublished essays and lectures, nine of which appeared by 2020. Since his death, Stroud also sponsored the annual James Hillman Symposium at the Dallas Institute. Stroud died in 2021 at the age of ninety-three.

Robert Sardello, with his late wife Cheryl, went on to develop a School of Spiritual Psychology, based in part on the principles of Rudolf Steiner. Sardello also authored numerous books.

Louise Cowan, who eventually returned to teach at her beloved University of Dallas, received the nation's highest award for achievement in the humanities, the Frankel Prize (now called the National Humanities Award) at the White House in 1991. "Louise's Ladies" gathered to honor her ninetieth birthday in 2006 in Dallas, where Louise spoke on "The Unique Understanding of Women in Western Culture"—filled with references to Homer, Virgil, Milton, Dostoevsky, and Faulkner— and received a standing ovation. The grande dame of Dallas's literary world died in 2015, at the age of ninety-eight.

Seven years prior to her death, Louise recalled in an interview: "It was one of the highlights of our lives to have Jim down here. What he provided was something that we, and the city, needed badly."[101] Later, she wrote: "It was not only that he was brilliant and original but that, unlike us, he had risked 'the big time,' and still seemed to appreciate and listen to our ideas. Like us, he seemed to think that imagining was the most important activity in which one could engage. Looking back, I see how different the general tone of the times was then: we knew somehow that we were caught in the midst of what Faulkner's characters called 'the end of an era' and we thought we might be able to help determine the new age. How differently it has all turned out!"[102]

NOTES

1. "a very special form of courage. . . .": Author interview with Ed Casey, November 2008.
2. "personal physical courage. . . .": Author interview with Randolph Severson, November 2008.
3. "Hillman was what UD pretended. . . .": Randolph Severson email to author, June 8, 2015.
4. "restless, angry, disappointed. . . .": Randolph Severson, "Seeing Red: A Tribute to James Hillman," a talk given November 20, 2013, at Dallas Institute annual symposium.
5. "I remember Hillman said. . . .": Author interview with Robert Sardello, November 2008.
6. "I wanted revenge. . . .": Hillman interview with author, January 2009.
7. Betty Graham and founding of the Dallas Institute: Author interview with Gail Thomas, November 2018.
8. "We all talked excitedly. . . .": Author interview with Louise Cowan, November 2008.
9. "to bring the imagination to bear. . . .": Author interview with Robert Sardello, November 2008.
10. "There was talk about affiliating. . . .": Author interview with Hillman, October 2008
11. "a wonderful old house. . . .": Author interview with Gail Thomas, November 2008.
12. "It had a hot tub. . . .": Ibid.
13. "a blank canvas. . . .": Author interview with Thomas Moore, February 2009.
14. "bringing something to Dallas. . . .": Author interview with Joanne Stroud, November 2008.
15. "unsightly people. . . .": Author interview with Lyle Novinski, November 2008.
16. "a place where intense conversation. . . .": Hillman quoted in *Dallas Morning News*, March 17, 1981.
17. James Pratt's background and quotes are all drawn from an interview with the author, November 2008.
18. "ultimately became a vision. . . .": Author interview with John Tatum, February 2009.
19. "The moisture that gives pleasure. . . .": "Souls Take Pleasure in Moisture," by James Hillman, in *Stirrings of Culture*, Robert J. Sardello and Gail Thomas, editors, The Dallas Institute Publications, 1986, pp.203–205.
20. "Well, he can sometimes say outrageous. . . .": Author interview with Joanne Stroud, November 2008.
21. "wonderful Renaissance idea. . . .very estranged": Author interview with Hillman, October 2008.
22. "I think he loved it. . . .": Author interview with Gail Thomas, November 2008.
23. "because it was very much. . . .": Author interview with Randolph Severson, November 2008.
24. "it turned out to be a dialogue. . . .": Author interview with Ron Schenk, November 2008.
25. "The time at Dallas was most valuable. . . .": Letter to Hillman form Kathleen Raine, May 5, 1982, Opus Archive
26. "I like being with similar spirits. . . .": Author interview with Hillman, October 2008.

27. "Because Hillman was there. . . .': Author interview with Joseph Cambray, September 2007.

28. "it's because after ten. . . .': Author interview with Hillman, January 2009.

29. Late night parties: Author interviews with Thomas, Berry, Severson.

30. "Some of us tried to recreate. . . .": Author interview with Sven Doehner, July 2007.

31. "a free-wheeling conversation. . . .': Author interview with Ed Casey, January 2006.

32. Sardello and Thomas quotes: Author interviews.

33. "could give things a gravitas. . . .": Author interview with Thomas Moore, February 2009.

34. "Interiors in the Design of the City: Ceilings," in *Stirrings of Culture*, pp. 78–84.

35. William Burford: Author interview with Gail Thomas, November 2008.

36. Robert Trammell: "Robert Trammell: 'The grass-roots poet in Dallas,'" by Jerome Weeks, Dallas Morning News, May 9, 2006. www.wfaa.com/cgi-bin/bi/gold Also, "Dallas poet's works dedicated to us all," *Dallas Morning News,* December 19, 1984.

37. "I think the Institute. . . .": Author interview with Gail Thomas, November 2008.

38. "Reagan runs the country. . . .": JH letter to Rafael López, undated, late 1980, Lopez private archive.

39. The quotes from "On Show Business Ethics" appear in *Philosophical Intimations: James Hillman Uniform Edition 8*, Thompson, Ct.: Spring Publications, 2016, pp. 75–82.

40. "Here's the letter paper. . . .": JH letter to López, López private archive.

41. "Dallas is the place of assassination. . . .": Hillman letter to Rudolf Ritsema, April 1, 1981, Eranos archive.

42. "Dallas does not worry. . . .": JH letter to Lopez, July 28, 1981,. Lopez private archive.

43. "My depressions were worse. . . .": JH letter to Lopez, Lopez private archive, summer 1981.

44. "If you just sit in your room. . . .": JH letter to Lopez, July 28, 1981.

45. "was always challenging me. . . .": Author interview with Joanne Stroud, November 2008.

46. "I love working with patients. . . .": JH letter to Lopez, July 28, 1981.

47. Hillman interview with author, January 2008.

48. "Now I go to Florence. . . .": JH letter to JP Donleavy, Donleavy private archive.

49. "He had somebody translate. . . .": Author interview with Pat Berry, February 2019.

50. "Each night, like tonight. . . .": Hillman undated letter to Charles Boer, 1983, Boer papers, courtesy of Jay Livernois.

51. "that amazing building that seems. . . .": JH letter to Robert Duncan, undated, Robert Duncan Archive, University of Buffalo.

52. "Men dressed in Renaissance vivid. . . .": JH letter to "Rafael and Valerie," López private archive.

53. "to speak as a psychologist. . . .": Hillman's talk on *Anima Mundi: The Return of the Soul to the World* first appeared in *Spring 1982*: 71–93. It appears again in *The Uniform Edition of the Writings of James Hillman, City & Soul, Volume 2*, pp. 27–49. .

54. "even farther from ego-psychology. . . .": *A Blue Fire: Selected Writings by James Hillman*, Introduced and Edited by Thomas Moore, Harper Perennial: 1989, p. 10.

55. "The temptation always. . . .": *A Blue Fire: Selected Writings by James Hillman*, Introduced and Edited by Thomas Moore, Harper Perennial: 1989, p. 167.

56. "We all recognized this as a radical turning point. . . .": Author interview with Ed Casey, January 2006.

57. "a clearer, more direct translation. . . .": Article "How the Soul is Sold," by Emily Yoffe, *New York Times*, April 23, 1995.

58. "Music in Therapy": Thomas Moore, *Spring Journal*.

59. Thomas Moore's background and the quotes are drawn from his interview with the author, February 2009.

60. "When my father lived in Dallas. . . .": Susanne Hillman, "Memories of my Father," sent author September 2020.

61. Institute "is very different than where. . . .": JH letter to Gail and Bob Thomas, Thomas private archive.

62. Education: Author interviews with Louise Cowan and Gail Thomas.

63. "I could sense a definite. . . .": Author interview with Judith French-Kelly, November 2008.

64. "with a wonderful actor. . . .": Author interview with Patrick Kelly, November 2008.

65. "Eventually they said. . . .": Author interview with Thomas Moore, February 2009.

66. James Hall controversy: Author interview with Ron Schenk, November 2008.

67. "who would gossip about Hillman. . . .": Author interview with Randolph Severson, November 2008.

68. "when we had those evenings. . . .": Author interview with Hillman, June 2009.

69. "He was like a conductor. . . .": Author interview with Ron Schenk.

70. Moore and "Sada" story: Author interview with Moore, February 2009.

71. "a healthy drinker and eater. . . .": Author interview with Randolph Severson, November 2008.

72. "I remember chauffeuring Hillman. . . .": Randolph Severson, "Hillman, Lopez, and Duende," talk delivered at 2017 Dallas Institute Symposium on *Mythic Figures*. Transcript provided to author by Severson.

73. "the conversation had wandered. . . .": Severson, "Hillman, Lopez, and Duende."

74. "all kinds of esoteric stuff. . . .": Author interview with Michael Sipiora, November 2016.

75. "Hillman was kind of like the older. . . .": Author interview with Randolph Severson, November 2008.

76. "so now am I the new one. . . .": Letter from Hillman to "Dear Rafael," January 18, 1983, Opus Archive

77. "forget any idea of a new edition. . . .": Letter from Rafael to "Dear Jim," January 25, 1983, Opus Archive.

78. "Rafael was incredibly demanding. . . .": Pat Berry email to author, December 2017, and interview with author.

79. "a weird thing. . . .": Author interview with Hillman, October 2008.

80. Rafael López-Pedraza, *Hermes and His Children*, Daimon Verlag, 2010, p. 50.

81. "There was a Xerox machine. . . .": Author interview with Dennis Slattery, March 2007.

82. "He said, "No I don't want. . . .": Author interview with Thomas Moore, February 2009.

83. "but I learned from other people. . . .": Author interview with Pat Berry, August 2008.

84. Cowan "an amazing person. . . .": Author interview with Hillman, October 2008.

85. Louise Cowan quotes: Author interview, November 2008.

86. "I am enormously indebted. . . .": JH letters to mother, Hillman private archive.

87. "Madeleine volunteered at a Jewish thrift. . . .": Pat Berry written communication with author, December 2017.
88. "My parents sat once a month. . . .": Author interview with Hillman, June 2009.
89. "I thought he was an extraordinary therapist. . . .": Author interview with Gail Thomas, November 2008.
90. "was so true but also so unbelievable. . . .": Randolph Severson email to author, December 14, 2017.
91. "He had really nice luggage. . . .": Author interview with Stella Rodriguez, February 2009.
92. "Japan had a huge impact. . . .": Hillman letter to Bob Stein, December 24, 1982, Hillman private archive.
93. "Where exactly is the money complex. . . .": Hillman, "A Contribution to Soul and Money," *Spring 1982*, reprinted in *Soul and Money*, Spring Publications Dallas: 1992.
94. Dallas as "the cultural challenge. . . .", *Inter Views*, page 129.
95. "Buffalo, like Dallas, is in the midst. . . .": "Buffalo's Inner City: A Conversation Between James Hillman and Paul Kugler," *Buffalo Arts Review* 1/1 (Spring 1983), Opus Archive F83.
96. Keynote address: "The Spirit of the City," James Hillman, published in *Buffalo Arts Review* 1/2 (!983), Opus Archive F84.
97. "What seems mainly on my mind. . . .": JH letter to Thomas Moore, Moore private archive.
98. "Here were all these people moving to Dallas. . . .": Author interview with Ron Schenk, November 2008.
99. "I believe it is a pattern. . . .": JH letter to Author, 2005.
100. "When we started the project. . . .": Author interview with Gail Thomas.
101. "It was one of the highlights. . . .": Author interview with Louise Cowan, November 2008.
102. "It was not only that he was brilliant. . . .": Louise Cowan email to author.

13

MOVING EAST, CLOSING CHAPTERS

"I think it's the vegetative life that I sought in Connecticut, the green trees only a representation of the going to seed, or the corn growing, or the vegetative disturbances in my stomach. The plant psyche is persistent but receptive at the same time; the animal psyche is so damned hungry."
—*James Hillman, undated letter to Pat Berry, late 1983.*

A new era in Hillman's life began with publication of *Inter Views*, the first (and only) work to offer details of his personal biography. It was a book he originally considered titling "Skirmishes at the Border" ("No footnotes, just talk back and forth with an Italian lady," he wrote Charles Boer prior to publication).[1] It contained, as he put it, "something more than the history of events." Weren't questions about one's life, as he put it in the book, "trying to get some lore, to break into myth?"[2]

The lore turned out to be more about Laura Pozzo, listed on the cover as the woman with whom Hillman held the conversations. One reviewer, Billy Porterfield of the *Dallas Times Herald*, suspected that Hillman created his Italian interviewer out of whole cloth. "No mortal can talk like that," Porterfield wrote. "Few philosophers can cogitate like that . . . surrounded by every arcane reference, much less at the drop of a journalist's question." But it didn't really matter to Porterfield, who found himself "stunned by its iconoclastic and visionary brilliance."[3] A Hillman critic, Walter Odajnyk, wasn't so generous: "Pozzo's questions are so perspicacious . . . that I suspect the interviewer is James Hillman himself or a very close colleague." Odajnyk believed it was part of Hillman's ongoing effort to avoid being pinned down and to escape the literally real, even his own biography.[4]

In Pozzo's Preface, she described herself as an "independent journalist" who flew from Rome to Zürich in the summer of 1980 to begin interviewing Hillman for the Laterza publishing house. Translations of Hillman were already popular in Italy; both *The Myth of Analysis* and *Pan and the Nightmare* had been bestsellers there. "We are now contracting with the Italians to publish four books a year,"[5] Hillman wrote in a letter. The Q&A sessions in English for *Inter Views* were said to have continued in Rome and Ascona, followed by transcription into Italian. Hillman's Preface notes that the idea and topics were Pozzo's: "As an interviewer, she kept to the spartan single voice, thereby graciously inviting multiple and luxuriant responses to come through from my side."

Pozzo drops a hint, writing at the book's opening: "I really did not foresee what I was getting into." That's apparently the truth. Laura Pozzo was a pseudonym. The only time Hillman is known to have mentioned her real name is in an undated letter to his mother, describing the sequence of interviews and transcription. Her name is Marina Beer, the same name appearing on the cover of an early English language edition of the book (listed in 2017 on eBay.) Beer's background was "mostly in literature, both Renaissance and modern . . . and in psychology— Freudian and Jungian."[6] She would later write the biography, *Primo Levi and Italo Calvino: Two Parallel Literary Lives.*

Pat Berry, asked in 2018 what she recalled, responded: "Yes, as I remember Laura Pozzo was actually a woman named something like Marina Beer. If you found that name, it is right. She didn't like JH going over the interviews and sometimes inserting what he thought she should have asked him and what he thought he should have answered. She got in a huff and I believe they worked it out by her saying he could publish it but under some other name. Apparently like Pozzo."[7] (The English translation of "Pozzo" is a well or underground shaft).

At any rate, Hillman's longtime friend Adolf Guggenbühl was impressed with the outcome. "In *Inter Views* you really reveal yourself as a person, not only as a man with ideas," he wrote Hillman. "It was very stimulating to read *Inter Views*, because part of your development which you describe there I witnessed or saw happening. When I first met you, you were still a very— should I say, literal, Jungian. Then came the tremendous development and the pouring out of ideas. Now it is very fascinating to read all that, to see it described by yourself in *Inter Views*."[8]

It's conceivable that the "poetic license" Hillman took with his interviewee's name on the book helped to inspire another project that emerged around the time of publication. He and Pat hadn't yet decided whether to resettle on the West or East coasts, but knew they wanted to go somewhere new. In the spring of 1983, Hillman wrote to Charles Boer asking if he might find a place for them to stay in New England to escape the summer heat of Dallas. Hillman had originally met Boer through Paul Kugler, who had been Boer's student at the University of Connecticut. Best known as an English professor, Boer was also a poet and translator. He was nominated for a National Book Award for his translation of *The Homeric Hymns* from ancient Greek, and more recently translated Marsilio Ficino's *Book of Life* from Latin.

Boer enlisted Jay Livernois, then working on his Ph.D. in Comparative Literature, to see what the university's housing office might have available for Hillman. Livernois, born and raised on a Connecticut sheep farm, was also acquainted with Hillman, having taken his graduate class in Alchemy at the University of Dallas three summers before. He and Boer found that the first house on the university's list, in rural Ashford, "much to our shock met all the requirements that Jim and Pat were asking for."[9] They moved in for the summer.

It seemed to be just what Hillman needed. "I need to find a new way of working: more contemplative and less rushing to the typewriter," he wrote to Wolfgang Giegerich in mid-July. "Perhaps that's what's going on this summer: I am doing nothing but play baseball and tennis, sitting and reading, and some letters. No project. Lots of drinking too with Charles Boer who found me this farmhouse where Pat works on her dissertation and we take 5 to 8 mile walks and sometimes watch television. I am not depressed but instead enjoying this 'absence' of my usual self. The projects sit on the table, quite moribund. Reading outdoors looking at green trees and cows and cornfield is a remarkable joy."[10]

Over lunch one day, Boer and Hillman cooked up an idea for a satirical work combining Freudian psychology and recipes, purportedly based upon "discoveries" among Freud's papers in Vienna. The idea, Hillman said, was "sort of a deconstruction of the history of psychiatry" through what they came to call *Freud's Own Cookbook*. "Through these recipes, I mention all the people in German and Viennese and Swiss psychiatry, who have been forgotten but are the real backbone of the field. They could be remembered through this comedy, rather than textbooks." [11]

When Hugh Van Dusen, Hillman's editor at Harper & Row, came to the farmhouse to visit, Hillman presented a Preface he'd put together—and Van Dusen offered a decent $15,000 advance. Boer was thrilled, as that would provide ample funding to get him to southern Italy for the Eranos gathering in August. Boer brought Livernois along, and they joined Hillman in the same small hotel for the conference. Afterward, they all moved into Casa Gabriella, where Livernois first encountered Hillman's oldest daughter Julia, with whom he started an initial "very casual friendship" (he would later become her steady boyfriend). Livernois and Hillman shared the same birthday, April 12, precisely thirty years apart.

Boer and Hillman then worked together on the cookbook through the winter, mostly by phone. By early 1984, it was done. "Glad to hear you have finished," Hillman's old friend Kenny Donoghue wrote him. "It *may* finish you as a serious thinker."

Freud's Own Cookbook, "Edited by James Hillman & Charles Boer," would open with an Acknowledgment expressing their "gratitude to the Sigmund Freud Archives for not considering the manuscript of this book important enough to be put under lock and key and thus not impeding in any way its being made available to readers in this century."[12]

The *New York Times* got the picture. "It is pleasurable indeed to come upon this compendium of Sigmund Freud's tried, tested, traditional recipes," wrote the reviewer. "Many, of course, are familiar. There are the Freud Clams that most of us have tried before, his Fettucine Libido, Erogenous Scones and splendid Paranoid Pie with its special Mesmer-Icing, as well as Incredible Oedipal Pie and Momovers . . . To this day, nobody but Freud has had the courage to define the matzohball for what it is—'the ego in the midst of the primal broth' . . . In addition to its luncheon interruptus and fettucism, it contains a number of well-tested legitimate recipes and is a valuable addition to any cookbook shelf."[13]

Freud's Own Cookbook would prove a hit. Hillman and Boer did interviews on national radio and in many big newspapers. In its first month, it became Harper & Row's best seller in that line of books. Eventually *Freud's Own Cookbook* would be translated into twenty-eight different languages, from Italian to Japanese.

Hillman's colleague, Wolfgang Giegerich, wrote him from Stuttgart: "I find it very helpful to look at psychoanalysis from this kitchen perspective, it frees one from taking the old masters all too literally and seriously. So it really opens a way for an unpartisan and not disciple-like relationship to our tradition, without being in any way too iconoclastic or unrespectful . . . I really think of this book in the first place as a different kind of history book."[14]

Guggenbühl seems to have had a different reaction. "That the cookbook shocked you a bit is fine," Hillman wrote him. "That is part of its intention. It is a transgression, as humour should be . . . It is 'deconstruction' as the term is nowadays, a taking down or taking apart . . . Yes, it must even be blasphemous."[15]

Yet some took the cookbook very seriously indeed—literally. On one of several lecture trips that Hillman and Margot McLean would take to Japan in his later years, they were invited along with two Japanese scholars to a restaurant in Osaka. "In honor of James Hillman's coming," Margot would recount, "they made us a ten-course meal using all the recipes out of *Freud's Own Cookbook*, a translation of which they had in the restaurant. One of these was Fettucine Libido. We laughed as we ate. The humor that came out of *Freud's Own Cookbook* at that meal was something I'll never forget. And I have to admit some of it was delicious."

In 1983, Hillman had also published *Healing Fiction*, whose title is an apt reflection of those aspects of *Inter Views* and *Freud's Own Cookbook*. The short book is Hillman's most elaborate exploration of three predecessors—Freud, Jung, and Alfred Adler—and the metaphorical or mythic nature of their differing psychologies. Hillman especially set out to "restore Adler to us,"[16] describing him as "a forerunner of what is now called post-modern consciousness."[17] While Freudian and Jungian psychologies try to answer the question, "What does the soul want," Adler pointed out that the most important thing is "not *what* the soul wants—but *that* it wants."[18]

Adler had understood the role of "guiding fictions," Hillman noted, adding that "successful therapy" is "a collaboration between fictions, a revisioning of the story into a more intelligent, more imaginative plot, which also means the sense of mythos in all the parts of the story. Unfortunately we therapists are not aware enough that we are singers. We miss a lot of what we could be doing."[19]

Like dining on Fettucine Libido in Osaka, perhaps?

FINDING THOMPSON

Hillman and Pat loved the Connecticut summer place so much that "they decided to find and buy a house in the area and move from Dallas."[20] In September 1983, they took a trip together to look at some properties that Livernois had scouted for them, but they decided not to buy. Then in November, Pat flew East a week ahead of a lecture Hillman had scheduled in Boston. Staying at Boer's home in Pomfret, Connecticut, she rented a car and drove north up the coast as far as Gloucester, Massachusetts and then down to southern Connecticut, looking nonstop for a prospective house. She found a good possibility in the working-class seaside town of Mystic but, when he arrived, Hillman didn't like it. He was about to give up when Pat called the realtor one last time. There was an old woman who lived alone in Thompson, the last town in northeastern Connecticut on the Rhode Island and Massachusetts borders. She had put up her house for sale, but then withdrew it. Still, James and Pat were welcome to come take a look.

A little more than an hour's drive west of Boston, Thompson remained a picturesque hamlet without a single industry. There was, however, irony in Hillman's being drawn to it. In 1646, the Reverend John Eliot began "civilizing" the Indians by teaching them Christianity, after which it became known as a "Praying Town." The term "Swamp Yankee" originated here during the American Revolution, and today its International Speedway hosts an annual "World Series of Auto Racing." Along Main Street was a row of rather grand colonial and Federal dwellings and public buildings. Just off the village green, down a long gravel driveway, stood an old and haphazardly elongated wooden farmhouse. Built in the mid-nineteenth century, it appeared quite rundown, with three different families filling its upstairs, front and back. Surrounded by oaks, maples, and a lone birch tree, the house lay on five acres of land—all woods, fields, and marshlands. In that sense, it was New England idyllic. Hillman knew they'd have to tear out parts of the house and rebuild, but the price was hard to beat: between $82,000 and $85,000 for the entire property, he would remember. Also, Livernois remembered, it "was close to the highway so they could attract [therapy] clients from Boston and other smaller cities."

Pat moved first, in May 1984, and hired Livernois as the contractor to oversee redesign and rebuilding parts of the house. His father, Joseph, owned a number of properties in a town nearby and regularly hired Laotian immigrants as laborers. Learning that Hillman and Pat would need help fixing things up and taking care of the property, Joseph suggested that once the house was finished, they take in a refugee Laotian peasant family that included three girls and a boy. The family, none of whom spoke much English, would have an apartment in the back part of the house with a third floor and attic rooms for the children.

The following month, Hillman recalled, "we shipped everything up from Dallas. Some of the boxes of books we hadn't unpacked since we left Zürich six years before." He followed in their wake. Before long, Sven Doehner arrived from Dallas and, in exchange for fixing some of the locks and other work, received free analysis and lived for a few weeks in a room on the second floor. Hillman's daughter Julia also arrived and bought a house next to Jay Livernois's cottage on a lake twenty minutes away.

Hillman was interviewed by cultural historian Nicholas Fox Weber, who described his new abode: "The diverse rooms and sloping floors of that farmhouse in Thompson offer much of what he has come to revere in his professional research. In his study, he uses a sideboard made from stair treads bought locally, while his desk is a wooden table, originally used for making gloves, that he brought from Switzerland. A heavy piece of local walnut spans two file cabinets to provide a second work surface. These objects 'have display'—an imperative if things are to have soul, according to Hillman. Full of character and history (natural as well as worldly), they will also age well."[21]

Hillman wrote to Rudolf Ritsema: "We are over our heads in this new place. 6 Laotians, two huge horses, chickens, a goat and a field of five acres just mowed and ready to be plowed and planted in the Spring, with what we do not know."[22] He added in another letter: "We have taken on an immense project, for no reason. As if the Dallas maniacal side infected us and we started something far too big up here."[23]

The outside world, of course, had no idea. And in that realm, Hillman was becoming a more and more recognized name in American psychology. Despite having spent most of his adult life in Europe—even ultimately becoming a Swiss citizen—now that he'd settled on U.S. soil and moved from the nouveau Texas West to the Connecticut Yankee East, the essential Americanness of the Atlantic City boy caught the attention of commentators.

For example: A doctoral dissertation by Dennis Walsh on "The Americanization of Psyche" contained an enlightening chapter on Hillman. It quoted Walt Whitman—"I contradict myself. I am large. I contain multitudes,"—and continued: "Hillman himself is thoroughly American in his restlessness, his pioneering spirit, his pluralism and in his unrelenting energy. American too in his affection for multiple cultures, his pushing of limits, his frontier consciousness and his perpetual need to be young, undefined and continually self-renewing and self-transcending. He is equally American in his colossal lack of piety toward most conventional institutions and established traditions."[24]

Might one even call Hillman archetypally American? Following their first six weeks of summer spent in Connecticut, he expressed the alteration of his psyche in a handwritten letter to Pat from Eranos in August 1983. This had to do with stopping over in Zürich while en route. "The soul sadness, no seeing the past in the streets of Zürich . . . Zürich itself physically is beautiful—no doubt. But not where my life is: no life there for me. I am a tourist and a familiar but not an inhabitant. What anyway is a human's relation with the world, with geography, with place. Are we really *at home* here?" [25]

In the American spirit of constant re-invention, Hillman continually reworked the underpinnings of his shape-shifting psychology. "'Soul-making' does not exist really in any language," he wrote an Italian editor who proposed translating one of his works, "and is a term invented, as the use of the word *insight* as a verb (to see into, to gain insight, to see through), and several other such awkward inventions . . . What I wish to emphasize is the activity of crafting, of refining, of an operatio (as in alchemy), that one works on the soul, that it is a poiesis, a making, a *psychopoiesis*. It is contrary to the organic notion of the soul as growing, or as developing, evolving, but more an emphasis that goes with the active loving (Plato's sense of Eros) which means that Christian grace is not enough, nor is faith; but one shapes, builds, works at, animation."[26]

Hillman's full-time period in Connecticut commenced as his popularity was on the rise— the first book-length study of his thought appeared (*The New Gnosis: Heidegger, Hillman and Angels* by Robert Avens) alongside the first lengthy critical evaluations of his ideas in scholarly journals: W. A. Shelburne's, "A Critique of James Hillman's Approach to the Dream" in the *Journal of Analytical Psychology* and Walter Odajnyk's, "The Psychologist As Artist: The Imaginal World of James Hillman" in *Quadrant*. Odajnyk, a Jungian analyst and author, wrote: "Were his imagination stronger, presumably he would have become a novelist." But it wasn't just Hillman's imagination Odajnyk found wanting—he also said Hillman's work depended "mostly on rhetoric, or making an impression, rather than on solid intellectual argument . . . Ultimately, I think archetypal psychology can easily be used to avoid a real encounter with the unconscious."[27]

Guggenbühl, after reading the critique, wrote Hillman: "At least the man takes the trouble to write about you and he has certainly read you too. To my knowledge it is the first attempt of anybody to present your ideas in a coherent way. That he has some criticism doesn't really matter. What this article really means is that you are even among the Jungians now one of the established recognized authors and psychologists. What I mean is: your psychology, your ideas have now become classic, part of the general scene, and have to be known by everyone wanting to study Jungian psychology."[28]

In 1985, Hillman was invited to serve as MC at an exclusive black-tie dinner honoring Joseph Campbell at the National Arts Club in New York. The guests included "Star Wars" creator George Lucas and singer Linda Ronstadt. "No one in our century—not Freud, not Jung, not Thomas Mann, not Levi-Strauss—has so brought a mythic sense of the world back into our daily consciousness [as Campbell]," Hillman was quoted in the *New York Times*.[29]

The *Times'* Science section also carried a long Hillman profile by Daniel Goleman headlined: "In Spirit of Jung, Analyst Creates Therapy Nearer Art than Science." It began by describing a

Chinese silk screen hanging over the couch in Hillman's analytic consulting room on the second floor of his Connecticut house, "depicting a sage sitting on a bamboo deck, casting a doleful, cantankerous gaze at some exquisite birds." This seemed fitting for Hillman, Goleman said, "proposing a main goal of therapy is to heighten people's aesthetic appreciation of the world around them."[30]

Hillman would hardly have argued that point. As he wrote his European colleague, Wolfgang Giegerich: "My interests have opened into new directions. Painting . . . I give a new course now on the images of anima, a phenomenology of anima moods and desires and states as witnessed in 19th and 20th century paintings, a long slide show with 200 paintings that takes all day to look at. I am enchanted by it."[31]

In the early autumn of 1985, Hillman would return to Dallas to give a seminar on this subject at the Dallas Institute, bringing in his friends Giegerich, Guggenbühl, and Kugler to participate. "More psychological presentation happened in two days than has happened here in over a year," Robert Sardello wrote him afterward, then went on: "You seem to have released the Institute from your imagination. Of course you like the people here, but are not and understandably cannot be engaged in the internal sense. But it brings home how little is here."[32] Sardello added that he himself was applying for teaching jobs around the country.

RELEASING ERANOS

In the early 1980s, Hillman forged connections with two prominent American thinkers, Rollo May and Norman O. Brown. May was America's most influential existential psychologist, whose ideas overlapped with Hillman's distant relation, and Jung's colleague, Ludwig Binswanger. May corresponded with Hillman while working on a book, *The Cry for Myth*—in which he proposed that without myths to make sense of their lives, contemporary individuals more readily fall prey to anxiety and addiction. May wrote Hillman: "You certainly have come across in a big way to my inquiry about myths! Your books will be of great help to me and I can scarcely wait to read them."[33]

Brown, the most popular philosopher of the era, had authored several books that resonated with the sixties counterculture: *Life Against Death: The Psychoanalytical Meaning of History* (1959), where he advocated overcoming repression to face death head-on and thereby affirm life, and *Love's Body* (1966), examining and extolling the role of erotic love over civilization throughout the human saga. He and Hillman had been featured speakers at Robbie Bosnak's 1983 conference on "Facing Apocalypse," where they engaged in a private conversation about Eranos' Henry Corbin.

"All the positive that you (or I) say about Corbin is true," Brown later wrote Hillman from the University of California Santa Cruz, "and yet there is a fatal inadequacy—his obstinate exclusion of the political-historical reality. I don't think he could ever have seen, as you did in your letter to me, cosmic significance in the victory of Khomeini."

What Hillman initially wrote to Brown about the Ayatollah Khomeini seizing power from the Shah of Iran hasn't been found, but Hillman's response sheds further light on his own intellectual relationship with Corbin. "That 'fatal inadequacy' in Corbin to deal with the political may itself be political, not in the best sense that the revisioning of the world is in itself a political act, but in the worser sense that as a Protestant with a tough row to hoe in France at the Ecole des Hautes Etudes, and four years of internment in Turkey during the war, and being a man innately of 'the Right,' he kept himself out, and back. He had a very strong bourgeois layer in him, what the French call a couche . . . My own minor and very modest struggle with him was over the pathological. He could not make place for it except as such (a fallenness.) . . . Whether political or pathological the turn is similar: can the visions of the spirit ever include the actualities of the psyche."[34]

Hillman also alluded to Corbin—his importance as well as their divergences—in responding to a letter he'd received suggesting that his Greek polytheism led to nihilism. "Remember, I am a psychologist: my attempt is to speak for soul in its ongoing life, needing no salvation or redemption, enjoying its pleasures, feeling its errors, and walking right on down the road . . . The nihilism is pragmatic not ontic. It is a nihilism that says you can't ever be sure of your sureties, safe in your safeties. There is always another God around and even this God here has various relations and myths in which he or she performs differently . . .

"This means that I am not trying to build a system or follow Corbin's vision, in its prophetic or emancipatory sense. He is crucial for re-imagining psychology, for the angelology, etc., etc. But theology is always a pitfall, even a Corbinian one.

"Christianity doesn't seem able to live without theology. It has sold its mythology and its literature and its ritual too I think, to theology. Everything else is handmaiden. So, you won't entice me into theology, not even Corbin's. For me, all theology, and here I think I follow Jung, is a form of psychology, statements of the psyche."[35]

There was discussion at Eranos that, in the event of Ritsema's death, Hillman would be asked to assume responsibility for the Tagung. He indicated he would be honored to accept. Hillman had written to Ritsema after the 1980 event that "you tried to do what must be done: keep the old and new together, and they are always in danger of splitting . . . You and Catherine carried a huge load, blotting up all the spillage before it leaked onto us . . . Eranos is as important as ever and it will always be fragile and questionable, because of its very spiritual nature." [36]

For his 1981 lecture, Hillman chose "The Imagination of Air and the Collapse of Alchemy," focusing on the decline of the alchemical imagination in favor of science at the close of the eighteenth century. He wrote to Ritsema that his lecture fit the theme of the "rise and decline" of the gathering. The biologist Adolf Portmann, Hillman's other Eranos mentor besides Corbin, remained the organization's president with the task of concluding and evaluating the proceedings, and summing up the individual presentations. But Portmann's personal decline was suddenly in dramatic evidence.

Christa Robinson, present at Portmann's last presentation, recounted what transpired: "He started his talk and then stopped, fiddled around in his papers, and started again, only to stop anew. In the audience there was deep silence as it became clear that he had lost the thread of his presentation. Then I saw Rudolf Ritsema, director of Eranos for over thirty years, walk over to Adolf Portmann and take his arm and gently lead him out of the hall. Meanwhile Wladimir Rosenbaum, a lawyer and in former times an analysand of C. G. Jung, took Portmann's place and presented a twenty-minute speech, summing up and appreciating the lifework of Portmann.

"When he finished, Gershom Scholem, a Jewish historian and philosopher, took the podium and spoke for another twenty minutes about the importance of Portmann's lifework. These were spontaneous tributes given by two men who were not necessarily friendly to Adolf Portmann's way of thinking and looking at phenomena. That was also Eranos—a place where Jung's concept of the completeness of life was realized and lived."[37]

Scholem, born the same year as Portmann (1897), would die a few months before him in 1982. When the Ritsemas' note about Portmann arrived in the mail that July, Hillman was at his summer retreat in northern Sweden. He was already working on his paper for the August conclave at Eranos, whose overall theme was to be "The Play of Gods and Men." Hillman's lecture would be titled "The Animal Kingdom in the Human Dream."[38]

He responded to the Ritsemas: "This morning I was finally able to put onto paper the way Portmann can come into my paper, overtly, expressly. Then a little later we were walking to the tennis court from the front steps, when a beautiful local snake crossed our path. We stood there, four of us watching it, following it glide through the grass, noting its markings and motions, amazed, and gratified to be given this lovely show. At lunch, a large black dog walked in: the neighbor's, we had seen it on the road, but suddenly it found its way into the house while we were eating. Then when I got the post, there was the announcement of Portmann's death."[39]

In his long essay, Hillman would write: "Portmann insisted that 'appearance, like experience, is a basic characteristic of being alive.' All living things are urged to present themselves, display themselves . . . Portmann brought many kinds of evidence for these 'unaddressed appearances.'"[40]

In the letter to the Ritsemas, Hillman continued: "He was a splendid guide in many many ways, devoted, undeviating, with a very fine sensitivity. I just hope I can live long enough to grasp all I want still to learn from him, from Corbin and Scholem, and from Kerényi (whom I have so far grasped most). A death tends to remind me of the terrible old feasts of 'eating the dead' in the sense that one has the strange task not just to carry on, but to 'incorporate'—maybe this is an inflation a megalomania that comes from Saturn himself, and my father complex, but that feeling is nonetheless there. Somehow Portmann must enter my 'bloodstream.'"[41]

The dead themselves would not go gently into that good night. Hillman wrote Ritsema again a few weeks later: "Though my intention with this lecture is to honor Portmann, and it was my intention even before I had heard he died, the result is that for the first time Jewish material has crept in—as if Scholem will not be left out! The Bible, not the Greeks . . . I am shocked."[42]

The following two summers, 1983 and 1984, Hillman would attend Eranos but not give a talk—as if Scholem's and Portmann's passings marked a kind of culmination. The death of Portmann in particular, who'd made most of the executive decisions for a while, left a vacuum. No new board members were named, and Ritsema basically had to keep Eranos alive on his own. The place itself still moved Hillman deeply. He wrote Pat that "as soon as I walked around the Gabriella houses and gardens, it was like never having left; I feel a 'belonging' here which is not only history but a place of 'thought.' My thought is favored by the genius loci [the protective spirit of the place]." Looking ahead, he corresponded with Ritsema about possibly claiming Casa Gabriella for himself starting in 1990. Hillman's daughter Julia had attended the Tagung for the third time, and they were talking of jointly putting together the funds. This conversation would continue for a while, and included a back-and-forth about Julia Hillman perhaps becoming sole owner of Eranos.

At the same time, weariness seemed to be overtaking Hillman. In 1985, he was planning a lecture called "On Paranoia" for the Eranos conference themed "The Hidden Course of Events." Ritsema, however, had his doubts about the lecture after Hillman wrote him that it was "on the subject of what I must call the negative aspect of the hidden, let us say, the paranoid aspect, and especially in its relation with suspicion and enemies and war. You know I have been concerned with the psychology of war (as well as with enmity) for a long time, and have been working on the syndromes of psychopathology in lectures."[43]

Ritsema responded: "It seems to me that paranoia is not the negative aspect of the hidden, but a negative *reaction* . . . People superimpose paranoid reactions onto anything unknown, no matter whether it is a hidden development or man-made secrecies. To my feeling, this year's theme refers rather to the actual qualities of what is hidden and with the immediately perceivable aspects of our inner and outer events."[44]

Hillman then begged Ritsema to allow him to retain his two-word title and added: "You needn't worry that I shall speak only clinically. It will have a 'cosmological' aspect . . . but my aim is definitely against Western paranoid Weltbild [worldview] and so I must be true to this theme as it has urged itself on me. Of course, I shall have to recover the 'values' of paranoia, not only discharge against it."[45]

While Ritsema wrote back that the title "is certainly the shortest of the whole history of ERANOS, you have stimulated my curiosity by saying a few words about your intentions. I shall have to cool down my impatience till August."[46]

By mid-summer, Hillman was having his own doubts about the whole enterprise. He informed Giegerich that he hadn't "a clue what to do in the second hour" of the talk and that "sometimes, I feel Eranos is too much now for me. Each year I go to the edge, over the edge, teetering. I feel too old to teeter."[47]

He then wrote Ritsema: "The lecture is coming very very slowly. It is still a great confusion having not found a thread out of the labyrinth. These Eranos labors are each one, year for year, 'too much' . . . either too ambitious, or too far to reach, or beyond my capacity. I fear that this will be not nearly as entertaining as [the more recent lectures on] animals nor as beautiful as heart nor as informative as gas . . . but paranoia is a heavy topic, as is the 'hidden.'"[48]

Yet when Hillman took the podium late that August, David Miller felt "On Paranoia" was among the most profound talks he ever delivered. "He raised the question of, what's the difference between a psychotic paranoid delusion and a believer who appeals to revelation?"[49] Hillman described paranoia as "a meaning disorder," at the edge where "psychology cannot be fully separated from religion." He used case histories of the mental illnesses of a Presbyterian minister as well as the famous Freud case of Daniel Paul Schreber, letting the men's accounts speak for themselves.

For two years, Hillman had been recommending English speakers to Ritsema who he believed "would make lasting contributions to Eranos, and could carry the mantle of some of the past people whose absence (and not only economic conditions) is reflected in weakened attendance." Among others, he suggested Norman O. Brown (who would never be invited).[50]

After the 1985 gathering, Hillman confided to Giegerich (whom he had earlier convinced Ritsema to include on the program) that now "Conversations with Ritsema about the lectures is not of much use. When I mentioned to him what [David] Miller said that originally Eranos brought together people of exceptional ideas (Otto, Jung, etc.) he pointed out from the early yearbooks how many 'other sorts' were there as well. His eye is on the mediocre, I feel, and whom he can 'form,' like a stable master taking in fillies to eventually become noble champions."[51]

Late in January 1986, Ritsema wrote Hillman that he agreed to cancel his registration at Eranos, adding: "It gives such a good feeling to look back upon 15 years of smooth cooperation."[52] Their relations remained cordial but, for the first time in twenty years, Hillman would not attend Eranos that summer. He explained to Ritsema from Connecticut: "There are duties here in the house . . . I am no longer able to accomplish in a day what I used to, and yet the small obligations pile up. I simply don't want to work as much as I did in the past. And now, as the final straw—and which made it clear to me, I have lost or mislaid my Green Card which allows me to enter the USA on return. Until this is found, or reissued by the Govt, I simply can't go out of the country."[53]

Hillman worked things out for the following year. He would call his 1987 lecture "Oedipus Revisited." One angle, he wrote Ritsema, "has to do with the father/son, and revisioning the family, and what 'killing the fathers is as a psychic phenomenon, in our culture, our myth of that culture, and in psychology."[54] Afterward Hillman wrote in a letter to Hayao Kawai, a Japanese colleague: "Did you know that this year at the end of my Eranos talk, my voice broke, and tears came. It is amazing the power of the daimon at that Eranos podium!"[55]

David Miller remembered Ritsema taking him aside after the conference and swearing him to secrecy until it was announced publicly—but the next summer would be the last in the classic style of Eranos. Boarding a plane in Zürich to return to the U.S., Miller cried all the way home. Ritsema had decided to turn Eranos into a platform for his personal passion, studies of the *I Ching*. Hillman hadn't been told, but seemed prescient in his decision not to return in 1988. "I live one day at a time and have lots of resistance to high-powered intellectual things and to formalities," he wrote Ritsema that June. "Many things are breaking up & through, and until new patterns are formed, I must just take it easy."[56]

The day Ritsema announced that the future program would be different, "a north wind tempest came up outside while he spoke, and when he finished the wind dropped in the same moment," according to Christa Robinson, who worked at Eranos.[57] Hillman initially couldn't even bear to respond to the news. Finally, early in 1989, he wrote Ritsema: "When I feel quiet enough and less angry, I shall attempt a reply. I too have that 'hopeless' or 'abstracted' feeling that 'what's over is over,' and there is absolutely no sense in my exerting myself at all about what you have set your mind on, else you would have years ago spoken with me. I do believe you truly wish no response.

"Despite this that I think and feel now, and where you are now, I do look back with great pleasure and humor, and also gratitude, to our years together, and with Catherine, and to Gabriella, and the friendship, which in my heart is still there."[58]

Hillman would go on in future correspondence to plead his case with Ritsema that his *I Ching* studies needn't replace Eranos itself. "A large and generous reconciliation," was still possible in Hillman's view—"a collaboration with the old guard, of whom I am" with "a new young group of direction and administration composed of those who are most traditionally associated with Eranos, like Hinshaw, Robbie, Giegerich, young [Hayao] Kawai." Wouldn't that ensure "that the property and the *spiritus loci* does not go to a bank and become another condominium. Those ghosts will not accept that, but those ghosts do not perform miracles. They are not angels."[59]

The next response from Ritsema ignored all that, dealing only with copyright arrangements concerning *Spring*'s publication of the Eranos Lecture Series. Allegedly, there was an omission in the catalogue—pointed out by Joseph Campbell's literary agent. Ritsema added: "There is another matter I should also mention: your closet in the piano room. Through all these years we have faithfully kept this closet for you, we are now both over 70 [sic: Hillman was just turning sixty] and I don't feel we can pledge ourselves to anything beyond the end of 1989. You should avail yourself of your presence in Europe to pass by and pack the material." Such were "the burdens of aging!"[60]

The empty closet . . . did this conjure images of Kate's packing up all of Hillman's belongings almost fifteen years before, shipping them to the apartment in the Tessin that Ritsema had provided him? Did Ritsema know this? At any rate, Hillman could not bring himself to follow up on the request. "My time in Europe was very tightly planned in advance," he wrote back. "So I rushed through, and could not empty that little closet. I suggest you simply open it up and put contents all in a storage box, and next time I have a chance I'll collect it. We still haven't settled the Dictionaries, and I have a deep nostalgic longing for the old RED one with the Latin Appendix I found so useful."

Ritsema said he'd send those along, and could ship the closet contents to a storage house in Zürich where Hillman's daughter Julia still had some belongings. He reminded Hillman in a subsequent letter that the closet would need to be emptied by the beginning of the next year, because "we are at present doing a thorough cleaning and renovation of Casa Gabriella."[61] Hillman wrote back: "Concerning the things left in the closet at Gabriella; I don't believe there is very much there—but who knows? So, why not junk it all into a cardboard box and post it to Carola [Hillman's daughter who still lived in Switzerland]." He added that he was "delighted to receive the red dictionary that I relied on for so many years."[62]

April 14, 1990: "Dear Ru, thank you so much for sending the box to Carola. So now the closet is empty; a chapter closed. I have so many memories of that room!"

One more letter followed from Hillman that summer. It indicated he'd like to meet with Ritsema and his wife, and acknowledged that he would miss "the idea or spirit of Eranos . . . Frankly, I would like to see an entire *renewal*, a fresh spirit with new people."[63]

Ritsema responded that this was "exactly what we have in mind for the upcoming Eranos Round Table Conferences" and enclosed the announcement, asking: "How do you feel about joining one of next year's conferences about dream and oracle?"[64]

There was no mention of the underworld. And after fifty years of Eranos, what had been was over. A revival would later be presided over by a gentleman who headed the Hilton hotel chain.

QUICKSAND

Pat had felt the shift happening with her therapeutic practice in Dallas. "I began to see how archetypal psychology got *mis*used," she recalled. "People would come in saying all the right things, talking about gods and goddesses, and be using it as a defense, hiding behind it, being afraid to talk about their personal lives or their relationships . . . Someone would excuse their behavior because they were a child of Dionysus . . . For me that was very upsetting because it meant that the idea could be used defensively . . . It was like a crisis of belief."[65]

She'd "worked a lot of it out" in her doctoral dissertation, examining what she called the "psychopoetics" of Jung's early writing, where he used scientific and medical language but came to very different intuitive conclusions. "But by the end of it I was sick, felt this is all words, all tricks.[66] There was something in me that was not sticking to what I was supposed to feel or think as an Archetypal Psychologist," she remembered. At the same time, Hillman "had to be true to his own thing, the psychology he had founded and wanted to extend into the world. His work turned in a way that I couldn't turn. I felt it was becoming more reified and literal than it had been in its early years. I was increasingly drawn to more depth and intimacy in relationships, both personal and therapeutic. When I began to dream of the walls of the house falling down, I knew we were in trouble."[67]

Finishing the dissertation had exhausted her, "like I had burned out my intellectualism and needed to be just an ordinary person, re-find something natural or physical," Pat said in our first interview. The farm in Thompson, where she could ride horses bareback, initially seemed to fulfill that need. "But I didn't want to write. And Jim kept wanting me to write, and be with him, and he was writing all the time."[68]

He was also aging, and reflecting on what that meant. In a letter, Hillman wrote: "In some ways one gets more efficient with age"—noting that he "cuts more easily right to the point, at the same time I find my resistance to work increasing so I don't really like sitting at the table for too many hours at a stretch.

"The relation to work, and therewith to the 'spirit' is a primary occupation. Strange, one would think it would be anima questions, sex, or death, or what have you . . . but it's not, it's the question of getting the 'mind' or the spirit in the right place."[69]

After they came to Connecticut, Hillman gave a more earthy life a good shot, even taking up driving again. "Pat and I took a ride in the woods and through fields on the horses for nearly two hours," he wrote Guggenbühl. "You cannot imagine how exhilarated . . . it makes one associate back to colonial horse times, and the mixture of the animal and keeping close to it, plus the passive sitting on its back as a pair of eyes and ears, this strange double sort of passivity and intense alert activity to the movements of the animal . . . but I also like driving the Honda."[70]

Pat worried about his new proclivities, and not without reason. "On horseback he tended to be wild beyond his abilities," she recalled. "One time galloping along out of control on one of the horses he went under a low hanging branch that knocked off his glasses and nearly himself. That wasn't a big thing [to him]. Another time we were riding in the woods when he let his horse (Justin) wander into a bog in which they began to sink. I yelled at him to get off the horse and hang onto a tree. Finally he did and we were able to urge this 1,200 pound horse to use his last effort to get himself up and out of the quicksand. He did, but it was a scary event."[71]

On February 2, 1986, the day Hillman and Pat celebrated ten years of marriage, he wrote to Guggenbühl: "I had thought that living here would make all sorts of virtues possible: exercise, nature, garden, reading, writing, friends, but I remain still trapped inside my intense Jewish urban mind, with its desire for more and more, still 'untamed sulphur.'"[72]

His and Pat's collaborations didn't disappear. They both had therapeutic practices in different rooms of the house. They continued to travel together and give talks and seminars, including a four-day gathering late in 1984 in Santa Barbara on "Fairy Tales, Dreams and the Journey to Elsewhere" and a three-day seminar on archetypal psychology in Oxford, England. They attended Eranos together in 1985, where "Pat says that here the spirits work with you, while in America you have to work against them to write something."[73]

Back in America, in addition to riding her horses, Pat began playing sports—baseball and then volleyball—and skipped accompanying Hillman to Italy because her team had a final game she felt she couldn't miss. Hillman wrote Guggenbühl resignedly: "Pat seems to have left the intellectual world altogether: horses, fences, grain, hinges, homework for the Laotian girl and interpretations for the Laotian man and his work at the factory. She also spends days on the Interregional [Jungian] Training System. Politics."[74]

THE ONCE-IN-A-LIFETIME BIRTHDAY

Hillman's sixtieth birthday party was slated for the Fourth of July weekend in 1986. In the month or so previous, several positive developments had occurred. Charles Boer had agreed to take over the helm of Spring Publications, which Hillman noted was now surviving with "better management. Bigger sales. But also bigger discounts so that profit is still a mirage." Profit, however, had been handsome on another front: "We sold Dallas house for ¼ million dollars!!! And I don't know how to invest it. I am scared," he wrote to Guggenbühl.[75]

The Laotian family had moved out ("the father wants his own place, among his own kind, a town nearby with ten families") and Kenny Donoghue arrived from Ireland to take over the apartment at the back of the house. He would handle care of the animals, while going daily to the library across the street—and translating Wolfgang Giegerich's paper, "Burial of Soul in Technical Civilization," for publication in *Spring*.

The farmhouse guest room had rarely been empty, but the property was soon to be overflowing. Hillman's birthday invitations were inscribed with "ON BEING HERE" and "ON GETTING HERE," and noted: "The bash begins sometime in the early afternoon, Saturday. Events. Sports. Towards evening: acts and music." As for clothing: "New England Country Informal, like colonial irregulars." He wrote one attendee: "Pat's organizing performances, so if you have a speech, an act, a dance, an imitation, a song—whatever, it's wanted. (Costumes included)."[76] And to another: "It will be *Gigantic*, like the 1920s."[77] Jay Livernois and Julia Hillman, who'd become a couple the year before, would be the primary organizers.

Altogether about 120 people would attend the party, many staying in nearby inns or bed-and-breakfasts. They flew in from Texas, California, Minnesota, England, and elsewhere. Adolf Guggenbühl and his wife Anne came all the way from Switzerland, Bianca Garufi and her husband Pierre Denivelle from Italy. A new friend, the poet Robert Bly, was there. Also in attendance was the daughter of the late CIA Director Allen Dulles, Joan Buresch—a friend of both Pat's and Hillman's from the Zürich years. Hillman's four children were on-hand, and twenty-six-year-old Laurence showed family movies and ultimately joined his father in a tap-dance. Some jazz musicians provided early entertainment, while a pig roasted over a spit in the backyard.

Hillman wrote Giegerich afterward, to tell him he was missed at the party, and to recount how it went: "The party was a festival lasting three days and it seems people came away exhausted by the extraversion (even if in the country with green all around) and at the same time renewed, refreshed. Pat and I were surprised how easy it went; how it flowed along without 'management' . . . I had spent three months learning to tapdance and to great surprise, danced with my teacher."[78]

His longtime friend Bob Stein found it a "fantastic" celebration where "the eros was terrific . . . highlighted by your spectacular dancing feat."[79] Anne Guggenbühl wrote Hillman afterward: "I have never experienced anything at all like it, and I feel that it somehow changed something deeply in me."[80] Robert Bly reflected on "all the zaniness, family, peacock generosity, 19th century warmth and lively conversation."[81] Ginette Paris wrote of his "very Zeus-like hospitality" and "Hermes-like vivacity," amid everyone "chatting and drinking delicious wine under the trees, with children playing around and horses moving in the background."[82]

An undercurrent was also moving through it—something Hillman felt compelled to reflect upon in a letter to Guggenbühl. It was "like a convocation of the blessed, a heaven-fantasy. And so it has a base in something transcendent and also manic. That's why it was so 'big' physically-geographically. Why everything was 'too much'—even the music far too loud . . . And of course our simple 'ego's' Pats and mine were not up to managing it properly . . . we just were carried away with the Great Idea of it. The little details like rooms and food and films and so on went without hitch, but there was a human failing all through."

Hillman had planned to introduce and welcome everyone, speaking about strands of the past and new babies and remembering the missing, including the dead. But that didn't happen, and he deeply regretted it. "And now after the event these mistakes, these lost moments, this opportunity eats me every morning . . . Here was good eros and bad feeling, and it is amazing how long feeling mistakes continue to eat at the heart afterwards.

"It's of course partly cultural: extraversion of a certain sort, performance (my dancing eclipsed my consciousness so much that I was utterly narrowed for two hours before worrying about being able to do it) . . . The wall-less picnic grounds, the fourth of July as explosion and riotous looseness, the pig . . . all this had an effect too of blocking that recollection that we were all here for something and that that something needed articulation and words were needed also to bring people together not only 'action.'

"So the opportunity is missed and the moment can never occur again. It is like a general who erred at a certain moment in a battle. It also shows that the 'Gods' can be present, as I feel they were in that lucky feeling that went on throughout, and yet something human is missing."[83]

The human element was missing in more ways than one. This was to be the first and only occasion that Pat's mother met Hillman's mother. Pat recalled: "My mother and stepfather had arrived a day before the party and were staying in their trailer parked in the driveway. When Jim's mother arrived, I was in my office, but looked out the window in time to see my mother walk across the lawn to Madeleine to introduce herself. What occurred then nearly killed me. Madeleine put her nose in the air and turned away, visibly snubbing my mother. I felt such anguish for my mother. It was like two parts of my being colliding. I am so glad my mother had enough sense of her own worth not to leave, but for the rest of the events she and my stepfather stayed in the shadows, discretely away from the party."[84]

Interestingly, Anne Guggenbühl's letter to Hillman said of Hillman's mother that she "has mellowed since I saw her last and is quite incredible—she remembers *everything*." Anne also "enjoyed meeting Pat's parents. I asked her mother 'and how long have you known Pat and Jim?' I never dreamt she was her mother as she looked too young."

DEPARTURE

A little more than a year later, his Saturn return was ending when Hillman began a letter to Guggenbühl: "As I write this on Monday Labor Day morning [1987], our local white church is still burning. It started at nine, and at eleven thirty, they are still trying to finish putting the fire out. No water. They have to pump it from trucks and ponds. Nearest pond is more than half a mile. The green is covered with people, cars, trucks, dogs. The minister's wife (our next door neighbor) is on the ground

shaking, Pat's with her. The children were 'kept from seeing it'
. . . why? A terrible thing to watch, the roaring orange flames
inside the belltower, the smoke coming from the steeple like an
inferno. I am still shocked in my solar plexus. I was close to tears
watching. The communal part—neighbors, the postmistress
pale as ash for she is like the 'keeper of the green,' the cop who
shoes our horses, clustered all of us. I talked with neighbors I
never see or ever speak with. The new organ is watered out, and
now Pat just came back in to get the trucks for they are going to
load the stuff in the church and move it to keep from looters.

"There was a big barn and farm burning two days ago where
we often ride. I went past the next day on the horse—a black
ruin, with a burnt out van, while in the field four horses just
gaze away as if nothing happened."

Early in the year, Hillman had wryly described returning from
a trip to Japan immediately after going to Milan: "It was all too
much, and I more or less collapsed. Now, home again, burdened
by my history of heroic accomplishments—too many activities requiring 'attention': patients, normal life and its ridiculous
complications, family, lectures, writing, and Spring. Publ.—this
business that puts into the bank now 250,000 dollars a year and
ships 50,000 books a year from the warehouse, we take more out
than goes in! Everything is too much. Especially editing *Spring*
each year. I shall give it up and just keep the publishing business
going, but the annual is such an effort . . . And, writing is a torture when one has to do other things too so that one can't enjoy
the freedom of it. My actual life is enviable in every way, but
this hero-daimon won't let me pleasureably live it. And at 60!"[85]

Amid all the shadows, in retrospect Pat's separation seems
inevitable. While possessing a tough exterior, she'd been
wounded by the kinds of remarks people would make to her. At
an event, someone told her: "Well, we wouldn't even be listening to you if you weren't James Hillman's wife." A close friend
of both Hillman and Pat recalled: "She was always worried that
people were relating to her because they wanted a way to him.
That made her very paranoid about people's loyalties." Her own

leaned more and more toward relationships with other women; it is not known how much Hillman knew about this.

Hillman wrote to a colleague in England in the summer of 1987 that, while he and Pat had loved recently visiting there, "that was her—for the time—swan song of lecturing. She now plays ball most of the time . . . baseball teams and volleyball teams and trophies, and horses too."[86] And in a letter to Ritsema: "Very different worlds & interests we each have: *classically Jungian*: I am more & more 'aesthetic' and she more and more *active, physical, local*, so we live more & more in our own worlds, tho' with ease & friendliness and share the work of our large place—neither dependent on the other, & it is satisfactory, tho' not altogether."[87] His longtime Eranos friend responded: "Your letter of December 2 moved me deeply. It is sad when the flow of life and libido takes a direction that parts from one's partner's river."[88]

Then in her early forties, Pat felt "at a different stage, still needing to explore and form." She said during an interview in 2011 that "at another time, there's no question I would have stayed. But at this time, with the women's movement, there seemed permission to go lead a different life, and that's what I wanted to do. I think I needed to explore other relationships and more kinds of psychology. Being with women I got closer to a part of myself that was more sensate, emotional, real and ordinary (like my mother) . . . aspects of life that were missing with me and Jim in our intellectualness and sophisticated lifestyle. Even though I loved him more than I've ever loved anybody." Pat added, tears in her eyes: "But my God, what it did to him!"[89]

As 1988 dawned, he knew it was imminent. He wrote in a letter: "Pat and I live in separate parts of the house. How the future will unfold for us each, who knows, but it won't unfold for us together. Our feelings, our interests and our lives are now—and have been for about two years more and more divergent."[90]

And in February, writing to Michael Ventura, he reflected: "I am at times in splendid shape, a world opening, a freedom

I never had, at times collapse and despair; I am coming to the end of the marriage"—concluding,. "Our ways go so different; mine to anima, hers to athletics, and our mutual intellectual life phases out. How strange."[91]

Pat recalled that when she told Hillman she wanted to move out, "We both collapsed on the floor in tears. He asked what he did wrong. I said, 'Nothing, absolutely nothing.' I think I want to be with women."[92] The date, she would remember almost thirty years later, was March 3, 1988. After Pat left for Cambridge, Massachusetts, to care for a friend's cats who was leaving the country for a few weeks, Hillman expressed his pain in a letter to Guggenbühl.

"Dear Adolf, I was glad for your call. I haven't written because I haven't been able to. I'm still not able to. So much goes on in my psyche every day and especially at night while I lie awake for hours. It is my kind of heart attack I suppose, one in the feeling-heart. I haven't been alone since age 22, and I can't bear it. And don't want it . . . The depth of the illusions lived with Pat, and the discoveries of my repressions and accommodations in order to live with Pat come daily to the surface, and their roots seem ever deeper. In this I am reliving all sorts of things with my time with Kate. It's a complete overhaul of my life."[93]

Donoghue was still staying in the house with him "and provides excellent companionship." Hillman also felt closer to Julia;. Carola was visiting, and Laurence had come through. By now Pat had found an apartment and, by June, would buy a duplex in Cambridge with additional rooms for renting out. Her analytic practice was growing, and she traveled back and forth to Thompson weekly—to see patients there and play volleyball with her team, the Blue Angels.

Hillman described Pat as "'on her own' and of course in the midst of a kind of breakdown herself." Two years later, she would write him: "Much of who I am was formed by, with and around you. I was so young when we met (23. 25 when we became involved in what was to prove fatefully). You grew me up through my 20s & 30s, educated me, shared thoughts, worlds, experiences—all of which formed me . . . made me rich in life and soul. I can never repay you for this in any direct sense. How I did pay you, I guess, was with my own life, our shared life. We both gave and gained from what we were together. I don't know how or why that ran out for me (despite the thousands of dollars spent in therapy the past 2 years trying to figure it out). I do know I can't go on living in guilt (right or wrong) and that I must go with the strength of new life that is now beginning to return to me."[94]

Hillman, looking through old letters on a trip back to Zürich, would recount to Pat reading snatches of his correspondence with Kate dating back to the very first in 1947. "They had so little content, so little actual particular relationship content," he reflected. "Looking at my images in fotos from 1947 through 1965—what a stupid bourgeois jewish boy. You've had quite a hand in 'what I am today.' Your perceptions and challenges and being so fucking difficult—all those early neurotic reactions in 1968–1971 were 'right' inasmuch as they were released by my unconscious bourgeois patterns of relating as 'consideration' and managing. Looking back, I think you did right to react as you did. Animal."[95]

In a letter to Guggenbühl, Hillman wrote: "In all this I dream and dream of radical changes: like all the books I've written no longer there . . . like big trees being cut down, and very small ones planted . . .

"Sometimes I'm glad for all this, that I can still be alive and find a new phase of life with new opportunities, new women, new perceptions and feelings and discoveries. Other times, I prefer to return to the stability of before, even if 'false.' Stability seems the main word I use with myself, and seem to have little of it. I go dancing 3 times a week, I write my articles and edit *Spring*, and carry on the usual life, except for letters. But I can't imagine what the future will be. This is a large and lonely life, this house in the country, and I am not connected to the people around here, as has always been my style. My friends, and as often in the past, my loves, live far away . . . so much is 'in the mind.'"[96]

Hillman would write again to Guggenbühl a couple of months later, and elaborate: "As for Pat and our deeper connection: it had the depth of our mutuality. It was very generative—after all *Spring* and archetypal psychology did come from it. It brought me back to America, and her psychopathic style loosened up lots of my paranoia."[97]

To another colleague, Hillman explained: "My life fell apart this winter and spring, though the underpinnings had crumbled long before, though I blithely preferred not to notice . . . I am in a phase of what might be called radical catastrophe and reorganization."[98]

Thirty years later, Pat reflected: "Our separation was actually ideological. We had these fights back and forth where he accuses me of making everything personal, and I'm accusing him of making everything ideological. What I came to in myself is, I'm a psychotherapist and I'm interested in people and like hearing people's stories, more than I'm interested in justice or beauty or truth. Those are abstractions to me. In letters I've come across recently, I kept asking him to talk and why can't we go to therapy. Of course that was anathema, because he's been writing against it the whole time!"[99]

He and Pat would remain friends, even confidantes, for a time. She had Thanksgiving with him and the (now-adult) children in 1988, and her birthday dinner with him and friends at the house the following January. Their divorce would not be finalized until 1991. But already for Hillman life was taking a very different direction. It wasn't long after Pat left that he stopped practicing analysis and turned down Ritsema's invitation to Eranos.

Hillman had earlier written Guggenbühl of having observed at an Inter-Regional Jungian gathering "how few of the members take any 'political' interest, or joy in thinking about what is going on. It is as if all this is 'not psychological.' That is the usual defense. But more deeply is a desire to be innocent. I am convinced that this is the theme of the American psyche—innocent means good, and means saved, and means the 'child.' It is said that innocence and its conversion to experience is the dominant theme of American literature from 1800 . . . It has to do with protection from sophistication and culture: as if these elements of life were per se sinful and unnatural.

"At the end of May," he went on, "I have three days in California with a group of aging puer men who meet regularly (through Robert Bly)."[100] He already counted himself among them, and the aging of the body did not sit well with him, perhaps for the first time. He mused: "That one must give oneself over to the deterioration process: this is so foreign to consciousness over here. Here, the older one gets the more one 'combats' ageing. Wherever you go, even here in the country, people are jogging, men out gardening at 84 (the old toothless man across the street.) It is not just a cult of youth, not a fear of dying. But what is it? On the one hand I refuse to do exercises. I just can't (although I love sports and games), and on the other hand I look at my skinny arms and legs, and my spreading stomach, and see the bodybuild of sixty to seventy appearing. I both like it and don't want it. It occupies my fantasy. I passed much of the winter dealing with new glasses (they are still not right), a new gold tooth and root canals (rot inside the root), poison ivy treatments, and four times a cold—including again now, after an airplane trip. I am used to hypochondria—all the pains and pseudo (?) heart anxieties and bowel cancer anxieties and so on, but that this deterioration real or imagined should be so much the focus of fantasy, this does disturb me."[101]

Sven Doehner, who'd been in analysis with Hillman, recalled going to see him after Pat left: "He opened up in a way that was very intimate. One of the subjects that came up was his own thoughts of suicide. He mentioned, when he'd written the book [*Suicide and the Soul*, 1965], he had no idea what he was writing about. That's the honesty of the man, that he could say that to me was extraordinary. I remember him also saying, 'Maybe what I should be doing is getting close to my friends, but I feel like getting as far away from my friends as I possibly can.' It was six months later that he joined with Robert Bly and Michael Meade, and started going into the woods with the men. I think his way of grounding, as they say nowadays, or finding some kind of stability, was not to go back to the old faces."[102]

Around this same time, Hillman had done a weekend seminar on Family, "a fantastic subject, and as a social fact rapidly disappearing." He'd also given a talk in Birmingham, Alabama, on the subject of white supremacy, "how the social problem is archetypally based in 'white consciousness.'"[103] He'd "started a new kind of lecture course: 'anima' with two hundred slides—a phenomenology of men's moods and desires—of paintings from the 19th and 20th century."[104] Each of these subjects would come to the fore in the next phase of Hillman's life, a profound exploration of masculinity that he first referenced in the letter about his aging physicality.

"Last week I did some 'teaching' . . . in a men's group (93 men) in an old CCC camp from the thirties in the redwood forest in remote northern California. The place was deep fern and forest, with stumps the size of houses where trees had been cut in the 1890s, and the new 'young' trees were larger than anything you see normally. I noticed that the deeper issues such as decline of body, the sexual anxieties, the actual and concrete got sort of passed over in conceptualized feelings and resentments about fathers and sons, about male bonding, and so on. Actually, I enjoyed it. It was a 'test': could I be among men on that level and yet remain the effeminate scholarly jewish person I am. I managed to be on the one hand as they were and also not as they were. It was sort of a redemption of my navy days and my camp days as a boy."[105]

It wasn't just redemption Hillman experienced, but renewal . . . rooted in the mythopoetic, aspiring toward a different culture. James Hillman was becoming, as the phrase goes, one of the guys.

NOTES

1. "Skirmishes at the Border. . . .": JH undated letter to Charles Boer, courtesy of Jay Livernois, Boer archive.
2. "something more than the history of events. . . .": *Inter Views*, Page 111.
3. "No mortal can talk like that. . . .": Column by Bill Porterfield, "The good Dr. Soul in a sick world," *Dallas Times Herald*, April 25, 1983.
4. "Pozzo's questions are so perspicacious. . . .": "The Psychologist as Artist: The imaginal World of James Hillman, by V. Walter Odajnyk, *Quadrant*, 1984.
5. "We are now contracting with the Italians. . . .": Hillman letter to Pat Berry, undated.
6. "mostly in literature. . . .": *Inter Views*, p. vii.
7. "She didn't like JH going over. . . .": Email from Pat Berry to author, December 15, 2017.
8. In *Inter Views* you really reveal. . . .": Guggenbühl letter to Hillman, April 19, 1983, Opus Archive.
9. "much to our shock. . . .": Jay Livernois written response to author's questions, August 2018.
10. "I need to find a new way of working. . . .': Hillman letter to Wolfgang Giegerich, arrived July 17, 1983, Giegerich private archive.
11. "sort of a deconstruction. . . .": Author interview with Hillman.
12. "gratitude to the Sigmund Freud Archives. . . .": *Freud's Own Cookbook*, Edited by James Hillman & Charles Boer, Harper Colophon Books, 1985, p. vii.
13. "It is pleasurable indeed. . . .": Review of *Freud's Own Cookbook*, by Fred Ferretti, *The New York Times Book Review*, May 26, 1985.
14. "I find it very helpful. . . .": Letter from Wolfgang Giegerich to Hillman, October 22, 1985, Opus Archive.
15. "That the cookbook shocked you. . . .": Letter from Hillman to Adolf Guggenbühl, undated, Guggenbühl archive.
16. "restore Adler to us. . . .": Hillman, *Healing Fiction*, p. 129.
17. "a forerunner of what is now called. . . .": Ibid, p. 110.
18. "not *what* the soul wants. . . .": Ibid, p. 129.
19. "Successful therapy. . . .": Hillman, *Healing Fiction*, Putnam, Ct: Spring Publications, Inc., 2004 4th edition, pp. 17–18.
20. "They decided to find and buy. . . .': Jay Livernois answers to Author's questions. 2019.
21. "The diverse rooms and sloping floors. . . .": "Habits and Habitations," by Nicholas Fox Weber, *Connecticut* magazine, March 1987.
22. "We are over our heads. . . .": Hillman letter to Rudolf Ritsema, November 9, 1984, Eranos archive.
23. "We have taken on an immense project. . . .": Hillman letter to Wolfgang Giegerich, November 14, 1984, Giegerich private archive.
24. "Hillman himself is thoroughly American. . . .": Dennis Walsh, "The Americanization of Psyche," Opus Archive.
25. "The soul sadness. . . .": Hillman letter to Pat Berry, August 1983 (undated), Berry private archive.
26. "'Soul-making' does not really exist. . . .": JH letter to Dear Mr. Rabu, Spring 1986.

27. "Were his imagination stronger. . . .": Walter Odanyjk, Quadrant.

28. "At least the man takes the trouble. . . .": Guggenbühl letter to JH, June 15, 1984, Opus Archive.

29. "No one in our century. . . .": "A Master of Mythology is Honored," by Leslie Bennetts, *The New York Times*, March 1, 1985.

30. "depicting a sage sitting. . . .": "In Spirit of Jung, Analyst Creates Therapy Nearer Art than Science," by Daniel Goleman, *New York Times* "Science Times," July 2, 1985.

31. "My interests have opened. . . .": Hillman letter to Wolfgang Giegerich, June 4, 1985, Giegerich private archive.

32. "You seem to have released the Institute. . . ." Robert Sardello letter to Hillman, October 29, 1985, Opus Archive.

33. "You certainly have come across. . . .': Letter from Rollo May to James Hillman, December 28, 1983, Opus Archive.

34. The Norman O. Brown correspondence comes from Robert Hinshaw's private archive of Hillman's papers in Einsedelen, Switzerland.

35. "Remember, I am a psychologist. . . .": JH letter to Emerson C. Fersch, May 29, 1986.

36. "You tried to do what must be done. . . .": JH letter to Ritsema, August 31, 1980, Eranos archive.

37. "He started his talk and then stopped. . . .": *Living With Jung*, chapter "Hearing a Similar Voice: Christa Robinson at 68," page 143.

38. "The Animal Kingdom in the Human Dream" is reprinted as the lead essay on *Animal Presences: James Hillman Uniform Edition No. 9*, Putnam, Ct.: Spring Publications, 2008, pp. 9–57.

39. "This morning I was finally able. . . .": Hillman letter to "Dear Ru and Catherine," July 7 or 8, 1982, Eranos archive.

40. "The Animal Kingdom in the Human Dream," p. 51.

41. "He was a splendid guide. . . .": Hillman letter to "Dear Ru and Catherine," July 7 or 8, 1982, Eranos Archive.

42. "Though my intention with this lecture. . . .": Hillman letter to Rudolf Ritsema, July 26, 1982, Eranos archive.

43. "on the subject of what I must call. . . .": Hillman letter to Ritsema, November 9, 1984, Eranos archive.

44. "It seems to me that paranoid. . . .": Rudolf Ritsema letter to Hillman, November 19, 1984, Eranos archive.

45. "You needn't worry that I shall speak. . . ..": Hillman letter to Ritsema, January 19, 1985, Eranos archive.

46. "It is certainly the shortest. . . .": Ritsema letter to Hillman, January 28, 1985, Eranos archive.

47. Hadn't "a clue what to do. . . .": Hillman letter to Wolfgang Giegerich, June 4, 1985, Giegerich private archive.

48. "The lecture is coming very very slowly. . . .": Hillman letter to Ritsema, July 17, 1985, Eranos archive.

49. "He raised the question. . . .": Author interview with David Miller, June 2008.

50. "would make lasting contributions to Eranos. . . .": Hillman letter to Ritsema, August 25, 1983, Eranos archive.

51. "Conversations with Ritsema about the lectures. . . .": Hillman letter to Wolfgang Giegerich, September 5, 1985, Giegerich private archive.

52. "It gives such a good feeling. . . ." Ritsema letter to Hillman, January 24, 1986, Eranos archive.

53. "The Laotians have moved out. . . .": Hillman letter to Ritsema, July 14, 1986, Eranos archive.

54. "has to do with the father/son'. . . .' Hillman letter to Ritsema, February 1, 1987, Eranos archive.

55. "Did you know that this year. . . .": Hillman undated letter to Hayao Kawai, Opus Archive.

56. "I live one day at a time. . . .': Hillman letter to Ritsema, June 25, 1988, Eranos archive.

57. "a north wind tempest came up. . . .": Author interview with Christa Robinson, October 2010.

58. "When I feel quiet enough and less angry. . . .": Hillman letter to Ritsema, February 19, 1989, Eranos archive.

59. "a large and generous reconciliation. . . .": Hillman letter to Ritsema, July 26, 1989, Eranos archive.

60. "There is another matter. . . .": Ritsema letter to Hillman, August 3, 1989, Eranos archive.

61. "we are at present doing a thorough cleaning. . . .": Ritsema letter to Hillman, November 29, 1989, Eranos archive.

62. "Concerning the things left in the closet. . . .": Hillman letter to Ritsema, December 15, 1989, Eranos archive.

63. "the idea or spirit of Eranos. . . .": Hillman letter to Ritsema, July 1, 1990, Eranos archive.

64. "exactly what we have in mind. . . .": Ritsema letter to Hillman, July 25, 1990, Eranos archive.

65. "People would come in saying. . . .": Pat Berry interview with Lyn Cowan; "Someone would excuse their behavior....": Pat Berry podcast with Michael Lerner, January 16, 2015.

66. "But by the end of it I was sick. . . ." Ibid.

67. "There was something in me. . . .": Pat Berry, Side by Side interview.

68. "like I had burned out my intellectualism. . . .": Author interview with Pat Berry.

69. "In some ways one gets more efficient. . . .": Hillman letter to Mary Watkins, undated, mid-1980s, Watkins private archive.

70. "Pat and I took a ride in the woods. . . ." Hillman letter to Guggenbühl, May 10, 1985, Guggenbühl private archive.

71. "He tended to be wild. . . .': Pat Berry email to author, December 30, 2017.

72. "I had thought that living here. . . .': Hillman letter to Adrolf Guggenbühl, February 2, 1986, Guggenbühl private archive.

73. "Pat says that here the spirits. . . .": Hillman letter to Wolfgang Giegerich, September 5, 1985, Giegerich private archive.

74. "Pat seems to have left. . . .": Hillman letter to Guggenbühl, May 10, 1985, Guggenbühl private archive.

75. Surviving "with better management. . . .": Hillman letter to Guggenbühl, June 6, 1986, Guggenbühl private archive.

76. "Pat's organizing performances. . . ." Hillman note to Gail Thomas, provided author.

77. "On Being Here. . . .It will be gigantic": Hillman invitation and note to Ginette Paris, Paris private archive.

78. "The party was a festival. . . .": Hillman letter to Wolfgang Giegerich, July 28, 1986, Giegerich private archive.
79. "a 'fantastic' celebration. . . .': Robert Stein letter to Hillman, Hillman private archive.
80. "I have never experienced anything. . . .": Anne Guggenbühl letter to "Dear Pat and Jim," July 29, 1986, Opus Archive.
81. "all the zaniness. . . .": Robert Bly letter to "Dear James and Pat," August 8, 1986, Opus archive.
82. "very Zeus-like hospitality. . . .": Ginette Paris letter to Hillman, undated, Paris private archive.
83. "like a convocation of the blessed. . . .": Hillman letter to Guggenbühl, July 1986, undated, Guggenbühl archive.
84. "My mother and stepfather had arrived. . . .": Pat Berry email to author, December 30, 2017.
85. "It was all too much. . . .": JH letter to Wolfgang Giegerich, February 20, 1987 postmark.
86. "that was her—for the time—swan song. . . .": Hillman letter to Peter Tatham, undated, summer 1987, Opus archive.
87. "Very different worlds & interests. . . .": JH letter to Rudolf Ritsema, December 2, 1987, Eranos archive.
88. "Your letter of December 2 moved me. . . .": Ritsema letter to JH, January 6, 1988, Eranos archive.
89. "at a different stage. . . .": Pat Berry interview with author, December 2011, and email to author, December 2017.
90. "Pat and I live in separate parts. . . .: Hillman letter to Ginette Paris, January 1988, Paris private archive.
91. "I am at times in splendid shape. . . .": Hillman letter to Michael Ventura, February 11, 1988, Opus archive.
92. "We both collapsed on the floor. . . .": Pat Berry email to author, December 2017.
93. "Dear Adolf I was glad for your call. . . .": Hillman letter, Guggenbühl private archive.
94. "Much of who I am was formed. . . .": Pat Berry undated letter to "Dear JH", Berry private archive.
95. "They had so little content. . . .": JH letter to "Peebee," undated.
96. "In all this I dream. . . .": Hillman letter to Guggenbühl, March 24, 1988, Guggenbühl archive.
97. "As for Pat and our deeper connection. . . .": Hillman letter to Guggenbühl, dated May 7 [1988], Guggenbühl archive.
98. "My life fell apart. . . .": Hillman letter to Michael Adams, undated, summer 1988.
99. "Our separation was actually ideological. . . .": Author interview with Pat Berry, December 2018.
100. "how few of the members take any 'political' interest. . . .": Hillman letter to Guggenbühl, May 10, 1985, Guggenbühl private archive.
101. "that one must give oneself over'. . . ." Hillman letter to Guggenbühl, Guggenbühl archive.
102. "he opened up in a way that was very intimate. . . .": Author interview with Sven Doehner, July 2007.
103. "how the social problem is archetypally based. . . .": Hillman letter to Guggenbühl, February 2, 1986.

104. "started a new kind of lecture course. . . ." JH letter to Guggenbühl, June 4, 1985, Guggenbühl archive.

105. "Last week I did some 'teaching'. . . ." Hillman letter to Guggenbühl, June 4, 1985, Guggenbühl archive.

14

MEN AND MYTHOPOETICS

"We live in a poetically underdeveloped nation. Men blame their own lives for a deficiency in the culture. For, without the fanciful delicacy and the powerful truths that poems convey, emotions and imagination flatten out. There's a lack of spirit, of vision. The loss in the heart appears as a loss of heart to take up the great cultural challenges that are part of every man's citizenship. It is in this sense that we have come to think that working in poetry and myth with men is a therapy of the culture at its psychic roots."[1]*

—from the foreword to* The Rag and Bone
Shop of the Heart, *edited by Robert Bly,
James Hillman, and Michael Meade.*

In mid-February of 1986, Robert Bly—recipient of the National Book Award for poetry—wrote to Hillman inviting him to be a teacher at his third annual Minnesota Men's Conference that coming autumn on Sebago Lake. Bly had long been an admirer of his work, and Hillman had spoken at his conference on the "Great Mother and the New Father" a year-and-a-half earlier. But this invitation took Hillman by surprise. Still, Bly's theme—"Men's Work in the World: Leaving the Father's House"—seemed along the lines he'd been thinking about himself. Hillman accepted.

About a month before the late September gathering, he wrote Bly: "We've got to get away from both the whiney young man whose 'father never loved me' and away from the compensatory young man who follows [Carlos] Castaneda and is full of 'power' eagle fantasies . . . so that we get some men with guts and honesty and intelligence into the community."[2]

That summer, for the first time in twenty years, Hillman had decided not to attend the Eranos gathering. Now he would suddenly find himself not among European scholars and American intellectuals exploring lofty esoteric ideas, but among American males from all walks of life delving deep into their personal lives together. Rather than overlooking Lake Maggiore and the nearby Alps, he would be staying in a North Woods cabin for five days at a rustic lakeside camp enclosed by more than a hundred acres of wilderness. The number of attendees was about the same as at Eranos, in this case limited to ninety men each paying a $400 fee, out of which came conference expenses and the teachers' compensation.

Hillman imagined that entering this realm would not be easy for him. Although he'd been back in the United States for eight years, he remained "very lofty, still very Swiss."[3] And this was "not academic America or rich America or protected America, but exposure to what you might call basic America. Some of these guys were Vietnam vets, and a lot of ex-alcoholics. Men in pretty dark places with their wives and their lives."[4]

One of the Minnesota conference organizers, Craig Ungerman, remembered the reaction as Hillman stood before the group reading formally from a paper he'd prepared on "Extending the Family." "The guys weren't quite used to this, because in these early days there was a kind of insane energy that mostly Robert brought to it. Jim was more reserved, brilliant ideas but the style was like oil and water—'what the hell is *this*?'" Illustrative of this difference, Bly had implemented some "organized mischief," what he called "coyotes" whose job was to "do a little hell-raising, mix things up." One of these, a short, thin fellow named Paul, met with some of the organizers after Hillman's opening talk, to discuss: "What can we do to kinda loosen him up?"

The next day when everyone filed into the room, Paul entered and took a seat. He was stark naked. Not yet having seen the "coyote," Hillman began to speak. Hearing some laughter, he asked if there were any questions. Paul raised his hand and, as he finished posing a seemingly serious query, Hillman said: "Would you stand up, please?" When the fellow did, the room convulsed with laughter. Ungerman remembered: "It was great, because after that James definitely loosened up and wasn't reading so much from the paper, and it made him more a part of the conference."[5]

Another of the organizers, Ed Groody, recalled that in the course of one of Hillman's talks, someone began mocking him as an authority figure offering wisdom and power instead of being "one of the guys." Groody remembered Hillman interrupting to say, in essence: "Now wait a minute, everybody, listen up right now. We're here for the next five days and this is the most important thing you're going to hear!"

According to Groody, "Everyone was like, 'Oh my gosh, what is Hillman gonna *say*?!' And he goes on, 'Everybody, everybody—Robert, Michael [Meade], me—*everybody* is fucked up!'" For Groody, "I must have been twenty-seven at the time, got into this at the same time I was working through depression in therapy, isolated from other people—and that was just a very valuable thing to hear. Everyone's fucked up, not only me."[6]

Pat Berry picked him up at the airport after the Minnesota event, and remembered, "Jim's considerable struggle, embarrassment, and feeling of failure, that he could not do it."[7] Yet during those first days in the North Woods, it had amazed Hillman to watch the group react as Bly read poems by William Blake: "They listened with such acuteness, their hearts were open, they wanted to know."[8] And so did he.

Hillman would recall: "I was like some of the men there who were in transition, whose life was fallen apart or changed." His second marriage was in crisis. Eranos was ending. He would give one final lecture there, which he conceived in the wake of that first men's gathering. In November 1986, Hillman wrote Ritsema: "The theme is beginning to 'awaken'; has anyone else suggested *Oedipus*? I think I would like to take a new look at the root metaphor of *psychoanalysis, family, father* and the Western central tragedy of 'killing the father.' It bears also upon the *heroic* upheavals (search for new paradigms or methods)."[9]

For Hillman, there would be further upheavals to come—not only separation from Pat, but closing his therapeutic practice and ceasing his editing of Spring Publications. As he would write to Bly: "My life is radically changing . . . Old things reveal new faces, and new wonderful things emerge in the midst of shock."[10]

The men's movement, as it was publicly known, lasted less than a decade in mainstream awareness. It was generally caricatured in the media as groups of shirtless adult males drumming-and-dancing in the forest, getting away from their wives and returning to their primal roots. "There was a huge misapprehension," Hillman reflected years later, "that we were all in the woods to be wild, savage, rude, crude, anti-woman. That was the way the world got it, and it was so different than that. It was weeping, it was dancing, it was struggling to say what you felt. What occurred was astounding."[11]

Over the course of the next decade, Hillman would teach at more than thirty such events all across the United States as well as in England and Ireland, from one-day workshops to six-day-long gatherings. He viewed it as "a psychological experiment, doing therapy in a new way."[12] At the same time, the men's groups would take ideas that he'd been thinking about for years and force him to embody and weave everything together—emotionally, intellectually, and practically. This would bear fruit in his last four books, including *The Soul's Code*. And Hillman's deepening personal involvement saw the forging of a number of friendships that would last the rest of his life.

ORIGINS

Bly remembered the exact date he first met Hillman, September 20, 1979 on the St. Croix River, at a conference where they were each speakers. Already a reader of his work, the acclaimed poet wrote Hillman several admiring letters. It turned out the two men had much in common. Both born in 1926, Bly had also been his mother's favorite, although the small Minnesota farming community where he grew up was a far cry from Atlantic City. They had joined the Navy the same year (1944), where Hillman felt his first therapeutic calling and Bly initially came into contact with poetry. Then, while Hillman was at Trinity College among the Irish poets in the late 1940s, Bly was at Harvard "in the midst of an intense group of beginning writers," and "one day while studying a Yeats poem I decided to write poetry for the rest of my life."[13]

In 1968, Bly had received the National Book Award for his poetry, along with mobilizing the literary community's anti-Vietnam War movement. During the seventies, Bly recalled, he "had a longing to learn something about mythology" and, in 1974, held his first Conference on the Great Mother. Bly didn't know it at the time, but the year before Hillman had written an essay titled "The Great Mother," that said: "When the father is absent, we fall more readily into the arms of the mother . . . The missing father is not your or my personal father. He is the absent father of our culture."[14]

It was a theme that would be taken up often during the men's gatherings a decade later, and in Hillman the seed had been planted long ago. Among the first courses he took after enrolling at Zürich's Jung Institute in 1953 was Erich Neumann's "Great Mother and Her Symbols." Another was Marie Louise von Franz's "Archetypal Patterns in Fairy Tales."

In the mid-1980s Hillman began giving a number of lectures around the country, on the psychology behind fairy tales, often with Pat Berry. The first time they went to California, they gave a talk that consisted of comparing dreams and fairy tales back-and-forth. Around the same time Bly, in relating a Celtic story at his initial men's conference in 1983, felt that "many of the classic fairy tales lay out stages of initiation into adulthood which we've entirely forgotten, that our ancestors apparently knew a lot about."[15]

Bly came across a German folk tale from the Brothers Grimm called *Iron John*, about a hair-covered "Wild Man" discovered at the bottom of a pond into which many hunters had disappeared. He is captured and brought to the king's courtyard, where one day the young prince's golden ball rolls into his cage. In the end, the prince rides off into the forest on the Wild Man's shoulders. Considered a parable about a boy maturing into adulthood, *Iron John* resonated with Bly's male audiences. "Every modern male has, lying at the bottom of his psyche, a large, primitive man covered with hair down to his feet," Bly said. [16] The point was not to *be* the Wild Man, which would be as foolish as a Greek today trying to be Dionysus, but rather to get in touch with this more "spontaneous, truthful" part of oneself.

Influenced by similar practices within the women's movement, by the late 1970s groups of men had begun organizing consciousness-raising groups. But where many feminists wanted men to learn from women about expressing their feelings, Bly's new "mythopoetic" approach emphasized the "deep masculine," honing in on the male's unique psychological and spiritual needs by retrieving wisdom from the past. "Certainly the patriarchy has suppressed women," Bly said. "The patriarchy has also repressed the open, generous side of men." Bly saw myth, poetry, music, and dance as "the original therapy" to help awaken men from emotional slumber. Bly spoke of "soft males" being influenced by the cultural upheaval of feminism—perhaps becoming more sensitized but also lacking "energy, assertiveness and the ability to make commitments."[17]

"Every family gives you a wound," Bly believed.[18] Men often carry reservoirs of unacknowledged grief and loss which, if tapped into, could serve as a doorway to feeling. His own woundedness stemmed from the alcoholism of his father and over-identification with his damaged mother, for which Bly had compensated by being "cheerful." He'd been in his mid-40s when he realized "the possibility that my life was not going to be a series of triumphs, that what was asked of me was not to ascend but to *descend*."[19] This was contrary to the upward-pointing American way and a society that honored victory, not loss; answers, not questions; pride, not shame. Yet, as Hillman once said, which Bly was fond of quoting: "The spirit is like fire; it wants to fly up—but the soul is like water: it wants to descend."

With the Industrial Revolution, Bly pointed out, fathers began leaving the home to spend their days working many miles away, their sons no longer alongside them. During the 1960s, the Vietnam War had exacerbated the rift between fathers who favored the war and sons who did not. Unlike the camaraderie and trust exhibited during World War II, "a new situation evolved during the Vietnam War which amounts to older men lying to younger men."[20]

After Bly laid out many of these ideas during a 1982 interview with Keith Thompson published in the *New Age Journal*, interest rapidly increased. Bly soon began hosting week-long men's retreats in the woods of Minnesota and California. For his second gathering, he invited Michael Meade to be a storyteller. They had met at one of Bly's Great Mother conferences. Twenty years younger, Meade was a gritty Irish-American who'd grown up among the street gangs of 1950s New York City. "I found another world on my thirteenth birthday when my aunt gave me a copy of Edith Hamilton's *Mythology*, an anthology of Greek myths and legends," Meade wrote in his 1993 book, *Men and the Water of Life*. "They mirrored the complications and dramas of the life I was experiencing."[21] His father was a Teamster and Meade drove trucks to put himself through college, majoring in literature and philosophy. Drafted into the Army during the Vietnam War, he began a pattern of resistance that led to imprisonment in solitary confinement. At the same time, Meade's ongoing "studies of ritual art and tribal music led to the practice of various forms of traditional drumming, chanting, and storytelling." He began performing stories before audiences while drumming and "the discussions developed into workshops on myth and symbolic imagining."[22]

Unknown to Bly, Meade was also an avid reader of James Hillman. Going through a rough period of divorce, with little money and basically scrounging for furniture, Meade had come upon a Goodwill box while walking down the street one night. Sticking out the top were two brass floor lamps and the nose of a hand-made Chinese junk ship, under which was a stack of books. Two of these intrigued him: an old volume titled *Wild Birds of North America* and a worn copy of *Re-Visioning Psychology* by someone named Hillman. Meade took it all back to his apartment and began devouring Hillman's text that same night, the first psychology he had ever read.[23]

Meade went on to read Hillman's essay on "Senex and Puer," learning these were Latin terms for "old man" and "young man." The Senex person was grounded, responsible, committed, disciplined, authoritarian. The puer was fiery, ambitious, desirous, flashing with insight, ascending like the winged Icarus. "These diverging, conflicting tendencies are ultimately interdependent, forming two faces of the one configuration, each face never far from the other"[24]—an archetypal and primary psychological pattern. Meade found that this essay "really opened up the masculine psyche and gave me insights into my father and my sons and all kinds of teachers in my own psyche."[25]

Meade and Hillman had met for the first time at the Bly conference in Maine on "The Great Mother and the New Father," where Hillman was invited to lecture in June 1984. Hillman's first presentation dealt with how nuclear weapons were part of Christianity's shadow—Meade recalled, "that really upset a lot of people." Afterwards, when Hillman went outside for some air, Meade walked over and said: "Excuse me, Dr. Hillman, but that was a great talk." Hillman raised his eyebrows and replied: "Do you mean it? People seemed very unhappy." Meade remembered saying: "But that's the *proof* that it was a great talk. If your job was to get at the shadow, you have provoked the shadow." They went off together for a glass of wine and conversed into the night.

Two days later, Hillman was scheduled to give his talk on "Senex and Puer." But as the audience began gathering that morning, he was nowhere to be seen. Meade, knowing where Hillman's room was, found him there—still in bed. Hillman informed him that he wasn't feeling well and so wasn't getting up. An exasperated Meade asked what Bly could tell the attendees. "You're familiar with this subject," Hillman said.

"Yeah, I've studied it," Meade replied.

"You go give the talk, I'm sure you'll be fine," Hillman told him.

And so, with considerable trepidation, Meade did. "The Doctor" was ill and had asked him to fill in, Meade recalled telling the audience: "This will be pathetic, so I recommend you read his essay, but let me give you some rough ideas." About halfway through his off-the-cuff remarks, Meade noticed some people looking elsewhere. He turned to see that Hillman had walked in and was standing in a corner of the hall.

"I said, 'Well, here he is—Doctor, take over.' And Hillman said, 'Oh no, this is *improving* what I wrote! You go ahead and finish it!'"

Afterwards, still stunned at someone having "that kind of relaxation, and such generosity and humility," Meade found Hillman again, who said he'd meant precisely what he said.

"Well, I was just using your ideas," Meade said.

"No, some of your ideas were in there," Hillman told him, "and they're damn good. I'd rather hear you talk about Puer and Senex than me." For Meade, then still in his thirties, it was "like a blessing confirming that part of myself."[26] He'd found the older mentor he'd been looking for.

It was Meade who suggested to Bly that Hillman be invited to the 1986 event in the North Woods of Minnesota. He would later reflect in an interview: "I knew the ideas could fit, but I didn't know if *he* could fit. But he was *in* it, right away."[27]

AMONG THE REDWOODS

When Hillman came to teach for a second time in June 1987, for a gathering of ninety men deep within a redwood grove near Mendocino, California, Bly's co-organizer Martin Keogh was worried. "I knew everybody else we brought on board, but not him, and I had talked to a couple people who said, 'Oh, that man is dull! And he doesn't care at all how he comes across.'" Bly tried reframing their perspective of Hillman by telling the men: "You will see the wheels turning as he thinks and speaks. Stay with it, he's brilliant!"[28]

The lodge hall, located in the crook of a creek that flowed through the trees, had been built by the Civilian Conservation

Corps during the Great Depression. Out front, in a large clearing where redwood had been milled from the surrounding grove, the event began with everyone standing in a "naming circle." One at a time, the men were to step forward and say their given name, after which the others would then echo them. According to Keogh, "It was a way to become acquainted with everybody's name, but it was also very powerful hearing this chorus of men saying your name back to you three times."

The ceremony was about to commence when Hillman showed up. "Having no idea what they did at these things," he recalled, "I thought everybody picked an odd or funny name when introducing themselves. I remember walking in after gathering up some ferns in the woods and putting them all over my checkered shirt and blue jeans and weaving them into a little tennis hat. When it came my turn I said, 'My name is Fern.' Completely off on the wrong track!"[29]

Not far from the camp was an organic meat farm, from which the kitchen staff had butchered a ram and a goat scheduled to be roasted on the last night. As Hillman and the fellow who'd picked him up at the airport walked down the path, they noticed the dead animals hanging from a rope. On the ground lay the ram's head with the horns intact. Hillman and the other man picked up the ram's head, passed through the circle of men, set it down in the center, then silently merged with the others.[30]

The ram's head . . . it was the symbol for Hillman's Zodiacal Sun and Moon conjunct in his birth chart. It was also (along with Pat Berry's Capricorn goat) the insignia of his Spring Publications. "The incident with the ram's head seems central to what was happening when Meade and Bly decided to bring Hillman into the mix. The U.S. is wounded around the intellect—the academic mind split from the working-class body, both forgetting that there's blood in the brain. The ram's head is not only primal, it's an image of the blood-filled head (the mind embodied, incarnated as the stubborn, driving, masculine head of the ram) re-entering the circle, bringing the pagan world with it—Zeus and Ares, Dionysian dismemberment and resurrection.

Not only for Hillman, but for the other men and for America, the head and the body, once severed, were now ritually reunited," as Hillman scholar Scott Becker elucidated to me.

"This idea of severing and reattachment also became relevant to the literal events in Hillman's life—withdrawing from Hera's world of marriage and leaving behind Apollo's academic detachment, he entered the fray with Ares and began crafting things of beauty with Hephaestos, not abandoning the intellect but attaching it to things that 'matter,' so that the 'guts' of intuition gain clarity of thought, and thoughts become bloody (visceral, vital to life). Also, the head brings in not only intellect, but authority, the vertical dimension that Bly noted is lost in a 'sibling society' where young men know only others their own age. Finally, Hillman's move with the ram's head introduced a cosmology in which the animal world, the spiritual world, the political world, the academic world, and the world of practical work are not separate. This reconnection is, in part, what others feared when they thought about half-naked men drumming in the woods. How do we reach back in time without returning there, losing our minds, so to speak? Hillman moved to bring rational clarity into a direct connection to animistic ritual—not a return to primitive, unthought action, but a fully imagined dialogue with the invisible powers—neither controlled by them nor cut off from them."

The men filed into the lodge. Its seating arrangement was semi-circular, with several rows of chairs, then tables to sit on, and behind those more tables with benches on top, creating a kind of intimate, three-level amphitheater. The attendees were mostly white, over thirty, and came from many different professions. "A lot of them had gone all kinds of routes looking for their pieces of the puzzle," recalled Joe Landry, a Massachusetts man who attended numerous gatherings—"to therapy, to EST groups, one who'd been part of Jonestown, and many like myself from the recovery movements. Some would really come apart at these events. The so-called absent father was a phrase tossed about in those days, along with the wounded child, and you had men with a lot of unresolved issues from childhood. Then many of them had added layers of their own pain— divorces, substance abuse, addictions, fuck-ups of various kinds, and had really fallen flat."[31] The oldest were invited to sit in the front, close to where the three teachers huddled close together on folding chairs.

Bly, a tall, large-boned man with unruly white hair, is wearing steel-framed glasses and a blue brocade vest. Next to him sits Meade, a round-faced Irish-American with heavy bangs, cradling a conga drum. To his left is Hillman, who has on running shoes with slacks. He would describe the gathering in a letter afterward to a woman friend: "An all-male attempt at 'discovery.' Very moving, touching—and amusing. It feels good to be accepted, even honored, as a 'strong male' by younger men after years of being such a Jewish Intellectual Snob."[32]

What it was like to witness the interactions can be derived from an audio recording of one of the Mendocino events during those early years. During the introduction, Hillman speaks of "keeping alive something . . . besides the usual ways that we live with other men, by watching TV or drinking beer or talking about cars and sports; there is no movement of the soul in that."[33] Bly follows by asking Meade to accompany him on the drum as he chants the first stanza of a William Butler Yeats poem in a nasal but resonant baritone. Next comes Meade with a poem by Rumi, then one that Hillman recites by D. H. Lawrence. The three of them take turns offering William Blake's *Proverbs of Hell*. "If they were around nowadays, Jim says they'd be 'Bumper Stickers From Hell,'" Meade says, and the roomful of men laugh.

Hillman quickly responds: "How about this one, Michael. You never know what is enough unless you know what is more than enough.'" Some of the men applaud. Bly recites another of Blake's *Proverbs*: "The road of excess leads to the palace of wisdom." Someone from the audience shouts out: "Pretty dangerous!" Meade says, "If you're here, you're willing to get involved in danger." This reminds him of an African proverb: "If you came here to get out of trouble, you're like the man who, trying to get out of the rain, jumped into the sea." Hillman reads a poem by Etheridge Knight, an African American whose debut book *Poems from Prison* had earned him critical acclaim.. The poem is called "Feeling Fucked Up."[34]

"Are you ready to start a story?" Meade asks. A booming "Yeah!" comes from the men. As Meade starts drumming, he instructs them not to try to catch the whole thing, rather some small detail—"an image that will open the door to the story." Story, after all, means storehouse, a place in which things are stored. Then Meade begins, rhythmically, physically, ferociously: "Once below a time—next to time—before time was made digital, made to glow in the dark, captured in sequential numbers . . . Once, in that time—in a land beyond this time—there was a king."

This is a Russian fairy tale called *The Firebird*. At intervals it would go on all week—about a hunter and a horse and the feather of a great bird, and the most beautiful woman in all the world riding in a silver vessel with golden oars on the endless expanse of the blue ocean. Hillman provides commentary as the story progresses, raising questions for the men to think about. "Desire has been reduced in the culture to needs," he says. "And the man in this story is not a needy boy, he is a hunter. To discover what the soul desires, and what fire is in the breast, is not an easy thing. I don't think psychotherapy has helped that much. Psychotherapy is very interested in needs, and not so interested in desires. You know, the image of the parrot lying on its back on a couch in the therapist's office with his claws up, and the therapist is saying to the parrot, 'Are you sure you don't *need* a cracker?'"

Many in the room laugh. "So our desires get reduced to needs," Hillman goes on, "as if they are some internal thing that didn't get taken care of forty years ago when you were in another city living with your mother or your father . . . Needs may come first, and that's a very important part of our lives— we need a lover, a blessing, protection, refuge, support groups, a leader, a good friend, and so on. But there is something beyond the neediness part. You know yourself the difference between a need and a want. If you're lying with your woman and you *need* her, you're putting her into a mother role and she's turned off; whereas if you *want* her, she's desirable. Very simple little thing—but that's a couple thousand dollars worth of therapy right there." The room erupts in laughter and applause.[35]

Rick Chelew, a sound engineer who audio-taped many of these gatherings for his Oral Tradition Archives, remembered that at some point, Meade "would stop and ask each of us where we are in the story. Then we would tell the story (or the story would tell us) and it would unravel (and unravel us) as each person, in short order, would answer three questions: Where are you in the story (or 'what is the image that grabs you'), secondly what is the feeling associated with this image, and thirdly how does this reverberate in your life (an image from your personal story)."[36]

Hillman recalled: "Everybody found themselves in the story at one point or another—crossing the river, meeting the monster, losing the shoes, whatever the fairy tale was. Michael would say, 'All the men who felt they'd lost their shoe and couldn't find it, go over there.' That created shared conversation, about why they didn't stop to pick it up, all such things. It released huge amounts of imagination."[37]

Chelew recalled a group once being taken so deep that they stayed on the redwood floor of the old lodge cabin for more than nine hours: "All scheduling went out the window and we were locked into this imaginal space together. No one seemed to want to leave that circle until the story (which included pieces of 100 men's stories) was concluded."[38]

Freud and Jung had believed that men feel through their *anima* or feminine side. "There needs to be a second act that acknowledges that men have a tremendous amount of feeling on their masculine side," Bly once observed, similar to what Hillman had been talking about for some years. Many archetypes or character models were seen as embedded in the male psyche: King, Warrior, Quester, Trickster, Lover, and Wild Man. Bly explained: "The fairy tales in which these archetypes occur can convey a tremendous amount of psychological information in a simple turn of a phrase. It would take a psychologist many pages to accomplish the same thing in scientific jargon."[39]

As the week progressed, Hillman would give his own talks, which Meade called "embodied ideas" that could "hold water and if necessary blood."[40] Hillman also participated in the various non-intellectual activities—dancing and mask-making and other rituals. "It had a profound effect on James," according to Margot McLean, who first met him during this period and would later become his wife. "I think he was not only a teacher, but was going through some sort of strange participation. He merged with these men. It was like being in the belly of the beast, and so private and personal. James respected the work on such a level that it was almost this sacred space. For men to all be together in this kind of intimacy doesn't come easily. This brought him down into a different realm, and I think it softened him."[41]

Thousands of other men felt similarly. Rick Chelew reflected more than twenty years later: "It was not only finding the courage to look at my deep longings in a new way, but the realization there are some things we cannot do *on our own*, that we need some kind of community." Luis Rodriguez, today one of the leading Hispanic writers in America (author of the best-selling memoir of gang life, *Always Running*), recalled: "When you look at the ghetto or barrio, they were talking about issues we embody but don't have the language for—because they were looking at mythology, at indigenous cultures, making this appropriate and relevant to the modern world."[42]

CREATING RITUAL SPACE

Orland Bishop, who went on to create the Shade Tree Multicultural Foundation in Los Angeles, attended these gatherings for twenty years as both a teacher and participant and reflected: "In that kind of space, it's an initiation. They created that kind of tension, five days of ritual-making where you actually go through years of unresolved locked thinking. Anything could happen, going towards some threshold of soul. It's about freeing the will from repetition. You cross all the breaking points and just surrender to what is inevitable—the descent into the uncertainty—and then you make a ritual."[43]

Hillman elaborated: "Where men are gathered together, it's fearful. For men to stand up and open their wounds to each other, in public and in small groups in their cabins, to talk about their marriages and fears and humiliations, their fathers and fighting their own sons: all those things were so difficult. So a hundred men brought in a gang to the woods need a structure right away. Each man has to find his place, and you don't do it by counting off and giving everybody a number or lining up like a military drill. We used very archaic modes of organizing, much deeper than a system: elements, animals, colors. It was really to put the men in a poetic metaphor for a week. If I belong to the element of water, I have to think in terms of fish, of flowing. And the water people are going to be different from the fire people. Thinking in these ways places the mind into another space, where you begin to imagine poetically about yourself. Seen from the outside, using animal names for little groups and having contests might sound trivial or like boy's camp. But they weren't, not when you were *in* it."[44]

Emphasis on animals played a big part; "Animal Truths, Imagination, and Danger" was the theme of a 1987 event. To forge the metaphoric ritual space, Bly, Hillman, and Meade would spend a considerable amount of time beforehand considering questions like: What do we know about turtles? As Meade recalled, "We would go from literal nature studies to the psychological and mythological. In mythology, the turtle is the name that many peoples have for the earth. Jim would say, 'The psychology of the turtle is not to stick your neck out.'"[45]

The trio would finalize their ideas and then post short essays about the various "totem animals," from which the men would select to form three clans. It might be hawks, bear, and salmon one time; turtles, trout, and vultures the next. For example: "Elephant Clan: Elephants are the oldest large people on earth. They remember where their friends died, and they will sometimes carry a bone for miles. In the dusk, their tusks shine with a strange lonely force, and no one trifles with them. They have made their peace with the earth, and they flap their ears slowly to cool themselves. Elephants carry the soul's cares to caves, hollows, desert, and waterholes. They are teachers; they walk for hours with the young."

Transposed to the men: "Elephant Clan (men with long memories, those who feed the poor, men who honor sweat, the keepers of ugly facts, men who sit on the ground together)."[46]

Bly, Meade, and Hillman would each lead different clans. "It was also important that these large groups have smaller and smaller units of affiliation," Hillman remembered. That was where the four elements came in—fire, earth, air, or water—and then sub-groups with names like Luminous Men, Resounding Men, Shadow Men, and Slow Men (Hillman said he particularly liked the last). They were not labels but again metaphors: Men with wings of pride and ambition, Men faithful to the wound, Men who hold the stones of their father, Men with one thing wrong. These were designed to raise philosophical questions: Is it good to have one thing wrong, or do I need more than that?

At mid-morning, in between the teachers' talks, the men would do some kind of movement together—a dance or martial arts or even animal-imitation. In the afternoons, they worked on crafting things like masks. According to Meade, "That notion comes from Africa, where the mask is a very powerful representation of unseen things." Other objects were fashioned out of cloth or candles. Sometimes shrines would be carved from hollowed-out tree trunks. Hillman remembered: "They were working at some particular symbolic image that carried soul for them. And they would use whatever they could find, things they would pick up from the woods."[47] Hillman eagerly took part in all of it. "I think this opened Jim in many ways," Meade believed. "He would move from the rigorous way he could be onstage, reading and extemporizing from a paper, to suddenly being in the world of immediate sensation."[48]

Meade was amazed at the men's inventiveness. On the way into lunch one day, a small group of masked men sat on the roof silently observing everyone else approaching the lodge. Another time, a warrior clan said that anyone who wanted lunch needed to bring a gift. It could be a piece of art, a dance, a poem, a massage, whatever. Some abstained and chose not to eat, while others confronted those seeking power over the lunch-line. There was only one rule, established on the first night: no physical violence. But some of the men had turned to violence before.

Hillman remembered: "Some had huge, terrible stories to tell. I used the idea in my talks that the Vietnam vets were *half*-initiated. They'd been through the training and the wounding, the physical initiation, but they'd never been taught how to make the transition back into the world. That's why they brought war back with them into society and beat up their wives and went crazy. Some were addicted to their guns. So we were losing the future leaders of the country. Michael Meade was really a genius at handling such people." [49]

At one event, Vietnam veterans were brought together in the same room alongside a group that had managed to evade the draft. "We argued out the entire generational war," said Meade, after which they held a welcome-back ceremony for both sides. "That is the third step of initiation, to be brought back in but with a recognition of where you've been."[50]

In a letter responding to someone who'd complained that "some men were laughed at and ridiculed for expressing their opinions," Hillman wrote: "I am convinced that the greatest form of respect is forthright and open challenge," and pointed out that being mocked had its place in tribal initiation rituals. Besides addressing "the deep grief and mourning over lost fathers and lost sons, over lost possibilities, and failures . . .

American life is filled with hardness, competition. A men's retreat
is not a retreat from that hardness, but a place where hardness
can become clearer and have spiritual value and import."

Before dinner, around five o'clock everyone would assemble
for "conflict hour." This took the place of cocktail hour, and
was a time when anyone could express themselves about the
events of the day. The idea originated with Bly asking the group
whether he'd done anything wrong. This evolved into three levels of "conflict hour." There might be conflict with one of the
teachers, where someone felt they were misusing their authority.
The conflict might be about something in the material itself that
needed challenging. Or the conflict might be cultural, involving
racism or homophobia. As Meade said, "The purpose here is not
to resolve the conflict, the purpose is to deepen the conflict."

Hillman described how, "People would take sides and shout
and argue and release a lot of animosity. Also against the teachers. Somebody would stand up and say, 'Robert, you put that
man down, his poem was as good as any other and you shamed
him.' Then somebody else would say, 'No, he deserved it!' The
point was, there would be strong presentations of aggression
without physically hitting each other."[51]

In their cabins at night, men who had never met would begin
to open up about their wives and sex lives and difficulties with
and as fathers. Also, at the close of day, the teachers would review
together what had happened for a couple of hours, sometimes
challenging each other ("What the hell did you do *that* for? That
seemed self-serving.") Occasionally, the men would do ritual
combat in the middle of the night. Bly, Hillman, and whoever
else was the oldest teacher present would be the judges. A circle was drawn on the floor, and each clan would send forth a
champion. The man entering the circle declared the challenge. It
might be placing hands on each other's shoulders, to see which
man could force the other to leave the circle. It might be who
could boast better, or do the best insults.

At one event, tension escalated between the teachers and the
younger men in the audience. Andy Castro, who today works

with troubled youth in California, recalled: "There was a lot of hurt voiced by the men who felt not only unprotected but assaulted by and exposed to brutalities from their fathers and grandfathers. The teachers huddled, and then structured the room with the wounded men to one side and the remaining men to the other. The latter group had put on plaster-of-Paris masks, held 'weapons' that looked like knives, and shouted insults and threatening epithets to the wounded throng. Jim, Robert, Michael, and Terry [Dobson, an aikido master] formed a kind of 'red-rover' line between them, interlinking arms and standing strong. A couple of the 'volunteers' attempted to launch themselves over, and were met with a surprising physical opposition by the teachers, the elders. The teachers held the line, inexpugnably so. But it was all just a ritual, not a literal threat, and very powerful for the men. The ritual was effective as it fit the moment and mood of the room, more than a prescription for providing a corrective emotional experience."[52]

Other rituals belonged to the realm of trust. "Whether men can trust each other to hold their back," as Hillman put it, "is one of the great problems in a competitive capitalist society."[53] One time, the men divided into fifty pairs. Half of them put on blindfolds. The others took the blind men by an arm and led them into the forest, up branch-covered paths and over rocks, through trees with leaves brushing their faces. Encouraged to take care of the other man, they were also told to take risks— "because," Meade recalled, "it was all about learning how to feel and trust other men. At the end you stand alone again, and you never know who guided you."

One time, while watching the ritual of trust, Meade was standing next to Hillman. When he glanced over, he saw that Hillman was crying. "I said, Jim, what's going on? He said, 'You know, I never talk about it much. But when I was in the Navy during the war, I worked with the ones who had been blinded. And I feel like I'm back there.'"[54]

For Hillman, "Doing something for the dead was a big piece of these rituals. There was great emphasis on grief, on burning away resentments, on letting go. Men built little shrines and altars, as part of this attempt to connect backward. We were trying to wash away, I would say, the personal baggage that people have. I often talked about the importance of the dead: Never mind your mother and father, think about your grandparents and what you're *really* carrying . . . The dead want to teach us something."[55]

John Densmore, drummer for the popular sixties rock group The Doors, had lost a brother to suicide and the band's lead singer Jim Morrison to heart failure at only twenty-seven. In his memoir, *Riders on the Storm*, Densmore recounted an experience in one of the sweat lodges at Mendocino. At first he felt cramped and wondered, "what the fuck am I trying to prove here?" He went on: "We go around the circle, passing a rattle, or truth stick, each man bringing into the sweat whoever or whatever he wants to work on. One of the guys says he's an alcoholic and would like to be healed." Densmore then evokes "the spirit of Jim Morrison to help me understand his death . . . and to use his knowledge of alcohol, another 'spirit,' to help you." According to Densmore, "The confessor on the other side of the glowing rocks seems to get a jolt." When Densmore crawls out of the sweat lodge after 45 minutes: "I feel cleansed . . . In these men's groups I've found not only the two brothers I lost, but a multitude of brothers sharing deep feelings."[56]

At Mendocino in 1992, Terry Dobson came for the last time. He had introduced the martial art of aikido to the U.S., and taught the skill at a number of the men's groups. For some time, Dobson's physical condition had been deteriorating from a rare illness. He called Meade and said "I'm gonna be leaving soon, and I want to do one more event." But Dobson couldn't specify a date, since he wouldn't know until two days before whether he had strength enough to travel. Meade said, "How about we'll put your name on every brochure, and one time you'll show up."

When he finally did almost a year later, it was clear Dobson wouldn't be around much longer. That summer, they happened to be exploring grief in ancient traditions and were holding

Buddhist and African funeral ceremonies. Meade remembers his friend, only 55, sitting in the back during the African rite. "I went over to see how he was doing, because he didn't look good. He said, 'No, this is great, this is the party I need.' Then he said, 'Now I want to make a deal. If I die tonight—don't stop this funeral.' He meant it. So much so that Terry never made it home from that trip. He went into a coma two days later. What can you say about events so deep that you want to *die* at them?

"I still carry a picture of him that I took that night," Meade once said in a whisper.[57]

EROS BETWEEN MEN

Hillman had always liked collaborating on projects—with Kenny Donoghue on Freud's *Cocaine Papers*, with Rafael López and Adolf Guggenbühl in Zürich, with Marina Beer on the dialogue book *Inter Views*, with poet Charles Boer on *Freud's Own Cookbook*. So working alongside Bly and Meade was not an unusual situation—but beyond doubt it was his most spontaneous venture.

Meade called it "a desire to change the culture without a program."[58] After the first couple of years, no schedule was ever posted on the wall. The cooks were told to be prepared to hold off serving meals if something else was happening. One time two meals were skipped in a day; nobody ate for some fourteen hours, and no one complained. A day that began at 7:30 a.m. often would not end until midnight. Nothing except the over-arching theme got worked out ahead of time, and it never turned into a routine where they would do the same thing twice. The teachers would often figure out their topics in the car on the way in from the airport. Beginning with poetry, stories and ideas, they'd simply see where the spirit moved them.

Their presentations were called "harangues," a term Meade borrowed from the African practice of giving short thematic speeches. Because they liked to keep things loose and surprise each other, some listeners compared them to a jazz trio, "jamming with language."[59] As Don Shewey, a journalist/participant, wrote in a 1992 article for the *Village Voice*, Bly and Meade were "like the rhythm section of this jazz band, relentlessly collaborative. But every so often . . . they concede the floor to Hillman, who's more eccentric, a one-man band who gives a dazzling, half-composed, half-improvised rap on whatever topic seems pertinent to the occasion."[60]

Richard Olivier (son of the British actor Laurence Olivier) described the three leaders: "Meade got you through the body, Bly got you through the heart, and Hillman got you through the brain. And with the three of them together, things moved very, very quickly. You saw them being themselves *and* being teachers at the same time."[61]

All Hillman's adult life, it was the erotic connection between the people that held different groups together from Dublin to Dallas. Eros is often considered to relate only to sexuality, but long ago Plato viewed Eros in much larger terms, as necessary for connecting to the beauty in another soul or in the world, or to the archetypal reality of Beauty itself—and so essential for wisdom. The Greeks had the idea that there could be no teaching and learning without Eros among the participants. Surrounding Hillman's intellectual activities was a consistently festive atmosphere—from the Irish pubs of his college days and the wine-filled Spring House discussions, to the evening confabs in his Dallas living room, and the sixtieth birthday celebration in Connecticut.

Hillman had studied psychologist Alfred Adler's idea of a communal sense, a *Gemeinschaftsschule*, and written about this in *Healing Fiction* (1981). And it was much in evidence in the relationship between Hillman, Bly, and Meade—something beyond mutual respect, something that the roomfuls of men watched unfold between them. As Hillman put it, "We fed each other. We weren't just blowing our own trumpets, we were fascinated with what the other guy said and really listening. This was genuine love for each other's minds and creations, spontaneities, powers, whatever it is."[62]

The Eros took many forms. Since the teachers stayed onstage together, they were always exposed and forced to react. When one seemed like they were being attacked, the other two would often come to his defense. Not that they let anything pass among themselves. Rick Chelew observed that "they had a huge respect for each other, and were being entertained by one another, but were also close enough as friends that they were willing to argue and sometimes very heatedly."[63]

The younger Meade enjoyed doing battle with the older Bly. He would insult Bly's Scandinavian-Viking heritage, who in turn would take on Meade's Irish-Celtic background. Their trading of insults was based on "The Dozens" in African American tradition, a preparation for life which sharpened your perspective and also made you aware of your weaknesses—something Meade had grown up with in his tough New York neighborhood. The audience, Meade said, liked to see "two grown men fiercely disputing without bloodshed." Hillman would pick his spots to join in the fray, often trading insults with Bly.

Fred Stephens, who organized southern gatherings in North Carolina and Virginia, remembered Hillman once saying, "There's too much complaining about the parents!" and Bly replying, "Yeah but I don't care, I'm gonna continue to whine about my father and mother"—and he did. One time, in an argument over poetry, Bly tossed one at Hillman: "What would you know, you're from New Jersey!" Hillman rapidly named off five New Jersey poets (including Bruce Springsteen), and shut Bly up.[64]

Because many of the attendees had grown up in homes with absent or alcoholic fathers, Bly said it was often difficult at first for the men to place confidence in the teachers. "So we were lucky in a way that James and I and Michael were all sort of powerful in our own areas, and didn't have any jealousy of the other two. That was a good model for men to see. In fact, they were astounded that we admired each other so much and had so much affection for each other. I think the men learned more from that than anything we said."[65] Indeed, men would come up afterwards and say how helpful it was to witness the camaraderie, because as participants expressed: "All I know is how to compete with other men" or "I have tremendous fear of someone being smarter."

Thus, the trio become mythical figures themselves. Don Shewey wrote: Bly was a "kind of dervish, constantly pounding on the poetic landscape . . . a lion, king of the jungle." Meade was seen as "the leprechaun in the forest" or "like a frog . . . close to the ground, a proletarian prince." As for Hillman: "Replace [his] tweedy wardrobe with a cape and staff, and you'd call him a sorcerer or holy fool."[66]

Describing themselves was another matter. Hillman felt that "Robert could be totally arrogant and I could be completely narrow-minded."[67] To Bly, while he and Meade were much more "cloddy and clumpy," Hillman brought a "playfulness and amazing ability to bounce around in the philosophical and religious culture." If the other two got stuck, Bly would often turn and ask Hillman what he thought.[68] Craig Ungerman remembered: "James was much more disciplined, cool and detached and probably held the three of them together because he wouldn't get as emotionally involved." [69] Rick Chelew observed them all "letting their hair down, taking chances, trying out material and getting instant feedback. They'd often write down what people said—especially Bly, who would read his works in progress and ask for comments, then cross out lines and change them right there during his talk."[70]

The relationships fed one another "off the court" as well. Meade recalled that sometimes the story he chose would change as he told it and he once asked Hillman, "I'm not sure if I'm doing something legitimate or am I violating some code?" Hillman replied, "No, it's your imagination engaging the story and I completely trust what you're doing." From this response, Meade felt, "I really got permission from him to tell stories in a spontaneous way, which turns out to be the ancient Irish method as well as the Griot practice in Africa and with certain Native American tribes too. I had stumbled into this but instinctively, and I needed some confirmation and blessing, which Jim gave me."[71]

Hillman once wrote Bly afterward asking him to recall an exercise he'd put the group through, saying: "It was excellent! I think useful for therapy, and I wish to recall the steps to give them some more thought. If therapy is to be conceived anew in terms of image & beauty (not only medical model on soul-saving), then we also need new ideas for *practice*."[72]

Bly's journals were filled with notes on Hillman's various lectures. In another letter, Hillman wrote him: "I want to tell you that I have the strongest & strangest feelings of protection in regard to you . . . When you get attacked & misunderstood, of leaping from my chair in your defense. Why do I feel this protective urge? You're a big boy and can, and do, handle yourself pretty capably. Sometimes, I feel you are 'lost' in the world, as if you are a son, a young man needing protection (or an old goofy father?) and that in Jung's terms—personality #1 doesn't know how to protect & explain the inspired behavior of personality #2."[73]

Over time, other teachers would be enlisted to join them. But according to Hillman, "We didn't call in sociologists or cultural historians or anthropologists to give us lectures on ritual. There was never another psychologist who came and talked about marriage or the mid-life crisis or other transitions in a man's life. Instead, we had major poets."[74] With three of those poets, Hillman developed lasting relationships. There was Gary Snyder, one of the original "Beat" poets and later a leading ecologist; Coleman Barks, a southern poet and translator of Rumi; and Etheridge Knight, a southern black poet who'd gotten addicted to heroin after being wounded in the Korean War and spent years in and out of prisons where he began to write. He went on to receive an American Book Award and a Guggenheim Fellowship. Bly had befriended Knight and coaxed him into coming to the predominantly white events. Now he and Hillman also became friends. "James, I'm glad we met. We/ Brothers/Be—Etheridge," the poet wrote him. Hillman also helped Knight out financially, who responded saying: "I'm back in Boston and doing okay. Thanks for your help. Will send you your bread . . . Love, Etheridge." After Knight died of lung cancer at age sixty in 1991, Hillman spoke at his memorial.[75]

From other fields, besides aikido master Terry Dobson, came dance instructor Ricardo Morrison, drummer Aidoo Holmes, Buddhist scholar Jack Kornfeld, and animal tracker John Stokes. But only the spontaneous combustion of the Bly, Meade, and Hillman trio resembled the Greek idea of theater. Don Shewey wrote, "as an opportunity for the community of citizens to gather and, in a formal way, discuss the things that matter to them . . . It feels like nothing so much as a town meeting, only the community in question exists not on the map but in the hearts of men."

"DOING THERAPY IN A NEW WAY"

From the men's gatherings, Hillman was gaining a new understanding of what counted as therapeutic: "It was exposure in a group, it was cultural, it was directly challenging, it was very physical, and it had an initiation aspect. That's quite different from just sitting in chairs and talking. It was learning things no one had thought about before, outside of the consulting room, a radically different learning."[76]

During one of Hillman's talks, a man stood up and said, "Well, we don't really know you, you don't tell us anything." Hillman asked him what he meant? "Well, we don't know who you really are." Hillman responded, "Here I am, standing up here and telling you everything I've got in my head. I'm completely exposed. And you say you don't know who I am. So what else is there, what do you want?" The man persisted and Hillman said, "Let me ask you a question. Are you a therapist?" He was. Hillman went on: "You only know someone if you know their whole personal story. In other words, you want a case history. You're not really interested in the person. You're not able to make judgments from what you're seeing, what you're living with. You want to put me in one of your boxes." Hillman added, with finality, "Six days here is better than five years in a consulting room for almost everybody."[77]

Most of the men had never heard a psychology talk in their lives and Bly marveled at Hillman's ability to reach them—coming in with "ten times the knowledge that anyone in the room had, and when it came time he'd modify it and tune it down and say things that were really helpful."[78] Hillman seemed to speak from a deep well of experience, and certain things he said stayed with the participants for years. Robert Carulo from Massachusetts remembered: "If you're visited in the night by demons, be sure to talk to them—because they have something to say."[79] When Hillman was asked a question during his talks, often he wouldn't answer right away and sometimes would respond, "I'm not gonna swing at that one today." Other times, he would flash with anger, for example when a man went on and on complaining about his wife and Hillman finally shouted out: "Get a maid!"

Hillman had a large collection of slides he used for lectures elsewhere that he called "The Anima in Painting." They were not necessarily paintings of women, but artwork from around the world that he felt in some way represented aspects of the soul. In the autumn of 1987, he decided to bring his slide show to the Mendocino Woodlands Camp in Northern California and called it "Anima House" (a spin on a popular film of the time, *Animal House*). It was the same night that a few groups were doing sweat lodges nearby. But since there was a drought that year and no outdoor fires could be lit, the rocks for the sweat lodges had to be heated in the lodge's large fireplace. Martin Keogh would never forget the scene—the projector flashing Hillman's anima images against the beams, while other men passed through with wheelbarrows into which they shoveled the glowing rocks.

"A group of about twenty guys stayed until after midnight, some who'd never been to a museum or looked at paintings," Hillman recalled. "Some became enraged, telling me 'You shouldn't have done this, you're showing us pictures of naked women, no more pornography!'"[80] Meade remembered others hooting-and-hollering at the images, and Hillman becoming angered. John Densmore recalled joking to Bly that Hillman should change "anima" to "enema," but added: "I think it was the first time a lot of people were exposed to the idea of an inner feminine." [81]

Fred Stephens said that Hillman was finally asked to "stop using all this jargon. He did not resist whatsoever. He immediately reframed things in everyday terms. That's where Hillman earned my respect. He seemed to take the challenge to reach out to this audience of men in the forest who were not necessarily interested in the Jungian language and still get his message across. I always thought, is this where he prepared himself for the wider audience?—a sign of his desire to reach the 'common man,' leading to the success of *The Soul's Code* and his later work."[82]

Keogh said: "James can be very eagle-eyed, you can almost see the feathers. But this night as he was showing the slides, I will never forget how he dripped and melted into his seat. He entered this anima state, it was like a weather system, it wasn't linear and it almost didn't have bones. Just to make sure that he got back to his cabin safely that night, I sent two of the men with him so that he could find his way."[83]

At the same gathering, Hillman gave his first presentation of a lecture on "The Asshole." It was daring and, for a group of almost all heterosexual males, frightening to many. Hillman said: "Part of it had to do with the fear of homosexuality, and another part with being uptight, tight-assed. What came out of that was, a couple of gay men in the audience talked very openly about asshole erotics. And two medical doctors spoke up about how shy physicians are to do the prostate examination, even though it's absolutely crucial because so much cancer starts there, and what a fault that is in medicine. So a whole world opened up."[84]

Meade recounted an end-of-the-day review among the teachers when Hillman made the comment: "It's not just the fear of sexual penetration by another man, but fear of intellectual penetration or emotional penetration are all part of homophobia." It was all about breaking down barriers. Craig Ungerman related that, when Hillman repeated the talk a year later in Minnesota, the initial snickering soon turned into a remarkable dialogue. "At one point a guy stood up who I'd never seen before, but he was gay and started talking about 'techniques' to make the asshole bigger, and of course everybody else in the audience was very uncomfortable. But again, James was very cool in saying, 'Thank you for that information, that's incredible. Next!' Then later we ended up doing exercises, it was a blindfolded situation and sometimes you'd have to have a partner, and I ended up attached to the guy who made this comment—because I had issues about him and I had to work through it."[85]

In an interview for a men's magazine, *Wingspan*, Hillman addressed the importance of involving gay men in these retreats. "One aspect that straight men admire the most is the dedication to feeling, taste, sensitivity," he said. "Their contribution to eating, style, dance, the arts, manners, is simply tremendous [and] much of homophobia is resistance to the power of beauty."[86] He also addressed, in a piece called "Love in Male Friendship," the fact that "Friendships are so hard to maintain because they continually demand accessibility, that you let yourself take in the other person, let your imagination be stirred by thoughts, approaches, feelings that shake you out of your set ways."[87]

The asshole was not the only taboo theme that Hillman took up with the men. He spoke about erections and masturbation. One lecture topic was titled "Cocks and Cunts." When men talk about sex, "it's usually jokes or adolescent boastings or action-packed machismo" and Hillman wanted to elevate the conversation, get away from four-letter words in which "the whole genital world is reduced to utter dumb simplicity." White American speech offered "hardly any phrases about places, rhythms, touches and tastes. We either have obscenities or we have scientific language like 'erogenous zones.' Yet listen to the marvelous language of foreign erotica—jade stalk, palace gates, ambrosia—it's endless." Because we lacked good language, we didn't speak about sex, and the lack of imagination "reinforces the image of love-making as a heroic performance." There was, in addition, the "romantic desire for fusion" with the woman, which "drives people into extremes of possession and identification." As an alternative approach, Hillman spoke of "imaginal sex," going beyond the heroic or romantic to a place of fantasy where "love itself changes" into something "larger, stranger, explorative, experiential. In which things come up, surprises, and ritual . . . There's a feeling of being close to terror and to beauty."[88] All this led to deeply frank group discussion about a subject that men are usually reluctant to address.

Coleman Barks, the poet who first met Hillman at a men's week in North Carolina, said that Hillman "would encourage people to reveal the parts of their body that they were ashamed of, often to do with the mid-belly. I still have a vision of James across the way, walking around with his shirt up to expose that part of himself. It was very beautiful, very freeing for people I think."[89]

Indeed, as Martin Keogh reflected: "Before James came to the men's conference there was never any nudity. Then men saw him sunbathing nude by the stream under the redwoods. It was hard to find a sunny spot in those tall trees. But he managed it. After that nudity was not a problem for the men."[90]

Especially freeing for the younger men, was Hillman standing up for the passionate puer energy. Countering the idea that the puer "must have his wings clipped, his energy roped and subdued," Rick Chelew has written, "Hillman says another way is to increase the passion, turn *up* the heat, and find one's way through via the excess. . . . The idea of defending and honoring want and desire was news to a whole generation of new-age, feminist-influenced young men who were ashamed and disgusted with the results of their fathers' desires: for money, domination of nature, their families, and other men. We turned, naturally, to our mothers, to eastern religions, and desirelessness became something to strive for, desire and ambition something to be ashamed of. In walks Hillman, tearing down all those ideals and showing us something else."[91]

It was freeing for him as well. In a letter written after the Wisconsin conference, Hillman said he "came home feeling an inch had been added to my shoulders, my deltoid muscle to be precise. A very strange sort of experience . . . I feel it still even as I sit here. My voice had also dropped. So I think I shall be continuing to go. They are quite extraordinary. Not just the men, but the teachers that Bly has inspired and assembled, the group itself, although this time 70% were new men who had not been there before."[92]

Even as the years passed, participation was never easy for Hillman. As Don Shewey wrote: "His patrician style of criticism strikes some men as 'caustic,' and his characteristically contrary thinking puts others' noses out of joint." One of his faults, Hillman admitted, was that he wasn't personal enough. Joe Landry, who some time later also became Hillman's barber, recalled, "A lot of people would say to him, 'You're in your head,' or 'You should be feeling things more,' and 'You're not genuine, these are only ideas.' I remember him ramming his fist to the table and shouting in true James-style: 'But the brain is full of blood—probably more than anywhere else!'"[93]

When he made mistakes, though, Hillman was prepared to acknowledge them. Roger Knudson, later a close colleague of Hillman's and now a retired clinical psychologist and Professor Emeritus at Miami University of Ohio, met him for the first time at a North Carolina men's event. To Knudson, Hillman was already a hero whose books he'd been teaching. When Hillman gave an assignment to the "turtle clan" that Knudson was part of, it turned out to be something which the other teachers felt he had not discussed with them—and so had overstepped his bounds. When Hillman came "crestfallen and openly apologetic" to remove the assignment, the group had already put so much work into it that Knudson blew up at him. Hillman listened and said, yes, he'd "really screwed things up." Then, at conference's end, while men were standing silently in a semicircle, Hillman walked up to Knudson and hit him in the chest with his open palm. Knudson followed by writing what he remembered as a "long tangled and confused letter" to the man he had long held on a pedestal.

Hillman wrote a letter in response: "My feeling about our connection is: one of those gifts in life. First of all we made it through the betrayal thing very well. You were, and your group, forgiving and understanding. I came off too quickly, and without enough thought 'ordained' your group *above* all others . . . I did not even guess you were an 'academic', let alone a psychologist! . . . Our connection also has that deeply male brother feeling that we talk of at these events—but do not always have happen, or feel, in fact. So thank you for your response, humor, straightness and self-containment."[94]

Hillman refused any mantle of authority and, Martin Keogh said, was the easiest of any of the teachers to get along with "because he wasn't at all invested in the people around him *changing*." One night, sitting with him on the riverbank near the staff cabins, Keogh spoke of all the "beautiful gems" that Hillman came up with during his lectures and asked him to "teach me how to mine, not just show me what you've discovered." Hillman leaned back and, after a brief silence, replied: "I have no interest in that whatsoever. That's your job. I'm doing my job." That conversation inspired Keogh to go back to the university from which he'd dropped out. When he told Hillman about this the following year, he responded, "Oh, what are you studying, psychology?" No, Keogh said, English literature. "That's great!" Hillman exclaimed.[95]

Another time sitting at a table in the woods, Meade remembered that Hillman kept literally turning over a rock as they worked on writing totemic descriptions about the various clans. He would always "look for the shadow side of it; he never wanted things to be too bright," said Meade. Buddhist teacher Jack Kornfeld tells a story about a morning when men were talking about their dreams and one stood to equate his nocturnal experience with one of the Greek gods. "And James, as if propelled by some force, rose out of his seat blazing and he said—'Don't you'—and then he looked at the whole room—'think that *you* contain the gods!' He paused for a minute, quite on fire, and then said something like: 'You don't understand, these are enormous forces, beings, archetypes, and they come and possess us, and there's nothing in our power that can stop it, and we become the channel for something so much greater than ourselves. It's your ego thinking you contain this, you're lucky if you can *stand* it!'" [96]

Hillman reflected: "We always had a banquet on the last night, and at one of these, Michael asked if I would do the blessing. I said, 'We bless the food with our appetites.' It was the idea that the food blesses itself, its presence blesses us, and the cooks bless us with their skills—but for a human being to bless the food is a *hubris*. This brings in the animal again. When the indigenous people shoot an animal to eat, they believe that somehow the animal accepts being killed. To have an appetite is a blessing; you relish the food, you give it highest value."[97]

Orland Bishop recalled: "When we finished all this deep ritual work, Hillman loved to toast. He introduced to us how to really pay tribute to a man's spirit in this way. It was his signature. I think in a certain sense he connected the Dionysian ritual of what it is that a person is going back into the world to do—where the banquet is about honoring life, honoring the return. It must be elegant. Find the poetry."[98]

After all was said and done, the men could cut loose. Beer was popular during the early retreats, but Hillman introduced wine before dinner. The only requirement for either beverage was, you couldn't drink unless you were willing to dance. Robert Carulo remembered Meade saying, "If men learned how to dance, maybe they'd put their weapons down." Former Doors percussionist John Densmore said that, at the first event he went to, when he heard Meade was going to teach drumming, "I started to take a walk. I'm not going to sit around and listen to fifty amateurs. But I was a few hundred yards away when, in like 20 minutes, he'd coalesced them into a simple ensemble.""[99] Meade had figured out a way of drumming in the air, with his back to the men, so they simply watched his hands and imitated it on the drums. After a couple of sessions, he could get a hundred people playing a traditional pattern. Later, it became men drumming in circles.

Densmore recalled: "Throughout all the years of the conferences, they'd have carnival or Mardi Gras nights and Michael would get everybody doing three different beats that would make a samba. If you weren't part of it, you might say, 'what the hell's going on here, are they a bunch of gays?, all these men hooting and dancing with each other.' But in fact, there was something incredibly freeing about it. And to see James Hillman take off his glasses and start jumping around like a fool!"[100] Rick Chelew said that Hillman "set the bar of how much you were willing to let go and give in to this experience. If he can do it, am I too cool to get involved?"

One night in Mendocino, a line was crossed. A "coyote" whose task was to invite trouble came into a roomful of men samba-dancing to different drum rhythms. He brought with him an inflatable sex doll, complete with large mouth, breasts and vagina, and started batting it through the air. Some of the men joined in, but Martin Keogh remembered that a "tangible tension came over the room, because the work we were doing was not at all about denigrating women, and this was way over the edge."

Suddenly, Hillman stepped out from the others. He walked over and plucked the doll out of the air. Then he started waltzing with it. Said Keogh: "He took a major energy, in a sense violent energy, raised it to another realm—and danced it right out of the room. The doll was never seen again."[101]

NOTES

1. "We live in a poetically underdeveloped nation. . . .": *The Rag and Bone Shop of the Heart: Poems for Men*, Robert Bly, James Hillman, and Michael Meade Editors, HarperCollins Publishers, 1992, p. xx.
2. Hillman letter to Bly, "We've got to get away from both the whiney young man. . . .", August 12, 1986.
3. Hillman on exposure to basic America: Ibid.
4. "not academic America. . . ..": Author interview with James Hillman, January 2009.
5. Craig Ungerman on Hillman's opening talk/the "coyote": Interview with author, March 2010.
6. "Everybody's fucked up. . . .": Author's interview with Ed Groody. February 2009.
7. "and Jim's considerable struggle. . . .": Author interview with Pat Berry.
8. Hillman on Bly reading Blake poems: Interview with author.
9. "The theme is beginning to 'awaken'. . . .": JH letter to Rudolf Ritsema, November 11, 1986, Eranos archive.
10. Hillman, "My life is radically changing. . . .":, JH postcard addressed to Bly, circa 1988, Bly archive.
11. "There was a huge misapprehension. . . .": Author interview with James Hillman, January 2009.
12. "doing therapy in a new way. . . .": Author interview with James Hillman, December 2007.
13. Bly among Harvard writers: Ibid.
14. Hillman Great Mother essay: in *Senex & Puer*, by James Hillman, "The Great Mother, Her Son, The Hero, and the Puer," Putnam, Ct.: Spring Publications, 2005, p. 121.
15. "many of the classic fairy tales. . . .": Robert Bly, private archive.
16. Bly on modern males: quoted by Trip Gabriel, *New York Times Magazine*, October 14, 1990.
17. "Certainly the patriarchy has suppressed. . . ..": Robert Bly quoted in *Austin American-Statesman*, April 4, 1989, "The Male Myth" by Carlos Vidal Greth.
18. Bly, "Every family gives you a wound": article by Don Shewey, "Town Meeting in the Hearts of Men," *The Village Voice*, February 11, 1992.
19. Bly on what he saw in his mid-forties: "A Gathering of Men," Bly Interview with Bill Moyers, January 8, 1990, PBS, available on YouTube.
20. 'older men lying. . . .': Bly quoted in *Austin American-Statesman*, April 4, 1989, "The Male Myth" by Carlos Vidal Greth
21. Michael Meade discovering mythology: Michael Meade, *Men and the Water of Life*, HarperSanFrancisco, 1993, p. 5.
22. Meade studies and performances: Ibid, p. 9.
23. Meade on discovering Hillman: Interview with author, June 2009.
24. Senex and puer defined: Introduction by Glen Slater, *Senex & Puer, James Hillman Uniform Edition No. 3*, Putnam, Ct.: Spring Publications, Inc., p. X.
25. Meade on Senex & Puer essay: Interview with author, June 2009.
26. Meade's first encounter with Hillman: Ibid.
27. "I knew the ideas could fit. . . .": Ibid.

28. Bly setting up Hillman's appearance: John Densmore interview with author, May 2007.

29. "Having no idea what they did. . . .": Author interview with James Hillman, November 2009.

30. Hillman entrance to Mendocino: Author interview with Martin Keough, January 2009.

31. "A lot of them had gone. . . .": Author interview with Joe Landry, September 2008.

32. "An all-male attempt. . . .": James Hillman letter to Ginette Paris, June 15, 1987, Paris private archive.

33. Hillman on "keeping alive something. . . .": Transcript of *Men and the Life of Desire*, Scottish Rite Temple in San Francisco, March 11, 1990 (Oral Tradition Archives).

34. Etheridge Knight: https://www.poetryfoundation.org/poems/48752/feeling-fucked-up

35. The quotes are derived from a transcript made by the author from an Oral Traditions Archive recording with James Hillman, Robert Bly, and Michael Meade, in Mendocino, California.

36. Rick Chelew: Email to author.

37. "Everybody found themselves in the story. . . .": James Hillman interview with author, January 2009.

38. "All scheduling went out the window. . . .": Rick Chelew email to author.

39. "The fairy tales in which these archetypes. . . .": Bly quoted in Austin American-Statesmen, "The Male Myth," April 4, 1989.

40. "embodied ideas. . . .": Author interview with Michael Meade, June 2008.

41. Margot McLean on Hillman and men's groups: Interview with author, April 2010.

42. Luis Rodriguez on men's groups: Interview with author, May 2009.

43. "In that kind of space, it's an initiation. . . .": Author interview with Orland Bishop, October 2016.

44. "Where men are gathered. . . .": Hillman interview with author, November 2007.

45. "We would go from literal nature studies. . . .": Author interview with Michael Meade, June 2009.

46. Clans: Bly archive, University of Minnesota.

47. "They were working at some particular. . . .": Hillman interview with author, January 2009.

48. "I think this opened Jim. . . .": Author interview with Meade.

49. "Some had huge, terrible stories. . . .": Hillman interview with author, January 2009.

50. "We argued out the entire. . . .": Meade, author interview.

51. "People would take sides. . . .": Hillman interview with author, January 2009.

52. "There was a lot of hurt. . . .": Andy Castro interview with author, April 2010.

53. Hillman on men and trust: Interview with author, January 2011.

54. "It was all about learning. . . .": Author interview with Meade.

55. "Doing something for the dead. . . .": Author interview with James Hillman, January 2009.

56. John Densmore on the sweat lodge: *Riders On the Storm: My Life with Jim Morrison and the Doors*, Delta re-issue edition, September 1991, pp. 303–304.

57. Terry Dobson story: Meade interview with author.

58. "a desire to change the culture. . . .": Author interview with Michael Meade, June 2009..

59. "Jamming with language. . . . Author interview with Rick Chelew.

60. "Town Meeting in the Hearts of Men," by Don Shewey, *Village Voice*, February 11, 1992.
61. Richard Olivier: Interview with author, July 2007.
62. "We fed each other. . . .": Author interview with Hillman, January 2009.
63. "They had a huge respect. . . .": Author interview with Rick Chelew.
64. "There's too much complaining. . . .": Author interview with Fred Stephens, June 2008.
65. "So we were lucky in a way. . . .": Author interview with Robert Bly, July 2007.
66. "If Bly comes off as a lion. . . .": Shewey, *Village Voice*.
67. "Robert could be totally arrogant. . . .": Author interview with "Hillman, January 2009.
68. "playfulness and amazing ability. . . .": Bly, author interview.
69. "James was much more disciplined. . . .": Ungerman, author interview.
70. "letting their hair down. . . .": Chelew, author interview.
71. Hillman confirmation: Meade interview.
72. Hillman asking Bly to recall an exercise: JH letter to Bly, December 5, 1988, Bly papers, University of Minnesota.
73. Hillman to Bly on feelings of protection toward him: JH letter to Bly, December 7, 1990, Bly papers, University of Minnesota.
74. "We didn't call in sociologists. . . .": Author interview with Hillman, October 2010.
75. "I'm back in Boston. . . .": Etheridge Knight letter to JH, December 30, 1987, Opus Archive.
76. "It was exposure in a group. . . .": Author interview with Hillman, January 2011.
77. "Six days here is better than five years in a consulting room. . . .":: Author interview with Meade.
78. "ten times the knowledge. . . .": Bly, author interview.
79. "If you're visited in the night. . . .": Author interview with Robert Carulo, March 2008.
80. "A group of about twenty guys. . . .": Author interview with James Hillman, November 2007.
81. "I think it was the first time. . . .": Author interview, Densmore.
82. The author interviewed Fred Stephens in Pittsburgh in 2006; this quote is also drawn from an email from Stephens to the author, July 25, 2013.
83. "James can be very eagle-eyed. . . .": Keogh, author interview.
84. "Part of it had to do. . . .": Author interview with James Hillman, November 2007.
85. "At one point a guy stood up. . . .": Ungerman, author interview.
86. Hillman on importance of gay men being involved: "Private Men; Public Psyche," interview with Hillman, *Wingspan*, September 1991.
87. Hillman on "Love in Male Friendship:" *To Be A Man: In Search of the Deep Masculine*, Edited by Keith Thompson, Los Angeles, Ca: Jeremy P. Tarcher, Inc., pp. 228–230.
88. Hillman on "cocks and cunts": Tape transcript from Mendocino Men's Conference, September 1988.
89. Hillman "would encourage people. . . .": Author interview with Coleman Barks, June 2009.
90. "Before James came to the men's conference. . . .": Martin Keogh email to author, January 2019.
91. "must have his wings clipped. . . .': Rick Chelew, shared with author.

92. "came home feeling an inch had been added. . . .": Hillman letter to Ginette Paris, undated.

93. "A lot of people would say to him. . . .": Author interview with Joe Landry, September 2008.

94. Hillman on connection with Knudson: JH letter to Roger Knudson, November 1, 1993.

95. Keogh and Hillman: Author interview with Martin Keogh, January 2009.

96. "And James, as if propelled. . . .": Author interview with Jack Kornfeld, March 2008.

97. "We always had a banquet. . . .": Author interview with James Hillman, January 2011.

98. "When we finished all this deep. . . .": Author interview with Orland Bishop, October 2016.

99. "I started to take a walk. . . .": Densmore, author interview.

100. "Throughout all the years. . . .": Ibid.

101. Hillman and the sex doll: Author interview with Martin Keogh, January 2009.

15

FATHERS AND SONS, MEN AND WOMEN, BLACKS AND WHITES

"Today we need heroes of descent, not masters of denial, mentors of maturity who can carry sadness, who give love to aging, who show soul without irony or embarrassment."
— *James Hillman,* Kinds of Power, *1995.[1]*

Early in 1990, Robert Bly was featured in a 90-minute PBS special with Bill Moyers called *A Gathering of Men.*[2] James Hillman sent Bly a note containing both praise and critique, and added that Bly's effort "did not damage the 'daimones' who invisibly take part in the men's workshops and retreats. I don't believe they will object." The broadcast was a landmark moment. Almost overnight, the little-known woodland events that Bly had initiated almost a decade before were turned into a "men's movement." By the end of the year, Bly's book *Iron John* was on its way to becoming an international bestseller. Suddenly, there were cover stories in *Time* and *Newsweek.* And interest in the workshops skyrocketed.

That March, a Sunday event at the Scottish Rite Temple in San Francisco sold out quickly by word-of-mouth, resulting in a small mob scene with men trying to get tickets and good seats in the morning. The topic that Bly, Hillman, and Michael Meade chose for the 750 in attendance was "Men and the Life of Desire."

Not long before this, Bly had recognized "the amount of anger [coming] from men who had been ignored by their fathers." It happened when he asked those who hated their father to move to the left side of the auditorium, and those who loved their father to stand on the right. The room divided pretty much in half. Bly then asked to hear from someone who loved their father. As one fellow began explaining what his father had done for him, from across the way another shouted: "You're a fucking liar, you know that? My father was a sonovabitch and so was yours!" The battle between the two sides went on for almost an hour.[3]

Now, in an afternoon segment, Bly noted that the fathers in TV ads were always stupid—ads largely "written by young men rejecting their fathers." When the father is gone, he went on, everyone becomes the sibling; young men look sideways, not up, knowing only others their own age. "In a sibling society, people do not want to change society, they want a higher standard of living."[4]

Hillman spoke on the "cry to be fathered," an ongoing concern in psychotherapy and the culture. "We all want a protector or teacher or noble institution of instruction, someone who knows, a roof, a truth, a place to be sheltered or unbroken word—a good father. We forget that in the myths, both the Greek and in the Hebrew Bible, the father is a murderer." From Oedipus to Abraham and ultimately Jesus ("Father, why hast thou forsaken me?"), a fundamental tenet of the father's world is that he is *not* reliable. Thus "our own complaints don't understand the shadow, which is archetypally given . . . it goes with fathering to be a 'bad father.'" But what else might we realize? Hillman made a point about standing by a bridgehead and waiting for the father to cross over, but all the while he was crossing at another part of the river—"because you insist he come where you want him to come, you never get to see what he is actually doing and how he is coming across."[5]

There were differences between the actual father and the mentor or teacher who often knows you better. "Maybe it is not the father's job to do the blessing. Or maybe the father did bless you in a way you haven't seen. Maybe the resentments keep you from the blessing. The longer you wish you had a good father, the more you repeat the damages your father did to you, the more you remain the wounded child." Yet, if men realize that the pain of the father's failings belongs to fathering, then: "The commonality—and commonness—of shared shadow can bond father and son in dark and silent empathy as deep as any idealized companionship."[6]

At the end of his remarks, Hillman shouted at the audience: "I'm enraged at you being outraged by your father, or your mother, and not being outraged about what else is happening in the world!" Some in the crowd applauded. Others howled in protest.

Hillman had noticed, "Early on, the men usually started off with this psychotherapeutic language about their fathers and not being loved. Where I had most of my fights was in trying to *dis*count their personal experience. Again and again, 'We've had that, we've had that, we know what your father didn't do. What *did* he do? What else, what else!' Your father is doing something that you don't even see because you're trapped in your own desires, your own complaint, your own soul. I ran into trouble with that, because they wanted to stay in their complaining position."[7]

Yet the results of having exchanges about fathers and sons could be profound. Richard Olivier, son of the famed British actor Laurence Olivier, was particularly affected by his experience in the men's groups. The day his father died in 1989 had marked a turning point in his life. As described on the jacket of his 1995 memoir, *Shadow of the Stone Heart*, "Unable to grieve and confused by an increasing alienation from family, friends and life itself, he found himself facing the crisis of an unresolved boyhood."

Someone gave Olivier a tape of a Bly lecture and he decided to attend the first men's event that the poet held in England. Olivier recalled: "He said something like, 'In modern society, a boy can't become a man until the day his father dies,' and it made a lot of sense about the struggle I was in." Bly ended up inviting Olivier to help out with organizing future events, and that was how he first encountered Hillman in London. "The first subject I ever heard him speak on was something about the persona and about fame. Having come from a famous family, it was something I'd been feeling a little oppressed by. This was the first time I had met anyone who, in a very concentrated period of time, could completely change the way you think about something. I believe he said once, 'I rearrange the furniture in your head.' I've never witnessed that kind of poetic intellect—in the sense that it wasn't arid, not just ideas, but somehow going into a fixed notion and being able to loosen it and shake it apart, then move you into awareness of a different possibility. I literally came away feeling that my head was on fire. We went out to dinner afterwards with a few people, and I remember saying something about growing up in a famous family and people fulfilling their purpose but they don't often make the families very happy. James turned to look at me and said, 'What makes you think you ought to be happy?'"[8]

In May 1991, Olivier traveled abroad to participate in the first multicultural men's conference at Buffalo Gap, West Virginia, living for a week in the woods with fifty white men and fifty men of color. Until then one of his concerns was that, if he revealed who his father was, that would become the sole subject of conversation. At Buffalo Gap, he found the courage to stand up and say, "I'm Richard Olivier and Laurence Olivier was my father." Catching himself, he went on to add, "I've never said that in public before." Olivier remembers, "One of the big black guys in the front row shouted out, 'Say it again! Say it again!' So I did. 'One more time!' the men said."[9]

Over the course of the week, Olivier took in Bly's powerful poem *My Father's Neck*, Meade's fairy tale called *The Six Companions*, and Hillman's recapitulation of the myths on which our culture is founded: "The Father has to betray the son, it's in the wiring; it's not in the wiring of the Mother. Smothering is in the wiring of the Mother. You may be angry at the universe because it put betrayal in the Father—and you may be angry at your father because he was not a good Mother!"

Olivier later wrote of hearing those words: "I was stunned. I had never been able to contemplate anything other than my father's failure to do (my perception of) a father's job. What if betrayal is part of that job? If father does not 'fail us' what inspiration do we have to leave his house?" At one point, Olivier revealed a long-suppressed realization to the group, "saying that I must be the only white man present whose first memory of his father was as a black man." He went on to tell the story of when, as a child, he had seen Laurence Olivier, "in his full power," onstage as Shakespeare's black Othello.[10]

That same year, Hillman's own son, Laurence, accepted his father's invitation to attend a men's week with him in North Carolina. He had recently turned thirty. Two weeks away from having his first child, Laurence had just been talking with his therapist about "working through the shit" about his father before he became one himself. "So I went," Laurence remembered, "and I didn't know if I wanted to beat him up, or if I wanted to just cry and have him hold me. It was clearly one of those two extreme emotions." He described the two of them as "dancing around each other" for a few days, because nobody knew that he was Hillman's son.[11]

Sitting in the audience as his father spoke, Laurence Hillman found himself thinking, "Boy, this guy is smart, this is great stuff, unbelievable." Talking to the men sharing his cabin afterwards, Laurence suddenly realized that, while his father's brilliance might go right over the heads of many of those present, *he* understood it. "It wasn't easy to grasp—complex deep stuff that I'd never seen him do in such a setting, but with a lot of beauty and compassion. I recognized his language as being mine; as someone once said, I was marinated in archetypal thinking. That was a gift."[12]

Father and son took a walk together the next day. Laurence remembered that "it was really awkward, one of the hardest conversations I've ever had. I said to him, 'Instead of having all this anger, I'm realizing what you *did* give me—which is this psychological ability. Being here has awakened that in me, the way of thinking and having that skill.' We stopped and we hugged and we both cried. And he said, 'You know, if you hadn't said that, I would have felt like I gave you nothing.' It was a huge revelation."

On the last day, at an all-male feast, Laurence stood up and said, "I want to make a toast—to my father—James Hillman." They hugged again while the room exploded with applause. Laurence Hillman went home to St. Louis, fired his therapist, and stepped into fatherhood with his new baby daughter. "I was very strong when I came back," he recalled. "I felt blessed."

The Life and Ideas of James Hillman

Asked how his relationship with Laurence changed, Hillman said: "Two things happened. One was, I admired him enormously for his courage in coming to this event, going through the whole thing, and then revealing himself at the end. Not many young guys would do that. As far as what happened to him, it was that he could see what I do and see me through the eyes of other men."[13]

At that same conference, as recounted by William Finger in an article called "Finding the Door into the Forest": "Hillman, the intellectual—not Bly, the poet—changed my view of poetry forever. Hillman started reading 'The Race' by Sharon Olds, about a dash to catch a plane to see a dying father. Hillman choked with emotion by the fourth line, continuing though until the man was racing down the long corridor to the gate. Then Hillman stopped, sobbing. Michael [Meade] reached his left hand around James's shoulder and held him. Then Hillman, who was in his sixties, resurfaced from his pool of grief and finished the poem. Tears were streaming down my face too, and I knew how it felt to have my heart opened at unexpected moments."[14] Participant Fred Stephens recalled: "I guarantee you there was not a single man there who doesn't remember that to this day."[15]

At Meade's urging, Richard Olivier and Laurence Hillman met for the first time at James Hillman's seventieth birthday party in New York. "I think you guys will really get on," Meade told them. They became fast friends and sometime co-workers. Olivier Mythodrama, using Shakespeare's plays as a basis of leadership training among business professionals, now runs workshops all over the world. Combining astrology with images from theater (including Shakespeare), Laurence Hillman has taught in many of the same countries.

BUFFALO GAP

Nobody knew what might happen during the first multicultural men's conference, held at a remote location in the hills of West

Virginia. The surrounding little town of Capon Bridge derived its name from the waterway it crossed, the Shawnee Cape-cape-de-hon, meaning "River of Medicine Water." Resting literally in a fissure between two mountains (Sandy Ridge and Slane's Knob), Buffalo Gap had been founded as a Jewish kids camp soon after World War II, based on the idea that children of all faiths would be welcome. There were later rumors that it also hosted meetings of the Ku Klux Klan. Now fifty white men came together with an equal number of men of color, mostly African American but also Hispanic, Native American, and Asian.

It had originated when the writer Michael Ventura, who attended some of the early events, said something that especially struck Michael Meade: "Is this men's work, or just white men's work?" Meade began compiling an address list of the small number of African Americans who had attended various men's gatherings. Then, at an event on psychology and men in 1990, Meade suggested taking a portion of their conference income and setting it aside to begin having programs that brought together men from diverse cultural backgrounds. With Hillman the first to agree, Meade created the Multicultural Foundation (today called Mosaic) and soon began visiting black communities in various parts of the country, recruiting and offering scholarships for a summit meeting. He and Bly spent months at organizing the first one.

Three black teachers were enlisted to join Bly, Hillman, and Meade: playwright and Howard University professor Joseph Walker, author of the award-winning *The River Niger*; Malidoma Somé, born and raised in West Africa and then teaching comparative literature at the University of Michigan; and Chicago poet/political essayist Haki Madhubuti. One of the architects of the Black Arts Movement of the 1960s, Madhubuti was the founder of Third World Press and had just published a new book called *Black Men: Obsolete, Single, Dangerous?* He and Bly had crossed paths before, but Madhubuti was surprised to receive the invitation.

"I'd worked with a group of black men at retreats in the Catskills a few times a year," he remembered, "but not at any level with white men or even the white community because I felt they had betrayed us. In terms of their dedication to a truly multicultural America, their word for the most part was not true."[16] Still, Madhubuti respected Bly's work and the request seemed genuine. So he'd decided to go.

The Buffalo Gap Camp for the Cultural Arts was a two-hour drive west of Washington, D.C., located on a manmade lake in the foothills of the Alleghenies. There, early in May of 1991, the men began arriving and finding their cabins. The opening ceremony took place in an octagonal, wood-paneled meeting hall adjacent to the dining room and kitchen, with a small raised platform at one end and just enough space to cram in folding chairs for the hundred men. Joseph Walker led the group in a chant to Papa Legba, African god of the crossroads. Aidoo Holmes, a master drummer trained in the African tradition of musician as spiritual healer, then began a libation ceremony. "We could call on the names and spirits of any friends, dead or alive, mentors, ancestors, guardians or allies to join us and share the water libation, which he would bless and pour into a bowl as a welcome," recounted Richard Olivier in his memoir.[17] After the first two speakers, both white, went further than names and offered a prayer to Jesus and a welcome to one's father, a black man cried out: "Malcolm X!" Another shouted: "Frantz Fanon!" The tone was set.

That night after dinner, as John Densmore remembered, Madhubuti opened his presentation by saying: "How am I supposed to trust a group that committed genocide against Native Americans?" Meade recalled Madhubuti continuing: "I'm not saying there aren't any good white people, I'm saying I never met any." Within fifteen minutes, an intense argument broke out in the room. A black man said, "When we're walking down the street, why do you people cross to the other side of the block?" A white man responded, "Because I'm afraid of being mugged, goddamn it!"

When Bly asked, "What in your life is urgent right now?" stories started pouring forth: A white man who worked in a drug unit at a large prison, haunted every night by the lost men and boys he dealt with by day, and the desperate need for some form of real initiation. The black man who worked in a hospice for AIDS babies, one having died in his arms, beseeching those present: "Where are the fathers? Where are the brothers?" The last speaker, introducing himself as Abati, said he didn't think black men were ready yet to take part in a group like this. "Any idea that we might work our way slowly up to the tension between blacks and whites had flown out the window," wrote Don Shewey.[18]

Hillman remembered how, "Buffalo Gap profoundly affected me. [When I was] in the Navy, black men were in a different barracks and trained separately. At Buffalo Gap, we shared sleeping quarters. I would say this was my first immediate, daily, one-on-one encounter with black people. We were face-to-face, living in the middle of the racial conflict. There was also a continuation of this fundamental strain that runs through my life—for example, earlier in Zürich with the calls for my resignation as Director of Studies: it was meeting the fears, going into the test. Not because the black men were aggressively attacking the whites, but I mean the fears that you bring with you, your racism."[19]

The next morning, Bly and Hillman opened proceedings with a discussion of how to imagine the father in a different way, followed by Meade commencing a fairy tale. Then came Malidoma Somé, wearing a modest dashiki over gray-and-white striped pants, a kufi on his head with five white stars on it. A mutual friend had recommended that Meade invite him to come here, but at the time Malidoma barely knew what a men's group was. Now he was being asked to talk publicly for the first time about his initiation, twenty years before, into the Dagara tribe in the West African nation of Burkina Faso. "Through pain, I became what I am today," Malidoma began. The men fell silent.

Malidoma's was a most unique story, one he would later relate in his first book, *Of Water and the Spirit*. He'd been taken from his tribe when only four by Jesuit missionaries, who wanted to some-day make him a priest. When he ran away at twenty and returned to his village, he was scarcely recognized by his own family and could not speak his native tongue. The only solution, a coun-cil of elders decided, was to put Malidoma through the tribe's initiation rites, several years later than the usual age (thirteen to seventeen). He revealed to the men at Buffalo Gap a few of the trials he endured, which included sitting naked in hundred-degree heat and staring at a tree for three days. "You either succeed and live, or fail and die," he said. His quest had included out-of-body journeys to "other worlds." Afterwards Malidoma was told he would fulfill his destiny by living in the West as a teacher of African ways and wisdom. He would emerge from twelve years of Western education with three MAs and two PhDs. The name Malidoma meant "be friends with the stranger/enemy."[20]

He had no idea how his story would be received in Buffalo Gap. Craig Ungerman from Minnesota remembered that "we were mesmerized, but we didn't know it was over. The whole room was quiet for what seemed like a minute, though it was probably only ten seconds. Then all of a sudden everybody just erupted, stood up and cheered. We were all crying and Malidoma was crying."[21] Richard Olivier described the moment in *Shadow of the Stone Heart*: "I had been transported into a new realm of possibilities. My spine was tingling with excitement at the tales of his trials, my mind mourning that there was no conceivable equivalent in my culture . . . Was it possible to develop a new model, suitable for the Western mind?"[22] Don Shewey wrote in *Common Boundary*: "For those of us harboring fuzzy ideas link-ing initiation with panty raids or secret handshakes, Malidoma's story arouses a recognition of the deep spiritual dimension of male initiation. It's so ironic, I think afterwards, and typical of American culture. We're dying of spiritual starvation, and the people who hold the cup of nourishment are precisely the ones we have despised, discredited and conspired to exterminate."

Something had broken open with Malidoma's tale. The camp was "bristling, kinetic," said John Densmore. That night during "community time," wrote Olivier, "Questions of trust, safe space and prejudice mingled with personal stories that sent arrows of emotion arcing across the room." Two hours later, Olivier "felt as if someone had cut into my chest, pulled my heart out and used it as a trampoline. Michael Meade stood to end the evening with a deep breathing exercise that restored a sense of external reason."[23]

It may have been that same night that Meade was awakened at two o'clock in the morning and remembered: "A white guy and a black guy equal in stature and size, in their thirties, both very vital, had gotten into an argument over racial issues that led to a fight—and now they were in a death-grip. This to me was quite symbolic, what are we gonna do? People were trying to pull them apart, but it was useless. So I lay down on the floor and talked to them. We talked it out until they let go."[24]

Madhubuti, who had been quietly getting "the lay of the land," gave the lead-off talk the next day. He spoke in an incantational style, of a father he never knew and a mother dead at thirty-five due to alcohol and drugs. "I've been on my own since I was sixteen," he said. "I learned what to do by seeing what not to do." Now he "upped the ante considerably . . . with a blistering report on black history in the West," to the present moment when one in three black men from ages of sixteen to twenty-nine were incarcerated. He spoke of the importance of culture, how it can lead to shared understanding, and be the "medium through which meaning is passed down generations." Yet black men had been "denatured," cut off from their own. While saying that "collectively I do fear white men, because of the amount of destruction they have caused," he also extended a hand to those who had come to Buffalo Gap. "I am here because this is history making—we're starting at a new level of history."[25]

Hillman followed him to the podium to give a talk he'd first delivered in 1986 called "Notes on White Supremacy." On the first occasion, he wrote in a letter, "at first I saw that it was the same sort of attack on Apollonic consciousness as I did years ago, combined with some of the same alchemical reflections of before, but then I noticed that the paper finally has a different cast, a different body of research, and a different complexity. One does not escape one's basic themes, but they do get elaborated differently."[26]

The elaboration five years later to this ethnically diverse group was something else again. Hillman observed that the very phrase "white supremacy" was embedded in our language and culture, starting with the *Oxford English Dictionary* definitions of white ("morally or spiritually pure or stainless . . . free from malignity or evil intent") and black ("soiled, dirty . . . having dark purposes, malignant, deadly, baneful, disastrous, sinister"). Associated with innocence, white maintained its supremacy by exclusion, by the absence of anything noxious or harmful. "Black becomes necessary to represent what is excluded from white" and so becomes "other," which in the Christian tradition is impure, opposed to good, and thus "evil." Hillman explained how Newton and Kepler, in developing optics, had reduced the visible spectrum of light to what exists in white, refracted through a prism. It was the "supreme color," while black was "the absence of light." Philosophers then proclaimed the "age of enlightenment." With depth psychology defining darkness as "the unconscious," (symbolized by dreams of Africa and "primitive" peoples), the exclusion of black was complete: the linguistic and religious "absence of good," optically defined as the "absence of light," philosophically defined as "without the light of reason" and psychologically defined as the "absence of consciousness." And so, "In social history, this equation promotes missions and colonization and suggests blacks are savage and stupid." Hillman's proposal was that we seek to move beyond black and white: "For we can't get out of our skins, but we can go out of our minds."[27]

Years later, Hillman recalled that, "The ideas were pretty abstruse for this audience. It was too subtle and it wasn't successful. Many saw me as an old white man laying out how blacks became evil, and defending white supremacy! I mean, that was part of the problem. The moment you use the word white, you set up a situation that puts white on top. My proposal was actually very simple: give up whiteness, get rid of the idea of being white. But it was too intellectual for most of them, I think."[28]

It wasn't for Malidoma Somé, who remembered being astounded to realize that "the whole idea of race is conceptual, something we are all stuck with. How James Hillman broke it down made so much sense."[29] And it wasn't too intellectual for Haki Madhubuti either, who had never heard of Hillman before Buffalo Gap and thought the talk was "quite defining and revelatory," to move beyond the term racism to the concept of white supremacy: "He, a white man, trying to bring some new understanding to those who were *not* white."[30]

Meade believed that Hillman offered "the intellectual backbone for what we were doing, of grasping this almost cosmologically." Indeed, two reports of reactions bordered on the cosmological. Olivier wrote: "As he finished . . . an image loomed in front of my inner vision; a white finger rubbing a black skin." Shewey wrote that Hillman's analysis "inhabits you in ways you can't control or predict. The next morning a dream-like vision appears to me in meditation: a basket lined in dark purple cloth is placed in front of me, and in it I place a drowned baby, completely black and lifeless. This powerful image conjures for me my unloved self, my unborn dreams, my disappointments. I wonder how much this rejected blackness has to do with the pain of separation from my African brothers." [31]

The next day, Madhubuti arose early and went to find Meade, who was staying in the next room. Meade remembered him saying: "I've seen something I never saw before—people working together and taking risks here, and it's in the music too." Meade had invited some "kick-ass drummers" of Caucasian, African American, and Latino heritage, and Madhubuti was stunned to realize that here were "a hundred guys who previously thought they might kill each other, all dancing like crazy. He said, 'This is something profound, I didn't know this was possible in a few days.'" Twenty years later, Madhubuti recalled: "What was very defining to me was the number of white men and others who had actually mastered African drumming."

When Madhubuti addressed the group that day, he spoke of how a lot of the emotional and intellectual baggage was gone, the "suspicion and apprehension about other men and other races, ancestral fears, guilts and passions we've been carrying because we had no place to put them, media-stoked impressions about men of other races and what a 'men's conference' might be like. All that created a thick atmosphere that we've been cutting through with honesty, courage, and articulate rage. Now we see each other more clearly. We've sniffed each other out and determined that we're not enemies. We agree that the world is in dire shape and needs drastic changes, and that part of our project as men is to put our warrior energy at the service of the larger community."[32]

Hillman described his impressions of Madhubuti: "In the beginning, he was annoyingly aggressive: 'I don't have to pay another minute of attention to white people.' You realized how deep this was and how long it had been going on. At the same time, Haki was very dignified. He was extremely interested in educating youth and had started four schools in Chicago. I came to respect him very much. Some time later, when he came to give a talk at a school gym in Worcester [Massachusetts], I went and sat in the audience."[33]

At Buffalo Gap, Madhubuti observed that Hillman "was one of the calm, very logical, very careful voices, impassioned at times and obviously very serious. His words were always healing at the conference, and that impressed me a great deal."[34]

As the week drew to a close, Meade said, "once we broke through all the cultural limitations, we were in this land of great imagination and depth." The last night, they decorated the lodge for a celebration, and all stood to the side to watch Hillman perform a tap dance accompanied by Densmore on the drums and a young Jamaican on saxophone. Olivier described the scene: "The sight of this gracefully ageing white man, elegantly tapping away to the harsh and urgent beauty of the young black man's saxophone, was extraordinary . . . As they finished, a hundred men cheered and swarmed onto the floor. We divided ourselves into drummers and dancers, and continued for as long as we could stand."[35]

Preparing to depart Buffalo Gap in the morning, a man came up to Meade carrying a big ceramic drum that had somehow been broken during the festivities. "He was really upset," according to Meade. "So I said, 'we'll collect some money and get you another drum. Leave it there on the ground.' I looked down and saw all these colored ceramic pieces and I put them on the drumhead. We had to close the week somehow. So I placed this broken drum in the middle of everybody and I said, 'We've had something great here. Either we're now going to leave feeling bad because we broke this, or how about if everyone takes home a piece of this drum? It might even break our hearts a little because we may never find this feeling again. But if we ever came back together, we could reconstruct that drum.' So today it exists in homes around the country, with men of all different types. And the name for my organization, Mosaic, comes from that broken drum."[36]

Madhubuti said that "West Virginia opened up possibilities and retuned my ear to listen to white men differently. I met many men there that I still have contact with today, Robert Bly being one and John Densmore who has helped me tremendously at Third World Press and with our schools." Today the author of twenty-eight books, Madhubuti continued to teach at numerous multicultural men's meetings.

After the week together at Buffalo Gap, Densmore remembered driving back in a van to Dulles Airport, with a mixed group including Madhubuti and several African Americans. "When we pulled up to where the skycaps are, we just sat there for like ten minutes. Nobody wanted to get out of the car." [37]

Later that same year, a dryer caught fire. The Buffalo Gap Camp burned to the ground.

MEN AND WOMEN

In the late eighties, a letter had arrived addressed to Hillman and Bly "of the men's movement." It came from Bly's ex-wife Carol (they had divorced in 1980 after a twenty-five-year marriage), and it took strong exception to one of the conference brochures. The imagery, she felt, was "excite-to-battle language." She found this "men's separatist movement" frightening and the notion of drumming ridiculous, wondering "is wild laughter what the world so desperately needs?" Her advice was: "Please seriously think of stopping all *male bonding*."[38]

Hillman took up the challenge. "Male bonding is crucial," he wrote back, "not because it is a separatism but because it is a response to the alienated and competitive state of male existence in our Western culture, which has terrible paranoid consequences. Men afraid of other men are not men anyone wants to be near, so they become more isolated and more paranoid . . . As for laughter, and wild laughter. Yes, the world sure does need it, and I suspect you do too. As for drumming: what in the name of the Gods exercises you about drumming. There is hardly anything more fundamental in human culture. It is like fire and eating and making babies and speech and dance." In conclusion, he said: "Finally, again, finally, ask yourself why are you personally so threatened by this announcement."[39]

Carol Bly was not, of course, alone in feeling threatened. Feminist leader Betty Friedan had no use for the movement, calling it "a definition of masculinity based on dominance."[40] Cultural critic Barbara Ehrenreich thought that archetypes like the Wild Man and the Warrior embraced longstanding models of the heroic male: "Whether they mean to or not, I think they are glorifying that essentially bloodthirsty tradition."[41] (Bly's response to such criticisms was, "To take a symbolic expression literally is what the fundamentalists in our culture do and a lot of unnecessary conflict results."[42]) Jill Johnston, writing in the *New York Times Book Review* on "Why *Iron John* Is No Gift to Women," conceded that perhaps the drumming and chanting "could be said to help them restore their sense of lost power. But the fact is that white men are not an oppressed group. These meetings smack of . . . paranoid and racist overreactions." What was needed was rather that "men needed to be initiated into primary parenting and real domestic responsibility, as well as the world."[43]

Margot McLean recalled having heated discussions with a number of her female friends about what these gatherings represented. "The premise where I took issue with them was, this is not increasing male aggressiveness toward women. If anything it was sensitizing men in a very different way. I think it was a painful journey for a lot of these guys. I was surprised at my friends' lack of insight. Men reading poetry to each other and engaging in tough conversations cannot be equated with the stereotype of male chest-beating and domination."[44]

The irony of the negative reactions was that, for many of the male participants, their wives had pushed them into attending. Hugh Van Dusen, Hillman's book editor in New York, came to several of the events. He recalled his introductory evening in North Carolina when "One man stood right up and said, 'My wife got my plane ticket, made a reservation at a motel, and drove me to the airport.' He was from Atlanta. Another man followed him, and said, 'I came home from a business trip three weeks ago and my wife said, 'You know, you're really boring.' I figured I better do something, so I'm here.'"[45] An organizer of some of the events. John Guarnashelli, reported that at first his wife "reacted the way many women did, as though they were being abandoned because I suddenly have men friends and am talking to these guys on the phone. It took me about a year to figure out that there was much more of *me* to be home with *her*, and after that she was fine with it."[46] Meade received many messages from women asking, "What did you do to my husband, or my son, that he is so different." Or saying, "The conversation has improved wildly, and the lovemaking, there is a new empathy present."[47]

Hillman remembered how the gatherings would conclude: "Michael would give a talk at the end about how to leave wherever we were meeting. You're going to get into your car now and on the road, and you're not going to know who or what you are, which is dangerous. So when you begin to feel a little bit out of it, just pull over. He was absolutely right. I mean, they *were* in another place, like going off to war or something. And a nice thing to do, Michael would say, is when you're in the airport, buy a little something to take home to your wife."[48]

Hillman believed that the idea of a men's movement being a counterpoint to feminism was "a false opposition, like so many things that are set up in America as two sides. In fact, women sent their lovers and husbands and supported it very strongly. And what we talked about was never anti-women, nothing about women as ball-busters or tyrant mothers who ruined you, none of that. But this wasn't a positivism, so that you get on better with your wife. That was deeply secondary. Fathers were more important than women."Indeed, John Densmore said, "We didn't talk about women much at all." When it did happen, it was generally at night in the privacy of the cabins.

Having already expanded horizons with a multicultural conference, Meade went on to organize an event with approximately fifty men and an equal number of women. After the sexes separated for the first several days, they came together with the men in a cluster of concentric circles on the floor and the women sitting in larger rings around them. "There was to be no dialogue between the two groups," Meade wrote in his book, *Men and the Water of Life*. "The men began to speak into the fragile silence . . . There were concerns and complaints. There was weeping. There was screaming rage, rage that went all the way back to Mother. There was careful thankfulness expressed by a man toward his wife, who was present. There was deep anguish over what daughters would experience in the chaos of the world. As the men went on, many women began to weep, and as the telling continued, more and more men and women were crying. Throughout the entire presentation, not one woman spoke. Then it came time to change places."

As the women moved to the center, their knees touching in close circles, and "began to express their feelings about men . . . a completely different thing happened. The men could not stop themselves from answering, correcting, and elaborating on what the women said. It was shocking. In order for the women to continue, the men actually had to link arms and hold onto each other to keep one another from bursting out with some statement of disagreement or even of agreement." As the women "got to say all that they wished to say," including "once again . . . the entire range of emotions," afterward the men were stunned "by their inability to listen . . . Throughout the rest of the conference, we all found it easier simply to hear each other . . . The ritual of listening had opened another ear inside, an inner ear that was intrigued by what the other gender group might say."[49]

As Scott Becker wondered years later, "what can be learned from these radically brave, culturally seismic encounters between white men and men of color, between men and women, beyond the usual notions of confronting social injustice, and engaging in honest communication and emotional intimacy (which are naturally critical to the process but don't necessarily lead to the kind of profound experiences described here)? Surely something more was happening than the sharing of personal information or even collective experience. Perhaps this: along with the requisite honesty, courage, and clarity, these encounters included a shift in the style of discourse from the literal to the poetic. What allowed, for example, black men and white men to hear each other beyond their literal, concretized differences, in a way that wasn't black-or-white, where black and white were not metaphysical categories but images lived within—alongside other ways of imagining? Wasn't it due to the way the men spoke and listened: not only with compassion but with imagination? Couldn't we say that the fairy tales Meade shared allowed the participants to enter the tales, so that their personal stories no longer sounded so personal or so literal? We could say that these encounters were so powerfully transformative because they occurred in a metaphoric, moonlit space:

> 'The obscure moon lighting an obscure world / Of things that would never be quite expressed, / Where you yourself were not quite yourself, / And did not want nor have to be.'
> —Wallace Stevens, 'The Motive for Metaphor' "[50]

A BOOK OF "POEMS FOR MEN"

Several years before the multicultural and gender events, a host of new magazines had appeared with titles like *Wingspan, The Men's Journal, Changing Men, Brother*, and *Making Waves*, along with books such as *The Liberated Man, The Myth of Masculinity, Men Freeing Men*, and *Beyond Patriarchy*. New Warrior weekends commenced, and Men's Quest Councils. Some two hundred American colleges were offering classes with descriptions like "The Psychology of Men" or "Sociology of the Male Experience."

"It seems surprising," one writer commented, "that in the late 1980s, when so many other liberation causes are barely treading water, the amorphous men's movement should be rising like a missile from the deep."[51]

Six months after Bly appeared on the Bill Moyers documentary in 1990, Hillman was having lunch in New York with Hugh Van Dusen, who had been his editor at Harper & Row (now HarperCollins) since publishing *Suicide and the Soul* a quarter-century earlier. When Van Dusen asked Hillman what he was up to, "he leaned back in his chair, and a faraway look came over his face. He said, 'I am doing these men's weekends with Robert Bly and Michael Meade, and they mean more to me than anything I've experienced in many years. But don't ask me to explain what they are and *don't* ask me to write about it.'"[52]

This piqued Van Dusen's interest, and he shortly wrote Hillman asking if he might attend "one of these mysterious men's weekends." He did, and eventually went to three more, meantime proposing to the publishing house that a book should come out of this. At that point, there wasn't much interest. But in November 1990, Bly's *Iron John* was published and went on to spend sixty-two weeks on the *New York Times* bestseller list. Sam Keen's book *A Fire in the Belly* joined it there, and HarperCollins took notice. Although writing a collection of essays didn't interest the Bly-Meade-Hillman trio, assembling an anthology of poetry did. They received a substantial $125,000 advance, and a willingness by the publisher to pay for rights to the selected poems.

So the three men set to work. Five times after a men's weekend—in New York, Boston, Washington, D.C., Minneapolis, and Santa Fe—they would hang out together for several days in a room, read poems to one other, and offer critiques. "We found an abundance of marvelous poems on all the questions we'd been talking about, the naïve male, the great mother, father's prayers to sons and daughters," Bly remembered.[53] Each brought their favorites and they would then vote on which poems would make it to the next round. Two out of three was the requirement. While Bly and Meade were aggressively opinionated about their favorites, Hillman became the negotiator.

According to Meade, "We'd get ones I wouldn't like and then Robert would go, 'Arrrggghhh, great poem!' Then it would often come down to Jim. So the pressure would be on him, which way are you going? Well, I find Robert trying to buy him off in the next room saying, 'If you let this one in, I'll go for the next one you like.' It was really funny. Also intense at times. Each occasion was almost like an opportunity for excess. I remember Jim saying to me, 'Boy, you're being tough on Robert.' And I said, 'Jim, if I don't knock him back, we're gonna have two-thirds Bly poems in this book!' But for the most part, this was a tremendous adventure. We had a pile of accepted poems and rejects, and you could change your mind the next day. This went on for almost a year."[54]

They had a hard time settling on a title. In the end, they chose a line from Yeats and called the 500-page volume *The Rag and Bone Shop of the Heart: Poems for Men*. In the Foreword, they wrote that, for years, they had "opened and closed the gatherings of men with poems" and these were the ones "which moved men the most." The edges of the cover listed Rumi, Lorca, Yeats, Frost, Lawrence, Neruda, Rilke, Sharon Olds, Etheridge Knight, and more.

Van Dusen recalled: "We published the book in hardcover in the fall of 1992, and without many reviews or much traditional publicity—no Oprah, no NPR—it sold an astonishing 16,000 copies. That may sound modest, but a runaway bestselling poet would kill for a 5,000 copy sale. Word of mouth—that most miraculous publication tool—just began and kept going and going. We put the book into paperback the following year, and it is still in print today, selling thousands of copies year in and year out." [55] He wrote to Bly that this book was "one of my proudest achievements as an editor." [56]

THE MEDIA AND THE MOVEMENT

John Densmore recalled Robert Bly saying at the very first men's meeting he attended, "If this ever becomes a movement, we're in trouble." Hillman remembered that "we were very suspicious of publicity, because there was a deeper inner and confessional aspect to this work. When we discovered somebody writing a piece, usually they were thrown out." [57] But once Bly's notoriety occurred in 1990, the men's groups were soon being parodied on *Murphy Brown*, then the country's top-rated TV show, and lampooned on the late-night talk shows. *Time* magazine denigrated Bly in a profile, calling the men's movement a "depthless happening in the goofy circus of America." Another *Time* piece noted that "they [the men] act out emotions in a safe haven where no one will laugh at them." [58] A writer for the *New York Times Magazine* attended an event in Texas and concluded in "Call of the Wildmen": "Enacted without a pre-existing system of beliefs, the drumming, dancing and vision-questing of the new masculinity feel pretty silly—at least they do to this camper." [59] *Newsweek* followed with a cover story depicting a fellow wearing a tie and blue jeans, holding a conga drum in one hand and a baby under the other arm. The article referred to Bly's conclusion "unsurprisingly, that we are sadly lacking in kings, wizards, and enchanted forests." [60]

Organizer John Guarnashelli recalled convincing a *New York Daily News* reporter that this was about more than "romantic primitivism" and in fact was addressing contemporary men's needs and issues. But when the story appeared, "There it was, the same old crap." When Guarnashelli called the reporter to ask what happened, the response was: "My editor wouldn't let me write it."[61]

Journalist Don Shewey, after attending several of the mythopoetic men's gatherings, gave a description of the media's role in *The Village Voice* early in 1992.[62] "The media—TV, magazines, newspapers—have picked up the scent of something fresh and wild and intriguing going on with these men, but they don't know exactly how to deal with it. The usual media handles are missing; the men with the ideas don't consider themselves celebrities, so they've mostly declined offers to go on Donahue and Oprah. Spiritual transformation cannot be televised. So the media basically make fun of the whole thing. Mock the leaders, mock their attire, mock their rituals, reduce their ideas to cartoon clothes, mock the clichés, ignore the content, chase the animal into a trap and kill it. How many articles have you read about 'guys out in the woods banging on drums and dancing around fires' that make it all sound like the most ludicrous kind of pretentious, self-indulgent, corny, macho bullshit behavior in the world?"

Shewey's article went on: "The media contributes to suppressing men's consciousness by its antispiritual bias. The men's movement is seen as silly because the substance is edited out. It's seen as trendy and superficial, because that's what can be shown on TV or described in Timenewsweekspeak—they get the soundbites, but not the Yeats poems. Men's work is seen as apolitical because the politics are censored." To Shewey, "the most impressive thing about the mythopoetic men's movement, as exemplified by Bly, Hillman, and Meade, is that it scrupulously avoids indoctrinating men with some est-like formula of behavior." Rather, it was about finding "the great creative potential in men working together for change . . . It has to be acknowledged, though, that American society does not want this consciousness to spread—perhaps precisely because it's an inquiry and not a movement, a process and not a product. Everything in America is about moving the merchandise. So get ready for the 15 minutes of Men."[63]

Bly recalled that, with the onslaught of publicity, applications to participate dropped 50 percent in a year.[64] "We used to have long waiting lists, months in advance," Martin Keogh remembered. But as soon as the *Newsweek* cover article appeared, "I knew that what we were doing was over. We had never called it the men's movement, we called it men's work. There weren't many who came that wanted to be part of a 'movement.' And we had more therapists getting involved. I remember James saying, 'You know, therapists by nature are much more spectators. The men coming aren't getting dirty like they used to.' So what went super-nova for a moment then collapsed."[65]

Richard Olivier believed that "it was a victim of its own success. Bly didn't quite know what to do with it. He was determined not to organize, but that lack of organization and control meant everyone could take it wherever they wanted. In retrospect, I think there probably needed to be something like a council of organizers who said, how are we going to deal with all the publicity. When you are in a zeitgeist moment with thousands of people wanting this, and you're the only ones who know what you're doing, they possibly could have been a little more thoughtful about how to lead people onward. Although James will always say, 'I don't do how-tos.'"[66]

To Hillman: "Others began to turn it into a training system, as if you could go for a weekend and really accomplish something. I felt there was getting to be something repetitive about it, I don't know quite what but my imagination didn't get captured in the same way. Also the men we were dealing with were changing. They were more middle and upper-class, men who easily had the money to pay for the week, they were not as broken in the same way. And I didn't feel as therapeutic toward these more conventional types. I liked the inter-racial part, but I didn't have the connection to working with youth gangs that Michael was beginning to go towards. Robert was concentrating on new forms of poetry, and my own writing work on new ways to do psychology also took over. Maybe there is an autonomous spirit where these things only last for a certain period anyway."[67]

> *"WHAT WE ARE ABOUT IS THE BROKEN HEART."—James Hillman.*

A second multicultural men's gathering took place in a beautiful, wooded canyon at Camp Shalom, near Malibu, California, January 25–30, 1992. This time Great Elk, a Native American leader, was invited to bless the event. Powerful confrontations between black and white men sparked intense dialogue on a variety of racial issues. The men suffered together, struggling with their collective pain and fear.

A privately-printed booklet was disseminated afterward to the hundred participants, each of whom contributed a poem or reminiscence. Hillman wrote a page-long essay. "The question that we began with, and it came up again and again, is: What is the conference about? What are we here for? And I think what we are about is the broken heart. And whether we feel the broken heart in our personal stories of our marriages, the deaths in the family, the Vietnam war, or the relationship with the father, there's a broken heart. And it's the broken heart of America. It's the broken heart of our society. I don't think that we should talk about the healing of the broken heart, but to realize that it is there, and that's what love is really all about. That's where love comes in, through the broken heart. Heartbreak is what it's all about. Heart-break. What has happened here is the experiencing of the heart-break of America. This has been something different than an 'experience.' We have been inside the heart-break of America. It has been personal. We each have our own piece of that heartbreak. But we also *are* the heartbreak. Broken, our hearts broken and the heart of the country, broken into fragments which we call our neighborhoods, ethnic colors and so on. And what has happened here has been that the spirits and the images that live in the heart, or connect with the heart, have met. And the souls have met. Maybe each of us as embodied ego people have not all met and there's huge resistances in that meeting but the souls have met and the spirits have met. It doesn't mean that they love each other. It doesn't mean that they all dance together but they've met. And that keeps the heart alive because it's only the heart that is isolated or sealed or complacent or self-content that isn't feeling that it is broken. It doesn't feel the heartbreak and that is the danger. So what I want to leave with is not healing. I want to leave with that awareness of heartbreak. And I thank you for making me feel *that* . . . intensely!"[68]

The last time Hillman attended a men's event was at Mendocino in June of 1993. Bly and Meade had already parted ways, because the multicultural gatherings that Meade wanted to focus on didn't hold the same interest for the poet. "I could see that things were ending, partially because of what I felt I had to do," Meade said. "I could not stay in a room of just white men anymore."[69] Hillman said: "He was always pushing against Robert, and I think he felt Robert's presence as an obstacle"[70] as time went on. Hillman continued to do engagements with one or the other of them, including with Bly in England in October 1993 and with Meade in August 1994. The latter was called "Village of Reconciliation, The First Mendocino Conference for Men and Women." It brought together Hillman, Meade, and Malidoma; and Malidoma's wife Sobonfu Somé, Ginette Paris, professor at Pacifica Graduate Institute, and dancer Anna Halprin as the team of instructors.

The idea of bringing together men and women from numerous races and backgrounds came from Malidoma's West African culture. But this was America, not Africa, and from the beginning the tension was palpable. During one "conflict hour," Hillman offered the metaphor that we were all on the Titanic, in terms of our sinking civilization. He preferred this as "a background that eliminates this constant redemptive futuristic thinking, that's constantly concerned with salvation and used . . . as a denial of where one *is*."

Considerable back-and-forth ensued with the audience, including some who viewed this as a despairing attitude. Hillman disagreed. Meade finally jumped in to say to him, "You're talking about your own death." Hillman then became angry, accusing Meade of explaining him. Meade countered that Hillman needed to "carry some personal responsibility for delivering the image." Hillman said that it wasn't about despair or hope, rather "the respect and the dignity of daily life and being alive and awake and responding in each moment . . . You have to have a sense of the reality of what's going on in the world." Meade said that "doesn't have to become everybody's reality."

Hillman turned to him in exasperation: "You don't think that there is some sort of collapse, avalanche, sinking, call it what you want?" Meade then spoke of the image being "actually bigger than the Titanic, it's shedding of culture and of nature." Hillman said he agreed with this. But Meade still clung to the hope that the crying child in the back of the room "will have something different," and Hillman replied: "But you see, you are in a different myth . . . a myth of rebirth . . . I'm talking about, how do you *live* when the ship is going down?"[71]

Margot McLean, who was in the audience, remembered: "Something pushed a button in Michael, and he became the attack dog unleashed as he turned on James. It was clear to a lot of folks that he was missing James' point. Michael created an atmosphere that killed the conversation."[72]

The argument did not resolve as men and women from the audience clamored to join in. Malidoma remembered: "Oh my God, it was a huge fight. Talk about clash of ideas! But there was something about Hillman that I really admired that day. Even when Michael was just beside himself, yelling and so forth, Hillman never raised his voice."[73]

This was to prove Hillman's final appearance at a men's gathering. Looking back years later, Meade said: "It became the 'Village of Wreckage.' The reconciliation part was minimal, the wreckage was major." He came to realize that "some of the things that work extremely well with men don't work as well with women, or when women are present," even though he couldn't explain why.[74]

Meade knew that his older colleague was offended by his belligerence. They did not see one another again for almost two years, when Meade came to Hillman's seventieth birthday celebration in New York. Toward the end, Meade rose and addressed his fellow teacher. Meade remembered saying something like this: "Jim, you're going to hate this, but I think it's necessary. Would you stand up so that we can all sing to you? I know your sentiment goes against that, but this is a culture that needs elders very badly, and a lot of us here feel that you *are* one, and sometimes these things have to be fully recognized."[75]

Hillman reluctantly stood, as the room joined in singing African verses about the ancestors that Meade had learned from Malidoma Somé, a man about whom Hillman said: "He has become one of my teachers. He knows."[76]

LEGACIES

In the wake of what Bly, Meade, and Hillman pioneered and the concomitant attention it received, there came the Million Man March, held on the National Mall in Washington in October 1995. Haki Madhubuti was one of the main organizers of that effort to "convey to the world a vastly different picture of the Black male." This was followed in 1997 by "Stand in the Gap: A Sacred Assembly of Men," organized by the Christian Promise Keepers group and reportedly even larger than the Million Man March.

Since that time, the Mankind Project evolved out of the New Warrior Training Adventure, "a weekend process of initiation and self-examination that is designed to catalyze the development of a healthy and mature masculine self." The Mankind Project conducted workshops around the globe. John Guarnashelli, another early participant in the mythopoetic events, went on to start some forty-five individual groups in New York and form a non-profit called On Common Ground.

In New Orleans, Project Return provided older ex-cons as mentors to young men coming out of prison. According to Bly, the recidivism rate is only 15 percent, compared with 85 percent in government-run programs. Bly himself continued to hold annual men's events in the Minnesota North Woods. To this day, Meade hosts annual gatherings for a hundred men each August at Mendocino; he also directs the Mosaic Cultural Foundation out of Seattle, Washington, where he started a program called "Voices for Youth" to work with homeless teens. Orland Bishop directs the ShadeTree Multicultural Foundation, with a focus on mentoring and forging truces among gang members in Los Angeles. Malidoma Somé holds workshops on African ritual around the world.

Many others who took part in the mythopoetic men's work—such as John Densmore and Craig Ungerman—continue to meet regularly with small groups of men in their local communities. The men who came out of those years speak of having male friends for the first time, or coming home to start doing art or getting involved politically or reciting poetry to their wives. Densmore says he had no idea what a mentor was, nor did he have role models, until he got involved. From Bly and Hillman, he found "the boundaries, the discipline" to write his memoir and more recently a novel. The work also provided organizer Martin Keogh a love of language. Keogh, who has taught what's known as contact improvisation dance in thirty-one countries, went on to write not only about dance but a book on bereavement and an anthology of essays, *Hope Beneath Our Feet*, concerning how to live one's life in the face of looming environmental catastrophe.

Newsweek magazine, in a cover story on rethinking masculinity in September 2010, noted that in seeking to "get back on track," some men today "have turned to old models and mores of manhood for salvation." Rutgers University anthropologist Lionel Tiger wanted to reclaim "maleness as a force, as a phenomenon." New books appeared with titles like *The Dangerous Book for Boys* and *Shop Class as Soulcraft*, while TV shows like *Dirty Jobs*, *Ax Men*, and *Deadliest Catch* are "re-romanticizing soot-collared work."[77]

Yet old stereotypes die hard. *Newsweek*'s summation of "The American Man" had this to say about the 1990s: "The New-Age Man. Feeling displaced, men respond with a full-scale retreat: weekends in the woods to hug and shoot stumps."

This missed the trees for the forest. Hillman said: "I remember once when everybody was weeping. You're sitting in a room and *ninety men* are weeping! I used the phrase then for the first time and Michael used it since: 'Let's take it out to the trees. They can hold what we can't.' But why was this so threatening to the media and others? What really was at stake here? Perhaps it was corporate America, which keeps men enslaved in a certain way. Ordinary men were increasingly being marginalized in American society—alongside women, gays, and people of color—so that the only power resides with an exclusive elite. The men's movement was not an anti-feminist movement. And it wasn't a Marxist movement, of brotherhood of the working class. It was really an anti-capitalist movement.

"It was also an erotic movement. It was to make men feel for each other and what they had gone through, and how they are being stupefied and stultified and abused by the money world, the ambition and the competition. We didn't attack it in that language, but we were encouraging a whole other world. The world of the arts, especially poetry, the world of the body and of doing things together—but not as a team in a business.

"In a capitalist society, what is the purpose of your life? It's to make money. And this is not ultimately satisfying. Look at today's men on the TV ads—they miss their chair and fall down, or spill their beer, or need their wife to tell them which medicine to take. And this making fun of the American man for being a dumb jerk—or just a good guy who throws a baseball with his son or takes him to the soccer games—was never enough for capturing the true vision of a man. He wants to do something

for his tribe, his society, not just his family. You've got to have
a spiritual goal of some sort that has to do with real values.
Women found ways; they had been abused and repressed and
ignored and the feminist movement gave them position—look
at all the women now running for political office, for example. But men have a terrible problem in our society. During the
civil rights movement and the anti-Vietnam period, there was
a strong purpose for men. But from the Reagan era onward,
it was about getting a business degree or going into high-tech
to earn a lot of money. I don't know whether there is anything
today which captures that basic desire for a greater purpose.

"In our work with men, there was a desire to awaken the
deep source of American strength, which is not just capitalism
or militarism. It's even deeper than politics. It's visionary and
mythical. We were trying to open the soul through story, myth,
poetry, talks, and rituals. It didn't cause a change in society. So
what did it do? What does art do? What do things do that truly
touch the soul? It's so hard to define.

"It's not a sociological effect. That misses the point. Whether
it continued or not is minor compared to the radical approach to
the education of the American man. What matters is, we came
up with a whole other way of education, outside of academia
and a curriculum—a whole method which was not based even
on method. It had to fail in a way, because this kind of radical
re-visioning always does.

"So yes, it was threatening. That's part of why I found it so
attractive, *because* it *was* threatening. Just like Bly's book *Iron John*,
and just like Michael Meade, the rebel who was once thrown
into solitary confinement. It's not only that we were playing jazz
together, we were also radicals. But we were not preaching revolution. We were preaching culture.

"The natural inclination is to say, it either failed or it affected
many men's lives. I'd like to get away from either of those perspectives. In general, Hillman's psychology doesn't develop into
the world, nor did this. It represents another world that we have
to constantly be reminded of: the world of culture, the world

of gods, of spirit, figures. Almost like a service to the other world, a service to the poetic. In that sense, the whole thing was a ritual. It wasn't concerned with converting people to another way. It was to keep the gods alive. And the effects may go into the underground and become invisible. We don't know."[78]

NOTES

1. "Today we need heroes of descent. . . .": James Hillman, *Kinds of Power*, New York: Currency/Doubleday, 2004 paperback edition, p. 49.
2. "A Gathering of Men": Transcript available on www.billmoyers.com, program viewable on YouTube.
3. The divided room over fathers: Author interview with Robert Bly. July 2007.
4. Bly and Hillman quotes on fathers and sons, unless otherwise noted, are taken from a transcript made from "Men and the Life of Desire," March 11, 1990, Oral Tradition Archive.
5. Father crossing the river: Hillman letter to Andre Kramer, 1990.
6. Hillman on realizing the pain of the father's failings: "Fathers and Sons," by James Hillman, in *To Be A Man: In Search of the Deep Masculine*, Edited by Keith Thompson, Los Angeles: Jeremy P. Tarcher, Inc., 1991, pp. 201–02.
7. Hillman on running into trouble over fathers: Interview with author.
8. "The first subject. . . .": Author interview with Richard Olivier, July 2007.
9. "I'm Richard Olivier. . . .": Ibid.
10. Olivier quoting Hillman and describing his experience at Buffalo Gap: Richard Olivier, *Shadow of the Stone Heart: A Search for Manhood*, Pan Books, 1995, p.
11. "working through the shit. . . .": Author interview with Laurence Hillman, July 2007.
12. "It wasn't easy to grasp. . . .": Author phone interview with Laurence Hillman, January 2018.
13. "Two things happened. . . .": Author interview with James Hillman, February 2009.
14. "Finding the Door into the Forest," by William R. Finger, in *Wingspan: Inside the Men's Movement*, Ed. by Christopher Harding, New York, St. Martin's Press, 1992, p. 105.
15. "I guarantee you there was not a single man. . . .": Author interview with Fred Stephens, June 2008.
16. The author interviewed Haki Madhubuti in February 2011.
17. "We could call on the names. . . ." Richard Olivier, *Shadow of the Stone Heart*, p. 101.
18. "Any idea that we might work our way up slowly. . . .": "At Buffalo Gap," by Don Shewey, *Common Boundary* magazine, October 1992.
19. "Buffalo Gap profoundly affected me. . . .": Author interview with James Hillman, January 2011.
20. Malidoma Patrice Somé's story is drawn from his memoir, *Of Water and the Spirit, Ritual, Magic and Initiation in the Life of an African Shaman*, Compass Books, 1995.
21. "We were mesmerized. . . .": Author interview with Craig Ungerman, March 2010.

22. Olivier on Malidoma: *Shadow of the Stone Heart*, p. 111.

23. "Questions of trust, safe space. . . .": *Shadow of the Stone Heart*.

24. "A white guy and a black guy. . . .": Author interview with Michael Meade, May 2008.

25. Madhubuti's talk: cited in Olivier, pp. 115–116.

26. "At first I saw that it was the same sort of attack. . . .":JH letter to Wolfgang Giegerich, July 28, 1986.

27. Hillman talk on white supremacy: cited in Olivier, pp. 116–117.

28. Hillman on the ideas being "too abstruse". . . .: JH interview with author.

29. "the whole idea of race. . . .": Author interview with Malidoma Somé, May 2008.

30. "quite defining and revelatory. . . .": Author interview with Haki Madhubuti, February 2011.

31. "inhabits you in ways you can't control. . . .": Shewey, *Common Boundary*.

32. Madhubuti address to the group: quoted by Shewey, *Common Boundary*.

33. Hillman on Madhubuti: Author interview, January 2011.

34. All Madhubuti quotes are from the author's interview.

35. "The sight of this gracefully aging white man. . . .': Olivier, *Shadow of the Stone Heart*.

36. "He was really upset. . . .": Author interview with Meade, May 2008.

37. "When we pulled up. . . .": Author interview with John Densmore, May 2007.

38. "excite-to-battle-language. . . .": Carol Bly letter to Robert Bly and James Hillman "of the men's movement," June 28, 1988, Bly archive, University of Minnesota.

39. "Male bonding is crucial. . . .": Hillman letter to Carol Bly, date unknown.

40. Betty Friedan on movement: quoted in "Drums, Sweat and Tears: What Do Men Really Want?" *Newsweek*, June 24, 1991.

41. "Whether they mean to or not. . . .': Barbara Ehrenreich.

42. Bly, "To take a symbolic expression literally. . . .": Letter by Bly, 1988, Bly papers, University of Minnesota.

43. "Why Iron John Is No Gift to Women," by Jill Johnston, *New York Times Book Review*, February 23, 1992.

44. "The premise where I took issue. . . .": Author interview with Margot McLean, January 2020.

45. "One man stood right up. . . .": Author interview with Hugh Van Dusen, August 2007.

46. Wife "reacted the way many women did. . . .": Author interview with John Guarnashelli. October 2009.

47. "What did you do. . . .": Author interview with Michael Meade, May 2008.

48. "Michael would give a talk. . . .": Author interview with James Hillman, January 2009.

49. Meade on the gender conference: *Men and the Water of Life*, pp. 279–280.

50. Li:WallaceStevens:https://hudsonreview.com/2013/03/the-motive-for-metaphor-2/

51. "amorphous rising" of men's movement: "Male Men," by David Roberts, *Boston Globe Magazine*, June 18, 1989.

52. Van Dusen on Hillman and men's groups: Talk given by Van Dusen at conference honoring Robert Bly.

53. "We found an abundance of marvelous. . . .": Author interview with Robert Bly, July 2007.

54. "We'd get ones I wouldn't like. . . .": Author interview with Michael Meade, May 2008.

55. "We published the book in hardcover. . . .": Author interview with Hugh Van Dusen, August 2007.

56. 'one of my proudest achievements. . . .": Letter from Van Dusen to Bly, February 25, 1999, Bly archive, University of Minnesota.

57. "we were very suspicious of publicity. . . .": Author interview with Hillman.

58. *Time* magazine on movement: "What Do Men Really Want?", By Sam Allis, *Time* magazine, Fall 1990.

59. "Enacted without a pre-existing system. . . .": "Call of the Wildmen," by Trip Gabriel, *New York Times Magazine*, October 14, 1990.

60. *Newsweek* cover story: "Drums, Sweat and Tears: What Do Men Really Want?" *Newsweek*, June 24, 1991.

61. *New York Daily News* anecdote: Author interview with John Guarnashelli. October 2009.

62. Media coverage of movement: "Town Meeting in the Hearts of Men," by Don Shewey, *The Village Voice*, February 11, 1992.

63. All Shewey quotes are from the *Village Voice* article.

64. Bly on applications dropping and why: Interview with author.

65. "We used to have long waiting lists. . . .:" Author interview with Martin Keogh.

66. Richard Olivier on "victim of its own success. . . .": Interview with author.

67. "Others began to turn it. . . .": Author interview with Hillman, November 2007.

68. James Hillman, in privately-printed booklet from The Los Angeles Multicultural Men's Conference, Malibu, California, January 25–30, 1992. Provided author by Miguel Rivera.

69. "I could see that things were ending. . . .": Author interview with Michael Meade, May 2008.

70. "He was always pushing against Robert. . . .": Author interview with Hillman, November 2007.

71. Quotations from Meade and Hillman at "Village of Reconciliation": Transcript made by author from Oral History Archives tape of August 1994 conference.

72. "Something pushed a button. . . .": Author interview with Margot McLean, January 2020.

73. Malidoma on "Village of Reconciliation": Interview with author, 2009.

74. "It became the 'Village of Wreckage'. . . .": Author interview with Michael Meade.

75. "Jim, you're going to hate this. . . .': Ibid.

76. "He has become one of my teachers. . . .': Hillman recommendation of Malidoma Somé, December 3, 1992, Opus Archive.

77. "Men's Lib," by Andrew Romano and Tony Kokoupil, *Newsweek* magazine, September 27, 2010.

78. The Hillman quotes are drawn from interviews with the author, November 2007, January 2009, and October 2010.

16

A POETIC BASIS OF MIND

> *"This business of language has me again gripped . . . I see too that this language concern has been on my agenda at least since 1967 at Eranos with the talk on the Speech of the Soul vs The Language of Psychology and my puzzlement as to how does one write psychology? How does one speak so that it touches, reaches, expresses psyche/soul?"*
> —James Hillman, from a letter to Robert Bly, 1998.

In the beginning, there had been Donleavy. J. P., author of the legendary *Ginger Man*, a first novel that sold 5 million (some say 45 million) copies worldwide since its publication in 1955. J. P., Hillman's best friend while at Dublin's Trinity College, a man with whom he stayed in touch for the rest of his life. J. P., who authored ten more novels, and whom Hillman called by the nickname of Mike. J. P., the writer Hillman had once longed to be.

Inside his great stone mansion in Mullingar, Ireland, in 2006, J. P. related this story about Hillman: "I remember on one occasion, he was coming down to New York, where I was staying at that rather nice place called the Ritz-Carlton on Central Park South. Jim arrived from Connecticut and he had a beautiful, brand-new, marvelous sort of attaché case with him. I said, 'Jim, I've never seen anything quite as beautiful as this leather case.' He said, 'Yes it is.' I said, 'Well, I guess you've got all your papers and documents and everything there.' He said, 'No, no—it's full of eggs.' Full of eggs. From his chickens."[2]

From a letter to "Dear Jim," September 11, 1975: "good news your book [*Re-Visioning Psychology*] up for Pulitzer—Although I have never been a great believer in prizes. I gladly take them if they come without strings."

From a letter to "Dear Jim," December 19, 1975, Levington Park, Mulls, Ireland: "Ah God the U.S.—often I pass by your hotel the St. Mortiz [sic] while there. This time I was running around desperately trying to get famous, or make believe that I used to be. But it is astonishing at how often one can repeat day after days one's salient facts and even indeed to be delighted doing it."[3]

From a Hillman letter to "Dear JP," June 1977: "You may note that I am in my cups . . .

"In the fuzz of this half-liter, I recall your long typed pages. My typists never approved of long pages. I find that pages extend as one gets going, but the typists get put off. You should worship the lady in the lodge, Epps, for her acceptance of the long page. PB was very moved by your method and has taken it to heart, for she feels she works as you do. A nugget of unworked-out clustered thought, that only through time and rewriting gets more and more expanded into intelligibility."

From a handwritten letter to "Mike," April 10, 1999: "In old age one clears the closet. Stuff from morgue. Perhaps you have an archive? An Institute in California collects all my papers in boxes and catalogues it in careful systems. I get it out of my wood flammable house, to be put down in their earthquake land. I got some money for it all. What did you do with yours?"

From a handwritten letter to "My dear Jim," November 18, 2003: "Misty day—great boughs of oak on the ground. Been looking through files—yours massive with best postcards of all time—investigating archives . . . Fond wishes, Mike."

On a visit to interview Donleavy in 2006, the Mullingar mansion is beginning to fall apart. In the dining room, the sills of the cobwebbed windows are green with moss. In the closet of a guest room are clothes from J. P.'s fox-hunting years. In the library, rows and rows of Bankers Boxes storing J. P.'s manuscripts. "My archive since I never threw anything away from the first days that I started to scribble takes up a whole room," he had told another interviewer.

Was success something you and Hillman foresaw? J. P. responded:. "Somehow it was almost a given that we both just thought, nothing could ever stop us in the world. In Jim's case, I guess this has happened because his reputation now has spread far and wide. When his name may come up with people, I say he's the inventor of Hillmanism—combining Jung and Freud."

J. P. listens to a story of Hillman dreaming constantly about Donleavy during his early years studying at the Jung Institute in Zürich—the same year *The Ginger Man* was published—and suddenly realizing while walking down the street one day that he could *write about psychology.*

"Really?" J. P. responds.

Yes, Hillman said he didn't have the kind of imagination that a novelist needed.

Taking a deep breath, J. P. continues: "I think, if he'd decided to become a novelist, without any doubt he would have become one of the most successful and richest novelists of all time. Undoubtedly. That often went through my mind, he just fitted the role so perfectly. But whatever stopped him—I had no idea ..." A pause. "There's no doubt in my mind that he'd have been immensely successful."

From a letter to "Dear Jim," July 24, 1958, from 20 Broughton Road, Fulham, London: "Book in New York was published May 8—last Sunday it moved on to *New York Times* bestseller list ... The amount of money now is vast ... How's things going with your own book—stick to your guns."

WRESTLING WITH THE ANGELS

"When for instance I am asked, 'How was the bus ride?' I respond, 'Miserable, terrible, desperate.' But those words describe me, my feelings, my experience, not the bus ride, which was bumpy, crowded, steamy, cramped, noxious, with long waits ...

"The appreciation of the anima mundi requires adverbs and adjectives that precisely imagine the particular events of the world in particular images, much as the ancient Gods were known through their adverbial and adjectival epithets ...

"This 'adjectival revolution' would overthrow the canon of good writing, the ascetic Puritanism—'plainness, simplicity, orderliness, sincerity'—of Strunk and White and of

Fowler (in English), that contemporary form of Protestant iconoclasm which bans the adornment of adjectives and adverbs in favor of bare nouns and verbs making definite assertions in the active voice—a grammatical world of heroic subjects doing things to objects, without ambiguity, passivity, or reflexiveness . . .

"Our way back to the bus thus leads back to the Renaissance insistence on rhetoric, incorporating along the way poetic methods of Imagism, Concretism, Objectivism, Projective Verse—modes of language that do not dwell in 'experience' and which instead enliven things, giving them back their animated faces."

—James Hillman, *"Anima Mundi: The Return of the Soul to the World"*[4]

"As part of the polytheistic enterprise, archetypal psychology sits on the back of various animals, tints it abstractions with differing colors, and works the mines of many metals, not only the depressive lead of Saturn and the quicksilver of Hermes. Imagine! Words not only angels with silver's trumpet, but descendants of the mammoth, tusked words, shouldering their way into our minds, shaggy and towering above our frantic actions, so close to the jugular."

—James Hillman, *"Silver and the White Earth, Part One"*[5]

In the early 1980s, Hillman and his young assistant, Randolph Severson, had walked around the corner from Hillman's home in Dallas for a *Spring* "editorial lunch" at the Dixie House, a local restaurant specializing in "southern' home cooking," where the two often ate together. As they walked the short distance back, they began discussing an article which in time became the influential book, *Jung and the Post Jungians*, by a young Jungian analyst in London, Andrew Samuels. The article accorded Hillman and Archetypal Psychology a prominent place in the fermenting Jungian landscape, joining him with Michael Fordham and others in a project of pluralizing and decentralizing the psyche so as to reflect multiple voices and backgrounds: "We are lived by powers we pretend to understand," a favorite Hillman quote from W. H. Auden.

Although appreciative of the scope and depth of understanding exhibited by Samuels, Hillman, as Severson recalls, believed that in grouping him with other "pluralistic" voices in Analytical Psychology, Samuels had missed the "main thing" about archetypal psychology: "It's the rhetoric," Hillman insisted. "It's the rhetoric. It's not my style. It's the Psyche's style. It's the speech of the soul. It's Psychology."[6]

Years later, Severson would reflect: "If you've ever edited Hillman, you know that the text often looks like a musical score: additions, arrows, insertions, underscores, blocks, circles. It was like he was writing for five different voices, five different musicians." Or, as the Brazilian psychologist Gustavo Barcellos put it: "Hillman's pages are constantly speaking among themselves, arguing, pushing, yielding, dissenting, persuading and betraying each other. It is this textual democracy that keeps Hillman's texts alive."[7]

Hillman's engagement with language, his wrestling with the Angel of Language, with winged words, with words as Angels, was lifelong, extending back to early efforts at creative writing, literary magazines and his abortive ambition to be a novelist. That occurred foremost during his years at Trinity College in Dublin, where the Irish language captured his fantasy. "It was not only the rhythms and the peculiar way they put a sentence together, but that it's imagistic," he reflected in 2005. "And my big fight with psychology is over the boringness of its language."[8]

As a psychologist, Hillman always displayed keen interest in and critical sensitivity to matters of language, style and genre, which he maintained to be always "full of gods": "The idea that there is a God in our tellings and that this God shapes the words into the very syntax of a genre is not new in literary studies even if it might come as a shock to my colleagues who really believe they are writing case histories."[9]

Freud didn't fit that mold. He once told an Italian interviewer that he was "really by nature an artist," that his books "in fact more resemble works of imagination than treatises on pathology. I have been able to win my destiny in an indirect way, and have attained my dream: to remain a man of letters, though still in appearance a doctor."[10]

Hillman viewed both Freud and Jung as "workers in story": "Why did Freud get himself into this tangle between the medical and literary when trying to write psychological case reports? Was he not struggling with a form of writing for which there are no existing models. His mind moved back and forth between the two great traditions, science and humanities . . . Freud tangled the two because he was engaged in both at once: fiction and case history, and ever since then in the history of our field, they are inseparable, our case histories are a way of writing fiction."[11]

To Hillman, Jung was a "Child of Hermes": "Jung's way of writing psychology seems to have been under the tutelage of Hermes in several ways: the concern for borderline conditions of the psyche; the engagement with psyche's hermetic secrets, and, third, his hermeneutical research along the borders of psychology, where odd fields touch each other."[12]

Mars and Venus, Shakespeare's Antony and Cleopatra, resound through Hillman's own style: "Mars who rides a lion, Mars, beloved of Aphrodite, demanding right"[13] and Aphrodite who "appears . . . as the manifest visible image, the displayed presentation."[14]

Not every reader swooned over Hillman's singular style. In a generally favorable Sunday *New York Times Book Review* (August 26, 1979), of *The Dream and the Underworld*, Edgar Levinson tweaked Hillman for "leaning heavily in the direction" of "purple prose."[15] A *Boston Globe* reviewer of *Re-Visioning Psychology* maintained that "he uses words as if they were NASA space boots specially recustomized for a clomp up Mt. Olympus— tromping over metaphors with unfeeling abandon."[16]

But Annie Gottlieb surely spoke for the majority of readers when, in a 1990 *New York Times* review of Thomas Moore's *Blue*

Fire, an edited selection of Hillman's writings, she wrote: "Mr. Hillman has an exciting, difficult, deeply cultured mind, one that ranges easily from the arcane of alchemy to the discomforts of a bus ride, just as his vocabulary ranges all the way from 'hermeneutic,' 'metaxy' and 'theriomorphic' to 'rube' and 'roly poly.' He can write as breathtakingly as a poet and, at times, as unintelligibly as a philosopher."[17]

For Hillman: "Language is the human way we take part in the world. Let your language learn to rise and fall—dance on the balls of your feet."[18] Every morning, up before daybreak, eating what he called his 'first' breakfast, typewriter keys soon in whirrs and spasms of clicking, Hillman did write on the balls of his feet, his style both modeling and advocating language that is "sharp as a claw, soft as down, with the beat of angel's wings."

If there is a secret to Hillman's style, it might be captured in his observation that our language badly needs examples of the power of exorbitant words. In its original meaning exorbitant meant lawless and literally 'off the track,' the style of the Dionysian Rogue—think of Falstaff, the Hermetic Highwayman, the Picaresque Knight Errant, who in *Revisioning* Hillman makes emblematic of archetypal psychology. Kindling with exorbitance, it "o'erflows the measure." (*Anthony and Cleopatra*, Act I, Scene I, line 2.) And as in Shakespeare, exorbitance sometimes foils the Grammarian in us, resisting punctuation and the other proprieties of the uniform usage, which for Hillman were the throttling monotheism of the King's English and the Freshman Composition teacher.

Interviewed by Jay Kugelman in November 1978, Hillman opined: "Well, what's going on is the breakdown of the language itself, so that we no longer know if I am a subject or an object, or if people are subjective or objective. That's all busting up *in* the language itself. So we try to get it all back into grammatical rules in school and tell people they're speaking wrongly and so on, but there's something happening already. Breakdown of punctuation is happening. It's happening in education. It sounds like the breaking apart of culture, but it's also returning language to its pre-punctuational state . . . This is anathema to American thinking, where everything is laid out in the laws. Or you read Hebrew or you read Chinese, the punctuation is very questionable, I'm talking about archaic languages. So the loss of punctuation may be to restore the imaginative use of language, where a word can be reversed or it can take another part of speech."[19]

As exorbitance may be said to be the secret of Hillman's style, reverberating powerfully in its combativeness, beauty, energy, and freshness, in the glory and gleam of Mars and Venus —so the secret source may be Shakespeare. Although references to Shakespeare run sparse in Hillman's work—two references only indexed in *Revisioning*, for instance—in a paper entitled obviously enough "You Taught me Language," Hillman somewhat sheepishly admitted: "I am an amateur Shakespearean, a sentimental idolizer and uncritical lover of the Bard. I was already bicycling to Stratford in 1946. I've been going to his plays for sixty years . . . When I was young and twenty, I tried seducing my wife to be with appeals from *Henry the Fifth*—'nice customs curtsy to great kings.' And, while a schoolboy I memorized my passages from *Julius Caesar*—'you blocks, you stones, you worse than senseless things.' 'Cry havoc and let slip the dogs of war,' shouting them up and down the wintry gray Atlantic shore, a little-boy Lear, my thirteen-year-old voice cracking at the strain, Shakespeare, 'you taught me language.'" Hillman later added: "It comes in my mind *all* the time, either the rhythms or phrases or something."

Dense, dazzling, daring, the style he both called for and demonstrated could also be termed deviant. As Levinson's *New York Times* review suggests, the style departs from 'peer-reviewed' APA (American Psychological Association) norms and professional decorum. According to Severson, Hillman once confided: "If I'd been forced to suffer through that peer review thing I would never have been published."

In a recorded conversation with poet Clayton Eshleman, Hillman stated that this "notion of the psychologist as man of science/observer—I think that's where the trouble is. And I think that psychologists have fallen into this. They have imagined themselves to be objective, outside critics. Or they have imagined themselves to be interpreters, or commentators, and in the scientific flow."[20]

In its uniqueness, Hillman's style expressed his insistence on the "poetic basis of mind."

"Following Jung I use the word fantasy-image in the poetic sense, considering images to be the basic givens of psychic life, self-originating, inventive, spontaneous, complete, and organized in archetypal patterns. Nothing is more primary."[21] As he put it more concretely to the Italian scholar Sylvia Ronchey: "We use words like fear and anger or exhaustion. But before that abstract word, fear, there are natural images of running, or peeing in your pants, or a tarrying image to run from. The great epics, and the poets today, don't use abstractions: they try to express the 'inner world' with very precise concrete images and sounds."[22]

The way Hillman saw it, the poets who came to prominence "parallel with psychoanalytical Newspeak" at the beginning of the twentieth century were its crucial counterweight. They included Ezra Pound, T. S. Eliot, Wallace Stevens and D. H. Lawrence. "Go in fear of abstractions," Pound had counseled, "use no adjective which does not reveal something." Stevens had warned against "rotted names" such as extraverted, narcissistic, borderline, and depressed that permeate psychology. To Hillman, "with the loss of the image we lose the real world."[23]

In the early eighties, *Spring* began to distribute the prestigious vanguard journal, *Sulfur*, a vehicle for Black Mountain, San Francisco Renaissance, Beat and other Modernist and Post-Modernist poets, many of whom, including the editor, Clayton Eshleman, were published by Black Sparrow Press. Like birds to wing, or ducks to water, the poets took to Hillman who welcomed them as like-minded fellow travelers in soul-making and the forging of a new poetics faithful to a poetic basis of mind. In the inaugural edition of this new version of *Sulfur*, Hillman contributed a seminal piece, "Alchemical Blue and the Unio

Mentalis," where he concluded "This turn to poet and painter tells us also who are the alchemists of modern day . . . The alchemical laboratory is in their work with words and paints, and psychology continues its tradition of learning from alchemy to learning from them."[24]

CHARLES BOER

> *"As the dead prey upon us,*
> *they are the dead in ourselves,*
> *awake, my sleeping ones, I cry out to you,*
> *disentangle the nets of being!"*
> —*Charles Olson*[25]

It was one of those curiously synchronistic moments. Paul Kugler, just arrived in Zürich in April 1971, had been in the Jung Institute library filling out paperwork to enroll when he engaged in conversation with another young fellow. They were discussing an American poet, Charles Olson, who had just died the year before. Kugler, it turned out, had known Olson personally as an undergraduate student in English. Olson was said to have coined the term "post-modern" and, as the last chancellor at the experimental Black Mountain College in North Carolina, had been a huge influence on the poetic sensibilities of two other "Black Mountain poets," Robert Creeley and Robert Duncan. Olson had integrated parts of Jung's oeuvre into his poetics, against a backdrop of the role played by imagination. In the 1950s, he was already talking about a "poetry of soul," incorporating the realm of the mythological gods. The poetic image, Olson believed, should not be merely a subjective expression of the ego, but a basis for our human acts of knowing.

Hillman happened to be the only other person in the Institute library the morning Kugler was there reminiscing about Olson with the student who then made the introduction. Kugler was soon to meet up in Zürich and then travel to Greece with his former English professor at the University of Connecticut, Charles Boer. Boer happened to be the co-executor of Charles Olson's estate (and a future biographer). Boer was an expert in mythology, his 1971 translation of *The Homeric Hymns* from ancient Greek had just been nominated for a National Book Award. So before Kugler headed off to Greece, he made sure that Boer and Hillman met.

That marked the beginning of a long collaborative friendship between Hillman and Boer (whom he sometimes addressed in letters as "Chuck"), one that would eventually overlap with a larger poetic circle, again through the younger Kugler's auspices. Upon returning to Connecticut, Boer read Hillman's latest book, *The Myth of Analysis*, which he loved. But, as he expressed in a letter to Hillman, Boer thought he was "a bit intimidated by classicists when you write on areas they have come to think are their province alone. You vastly overestimate the acumen of classicists!" Hillman's work, Boer believed, was "among the most interesting and capable to come along on the subject of classical myth in years." In return, he sent Hillman a copy of *Homeric Hymns*.

Hillman replied: "Music. Sitting at this desk, arid, papers spewn with wrong words, music from your letter. Thank you indeed. If only it didn't take so fucking long to find out what I want to say and then to say it. Everything crafted, overcrafty. But letter from you has brought reward, and I thank you for it, and for your sending of your Hymns, which after reading, I shall use, rely upon, quote.

"The classicists are not the men 'out there' but the little senex band of doges in purple robes and Venetian skull caps who peer over my shoulder always 'making sure.'"[26]

In September 1974, Hillman wrote Boer proposing that when he toured the country promoting *Re-Visioning Psychology*, they should hold a three-day symposium on Greek Literature and Archetypal Psychology. Boer shied away from that invitation, but read *Re-Visioning* twice in a row from cover to cover and told Hillman that it was "stunning, endlessly provocative, beautifully written, terribly disturbing (for me anyway) on various moral questions, and there is nothing else like it. I'm stealing all kinds of things from it for my own purposes."[27]

Hillman replied: "As for stealing from it: we are all thieves, and in broad daylight; as for moral worries, I should hope so, I should bloody well hope that I've tortured and mortified proud remnants of the Christian armour. But that *you* find it beautifully written, *you*, that's a big beeloud glade and I thank thee from the heart." In a handwritten P. S., he added: "Harper's says that the book has been submitted for a Pulitzer Nomination, but I do not quite know what that means. Aren't Pulitzers for producing plays and journalism. Is this a put-on?"[28]

Boer also wrote Hillman to tell him there was a rumor going around he might be working on a book about "the poetic mind." He sent Hillman his own long biographical poem "The Soul of Pierpont Morgan," along with essays, "which I have filtered, barbarized, stolen, raped, fantasied, mutilated and plagiarized from several of your books."[29] At the time, Boer was dreaming up a detective novel about a female analyst who solves crimes with the help of Jung.

This time, Hillman responded at length: "Your letter made me green and yellow with envy. I want so desperately to do what you do: US history, poems, humour. I can't. I have been reading, for instance, the biography of General Sherman, who deserves a place in your Ulysses!" [Boer was writing the Foreword to *The Ulysses Theme* by W. B. Stanford, whose second edition Spring published]. And I have been this very day, which prompts in part this letter, going through the entire box and bundles of my own family history, pictures, diaries, letters from the civilwar period and after of the mad Hungarians whose blood I carry, and the little Jewish merchants in Tennessee and West Virginia, and the pretentious elders of the twenties strutting in spats with walking sticks down the Boulevards of Paris. Also, to pass on to you a tidbit: do you know that the man who invented baseball, Mr. Doubleday, was not only a Westpointer, the Westpointer in fact who pointed the first gun that shot the first shot at Fort Sumter on April 12 (my own birthday in fact), but was a Theosophist, so that in our National Sport there is an infiltration of Blavatsky. Thomas Edison was also an early member of the theosophical society."[30]

Boer made arrangements to attend the Eranos conference in 1976 and wrote Hillman afterward about the paper on dreams he'd presented: "Can it be that not since Freud have we had so *sensuous* a look on the topography of the dream? . . . You warn of sentimentalizing, and of the coldness of the Styx, but you write so warmly, and so invitingly, of its visions. I think of Dante, whom, like Virgil, you would have accompanied, but only so far. And rightly so."[31]

While offering to do book reviews for *Spring*, the 1977 issue published Boer's essay co-authored with Peter Kugler (Paul Kugler's identical twin brother and also Boer's former student at the University of Connecticut) titled, "Archetypal Psychology Is Mythical Realism." That same year, at the First International Seminar of Archetypal Psychology held at the University of Dallas, Boer presented a paper on "Poetry and Psyche" focusing on Olson. In 1979, upon Hillman's request, Boer translated Marsilio Ficino's *The Book of Life*—published the following year.

Boer helped Hillman broaden his understanding of how attending to the image related directly to archetypal psychology. And Hillman continued, in a sense, to wish that he was Boer. In a 1981 letter, Hillman wrote: "What are you writing, you lucky bastard. I write, sporadically, under dreadful clouds of thunder, without joy. 'MUST' and 'SHOULD' are the ZEAL and FORCE that chain me to the rock. Eranos, once a joy, now a curse." This mood carried over to the home front: "Our garden is a jungle of fire ants, red spiders, asps—and weeds. Rains flooding everything, grass pales from lack of minerals."[32] In a self-deprecating tone, he also wrote Boer of an upcoming talk: "I'm going to stand up with two oldtimers from the George Burns period (Bly and Campbell) all day long in a huge temple theatre in SF and deliver same as we three stand around garrulously all day talking to the 'crowd,' who come out to the show and be scolded and inspired for some 30 bucks a shot. I'm an oldtimer now myself, it's no longer the Hillmaniacs but over-the-hill-man."[33]

Shortly thereafter, not only would Boer help Hillman relocate to Connecticut from Dallas, he'd become his co-author on *Freud's Own Cookbook* and take over the editorship of *Spring Journal*. Living in adjoining towns, they would often see one another socially. "Charles was a wonderful cook, great with wine and entertainment," Pat Berry remembered. "He used to have us over for movie nights, with programs and reviews which we'd read, while sharing a wonderful five-course meal."[34]

Boer presided over a significant moment in the annals of archetypal psychology, as the moderator of the January 1979 conference held in Niagara Falls—titled (in a line taken from Shakespeare's *Midsummer Night's Dream*) "The Lunatic, The Lover and The Poet." Its watery conception had occurred during a conversation among Paul Kugler, Hillman, and David Miller, while swimming in the lake, Lago Maggiore, at the previous Eranos gathering. It was organized by Kugler, who sold Spring books at Eranos and was an adjunct professor teaching at the State University of New York-Buffalo (while working on his Ph.D. in literature—the requisite degree level for becoming a Jungian analyst). Kugler called the conference "an attempt to bring the anti-psychiatry movement that Thomas Szasz represented together with some of the sensibilities of archetypal psychology on the one hand and the writer's imagination on the other."[35] Besides Szasz and Hillman, the presenters were Rafael López-Pedraza, David Miller, Charles Boer, and the poet Robert Creeley, who knew Kugler through the university and his friendship with Boer. In the audience were several of Hillman's colleagues from the University of Dallas.

Hillman opened his lecture on "Silver and the White Earth, Part One" by saying, "I've been very nervous about this conference. This is a sobering place to stand . . . as a defrocked lunatic, that is an analyst. It's hard to talk in this company because I'm so often grouped with jerks, I mean the therapy trade . . .

I feel humbled to share words with you." He named the other participants, then began by quoting from a Creeley poem titled "Waiting."

While Hillman's relations with Creeley would remain mutually appreciative and civil, a tension lapped at the edges. Later responding to a request to blurb one of Hillman's books, Creeley wrote him: "Many thanks for your remarkable lecture 'The Thought of the Heart' . . . Meantime I've had a letter from your editor at Harper's, and then a copy of the ms [manuscript]. of your extended interview with the Italian analyst. In short, I'm asked for some comment that can be used for advertisement of the book. I'm going to demur, like they say, just I'm so backed up with work . . . There's no possibility of reading it for months, and I'm also in no sense a responsible qualifier of the material involved to begin with. So don't please think it's lack of interest—just that I feel altogether irresponsible providing some pat 'terrific'—ok."[36]

ROBERT DUNCAN

> "The poem
> feeds upon thought, feeling, impulse,
> to breed itself,
> a spiritual urgency at the dark ladders leaping"
> —Robert Duncan, "Poetry, A Natural Thing"[37]

He stood as one of the most esteemed poets of the latter half of the twentieth century, a leading figure in the literary movement known as the "San Francisco Renaissance" along with Olson, Creeley, and Kenneth Rexroth. Charismatic and kinetic in presence and speech, Duncan was a diminutive man, handsome, dapper, elegant, tailored. Nor Hall, later to become a close friend of Hillman and his wife Margot McLean, had met Duncan while a graduate student at Santa Cruz University, and credited the poet's influence with changing her life. "He had a very unusual, manic kind of mind," she recalled. "He would come in, always with this big cape on, open his briefcase, take out a big alarm clock, plunk it down on the table and set it for four hours—to stop himself from talking. Then he would start, walking as he talked, reciting poetry and telling endless stories about all the poets he had known." According to Hall, Duncan didn't care much for Jung and Jungians, believing Jung viewed angels metaphorically while *he* saw angels as real. The English poet and critic Kathleen Raine, herself am admirer and friend of Hillman, called Duncan a great "visionary poet." Hall said, "He lived in mythology."[38]

Paul Kugler "thought he would be particularly interested in Jim's work because of his interest in Neoplatonism. He was probably the most articulate voice in America on visionary poetics, transcendental imagination."[39] As Duncan later recounted, "Before I met or even started reading James Hillman, I paid my $90, or whatever it was, because James Hillman was announced at the Jungian Center in San Francisco as giving a weekend on the underworld of the gods."[40]

In 1979, the year Hillman's *Dream and the Underworld* appeared, soon Duncan's notebooks would contain numerous references to it. He wrote down Hillman quoting Heraclitus ("Sleepers are workers and collaborators in what goes on in the universe.") And quoting Hillman in bringing to light one of Duncan's dreams. ("It is better to keep the dream's black dog before your inner sense all day than to 'know' its meaning.") In the morning dream fragment that lingered for Duncan, "there remains the host changing himself into a bull calf and running thru the suite of rooms."[41]

It would be Kugler who introduced them, and Duncan who invited Hillman over to dine with himself and his life partner, an artist who went by his first name of Jess. Perhaps they talked of H. D. (Hilda Doolittle), the imagist poetess of whom Duncan was a devotee: "It was a responsibility to glory that she touched in me."[42] She had resided on the same street where Hillman had his analytic office in Zürich. Perhaps

Hillman spoke of a Duncan poem that he'd "hand copied from a friend's magazine some years ago . . . about the moon coming to a close."

Hillman wrote to "My dear Duncan, and Jess" in February 1980 from Dallas: "This long while I have not written to thank for the fish, the evening, the visit through Neoplatonism, and the welcoming charm and pleasantness. This letter isn't proper thanks either . . . but at least an awareness to you that I am here, and your images are here."[43]

At the end of March, Duncan sent Hillman poems he'd written in the late 1940s, when he'd discovered Robert Browning's references to soul-making. That November, Duncan appeared at another Kugler-organized event in Buffalo, "Anima, Animal, Animation: A Conference on the Poetic and Bestial Faces of the Soul," presenting along with Hillman, Pat Berry, David Miller, Robert Creeley and animated filmmaker Suzan Pitt. Hillman spoke on "Going Bugs." Duncan gave a lecture and did a Saturday evening performance alongside Creeley for the first time in more than twenty years—before an audience of six hundred.

Hillman was blown away, dashing off a handwritten letter to Duncan: "Thank you for your tour-de-force marvelous riotous speech at the end of the Buffalo shoot-out. The *intelligence* especially—and the multi-levels and the absurdity. To say nothing of the beauty. Just grand." Referencing the event several months later, Hillman wrote: "Last night I played the tape of the Buffalo Bug lecture. Draggy in rhythm, but good in content. Recalled Buffalo. Thought again of your splendid performance. Lordy, lordy, that was sumpthin!

"You read a poem 'Styx' there. Would you allow us to print it in the present issue of *Spring*? It's the right place for it. If it's money, well then we'll pay."[44]

The poet agreed, and responded by saying his collection of *Spring* meant: "I begin to gather leads as to ferments, catalysts, departures and returns, infections as well as resistances—the richness in thought in the Jungian domaine."[45] He proceeded to ask Hillman to write a piece on "Robert Duncan and Psyche" for the journal *Ironwood*. Hillman said he was honored, but declined: "I don't know the work well enough and fear damaging something." He wrote again to Duncan asking if he would consider writing something for *Spring* as part of "the collection of pieces we would publish by poets on Jung . . . The Whole Bloody Field needs poetic redemption," Hillman went on, "that is, picked up by the poetic sense, turned over, and handed back to psychology, saying look here, look again, see what you missed."[46]

Duncan began a long handwritten reply: "If 'the whole bloody field' depth or debt has come to be in hock, can the poetic redeem the pledge? But let us start as Confucius does with 'No ought'—nothing owed. Would the soul be deprived of its essential life drama? Is it poetic 'redemption' you speak of, or the irredeemable, the formal or fateful imperative in which the poetic is compelled to realize itself in the poem? The modern poem [poet—poetics] at large *uses* depth psychology; zen religion; myth structuralist, vegetative, cosmic, comic; linguistics; logical positivism, illogical negativism; avant gardeism; ethno-anal-itical orality—whatever to temper its own furor. And one wonders where there is so little fire at the vast expansion of the Fire Department." He expressed "delite in your and Pat's being trouble agents."[47]

He wrote again early in 1982: "How fruitful I find your current work, Jim." Duncan was referring to having received *The Thought of the Heart*, and discovering that Hillman's section on the "Alchemical Heart" mirrored his having brought William Harvey's anatomical dissertation into his poetics in 1949; "but I did not find, as you have, a 'mechanical heart' but a 'vital' heart."[48]

Two ensuing letters crossed in the mail:

February 15, 1982, Hillman to Duncan: "The issue is one of cosmology, and it is that which made Corbin a figure for me, and in that place you are too . . . The principle and powers speak through your long lines, those lines like a score, the rhythm comes off the page, almost as melodies, another sense of the lyric there, not the short lyric as a finished piece but *lyrical*, sweettuned—but back to cosmology. That is what I am about now, beginning the cosmological work that shall have to be written from psyche, and therefore saved from confusion with metaphysics and ontology.

"The north turned cosmology into ontology, as they turned *cosmos* into universe. Lost the 'face' of things, the cosmetics, the anima mundi . . .

"I am working at reconstructing a cosmology which starts from psyche's need rather than from spirit's pronouncements, a peopled cosmology, pathologized too, and one which will drive the Lacanians and Heideggerians and Levi-Straussians into the wilderness of their linguistic ontologies where there are no burning bushes, and no pillars of fire to lead them from their nightwood. Here comes Pharoah's troops chasing Heidegger, they are going to drag him by his few wisps of hair back into the land of Dread.

"Oz and Alice and the children's books you showed me in your upstairs rooms are the necessary recipients, the vessels for the imaginal—but so is everything else from pornography to popculture . . .

"Jung did grasp that. He said start with whatever is in your mind. Start with the symptom. Don't purge yourself of the images . . . let them be the start. We return to the imaginal through the fortuitous angel in the image, whatever it is, whatever its face, it is a mirror, even the cracked mirror of an Irish servant girl."[49]

February 17, 1982: Duncan wrote an entire letter to Hillman about his just-published *Thought of the Heart*. After quoting a passage, Duncan added: "No wonder—every wonder!—Jim, that wherever I find young readers of my work, they are followers of yours . . . This passage on 'they who are they' I will be bringing forward into the work of the seminar on Poetics on Person."[50]

From Duncan's Journal, February 19, 1982: "Note—correspondence with Hillman has just opened up the ways for me.

I had been holding back from the sublimation/sublime, the subliminal inflation in which the start I knew waited . . . I had thought I had had the courage of this unwarranted 'glory' or 'grandeur' or 'arbour'—but clearly now the way lies farther out from shore, all the way into the eddies and 'high-flown' wintry passages."

Later, Kugler, ever the catalyst, invited Duncan to give the annual lecture for the Analytical Psychology Society of Western New York, suggesting that he might want to talk about Hillman's work. In Dallas, when Hillman caught wind of it, he wrote the poet: "Dear Robert—Seeing is believing. I see in the Buffalo Newsletter that in April you are to 'speak on' J. H.! What's goin' on—as we say in Dallas. I was supposed to write on R. D. [Duncan] (and Neoplatonism); still wish I could. But just can't.

"Amazed, flattered—but mainly *envious* that you can take on (me) what I couldn't (you). Though you have the far easier task."[51]

In Buffalo, on April 14, 1983 in a lecture entitled "Opening the Dreamway" (later transcribed and published in *Spring* 59, 1986), Duncan played Hermes to his imagined Hillman as Apollo, in a playful, wide ranging, divagating, teasing, taunting, alchemical blend of quicksilver and sulfur kind of mesmerizing, spellbinding speech. In his talk, Duncan firmly rejected the core notion of archetypal psychology as a poetic psychology. To Duncan, a "poetic psychology" would be a psychology of images, but the poet's experience of image is direct and unconcerned about fact-checking. "I mean Plato knew that there better not be a poetic republic," Duncan wrote and added: "Since a poetic psychology cannot exist, what then is Hillman?— A poet? A psychologist? A philosopher like Nietzsche or Heidegger? A would-be poet, perhaps, with something hindering, holding him back? A fear of Osiris-like, Dionysian dismemberment?"

Towards the end of the lecture Duncan zooms in with a kind of photographic lens intensity, on Hillman's essay "Alchemical Blue." As he races towards his final paragraphs, Duncan links Goethe and Hillman in their amazements about color and asks:

"Hillman and Goethe: are they both psychoanalysts, are they both poets?" For Duncan, notwithstanding his fascination with Hillman, his at times complete absorption in and profound appreciation for his work, the answer is: No. Beautiful prose, yes. Stunning, even staggering insights, yes. But, never poetry, never the willingness, never, perhaps, the courage, to suffer the Dionysian dismemberment.

One scholar called "the most complicated fullest lecture that Duncan had ever given," and afterward Kugler remembered him being "very concerned about whether he had said something inappropriate."

Hillman wrote afterward, in an undated letter:

"Robert,

"They've sent me tapes of your Buffalo talking and I'm being interrupted in my listening so that I'm not through, as if I'd ever be through, though I keep from getting closer to the second tape by playing parts back. It is such an excitement to hear how you can 'expand' upon this 'Hillman' and *let in light*."

Then this crucial paragraph:

"I do not expect to go beyond, surpass what I have been working at, because I may not be able to admit as much as you, because I am less than even a poor poet in delivering myself to the fact or image there, because I still do get caught in addressing the imaginary audience of positivist, sociological secular colleagues (my heroism as salvador of the damned rather than as visionary), because as a Parisian girlfriend in 1948 said to me 'You'll never be a writer because you care too much about your laundry'—literal laundry she meant, and finally because, there is that eye that the psychologist must keep on his plebian pedestrian tradition, over his shoulder, the world of normalcy (that requires actual life to be discussed as 'pathology')."

He had just come from San Francisco, Hillman noted, where he MC'd for two days "at the Jungian SPACE SHOT—Ursula le Guin, [*Star Trek* creator Gene] Roddenberry, Frank Herbert . . . and the astronaut [Rusty] Schweikart who did let 'the universe in' and is a remarkable man despite my bias against him before

I met him. It was an unsatisfying event in that it became mainly an 'experience' in that California way. Little hard thought. Too many spaced out fantasies . . . *Your* tape strikes me as *real* cosmic talk . . . Listening to you teaches me how to listen to you."

However, in San Francisco, "there wasn't one free moment, and I couldn't extend my time there, to have met with you." Now he and Pat were "off to Rhode Island soon for the Apocalypse conference." So Hillman offered a hand-written close: "Fond good wishes, and *thanks* for your Buffalo words."

There isn't any record of Duncan writing to Hillman in response. One final letter from Hillman (June 12, 1985) indicates that Duncan had fallen ill (he would die of kidney failure in 1988). Hillman informed the poet that he now lived in rural Connecticut. He was writing because he wished to publish Duncan's Buffalo talk "that touches off from 'James Hillman' and has much that is *telling, amusing,* and *extraordinary.* I see no reason to edit it . . . It gives a fine view of your notion, and the Neoplatonic notion, of poetry and the poet—as well as knocking 'Hillman' on the head for foolishness regarding myth, etc."

In his lecture on Hillman, Duncan read from his poem, "The Recital of the Pindar" (fragment 131 (96)) July 7–8, 1979:

Companion, hold steady the beat of the fire that
    burns me out . . .
Deep we go down to die in the beast by the stream
    where the flow
of tears has never ceased we thirst and would perish
    the human
yearning blossoming up, beautiful bud and full flower,
    from the stem
of remorseless hunger. Do you not see that my glare
    would be toucht by
you seeing me again? And yet, when we sleep, this
    fierceness re-

turns before us, waking in dream and in the spell of
    speech the
trance of deep poetry his roar the water roaring
    lion-rose-flame
rising round as the flood rises[52]

Compare these lines to so many themes and passages in Hillman: death, sleep, the Underworld, Aphrodite with her flowers springing up beneath her feet, the glare of red-faced Mars, sleep . . . "sleep, ah, perchance to dream" . . . poetry as the lion's roar, Poseidon's waves and thunder, the deep trance of poetry, the imagination, the 'lion-rose-flame' of the thought of the heart.

Was Hillman's work through the late seventies and eighties a commentary on Duncan? Or, is the magnificence and beauty of Duncan's poetry an anticipation and outcome of reading and knowing Hillman? Or, as Jung might say, perhaps both were under the sway of the spirit of the depths, and in their own way gave voice to its efforts to address the historical moment—the spirit of the times? Who is to say?

ROBERT BLY

"When we stride or stroll across the frozen lake,
We place our feet where they have never been.
We walk upon the unwalked. But we are uneasy.
Who is down there but our old teachers"
—*Robert Bly, "Gratitude to Old Teachers"*[53]

As poetics moved Hillman from his Eurocentric sensibilities and more deeply into the American scene, his relationship with Duncan came to its denouement—and along came Robert Bly. Like Duncan, Bly is considered among the greatest poets of the twentieth century, and was deeply affected by Hillman and vice-versa. They were born the same year, nine months apart. Their friendship mostly revolved around poetics and language and antedated and continued through their much more widely known association in the Mythopoetic Men's Movement. Bly was of Norwegian ancestry, burly and bearish, often poncho clad (as opposed to Duncan's cape), shamanistic, radiant with what he called "Zeus energy," a *skald* who could have comfortably sat beating a drum at the stern of a Viking ship, tufts of silvery white hair topping his always animated form.

Bly introduced himself in a letter to Hillman. Their friendship warmed. True affection sprang up between them. Their letters abound with consolations, cheers, endearments, and encouragement. In one instance, even their identities were confused. A librarian at the Jung Institute in New York responded to Bly during a phone call, saying "Certainly, Dr. Hillman." Bly wrote Hillman: "What is happening?"[54]

That was in 1977. Seven years later, Bly wrote Hillman after bringing him to his first men's "enclave" in Minnesota: "When you begin to speak, I feel something coming over the horizon that I have never experienced, flocks of some sort, winged, persistent, flamboyant; and I feel myself to be a small herd of mangy buffalo . . . So if you ever want me to teach with you, call. Or be."[55]

The sentiment was reciprocated. Hillman wrote to Bly: "Just preparing notes for our course at Schumacher in September . . . and I was searching my shelves for your poems ala [Francis] Ponge . . . two times thru, couldn't find them, then did, and then found the dedication, and am writing to thank you again for your piercing eye of the heart . . . Anyway, you have done it for years in your poems, and this is a note to thank you for them, and wish you would keep on doing this, like [William] Stafford day after day after day."

Hillman penned several of his own poems for a Festschrift book celebrating Bly's sixty-fifth birthday, saying: "Thank you, Robert, for your foolhardy courage, and your intelligent carefulness, from your friend and companion of that superb year, 1926."[56] And Bly often sent Hillman new poems in typescript, especially as the two entered their twilight years. As Duncan had, Bly inscribed quotes from Hillman's work in his handwritten notebooks.

Some years later, Margot McLean commented on their relationship: "With James and Robert, there is mutual love and respect. They meet in their work—through Robert's poems, and James' ideas. They also enjoy partaking in good meals together. But they are very different in personality. Robert is more of a guru, as he can handle all the followers and has his devoted entourage. James dislikes the guru idea and works against it. James feels Robert is one of our greatest poets and respects on a deep level his political engagement, especially during the Vietnam War."[57]

In an interview for the biography in 2007, Bly read aloud from Hillman's work on his Minneapolis porch and reflected: "You know at most parties, dinners and so on, the blade doesn't go down into the earth. And when the blade goes into the earth, that's when Jim begins to talk. And his prose, the stuff we were reading today, wo! The blade is really *in* there. So he's a genius, one of the few geniuses in my generation."

While musing pensively upon Hillman's influence on his poetry: "Well, I'd say in poetry, what you do is you really move from one detail to the next. A detail of a bird with a wounded wing. You move from that outward into the world, so that the poem itself is like a plant that's rooted—from underneath the seed you got a root in there—and so the question in poetry is, how can you keep that root by actually honoring the physical world and the detail of the dirt . . . around the plant. And at the same time begin to move outward into the area of affection and mythology and the old loves of men. Jim was tremendous help there, in being able to take that second step, which after you have a firm base in the object itself—I was writing these things called Object Poems—then what do you DO? Most of the object poets stop right there. But Jim understood something about this moving out into the aura of the human being, and then you go on into the aura of the earth and then the aura of God, you know what I mean? And he seldom made a misstep with that."

It may be too much to say that Bly and his poetry brought Hillman back to earth, down to earth, to the land of the shaggy buffalo, the body voice. But it may not. Whether fairly or not, Hillman was sometimes accused of neglecting the body. Bly cured him of that: exhibiting both the tenderness of the doe rising from the grass at first light and the straining grunts and growls and groans of the "shaggy buffalo," "the heavy bear that goes with me," gawking, squabbling, contesting in a "scrimmage of appetite" as the poet Delmore Schwartz described it. Under the influence of Bly, Hillman began to listen to and listen through the body more. To a brother in the Men's Movement, a participant in one of the Weekend Retreats who in dissatisfaction had raised a question, Hillman responded: "Regarding the head and the emotions . . . very much depends on which part of the body you *listen* with. If you listen with a detached head and try to figure things out, then you will feel it 'only in the head.' The head is, however, full of blood and the passionate intellect is the fiercest instrument we have for affecting the world."[58] Thanks to Bly, in Hillman's writing, while blood went rushing to the head, it also descended, and in the depths, the animal heart began to beat. "Writers and poets are the tigers, moles and giraffes who display the animal powers of language . . . Speech is animal display. Language is biological and instinctual."

Under Bly's enthusiastic influence, Hillman's style did alter. A new breath and pulse emerged. The style became a little easier and breezier, more American. In a spirited exchange with the Jungian Analyst Wolfgang Giegerich, Hillman asserted: "So as an American, I am out to affect vision . . . Therefore, sweet-talk your way as you go and anything goes, providing the vision helps life in the woods. Anima Mundi is a right idea not because it is sound in logic, but because it sounds a song that makes time and the earth where we spend it more beautiful, easier to enjoy, offering a feeling of communion among souls. The subject-object split, alienation, logic—just a passel of European troubles. What does matter is to speak in the belief that these troubles are overcome, as if the rhetoric makes the vision really so, or the vision makes the rhetoric really work, like our advertising, our preaching, our singing. Aufgehoben has already been translated into American: haven't you heard? 'We shall overcome.'"[59]

To the melancholic senex scholar, the Dionysian Rogue, the Hermetic Highwayman, the Picaresque Knight Errant, now was added a touch of Mike Fink and Davy Crockett, Johnny Appleseed, street preacher and poet, a bit of the jazz musician. During most of the fifies, sixties, and seventies, Hillman had been abroad, the young, aspiring would-be novelist, and then the buttoned up, tweedy Director of Studies at the Jung Institute, so that he largely missed the revolution in American culture and politics that occurred in the ferment of those decades. Thanks to Bly and to a decade back in the USA, for Hillman both the times and the style were a-changing.

COLEMAN BARKS

"Beyond our ideas of right-doing and wrong-doing,
there is a field. I'll meet you there.
When the soul lies down in that grass,
the world is too full to talk about.
Ideas, language, even the phrase 'each other'
doesn't make sense any more."[60]
—*Coleman Barks*

June 2009: The two are onstage together at the annual Great Mother Conference in Maine. Barks, pre-eminent translator of the thirteenth-century mystic poet Rumi, reads aloud from a poem by Ireland's Patrick Kavanagh—a man "with hayseed in my hair." Hillman said: "He was that kind of a person, because he was a farmer. He was of that hayseed earth, soil." When Hillman was attending Trinity College, Kavanagh had been a mentor. He proceeds to read another Kavanagh poem, "In Memory of My Mother."

Then Hillman read Wallace Stevens to the audience. Barks read a poem about an old man who walks around his neighborhood. He spoke of how much he loved Plotinus' emphasis on beauty. "When you begin to recognize beauty, you become beautiful," he says. Hillman responds: "How do you know when you become beautiful? Send me a postcard when you become beautiful."

Robert Bly had convinced Barks to translate the eleventh-century Persian poet Rumi in 1976, handing him a stack of pages saying, "these poems need to be released from their cages"—meaning take them out of academic jargon. Barks did so for eight years—a kind of daily spiritual practice after teaching several classes at the University of Georgia—before he published what became the best-selling *Essential Rumi*. He discussed his work on Rumi in an hour-long special with Bill Moyers.[61]

Barks and Hillman had first met when they shared a microphone in Seattle, then spent time together at men's retreats in Brevard, North Carolina. They used to imitate two old Southern ladies, who they dubbed Lydia and Edith, sitting on the verandah gossiping. Barks remembered: "Somehow we just fell into this role-playing without any preconception at all—'I don't know why you would say *that*, Lydia!' We'd probably be shot in feminist circles!, but nobody seemed to mind because we were so respectful. We loved being the women, is what it was. I've seen James actually in long black hair at the men's groups. He turned out to be a gorgeous woman, and I was very attracted to him! And I wasn't the only one."

Barks went on to reflect: "His writing style is lusciously sensual. A page of James Hillman's prose is like poetry to me, so beautifully crafted and sensuous. He thinks of his essays as free-wheeling paragraphs put together. He's able to condense grand trends of thought and make them clear so people just say, 'Ohhhh!' He's able to put such depth into our ordinary language and help us understand what kind of patterns we're thinking in, in making our judgments. He just gives depth to the condition

of being alive. Particularly his noticing of language is so important. He quickens us, I think. Poets love him and the poesis,
that he's always in the midst of it, always fiddling with words.
Language as a material, almost something to look at, like you'd
look at a piece of wood that you're gonna use—turn it over and
find out where you're going to put the grain." [62]

In a letter dated January 28, 2006—typed on an odd-shaped
piece of green paper, addressed to Coleman—Hillman wrote:
"Dear Man—I miss seeing your frizzled head and small twin-
kly eyes, are you well, I'd like to hear that voice of yours saying
any old thing from 600 years ago . . . You've got a freedom of
phrase or rhythm or an access to a little pile of Georgia kindling wood that is light weight and touches off big logs burning.
Lucky man. Let me know when you get North and East. We
have not danced together for ten years!"

Barks remembered: "I had a press called Maypop, after
the flow and the vine and the wine. James merrily renamed it
Nincompop."

November 18, 1992, Barks wrote Hillman upon publication
of *The Rag and Bone Shop of the Heart*, the book of poetry edited
by Bly, Hillman, and Meade: "I want to congratulate you three
hoodlums on the best damn anthology in existence. Really, so
magnificently put together and lovingly selected."

January 7, 2006, on a postcard with a picture of a wolf pup
howling, Hillman asks Barks: "My man: I'm to do a thing on
dogs—did your friend Rumi ever mention a dog in any way in
all his jillions of inspirations? I am especially interested in BAD
DOGS, evil, smelly, shit-eating fuckers, who kill babies and bite
achilles tendons, and lead the soul to death . . . Love & Kisses,
James."

April 10, 2007, on a fax from Hillman about a panel discussion he and Barks were to be part of, themed "Poetry in Times
like These": "We are always *in times like these*, when poetry *seems*
vagabond and homeless. Cheerio."

In *Hummingbird Sleep: Poems, 2009–2011*, Barks would include
several of the above excerpts from their correspondence and

write a series of poems he called "The Gift of the Comeback: For James Hillman."[63] Barks also wrote: "Toward the end James said he could not tell much difference between living and dying, his collaboration with spirit so seamless. Soul is consciousness, and that is still here."

WILLIAM KOTZWINKLE

> *"He was tall, lean with a hawkish profile, his nose strong and sharply arched" (p. 61); quoting the doctor, "The ego is the real tyrant, you know. Gives all the orders and hates change . . . Some wise men have said that psyche creates the world" (p. 97); quoting the doctor: "Our infirmities make our soul. I'm not trying to lift you out of your pathology. I'm trying to make you comfortable with it" (p. 115).*
> —From *William Kotzwinkle's novel* The Exile,
> *1987 (A description of the fictional analyst Dr. Gaillard—James Hillman become the stuff of novels.)*

Bill Kotzwinkle, as Hillman called him, is a prolific author of adult fiction, children's books, short stories, and screenplays. He was enlisted by Steven Spielberg to write a novelization of *E.T. the Extra-Terrestrial* and a sequel. His book *Doctor Rat* won the World Fantasy Award for best novel. A quirky genius, there's something timelessly counter-culture, counter-East Coast Literary Establishment about him, a kind of gentle Magus in the woods. Bill Kotzwinkle makes no bones of the fact that the character of Dr. Gaillard is modeled on the man he considered a sort of sorcerer.

In the early 1970s, he'd been reading his way through the Jungians—Von Franz, Esther Harding, and Eric Neumann—when Kotzwinkle came upon Hillman. "I saw the difference immediately," he reflected in 2019. "While they were steeped in Jung, they weren't alive to language the way Hillman was. I suspected he was a poet in disguise. He saw the vibratory power in words, and he balanced his phrases very carefully, obviously unsatisfied with erudition only but desirous of casting his thoughts in poetic modes."[64]

Kotzwinkle corresponded with Hillman a few times, sent him a copy of his first book (*Elephant Bangs Train*) and, while in Zürich researching a novel, dropped by the Jung Institute. Hillman was out of town. They met for the first time in 1976, when Hillman and Pat Berry were teaching in Syracuse. He was accompanied by his novelist wife Elizabeth Gundy (and later co-author with him of the best-selling children's series, *Walter the Farting Dog*). Kotzwinkle recalled: "By that time he'd read several of my books and I'd read all of his. I remember something interesting from that meeting. I asked him to elaborate, for my wife, on some aspect of his work. He said, 'I think not.' That was a strong position for him to take in a social context but he'd caught me in the typical novelist's game of manipulation, to get the subject talking along the lines I wanted, because novelists deftly try to get people talking about what the novelist thinks he can use, but Hillman wasn't having any. He was just as deft from listening to the manipulations of his patients. Nonetheless, it was a promising first meeting and a friendship began to form."

Kotzwinkle wrote Hillman after their initial visit: "A beautiful goldfinch just landed on the lawn—most unexpected and dazzling. That is how the poetic spirit enters your work."[65]

Kotzwinkle said Hillman had "a brilliant mind encased in an easy-going manner. He had dealt with the shadow of being important and knew it was a ridiculous pose for anyone engaged with psychic reality, for the psyche's enormous power makes supplicants of us all. He was aware of the mystic liveliness in every encounter, aware as well of the invisible forces that bear on the simplest conversation. To handle such high-octane power he had developed an easeful manner. If he hadn't done this, self-importance would've devoured him. But this meant that you felt the hidden part of him watching and waiting. Waiting for what? The sign of the spirit. It's why I thought, from the very first, that he was a poet—for a poet, if he's the real thing and not a pretender, lives for the signs of the spirit. But he chose instead to bring this kind of awareness into the analytical hour, where it makes different demands and brings about different results.

"He had a sister living in Maine which allowed us to get together again on my homeground on the coast, where Hillman threw himself wildly into the cold North Atlantic after a sauna, shouting, 'This is how we do it in Switzerland!' He plunged into life, hot or cold, high or low. It was what was endearing about him."

The Kotzwinkles then visited James and Pat when they lived in Dallas. "He told us he had no idea why he was living there, referred to Texans as Meanderthals, meaning they rambled on and on, but he said it with affection." Upon learning that the couple was moving to rural Connecticut, Kotzwinkle wrote to them: "I know that you are going to love the life. As one who has lived in the forest for almost fifteen years, I can promise many mysteries, with the exquisite voice of songbirds at evening, which is the most provocative sound on earth."[66]

Not long after Hillman settled into Thompson, the Kotzwinkles came again. "My car broke down in their town and I was depressed over it. As we drove to the garage he said, 'When I'm depressed I feel like a rusty anchor at the bottom of the sea.' This was typical Hillman, instructing me that my situation would benefit from some imagination, that I should sink like the rusty anchor to the bottom of my feeling of frustration and helplessness."

Kotzwinkle went into analysis with Hillman. He recalled that he couldn't have written *The Exile* without having done so. "He seemed amused by my effort. The analyst in the novel fails to provide a solution to the central character's problem, and maybe that disappointed him and he was gentleman enough not to mention it."

In 2019, Kotzwinkle recalled: "Jung had already shaped me as a thinker. And other forces had shaped me as a writer. Hillman's impact on me had to do with the dream world. We analyzed hundreds of dreams together. I still dream of him, always as a powerful figure, but the most powerful dream of him I ever had was when I encountered a caravan in the dream world, tinkling across the desert by night. I went to the head of the caravan and found Hillman there. He was the leader of the caravan. And that's what he was in life, the leader of a caravan of those who trade in dreams. And I can say that he led me through the dream world with consummate ability."

Hillman stopped practicing analysis in 1987, coincidentally the year *The Exile* appeared. "I was one of his last patients. Perhaps the very last, because during our final analytical hour he said, 'I can't do this anymore. It almost makes me ill.' This was a shocking moment for me but I thought I understood. There'd been too many repetitions of the familiar scenarios, and analysis was no longer carrying him to the depths of the psyche. His will to explore those depths had carried him out of the formal practice of analysis."

With a lifelong interest in mythology that had begun in his twenties amid the old stone figures on display in New York's Metropolitan Museum of Art, Kotzwinkle later compared notes with Hillman on the subject. Perhaps he shared an experience from when he and his wife first visited Zürich: "We were walking along the street toward the cemetery where Jung is buried and there, in the middle of the street was a perfect rose, wrapped in cellophane. It must have fallen from a florist's delivery truck, provided by the gods so we'd have something to put on Jung's grave."

As with so many readers, the "Hillman effect," like a storm or earthquake, like a deep sea volcano, Poseidon striking with his Trident as it were, deepened Kotzwinkle's insights into the rumbling, radiant presence of the gods. He wrote Hillman: "I've been thinking of you so much lately, and the other night I went to the bookshelf and took down Ficino. I thanked you for publishing this strange book, and for sending it to me, for it gave me a powerful illumination, one that had been building for some time. And I felt Minerva's grace suddenly, and had a tremendous surge of understanding concerning these gods he mentions—Mercury, Apollo, and Venus. They seemed more real to me than ever before, and their court all around me. Later in that day I was driving, thinking of Apollo, and a fisherman's cottage by the roadside was suddenly struck by sunlight, all the windows ablaze with reflected gold, and I saw—this is Apollo, this sun."[67]

This recognition of Apollo, and the perception of darker deities too—was, for Kotzwinkle, a consequence of Hillman's sorcery: "When we went to New York, a city I never thought I'd have to see again, I looked out the hotel window and saw the wrathful deities in all their dark array."[68]

As with the gods, Hillman awakened Kotzwinkle to the beauties of alchemy. In a letter to Hillman, Kotzwinkle wrote, "Thanks for the exposition in *Spring* ("Silver and the White Earth, Part Two," *Spring 1981*). Your struggle for clarity and the honesty in that work gave me a focus I'd never had before." In his 2019 reflection, Kotzwinkle returned to Hillman's alchemical work. "Hillman used his poetic power to portray the naïve medieval intellect, which was cloaked in moonlight and magic. Somehow Hillman traveled back to that world, assumed that cloak, and invoked the silvery moon. In this he was a necromancer, communing with the dead and at the same time instructing us as to what the dead were saying. He was there with them, in an astounding bit of time-travel made possible by his great erudition and his own magic soul."

In his letters, the sincerity and depth of Kotwinkle's admiration and gratitude shines through, but he could be searchingly critical as well. *Inter Views* excited his praise—"truly a brilliant and remarkable book."[69] But in an earlier pre-publication version, Kotzwinkle disliked the chapter on Writing: "The section on writing is dry—and your ideas aren't flashing there."[70] His criticism was straightforward and constructive, such that in the final version of the book Hillman revised the chapter, which Kotzwinkle surmised had been done in response to his suggestions.

By accepting Kotzwinkle's critique, Hillman embraced another *writer* on writing, a well-known and widely published *fiction writer*, for whom Hillman had not only real affection but also real respect . . . a *fiction writer*, like Donleavy was and like he had once dreamed of being.

On the poetic basis of mind in Hillman's work, Kotzwinkle commented: "His books are filled with entertaining pieces of medical and social history. In *The Myth of Analysis* he gives us a picture of Madame Tussaud touring England with the wax heads of decapitated French leaders. (She'd sculpted the heads when the leaders were still alive). Hillman explains how at that time the human head was carrying an archetypal fantasy which eventually developed into the strong ego of modern psychiatry. What a tour de force, from Madame Tussaud to Sigmund Freud's couch! The whole section has the flavor of Baudelaire's 'Flowers of Evil.' It's dark in the psyche, and its movements are strange and terribly complicated and Hillman used a poetic mirror to enliven his narration, so that we didn't drown in detail or the deadening language of psychiatric science. He saw the same poetic necessity in the narrative of everyday life. He knew that life comes at us loaded with irrationality whose peculiar gifts would be lost to us unless we could employ imagination in something so simple as feeding the chickens. It's this that made him such a lively man, ready to learn tap dancing so he could tap out the time on his sixtieth birthday."

From the psychological depths and spiritual ascensions of myth and alchemy to the exigencies of everyday life—in one letter Kotzwinkle thanks Hillman for teaching him a better way to hang clothes to dry. For Kotzwinkle, 'soul-making'—its novelties, renewals, aspirations and differentiations—articulated by James Hillman in archetypal psychology really was a 'god-send' or, better said, a gift from the gods, a gift as exhilarating and defining as a rosy-fingered dawn and golden chariot rising on a wine dark sea.

* * *

Randolph Severson wrote in 2020: "What is psychological writing? For me, it is as Hillman said, the archetypal psychology of the twenty-first century will be 'responding with intensity to depth' and 'images . . . images.' Intense feeling finds its own form through objectification in images, rhythms, words that convey the shape and sound, the life and nature of that feeling. Feelings were once called by the Church Fathers, 'spiritual senses' . . . Spiritual Senses, Psychic States. The objectification is not so much a discipline—that would be poetry. No, not through discipline but through desire—from the baby's cry to the death rattle a desire *to make ourselves by making ourselves heard*. In the Beginning was the word. Like Caliban, we all are born upon an Isle of noises. The 'poetic basis of mind' upon which Hillman founded his psychology requires as its most faithful expression a poetic speech. Poetic, not poetry. Poetic—imagistic, rhythmical, the free play of metaphor, heightened diction. More Stream of Consciousness than the well wrought urn. More Spontaneous Prose than sonnet. It all goes back to the patient on the couch, doesn't it and free association as the Gateway to the Psyche? Otherwise one can write about psychology but Psychological Writing?—that's a horse of a different color. And one like Joyce, Faulkner, Kerouac, Albert Murray, James Dickey and James Hillman discovered, not so easy to ride. To write about psychology and to write psychologically? James Hillman, alone, did both."[71]

"I imagine that when I'm writing it's got a form, a shape or that it's like a musical composition and certain themes have to come back in a different way and be disguised. And that holds the whole thing together. There will be subtexts that are thematic like music without quoting that necessarily in an overt way. In the last book I wrote, there are many passages that are Shakespeare but they're woven into the language. Or in another book it was Heraclitus woven all the way through. Once I was working on something and it felt like I was inside an enormous sculpture—a huge thing that was wrapped around me. The problem was how to write my way through this thing—like a giant. There's a feeling of

form that goes along, an actual palpable sense of form where a paragraph should stop. So you see, there is a dimension beyond the dimension of thought."

—*James Hillman, 1996.*[72]

NOTES

1. "This business of language has me. . . .": Hillman letter to Robert Bly, August 15, 1998, Bly personal archive.
2. 'I remember on one occasion. . . .": Author interview with J. P. Donleavy, October 2006.
3. "Ah God, the U.S. . . .': Letters from Donleavy to JH, Donleavy private archive.
4. "When for instance I am asked. . . .": Hillman, *The Thought of the Heart and the Soul of the World*, pp. 116–118.
5. "As part of the polytheistic enterprise. . . .": *Uniform Edition of the Writings of James Hillman, Volume 5*, p. 150.
6. Severson on Hillman and language: Communication with author, 2018.
7. "If you've ever edited Hillman. . . ." and Gustavo Barcellos quote: Randolph Severson, "Puer Phenomenology: A High Note," a talk delivered at the Hillman Symposium, Dallas Institute, October 20, 2014.
8. "It's not only the rhythms. . . .": Author interview with Hillman, May 2005.
9. "The idea that there is a god. . . .": Hillman, *Healing Fiction*, p. 23.
10. "I am really by nature an artist. . . .": Interview by Giovanni Papini, quoted in "The Psychologist as Artist: The Imaginal World of James Hillman," by Walter Odajnyk, Opus Archive.
11. "Why did Freud get himself into. . . .': Hillman, *Healing Fiction*, p. 5.
12. "So Jung's way of writing psychology. . . .": *Healing Fiction*, p. 34.
13. "Mars who rides a lion. . . .": *Thought of the Heart, Soul of the World*, p. 56.
14. "appears. . . .as the manifest visible. . . .": Ibid.
15. "leans heavily in the direction. . . .": *New York Times*, August 26, 1979.
16. "he uses words as if they were NASA. . . .': "A Plea to free the imagination," by Christina Robb, *Boston Globe*, May 9, 1975.
17. "Mr. Hillman has an exciting. . . .': *New York Times Book Review*, March 11, 1990.
18. "Language is the human way. . . .": Hillman speaking at a conference on "Words Alive! Awakening the Language of Soul," November 24, 1985.
19. "Well, what's going on. . . .." Hillman's interview with Jay Kugelman, KPFK Radio Los Angeles, November 1978 was transcribed by the author from Hillman's private archive.
20. Clayton Eshelman interview with Hillman is in the Opus Archive.

21. "Following Jung I use the word. . . .": *Re-Visioning Psychology*, p. xi.

22. "We use words like fear and anger. . . .": Transcript provided author by Sylvia Ronchey.

23. "With the loss of the image. . . .": Hillman, "Puritanical Iconoclasm and the American World Order," a talk delivered at the International Literary Conference in Ferrara, Italy, May 1999.

24. "This turn to poet and painter. . . .": *Alchemical Psychology, Uniform Edition*, Voi. 5, p. 124.

25. "As the dead prey upon us. . . .": www.poetryfoundation.org.

26. "Music. Sitting at this desk. . . .": JH letter to Charles Boer, December 17, 1972, used with permission of Jay Livernois, Executor, Charles Boer Estate.

27. "stunning, endlessly provocative. . . .": Charles Boer letter to JH, August 8, 1975, Opus Archive.

28. "As for stealing from it. . . .": JH letter to Charles Boer, September 1975, used with permission of Jay Livernois, Executor, Charles Boer Estate

29. "essays which I have filtered. . . .": Boer letter to JH, September 29, 1975.

30. "Your letter made me green and yellow. . . .": JH letter to Boer, October 20, 1975, used with permission of Jay Livernois, Executor, Charles Boer Estate.

31. "Can it be that not since Freud. . . .": Boer letter to JH, November 5, 1976.

32. "What are you writing, you lucky bastard. . . .": JH letter to Boer, June 17, 1981, used with permission of Jay Livernois, Executor, Charles Boer Estate.

33. "Im going to stand up with two oldtimers. . . .": Hillman letter to "Dear Charles," undated 1981, Boer papers courtesy of Jay Livernois.

34. "Charles was a wonderful cook. . . .": Author interview with Pat Berry.

35. "an attempt to bring the anti-psychiatry movement. . . .": Author interview with Paul Kugler, June 2006.

36. "Many thanks for your remarkable lecture. . . .": Postcard from Robert Creeley to Hillman, March 12, 1982, Hillman archive.

37. Robert Duncan poem: www.poetryfoundation.org.

38. Robert Duncan: Author interview with Nor Hall, July 2007.

39. Kugler "thought he would be particularly. . . .": Author interview, June 2006.

40. "Before I met or even started reading. . . .": Robert Duncan, 'Opening the Dreamway," published in *Spring 59, 1986*.

41. Duncan's notebooks: copies provided author courtesy of Robert Duncan Archive, The Poetry Collection, University of Buffalo.

42. "It was a responsibility to glory. . . .": "Duncan's Divagations," by Ange Mlinko, *The Nation*, February 21, 2011.

43. "about the moon coming to a close. . . .": Hillman letter to "My dear Duncan, and Jess," February 8, 1980, Robert Duncan Archive, The Poetry Collection, University of Buffalo.

44. "Last night I played the tape. . . .': JH letter to "Dear Robert," March 6, 1981, Duncan Archive.

45. "I begin to gather leads. . . .": Duncan letter "To Jim," March 15, 1981, Opus Archive.

46. "the collection of pieces we would publish. . . .": JH letter to Duncan, August 1, 1981, Duncan Archive.

47. "If the 'whole bloody field. . . .": Duncan letter to "Dear Jim," August 6, 1981, Duncan Archive.

48. "How fruitful I find. . . .": Duncan letter to Jim and Pat, January 30, 1982, Opus archive.

49. "The issue is one of cosmology. . . ." Hillman letter to Duncan, February 15, 1982
50. "No wonder—every wonder!...." Duncan letter to "Dear Jim," February 17, 1982, Duncan Archive.
51. "Dear Robert—Seeing is believing. . . .": Hillman letter, undated, to Duncan, Duncan Archive.
52. "The Recital of the Pindar": *Robert Duncan: The Collected Later Poems and Plays.*
53. Bly "Gratitude to Old Teachers": https://www.loc.gov/poetry/180/072.html
54. "Certainly, Dr. Hillman. . . .": Bly letter to Hillman, June 4, 1977, Robert Bly Papers, University of Minnesota Libraries.
55. "When you begin to speak. . . ." Bly letter to Hillman, July 21, 1985, Bly Papers.
56. "Thank you, Robert, for your foolhardy courage. . . .": *Walking Swiftly: Writings & Images on the Occasion of Robert Bly's 65th birthday,* Edited by Thomas R. Smith, St. Paul: Ally Press, 1992, pp. 245–249, "James Hillman."
57. "With James and Robert. . . .": Author interview with Margot McLean.
58. "Regarding the head and emotions. . . .": Hillman letter undated.
59. "So as an American, I am out to affect vision. . . .": James Hillman, "Hegel, Giegerich and the U.S.A.," *Spring 1988.*
60. Coleman Barks poem: https://www.goodreads.com/quotes/538827-beyond-our-ideas-of-right-doing-and-wrong-doing-there-is-a
61. The full Moyers-Barks interview is watchable on YouTube.
62. "Somehow we just fell into this role-playing. . . .": Author interview with Coleman Barks, June 2009.
63. Barks' *Hummingbird Sleep*, published in 2013, is available on Amazon.
64. "I saw the difference immediately. . . .": All Kotzwinkle quotes are from written response to the author's questions, received June 12, 2019.
65. "A beautiful goldfinch just landed. . . .": Kotzwinkle letter to Hillman, June 21, 1976, Opus Archive.
66. "I know that you are going to love the life. . . .": Kotzwinkle letter to Hillman, January 17, 1984, Opus Archive.
67. "I've been thinking of you so much. . . .": Ibid.
68. "When we went to New York. . . .": Kotzwinkle letter to Hillman, June 20, 1984, Opus Archive.
69. "truly a brilliant and remarkable book. . . ..": Kotzwinkle letter to Hillman, May 9, 1983, Opus Archive.
70. "the section on writing is dry. . . .": Kotzwinkle letter to Hillman, March 25, 1982, Opus Archive.
71. "What is psychological writing?". . . .: Randolph Severson email to author, October 20, 2020.
72. "I imagine that when I'm writing. . . .": *Visual Art & The Environment, Conference Report*: Margot McLean and James Hillman, privately published 1997, p. 89.

17

EMBODIED: FROM HERMES TO PAN

"Hillman was aware of the theatrical quality in human life. Once you've realized this, there is no way of forgetting it. Jung drew the veil for me back in the early sixties, and somehow it increased the energy with which characters appeared in my stories. They seemed to arrive from a greater depth and cast darker shadows. Naturally I saw the same forces at play in people with whom I interacted socially. Not that I was an armchair analyst, only that I saw us as actors in a play we didn't quite understand, and that sometimes our cues came from a voice offstage. When I met Hillman he was quite consciously stage-managing the play."
—William Kotzwinkle.[1]

"Night Music Slanted
Light strike the cave of sleep. I alone
tread the red circle
and twist the space with speech."
—Opening lines of Cell Song, *a poem*
by Hillman's friend Etheridge Knight.[2]

Before Hillman came to sit alongside African Americans at the men's groups, before he took up the tap tradition of Master Juba, Mr. Bojangles, Sammy Davis, Jr., and Gregory Hines— before these auspicious moments had been the first conference devoted to archetypal psychology in January 1977 at the University of Dallas. There occurred the nightly Disco dances at a gathering over which Hillman presided, Disco itself (in the wake of the movie "Saturday Night Fever") a form of syncretic urban Venusian elegance never seen before. Hillman, too, was— different from anything prior in the academic or Jungian worlds.

In the curious way that Hillman's life often took years to catch up with his inspired words, the same was true with theater and dance. He had first assessed a certain goat-footed god in his 1972 "Essay on Pan." A wild child sired by Hermes, "as master of instinctual soul, he has something to teach about rhythms and range. Pan was a music man and called a great dancer. He made his appearance felt in choral gatherings, in the beat of rhythmic clapping, bringing communal order to private panic . . . Dance comes from out of the wild, and its intoxication leads us back into it . . . It is not Pan who is mad and must be healed, but the society that has forgotten how to dance with him."[3]

A decade later, on a rustic communal setting in the south of France, Enrique Pardo was "calling for Pan." Pardo, scion of a wealthy Peruvian family, widely-read and classically educated, had studied and taught painting before joining a unique acting troupe known as the Roy Hart Theatre. He was familiar with Jung, but had yet to encounter Hillman's work. Living in London in the late 1970s, he discovered atop a pile of books put aside for his next year's reading, Rafael Lopez-Pedraza's *Hermes and His Children* and, underneath that, Hillman's *Pan and the Nightmare*.

"At the time I was studying the rapport between voice and movement and between singing and dancing," Pardo wrote later. "I saw in Pan *the* singing-dancing god, leading the Dionysian retinue." Here was "the meeting of images and animality. I saw his pursuit of elusive nymphs like Echo and Syrinx as the birth of imagination, where compulsion borders on art." He linked Pan's presence in theatre "to what Hillman calls 'the spontaneity of instinct.'" Pardo's desire became "to return theatre to its religious origins, to ritual, the mysteries, initiation." His *Recherches Pantheatre* study focused on the importance of images, how "dreams and fantasies are reflected against their cultural, imaginal sources, particularly in Greek mythology, in the Judeo-Christian tradition, and in the revisioning of the psychology of Neoplatonic thought." [4]

In the archetypalists, Pardo found the mentors he was looking for. He devoured *The Dream and the Underworld*, wrote enthusiastic letters to López and Hillman and, before long, reached out to Charles Boer asking permission to incorporate his translation of *The Homeric Hymns* into a performance piece on Pan. As it happened, in the late summer of 1983, the theatre group was to present an open-air evening performance at the Palazzo Moretti in Locarno, Switzerland. Hillman and Boer were at the Eranos gathering nearby and saw a poster about it. Accompanied by Hillman's daughter Julia and her boyfriend Jay Livernois, they decided to attend the Italian opera "Pagliacci."

Hillman wrote to Pat Berry afterward: "This group begins with the *VOICE* and reads all of *Spring* articles & books. Uses us for its philosophy . . . López visited them in March for a week in France. So by coincidence they were here! An extraordinary wonderful evening—delightful, moving, thrilling. They were enchanted that we had come: 'Their heroes.'" Yet something puzzled Hillman: "I can't find the connection between what I write & what they do. Here were the fruits of years of work in these people, a whole theatre troop, yet I couldn't see the relation. It felt 'depersonalized.' In other words: '*I don't know what I am at.*'"[5]

Perhaps the not-knowing intrigued him enough to accept an invitation from Pardo to teach at a small workshop/conference at the Theatre's home-base in Malérargues the following January. Hillman, Boer, Livernois, and Hillman's longtime friend Joan Buresch arrived by train from Paris, "wearing these long winter coats and looking like people out of the Forties," Pardo thought. The visitors would stay for almost two weeks. Boer later recounted how the theater group had moved from London into "the ruins of a French chateau," where "it painstakingly rebuilt, regrouped, and revived" following the death of impresario Roy Hart in an auto accident. "Some of its forty or so actors took jobs harvesting grapes, paving roads, and working factory lathes to get money to restore the property and build their theater. Malérargues is a stubbly village of stone cottages, a theater and workrooms centering around the main chateau, with occasional lunchtables strewn in the middle of fields. To stroll the grounds at almost any hour of the day is to hear boffo screams, long profuse belly laughter, and falsetto top notes, while bodies everywhere go through humanly impossible contortions."[6]

In this Pan-possessed pastoral setting, Pardo and company set about "dismembering Dionysus" in studying the actors' relationship between voice and movement exercises explored "a land of exceptions" with image as the main character. "The most dramatic objective event is the precise moment when the body weight leaves the floor and defies gravity." Pardo recalled that Hillman, watching a work session, "remarked that the drama and difficulty of 'following through' had probably much to do with what is called in Jungian psychology 'facing shadow,' the unknown in the actor that the image recognizes."

Pardo remembered saying to Hillman: "'What your work implies for artists is incredibly important.' He was at that time seeking contact with artists, saying in a sense that 'my work is poetical, poesis-based, it's not clinical or scientific.' He was wishing for bridges with artistic creators. I think I came to him at the right moment with that. I believed art was too bound with politics and ethics. I said to everybody I knew, read this book *Dream and the Underworld*, it will free your perspective on creativity."[7]

Hillman invited Pardo to write a piece for *Spring* and spread the word among his colleagues. He brought into the mix Pat Berry and Ginette Paris, then Paul Kugler and Nor Hall. At his suggestion, Pardo started a Mythic Theater Festival. He attended several of the Eranos conclaves and also came several times to visit Hillman in Connecticut. At Hillman's sixtieth birthday party in 1986, Pat Berry recalled of a Pardo performance: "What he could do with his voice was amazing. He was able to make multiple sounds at the same moment with his vocal cords, as if he was playing a reed instrument—a way-out exploration of Pan. I'd never heard anything like it."[8]

Nor Hall, a post-Jungian psychotherapist who in 1980 published *The Moon and the Virgin: Reflections on the Archetypal Feminine*, found her participation in Pardo's events life-changing, fueling her ongoing interest in dramaturgy. The first time she attended, "he was working on what he called the theater of boredom. He had his people walking from one end of the room to the other carrying a long pole, trying to do it in the most boring way possible. Watching this and then listening to Enrique's comments,

I thought, 'my God, this is the best therapy I've ever witnessed in my life!'"[9]

Pardo described himself as "militant about Hillman's work" with his young actors. "I always obliged them to read Hillman, do their catch-up intellectually because there is a tendency sometimes to say, 'well, it's just in our bodies.'" He recalled, too, Hillman pushing him in that direction, "at one point saying to me, 'beware of a kind of idolatry of images. Images are also ideas and ideas are images.' What is the relationship between narrative and image and theater? What kind of theater do you do in terms of narration? What's the logic of narration and what is the psychology of narration?" Hillman's form of mentoring did not let Pardo off the hook. "I remember very clearly during a laboratory workshop, when I spoke rather harshly about sentimentality in a criticism of some actors. And he went at me afterward. He said, 'you have to watch the focus of your elitism.'"[10]

Hillman gave his slide lecture on "Anima" at Malérargues in 1987, later spoke on alchemy and gave a series on Aphrodite. And Hillman invited Pardo to several men's gatherings in California and twice in England, where Pardo was fascinated by the interaction between Hillman and Bly. "I adored being harangued by these two grandfathers," he recalled.

Hillman's relationship with Pardo's Mythic Theater helped trigger a major shift in his life. As Nor Hall described it: "I believe his involvement corresponded to concluding his work as an actual therapist in the office. I think he saw how deeply the psyche was touched and moved by theatrical directing of movement and expression of feeling and meaning—how much more happened in an hour or two observing Enrique work with his actors than generally happened in therapy. He had a similar feeling towards theater as he did to poetry, that both were a way of working with images. And it was about his understanding of embodiment. Poets and actors embody their work, as do artists because they're moving their hands. All that began to have a kind of imaginal coherence that was really important to James."[11]

JOINING THE DANCE

Murray Stein, a Jungian analyst who first met Hillman in Zürich during the Spring House days, put it like this: "He plays with ideas. He juggles. He's a dancer and very light on his feet, rhetorically very deft. You don't want to be in an argument with him on a platform, because it's very uncomfortable. But it isn't because of his robust intellect so much as another kind of gift, artistic really."[12]

Though he'd grown up watching many performers, including dancers along the Atlantic City Boardwalk, Hillman himself never danced until he attended a "Carnival of Nations" in Dublin's Trinity College gymnasium in 1950. After appreciatively observing the dancers from African and Asian countries, at the end he felt compelled to take the stage. A local columnist for the *Irish Times* would write that the festive night was "rounded off with some incredible jive dancing, in which . . . the male dancer was John [sic] Hillman."

As young Hillman described what transpired in letters to his family, he was often looked upon "with great suspicion as I talk differently and dress differently, and the first day they gave me the part of a British Colonel because they said with nasty smiles, you can do that fine . . . Everybody laughed for I wore short pants and was stupid and had a big accent. But then I jitterbugged with a girl like they do in Hollywood pictures and we brought the house down and were the only ones to get an encore . . .

"The next night we tried harder and of course it wasn't as good. Besides I did a terrible thing. Changing my clothes so fast, I forgot to close my pants . . . I came on stage and did the whole dance in front of professors and pastors and parents . . . with every button of my flies opened." He'd buttoned up for the encore, and "now people who said I was an intellectual snob, smile at me and one African asked me to teach him how to dance!"[13]

While going on to study at the Jung Institute in 1950s Zürich, friends would remember Hillman and his American colleagues

Marvin Spiegelman and Robert Stein livening up occasions with impromptu dances. Anne Guggenbühl-Craig, whose own husband Adolf didn't like to dance, remembered taking the floor with Hillman at a Jungian Congress and being "quite surprised to realize he could dance extremely well. It was a side of him I didn't expect."[14]

A generation later, in 1985 Hillman placed a phone call to Leslie Snow, who had a dance studio not far from his Connecticut home in the nearby town of Putnam. "I didn't know who he was or anything about him when he called asking to take some lessons," Snow recalled. "He said he wanted to develop a performance piece for his 60th birthday. He was inviting people from all over the world to an outdoor event in Thompson, and he wanted to surprise them. The element of surprise seemed extremely important to him. Well, in my school I'd get a certain percentage of crank calls from older men. As he remembered, I questioned him suspiciously, asked how much he weighed and so on, before I finally relented and set up an appointment. He walked in—and stayed for twenty-five years."[15]

Snow's school, then called Connecticut Young Artists, was the outgrowth of a lifetime in dance. Her studio at the edge of town occupied an old mill whose top floor held chestnut beams and pillars. The room had been renovated to overlook a waterfall on one side. It was a fitting space for Hillman, about to simultaneously immerse himself in sylvan settings with the men's groups. "He really had a feel for a kind of performance style," Snow recalled, "harking back to what he remembered on the Atlantic City Boardwalk as a boy. He admired Fred Astaire and Gene Kelly and Donald O'Connor, and we would explore a lot of those styles."

Snow quickly realized how seriously Hillman took this. They would spend some six months, meeting more than once a week when Hillman wasn't traveling, working up a 1930s-style Fred Astaire and Ginger Rogers tap dance routine to do together. "He was a wonderful student, very humble and inquisitive," according to Snow. "And after we performed before a very astonished crowd of people [at the birthday party on April 12, 1986], that was the initiation of his exposure to dance and he really wanted to keep it going. He loved tap, but more than anything he loved the process. He wanted to learn how to become an improvisational performer with movement. So we did all kinds of things—incorporating ballet and modern techniques, many different approaches to open that window. He always had goals in mind, but he never wanted to have a fixed routine. Finally he began to have his own little vocabulary of movement, which is what he really wanted."

Snow was pregnant when they began, and found Hillman to be "a terrific help"—to such a degree that upon her arrival he bought Laura, the new baby, her first pair of tap shoes. Snow "consciously did not pursue finding out too much about his background," and Hillman liked it that way. "The desire to express through movement had always been there in him," Snow reflected. "So we basically spent a long time just lifting the layers and building the confidence to get rid of the self-consciousness. Yes, there was frustration at times but always with great humor. We had more laughs over those difficult moments. We'd talk through them and physically walk through them and return to them. All the things we feel when we're up against a wall—but after another couple of sessions we'd always manage to get to the other side. Then he would trust me. And this trust is something I treasure, because he was willing to go to that place of vulnerability. If things were getting too intellectualized, I could tease him and we could get right back to the essence."

In certain ancient societies, as Robert Bly had explained to Bill Moyers in 1990, men who didn't or couldn't first learn to dance and recite poetry were deemed unfit to be warriors. Michael Meade, in his book *Men and the Water of Life*, described the Irish idea that you shouldn't give a man a sword until you've taught him to dance. Thus would one of the men's gatherings come to be called "Men and the Dance of Desire." Hillman added: "Pan often wears a pine wreath or a chaplet made of fir."[16] Perhaps it was no accident that, when he attended his first men's conference in the woods of Minnesota in September 1986, he showed up with a wreath on his head and calling himself Fern.

At these retreats, it wasn't long before Hillman's robust intellect merged with nascent rhythmic excursions to inspire others. As participant Rick Chelew put it: "Something that gave me a lot of respect for Hillman was his ability to go into the experiential, the body. This wasn't his natural forte, because he lived in his mind a lot. But he was so willing to jump in with both feet and be involved with the dancing and drumming. It could appear ridiculous to the outside, but for a lot of us, it set the bar of how far you're willing to go."[17]

Hillman always brought along his tan tap shoes and, at several men's gatherings, the grandson of Frank Lloyd Wright played saxophone to accompany his soft-shoe routine. Sometimes the men would initiate a verbal call of "tap, tap, tap," and Hillman would rise to the occasion. Other times, it might be foisted upon him. "Apparently he was well-known through the years at Mendocino for doing bad puns," attendee Barry Spector remembered. "And when he did, he was 'penalized' by having to get up and tap dance."[18]

At the multicultural men's gathering in West Virginia, Malidoma Somé recalled being stunned by "discovering another layer of this intellectual giant—the agility, the way he was moving his body" after Hillman asked onetime Doors drummer John Densmore to accompany his effort. [19]

"Jim was fantastic on that tap dancing," Bly would recall. "I think it's one thing that kept him going so beautifully. You try to pin him down to a doctrine, the sonofabitch will say the opposite of what he just said. And that's like tap dancing. I consider him a cultural thinker and a cultural player and a cultural tap dancer, more than I would either a psychologist or a philosopher."[20]

Jack Kornfeld remembered the last time Hillman came to the Mendocino gathering. "On the final night, after an Arthurian kind of banquet where people were making toasts to the ancient gods and the collaboration of men, it was time for James to leave. He got up, dressed quite impeccably after a week of sweaty initiation deep in the forest, and gave us his own ritual offering as his departure. It was beautiful. He tapped his way out of that room."[21]

MYTH AND MOVEMENT

Around the same time that he began taking tap lessons, Hillman received a letter from Debra McCall. Then in her mid-thirties, McCall had been a dancer her entire life. She was best known for her reconstruction of the 1920s Bauhaus Dances, which toured to sold-out venues in the U.S., Europe and Japan. Earlier she had majored in psychology and spent eight years working at Bellevue Psychiatric Hospital. McCall had been certified in Laban Movement Analysis, "a recognition that movement is a psycho-physical process, an outward expression of inner intent."[22] Hungarian-born Rudolf Laban had described four motion factors based on fundamental psychological attitudes—either resisting or accepting the physical conditions that influence movement. A contemporary of Jung, Laban correlated this hypothesis to the depth psychologist's four functions of consciousness (sensing, thinking, feeling, and intuiting).

Herself a student of Jung's work, McCall had also embarked on a series of workshops she called "The Body of Myth." In 1984, she initiated a program of expressive arts therapy in several cities in Italy. It was there she first heard of Hillman and, starting with *The Myth of Analysis*, began reading him voraciously. From New York came her letter inviting him to consider becoming the clinical supervisor to a group of creative arts therapists who loved his work. Intrigued by the synchronicity, Hillman invited McCall to come to Connecticut and discuss the possibility. "We would bring cases and present them, move them, and draw them," she told him. Hillman agreed. For the next two years he would alternate supervising the group between his Connecticut home and a location in Manhattan, "and he was flying with it!" McCall remembered.[23]

Pat Berry was in the process of leaving Hillman when, in October 1987, McCall decided to move full-time to Rome to teach. Not long after she arrived, Hillman wrote her that he would soon be coming to Rome to lecture at a Jung conference. They arranged to meet there in early March 1988. Hillman landed the day after Pat moved out.

Inside the Vatican, he and McCall spent time together in the Hall of the Muses, discussing how the muses each had a role in raising Dionysus. Hillman would remain in Italy for more than a month, speaking also on "Anima" in Florence. He and McCall ended up making a trip to Sicily. "I believe it was Easter," said McCall, "because we saw the ritual of the running with crosses from different corners of the piazza and then doves being released."[24] They visited the ruins of Agrigento, one of the main ancient cities of Magna Grecia, viewing the temples of Demeter. "We both had the same dream one night—these beautiful vases that we'd been seeing, overflowing with pomegranate seeds."

Hillman had traveled in Sicily once before, bringing Pat for a four-week vacation in 1974. Now, McCall sensed, he "was coming off of Pat leaving and seemed very raw and vulnerable, trying to hang on and make sense of everything. What both of us felt, and we talked about this, was the presence of the Plutonian—Hades—and really being dragged into the underworld there. We were exploring the collective unconscious together."

Hillman came home to attend a men's conference in Mendocino, where one of his presentations was titled: "Receiving love over many bridges." He wrote in early May, "I shall put on my tap shoes (after two years of lessons) and dance in public at the [Putnam] High School with 14 year old girls, in a theatrical show."[25]

He reflected further, on what he was going through personally, in the same letter to Guggenbühl. "I am wrestling with loneliness, with ageing, impotence, and especially with love whatever that is. Also with anger over self-betrayal regarding the past and my self-deceit in not 'getting what I want' with Pat but accommodating, complying . . . I am glad it's over and she is gone, but the space left, the torn tissue of symbiotic life style, of habits, leaves me with a great wound in the solar plexus. It is better today than six months ago. I have a young girl here in her 20's I have seen in the winter, and from time to time, and I have another woman in her thirties who will be staying here in the house in the summer, tho I fear our connection is mainly collaboration rather than physical closeness which is what I feel desperately in need of. Whatever is going on inwardly seems tied completely to the 'women', so classically I am suffering from an immense attack of anima. Nothing new here, except that it comes late after 20 years of monogamy, strict." [Hillman had just turned sixty-three]

"The only clinical thing I can say is that the area of disaster seems contained, like the tree can hold the bleeding wound. I am not the wound. I am wounded. I have had remarkable dreams. On my birthday, among other dreams, I had a new license plate for an old black car: AD1 (and this was in Sicily, after much time in Greek temples, underworld deities, a return to the 'religion' if that is what it is that moves me so profoundly) where AD means also 'Ades (Hades) and Adonai. I am therefore in my first year of a new life, and feel still in breakdown condition: ruins and flowers together. Hades/Pluto and Persephone together."[26]

AD1 meant, too, a coming into his body in a whole new way. It didn't seem coincidental that Hillman's acknowledgment of a willingness to change had occurred in Italy. As McCall observed: "Everyone over there walks using their shoulders. They're sinuous, sensuous, serpentine. There's a three-dimensional quality of movement, where all the joints seem liquid." This phenomenon fascinated Hillman. As they analyzed it together, "he understood completely what I was talking about and contrasted it to his own body image."

McCall remembered Hillman saying to her: "When I think of my body image, I think of myself like a Herm—a head, a penis, and a slab of concrete between the two." The Herm, a standard element in classical architectural style, is a tapered, rectangular stone post crowned by a portrait bust. Hillman often mentioned how herms were found at crossroads. In ancient Greece, it was associated with the god Hermes, with whom Hillman had long identified. "He had a hard time grounding himself," McCall recalled. "The part of his body below the neck was very rigid, so much tension, and it bothered him. We worked a little on how he sat at his desk. In his sitting posture he was cutting off the downward flow, always leading with his chin and his beak, as he put it."

Many of McCall's workshops had been influenced by Jungian publications, and recently by archetypal psychology. One was called "Women Waiting," harkening back to Greek myths that featured Penelope weaving or Demeter refusing to allow things to grow. In autumn 1988, McCall received a Fellowship in Advanced Design at the American Academy in Rome. Late that same October, Hillman came to Rome to give a lecture titled "From Mirror to Window: Curing Psychoanalysis of its Narcissism," and stayed for a week. McCall showed him photographs she had taken in private collections in southern Italy and Sicily while doing research for her choreography, "Psyche's Fourth Task." These were clay tablets called "pinakes" that depicted Persephone in the underworld. Yet these tablets portrayed Persephone in unusual fashion with her marriage chest, little baby, and other gods coming to offer her gifts. Hillman had never seen that imagery before. It resonated with his view of how the shadow may be denigrated, yet underneath contains all the riches.

McCall also took Hillman to one of her favorite places, Ostia Antica, just outside Rome. Examining an exquisite shrine dedicated to Eros and Psyche, McCall explained the rich three-dimensional spiral in which they were entwined. "I remember him spending a lot of time looking at it. They were depicted in a spiral form, and now he had the language to describe it. Thereafter, he saw three-dimensionality everywhere."

She observed that "he felt more free, particularly when we were in Italy. He was away from America, away from judgments. The Italians loved him, he felt very welcome, and I think loved the language, the flow, just being loose. I remember him throwing his head back, laughing and relaxing; all the tension he carried around would leave him."

McCall and Hillman decided to combine their specialties on occasion. She would engage workshop participants in "The Body of Myth," while he would lecture on "The Meaning of Myth." Then they would team for "The Feeling of Myth," including one workshop in Connecticut at Leslie Snow's dance studio. He would also join in McCall's predominantly female gatherings to the curiosity and delight of the others. At one point, McCall even did a session *for* Hillman; she was the therapist and he, her analysand.

Both viewed the customarily four-day events as inviting people to allow the unconscious to move them. McCall didn't give directives. "I would say, 'wait . . . allow yourself to be moved.' Sometimes people would lie there and nothing would ever come and that was fine with me. Because it can't come from the ego. But once it starts, if it comes from that deeper place, it's so beautiful. As [her teacher] Martha Graham used to say, 'Wherever a dancer stands ready, that spot is holy ground.'"

McCall emphasized the importance of shaping or sculpting space to feel three-dimensional volume, as people had experienced a century earlier working the fields and riding horses. With the advent of the machine age, movement had become more mechanical and thus two-dimensional. Now in the digital age, everything is one-dimensional. The shaping interaction with space had been lost along the way. Particularly for women, McCall focused concentration on the pelvic area, picking up on Martha Graham's technique that the essence of movement is contraction and release.

"James loved that about my work," said McCall. "We would do a lot of exercises on the floor, with the pelvis in space, moving like you do in yoga with these tilts and shifts." In the Laban technique, "if you think of yourself moving a refrigerator or pushing someone, you would emphasize what's called the heel-coccyx connection. You do this in 'the Bridge' in yoga, but work it in a different way."

This was difficult for Hillman, but further parallels between Laban and Jung interested him. Laban had emphasized qualities of exertion and recuperation, which McCall related to Jung's theory of amplification. When Hillman couldn't flow with the heel-coccyx connection,

McCall would suggest that he simply amplify his own natural lightness, in order to rise upward in space. The body would "recuperate" with grounding because it can't stay up there forever. For James to ground himself, he had to first amplify his natural lightness. The recuperation necessary after that amplification would be the groundedness he was lacking. As he tried this, the revelation made Hillman burst out laughing. "Now I know what you're talking about!" McCall remembered him exclaiming.

In the workshops, they explored the "alchemical body" and various archetypes, with the attendees sometimes partnering up. What would happen if Apollo and Dionysus moved together? Or Apollo with Apollo? Dionysus with Dionysus? McCall herself "always liked the Dionysian because it was so three-dimensional; James could relate to the Apollonian."

Aphrodite, on the other hand, was "something he desired, but always out of reach—even though his writings were poetic, so imbued with Aphrodite, and love, and anima. As far as I was concerned, he had Aphrodite's blessing. Anyhow, he conveyed he had not felt Aphrodite for a long time in his life."

For her part, McCall "thought the world of him, but more as a mentor than anything else." Looking back in 2018, McCall reflected on her relationship with Hillman: "I think we walked together, helped guide each other through a deep, rich time in both our lives."

IN THE AUDIENCE

"I feel I shall perish from the senex unless I can maintain mirth. I get into such narrow, tight, despairing conditions sitting at my table trying to write sometimes, that I yearn for the French light of Matisse, hence the new attention to painting, painters and anima."
—James Hillman, in a letter to Wolfgang Giegerich,
September 5, 1985.[27]

"My life lives in the same cage of 'ideas' . . . they come at me from everyside, and I have it seems little else but being their victim or whatever. I am not happy without them and I am angry at them. Tho I live in the country, there are days I don't even set foot out of the house. A dumb way of being, and something's gotta give, as they say over here.

"I wish I were a painter rather than a person with a type-writer. It's better for the melancholy of ageing to paint with colors and models and landscapes and dead fish and fruit."
—James Hillman, in a letter to Peter Tatham, summer 1987.[28]

On November 22, 1986, Hillman spoken at a conference on "C. G. Jung and the Humanities" at New York's Hofstra University. Among the other participants were eighty-two-year-old Joseph Campbell, the world's foremost expert on mythology, and Robert Bly. The three men dined together the evening prior. Hillman remembered "being my normal neurotic, fearful self—worried about what I should eat the night before I was to be on the stage. But old Joseph Campbell sat down and had a great big steak . . . a couple of drinks before dinner, black coffee and pie after dinner, and went up to bed and slept soundly."[29]

Sitting in the packed auditorium the next day was Margot McLean. Then in her early thirties, the artist lived in a downtown Manhattan loft and had begun to develop a reputation for creating art installations with powerful environmental themes. Her first, "Portal of the Corporate Gods," was an exhaustive piece on toxic waste. Another called "Silent Partings" used darkly painted gallery walls and dramatic lighting to slowly seduce the viewer into what at first appeared beautiful but at closer examination revealed the devastation and horror of environmental degradation.

Margot's older sister Kathleen, who had attended a couple of Joseph Campbell's prior talks, had gotten wind of the Hofstra conference and suggested they go. Both were interested in Jungian psychology, and Margot considered Jung's *Man and His Symbols* an excellent art book. At the conference, she would find Campbell's lecture "incredibly inspirational, almost as if he had transcended into another realm." (It would be one of his last appearances; Campbell died in October 1987). Margot had read several pieces about animals written by Hillman, which held an important place in her life and work. Watching him standing behind the lectern appearing "tall, wiry, and cocky, he had a kind of Dionysian energy and creativity," she would recall.[30]

More than two years went by, when she saw an announcement that Hillman would be speaking in the city again, at Columbia University, and decided to attend. She took the subway uptown to the auditorium by herself—a full audience was on-hand for Hillman's talk on "The Feeling of Myth." It was late February 1989. Margot returned to Columbia the next day for a smaller day-long seminar. When she arrived late, Hillman could not help noticing the tall attractive woman wearing a long tweed coat. Margot noticed him, too. "He was wearing a sweater that he still had twenty-five years later." In the course of the day, they engaged in conversation. He was interested to learn she was a painter as he loved visiting artist's studios whenever he could.

A follow-up several-day-long workshop on "Myth and Movement" was announced for the ensuing week, at the Open Center on Spring Street, not far from where Margot lived. Intrigued by everything she heard so far, she joined the twenty-some other participants. Debra McCall led the movement exploration. Hillman read aloud passages from *The Homeric Hymns*, to which the group responded. McCall's slide lecture depicted images of gods and goddesses in stone, temples, and landscape. Each bore unique characteristics: Dionysus was "free-flow and multi-directional," Artemis "direct focus," Aphrodite "serpentine around the central body axis." Therapy literally meant "to attend to," the group was told. "Therapia" was an attendant at the altar—not healing or getting rid of the problem, but attending to it. All this and more the group put into practice—moving with a body part they felt was dependable, and with another they felt wasn't, then allowing these two choreographies to interact "on stage" together and drawing an image of the interaction. Hillman described the event in a letter to London filmmaker Stephen Segaller: "We showed slides of places and fields of flowers and landscapes and read Greek texts as part of getting the physicality of the myths. It had a very powerful effect, and has not been done before."[31]

Margot recalled: "In the workshop we were all moving at the same time as if in a group flow around the room. When James and I came in contact with each other, there was an inhibition that I felt, and he later said the same thing to me, a little bit of 'don't get too close.'"[32]

Several weeks later, Margot sent Hillman an announcement for a show she was having in Hartford, Connecticut, a little over an hour's drive from his home in Thompson. She wrote: "I hope you can make it, Margot." It was an installation in the windows of the Real Art Ways gallery that she titled "Metaphorical Forest." The space was a converted brownstone and storefront, where Margot's installation could only be viewed from the outside looking in.

Hillman was out of town for the opening, but the installation remained up long enough for him to eventually see it. Arriving on a late spring afternoon, Hillman was struck first by the unique feeling of looking into a window much like dioramas in natural history museums. The space was filled with earth, leaves, rocks, trees, flowers and paintings of small animals that were not obviously apparent until you looked very carefully.

Neither art nor animals had been far from Hillman's mind. He often dreamt about paintings, and wished he had such a talent. At every museum he visited, he purchased slides of the art work. Shortly before meeting Margot, he turned his large collection into a slide lecture on "Images of Mood and Desire: Anima in 19th and 20th Century Paintings," given to groups ranging from men in the woods to the Institute of Jungian Analysts. He published "Let the Creatures Be: A Conversation with Thomas Moore" in the summer of 1983 in *Parabola* magazine, an article that Margot was familiar with, and "Human Being as Human Animal: A Conversation with John Stockwell" in *Between the Species: A Journal of Ethics* (1985).

What Hillman came across in Margot's "Metaphorical Forest" was unlike anything he'd encountered before—especially one small painting that his eye had to search out to identify, a miniscule cheetah nestled in among the trees and rocks of the installation. Years later, the two of them would collaborate on a book called *Dream Animals* and he would reflect on that moment: "It was the tenuous reality of the animal, that it was there and not there, much like the animals in our dreams that can be so terrifying, so startling, and yet are 'only dreams.' [She] seemed to have caught in a painting something I had been working on, teaching about, trying to put into words for thirty years."[33]

TO BE CONTINUED . . .

NOTES

1. 'Hillman was aware of the theatrical. . . .:" William Kotzwinkle written communication with Author, June 12, 2019.
2. "Cell Song," Etheridge Knight: www.poemhunter.com
3. "as a master of instinctual soul. . . .": James Hillman, *Pan and the Nightmare*, Putnam, Ct.: Spring Publications, Inc., 2000, pp. 80–81.
4. "At the time I was studying. . . .": Enrique Pardo, Dis-Membering Dionysus: Image and Theater," *Spring 1984*.

5. "This group begins with. . . .": Hillman letter to Pat Berry, 1983, undated. Berry private archive.

6. "the ruins of a French chateau. . . .": Charles Boer introduction to "Dis-Membering Dionysus: Image and Theatre" by Enrique Pardo, *Spring 1984*, pp. 163–4.

7. "the birth of all my work in many ways. . . .": Author interview with Enrique Pardo, March 2009.

8. "What he could do with his voice. . . .": Author interview with Pat Berry, June 2019.

9. "He was working on what he called. . . .": Author interview with Nor Hall, June 2019.

10. "I always obliged them to read. . . .": Author interview with Enrique Pardo, March 2009.

11. "I believe his involvement corresponded. . . .": Author interview, Nor Hall, June 2019.

12. "He plays with ideas. . . .": Author interview with Murray Stein, October 2006..

13. Looked at "with great suspicion. . . .": Hillman personal archive.

14. "quite surprised to realize. . . .": Author interview with Anne Guggenbühl-Craig, September 2006.

15. Background on Hillman and dance lessons: Author interview with Leslie Snow, October 2018.

16. "Pan often wears a pine wreath. . . .": author interview with Hillman.

17. "Something that gave me a lot of respect. . . .": Author interview with Rick Chelew, July 2010.

18. "Apparently he was well-known. . . .': Author interview with Barry Spector, October 2018.

19. "discovering another layer. . . .": Author interview with Malidoma Somé, May 2008.

20. "Jim was fantastic on that tap dancing. . . .": Author interview with Robert Bly, July 2007..

21. "On the last night. . . .": Author interview with Jack Kornfeld, March 2008.

22. "a recognition that movement. . . .": Ed Groff, *Laban Movement Analysis: Charting the Ineffable Domain of Human Movement*, JOPERD, February 1995.

23. Debra McCall's background and account of her relationship with Hillman is drawn from an interview with the author, July 2018. All McCall quotes, unless otherwise noted, were recorded in that interview.

24. "I believe it was Easter. . . .": Debra McCall email to author, October 10, 2018.

25. "I shall put on my tap shoes. . . .": Hillman letter to Adolf Guggenbühl, May 7, 1988

26. "I am wrestling with loneliness. . . .": Hillman letter to Adolf Guggenbühl, May 7 [1988], Guggenbühl private archive.

27. "I feel I shall perish. . . .": Hillman letter to Wolfgang Giegerich, Giegerich private archive.

28. Hillman letter to Peter Tatham: Hillman private archive.

29. "being my normal neurotic. . . .": Transcript of interview with Hillman by Andrew Dick, for an article in *East-West* magazine, February 1990, Opus Archive.

30. "incredibly inspirational. . . .": Author interview with Margot McLean, April 2010.

31. "So many came we had to do it twice. . . .": Hillman undated letter to Stephen Segaller, Hillman private archive.

32. "In the workshop we are all moving. . . .": Author interview with Margot McLean, January 2020.

33. "It was the tenuous reality. . . .": "Now You See Them, Now You Don't," in *Animal Presences: The Uniform Edition of the Writings of James Hillman, Volume 9*, pp. 188–189.

ACKNOWLEDGMENTS

The death of James Hillman on October 27, 2011, marked a turning point for this biography. He was no longer here to offer suggestions and provide psychological insights about his life and ideas. Thankfully, we had already covered in our interviews much of what appears in this volume. Yet as an investigative journalist, it was incumbent upon me to mine the ore and unearth the riches. This proved no easy task, nor one that could be completed in two volumes as I had anticipated. And I owe a debt of gratitude to many who played a part in opening new doors and filling in important gaps.

First, my thanks to those directly involved in production of the book at Skyhorse: Publisher Tony Lyons and my astute editor Jason Katzman, who suggested enlisting a copyeditor knowledgeable of the field that led to a remarkable "find"—Dylan Hoffman of the Pacifica Graduate Institute, where Hillman taught for many years. For her consistent support for over three decades, my literary agent Sarah Jane Freymann.

Margot McLean's help proved invaluable, including her directing me to new sources as James once had. Randolph Severson's eloquent and enthusiastic responses to each chapter consistently buoyed my writing spirit, along with incisive comments from Sonu Shamdasani, Alice Faber, George Peper, Laurence Hillman, and Susanne Hillman. And I can't imagine a more thorough and devoted indexer than Ellen Kaplan-Maxfield.

For providing photos from their archives, I am indebted first to Margot and also to Robert Hinshaw, Patricia Berry, Stanton Marlan, and Paul Kugler. For their transcription of some of my interviews, thank you to Pacifica students Erin O'Halloran, Miles Carroll, Myriesha Barber, and Maryam Tahmasebi.

For elucidation about the men's groups, Miguel Rivera and Andy Castro; and into the complexities of James Hillman's astrology, his son Laurence Hillman, Richard Tarnas, Jean Lall, and Joey Goldfarb. For many insights into Hillman's ideas, my thanks to Dr. Scott Becker, of the Great Lakes Psychology Group and the editorial board of Spring Publications.

It was a great gift to be able to include excerpts from literally hundreds of James Hillman's letters written over the years. This would not have been possible without the willingness of many of his friends and colleagues to send me copies of the correspondence that they'd saved. I am grateful to Patricia Berry, Adolf Guggenbühl-Craig, J.P. Donleavy, Wolfgang Giegerich, Marvin Spiegelman, Robert Hinshaw, Stanton Marlan, David Miller, Thomas Moore, Ginette Paris, Mary Watkins, Ed Casey, Murray Stein, Roger Knudson, Coleman Barks, Rafael López-Pedraza and Charles Boer. As well to the Robert Duncan Archive at the University of Buffalo (James Maynard) and the Yale University archive of William Coffin, and the archivists who hosted my research at the Eranos Foundation in Ascona (Gisela Binda), the Robert Fly Papers at the University of Minnesota Libraries (Ann Mulfort), and foremost the extraordinary custodians of the James Hillman papers at the Opus Archives and Research Center in Santa Barbara, California (Safron Rossi and Jennifer Maxon).

Last but certainly not least, for their personal encouragement and support on many levels, my heartfelt thanks to Jessie Benton, Wendy Orange, Barry Miller, and Orland Bishop.

This biography has taken the better part of two decades to bring to culmination, and to anyone whose assistance I have inadvertently failed to mention, my apologies and thanks to you.

INDEX

The abbreviation JH stands for James Hillman; PB = Patricia Berry; AP = archetypal psychology; DU = The Dream and the Underworld; *RP* = *Re-Visioning Psychology;* UD = University of Dallas; DI = Dallas Institute of Humanities & Culture; JAP = Journal of Analytical Psychology. References to the "Institute" refer to the Jung Institute (Zurich). Note that subentries under "Hillman, James" and "Berry, Patricia" are subdivided by paragraph headings, given in small caps. Also note that *Spring* is italicized when referring to the *Journal.* Spring with no italics refers to Spring Publications.

1960s *See* sixties
1968, 17
1970s *See* seventies

"Abandoning the Child" (Hillman), 117, 135–136, 138
abortion, 70
academia
　as Apollonian detachment, 419
　DI as public alternative, 320–322, 344–345
　as mind split from working-class body, 418
　specialization vs. mutual scholarship, 225, 293
　"verbiage, imagelessness, constriction," 263
"Achelous and the Butterfly: Toward an Archetypal Psychology of Humor" (Miller, *Spring 1973*), 205
Achilles, 68
acting out, 335
active imagination
　dialogue between "Voice" and "I," 20–21
　as "the *mirror par excellence*," 238–239

　as "a form of prayer" in Jungian dialogues, 235
　reading *RP* as essay in, 219–220
　ego implied in introverted technique, 32
　as Jung's private vision in "Seven Sermons," 114–115
　partial Bosnak basis for re-entering dreams, 119–120
　via 16th-c. Memory Theater system, 124
Adam (biblical figure), 64–65
adaptation
　as self-preservation function, 241
　to the expectation of others, 212
　as a cultural gift, 197
　as evolutionary reason, 240
　as existential, 178
　to Hera's culture, 79
　as "the real Jewish difficulty," 178, 179–181
　as real only via imagination, 236
Adler, Alfred, 374, 431
Adler, Mortimer, 303–304, 344
aesthetic response
　as response from the heart, 339–340
　to self-presentation via "animal eye," 241
　as active participation in world, 253, 319

fragmentation
  of AP community, 269
  of consciousness, 66, 140
  of JH 's cut-and-pasted notes, 230, 297
  as new symptom, 339
"Fragments from a [Jung] Talk with Students" (Hillman), 85
Fredericksen, Don, 304–310
freedom
  as "Dionysian experience leading women to frenetic freedom," 160
  freedom of styles, freeing individuation from ego stereotypes, 85
  in free exchanges of evenings at Dallas House, 347
  "freeways" as reinforcing fantasies of unburdened freedom, 302
  in JH–PB relationship, 175–176
  JH's "freedom I never had" coupled with "collapse and despair," 396–397
  via "getting rid of images of how lives should be lived," 88
  G. Scholem as embodiment of freedom to forge new paths, 227–228
  of Hungarian freedom fighter, JH's ancestor, viii
  "There was an incredible freedom, leaving Zürich behind," 289
  UD's "censoring of academic freedom," 306
  of writing—and "torture" of obstacles, 395, 515
'French Exodus,' 190–191, 192
French-Kelly, Judith, 302, 304, 345
Freud, Sigmund
  as a "rather large figure, in a time of large men," 269
  "really by nature an artist," 492
  showed mythological basis of psychology, 154
  via psychopathology, notes "psyche's propensity to personify," 149
  believes along with Jung that men feel via feminine side, 422
  misogynist perspective of, 64

pioneer of depth psychology whom Jung takes to a deeper level, 48
AP as a deviation and resemination of Jung and Freud, 203
JH's oedipal rejection of Jung compared to Jung's of Freud, 112–113
how does AP interpretation of dreams differ from Freudian? 274
how well Freud took his transference defeat with Fleiss, 114
learning from Frau Lou that "love requires personifying," 150
and reductive atmosphere of Freudians, 161
sympathy with Freud's pathological incident on Acropolis, 113
"tangled science, humanities in writing fiction plus case history, 492
as "tending to denigrate the psyche" as inferior to ego, 94, 151
  See also Freud's Own Cookbook
Freud and Philosophy (Ricoeur), 146
Freudians See psychoanalysis
Freud's Own Cookbook (ed. Hillman & Boer, 1985), 372, 430, 500
  See also psychoanalysis
Frey, Liliane, 12, 113–114
friendships
  as demanding "feelings that shake you out of set ways," 438
  changes afoot for JH in mid-seventies, 212
  with J. P. Donleavy, begun at Trinity, 271
  long collaboration with T. Moore, 341–342
  long collaborative friendship with C. Boer, 497
  with R. Bly mostly revolved around poetics and language, 412–413, 509–510
  See also Hillman, James: CORRESPONDENCE WITH
functionality
  for Jung via four functions of consciousness, 164, 538
  Portmann insists dispay not reducible to any single function, 241

"The Problem of Fantasies and the
Fantasy of Problems" (Hillman), 79
The Problem of the Puer Aeternus (von
Franz), 79
problem-solving, 153–154
"A Processional Exit" (Terry Lectures'
end), 164–165, 357–361
profit motive, 327
progress, 94
projections, 93, 110, 162, 351
Project Return (New Orleans), 479
Protestantism, 32, 111–112, 263, 380,
489–490
"Proverbs of Hell" (Blake), 420
psyche
archetypal background of, 49, 93
its life (soul) vs. ours (ego), 273–277
pathologizing tendency of, vii–viii
as embedded within collective
unconscious, 337
the Gods as archetypal forces in, 65
"a cosmology from psyche rather than
spirit," 504–505
as a multiplicity of selves, 94, 211
as "the forming idea of a living body,"
246
how does one speak so to express
psyche? 487
innocence as theme of American
psyche, 399–400
beyond the consulting room, 84–85
new sense of reality via world
expressions, 339
appreciating "the range of . . . the
fringes," 343–344
perspective of vs. social history, 160
plant psyche vs. animal psyche, 369
RP "explor[es] the non-human reaches
of," 219
self-presentation as *sui generis* aim of, 242
spontaneous expression of via
Eranos, 225
See also personifying
psychoanalysis
as Freudian analysis, 5, 85, 145
psychoanalytic theory, 159–161
root metaphor of, 411
"after one hundred years of solitude
of," 339

importance of pathology in, 146
psychology of "conation, a will
job, ego control or relaxation,"
177–178
vs. Jungian psychology, 177–178, 274,
294–295
father-son tradition of, 114
and femininity acceptance, 66
JH breakdown in practice of, 211
as early treatment for hysteria, 64
language of as "Newspeak" vs. poetry,
495
looking at via "this kitchen
perspective," 373
and reduction, 161
of—and for—the street, 339, 340–341
work with R.D. Laing in existential,
106
See also analysis; anti-psychiatry
movement
"On Psychological Creativity" (Hillman),
xv, 41, 88
"psychological faith," 208
"On Psychological Femininity" (Hillman,
1969), 58, 59, 67
*A Psychological Interpretation of The Golden
Ass of Apuleius* (von Franz), 79
"On Psychological Language" (Hillman,
1968), 41, 120
psychological thinking, 125–127, 152, 153
"Psychological Traditions" (Hillman
course), 49, 296
psychological writing, 522
"The Psychologist As Artist: The
Imaginal World of James Hillman"
(Odajnyk), 378
"Psychologizing," Terry Lecture 3
(Hillman), 152–155
psychology
AP focus is beyond interior
subjectivity, 337
and interrelation with mythology, 60
method moving from cognition to
aesthetics, 339
"my big fight over its boring
language," 491
religious perspective on, 219
speech of soul vs. language of
psychology, 487